THE CHALLENGE OF INTER-LEGALITY

The sovereignty of states to enact and enforce laws within their jurisdictions has been recognized since the Treaty of Westphalia in 1648. There are now, however, accepted global legal norms that transcend national sovereignty and hold states accountable for not including these in their domestic legal regimes. This volume is the first book-length treatment to describe and explain how legal orders can be interwoven and what to do about it. Coining the term "inter-legality," this volume provides essays on the history of inter-legality, the primary areas of inter-legality, the concept of jurisdiction, and the normative developments prompted by inter-legality. Bringing together a wide range of contributors who stem from a variety of different academic backgrounds, this book aims to answer three questions: Does inter-legality occur with some regularity? How does it affect traditional legal concepts such as "jurisdiction," "legal order," or "responsibility?" And what are the normative implications?

JAN KLABBERS is Professor of International Law at the University of Helsinki, Finland.

GIANLUIGI PALOMBELLA is Professor of Law and Applied Legal Theory at the Sant'Anna School of Advanced Studies, Pisa.

ASIL Studies in International Legal Theory

The purpose of the ASIL Studies in International Legal Theory series is to clarify and improve the theoretical foundations of international law. Too often the progressive development and implementation of international law has foundered on confusion about first principles. This series raises the level of public and scholarly discussion about the structure and purposes of the world legal order and how best to achieve global justice through law.

This series grows out of the International Legal Theory project of the American Society of International Law. The ASIL Studies in International Legal Theory series deepens this conversation by publishing scholarly monographs and edited volumes of essays considering subjects in international legal theory.

Books in the Series

The Challenge of Inter-legality Edited by Jan Klabbers and Gianluigi Palombella

The Nature of International Law Miodrag A. Jovanović

Reexamining Customary International Law Edited by Brian D. Lepard

Theoretical Boundaries of Armed Conflict and Human Rights Edited by Jens David Ohlin

Human Rights in Emergencies Edited by Evan J. Criddle

The Theory of Self-Determination Edited by Fernando R. Tesón

Negotiating State and Non-State Law: Global and Local Legal Pluralism Edited by Michael A. Helfand

Normative Pluralism and International Law: Exploring Global Governance Edited by Jan Klabbers and Touko Piipaerinen

Jus Post Bellum and Transitional Justice Edited by Larry May and Elizabeth Edenberg

The Future of International Law: Global Government Joel P. Trachtman

Morality, Jus Post Bellum, and International Law Edited by Larry May and Andrew T. Forcehimes

Parochialism, Cosmopolitanism, and the Foundations of International Law Edited by Mortimer Sellers

Global Justice and International Economic Law: Opportunities and Prospects Edited by Chios Carmody, Frank J. Garcia, and John Linarelli

The Role of Ethics in International Law Edited by Donald Earl Childress III

The New Global Law Rafael Domingo

Customary International Law: A New Theory with Practical Applications Brian D. Lepard

International Criminal Law and Philosophy Edited by Larry May and Zachary Hoskins

The Challenge of Inter-Legality

Edited by
JAN KLABBERS
University of Helsinki

GIANLUIGI PALOMBELLA
Sant'Anna School of Advanced Studies, Pisa

CAMBRIDGE
UNIVERSITY PRESS

CAMBRIDGE
UNIVERSITY PRESS

University Printing House, Cambridge CB2 8BS, United Kingdom

One Liberty Plaza, 20th Floor, New York, NY 10006, USA

477 Williamstown Road, Port Melbourne, VIC 3207, Australia

314-321, 3rd Floor, Plot 3, Splendor Forum, Jasola District Centre, New Delhi - 110025, India

79 Anson Road, #06-04/06, Singapore 079906

Cambridge University Press is part of the University of Cambridge.

It furthers the University's mission by disseminating knowledge in the pursuit of education, learning and research at the highest international levels of excellence.

www.cambridge.org
Information on this title: www.cambridge.org/9781108425476
DOI: 10.1017/9781108609654

First published 2019

A catalogue record for this publication is available from the British Library

Library of Congress Cataloging in Publication data
NAMES: Klabbers, Jan, editor. | Palombella, Gianluigi, editor.
TITLE: The challenge of inter-legality / edited by Jan Klabbers, University of Helsinki; Gianluigi Palombella, Sant'Anna School of Advanced Studies, Pisa.
DESCRIPTION: Cambridge, United Kingdom ; New York, NY, USA : Cambridge University Press, 2019. | Series: ASILstudies in international legal theory | "The general idea underlying this volume has been presented at workshops and dedicated seminars in various places, including the University of Edinburgh, Erasmus Law School Rotterdam, the European University Institute in Fiesole, the University of Milan Bicocca, and the 2017 annual meeting of the International Society of Public Law at the University of Copenhagen." –ECIP preface. | Includes bibliographical references and index.
IDENTIFIERS: LCCN 2018060515 | ISBN 9781108425476 (hardback)
SUBJECTS: LCSH: Conflict of laws–Congresses. | BISAC: LAW / International.
CLASSIFICATION: LCC K7041 .C422 2019 | DDC 340.9–dc23
LC record available at https://lccn.loc.gov/2018060515

ISBN 978-1-108-42547-6 Hardback
ISBN 978-1-108-44238-1 Paperback

Contents

Preface

The general idea underlying this volume has been presented at workshops and dedicated seminars in various places, including the University of Edinburgh, the Erasmus School of Law in Rotterdam, the European University Institute in Fiesole, the University of Milano-Bicocca, and the 2017 annual meeting of the International Society of Public Law at the University of Copenhagen. The editors are indebted to participants and commentators on those occasions, including Cormac Mac Amhlaigh, Maurizio Arcari, Nehal Bhuta, Mikael Rask Madsen, Dimitri van den Meerssche, Claudio Michelon, Hans Micklitz, Stefania Ninatti, the late Wibo van Rossum, Sanne Taekema, Rodrigo Vallejo, Neil Walker, and Tleuzhan Zhunussova. An authors' meeting was organized at the Scuola Superiore Sant'Anna in Pisa, where useful non-authorial comments were received from Lorenzo Gasbarri, Christian Joerges, Tuomas Tiittala, Orlando Scarcello, and Maria Varaki. The meeting was supported by the Scuola Superiore Sant'Anna and the Academy of Finland; the editors are grateful to both, as well as to Mortimer Sellers and John Berger for publishing this volume in the ASIL Studies in International Legal Theory series. The editors are also grateful to the contributors to this volume for their endorsement of inter-legality as a subject of advanced research and not least for their patient cooperation in preparing and finalizing this book.

Contributors

Samantha Besson
University of Fribourg

Edoardo Chiti
University of La Tuscia, Viterbo

Sergio Giuliano
Unaffiliated

Poul F. Kjaer
Copenhagen Business School

Jan Klabbers
University of Helsinki

Dimitry Kochenov
University of Groningen

Panos Koutrakos
City, University of London

Friedrich Kratochwil
European University Institute, Fiesole

Alberto di Martino
Sant'Anna School of Advanced Studies, Pisa

Gianluigi Palombella
Sant'Anna School of Advanced Studies, Pisa

Laura Pineschi
University of Parma

András Sajó
Central European University, Budapest

Yuval Shany
Hebrew University, Jerusalem

Sanne Taekema
Erasmus School of Law, Rotterdam

Antonello Tancredi
University Côte d'Azur Nice/University of Palermo

1

Introduction

Situating Inter-Legality

JAN KLABBERS AND GIANLUIGI PALOMBELLA

1 THE INTER-LEGALITY APPROACH

When two (or more) rules come from different jurisdictions, all of them are potentially applicable to the case at hand yet pointing to different substantive solutions, the question inevitably arises: What is the relevant law in such a case? Conflicts originate between rules stemming from different and overlapping legal orders (e.g., international law on the one hand and a particular domestic legal system on the other). An individual or a company may be prohibited from doing something by domestic law while entitled or empowered to do the same thing by international law or EU law – or vice versa.

This volume is inspired by empirical developments, registering the proliferation of such questions and situations, and by a few intuitions. First, interpreters might increasingly be inclined in such cases not to resort to solutions on a purely formal basis (is one of the legal orders concerned hierarchically superior?), but on a more substantive basis, aiming to do justice in the case before them. Second, regulators and lawmaking authorities, in many diverse domains, are becoming aware that inter-legality affects their own spheres of action, and that they shall have to confront the event of complex regulatory matters involving several competing legal rationales.

Notably, and accordingly, our conception of inter-legality differs from the conception as used by others. To us, inter-legality captures and describes the ways through which legal domains end up overlapping due to the interconnection of their substantive, material objects. It looks at law by changing the usual, traditional perspective, a perspective that is limited by the political, legal, and cognitive borders of a single self-contained system. One does not need the ascent to a juridical heaven of ready-made and principled justice – a deracinated, universalist standpoint – to realize that different legal orders may overlap normatively and reach beyond their own limits. On the contrary, an inter-legality perspective simply happens to be taken as soon as the vantage point of the concrete affair under scrutiny – the case at hand – is taken seriously. Looking at the demands of justice stemming from the case is rather different from "solving" an issue from the unilateral perspective of one of the legal regimes that actually compete in controlling and regulating the same issue. Various chapters in this book will help clarify and elaborate on the possibility and the nature of such a perspective about law.

In such a sense, inter-legality is not to be proposed as a "final" solution for our current legal problems, simply because inter-legality does not on its own represent a substantive set of legal principles from which any good answers can be derived. Nonetheless, inter-legality *recommends* something: it exhorts to approach the legal reality through a larger path, embracing the law as comprehensive and composite, understanding the normative complex as it surfaces through the circumstances and issues under consideration and awaiting (legal) justice.

Accordingly, the shift toward the construction of law from the angle of the case is essential to an inter-legality approach. Nonetheless, one does not have to take a realist and casuistic understanding of law – not necessarily. What is of primary relevance in the inter-legality discourse is that the text of the law is understood as being composed of more than one system-sourced positive law, and that the resulting texture of legality could not be what it is without this interplay. The premise for inter-legality reasoning is that the law of one single legal regime might not have unconditional primacy in given circumstances, not if the issue it regulates is also controlled by the law of another entitled and recognized legal regime. Consequently, inter-legality draws the path on which the search for a legal solution can be started. The point to note is that this solution is embedded within the law and justified by the law.

Inter-Legality does not suggest that legal conflicts should be solved by political means; it does not offer a *political* solution to be taken by legal actors. Among the relevant premises for an inter-legality approach is, in fact, the idea that where legal justice is at stake, solutions are requested of the law, not of politics. Certainly, politics can successfully work in solving disputes between states, or between states and regimes stemming from the work of international organizations, or other global regimes. And certainly, the International Court of Justice might believe that in a dispute related to war crimes, say, between Germany and Italy, the law can give no answers, and that its duty as a court translates into recommending the reopening of political negotiations between the states concerned. But this is not so from an inter-legality approach. Inter-legality stays firmly within the law, within legal thinking, within legal practice. Put differently, the understanding of law in inter-legality does not step outside the law (as in many versions of legal pluralism), but stays within its limits, although it considers those limits as drawn, if and when appropriate, by a plural concurrence of legalities.

For the purposes of this volume, inter-legality is not a matter of forum-shopping, of discontented individuals and groups being able to seek the jurisdiction most favorable to their claim (although, as will be discussed, the term was probably conceived with this in mind by the sociologist who made it famous). Indeed, in an important sense for us, this is precisely what inter-legality might help avoid: the very point of inter-legality is that the law will possibly indicate the solution to a dispute not by taking the one-jurisdiction-at-a-time perspective – the perspective of mutual alternative or exclusion – but by showing the relevance of – and the caring for – all the relevant normativities actually controlling the case. The choice, at the end, depends on how real circumstances allow for an equilibrium of justice between the positive law(s) competing in regulating the issues.

In a sense, one might call this the search for a "more just" solution, but our conception of inter-legality is not a kind of appeal to natural law or to some grand theory of justice. It is the inter-legal sense of complexity that requires the legal decision-maker to account for as many normativities as those involved in the case and to draw the "just" solution from a composite perspective that is not merely one-sided. And if that is so, then "forum-shopping" becomes a less useful activity for the forum-shopper.

Of course, all of this implies that the focus rests on individual cases, and therefore places judges (and other decision-makers exercising a quasi-judicial capacity) at the forefront. However, inter-legality does not demand that judges forge their verdicts upon their own thick background theories of justice. The ethics of a judge is inevitably a factor when it comes to delivering justice.[1] But the focus on cases only requires that a judge (or college of judges) is able to distinguish between several possible outcomes to find the ones that would better account for the plurality of reasons and claims involved in the issue. Hence, inter-legality is a highly contextualized setting, philosophically hinting at the qualities of practical wisdom in the consideration of the issue from non-unilateral standpoints and available to critical scrutiny from the perspective of "others."

Thus, if needed, the association would be with Aristotle rather than Kant, with Dewey or Sen rather than Rawls. There are, no doubt, outstanding philosophical questions that remain to be answered, but a full-fledged idea

[1] Think of the idea of doing justice in individual cases, the notion of case-by-case justice, and, e.g., the conception endorsed (if not invariably under the label "casuistry") by S. Toulmin, *The Place of Reason in Ethics* (Chicago: University of Chicago Press, 1986 [1950]).

of substantive justice is not essential to the practice of inter-legality. First, it would prove to be far from generally accepted; second, it would prevent the fair way of proceeding that inter-legality recommends (i.e., by considering the reasons and ideas of justice embedded in conflicting legal claims); and finally, it would be inappropriate in the context of a legal order, in which the decision-making does not depend on an autonomous and self-standing conception of morality and substantive justice, but on positive law.

2 CONSTITUTIONAL INSPIRATIONS

About a decade ago, international lawyers – and many domestic lawyers with an interest in public affairs – were in the grip of a seemingly new idea: the idea that the international legal order could be seen as a constitutional order. The idea had many inspirations. For some, constitutionalization was the answer to the fragmentation of international law, widely seen as a threat to the integrity of the system – constitutionalization would be the glue to hold the fragmenting system together. For others, it marked the liberal end of history, with a world finally united on the basis of shared values, typically Western civil and political rights, or even the ordo-liberal rights to trade, own property, and do business. And many embraced constitutionalization as an ideology required to accompany that other great ideology of globalization. For in a globalizing world without overarching political authority something was needed to sell the idea – and that something could be constitutionalization.[2] Indeed, the election of Donald Trump in the United States and the Brexit decision in the United Kingdom may well be signs that the salesmen have stopped their work: globalization meets with resistance because it is not met with a partner discourse to legitimize it beyond the unsubstantiated claim that globalization makes us all better off, that "a rising tide lifts all boats," neglecting the awkward circumstance that some boats are lifted far higher than others. It is appropriate to think that in the present times some counter-constitutionalism has started, and many indices are testament to this: some backlash against the language of constitutionalization has surfaced, even in the EU order, while resorting to the idea that, aside from the EU limits of competence, the notion of states' constitutional identity had to be valued and defended.[3]

[2] See generally J. Klabbers, "Setting the Scene," in J. Klabbers, A. Peters, and G. Ulfstein (eds.), *The Constitutionalization of International Law* (Oxford: Oxford University Press, 2009), 1.

[3] M. Arcari and S. Ninatti, *Exploring Counter-Constitutionalism: The Backlash Effect of Constitutional Vocabulary of the European Court of Justice and the European Court of Human Rights*, Workshop Draft Paper, July 2017, on file with the authors.

Indeed, it seems the conversation has calmed down considerably. International lawyers debate all sorts of things these days, but they do not debate constitutionalization with quite the same energy and passion as a decade ago, and when they talk about constitutionalization, it is more often in comparative terms than in terms of overarching principles – comparing judicial review in various states rather than positing a principle of judicial review on the global level, for instance. So, what happened? Why has constitutionalization become a less prominent staple of discussion? Obviously, the different attractions have met with different sorts of disappointment. Die-hard liberals may have started to realize that human rights, even if universal, may be contextual, and may be just a little too open-ended. They may have even started to realize that human rights come with their own bureaucracies that may not always be unequivocally good or human rights–oriented. Those who worried about fragmentation may have stopped worrying a little; they may have been appeased by the invention of the principle of systemic integration laid down in the Vienna Convention, and they may have found that the world does not collapse if trade lawyers and environmentalists talk past each other.[4] It may be inconvenient if regime representatives cannot communicate, but it is hardly cause for hysteria. Those who reimagined a *civitas mundi* may still be working on their reimagining, and if globalization has lost some of its glamour, so has constitutionalization.

But perhaps the main reason for this is that most of the attempts to look for constitutionalization have aimed to posit a thick, monolithic version of constitutionalization, implicitly (and sometimes explicitly) based on global unity, on a worldwide convergence of values.[5] This now has proved fallacious, as various theorists have pointed out. The world is a pluralist place, with pluralism existing on various levels, from the epistemological pluralism identified by someone like Neil Walker[6] and the conceptual pluralism of the

[4] The principle of systemic integration was popularized upon the discovery of article 31(3)(c) of the Vienna Convention on the Law of Treaties, suggesting that in interpreting a treaty, all rules of international law applicable between the parties ought to be taken into consideration. See M. Koskenniemi, *Fragmentation of International Law: Difficulties Arising from the Diversification and Expansion of International Law. Report of the Study Group of the International Law Commission* (Helsinki: Erik Castrén Institute, 2007).

[5] In addition, its explanatory force remained very limited, which fed the suspicion that constitutionalism was more ideology than theory. See J. Klabbers, "Constitutionalism as Theory," in J. Dunoff and M. Pollack (eds.), *International Legal Theory* (Cambridge: Cambridge University Press, forthcoming).

[6] See N. Walker, *Intimations of Global Law* (Cambridge: Cambridge University Press, 2015).

philosophers[7] to more mundane pluralities spotted by Nico Krisch.[8] So, it turned out, much of the debate was based on rather aspirational premises, on the unwarranted presumption of planetary unity, downplaying clashes of civilizations and happily ignoring above all the political economy of (international) law: whatever is done, whatever is proposed, it comes with winners and losers, and the identity of those groups remains remarkably constant over time. Legal and political decisions are rarely "neutral"; they tend to have distributive effects, even if sometimes unintentionally so. The West wins – and would have gained most from constitutionalization, cementing Western values and Western political practices – and the global South loses – and continues to lose.[9]

Still, while constitutionalization did not answer many questions and the entire decade-long debate may have been based on questionable premises, nonetheless it did tap into something real and of significance: the idea that it is no longer clear who exercises international authority, how authority is exercised, and with what justification. Clearly, the old Westphalian state system, built around keywords such as sovereign equality, national democracy, dualism, hierarchy, and state consent, no longer did the trick; sovereignty remains an important ordering principle, often clung to by governments, but it is not particularly accurate as a description of economic, social, and political processes. Authority, so we started to think, could come from all angles and directions, and seemed increasingly problematic to legitimate. If traditionally states could claim legitimate authority based on their internal structures, and international law could claim legitimacy because it was made by those same states and by definition and necessity based on their consent, this story no longer held good. It could not explain why all of a sudden banking standards would be set by the highly selective (and self-selective at that) Basel Committee and in the form of guidelines rather than legal rules. It could not explain the legal significance of "standards" developed by the International Organization for Standardization (ISO), or the Forest Stewardship Council, or the private agreement between workers and employers concerning safety in the garment industry. It could not explain why states would get all worked up whenever the Organisation for Economic Co-Operation and Development (OECD) would publish its annual Programme for International

7 See, for example, H. Putnam, *Ethics without Ontology* (Cambridge, MA: Harvard University Press, 2004).

8 See N. Krisch, *Beyond Constitutionalism: The Pluralist Structure of Postnational Law* (Oxford: Oxford University Press, 2010).

9 For a forceful critique, see B. S. Chimni, *International Law and World Order: A Critique of Contemporary Approaches*, 2nd edn. (Cambridge: Cambridge University Press, 2017).

Student Assessment (PISA) rankings – not even recommendations, but mere rankings. It could not explain how athletes convicted of doping use by their own sports' governing bodies could appeal to national or supranational tribunals.[10] And it could not explain why individuals would be bound to respect sanctions imposed on them by the Security Council, all the more so if those sanctions were taken in disregard of fundamental norms prevailing in their own political communities.

In other words, behind the challenges mentioned above lay another, deeper and possibly more fundamental issue: how to come to terms with changing patterns of authority and legitimation in international law. If there was one thing constitutionalization promised, it was the idea of structured order: the wide variety of norms could fall into place in a constitutional global legal order, with some at the apex and others below it, following some hierarchical pattern or other. Obviously, one might quibble (and one might expect there to be quibbles) about which norms would occupy which positions, but such debates notwithstanding, constitutionalization circa 2006 offered a glimpse of a well-arranged international legal order, with a beginning, a middle, and an end – and in that order, too.

This promise, needless to say, has not materialized, but the problematique has not been resolved either. In fact, it has only become more visible. The *Kadi* decision of the Court of Justice of the European Union (CJEU) in 2008 illustrated things nicely, presenting the intricate interdependence between three distinct categories of legal orders (the international, the EU, and the various national orders) and, what is more, suggesting that old solutions would no longer be workable.

The *Kadi* case hit a nerve – in fact, it hit several nerves; few judicial decisions have occupied so many legal minds in recent years as the *Kadi* decision. And yet, for all the hoopla, *Kadi* too has fizzled out, much like the constitutionalization debate. The very circumstance made so visible by *Kadi* (the interdependence between legal orders) has largely been left unexplored. There has been much debate about technicalities and much searching for practical solutions either advocating or opposing *hierarchy*,[11] and some looking further into review procedures and their relative merits and demerits.[12]

[10] On this problematique, see J. Klabbers and T. Piipariinen (eds.), *Normative Pluralism and International Law: Exploring Global Governance* (Cambridge: Cambridge University Press, 2013).

[11] A. Tzanakopoulos, *Disobeying the Security Council: Countermeasures against Wrongful Sanctions* (Oxford: Oxford University Press, 2011).

[12] D. Hovell, *The Power of Process: The Value of Due Process in Security Council Sanctions Decision-Making* (Oxford: Oxford University Press, 2016).

But little attention has been paid to the circumstance that perhaps *Kadi* was not an incidental case bringing a strange and unusual configuration to the fore, but could rather represent "the new normal." And yet, this is precisely what *Kadi* represents: the interwovenness of legal orders is not unique and special anymore, but rather represents a quite common state of affairs.

More recent cases confirm this state of affairs in various ways. Human rights lawyers may think of the *Al Dulimi* decision of the European Court of Human Rights, first rendered in 2013 and confirming the interdependence between the UN, European, and Swiss legal orders.[13] Investment lawyers may be reminded of the *Yukos* saga, decided by an international arbitral panel but subsequently set aside by a Dutch court – appeal is pending at the time of writing – and involving issues of procedural and substantive international, Russian, and Dutch law (and that is not even counting related proceedings taking place before domestic courts in various other national jurisdictions). Italy's Constitutional Court saw fit not to give effect to a decision of the International Court of Justice upon the defense of supreme constitutional principles concerning access to justice and fundamental rights, thereby spreading the debate about the rationale of international law and whether those very principles should have been interpreted as integral to any international law decision as well.[14] And the US Supreme Court did much the same in *Medellín*, but this time claiming to protect the integrity of US domestic law.[15] Lists of examples make clear that various legal systems can come into uncomfortably close contact with one another, and each of them can claim supremacy over competing legal orders. And these are just examples drawn from legal orders whose legal status no one would deny – the examples do not even involve soft law, or normative systems that not everyone would consider as "law."

3 INTER-LEGALITY IN THOUGHT AND ACTION

Among the first to use the term "inter-legality" was the Portuguese legal sociologist Boaventura de Sousa Santos, who referred to inter-legality during

[13] G. Palombella, "The Principled and Winding Road to *Al Dulimi*: Interpreting the Interpreters," (2014) *Questions of International Law* 16.

[14] On this at more length, see G. Palombella, "German War Crimes and the Rule of International Law," (2016) 14 *Journal of International Criminal Justice* 607, and especially G. Palombella, "*Senza identità*. Dal Diritto Internazionale alla Corte Costituzionale tra Consuetudine, *Jus Cogens* e Principi 'Supremi'," (2015) 35 *Quaderni Costituzionali* 815.

[15] *Medellín* can be, and regularly is, explained as a manifestation of American exceptionalism, but this does not preclude an analysis in terms of inter-legality.

a keynote address presented in the late 1980s. de Sousa Santos noted that inter-legality was a dynamic process due to the circumstance that "different legal spaces are non-synchronic," but his use of the term did not go much further. He observed, three decades ago, that we should start to conceive of law as "different legal spaces superimposed, interpenetrated, and mixed in our minds, as much as in our actions," explaining that we "live in a time of porous legality or of legal porosity, multiple networks of legal orders forcing us to constant transitions and trespassing." And this was different, he warned, from what legal anthropologists had traditionally referred to as legal pluralism, for legal pluralism suggests much more a side-by-side existence of legal orders coexisting in the same space.[16] For de Sousa Santos, inter-legality posed not so much a challenge as an opportunity: the porosity of legal orders would allow people to pick and choose which legal order to employ, and typically, they would employ the one most attuned to their claims or grievances.

The notion of inter-legality was picked up by William Twining on various occasions, but again without connecting the word to some actual innovation in the descriptive or normative fabric of legal discourse. In his *Globalisation and Legal Theory*, Twining suggests that inter-legality might provide a useful framework for further research, and then presents something of a broad outline before delving into a different debate.[17] And in a later brief article, Twining devotes some attention to classifying inter-legality, observing (among other things) that different orders or spaces can live in conflict but also in harmony with each other.[18] In support, other authors, without utilizing the inter-legality vocabulary, having suggested that, for example, much international law depends on national law for its implementation, and thus that international and domestic law can together build a strong legal argument in favor or against particular practices.[19]

It is necessary to specify wherein the utility of the notion of inter-legality may lie. We take the term as referring mostly to situations where actors are confronted with a variety of norms stemming from a variety of legal orders (or

[16] B. de Sousa Santos, *Toward a New Legal Common Sense*, 2nd edn. (London: Butterworths, 2002), at 437. The chapter was first separately published in 1987. See also A. Fischer-Lescano and G. Teubner, *Regime-Kollisionen: Zur Fragmentierung des Globalen Rechts* (Frankfurt am Main: Suhrkamp, 2006), at 34–40, distinguishing inter-legality from traditional legal pluralism.

[17] W. Twining, *Globalisation and Legal Theory* (London: Butterworths, 2000), at 230.

[18] W. Twining, "Diffusion and Globalization Discourse," (2006) 47 *Harvard International Law Journal* 507, at 513. The piece is perhaps best known for his wry observation that he aspired to start a self-critical legal studies movement – probably without much success (at 511).

[19] See, e.g., J. King, *The Doctrine of Odious Debt in International Law: A Restatement* (Cambridge: Cambridge University Press, 2016), demonstrating that some international rules require the help of domestic law in order to be enforced.

spaces), and all are valid and applicable in principle. Sometimes rules may point in the same direction, but the more interesting cases are where they do not. Thus, Mr. Kadi enjoyed certain rights under EU law (derived from both EU law and the human rights obligations of its member states), but a different set of rules emanating from the Security Council interfered with his enjoyment of these rights. In Italy, war crimes victims were thought to have certain rights against Germany as valid under Italian law, but as the International Court of Justice held, these were unenforceable against Germany under international law – something Italy's Constitutional Court found difficult to swallow. The defining elements for inter-legality to operate then are threefold: first, it must concern a variety of norms from different systems; second, these must all be valid within their own legal spheres; and third, they must in principle all be applicable to a particular set of facts. Hence, the state of affairs on the basis of which an elaboration of inter-legality has to develop involves a choice for the application of one set of rules over another, equally valid, set of rules.

This is all the more imperative given the difficulties involved in presenting such issues in neutral ways. Above, for instance, we referred to Mr. Kadi as enjoying rights under domestic and EU law, rights that were interfered with by the Security Council. We could just as easily have put it differently: under UN law, Mr. Kadi was obligated not to engage in specific activities; his rights under EU law and domestic law interfered with these obligations. The first rendition sides with human rights, the second with the UN and the maintenance of international peace and security. The point to note is that it is difficult to describe such situations with some precision and yet in neutral language: much of the language at our disposal is already evaluative,[20] and if that is the case, justice can only be served by an awareness of the partisan nature of the way we frame our issues – and therewith by inter-legality.

It is also useful to point out that inter-legality does not, in and of itself, clarify much about what others refer to as transnational law: it may be the case that there is law originating from, say, the Basel Committee, or that what some deem "soft law" is really hard law under a different name, but this is not something inter-legality addresses. It works, so to speak, on existing ontological foundations of law, but does not amend these as such. In other words, it speaks to contacts between legal orders or spaces, but does not itself decide what counts as a legal order. It aims to describe and perhaps explain legal relations,

20 See generally F. V. Kratochwil, *Rules, Norms, and Decisions: On the Conditions of Practical and Legal Reasoning in International Relations and Domestic Affairs* (Cambridge: Cambridge University Press, 1989).

not legal orders or systems or spaces. In this sense, its next of kin are the classic doctrines of monism and dualism.

Yet monism and dualism are no longer sufficient. For one thing, both doctrines were always premised on the thought that there were only two relevant legal spaces to consider: the international and the national. This is no longer tenable, with different legal orders in-between asserting a role: this applies to EU law, but also, quite separately, to the European public order established under the European Convention of Human Rights. And while Europe might be most pronounced here, the matter is not limited to Europe: one may discern an American public order based on the Inter-American Convention of Human Rights; UN missions in Africa are often intersected by regional organizations such as the African Union or the Economic Community of West African States (ECOWAS) – it is too simple these days to merely proclaim the relevance of the national and the international.

To this a second factor may be added: it is likewise too simple these days to invoke notions of normative hierarchy in order to decide which law should be applied to which set of circumstances. There are various reasons why this is so. First, it is increasingly being realized that facts rarely speak for themselves; instead, they require some kind of classification before they can meaningfully be discussed, and even then, our language is (as noted) often an impediment, in that neutral classifications are often out of reach. This classification is a human act, and thus a political act: hence, the so-called "politics of framing" assumes increasing relevance. The upshot of this is that the validity of a particular legal approach is only ever provisionally accepted: applying *this* norm to *these* facts is only accepted if the result is not too obnoxious. Should the result be obnoxious, then the legitimacy of the earlier decision dissipates, and it will be suggested that a different frame should have been applied. Thus, approaching the HIV/AIDS problematique as a matter of intellectual property law is not problematic per se, provided it results in a decent solution. If not, people will suggest it should have been approached as a health issue, or a human rights issue, or perhaps even a security issue.[21] This is a clear indication that the notion of inter-legality should get pride of place, precisely because alternative framing options are available. Concrete cases may present multiple substantive profiles and may fit different classifications, and thus cannot be decided mechanistically. What inter-legality eventually clarifies is that the interplay matters and should surface as such in legal arrangements, in legal assessments and in legal decision-making.

[21] The example is derived (with some liberties) from Fischer-Lescano and Teubner, *Regime-Kollisionen*.

Whereas in earlier days frames were by and large uncontested, this is no longer the case, and the contestability of the frame sets additional normative demands on the law. The legal solution must not only be technically competent (proper, solid application of intellectual property law to AIDS medication, to stick to the example), but also be considered normatively acceptable, for when other frames are available, the chosen frame must be able to convince on grounds of fairness or justice – lest it be considered a mere exercise of naked power.

Again, the *Kadi* case is a useful illustration. Technically, it would have been perfectly acceptable for the CJEU to declare the supremacy of the UN Charter and ignore human rights standards – in fact, the argument could be made that, technically, this would have been the most warranted solution, with the EU institutions simply implementing verbatim a Security Council resolution adopted in the fight against global terrorism – and if this results in human rights violations for the individuals blacklisted, then the onus is on the Council to get its act together, but not on the implementing entities to prevent implementation. Or so the argument could have gone.

And why it is no longer considered possible to simply apply notions of hierarchy and "damn the torpedoes" is a consequence of multiple factors. One factor can be identified as the well-known fragmentation of law beyond the state. Fragmentation, regardless of whether it is considered good or bad, suggests that there exists a rich variety of legal actors, authorities, and regimes that would grant voice and would promise the emancipation of the production of law from the presupposition of substantive coherence under a monist structure of international law. A further factor could be the geological pluralization of "layers"[22] of international law: the proliferation of a regulatory layer, the development of what is now named "global administrative law," and finally the unstoppable formation of a "community layer" and the rise of common public goods irreducible to the sheer bilateral interests of states. All of these expose a multiplication of the ideas concerning the raison d'être of law beyond the state: all these layers, including the conventional and original layer, pretend to represent the fundamental core – the key-vault – from which to understand and interpret the entire legal sphere beyond the states. But no layer can stand apart; they are not fossils but, instead, exist in dynamic interplay with each other.

Another factor itself deserving of separate appreciation is the inexorable rise of the individual, or humanity, as the "alpha and omega of international law,"

[22] J. H. H. Weiler, "The Geology of International Law – Governance, Democracy and Legitimacy," (2004) 64 *Zeitschrift für ausländisches öffentliches Recht und Völkerrecht* 547.

as it was recently been put.[23] What we mean by this is not the sterile position that says that the individual has become a subject of international law – this means very little in the absence of concrete rights and obligations. Instead, what is relevant is the realization that even if much international law is made by states to regulate relations between states, and even if much of this takes place within international organizations, nonetheless most of this international law ends up affecting individuals one way or another. Put differently, there are actually not that many substantive rules of international law that only apply to states in their international relations: there are the rules on diplomatic relations, and arguably rules on aggression and self-defense, but many rules of international law these days directly or indirectly, actually or potentially, affect individuals and legal persons. This is obviously the case with human rights law, refugee law, and the like, but applies equally to trade law, or investment law, or the law of the sea.

This has, arguably, always been the case, and it is possibly no coincidence that early observers of the first international organizations in the nineteenth century already captured glimpses of *Weltrecht* (or "global law") in entities such as the International Copyright Union.[24] Likewise, it is on reflection rather nonsensical to think of the work of the International Labor Organization as somehow unconnected to the rights of workers, or that the economic and social activities of the League of Nations would be limited to state relations only[25]: the interdependence of international and domestic law has remained hidden behind a layer of misguided international relations realism, and as so often, the lawyers have stopped thinking and simply embraced the realist assumptions.[26]

The upshot is that it is no longer considered acceptable when the law is applied in such a way as to negatively affect individuals. As Italy's Constitutional Court suggests, even the law on state immunity – traditionally the epitome of a state-centric international law – will come to affect individuals, and if that is the case, it should be interpreted on a less formal or procedural

[23] A. Peters, "Humanity as the Alpha and Omega of Sovereignty," (2009) 20 *European Journal of International Law* 513.

[24] See F. Meili, *Die internationalen Unionen über das Recht der Weltverkehrsanstalten und des geistigen Eigentums* (Leipzig: Duncker & Humblot, 1889).

[25] The impact of the International Labor Organization on domestic affairs is well sketched in G. F. Sinclair, *To Reform the World: International Organizations and the Making of Modern States* (Oxford: Oxford University Press, 2017).

[26] This is a recurring phenomenon: international lawyers have tended to be in awe of realists, for no other reason than that realists have tended to proclaim that they know that all is about power, and thus all should listen to them.

basis and in more comprehensive or systemic terms, accounting for those values of legal civilization that have come to imbue national constitutions as much as international law itself. Thus, the law must be applied with a sensitivity to the plight of those individuals.

In yet other words, it is not the case that the law opts for a solution based on formal hierarchy; nor even is it the case that it opts for a solution based on substantive hierarchy; instead, what one sees emerging is a contextual analysis of the facts of the case based on, one might say, the epistemological surfacing of the protection of the individual as a normative principle that not even international law now, as state legal orders, can ignore.[27] Or, to adopt the language of another legal sociologist, Gunther Teubner, it is the individual who has become the "constitutional irritant" of each and every legal order.[28]

That is why the answer to the question of justice in individual cases cannot any longer reduce itself within the prefixed parameters of hierarchy between normative systems. The well-known monist architecture of the legal world under international law, according to the Kelsenian design, was construed upon formal primacies and delegations of authority: such an edifice is challenged and can easily fall apart if "superior" norms are no longer superior by that fiat, but are to be validated on the basis of their substantive content and their respect for material principles and values. And when it comes to substantive principles in the extra-state realm, a final coherence of universally shared contents is still out of sight, while in many respects, substantive assessments require balancing and contextual analysis, being at odds with a priori authoritative supremacies.

It follows that our classic notions of monism and dualism are no longer particularly useful, a circumstance recognized by pluralists; intuitively, it is assumed that legal orders move from one to two to many: from monism to dualism to pluralism. Intriguingly, however, it may well be that this rests on a cognitive path dependency. Historically, at any rate, the sequence seems to have gone differently: the leading dualist, Heinrich von Triepel, posited his dualism well before[29] the leading theoretical monist (Hans Kelsen)

[27] Of course, this affects the narrative of international law as caring for states, while domestic law cares for individuals: see, e.g., G. Arangio Ruiz, "International Law and Interindividual Law," in J. Nijman and A. Nollkaemper (eds.), *New Perspectives on the Divide between National and International Law* (Oxford: Oxford University Press, 2007), 15.

[28] G. Teubner, *Constitutional Fragments: Societal Constitutionalism and Globalization* (Oxford: Oxford University Press, 2012).

[29] Triepel wrote his main work at the close of the nineteenth century, around the time Kelsen graduated from Vienna's gymnasium. See H. von Triepel, *Völkerrecht und Landesrecht* (Leipzig: Hirschfeld, 1899).

responded,[30] and it is often also conveniently forgotten that von Triepel presented his dualism not so much as a normative claim, but rather as an empirical claim. In his days, international law and domestic law were regarded (not always plausibly perhaps) as rarely meeting, dualism presented a convincing story, and it made sense to insist on the need to transform the commands of one legal order – the international – into commands recognized by the other – the domestic – insofar and to the extent that the subjects of the domestic order could directly be affected by the international order. Von Triepel himself held that such commands hardly existed, but acknowledged the possibility that the minority treaties, a recent phenomenon at the time he returned to the issue in the 1920s,[31] might grow into instruments of international law directly affecting domestic law – a position that would be strengthened a few years later by the analysis of a "Beamtenabkommen" by the Permanent Court of International Justice.[32]

In short, historically, the sequence was not "one, two, many," but rather counted backwards starting from two. The question is: What follows after "one?" We posit that what follows is not pluralism as commonly understood, but a different perspective on law: inter-legality. If classic Kelsenian monism posited the existence of a single legal order with different branches and with one of these – the international – being hierarchically superior as a matter of form,[33] our claim, in a nutshell, is that such hierarchical supremacy cannot be issued as a matter of form or pedigree, but has to be earned. In a world of inter-legality, courts will apply those rules that they deem most conducive to doing justice according to the legal premises available in the individual case. This will sometimes be a rule of international law, and sometimes it will be a rule from domestic law, or EU law, or any other appropriate legal order as may be identified. This may come to be a useful way of understanding what courts will do in cases where various conflicting commands may be present, and this volume contains our preliminary findings and attempts, with knowledgeable colleagues, to think things through.

A related point is this: the present volume is set up predominantly as explanatory theory. Admittedly, in legal matters, the descriptive and the

[30] Kelsen's monism was developed at some point in the 1910s, but is set out with clarity in H. Kelsen, *Principles of International Law* (New York: Rhinehart and Co., 1952).

[31] H. von Triepel, "Les Rapports entre le Droit Interne et le Droit International," (1923) 1 *Recueil des Cours* 75–121.

[32] *Jurisdiction of the Courts of Danzig*, advisory opinion, [1928] Publ. PCIJ Series B, no. 15.

[33] Kelsen's monism has been linked to his social-democratic cosmopolitanism in the splendid study by J. von Bernstorff, *Der Glaube an das universale Recht: Zur Völkerrechtstheorie Hans Kelsens und seiner Schüler* (Baden-Baden: Nomos, 2001).

normative are never strictly separate, and the same applies here: normative and explanatory uses of inter-legality may shade into each other. For instance, as normative theory, the current volume suggests that inter-legality is taken as the cognitive premise for the work of the interpreter. In taking inter-legality seriously, the interpreter should consider the variety of norms sourced in different systems that overlap in disciplining the case at hand: the solution for the case should obviously aim at avoiding injustice, and can begin to be seen as just if it accounts for the plurality of legal normativities actually interwoven in the case at hand and fairly considers through a comprehensive (as opposed to one-sided) perspective the countervailing normative claims involved.

This might lead to results that may sometimes be inconsistent with what a monist would expect, and may some other times be inconsistent with what "dualism" would require. If read through inter-legality lenses, what should be made to count is not how the dispute concerning the primacy between legal orders has ended, but how the normative claims issued by both of them have been valued and accounted for, making the most of them as a normative contribution to decide the case. From such a different point of view, resistance to international law imperatives may well be accepted, provided that on balance all things have been considered.[34] The CJEU "resistance" vis-à-vis international law in the *Kadi* case was deemed a victory for justice and human rights, but at the same time was viewed as undermining the authority of international law.[35] Yet achieving a victory of human rights does not, in and of itself, legitimize the undermining of international law. Taking a dualist attitude, the reasoning of the Court worked through a separation line between the two orders; it conjured up a world without international law, without the UN, and was accordingly in no position to explain, justify, or legitimize its prioritization of human rights over international law. The point here is not – emphatically not – that its outcome was somehow wrong; it was rather the process of identifying the relevant circumstances and the process of reasoning that remained incomplete. After all, particular outcomes should be clarified

[34] Tantalizingly, the CJEU has in several cases seen fit to set aside international law under reference to EU law offering a higher level of protection to individuals. The CJEU may have many motives for doing so, and it cannot categorically be excluded that one of them is a desire to do justice in individual cases. For an overview, see J. Klabbers, "The Reception of International Law in the EU Legal Order," in R. Schütze and T. Tridimas (eds.), *Oxford Principles of European Union Law. Volume I: The European Union Legal Order* (Oxford: Oxford University Press, 2018), 1208.

[35] G. de Búrca, "The European Court of Justice and the International Legal Order after *Kadi*'," (2010) 51 *Harvard International Law Journal* 1.

and justified in light of the law applicable to the case on the basis of understanding and working through the inter-legality situation at hand.

4 THE ESSAYS IN THIS VOLUME

The contributions to this volume directly address inter-legality and are committed to making sense of legal realities from such a perspective. They offer rereadings of known states of affairs by focusing on the legal consequences of inter-legality, enhancing the interconnections, and aiming to provide a more comprehensive standpoint from whence to understand contemporary law. This, of course, entails a number of theoretical assessments as well. Insofar as inter-legality reflects the current transformations of law, it prompts innovative research on the received categories that might hinder both the understanding of contemporary legal problems and the search for new and more credible solutions.

Accordingly, Part 1 of this volume starts by opening up the field and by suggesting some background reflections concerning fundamental issues. Gianluigi Palombella examines a variety of fundamental ideas and organizations of legality: diverse structures, patterns, or "formats" of legality whose birth is originally placed in different historical times. "Law as Esprit," jus gentium, medieval law, and global administrative law are chosen as relevant to explain resilient features encountered in the present transformations of contemporary law. At the root of our inter-legality challenge lies the realization that we seem to live in each and all of such different formats at the same time and that the continuous reshuffling of their concurrent or competing rationales generates complexity, contradictions, and theoretical obstacles, as well as a new potential whose understanding requires that we overcome some preconceptions mostly attuned to each of those formats separately, but unfit to make sense of, and cope with, their enmeshing and interplay.

Inevitably, the attitudes toward law, scholarly apprehension, and especially judicial tasks in such a transformed horizon involve matters invoking our practical and theoretical responsibility. Friedrich Kratochwil uses the concept of responsibility by explicating its contextual character, enhancing the limits of the idea of the self-sufficiency of law to solve its own hurdles and to face the complexity of the social world. As he maintains, the inter-legality perspective promises to recollect the multiple blind spots that every perspective creates and illuminates law critically, reflecting on the diverse practices it is made of instead of elaborating on some systemic, a priori model of it. Like thinking, responsibility appears to entail a constant process of overcoming one-sided angles.

Sanne Taekema, in the fourth chapter, concentrates on the other pillar of our legal discourse: that is, the legal order and its picture as a closed system. Taekema suggests that plurality and tensions are due to and can best be seen by an interactional view on law, typically described in the work of Lon Fuller. The challenge that inter-legality presents, though, does not stem from the disconnection of law from the order it requires, but lies in integrating the frames of the systemic order with interactional practice as the blueprint of law.

The second part of the book is devoted to inquiries into relevant fields, viewed in the light of the inter-legality structures that they can display, and thereby presented under new lenses. In this vein, Samantha Besson engages with one of the most sensitive issues for inter-legality discourse: that is, jurisdiction. After reconstructing its lineages and fundamental features and by defending its value and its resilient strength, Besson argues for a reconceptualization of jurisdiction as an asset for international law and international intercourse based on the recognition of the equality of states and individuals amid the increasing and pervasive pluralization of legal authorities.

Dimitry Kochenov examines the unavoidable interconnectedness of legalities through an analysis of the global rise of inter-citizenship(s), a non-Westphalian notion spreading through interterritorial extensions of rights (like work rights or residence rights) outside the countries granting the citizen status.

Another, most outstanding case in point relates to trade and the evolution of the World Trade Organization (WTO). Antonello Tancredi highlights the inherent relevance of the trade sector to the problems of inter-legality and focuses upon the relations between the WTO and its members, stressing the lack of direct effect on one side, and on the other the interaction between the WTO and the "outer" international law system, as well as the jurisdiction of the WTO dispute settlement bodies and those of other international and regional tribunals.

A further, and certainly not minor field, considered by Laura Pineschi, concerns the protection of global common goods, namely through the instance of marine ecosystems, where the inter-legality state of affairs is explored in areas beyond national jurisdictions. Here, the fragmentation of regulatory regimes and the bilateral scheme of treaty-based arrangements, along with the implausibility of hierarchically ordered solutions, show the need for integrating practices on behalf of both legislative authorities and judicial reasoning.

Regarding such challenges, Panos Koutrakos re-enmeshes the general problem, itself jurisdiction-related, into the legal challenges raised by inter-legality in the very area of EU law, instantiating its complex interplay with international investment law. Relevant issues here include the exclusive jurisdiction of the CJEU, the primacy of EU law, and the role of domestic courts.

Exploring cases connected to a politically charged environment where investment arbitration is viewed by many with skepticism, Koutrakos draws on the practice of EU institutions in order to better conceptualize the management of inter-legality issues in such areas and reflects upon different approaches to these inter-legality issues: conflict, integration, and harmonious coexistence.

Andras Sajó and Sergio Giuliano address inter-legality by stressing the consequences of its enduring persistence in the realm of human rights. For the enterprise of adjudication, inter-legality is still a problem, not a solution: in order to avoid the risk of lowering human rights standards because of overdue deference to states' margins of appreciation, a meta-theory applicable to arranging the fragments should avoid the sheer logics of compromise, and "vigilant actors" (judges, scholars, citizens) should better defend the aspirations of liberal (multilevel) constitutionalism vis-à-vis the danger of the populist appeal to majoritarian democracy.

The final chapter of the second part of this volume is by Alberto di Martino and covers a further and increasingly relevant side of inter-legality. di Martino discusses inter-legality's recurrent appearance in criminal law, the branch of law most inherently conceived of as linked to sovereignty. di Martino revisits criminal law in the new context that he sees as being generated by transboundary criminality and the internationalization of penal choices, and he pays attention to the interplay between supranational orders and domestic provisions and the resulting interfacial role of judges. At the forefront of our concerns, one registers the revision of the principle of (national) legality, the novel inter-legal definition of the power to coerce and punish: all are emerging issues whose import for inter-legality and criminal law deserve attentive reflection.

The third and last part of the book represents the challenge of inter-legality in a different manner. It neither prepares and plows its background (the first part) nor samples and displays its mounting relevance through field inquiries (the second part), but aims to fine-tune our views on law in the transformed occurrences. Edoardo Chiti delineates how administrative law – in the wider global sense – restructures the interactions between the processes of administrative implementation of its own first-level measures and the implementing processes of other legal orders through joint responsibility, coordination of responsibilities, or conflict of responsibilities, eventually suggesting inter-legality as being based on the preservation and promotion of plurality and as an alternative both to the representation of the world legal space through traditional public international law and to the main understandings elaborated by global administrative law scholarship.

Poul F. Kjaer, while focusing on contemporary global governance law (defined by him as a post-imperial type of law that grew out of imperial law), recommends that lawyers aim to overcome a theoretical–conceptual deficit due either to an understanding of law as unitary norms with a global reach or, alternatively, due to radically pluralist perspectives dismissing the existence of unitary global legal norms. Inter-Legality, seen also in terms of inter-contextuality, however, opens the door for a third position through an understanding of global law as a decentered "in-between worlds" phenomenon constituting a "third space" characterized by material interconnectedness between different legally structured societal contexts.

Yuval Shany brings the challenge of inter-legality into international relations and discourses managed through courts and tribunals. Such courts and tribunals serve as inter-legality hubs: reconciling situations of inter-legality requires them to construct normative and institutional "bridges" across different regulatory frameworks – in other words, to engage at different levels with external legal orders and external institutions. However, until now, the engagement of international courts and tribunals with the concept of inter-legality has often been superficial, and the institutional configuration of international courts exacerbates some of the normative and practical challenges of inter-legality.

That leads us to the chapter by Jan Klabbers, which focuses on judging and inter-legality (i.e., on situations where technical competence in only one of the overlapping legal orders is no longer sufficient). Inter-Legality demands a receptiveness to and an understanding of rules across jurisdictions, and the application of rules and principles stemming from other legal systems, if judges have to do justice in individual cases. For Klabbers, to concentrate on the very demands stemming from inter-legality implies discussing the qualities of a virtuous judge. He develops a perspective largely on the basis of virtue ethics and suggests that it needs to be carefully tailored to the inter-legality context, since the point is not merely that the judge should uphold the law; it is also a question of how best to do so, and what doing so means in different circumstances.

Finally, Gianluigi Palombella concludes the book by presenting a general manifesto, intended as a full-fledged presentation of inter-legality, addressing normative problems as well. It starts by asking whether in conflicting and overlapping inter-legality occurrences, hardly arbitrated by hierarchy, the system-based paradigms are still capable of reflecting the present complexity and the material interconnectedness affecting the nature and functioning of legality. Inter-Legality entails a change in the epistemic perspective on law and presents a new scenario for delivering justice. While discussing milestone cases, Palombella designs a theoretical frame on the law, not only avoiding the monist/dualist alternatives, but also offering an appreciation and relocation of the achievements of legal pluralism. Inter-Legality, he concludes, reaches beyond both.

PART I

Opening the Field

2

"Formats" of Law and Their Intertwining

GIANLUIGI PALOMBELLA

1 INTRODUCING THE ISSUE

In what follows, the hypothesis is described that the present circumstances of inter-legality, at their very roots, are better understood as the simultaneous surfacing of diverse structures, patterns, or "formats" of legality whose birth is originally placed in different historical times. Our received ideas about law often reflect concrete organizations and features of legality whose development dates back to the periods of their more prominent life. One thousand years of medieval legality seemed to have been largely superseded by a state-based law paradigm, and both implied a characterization of law barely compatible with each other. The constant invocation of *ius gentium* has crossed and flanked the idea of legality, for centuries competing against law as a situated, territorial production, as well as against a varied overlapping of multiple regimes and medieval orders. The contemporary scene is hosting the overwhelming development of what has been called global administrative law (GAL), conceived itself as a flat layer of horizontal law crossing frontiers and organizing diverse fields of human action on a supranational scale. The state-based format of law, once pivotal in controlling the "external" world through inter-state law or international law, is at pains to make for a general unity capable of subsuming the proliferation of regulatory and normative regimes, often far from states' logic of international law and issuing non-treaty law, under a common label that does not exist. Among the failures of the recurrent attempts at the constitutionalization of international law is in fact the desire to keep the new GAL format within the narrower boundaries of inter-state law, which in truth had a different "format," raison d'être, and structure. In a sense, the constitutionalization of the legal world, be it as it may, underestimates, among the rest, the importance of differences. In our real world, the vertical overlapping of legalities, reluctant to hierarchy, the horizontal dissemination of juris-generative authorities exceeding and piercing the states, the awareness of a common layer and language of law belonging to all systems and peoples, and the repeated and relentless interaction among these complex factors can better be understood as the simultaneous recirculation of formats of law that bear different ideal-type logics and natures, and resurface to contaminate each other, regardless of their date of origin, at a time when it is vain to try and impose one single paradigm. The understanding of inter-legality can thus be better supported by the understanding of the *formats* of law that have become ideal-type components: through them, inter-legality makes sense as inter-formats as well.

The following pages are modestly devoted to bringing to the fore and describing in more detail some characters belonging to different legalities and times and grouping them as "formats." Law as esprit, *ius gentium*, medieval law, and GAL are chosen as relevant to explaining resilient features encountered in the present transformations of contemporary law. Each shall be given a dedicated – albeit brief – overview. Those formats' identities can be taken as a memorandum, a guide that may be of help in facing and interpreting the present inter-legality, as well as a consequence of such formats' interweaving.

2 LAW AS ESPRIT

For the sake of reconnaissance, one is brought to a preliminary insight into ideas of law that would otherwise be overlooked from a standard legal theory perspective. Law can be seen through the "volume" (as the property of geometric figures bearing depth; that is, the third dimension) that it occupies, and one can think of different "formats," despite their fabric being the same, formally made of norms.

Thus, one encounters "*l'esprit des lois*," for instance. The general premise appears to be that the legal world reflects and reshapes idiosyncratic combinations of outward simple elements. Starting from a huge amount of data and experience among diverse peoples, Montesquieu's enquiry follows the method of close observation of the lives of several countries. Power, commerce, laws and education, climate and territory, social conditions and religion, and common sentiments are necessary to understand how any form of government works – its corruption, survival, or flourishing. Governmental typologies themselves are drawn on qualitative criteria (not the Aristotelian divide). Every polity shows a "nature" and a "principle."[1] Montesquieu

[1] "There is this difference between the nature and principle of government, that the former is that by which it is constituted, the latter that by which it is made to act. One is its particular structure, and the other the human passions which set it in motion." Montesquieu, *The Spirit*

pointed to the "principles" that "set in motion" and make a structure to "act." Passions (not private, but public) toward common "institutions" are objective components of the polity.[2]

Laws themselves are "relations" that connect social, cultural, and geographical factors, commerce and economy, and manners and costumes, as much as the sound (or unsound) role played by political rule. "Relations" involve diverse contextual vectors and tensions among coexisting factors. In the reign of diversity, law both reflects and redetermines, as a factor among others, a fabric of interdependence and meanings, embedded in the "nature of things";[3] and the general "*esprit des lois*" takes shape as such a representation of the "whole," a rationale that would be missed should outward factors be overlooked.[4] Not a naturalist, and I believe not a determinist, Montesquieu explains in this sense the "volume" of law as a situated notion: not simply its logic, nor its ultimate connection and dependence upon nature or will. One can take this pattern to fairly reflect some part of our received ideas on law – let us call it "esprit" or the "esprit" matrix of law.

As a consequence, laws are hardly detachable from what they are supposed to regulate: accordingly, "[A] thing is not just because it is the law, but it should be the law because it is just."[5] In a sense, this redetermines and reshapes the interplay between reason and law, at least because it assumes that it is not some abstract optimal reason to determine the things. At the same time, the notion of will loses its ultimate strength: it does simply take its place within a determined context (i.e., within a somewhat constraining tale that is made of many more factors and protagonists on the scene).

of Laws, Volume I (Cincinnati, OH: R. Clarke & Co., 1873, Nugent trans.), at 22. According to Montesquieu, virtue is necessary in a republic, honor in monarchies, and fear in despotism. I cannot deal here with further classifications and issues. One would be, for instance, the relevance of what Montesquieu calls the "object" (e.g., for England, the object was "liberty," requiring a mixed structure, belonging to monarchy, aristocracy, and democracy). Another could be the separation of functions in government, famously reflected upon by one of Madison's Federalist Papers, and his interpretation in terms of checks and balance, and so forth. See A. Hamilton, J. Madison and J. Jay, *The Federalist Papers* (New York: Bantam, 1982 [1788]), no. 47.

2 For popular governments essentially, and in part also for aristocracies (where moderation is asked of at least the "optimates"), virtue is the required principle, as a functional, objective element of the complex system: Montesquieu, *The Spirit of Laws*, at 22 ff.

3 Ibid., at XXXII.

4 This is suggested by E. Ehrlich, "Montesquieu and Sociological Jurisprudence," (1916) 26 *Harvard Law Review* 582, 589.

5 Montesquieu, *My Thoughts (Mes Pensées)* (Indianapolis, IN: Liberty Fund, 2012, Clark trans.), *Pensée* 460.

Tellingly, such a stance could only attract the criticism of the founding fathers of legal positivism. With the "imperativist" legal view of John Austin, laws concerning societies[6] cannot be those Montesquiean "relations." The positivism and the hubris of modernity sharply separate factual relations and natural connections from law, and *ius* simply equates with *iussum*, an unconstrained issue of command. For Montesquieu, by contrast, monarchic despots, for example, erroneously think of laws as their own will.[7] Political rule truly belongs as a part in a complex of factors. Thus, while it would prove unlikely that natural law (or deterministic elements) governs of itself, law is other than mere sovereign "will."

Famously, the great sociologist Eugen Ehrlich[8] understood the social and multifactorial embeddedness of law in Montesquieu as standing neither within naturalist views nor within command notions of law. And the importance of diversity is a recurrent Montesquiean caveat: the same rules do not always have the same effect, or the same spirit, the same motives – and sometimes, they might actually be not the same at all.

In conclusion, laws and "relations" have depth, and the geo-territorial idiosyncratic richness should be put to the forefront and prevent indulgency to "similarities" among polities, orders, governments, and peoples. For sure, it is true that with Montesquieu prejudices and political rule are sometimes more likely relevant causes than "climate or culture," that conquest and commerce alter those causes and promote change, that local diversities can coexist with wider or even universal features in legal systems.[9] However, this horizontal continuity, the universality of some shared rationales of law, if any, can only "come after" and cannot be used to prevent enquiries upon law's *depth*, connotations that must be studied in order to understand different answers to questions about what the law is, how it works, and what it does (and eventually why it does so).[10]

This "esprit" format of law is often seen as a precedent to the later-flourishing cultural or linguistic views of law,[11] opposing the Enlightenment

[6] J. Austin, *The Province of Jurisprudence Determined* (Cambridge: Cambridge University Press, 1995 [1832]), at 210.

[7] Montesquieu, *My Thoughts, Pensée* 670.

[8] Ehrlich was recognizing Montesquieu as a precursor of legal sociology, as well as the various limits of his scientific work: see esp. Ehrlich, "Montesquieu," at 583, 596–600.

[9] Robert Howse has advocated a more universalist Montesquieu in his "Montesquieu on Commerce, Conquest, War and Peace," (2006) 31 *Brooklyn Journal of International Law* 693.

[10] This squares with what was recalled at the outset: laws live close to that by which polities are "made to act."

[11] One might recall, for example, von Savigny and his Historical School, in the German tradition from G. W. F. Hegel to the idea of *Volksgeist*. The German private law code took one more century (1900) after the Code Napoleon (1804) to be enacted.

creed according to which the universal rationalistic codification model was to be extended as far as the French army and dismantling the "national" character of law.[12] Here, I take "esprit" as a comprehensive matrix, where will and reason (the pillars of the two ideologically conflicting constructions of "legality") along with outward ingredients of law, as well as political and institutional passions along with formal and material components, in some distinctive combination lead to the comprehension of the "difference" of the "wholes." Despite many components being equal, this matrix sheds a cautious light over the quick tracing of similarities and removal of diversities or disagreements.[13]

3 *IUS GENTIUM*

Admittedly, "esprit" seems to leave some gaps. One example is *ius gentium*. It is different: it makes sense, and is seen to make sense of what is *common* to many legal orders, to diverse peoples. From Roman ages, to Grotius, and to the contemporary legal comparative doctrines, its nature oscillates between reason, morality, and consent. Though it is sound in itself, the format "esprit" might divert us from a different aspect that inheres in the reality of law as well.

"Esprit" is challenged first when the ordinary coupling of people/territory decouples through "dynamic" phenomena, like migrations, and in general the abandonment by social groups of their territorial birth places: in brief, the detachment of thought, language, and practices from their traditional homeland.[14] Roman *ius praetorium* developed so as to cope expediently

[12] That was until the second half of the twentieth century: thereafter, the opposite project of the "inherent unity of law" started to be pursued. See R. Sacco, "Diversity and Uniformity in the Law," (2001) 49 *American Journal of Comparative Law* 171, 171–172; A. Gambaro, "Western Legal Tradition," in P. Newman (ed.), *The New Palgrave Dictionary of Economics and the Law* (London: Palgrave MacMillan, 1998).

[13] See P. Legrand, *Fragments on Law as Culture* (Deventer: Tjeenk Willink, 1999), 10 ff. See also R. Cotterrell, "Comparative Law and Legal Culture," in R. Zimmermann and M. Reimann (eds.), *Oxford Handbook of Comparative Law* (Oxford: Oxford University Press, 2008), 709. The alternative attitudes of scholars in comparative law and in legal sociology are typical, whether their explicative focus enhances invariable archetypes of law, the common denominators, or the "intangibles" that culturally support and distinguish a non-transplantable legal language (like the good faith concept exported toward English law from continental Europe by a EU directive and transformed into something of unpredictable meaning). See G. Teubner, "Legal Irritants: Good Faith in British Law or How Unifying Law Ends Up in New Divergencies," (1998) 61 *Modern Law Review* 11.

[14] I refrain here from the further (but too simplistic) argument about the migratory fluxes of our centuries or the denationalization of contemporary societies.

with the legal habits of non-"citizens" (*peregrini*) reaching Rome.[15] That was originally *ius gentium*: born out of a "political necessity" and less perfect than *ius civile*, it assumed, for Sir Henry Sumner Maine, a dignified status through the support of *aequitas*, being then equated with the law of nature, common to mankind.[16] But in the words of Cicero, it was deemed to be law of reason and of nature: "*Est enim unum jus, quo devincta est hominum societas et quod lex constituit una. Quae lex est recta ratio imperandi atque prohibendi.*"[17]

Out of the ambiguous limbo, between reason, positivity, and nature, with Gaius *ius gentium* referred to the laws that are present in diverse societies and are held to be common to humanity (or vice versa).[18] Far later, Grotius clearly paralleled it with *ius civile commune* or "*non scriptum*": "when many at different times, and in different places, affirm the same thing as certain, that ought to be referred to a universal cause; and this cause ... must be either a correct conclusion drawn from the principles of nature, or common consent. The former points to the law of nature, the latter, to the law of nations."[19]

The main strand of *ius gentium* was later mainly referred to as underlying inter-state law, and also transnational commercial intercourses. In both senses, it was also present in the writings of Immanuel Kant.[20] Again, the father of the

[15] Pomponius, *Digest*, Liber singulari enchiridia (D. 1.2.2.28), English edition available at https://droitromain.univ-grenoble-alpes.fr/Anglica/D1_Scott.htm#XIV. See also G. Sherman, "*Jus Gentium* and International Law," (1918) 12 *American Journal of International Law* 56; G. Trnavci, "The Meaning and Scope of the Law of Nations in the Context of the Alien Tort Claims Act and International Law," (2005) 26 *University of Pennsylvania Journal of International Economic Law* 193, 199–222, and H. S. Maine, *Ancient Law* (Project Gutenberg 2007 [1917]) 29 ff., 36 ff.

[16] Maine writes: "Whenever a particular usage was seen to be practised by a large number of separate races in common it was set down as part of the Law common to all Nations, or *Jus Gentium*" (*Ancient Law*, supra note 15, at 29). Cfr. also Sherman, "*Jus Gentium* and International Law," supra note 15.

[17] Cicero, *De Legibus*, I, xv, 42, available at www.thelatinlibrary.com/cicero/leg1.shtml#15.

[18] Such a meaning can be traced back to Gaius, *Institutiones*, I, 1: "*Omnes populi qui legibus et moribus reguntur partim suo proprio, partim communi omnium hominum iure utuntur; nam quod quisque populus ipse sibi ius constituit, id ipsius proprium est vocaturque ius civile, quasi ius proprium civitatis; quod vero naturalis ratio inter omnes homines constituit, id apud omnes populos peraeque custoditur vocaturque ius gentium, quasi quo iure omnes gentes utuntur.*" Gaius, *Institutiones* (London: John W. Parker & Son, 2nd edn. 1859, C. Sanders ed.).

[19] Grotius continues: "The distinction between these kinds of law is not to be drawn from the testimonies themselves (for writers everywhere confuse the terms law of nature and law of nations), but from the character of the matter. For whatever cannot be deduced from certain principles by a sure process of reasoning, and yet is clearly observed everywhere, must have its origin in the free will of man." See Grotius, *The Law of War and Peace* (New York: Oceana 1964 [1625], Kelsey ed.), 23–24.

[20] For example, I. Kant, "To Perpetual Peace: A Philosophical Sketch," in I. Kant, *Perpetual Peace and Other Essays* (Indianapolis, IN: Hacket, 1982 [1795], T. Humphrey trans. 1983), 107.

positivist law as will returned *ius gentium* to *nature*: for Austin, indeed, universal "*leges et mores*" are other than positive law ("distinguished from those peculiar to a particular nation"). Law of nature indicates "dictates of utility" that "are always and everywhere the same," and "hardly admit of mistake": "there are legal or moral rules that are nearly or quite universal, and the expediency of which must be seen by merely natural reason, or by reason without the lights of extensive experience and observation."[21]

By assuming that *ius gentium* exposes "common answers to common problems" throughout various legal systems,[22] Jeremy Waldron theorizes a *ius gentium* directly sustained by a natural and moral quality, endowed with a "scientific" justification, cognizable through reason. As a concession to positivist perspectives, he requires that such a quality be acknowledged by some large consent. However, one can find such a mixed conclusion slightly ambiguous: what is the truth value of *ius gentium* founded on? Is it founded on reason or on consensus? On the one hand, it is to be recognized through a kind of a posteriori methodology (truths are inferred from *id quod plerumque accidit* – that is, from that which happens in most places – and depends accordingly on a consensus-based pattern). It sits firstly on the premise that a large diffusion (even if not majoritarian) is needed. On the other hand, Waldron requires that nonetheless it should be accompanied by a moral (supplementary) soundness.[23] Accordingly, a "scientific" measure of reason is essentially required: Waldron insists that here is a *repository of legal science* that it would be obtuse to ignore,[24] unless one thinks of law as "will" instead of "reason" (in a "scientific spirit").[25]

Evidently, *ius gentium* navigates between the two mythological monsters, Scylla and Charibdis. However, if law is reason (scientific), why not dream of a "unitary system of law"? Tellingly, James Gordley had maintained himself that a domestic lawyer should not ignore what foreign lawyers say, no more

21 Austin, *Jurisprudence Determined*, at 210. It is not displacing law, though: see ibid., 151–152.

22 J. Waldron, "Foreign Law and the Modern *Jus Gentium*," (2005) 119 *Harvard Law Review* 129, at 133: "But I shall use the Latin phrase '*ius gentium*' to refer to the law of nations in the more comprehensive sense – a body of law purporting to represent what various domestic legal systems share in the way of common answers to common problems."

23 J. Waldron, "Ius Gentium: A Defense of Gentili's Equation of the Law of Nations and the Law of Nature," *Public Law and Legal Theory Research Papers Series*, 08/34, at 9.

24 Waldron, "Foreign Law," 144. Moreover, we should look at countries whose consensus we would share as epistemic authorities, and at the same time selecting their solutions on the basis of our sense of the "right," in a "reflective equilibrium."

25 Ibid., 145.

"than a physicist should ignore a German or an Italian."[26] Thus, as a consequence of the "scientific" character of law, he worked – consistently – on the view that there is *one* legal system precisely as there is only *one* physical system.

Indeed, *ius gentium* should not be taken to lead us so far. Commonalities and diversities coexist, and law is partly reason, and partly not. *Ius gentium*'s pedigree simply provides for a format where "commonalities" are put to the forefront: we can learn from similarities, project transplants, and support our choices by reference to their popularity in different systems, criticize or limit their strength and plead for their reform, or adopt some fundamental normative ideas as criteria of the validity of legal norms, as in international law.[27] Nonetheless, *ius gentium*, as resilient as it is, may not be equated with the structure and contents of a legal order in itself. Conflating the two things would mean to advocate a global system of law, thereby overlooking the connection between law and situated social communities.

4 MEDIEVALISM: LEARNING FROM A FALSE FRIEND

One might consider that medievalism is less a format of a legal order than a complex geography of orders, where plurality and conflicts, duplications, and fragmentations flourish. This is only partially true. Medievalism has become the template of a complex legal universe in which the multiplicity of orders is managed through a series of peculiar paths ranging from case-centered interpretation of law to *aequitas* and a concrete focus upon justice. An elaboration of practical legal wisdom replaces abstract hierarchies and prevents one single legal order from assuming the ultimate say.

It was maintained by Hedley Bull[28] that the extra-states environment resembles a medieval structure, being made of a number of discrete worlds. The analogy is often referred to in explaining the European legal order. However, the apparently multileveled European legality achieved legal integration

[26] J. Gordley, "Is Comparative Law a Distinct Discipline?" (1998) 46 *American Journal of Comparative Law* 607, 611.

[27] A. Verdross, "*Jus Dispositivum* and *Jus Cogens* in International Law," (1966) 60 *American Journal of International Law* 55. The reference is to art. 53 of the Vienna Convention on the Law of Treaties ("A treaty is void if, at the time of its conclusion, it conflicts with a peremptory norm of general international law. For the purposes of the present Convention, a peremptory norm of general international law is a norm accepted and recognized by the international community of States as a whole as a norm from which no derogation is permitted and which can be modified only by a subsequent norm of general international law having the same character" (and for the *superveniens jus cogens*, see art. 64).

[28] H. Bull, *The Anarchical Society* (Basingstoke: Palgrave, 1977), 254–265.

through one "autonomous legal order"[29] and several institutional and political infrastructures. The analogy seems to perhaps better fit a larger realm (i.e., the not yet integrated array of orders including national, subnational, international, supranational, or global regimes and legalities on the world setting). Here, though, instead of providing an ultimate unifying paradigm, medievalism can be a sound example of the closest thing to a legal multiverse not unified under the overarching pivotal template of the state. A legal world that lasted a thousand years (after the decay of the Roman Empire) might at least prove to be a heuristic tool for us to approach the idea of a vague universality in conjunction with the plurality of orders, particularism, localism, and multilevel loyalties. The fundamental ordering instrument for it is held to be law. While the modern political law, as *instrumentum regni*, doesn't belong in the medieval institutions and mind-set,[30] law develops to regulate horizontal relations among circles and groups, statuses, private powers, and individuals: social practices are disciplined through Roman law as much as the merchant law that do not concern monarchs, local sovereigns, princes, and cities/municipalities.[31] The law is produced as a self-driven societal practice, given the relative indifference to it of the constituted power.

Medieval law interweaves *iura propria* and *ius commune*, local law and the universalized law elaborated on for centuries by jurists and scientists on the basis of the Roman law and canon law, merchant law, and the like.[32] The unifying substratum is "*aequitas*"[33]: "*leges*" are an authoritative recognition of a preexisting "*convenientia rerum*" and are justified by things in themselves.[34] Of course, the fragmented plurality of laws in the very background is premised on the metaphysic presupposition – the Augustinian and

[29] See Case 26/62, *Van Gend en Loos*, ECLI:EU:C:1963:1 and Case 6/64, *Costa v ENEL.*, ECLI:EU:C:1964:66, where the European Court of Justice (now Court of Justice of the European Union) stated: "By contrast with ordinary international treaties the EEC Treaty has created its own legal system which, on the entry into force of the Treaty, became an integral part of the legal systems of the Member States and which their courts are bound to apply."

[30] P. Grossi, *L'Ordine Giuridico Medievale* (Bari: Laterza, 2000), 31.

[31] The law made by the sovereigns was mainly organizational, drawing borders (e.g., vis-à-vis the ecclesiastical power), or meant to self-describe power's prerogatives: ibid., 50

[32] Ibid., 54.

[33] Ibid., 177; also E. Cortese, *La Norma Giuridica. Spunti Teorici nel Diritto Comune Classico* (Milan: Giuffrè, 1962), 295.

[34] *Reicentrism* here means the complex factual mixture of social meanings relevant to the legal assessment of the concrete situation: things in themselves, in other words, were logically prior to the *regula juris*, considered as a further distillation of concrete knowledge.

Thomistic idea – of some predefined universal order: nothing is in itself unless it is part of a universe ordered in the shape of God.[35]

Importantly, the many centuries generated the need for adaptation and change, for reinterpretation of the past: this pivotal role was played by legal science.[36] The relatively minor role of political power is paired with the prevailing of some "juridical civilization." The *corpus iuris* of Justinian was revived through centuries by relying upon the undisputed authority of *sapientia iuris*: the power of bridging universal principles and changing realities is called by the word "*interpretatio*."[37] Science and interpretation, as in the words of Bartolo da Sassoferrato, bear the highest task of ordering the world: from *aequitas* and through legal expertise and competence, the legal scientist finds an answer that he might (simply even ex post) trace back to the relevant "texts" (i.e., those *corpus iuris* passages that could better fit). While there is no *hierarchical* rule and no unique (immanent) single order, things "hold" due to confidence in the legal medium, which allows for open, interconnecting relations: in given circumstances, "spontaneous" law or scholarly law prevail over the rules of higher orders, despite their alleged (and somewhat illusory) universality.

While resisting any mirroring of the global contemporary structures of law, we learn from medievalism about the contingent nature of the modern state as a unifying institution and of the hierarchical ideologies about law and the *will-based* political culture supporting it. All in all, as Paolo Grossi has shown, the medieval setting represents a social environment ordered by law, not by politics (in the modern and contemporary sense of the word).[38]

[35] Within it, the prince pursues the common good. Aquinas, *Quaestiones*, 90, art. 1 e ff.; *Quaestiones*, 91 ff., available at www.corpusthomisticum.org/sth2090.html.

[36] But it is not that simple. Thomas's magister, Albert the Great (Albertus Magnus), taught that lex is a composite production. Since law has an autonomous status beyond political power and is a constraint against holders of power, in the reality of common life it depends on the cooperation of three actors: the people for whose welfare it is given; the legal scholar and master – the jurist – who writes it down and takes care of its technically appropriate form; and the prince whose authority and sanction are required as supporting it. Albertus Magnus, "De Bono," Tract. V, *De Justitia*, q. II – *De Legibus*; art. I – *quid sit lex*, available at www.albertus-magnus-online.de.

[37] It was in fact meant to be the challenging endeavor of dealing with an increasingly complex reality by a primarily creative activity that neither the princes, uninterested in the everyday business of societal intercourse, nor the often unlearned custom alone could bear and afford. For interpretation, see the *Glossa Magna* (i.e., the self-understanding of the interpreter's activity): "*interpretor, idest corrigo ... Item verbun apertium esprimo ... item arrogo, item prorogo, sed econtra corrigo, idest addo*" (*Glossa, Corpus Juris*) – as referred to in Grossi, *L'Ordine Giuridico Medievale*, at 165.

[38] Grossi, *L'Ordine Giuridico Medievale*.

After Grotius's "*etiamsi daremus non esse Deum*," and the Kantian connection of law to intellectual legislation, we seem to have lost most of the paths that made for the legal features of medieval times. This is the price of modernity. Having considered "esprit," "*ius gentium*," and medievalism, however, we are better prepared to admit also of legal perspectives that do not necessarily start from the cognitive political and organizational angle of the state.

5 BETWEEN INTERNATIONAL AND GLOBAL (AND ADMINISTRATIVE) LAW

The three formats of law in the previous sections belong to the world as we have known it for centuries. The world is still inhabited by the stable law of our communities (and states), with recurrent general constants. The format "esprit" has features that are large enough to also embrace the modern state-based political and social units. States have been powerful producers of an increasing amount of inter-nations or *inter gentes* law. Often, the main customary or generally recognized principles are here also deemed to belong, in this sense, to all, as *ius gentium*. Nonetheless, some other law has been generated.

To get into this matter, metaphors can be illuminating. The metaphor of international law as a progressive formation, in vertical cross-section, of "geological" layers has revealed that the flat view from the surface would miss the actual complexity. Joseph Weiler[39] has looked at how the layers developed and how conventional law, community law, and regulatory law have consecutively enriched the significance and spectrum of international law. The metaphor holds together parts that would be otherwise divergent and meant to embody different logics, natures, and fundamental rules. The suggestion is that we cannot make sense of the same thing unless through the layers of which it still consists; that is, which its "consistency" is made of. The untold part here is that those layers are bound to interact.

Other views have a different dynamic concern: they mainly see one of the layers above as explaining the others, revealing the real fulcrum, the governing principle. The *clavis universalis* is rather elusive, though: does the "human dimension,"[40] the development of a *super partes* law (in the community

[39] J. H. H. Weiler, "The Geology of International Law. Governance, Democracy and Legitimacy," (2004) 64 *Zeitschrift für ausländisches öffentliches Recht und Völkerrecht* 547.

[40] A. Cassese, *The Human Dimension of International Law: Selected Papers* (Oxford: Oxford University Press, 2008).

layer), ultimately explain present international Law? Or does the holding of the Masters of the Treaties, the conventional nature, still control the fundamental generative root of international law? And why not consider as a new fundament the further engine of regulatory and administrative rulemaking, one that is spreading through a large array of entities endowed (or self-endowed) with massive jurisgenerative power?

One can say that the progressive transformation of old concepts toward the meta-rule of "humanity" clarifies the trends and the hierarchy of "contents" and redefines sovereignty[41] or perhaps trade law.[42] On the other hand, from the "regulative" layer, even stronger claims are raised. It interconnects, horizontally and vertically, traditional and new entities developing rulemaking and administration in all fields of peoples' and individuals' lives (from human rights to commercial standards, from sport agencies to forest conservation, from environment to agriculture, form cultural heritage to energy, trade, and security). Accordingly, it pretends to have changed the light that can make real things visible. Its processes are inexplicable through the lens of the conventional layer, and therefore they are sampling not the traditional *inter gentes*, but rather a clearly different supranational and transnational global law. This is a paradigm shift for one general reason at least: that what was a layer of the same whole (called "international law") becomes the general frame for the true representation of the transformed nature of the law beyond the state. This is a prescriptive assumption, though, and as such it exceeds the descriptive task of this chapter. As things stand, the idea of a unique, integrative, global administrative regulatory law legitimately exposes a factual format of legality that is spreading in the current circumstances of the globalization of law. It does not seem, though, to replace anything prior to

[41] A. Peters, "Humanity as the A and Ω of Sovereignty," (2009) 20 *European Journal of International Law* 513. See also R. Teitel, *Humanity's Law* (Oxford: Oxford University Press, 2011).

[42] This last issue lends itself to ambiguity as to the role of human rights law. I agree with Robert Howse: "Instead of international human rights law enhancing the purported function of WTO legal norms as protections for private economic actors against the activist state, consideration of human rights implies flexibility under WTO law for the state to take positive action to protect individuals and communities against the excesses of economic globalization. For example, if states are fully to discharge their obligations with respect to the right to food or the right to health under the CESC, they may need to rely on various exceptions or safeguards provisions in WTO treaties. Interpreting such treaties in light of the human rights obligations in question would help to ensure that the exceptions or limitations provisions in question allow states the policy space to fulfill these obligations." See R. Howse, "Human Rights, International Economic Law and 'Constitutional Justice': A Reply by Robert Howse to Ernst-Ulrich Petersmann's Article in EJIL Vol 19:4," *EJILTalk!*, 9 December 2008.

it, up to the point of concealing under its predetermined coherence the resilience of other formats of law.[43] Such a kind of global law[44] escapes the coordinates of "situated" system-related practices, and its full-fledged profile now mirrors an unearthed template, where self-supporting law and regulation develop outside the remit of the will of states.

In a new regulative–administrative[45] dimension, a de-territorialized law emerges: if some earlier *ius gentium* was shaped by the Roman praetor to treat individual noncitizens who were far away from their homeland, here the point is not about the law for migrating and deracinated peoples, but about deracinated law: bodies of specialized regimes' law inhere in no location, but reach distant individuals, piercing the veil of states and the borders and shelters of social communities. Medievalism would not fit either: the paradigm of a global administrative regulatory format of law flattens the variety of legal orders and their differences because it develops as a flat body of regulatory law depending on a variety of horizontally ordered sources. For some it can still be included within a revised international law sphere, whence it has taken partly its start. But the point is that it alters the distinction between domestic and international law and the ultimate role of the latter, and gradually undermines sovereign equality among states.[46]

Specialized regimes' imperatives appear often to eventually detach from the root of international law, or to be barely explicable by its legal chain:

> Instead of neatly separated levels of regulation (private, local, national, interstate), a congeries of different actors and different layers together form a variegate "administrative space" that includes international institutions and transnational networks, as well as domestic administrative bodies that operate within international regime or cause transboundary regulatory effects ... [and private, public, domestic, and international] transnational networks of rule-generators, interpreters and appliers cause such strict barriers to break down. This global administrative space is increasingly occupied by

[43] See, e.g., Chapter 12.

[44] The expression is used often today, and has been invoked as a comprehensive label in the title of the book by S. Cassese, *Il Diritto Globale* (Turin: Einaudi, 2009).

[45] B. Kingsbury, "The Concept of 'Law' in Global Administrative Law," (2009) 20 *European Journal of International Law* 23, 25: "Global administrative law is emerging as the evolving regulatory structures are each confronted with demands for transparency, consultation, participation, reasoned decisions and review mechanisms to promote accountability. These demands, and responses to them, are increasingly framed in terms that have a common normative character, specifically an administrative law character."

[46] See B. Kingsbury and N. Krisch, "Introduction: Global Governance and Global Administrative Law in the International Legal Order," (2006) 17 *European Journal of International Law* 1; and 10–13 on the challenge of global to international law.

> transnational private regulators, hybrid bodies such as public private partnerships involving states or inter-state organizations, national public regulators whose actions have external effects but may not be controlled by the central executive authority, informal inter-state bodies with no treaty basis (including "coalitions of the willing") and formal interstate institutions (such as those of the United Nations) affecting third parties through administrative-type actions.[47]

In fact, even the law of UN-related institutions (UNCHR, FAO, ILO, WHO, WIPO, etc.) or of further entities generated by global authorities of a public nature, like the Codex Alimentarius Commission (a joint venture of the FAO and WHO), express substantively autonomous governance. And albeit born of traditional treaty-making, the most outstanding example – the World Trade Organization (WTO) – is taken to exemplify "the pervasive shift of authority from domestic governments to global regulatory bodies." Such a "shift of authority" also includes "transnational networks of domestic regulatory officials, private standard setting bodies, and hybrid public–private entities."[48] And what is equally relevant is that such separate functional regimes more often address private actors than simply states[49]: as with the international climate regime, regulations take effect "behind the national borders, within the national societies," and the ultimate addressees in various fields of global regulatory institutions are consumers, companies, and societal actors.[50]

The relevance of other "informal" entities of a supranational nature like the Basel Committee (on Banking Supervision) or of the International Association of Insurance Supervisors (IAIS) is undoubted. There are not only public entities: International Organization for Standardization (ISO) or Internet Corporation for the Assignment of Names and Numbers (ICANN) achieve global effectiveness despite lacking formal public authorization processes behind their birth. ISO, through standards affecting any kind of production, also undermines the ultimate effectiveness of national authorities on the same issues, and it has achieved worldwide respect, having been adopted in the

47 B. Kingsbury, "The Concept of 'Law'," at 25.

48 R. B. Stewart and M. Ratton Sanchez Badin, "The World Trade Organization and Global Administrative Law," *NYU Institute for International Law and Justice Working Paper* 2009/7, at 1.

49 See the GAL manifesto: B. Kingsbury, N. Krisch, and R. B. Stewart, "The Emergence of Global Administrative Law," (2005) 68 *Law and Contemporary Problems* 15. See also S. Cassese, "Administrative Law without the State? The Challenge of Global Regulation," (2005) 33 *NYU Journal of International Law and Politics* 663, 677.

50 M. Zürn, "Global Governance and Legitimacy Problems," in D. Held and M. Koenig-Archibugi (eds.), *Global Governance and Public Accountability* (Oxford: Blackwell, 2005), 144.

WTO-related Technical Barriers to Trade Agreement. Given its general acceptance and viability, it has de facto lost its voluntary character.[51]

Given the increasingly refined account of the different types of regulatory authorities producing "non-treaty law," traditional state and inter-state understandings "are inadequate to ensure that these diverse global regulatory decision makers are accountable and responsive to all of those who are affected by their decisions".[52] Moreover, the massive production of regulatory norms clearly transfers a considerable amount of power "to technical experts well-positioned in the specialised bodies administering those branches."[53]

As Carl Schmitt wrote, the admonition to silence, once pronounced by jurists against theologians of the "just war" (Gentili's *silete teologi in munere alieno*), is now pronounced against jurists themselves in order to keep them out of the realm of the superior necessity of technique.[54] For him, many indicia showed that the time had come for legality to be neutralized and reduced to silence by technocracy, with silence being commanded by the "new objectivity of pure technique."

The compensatory effort – vis-à-vis the self-referentiality of global regimes – has been to focus on and to harden measures of accountability.[55] And the GAL project has elaborated on a model of normative requirements based on transparency, participation, reasoned decision-making, and review. These should affect "the accountability of global administrative bodies,"[56] as they already do in many cases.[57]

51 For an analysis of ISO and legitimacy, see E. Shamir-Borer, "Legitimacy without Authority in Global Standardisation Governance: The Case of the International Organization for Standardization (ISO)," in S. Cassese et al. (eds.), *Global Administrative Law: The Case-book* (e-book 2012, I.C.1), available at www.irpa.eu/en/gal-section/global-administrative-law-the-casebook-2.

52 As Stewart and Sanchez Badin, "WTO and GAL" add (at 2): "At the same time, we believe that the divisions and differences in regimes, interests and values are too wide and deep to support, at this point a constitutionalist paradigm for global governance."

53 M. Koskenniemi, "Global Governance and Public International Law," (2004) 37 *Kritische Justiz* 241.

54 C. Schmitt, "Ex Captivitate Salus," in C. Schmitt, *Ex Captivitate Salus: Experiences, 1945–47* (Cambridge: Polity, 2017, Hannah trans.).

55 See also S. Cassese, "Shrimps, Turtles and Procedures: Global Standards for National Administrative Procedure," (2005) 68 *Law and Contemporary Problems* 109.

56 ". . . in particular by ensuring these bodies meet adequate standards of transparency, consultation, participation, rationality, and legality, and by providing effective review of the rules and decisions these bodies make" (B. Kingsbury, "International Law as Inter-Public Law," in H. R. Richardson and M. S. Williams [eds.], *Nomos XLIX: Moral Universalism and Pluralism* [New York: New York University Press, 2009], 167, 190.

57 Kingsbury referred to the Shrimp and Turtle case, when the WTO Appellate Body found the US ban arbitrary for failing to provide India with notice in advance and opportunity for

The global spreading of such a regulatory law format neither replaces sub-global legal orders, nor does it subordinate them: it has no necessary role in granting the validity of their norms (in other words, they do not become part of a universal, Kelsenian legality, and states' legal orders are not seen to depend on the higher supranational order's authorization). Such an autonomous self-standing format is not *the* overarching legality to which everything else ultimately belongs, although its ambition is to superimpose its general coordinative and rationalizing role onto the multitude of different orders, actors, and players to which its reach extends.

6 THE FORMATS' COPRESENCE AS A SYMPTOM OF INTER-LEGALITY

Taking stock, one ends up recognizing that the global (and administrative) law is a legal reality *of its own*, unmatched by other patterns. The knowledge we have of different matrices, like the "esprit" or *ius gentium*, teaches us how large their distance is from such a globe-concerning law, as described in Section 5. And it is for this reason – which depends on the diversity of formats, on the difference of shapes – that one cannot think of one law for the globe as a grand box holding other smaller-sized boxes. For sure, its global reach and the extent of its addressees' domains call any other legal order to compliance, to surrender harmonization, to expect inclusion. However, albeit "smaller" legal *Matrëška* do not necessarily fit into one another – their "volumes" and, say, form and figure were born instead not to fit. Accordingly, such an alleged global law is not apt to become *the general legal order capable of embracing everything else*; that is, the normative order to which all the others end up belonging. This holds true despite the increase of inter-order functional connections, the transformed relations between public and private, international and domestic, state and non-state law. Working on perfecting global law promises neither: (i) to change its "deracinated nature" devoid of territorial, cultural, and social embeddedness; nor (ii) to transform it into a universal *ius gentium* belonging to all peoples. Although the latter label would infuse the concurring laws of global regimes with a supplementary (but misleading) halo of universal consensus, the similarity is mostly ill-drawn: as we have seen, *ius gentium* always partakes in something else – it is deduced from law's institutes present in different systems, and we do not *see* it as a free-standing,

contestation. Notice was due since US Turtles policies were affecting a public other than its own. See Kingsbury, "The Concept of 'Law'," at 37. See also Cassese, "Shrimps, Turtles and Procedures."

self-contained, ordering structure. Moreover, one should consider that such a global administrative and regulative format is not only made of the safeguards affording procedural or substantive limitations for the exercise of regulatory powers: of course, beyond providing for those requirements of a "*ius gentium* kind" (respect for basic human rights, the rule of law, the principle of legality, access to justice, reasonableness, proportionality, and the like), the format is essentially made of massive amounts of substantive regulatory norms and is characterized by the exercise of rulemaking power by a wide range of newly forged authorities. The overwhelming amount of "substantive" provisions is its ultimate raison d'être.

Evidently, although a sui generis format of its own, the GAL too does not match or replace law as "esprit." It rather confirms the stance that Robert Post described: those international legal institutions "cannot be understood from the perspective of any single national tradition. They would thus-appear to elude the forms of comparative analysis that have been a mainstay of American legal scholarship . . . The new global legal order seems to subsist within an almost free floating melange of legal organizations . . ."[58] In a more refined stage of understanding, Kingsbury has written: "If a claim to 'law' is made in applying the label GAL . . . it is a claim that diverges from, and can be sharply in tension with the classical models of consent-based inter-state international law and most models of national law."[59]

While on the one hand the global regulative–administrative law is a law that crosscuts political allegiances and territorial meanings and somehow looks at the world as flat, on the other hand the globe hosts today a plurality of formats of legalities that are bound to overlap, interact, and produce tensions and divergences among different rationales. Nothing is impossible. Another world thrived for a thousand years on an open variety of legal orders, and it also considered the *juris prudentes* job as definitely controlling. However, medievalism – leaving aside its theological pull to unity – was not yet complicated by the evolving gifts of modernity, like the idea of legislation as political control, the strength of the state, its ethos, the "civilizing" force of international law, and the self-driven authority of technical efficiency. Medievalism – certainly a false friend if taken as the exhaustive representation of contemporary law – nonetheless exposes the ideal type of a complex format of legalities and, at the same time, in the present scenario, is itself just *a part of it*.

58 R. Post, "The Challenge of Globalization to American Public Law Scholarship," (2001) 2 *Theoretical Inquiries in Law* 323, 330.

59 Kingsbury, "The Concept of 'Law'," at 26.

The increasing request to tame the uncontrolled spreading of legal fragmentation through a more progressive, responsible, and transnational epistemic community of judicial authorities is a clear symptom of such a state of affairs.[60] Fragmentation, be it pathology or physiology, is a value-laden perspective. It depends on the relevant dispersed unity: not just the lack, but properly the (ontological) loss of a reassuring unified legal world. So the label "fragmentation" tells us more about our cognitive premises or pre-understandings than about the world itself. Fragmentation is often discussed as a matter of increasing numbers of international tribunals, whose proliferation is neither curbed nor hierarchically controlled by the International Court of Justice.[61] But the proliferation of courts or quasi-jurisdictional bodies is not purely artificial, because it follows the proliferation of legalities and sources.[62] Accordingly, the issue is to be framed and reassessed from a *reversed* perspective.

The anxiety about fragmentation should be replaced by a concern for the quality and adequacy of our cognitive and legal categories. At stake is a metamorphosis of law in the global, regional, and national scenarios, and the potential frustrating effects of the artificial fractures produced as a result of legal–technical boundaries protecting each legality against the complexity of interconnections. It is difficult to deny that different formats of law are claiming their share in both the explication and the resolution of any single, concrete affair.

The present circumstances make it hard to draw lines of in-depth separation between different domains: the material overlapping of economy, trade, environment, rights, security, etc., and the extent of their determinants and factors beyond rigidly delimited territorial spheres, along with the resilience of legal organizational forms endowed with distinctive and irreconcilable rationales, produces the non-tenability of the self-containedness of orders, regimes, and legalities. At the same time, those very regimes and orders are partaking in and contributing to spurious logics belonging to simultaneously resurfacing formats of law: we are living in a neo-medieval concurrence of legalities, further complicated by the different incarnations of "esprit," especially through the achievement of the state and by the overwhelming appearance

60 See S. Cassese, *I Tribunali di Babele* (Rome: Donzelli, 2009); and C. Brown, *A Common Law of International Adjudication* (Oxford: Oxford University Press, 2007).

61 ICTY, Prosecutor v Tadic, Case No. IT-94-1-l, Appeals Judgment, 34–75, para. 11.

62 As a preliminary study report had already stressed: G. Hafner, "Risks Ensuing From the Fragmentation of International Law," in *Official Records of the General Assembly*, 566 session, Supplement no. 10, 321 (UN Doc A/55/10) and G. Hafner, "Pros and Cons Ensuing from Fragmentation of International Law," (2004) 25 *Michigan Journal of International Law* 849.

of deracinated global rulemaking. We keep relying on some law of all the peoples that should make sense of disagreements and suggest an albeit limited amount of shared principles or institutions (the *ius gentium* type). The first task of the oft-mentioned "epistemic community" is to shoulder its adjudicative role at the crossroads and knots of such overlapping nets by fostering revisions of ideologies and categories proving to be unsuited and having been created some time ago to solve only older intra-systemic questions, both on the material and on the juridical plane.

The increasing value of naming such phenomena as "inter-legality" (not just "legality") lies in the realization that we are to live in each and all of such different formats at the same time, and that the continuous reshuffling of their concurrent or competing rationales demands a revision of our received understanding of law, especially in its "systemic" frames – an understanding that at best is attuned to one of those formats, but is unfit to make sense of their enmeshing and to cope with it.

3

Summum Ius, Summa Iniuria

Critical Reflections on Issues of Responsibility, the Legal Form, Inter-Legality, and the Limits of Law

FRIEDRICH KRATOCHWIL[1]

1 INTRODUCTION

The concept of responsibility – of having to "answer" to some other(s) for one's deeds – plays a central role in our vocabulary of agency and freedom, which in turn is constitutive for our understanding of how the individual links to society and the source(s) of legitimizing its "order." As a fundamental notion, "responsibility" thus touches upon important issues in philosophy and ethics, but also in theology, sociology, and psychology – to name just the most obvious – which, over time, have engendered fierce debates both within and across these fields. As the checkered pattern of the above-mentioned disciplines suggests, there seems to be a discernible move from phrasing the issues as theological problems to problems of philosophy and later of law.[2]

Charting these changes in the semantics of "responsibility" involves us, therefore, in some form of interdisciplinary undertaking, as we realize that the usual procedure of starting with an "operational" definition and then finding the cases serving as instantiations of the more or less free-standing concept will hardly do, as their meaning derives from their place in overlapping semantic fields. A definitional move not only assumes the coincidence of key concepts with traditional disciplinary boundaries, but is also entirely oblivious to the constitutive role of the vocabulary we use in constructing the social world, as here the idea of language as a "mirror" of a pre-existing reality quickly breaks down. As Aristotle reminded us, the social world is one of artifice, not of

[1] I gratefully acknowledge the suggestions by Mariano Barbato, Nicholas Onuf and Rodrigo Szuecs, who commented on an earlier version of this paper.

[2] This is not to say that there is only one sequence, as phrasing the issue of responsibility in legal rather than theological terms occurred in Roman law long before the assignment of responsibility became, in modernity, the domain of "positive" law.

"nature," and he also raised the issue of whether the world of praxis can be understood in terms of ontology buttressing a "theory," or whether praxis needs a different way of comprehending what is at stake.[3]

These initial observations have two further methodological implications, which the epistemological debates of modernity and post-modernity have vetted: one is that the traditional vocabulary of "perception" treats concepts as "impressions" whereby the causal arrows go from "the world" to the "mind." In social orders, however, most of the arrows go from the "mind" to the "world," since our most important concepts are "mind dependent" rather than existing independently of the intersubjective understandings of the actors who "use" them. Thus, what serves as "money" cannot be ascertained by what it "is" (e.g., examining the make-up of a coin or a banknote), but by understanding what type of actions thereby become possible (purchasing, saving, investing, paying taxes or penalties, donating) or are forbidden (bribing, forging, money laundering, buying illicit drugs or stolen goods, etc.).

The other implication is that numerous if not most concepts we use in the realm of praxis point to *particularities that interest us*. They place us in time and in a social space, rather than in an atemporal, universal theoretical limbo in which present, past, and future are essentially the same, as the logical symmetry of prediction and retrodiction suggests. There are, of course, in our vocabularies also generic concepts, such as "actor," "subject" or "human," but many of our concepts mark a particular status of the actors, such as "buyer" or "client." There are also concepts like "son" or "daughter," "friend," or even "senator" or "enemy" that emphasize a particular relationship that is not conveyed by generic concepts, such as "human." In short, nongeneric concepts are either "tensed," as Danto has called them, and/or "typed." The latter contain "status markers," while the former, in addition, call attention to actions or events that must have occurred before this status has been attained. Consequently, they also locate us "historically"[4] and thus cast just

3 Aristotle's distinction is centrally related to his distinction of "voice" (*phone*) and language (*logos*) that allows us not only to indicate via "signals" the dangers or pain and pleasure, but allows to communicate on the basis of conceptual distinctions that are not part of a given world but that come only into existence by the common use of concepts: "Speech is something different from voice which is possessed by other animals also and used by them to express pain or pleasure ... Speech (language) on the other hand serves to indicate what is right or wrong. For the real difference between man and other animals is that humans alone have the perception of good and evil, right and wrong, just and unjust. And it is this sharing of a common view that makes a household or a city." See Aristotle, *The Politics* (London: Penguin, 1962, Sinclair trans.), 1253a 11–13.

4 Thus, an "orphan" can only be someone whose parents are deceased and who is not yet a "normal" adult.

another doubt on the common epistemological tenet that "knowledge" – whether it concerns the natural or the practical world – has always to satisfy the "theoretical" criteria of universality, ahistoricity and necessity.

These issues need not be rehearsed here further,[5] save to serve as a warning that such an inquiry also involves us then necessarily in an "archeology" of the concepts, and this, in turn, makes an examination of the limits of "systemic" thinking necessary that is based on a functionally and atemporally conceived part/whole distinction. Much of our social world is, however, more like a patchwork of historically accumulated parts, rather than closed systems in which the different parts are related to each other according to the logic of part and whole. Instead, since the systems of the social world are neither natural nor mechanical, they have to generate themselves and interpenetrate each other so that what can be perceived from within a system has to be recast in terms of the system's own logic of reproduction.[6] Such an approach then replaces interdisciplinarity with a "translation" and creates, when applied to law, an *inter-legal* discourse that allows for greater pluralism without sacrificing the particular "take" that law brings to the exploration of the social world. Whether such "translations" are successful and can be done without reminders is, of course, another question.

The editors have hinted in their instructions to the contributors at this latter possibility. They noted that they did not expect that by accepting "pluralism" as a baseline, the ensuing debate would eventually lead to a convergence. But they were quite explicit in their "nudge" to the authors to avoid the barren traditional dichotomies in their explorations, such as the long-lasting dominance of the monist/dualist opposition (e.g., emphasizing the emergence of "functionalist" orders – or what are today also called "free-standing" regimes – that increasingly overlay the order imposed by territoriality).

While I fully agree that this secondary carving up of the social world can no longer be ordered by finding a "constitutional solution" – save perhaps in a global empire – the existence of the state as an "all-purpose organization" with its competence to determine its own competence and to establish a clear political and legal process is still indispensable, especially for governing *beyond the state*. Consequently, something more on the role of law in this transformative process and its social preconditions has to be said. This not only points us to the role of law in providing us with a language in which matters of

5 For an extensive discussion of these problems, see F. Kratochwil, *Praxis: On Acting and Knowing* (Cambridge: Cambridge University Press, 2018).

6 N. Luhmann, *Soziale Systeme* (Frankfurt: Suhrkamp, 1984).

common concern can be vetted, but also confronts us with the "limits of law" in accomplishing this task.

In this chapter, which uses responsibility as a prism, I shall focus more on the conceptual difficulties facing law in this context, rather than on those that arise in realizing the project of a cosmopolitan order, which has been the main focus of the debate addressing issues of reforming or designing institutions.[7] The reason for revisiting instead the crucial conceptual issues of the legal form and of the limits of law seems particularly advisable in view of the recent attempts in legal theory to eradicate the traditional distinction between setting priorities through legislation or agreement and limiting the courts only to "interstitial lawmaking."[8] Instead, some form of judicial activism and an expansion of "human rights" are advocated for solving social order problems under conditions of increasing interdependence. Despite its popularity, I consider this strategy of entrusting a bunch of eager and well-trained "Herculi" of law to be rather naive. Since it is entirely doctrinally driven, it makes little reference to either legal or political practice, and what one often sorely misses is not only the lack of engagement with the realizability issue of such blueprints, but also the examination of what such a change would mean for some fundamental *principles of the rule of law itself* (such as the separation of powers or issues of legitimization). Thus, while all people on the globe are obviously touched by law, the implied argument that a new "global" order can be built by just the gavel and pen of juristocrats suffers from all the myopias of "legalism."[9] True, law can be "declared" or created by fiat, but not all speech acts or declarations will do, and there might be more to the legal "form" than meets the eye, as we shall see.

Besides, such visions or projects are of interest mainly to theorists of law and to armchair philosophers, but have little allure for practitioners of law. The latter are familiar with the perplexities of law, which does not, however, prevent them from trying to do the best for their client by using the tricks of the trade, even if the "one right answer" à la Dworkin eludes them. To that extent, practitioners also know that an expansion of "rights" usually fails to provide the expected "solutions," since the values these rights protect cannot be ordered once and for all – no secret at least since Nietzsche and

7 E.g., see D. Archibugi and D. Held, *Cosmopolitan Democracy: An Agenda for a New World Order* (Cambridge: Polity Press, 1995); D. Held, *Cosmopolitanism: Ideals and Realties* (Cambridge: Polity Press, 2010).

8 See Justice Holmes in *Southern Pacific Co.* v *Jensen*, 244 US 205 (1917), dissenting.

9 For a seminal discussion, see J. Shklar, *Legalism: Law Morals and Political Trials* (Cambridge, MA: Harvard University Press, 1986).

Weber – and that the appeal to higher-order principles does little to abate conflict and often exacerbates it.

Thus, much of our thinking about social "order" along these lines is probably misguided. It is misguided because we tend to think that the reasons for social order lie in the clarity and systematicity of law. Only if everyone sees the world in exactly the same way is social peace guaranteed. In short, behind the above inference lurks the old "order of things" argument "explaining" how evil came into this world and is wreaking havoc. Remember that even before the "fall" of man in paradise, the rebellion of Lucifer against God occurred and his banishment to "hell" made "devils" out of the fallen angels. So the devil is not a "force" on the same footing as "being," but can only be thought of as a "privation" and as a "perversion" of the natural order of being. After all, does not the name of the devil (*diabolus*) indicate that he is the agent or force that turns everything topsy-turvy by spreading confusion?

The powerful hold of the conceptualizing evil as a perversion and "error" can be seen in European history, ranging from the Socratic argument that nobody can knowingly do evil[10] to the enlightenment discourse. In the latter, the light finally has overcomes the darkness of prejudice, and we, as free, responsible subjects, can see things now as they *are*, and we can now also trust the incontrovertible foundations of and the method that lead us to warranted knowledge. For law, this means that legal prescriptions have to be public, clear, and systematic, and it suggests also all rights as "trumps" have to be of one cloth.

But could it be that this view is mistaken since it misunderstands what public announcement and clarity can deliver and how language actually functions? This would not only be the case in the "natural world" – because this descriptive ideal is based on some theological assumption about natural kinds and on the "matching" of concept and object being guaranteed by God (Descartes) – but especially in the social world, in which "meaning" simply does not coincide with "truth." After all, legal "propositions" are not true, since they are counterfactually valid, and the law itself might not be all of one cloth. What the solicitor does and pays attention to are not the same as those that have to interest the judge or the professor teaching law, quite aside from the fact that laws "making us behave" is a metaphorical expression, not a causal statement. Thus, if law is to be best thought of as an agglomeration of

[10] See Plato, *Apology* 26 a. See also the Socratic paradoxes *arete episteme estin* (virtue is knowledge) and *oudeis hekon hamartanei* (nobody willingly does the wrong thing). See also Aristotle, *Nichomachean Ethics* (London: Penguin, 1976, Thomson trans.), 1145b 25–27, where he criticizes this Socratic argument about the necessary connection of knowledge and will.

different practices concerning the handling of rules – rather than as a full-fledged system that follows a systemic logic – then critically reflecting on these practices by taking different perspectives might be more fruitful than starting with an a priori model, provided by a view from "nowhere" and elaborating on it. It is here that the notion of "inter-legality" shows its promise.

There is a second benefit to following such a procedure of multiple perspectives and of their mutual critical vetting: it allows us to bring the "blind spots" into view that every perspective creates. Thus, instead of a taking a "transcendental turn," the actual examination of how concepts function in a semantic field makes visible their interconnection, their historical character, and their limits. Such a mode of analysis shows the interdependence of legality with other semantics, without subjecting it to "colonization," such as importing a new methodology taken from another field or by "dis-recognizing" the differences that exist. Examining, for example, "responsibility" and engaging in this way the "concept of law" clarifies not only law's deep involvement in constituting our rather imperfect social order, but also shows its "darker side," such as creating impunity for certain harms, although the damages caused thereby are well-known. Examples come easily to mind, such as environmental degradation – caused by our doing business as usual or by the pathologies of compartmentalized organizational decision-making both in the public and private sector leading to suboptimal results. Precisely because everybody works "by the book" but no one is responsible for the overall outcome things can – and frequently do – go awry.

Finally, by looking at the blind spots of law, we are not dealing with the usual miscarriages of justice that result from "corruption," mistakes, or the incompetence of the rule-handlers, but rather from *the very constitution of our social order*. This is a problem that deserves further attention rather than being passed over. To that extent, the old Roman adage – which provides the title for this paper – might be an embarrassing paradox for our modern, systemic understanding of law – which explains perhaps why it is now usually "forgotten" or rather "repressed" – but its importance was well-recognized by some of the earliest masters of the legal form.

From these initial remarks the further steps of my argument can be derived. The next section provides a broad-brush overview of some of the contexts and debates in which "responsibility" figured prominently, even if it was originally embedded in a wider conceptual grid provided in the Western tradition by theology and ontology. Thus, despite the rather broad scope of my inquiry, I have to admit its limitations. Consequently, legitimate questions can be raised as to the validity of the conclusions (or lack thereof) of this chapter.

While I accept this criticism, I do not think that its limitations are disabling – not because I think that "universal reason" has found its emblematic expression in the Western tradition, so that no others need be consulted, but because I believe the search for universal truth is most of the time a meaningless and "irresponsible" endeavor. It pretends that we are not limited historical beings, but can, like God (or his later stand-in, the philosopher of reason), look at the world *from a point outside of it.* Since this world is now finished and ready for inspection, no further questions can arise, unless one is stubborn or demented.

In Section 2, I investigate the assignment of responsibilities, examining more closely the paradox that points to the "dark side" of law. Section 3 then elaborates on the "logic" of the juridical form by first analyzing its genesis and then providing some illustrative cases from international and domestic law. Section 4 is then devoted to a discussion of the limits of law. A brief recapitulation of the argument and some further questions it raises can be found in Section 5.

2 LOCATING RESPONSIBILITY

One of the reasons for tasking law in modernity with the assignment of "responsibility" has to do with the breakdown of the old ontological order and the loss of pull of the old transcendental notions of *unum, ens, verum, bonum.* The "good" aimed at in action could then no longer be read off the "place" or position in the order of things. But some of the questions surrounding "responsibility" and of justifying one's actions have an even older pedigree. They arose out of the tension of a God who brings the world into existence by an act of his will, and the other ontological conception of a Platonic *demiourgos*, who imparts order to an existing *kosmos*, thereby providing us with a template of how we are to order ourselves (souls) and our communities.[11]

The "answer" to the question why God created the world and allowed us to do the "wrong thing" – and not only arranged the cosmos – was the one provided by the Augustinian *quia voluit* (because he wanted it), which engendered a "will" *problematique* with its own dynamics. Thus, the "will of God" and the problem of the "theodicy," and that of the individual's "free will," are situated in a semantic field that emerged from the interaction of theology and ontology, until the human subject and its capacities (nature)

[11] For an interesting elaboration of this point, see E. Castrucci, *On the Idea of Potency: Juridical and Theological Roots of the Western Cultural Tradition* (Edinburgh: Edinburgh University Press, 2016).

replaced in modernity the ontological and theological framework. This conceptual shift has important implications for the issue of responsibility, as we shall see.

Let us begin with the original semantic. It concerned – on the surface – the issue of "free will" and of role of "grace," but it was framed by the question of why there is evil in the world and by the problem of justification of one's acts, given the flaw of the original sin. The *problematique* pitted first the Pelagians, who insisted on man's natural reason to recognize what is good and should be done, against the fathers of the Church,[12] who stressed the need for "grace" because of the *natura corrupta* resulting from the original sin. The issue of "justification" became virulent again in the Reformation after some dormancy during the Middle Ages, where theologically oriented movements could be successfully suppressed by the alliance between rulers and theologians, and this problem could then be dealt with by the remedies of the sacraments and a quasi-juridified system of penalties and indulgences.

But if man cannot be "good" and follow the commands of God without the latter's bestowal of grace, then the issue of the freedom of choice – intrinsic to our thinking about responsibility and the justification of our acts – becomes moot. It is this problem with which Paul wrestled in his letter to the Romans. The more general question of the theodicy (i.e., how evil came into the world) is linked to the issue of why God bestows grace on some and "hardens the heart upon whomever he wills."[13] From Paul's answer both Calvin and Luther drew different conclusions, relying thereby on different parts of his letter: Calvin bases his answer on the predestination part[14] and Luther on Paul's argument about faith[15] (which he makes into the *sola fide* doctrine).[16] Both, in a way, rejected the view that doing good works and living according to the law were sufficient for an "existential" justification. Here, perhaps, the issues of legality versus legitimacy raises its ugly head – although, in a different (i.e., theological) register.[17] It is not only that the action had to be good, but that it had to be done in a specific habitus. Of course, consideration of the

[12] Pelagius (360–418) had propagated a "naturalist" free will argument dispensing with both the original sin and the need for God's grace for acting rightly. His teachings were considered heretical by the council of Carthage in 418.

[13] Roman 9:14.

[14] Roman 8:28.

[15] Roman 3:27 and 9:30.

[16] *Sola fide* (i.e., by faith alone) – relying on God's grace, man is "justified."

[17] M. Luther, *De Servo Arbitrio* (*On the Bondage of Will*, 1525): "Therefore, free will, if it exists is sin because it is opposed to faith and gives no glory to God" (Argument 5). Available at www.chapellibrary.org (accessed July 1, 2017). Luther answered in this pamphlet Erasmus of Rotterdam's *De Libero Arbitrio* (*On the Freedom of Will*) of 1524.

intentions of an act was not new to law, as the arguments in Roman law about *dolus specialis* show, but they had been limited to *particular typified actions* and were not part of a general justificatory "theory" of human actions. In any case, if a person's deeds have to be attributed to God's mercy – which for Luther God grants more willingly to the faithful than the inscrutable God of Calvin – then the actor deserves neither praise nor punishment for his or her actions. This seems at first a rather strange conclusion, showing that issues of general justification derived from a theodicy sit quite uneasily with the freedom of will argument that had become part of assigning responsibility, particularly in criminal law and in dealing with professional misconduct.

It is then perhaps not surprising that the philosophical debates in modernity concerning the link between free will and responsibility leave the theodicy problem and the question of grace behind. Rather, such attributions are now "secular" matters in that human nature, rather than ontology or the theodicy, provides the frame. Furthermore, the attributions involve now not only cognitive issues, but more specifically *sentiments*, which are formed through "commerce and conversation" from natural "passions," as Hume observed. Unfortunately, this part of the Humean argument did not enter the subsequent public discourse, and most people remember therefore only Hume's argument that "reason cannot be but the slave of passion," or that one cannot argue about tastes (*de gustibus non est disputandum*), both of which led to a rather impoverished "theory" of choice in utilitarianism. But such a selective interpretation of Hume forgets that, for Hume, "imagination" and not reason is the most important part of the "mind," and that the "sentiments" are not physical "drives," but are acquired through moral training and participation in the practices of a society. They are therefore not "psychological" and idiosyncratic, but have an intersubjective or public standing.[18]

Hume was thereby answering the challenge that Hobbes and his brand of "naturalism" had introduced. It was the Hobbesian attempt to ground our understandings of the social world in physical "givens" and to use a scientific method to explicate – as he claims, *more geometrico* (in the fashion of geometry) – the implications of these "natural facts." As he argues, such a procedure should then dispense with the errors arising from our imprecise

18 As for the argument that one cannot argue about taste – similar to Bentham's later argument that "pushpin [a card game] is as good as opera." See Hume's objections in his essay "On the Standards of Taste," in which he grapples, like later Kant in his Third Critique, with the problem of "reflective judgments": these are not "determinate," but are also far from being only idiosyncratic indications of personal preferences. D. Hume, "On the Standards of Taste," in D. Hume, *Essays Moral, Political and Literary* (Indianapolis, IN: Liberty Fund, 1985, Miller ed.), 11.

everyday language, which become the "causes" of quarrels and inhibit or prevent social reproduction. Hobbes also no longer relied on reason, but on the manipulation of the passions, particularly fear (in opposition to envy), for solving the problem of the "war of all against all." For him, social reproduction was being undermined by the theological issues of to whom we, as persons, are "ultimately" responsible. To that extent, the still prevalent "religious" belief that the highest evil – the *summum malum* – is not death but eternal damnation, undermines for Hobbes the authority of the sovereign and his ability to govern by the laws he makes. As Hobbes observes in his *Elements of Law*:

> This difficulty hath not been of very great antiquity in the world. There was no such dilemma amongst the Jews: for their civil law, and divine law was one and the same law of Moses. . . . Nor is it a controversy that is ever taken notice of amongst the Grecians, Romans, or other Gentiles. Also those Christians that dwell under the temporal dominion of the bishop of Rome are free from this question. This difficulty, therefore, remained amongst and troubled those Christians only to whom it is allowed to take for the sense of the Scripture that which they make thereof, either by their own private interpretation, or by the interpretation of such as are not called thereunto by public authority.[19]

Thus, Hobbes's "solution" to this problem, allegedly relying on naturalism, was, however, part of a political project, which he attempted to legitimize by an appeal to a "scientific" method, very much in the same way as Descartes had tried in 1637 and 1641 in his *Discourse on Method* and his *Meditations on First Philosophy*. That Hobbes, like Descartes, failed in this endeavor – as both had to rely on rather traditional rhetorical means of persuasion instead of compelling "demonstrations"[20] – is of course another matter.

Here, Hume's amendment that our judgments about "good" and "bad" are appraisals involving *intersubjective feelings* of praise or resentment was important and became a standard *topos* of the Scottish enlightenment. However, the subsequent "psychologization" of feelings as "private" phenomena in liberal utilitarian thinking turned the debate in another direction, which we cannot not follow here.

In more recent times, the free will *problematique* is framed by objections to the Kantian "solution" that had appealed to the allegedly universal intuition of the subject that s/he could set in motion new chains of events and that this

19 T. Hobbes, *The Elements of Law* (Oxford: Oxford University Press, 1994 [1640]).

20 E.g., see Q. Skinner, *Reason and Rhetoric in the Philosophy of Hobbes* (Cambridge: Cambridge University Press, 1996).

choice was not "causally" determined, but resulted from an act of free will. This construction generated over the years debates first among "materialists" and "idealists," and more recently between the "incompatibilists" and the "compatibilists," in which causal determinations of actions and the issue of "responsibility" hinge on the question of the availability of realistic alternatives to the agent.[21]

Here, of course, the issue of an infinite regress lurks in the background, since a "bad person" has bad "tastes" and acts, therefore, differently. Then the issue arises as to why and how these bad tastes arose and whether the assignment of responsibility boils down to some mythical "original" choice – the old theological notion of an "original sin" – or to Aristotle's argument that you can be held responsible for choosing bad ways of life that deform your character.

But while the notion of an original sin makes sense within a theological discourse – even if the notion of guilt that is transmitted to future generations without any conscious choice on their part strains the concept – the idea that one can somehow autonomously choose one's character is less than persuasive. After all, characters are "formed" (i.e., are the result of many choices and experiences), and they have to be tested in daily life and in crises. But if this is so, then they cannot be chosen once and for all as if they were available to be picked "from the shelf" and then simply take over. The various choices "on the way" make the argument of a deterministic causal chain rather specious, even though within a narrative all the points in-between can get connected and can thus appear as the "antecedent causes" of the subsequent choices.[22]

Whatever we think of these speculations, one thing seems to be uncontroversial: that an entirely new order of *problematique* arose for law in modernity, which could no longer be based on a common vision of the individual or "common good," but whose determination had to be "above" the actors claiming on the one hand the "competence of competence," and also had to appear "neutral" as to the more substantive personal and political projects of its subjects.

The metaphor of a social contract fundamentally changed the conception of obligation for both the sovereign and the individual. The sovereign was now to derive his legitimacy from the respect for and enforcement of the rights of his subjects, rather than being the "representative" of God – even if Hobbes's quasi-religious justification of the sovereign and the later *Dei gratia* invocation showed the considerable staying power of theological foundations. Furthermore, the subjects could choose certain obligations and responsibilities by

[21] E.g., see K. E. Boxer, *Rethinking Responsibility* (Oxford: Oxford University Press, 2013).

[22] For a further elaboration of this point, see Kratochwil, *Praxis*, chapter 10.

availing themselves of certain institutional rules (contracts) for their undertakings. While lawyers were the clear winners of the new legitimacy game, philosophers hung on to the argument that a universal "theory" of obligation was necessary in order to "ground" particular responsibilities and obligations.

In law, such speculative derailments are less common, but not unknown, particularly when the analysis imports its conceptual tools from economics or hinges (in another more hermeneutically oriented approach represented by Dworkin) on the "one right answer" thesis. It carries with it a special responsibility for the judiciary, especially those of the higher courts. Since I have argued that both approaches (general theory of obligation and right answer thesis) are conceptually flawed,[23] I shall leave them aside here and just note such an interpretation paired with the liberal emphasis on "rights" and their proliferation through various "generations of rights" – often without even bothering about who the respective duty-bearers of all these rights are – has led some observers to argue that the legal discourse is increasingly replacing the political one, based on "interest" and "power."

While such a judgment might be somewhat myopic since it relies on a "biased" sample by only considering "liberal states" and – to paraphrase Rawls – "peoples" like "us,"[24] much of the persuasive pull comes from the analogy to the discursive formations in the politics of Western states.[25] As Habermas noticed some time ago, the juridical form permeates these societies and has become the "only way" in which "it becomes possible reliably to establish morally obligated relationships of mutual respect even among strangers."[26]

Habermas's statement is interesting for two reasons. On the one hand, it articulates the hegemonic discourse in which law is credited with having replaced other sources of legitimacy by institutionalizing a foundational but secular notion of morality and obligation. In other words, law can now assign, so to speak, on the basis of speech acts, "responsibilities" without recourse to a religious justification or even without relying on the "moral point of view" of modern ethics. This line of thought is then carried further in Habermas's

[23] Dworkin's theory is faulty since he mistakes determinacy with uniqueness (which has different logical requirements), and the law and economics approach assumes "complete and costless" information, as otherwise no maxima can be calculated. For a further discussion, see F. Kratochwil, *The Status of Law in International Society: Meditations on the Role and Rule of Law* (Cambridge: Cambridge University Press, 2014), chapter 11; see also Kratochwil, *Praxis*, chapter 5.

[24] J. Rawls, *The Law of Peoples* (Cambridge, MA: Harvard University Press, 1999).

[25] E.g., see Jean Cohen's criticism in her *Globalization and Sovereignty: Rethinking Legality, Legitimacy and Constitutionalism* (Cambridge: Cambridge University Press, 2012).

[26] See J. Habermas, *Between Facts and Norms* (Cambridge, MA: MIT Press, 1996, Rehg trans.), 452.

argument about a "constitutional patriotism" that is part of the multicultural agenda for domestic politics. It also can then be extended to some form of "constitutionalism" for the reform of international institutions in accordance with a (Kantian?) cosmopolitan intent.

On the other hand, Habermas is a more critical thinker than most of the cosmopolitan advocates who just assume that a viable global order can be achieved by a conceptual "stretch," such as by making the existing international institutions more "statelike" or by arguing on moral grounds for a more "inclusive" form of solidarity. But by concentrating on principles and general blueprints, those speculations mostly avoid the practical problems of execution. Instead, these proposals make it appear that building the "city of man" is something like fabricating Russian dolls, where the smaller one is always housed in a larger one, and that the extensions are rather easily manufactured. Such a stance assumes that because something can be thought of it must also exist (the unicorn problem) or that it can be brought about by human intervention. Problems of realizability are for such "ideal theories" just subordinate details that create problems only at the stage of application and need not be taken into account at the planning stage, where "assumptions" provide the starting points.

Here, Julia Kristeva's cosmopolitan manifesto is instructive. She is taking her cue from Montesquieu, whose statement, she suggests, should be "engraved on all walls of all schools and political institutions"[27] – as if such a propagandistic display, familiar from all dictatorships, were able to do the trick! But let us look more closely at Montesquieu's "inspiration." He had postulated in his *Pensées* a moral yardstick by which actions could be evaluated in order to bring about a cosmopolitan order. Unfortunately, this yardstick – of a universal responsibility for the welfare of mankind – is bereft of any relationship to social reality by simply passing over the common experience of conflicting duties, which are addressed, for example, in Sophocles' *Antigone*, or by Sartre's student (who faces during the occupation of France the choice of staying home and caring for his mother or joining the French forces in Britain to fight the Nazis).[28] Instead, the quote from Montesquieu reads:

> If I knew something useful to myself and detrimental to my family, I would reject it from my mind. If I knew something useful to my family, but not to

[27] J. Kristeva, "Open Letter to Harlem Desir," in J. Kristeva, *Nations without Nationalism* (New York: Columbia University Press, 1993), 49, 63.

[28] See Sartre's lecture of 1946 using this example, which later was translated and appeared in 1986 as J.-P. Sartre, "Existentialism Is a Humanism," in W. Kaufman (ed.), *Existentialism from Dostoyevsky to Sartre* (New York: Plume Books, 1986), 345.

> my homeland, I would try to forget it. If I knew something useful to my homeland and detrimental to mankind, I would consider it a crime.[29]

Habermas is far from such wishful thinking when he takes up again problems of politics and of practical action at the turn of the millennium. He is now interested in the potential of a semantics inspired by religious thought that could lend support to a public order in a post-secular era. Far from the enthusiasm of convinced cosmopolitans who, as children of the enlightenment, are mostly secularists, he surmises that within religious communities there might "still exist something that has been lost and that cannot be restored by professional knowledge or experts."[30]

The two strands in Habermas's thinking and their – at least at first blush – rather contradictory implications have not escaped the attention of some critics,[31] but they raise a further question that goes far beyond Habermas's particular proposal of mediating the tensions between the "life world" and the law's monopoly of assigning rights and responsibilities. These questions go to the very nature of the juridical form and its limitations, as well as to the issue of whether the deficiencies can be cured by a "theory" with a better "fit."

The first question addresses the problem of whether displacement of the political discourse by a new form of legalism,[32] containing both law-fare of the military and speculations concerning "humanity"[33] – cast this time in a legal rather than theological or philosophical garb – is indeed able to create a vocabulary that allows us to address the "big problems" of our times. They range from the nuclear threat to environmental degradation, to mass poverty, or to the "externalities" that come with the exploding connectivity of contemporary life, such as systematic fraud, identity theft, and fake news.

The second question appears – at first blush – equally disheartening: that the hope of finding or inventing such a vocabulary might be misplaced, since it seems to turn back to the notion of a general "theory" of obligation that assumes as a precondition a standpoint outside of social reality.[34]

29 As quoted in Kristeva, "Open Letter," at 63.

30 J. Habermas, *Zwischen Naturalismus und Religion* (Frankfurt: Suhrkamp, 2005), at 247.

31 E.g., see I. Roele, "The Vicious Circle of Habermas' Cosmopolitanism," (2014) 25 *Law and Critique* 199.

32 For a critical discussion of this form of professionalism, see D. Kennedy, *A World of Struggle: How Power Law and Expertise Shape the Global Economy* (Princeton, NJ: Princeton University Press, 2016).

33 R. Teitel, *Humanity's Law* (Oxford: Oxford University Press, 2011).

34 In the case of Habermas, this could be a reflection of earlier dreams of a transcendental pragmatics by which the historical contingency of our understanding is "derived" from the specification of an "ideal speech situation" allowing for unimpeded communication.

This vocabulary then has to be "objective" (i.e., must be perspicuous to all) and has to be comprehensive so that it is able to show us how things really "are." Such a "decontextualization" of meaning, as I shall argue, is unavailable to us, however, as we are always situated in a particular context and face situations in which we are confronted by a "problem" (that is literally "thrown before you or us," as the original Greek meaning of *to problema* suggests). It is these two issues that the next two sections address. If anything, coming to this realization provides perhaps the strongest justification for a critical inter-legality.

3 THE LEGAL FORM

The upshot of my argument so far, which has tried to situate the concept of responsibility in different debates and semantics, was based on the hunch that the attempt to provide a comprehensive or even "operational" definition of responsibility will be – in its abstractedness – less than illuminating and that, therefore, it might be better to understand the concept as "a language game" going through and informing different forms of life. It becomes perspicuous to us not by developing a general theory of obligation or responsibility – thereby making law into some form of morality at basement prices – or by providing us with the universal hammer that makes out of the world a simple nail, but by distinguishing paradigmatic cases in which issues of responsibility are raised and by investigating then their embeddedness in different semantics. In this way, the changes in ascribing responsibility become accessible to us through the archeology of the discourses (practices constituted by certain normative understandings and the critical reflection on them).

In my plea for a "contextualization" of responsibility, I want to follow up on an old idea that Aristotle brought into play by objecting to Plato's assignment of general responsibilities in his advocacy of the community of wives and children,[35] as well as his in his skepticism toward a universal duty of charity, at which he hints in the section on private property.[36] In the latter case, he argues that dispensing freely one's possessions is – aside from being at odds with the experiential basis of the self-interestedness of human nature – problematic because such a "good soul" is likely soon to be overwhelmed by seemingly unlimited demands and will quickly run out of the means for helping others.

The former problem arises in that if everybody has a responsibility, then nobody is obliged in a concrete case (since there are so many others who

[35] See Aristotle, *Politics* Bk. II, 1262b16–1262b37.
[36] Ibid., at 1262b37–1264b25.

should chip in), so that additional criteria for the assignment of responsibility become practically inevitable. Thus, traditionally parents are held responsible for their children, keepers of animals are responsible for the damage done by their cattle or pets, property arrangements assign specific entitlements (and correlative duties), particular rights and duties are created by contractual undertakings, and only gross violations of the legal order, such as capital crimes that involve "culpability," entail (aside from some liability) punishment. And finally there is, as Hart pointed out, "role responsibility," which deals with the duties and responsibilities attached to a status or specific offices in a society.[37] Thus, for example, doctors owe specific duties to their patients, and civil servants have to exercise their powers within the limits prescribed by the law and the network of other offices.

These cursory remarks have two corollaries: one is that we again have to notice that the language game of responsibility is closely linked to other crucial concepts in the semantics field of praxis: agency, power, authority, capacity, identity, knowledge, risk and foreseeability, consequences, and state of mind (mens rea), to name just the most obvious ones. While this might seem at first blush just another way of touching upon different "disciplines," something else is going on, to which I want to call attention and which traditional "interdisciplinarity" keeps out of sight.

It is the capacity of language to create virtually ex nihilo the social world in terms of speech acts and institutional rules to which I have already referred, but which I want to interrogate again from a different angle.[38] As we have seen, it was Hobbes who first made the argument of the constitutive function of authority, articulated by speech acts. As he puts it bluntly in his second edition of *Leviathan*[39]: "*Auctoritas, non veritas, facit legem*" (authority, not truth, makes the law). Here it is no longer "truth" and the logic of assertions, not even the slow accretion of "doing things" in a certain way – as is the case in "custom" – that provide the deontic pull,[40] as law's aspiration is to monopolize issues of validity by assigning "meaning" to something,

37 H. L. A. Hart, *Punishment and Responsibility* (Oxford: Clarendon Press, 1968), at 212ff.

38 For a further discussion of Humean conventionalism, see F. Kratochwil, "Re-Thinking Inter-Disciplinarity by Re-Reading Hume," in N. Rajkovic, T. Aalberts, and T. Gammeltoft-Hansen (eds.), *The Power of Legality* (Cambridge: Cambridge University Press, 2016), 29.

39 Hobbes's Latin translation of his *Leviathan* (1651), which appeared in 1668, contains significant changes from his first edition, as the recent publication of the English and Latin version of *Leviathan*, placing them side by side, demonstrate. See T. Hobbes, *Leviathan*, 3 vols. (Oxford: Clarendon, 2012, Malcolm ed.).

40 As Hobbes surmises: "When long Use obtaineth the authority of a Law, it is not the Length of Time that maketh the Authority but the Will of the Sovereign signified by his Silence": T. Hobbes, *Leviathan* (London: Penguin, 1981, Macpherson ed.), Bk. II, chapter 26, at 313.

To a certain extent, this had already been recognized by the old formula that juridical decisions are not "true," but rely on the construct that something, established by law, is "held" to be true (*pro veritate habetur*). But this formulation still gives "truth" its pride of place by offering, so to speak, a "second-best" solution to the problem of validity – still linking it to "truth" – which then provides the "backing" for the assertions. While certainly evidentiary matters are subject to factual assessments – even if the "interpretation" of "data" always creates difficulties[41] – some "declarations" of law do not have this link to "reality," but bring, strangely enough, (social) reality into existence by the pronouncements. Here, the theory of speech acts and institutional rules, as pioneered by Austin and Searle in the last century, provide the necessary clarifications.[42] When, for example, a piece of paper says "this is legal tender," all debts public and private must accept it as a means of payment. In general, the assignment of a "status function" (i.e., the stipulation that an "x counts in circumstances y as a z") enables and obliges the "subjects." In other words, it is the specific role of law in the modern state to supply these "status functions," even if their actual assignment might be entrusted to certain members of the society, such as a university or a profession, which can "vest" persons with certain powers or judge their performance (as in the case of medicine or law).[43]

While these enabling and restraining functions have been duly noted, there is another side to this status assignment that often remains opaque, because it is also the function of law to "hide" certain ills by not "recognizing" them as legal causes of action. Thus, if some owner of an established shop, who just enlarged his business because of customer demand, is suddenly faced with a

[41] Hobbes is well aware that even a command theory of law that tries to counteract the confusion and imprecision of ordinary language by making the sovereign the "fixer of signs" is in need of a functioning "community of interpreters," as his discussion of the importance of the Laws of Nature and the "fidelity" to law's purpose in the Second Part of his *Leviathan* (1651), chapter 26, shows.

[42] See J. L. Austin, *How to Do Things with Words*, 2nd edn. (Oxford: Clarendon Press, 1962); J. Searle, *Speech Acts* (Cambridge: Cambridge University Press, 1969); J. Searle, *The Construction of Social Reality* (London: Penguin, 1995).

[43] This might seem like a happy pluralism, but actually the "fiction" of law of "incorporating" other sources of authority, and even Hobbes's own admission of the "independent" authority of the laws of nature – which are "unwritten" and need no proclamation – show the tensions that are better captured by the term "inter-legality": "The law of Nature and the Civil Law contain each other and are of equal extent . . . And therefore Obedience to the Civil law is part also of the Law of Nature. Civil and Natural Law are not different kinds, but different part of Law, wherof the one part being written, is called Civill, the other unwritten Naturall. But the *Right of Nature* [emphasis added] that is the natural Liberty of man, may by the Civill law be abridged, and restrained." Hobbes, *Leviathan*. Bk. II, chapter 26, para. 4, at 314–315.

competitor moving into his neighborhood, his "business" will indubitably suffer. But the original storeowner cannot claim "injury," even if the damage to his business becomes rather obvious as time goes by. Here, Hobbes's analysis is as clear as it is brutal, insisting that *without law there is no injury*.

Two problems derive from this argument, of which only the first has been extensively discussed. It concerns the problem that every entitlement assigned to a right holder thereby also imposes duties of at least noninterference on all others – according to the correlativity of right and duties. This problem has been addressed by some of the alleged "human rights," particularly the "later generations" of human rights, which frequently pass over the assignment of duties.[44] The result is the proliferation of purely aspirational goals, which are put in the garb of "rights." Because of their conceptual flaws, it is, however, not surprising that they are then frequently "operationalized" in terms of "only" some minimum requirements, without, however, solving thereby the problem of the assignment of responsibility to a definite group of duty bearers. It is in this context that the "right to food" or the "right to movement" has been dominating the discussions. The former entails entitlements requiring actual transfers[45] (not only the supply of public goods); the latter presupposes "duty bearers" who also provide, aside from the Kantian notion of a "cosmopolitan right to visit,"[46] the right to residence and social rights for noncitizens, perhaps even the actual bestowal of citizenship on the claimants. Obviously, these rights can hardly "function" according to the template of basic human rights, which merely safeguarded free agency and the natural liberty of all agents. It imposed only a duty of noninterference on all others, and on the government the responsibility to supply the public goods of safety and the administration of justice. While obviously public goods are not "free," as is sometimes alleged – mainly by libertarians (when comparing Public goods to entitlements that entail transfers) – it is also clear that responsibilities for actual "transfers" imply that – aside from voluntary charitable donations – some forms of "tax" are necessary, be they assessments charged to the relevant "members," licensing

44 See the searching critique of O. O'Neill, "The Dark Side of Human Rights," in T. Christiano and J. Christman (eds.), *Contemporary Debates in Political Philosophy* (Chichester: Blackwell-Wiley, 2009), 425.

45 Such transfers need not involve only "handouts" of the surpluses in the developed world (which impact detrimentally the food production in the poor regions of the world), but could entail a whole host of measures such as "fair trade" of commodities, insurance schemes, transfer of technologies (water), etc. But whatever it is, it will not be limited by the "capacity-building" measures for supplying public goods.

46 See I. Kant, *Perpetual Peace*, in I. Kant, *Political Writings*, 2nd edn. (Cambridge: Cambridge University Press, 1991, Reis ed.), 93, 105–108: Third Definite Article of a Perpetual Peace: "[The] Cosmopolitan Right shall be limited to Conditions of Universal Hospitality."

fees, charges on transactions, user charges on the global commons, or whatever. Needless to say, such "responsibilities" have been fiercely resisted by the states and by many members of the "global civil society."

The other problem exposing the "darker side" of law is, however, much less visible. It derives from the fact that law also bestows "immunities" to right holders that make damages "injusticiable" – should they occur outside of legal relations among the parties concerned or when the actions taken were within the limits of the law. The foundation of this argument is, of course, Hobbes's claim that in the absence of a "common power, there is no law: where no law, no injustice."[47] To the extent he suggests that "the definition of INJUSTICE, is no other than the not Performance of Covenant. And whatsoever is not Unjust, is Just."[48] Hobbes reiterates here the distinctions between a *harm* (damage), which is not recognized as a cause of action, and an *injustice*, which has as a defining element that some law has been transgressed. In his work *Of the Citizen* (*De Cive*), he argued:

> IV. From these grounds it followes, that an injury can be done to no man but him with whom we enter Covenant, or to whom somewhat is made over by deed of gift, or to whom somwhat is promis'd by way of bargain. And therefore damaging and injuring are often disjoyn'd: for if a Master command his Servant, who hath promis'd to obey him, to pay a summe of money, or carry some present to a third man; the Servant, if he doe it not, hath indeed damag'd this third party, but he injur'd his Master onely. So also in a civill government, if any man offend another, with whom he hath made no Contract, he damages him to whom the evill is done, but he injures none but him to whom the power of government belongs:
>
> V. These words just, and unjust, as also justice, and injustice, are equivocall … When they are attributed to Actions, Just signifies as much as what's done with Right, and unjust, as what's done with injury: he who hath done some just thing is not therefore said to be a just Person, but guiltlesse, and he that hath one some unjust thing, we doe not therefore say he is an unjust, but guilty man.[49]

The result of these deliberations is that "responsible action" (i.e., action in accordance with legal obligations) cannot be injurious or "irresponsible" even if, as already stated, they do inflict some (unrecognized) damage on the parties of a transaction or even on uninvolved "innocent" bystanders. Hobbes seems

47 Hobbes, *Leviathan*, 188.

48 Ibid., 15, 1–2.

49 T. Hobbes, *De Cive* (1642), chapter III: "Of the Laws of Nature," available at www.unilibrary.com (accessed July 24, 2017), quote at 18ff.

to be blind to, or not disturbed by, this "darker side" of law, a problem that was, however, well-captured by the old Roman adage *summum ius, summa iniuria* (the highest justice is the highest injustice). He is satisfied in making a further distinction between just actions and just persons, the former immune from criticism when s/he acted in accordance of the law, the latter turning on the character of a person and his/her motives in "doing right," but being well aware that "innumerable actions of a just man may be unjust, and of an unjust man just."[50]

The fact that persons causally involved in doing damage *cannot be called to "respond"* when acting within the law as they are "free from punishment," enjoying impunity (*in-poena*) has, of course, ominous implications for "political responsibility" as its "judgment calls" are hardly ever subject to review – save perhaps in the sense that a minister has to resign if something terrible has happened on his or her watch, for which s/he is – quite ironically – frequently not "causally" responsible at all, or that the government falls and has to call new elections.

Perhaps the worst part of this analysis is that the widely shared notion of law's responsibility of insuring some form of "overall responsibility" might not be too optimistic but actually wrong, and requires at a minimum some further scrutiny and soul-searching. In short, law creates its own blind spots and is complicit in creating suffering, making it "invisible" by passing it over and by providing for the freedom of action for officials within institutions that "facilitate dispersals and disavowals of responsibility ... in consistent and patterned ways,"[51] as Scott Veitch has persuasively argued in his seminal analysis. But the conclusion that therefore some form of universal responsibility has to provide the appropriate cure is a tall order to fill, both conceptually and practically.

4 THE LIMITS OF LAW

The constitutive complicity of law in creating systematic injustices by dispersing responsibility, despite creating substantial harm – not just by miscarriages of justice through corruption or incompetence, but "systematically" – usually becomes visible when revolutions provide the catalyst of inquiring into the nature and the (continued) existence of the legal system,[52] or when in the

50 Ibid., 19.

51 S. Veitch, *Law and Irresponsibility: On the Legitimation of Human Suffering* (Abingdon: Routledge, 2007).

52 H. L. A. Hart, *The Concept of Law* (Oxford: Clarendon Press, 1961), chapter VI.

aftermath of internal war and mass violence issues of "transitional justice" have to be addressed.[53] In both cases, the legality of amnesties has to be ascertained and questions of the culpability of the old political apparatus and its legal support structures have to be decided (e.g., Chile, South Africa, Eastern Europe), or warlords or perpetrators of mass killings have to be "brought to justice."

Of course, here the problem of "many hands" arises, as everyone "doing his job" is somehow implicated but also excused. After all, authority is granted in modern society to individuals on the basis of some qualifications (knowledge, know-how), and the exercise of specific powers is limited further by hierarchies so that no one, save those at the apex, seem to be responsible overall. In this way, the immunities for the "many" are kept intact by the *respondeat superior* principle, while the top leadership is either "guilty" – as the buck has to stop somewhere – or it is "not guilty" if it claims the immunity granted through the occupation of an "office." But the latter position is difficult to maintain since the discretion granted thereby cannot be limitless, as it is granted for the exercise of specific duties even if its stands in tension with some general notion of accountability that is always part of the discretion and immunity granted. After all, even the Chinese emperor could lose his mandate from heaven, although ascertaining the limit was as difficult as determining when in the Lockean theory a "long train of abuses" justifies resistance against the government, and remains beset by theoretical and practical problems.

The invention of limiting criminal responsibilities to the "kingpins" nevertheless seems to provide an answer to some of the difficulties arising out of such assignments of broad discretionary powers. Similar to racketeering law – where the membership in a criminal organization is taken as proof of criminal intent (not only of liability) – membership in the top circles makes a member liable to be prosecuted. But as the Tokyo trials and the recent discussions in international criminal law show, "clear rules" for ascribing responsibility are hard to find and even harder to apply. What is one to make of a person who joins the inner circle of the government in order to end a war (rather than planning and waging it)? This was after all Judge Röling's point in dissenting from the majority decision of the Tokyo Tribunal in the case of Japan's Foreign Minister, Tojo.[54]

Furthermore, a breakdown of rules resulting in "indeterminacy" cannot be remedied by drafting the rules more carefully, as is sometimes suggested, because the near-automaticity to which "clear rules" are linked creates exactly

[53] R. Teitel, *Transitional Justice* (Oxford: Oxford University Press, 2000).
[54] B. V. A. Röling and A. Cassese, *The Tokyo Trial and Beyond* (Cambridge: Polity Press, 1993).

the problems Judge Röling had to face. The difficulty is due to the open-ended nature of our concepts (e.g., the rule may be "no vehicles in the park," but is a motor-driven wheelchair or toy car a vehicle?) and to the necessary appraisals in applying even the "clearest" rule. Thus, the "no swimming" rule posted at the edge of a reservoir seems clear enough, but we would consider a judge who fines a man for jumping into the water in order to rescue a child to be a person lacking in judgment.

Kant identifies such an application of a rule by rote as a peculiar form of "stupidity" (*Dummheit*), which – as he notes – can often be found even "among professors and people who do not lack logical capacity."[55] For Kant, such people suffer from a flaw (*Gebrechen*), as they do not possess common sense (*Mutterwitz*), which the "apprentice" of rule-handling (*Lehrling*) must possess and can only be trained by experience and analogical and exemplary reasoning. It cannot be derived from some further specifications of how to apply rules, as the threat of an infinite regress dashes our hopes for finding an algorithm. If at all, the problem has to be "solved" by a judgment call, which is quite different from a simple subsumption, since it attempts to find or see "the point" of a rule and to weigh its impact on other concerns. Such a process of deliberation requires imagination and dexterity in analogical reasoning rather than a strict logical inference.[56] It has to look for similarities while also assessing the weight of disabling dissimilarities, which can then be used for "distinguishing" cases (as in common law). In our above example of "no swimming," such an examination justifies the making of an "exception," which, however, neither invalidates the rule, nor subsumes this "case" under it.[57]

These considerations are of particular relevance in international law, which mostly deals with "singular" situations that are unclear and where "distinctions" are both factually (incomplete information) and normatively difficult (is it an "attack" or an accident?). The "normal" in international law is the abnormal in domestic law. There, crises involving war and peace or crimes that "shock humanity" are at issue rather than the numerous recurrent situations such as traffic problems, building codes, and standard contracts that rule in domestic law address. As Koskenniemi points out:

[55] I. Kant, *Kritik der Reinen Vernunft*, A174; B133–B135.

[56] The conceptual distinction between identical sameness (e.g., as created by a punch-hole device) and the ability to "go on" by finding the "sameness" through authoritative interpretation – thereby allowing also for change – is very important.

[57] For an interesting collection of essays on "exemplary" reasoning, see M. Lowry and S. Luedemann (eds.), *Exemplarity and Singularity: Thinking through Particulars in Philosophy, Literature and Law* (Abingdon: Routledge, 2015).

> In domestic normality it is possible to live with automatic rules because the alternative is so much worse. The occasional injustice is not too dramatic and will be dispelled. . . . But this is otherwise in an international emergency of some gravity. An injustice caused by the law immediately challenges the validity of the legal system . . . The point of the rule (that is, the need to prevent serious and large scale violations of fundamental human rights) is more important than its formal validity . . . the need to uphold the formal validity of the law cannot be compared to the weight of the impulse to act now . . . Any appeal for passivity in the interest of upholding a general sense of law obedience will ring hollow, even cynical.[58]

There are several points that need further unpacking. Take the last sentence, which points to a genuine dilemma of action in general (i.e., when and how to act), given that neither doing nothing nor trusting in chimerical grand designs are usually the available options. In this fog of uncertainty, withdrawal or wishful thinking, rather than critical reflection, tends to take over. While Koskenniemi certainly characterizes well the outrage that certain acts of pure rascality engender in us – and it would indeed be strange if lawyers were exempt from such reactions – the problem remains that international law frequently has to address situations not comparable to those "routine problems" in domestic law, and that the remedies, such as using force, are not comparable to ticketing a lawbreaker or even putting him or her in jail, but might involve "armed conflict."

Furthermore - and this is my second point – given the exceptional character of certain situations and applying "the law" to them brings out the "politics" of international law, as political choices, different from administrative decisions, are necessarily "selective" and particular. They claim our attention by their exceptionality even if the choices aim at "normalizing" the situation that seemed to be getting out of control. On-the-spot visits or crisis summits create new documents and slogans, even if not direct agreements (as one often converges on the lowest common denominator or resorts to circumlocutions). But, above all, those meetings provide for ample photo opportunities by which the decision-makers and other "celebrities" can display their "concern," as well as signal to the audience that they are on top of things, even if the event is more a public relations than a problem-solving exercise.

Here, Kosovo is just one example in a "long train" of policies that were more concerned with demonstrating that one is a "force for good" than with

58 M. Koskenniemi, "The Lady Doth Protest Too Much: Kosovo, and the Turn to Ethics in International Law," reprinted in M. Koskenniemi, *The Politics of International Law* (Oxford: Hart, 2011), chapter 4, at 123.

forging a viable strategy that fit the "local" problem. Since the clarification of the principles seemed the most important thing preoccupying the media and the foreign ministries alike (since who in his or her right mind could disagree with promoting human rights?), their application to a concrete situation could be left hanging. After all, were we not already in possession of a solution, codified in the manual of "best practices," which was just waiting to be applied by eager peacekeepers and helpers on the ground? If such an analysis prevails, the pathologies of organizational decision-making are likely to abound.[59] As in bad medicine, the disease you have is more likely to be a function of the apparatus the doctor just purchased than of a thorough diagnosis. If you are lucky, the procedures at least do not hurt you, but are only useless.

This leads me to my third and last point: that less might often be more. This realization – that the grand visions of law have not succeeded that much better than former philosophical speculations of progress and destiny – is certainly a "downer," but might also cause us to lose sight of the modest but important contribution of international law and its "problem-solving" routines. Scholars such as Henkin[60] and the Chayeses[61] have stressed this role, even if their confidence that form will follow function, or that "process" will win out "in the long run" over atavistic assertions of sovereignty, was not only overly optimistic, but, in a way, misdiagnosed the problem by "ruling out" possible dramatic reversals of the observed trends. Nevertheless, international law still "works" and allows us to communicate, exchange goods and ideas, and even move around, even if all these privileges are rather unevenly distributed. Obviously, the "right to movement" is cold comfort for those who want to leave but find no takers. As these examples suggest, the simplistic narrative of progress or the "end of history," in which law has taken over the role of the Kantian *natura Daedala*[62] pushing and shoving mankind to its *telos*, is a poor guide in dealing with actual problems, particularly if we think that our work is done by superficially labeling them instead of analyzing them, not to speak of the problem of commitment that flows from the decision to tackle them.

59 See M. Cohen, J. March, and J. Olsen, "A Garbage Can Model of Organizational Choice," (1972) 17 *Administrative Science Quarterly* 1.

60 L. Henkin, *How Nations Behave* (New York: Praeger, 1968).

61 A. Chayes and A. Handler Chayes, *The New Sovereignty: Compliance and International Regulatory Agreements* (Cambridge, MA: Harvard University Press, 1995).

62 Kant, *Perpetual Peace*, at 112: "For if I say that nature 'wills' this ... this does not mean that nature imposes on us a duty to do it, for duties can only be imposed by practical reason ... On the contrary, nature does it herself, whether we are willing or not: *fata volentem ducunt nolentem trahunt*."

5 SOME FINAL THOUGHTS (IN LIEU OF CONCLUSIONS)

It is the bane of conclusions that they are supposed to summarize the argument and also provide some "solutions." I shall decline this charge, even if not meeting those expectations might have the odium of a trespass. As an excuse I can provide only one reason: that those expectations reinforce some of our worst tendencies and that meeting them is incompatible with my responsibilities as an academic – taking up still another facet of responsibility!

It seems to me that those expectations fundamentally misunderstand what thinking about practical choices entails i.e., that it has to do with an active engagement with different ways of looking at a problem and of vetting arguments. This is quite different from assuming that all we need are some general concepts and the collection (and re-collection) of some "boiled-down" conclusions. Thinking is above all activity and thus more like a performance than making a product (although the emphasis on books and articles and their impact measures by bibliometrics seems to push us in this direction). To that extent, having argued against ready-made solutions based on dubious generalizations or "ideal theories," I do not want to involve myself at the end in a performative contradiction.

Thinking needs to be enacted by going again through the steps, since this is how we learn and acquire new capacities. The aim here cannot be a reproduction of a set of instructions or memorizing certain "results." Nobody "learns" mathematics by remembering the solutions of the previous problems, which are then normalized into data in order to generalize from them. Rather, the proof that we have "learned" something is that we can now do something that we have never before encountered, even if all the elements are familiar, such as the numbers or the words we use. Thinking is like being able to speak a language, which is not just the ability to repeat the "model" sentence that we picked up in the language lab, which a halfway-intelligent parrot can learn.

So having spent considerable time in this chapter warning the readers against putting their trust in the old epistemic system requiring clear definitions and disciplinary understandings and following their respective methodologies, I do not want to give people now the marching orders for a new research program, as disciplinary "primers" so often suggest. If I tried to convey any message, it was the one that thinking has to be critical, not only challenging traditional wisdoms, but also showing why certain ways of thinking about problems are misleading, such as when Kelsen tries to "prove" that, for a legal system, *non liquet* cannot exist. Although no formal proof can be found in his writings – I at least have not come across one – making the point in formal terms does not distort Kelsen's "theory." It would have to take the following form:

(I) In logically closed systems of norms, a case of non liquet (in the sense of non-decidability of a concrete issue) is impossible;
(II) Law is such a system;
(III) Therefore, non liquet is impossible in law.

But this is simply a sophism. The major premise (I) is not a law of nature (e.g., all men are mortal), but rather an analytical truth having defined a system as closed and complete. Of course, the fact that even logic is not such a "closed" system, as the liar's paradox shows, should already give us some pause. The minor premise (II) is not a factually established truth, but just an assertion, and thus not analogous to "Socrates is a man." Consequently, the conclusion does not follow (unlike "Socrates is mortal").

In short, there might be "gaps" in law, and law itself might be much less orderly than assumed. Whether these gaps should be filled and whether this "filling" should be done by courts or law experts, especially if it occurs in such a contentious area as international politics, is of course another question. Here, the *Nuclear Weapons*[63] case and the voluminous literature it engendered provide much food for thought.[64] In this case, the often-criticized "majority opinion" – backed only by the casting vote of the president in order to break the tie – seems to have been that this gap should be acknowledged and filled by "legislation" through the political organs of the international community rather than the Court.

The opposite gambit is that lawyers have to acknowledge the politics in law and take responsibility as "professionals," particularly at a time in which the allure of the former expert is on the wane.[65] But this raises three further problems: What type of political action? To whom is this new professional supposed to be "responsible"? Finally, where are the levers for moving things? True, there is an increasing number of activists and of social "movements" that has added new themes to the political agenda and is conveying them to us by often carefully staged spectacles. However, making the evening news might be good for mobilization, but not for sustained political action. The problem

[63] *Legality of the Threat or Use of Nuclear Weapons*, advisory opinion, [1996] ICJ Reports 226.
[64] E.g., see the collection of essays edited by L. Boisson de Chazournes and P. Sands, *International Law, The International Court of Justice and Nuclear Weapons* (Cambridge: Cambridge University Press, 1999).
[65] E.g., see Kennedy, *A World of Struggle*. See also the more "existential" argument made in several of Martti Koskenniemi's articles, collected in Koskenniemi, *The Politics of International Law*, especially those collected in parts IV and V.

is simply that the most durable organizations of "civil" society are mostly one-purpose organizations, such as Amnesty International or Oxfam. They are good at what they are doing precisely because they are *not* political in the sense of taking responsibility for an overall political program that would have to address a comprehensive list of issues, establish priorities among them, and win support for their realization. In the absence of such an institutionalization, the "discourse of the 'global good'" remains elusive and prone to propagandistic cant. However, these are issues that will have to be taken up on another occasion.

4

Between or Beyond Legal Orders

Questioning the Concept of Legal Order

SANNE TAEKEMA[1]

1 INTRODUCTION

A generally recognized feature of the modern legal world is the existence of multiple bodies of law that coexist, interact, and conflict in various ways. The concept of inter-legality – the central theme of this project – generates a specific perspective on the relationships between the various guises of law. In his seminal piece, "Law: A Map of Misreading," Boaventura de Sousa Santos puts forward the idea as follows: "We live in a time of porous legality or legal porosity, multiple networks of legal orders forcing us to constant transitions and trespassings. Our legal life is constituted by an intersection of different legal orders, that is, by *interlegality*."[2] Sousa Santos emphasizes the diversity of the phenomena of law and the overlapping and intermeshing that goes on between them. However, he also makes use of the concept of legal order, a concept that can mean different things, not all of them amenable to the use he makes of it. In this chapter, my purpose is not to scrutinize the idea of inter-legality as such, but to investigate the underlying concept of legal order in its light: What possible meanings may that concept have if it needs to make room for inter-legality? Such an investigation cannot escape linking to underlying discussions on the concept of law. However, the goal of this paper is to try to get a grip on the slightly elusive quality of the concept of legal *order*, which possibly has a more restricted meaning than the concept of law.

My approach to this investigation is to reconstruct two conceptions of legal order as ideal types – a systemic view and an interactional view of

[1] Many thanks to Samantha Besson, Wibren van der Burg, Thomas Riesthuis, and the editors of this volume for their comments.

[2] Reproduced in B. de Sousa Santos, *Toward a New Common Sense: Law, Science and Politics in the Paradigmatic Transition* (Abingdon: Routledge, 1995), at 473 (emphasis in original).

legal order – and to trace the way these two conceptualizations make sense of the interrelations between legal orders. Additionally, it seems worthwhile to see whether there are other aspects of law that can illuminate why the notion of order differs in the two conceptions. The avenue that will be pursued here is the role of legal values, more particularly the value of coherence as the legal value that calls for order most directly. The different interpretations of coherence that suit the systemic and the interactional view can be explained by their link to the other different values highlighted in these two conceptions. However, I contend that including the value dimension makes it easier to see how the different conceptions of legal order combine.

As a preliminary note, I should clarify that the background of this chapter is in discussions within legal theory and legal philosophy. I am aware that there are close links between the views discussed here and debates in international law, and particularly international relations.[3] This is not the focus of the chapter, but there is a continuity between the interactional view of legal order and constructivist positions in international relations theory. I briefly address that link through discussing the work of Brunnée and Toope.[4]

2 THE NOTION OF LEGAL ORDER

Most legal scholars are familiar with the concept of legal order as a rough equivalent of "legal system": a body of law that can be identified, like the Indonesian legal order, the Dutch legal order, the international legal order, or the European legal order. Often, the term is used very loosely to denote a specific kind of law, merely specifying a subcategory of law in general. The European legal order, for instance, can mean different things, depending on whether you link it to the European Union (EU), the geographical territory of Europe, or European history. This loose sense of legal order invites discussions such as the fragmentation debate, which questions whether the international legal order really counts as such.

3 In particular, international relations has much more extensively discussed the notion of practice underlying this discussion, using the work of Wenger and Adler, than nationally oriented legal scholarship in particular: see E. Adler and V. Pouliot (eds.), *International Practices* (Cambridge: Cambridge University Press, 2011). The influence of (theories of) pragmatism, too, is limited in legal scholarship, but clearly recognizable in international relations scholarship. This pragmatist view resonates with my ideas on the importance of developing a pragmatist legal theory.

4 J. Brunnée and S. Toope, *Legitimacy and Legality in International Law: An Interactional Account* (Cambridge: Cambridge University Press, 2010).

As a matter of terminology (and reflecting a deeper theoretical point), it is interesting to note that lawyers' casual use of "legal order" almost invariably refers to an order as an object – something out there in the world of law (even if this world is an artificial one). There is, however, an equally important use of the term "order" that expresses the idea that ordering is an activity – the activity of bringing structure and regularity to a messy environment. Although the first notion of order dominates legal thought, the point of departure for this chapter is that both notions of order can be fruitfully used to think about legal order and that they lead to very different conceptions of legal order. An additional reason for investigating a second notion of legal order is that there is a rich tradition in socio-legal work – especially legal anthropology – that does not use a legal doctrinal notion of legal order, but studies legal order as an empirical phenomenon. Although the purpose in this chapter is not to explain how legal order is used as a concept in socio-legal studies, the use made of legal order in that field is relevant as input for a theoretical construction of the second perspective on legal order.

An important theoretical tool for the distinction between two types of legal order is Wibren van der Burg's idea of product versus practice models of law.[5] The product model of law is exemplified in the way we think of law as a set of authoritative texts or as a "coherent body of norms."[6] The practice model is recognizable when we think of doing law – the activity of interpreting, applying, and generally using law. An important characteristic of the product model is that law is seen as something we can describe, something that has a stable existence. This does not preclude change, but at any given time and place we can present a picture of the law. The practice model, on the other hand, is characterized by a dynamic and fluctuating account of law: people continually shape their legal expectations and norms in the process of acting legally. In the practice model, it makes little sense to speak of the law as if it is something with a separate existence; law is rather an aspect of our social life.

Whereas the two models represent general conceptions of law, a more specific notion of legal order can be developed on this basis. A product model of law generates a systemic conception of legal order, while a practice model of law generates an interactional conception of legal order. In the context of this paper, it is most fruitful to see them as ideal types in Weber's sense. The core of the systemic conception of legal order is that a legal order is seen as a structured whole, usually as a set of norms in which the relationships

[5] W. van der Burg, *The Dynamics of Law and Morality. A Pluralist Account of Legal Interactionism* (Farnham: Ashgate, 2014), at 21–26.

[6] Ibid., at 23.

between those norms are specified. The theoretical position that one can most closely associate with the systemic conception is Kelsen's pure theory of law.[7] Every legal system is built up of discrete identifiable norms that derive their validity from authorization by other norms, culminating in the basic norm at the top of the pyramid. Generalizing from Kelsen's position, we can see that such a systemic view of legal order has a number of characteristics: it is closed with clear boundaries; it has a focus on validity of norms; and it has a foundational structure.

In contrast, the interactional conception of legal order presents legal order as a social practice of legal activity, as a web of interactions between people giving rise to legal expectations. The legal theory most closely associated with the interactional conception is Lon Fuller's theory of implicit or interactional law.[8] Interactional law is a process of reciprocal adjustment of conduct on the basis of expectations; law is implicit in the conduct of people toward one another. Legal order is therefore the practice of intermeshing actions and expectations. Customary law is the traditional category we can most easily associate with this view,[9] but the claim for interactional law is broader: all of law eventually depends on horizontal reciprocal expectations.[10] The following characteristics of an interactional view of legal order can be derived: it is open to, or even part of, social practices more broadly; it has a focus on the efficacy of norms; and it has an organic form of arising implicitly.

If we focus on the differences between the two types, maybe the most striking difference is that of the boundaries of legal order. In systemic legal order, it is in principle very clear what belongs to the legal order, because there are norms specifying what qualifies as such. In interactional legal order, the difference between legal order and other social practices may be gradual and shifting. What holds an interactional legal order together is not immediately clear. This may be the stability of the group of people involved; for instance, a traditional customary legal order seems to survive most easily in isolation, without contact with other groups. It may also be a certain place

[7] H. Kelsen, *Pure Theory of Law* (Berkeley: University of California Press, 1967, Knight trans.).

[8] L. L. Fuller, *The Principles of Social Order. Selected Essays of Lon. L. Fuller* (Durham, NC: Duke University Press, 1981, Winston ed.).

[9] Ibid., at 213.

[10] Fuller uses two contrasting concepts in his work: made or enacted law and implicit or interactional law; see L. L. Fuller, *Anatomy of the Law* (New York: Praeger, 1968). There is debate on the exact place of the two forms of law in his theory – I take interactional law to be primary; see S. Taekema, "Private Law as an Open Legal Order: Understanding Contract and Tort as Interactional Law," (2014) 43 *Netherlands Journal of Legal Philosophy* 140. For extensive elaborations and interpretations of his work, see Brunnée and Toope, *Legitimacy and Legality*, and van der Burg, *Dynamics*.

in which the practice is rooted. An obvious example relates to local traffic rules: taking part in traffic in a certain city entails adjusting your expectations to those of the people you encounter. It may also be the purpose of the practice that holds it together, in which norms serve to further that purpose. Sports clubs may serve as an example. There may be various principles that provide a sense of unity to an interactional legal order.

The second difference – the focus of the validity or efficacy of norms – is closely related to the foundational versus the organic. Systemic legal order can derive its criteria of validity from the highest norms of the system: a constitution or other foundational norm usually provides such criteria. Predominantly, but not necessarily, such a foundation specifies formal criteria of validity: authorizing parliament to make law in accordance with a certain procedure; or authorizing courts to invalidate faulty legislation. Thus, the systemic conception seems to echo legal positivist theory.[11] It is, however, also fairly easy to think of a natural law foundation that forms the basis of the system. In that case, substantive criteria are included to determine validity. Interactional legal order evaluates norms differently by asking whether the norms in question contribute to the smooth operation of the interactional practice. A norm that effectively coordinates conduct is part of the legal order. Such norms can emerge, change, and fade away spontaneously, exemplifying the organic nature of interactional legal order.

A possibly less visible, but more crucial difference is the relationship between legal order and the actors involved. The ideal-typical systemic order is an order of legal norms: the norms specify who has an active role to play in the legal order and also who is subject to the legal order. Actors are important in the legal order because they are authorized to make decisions and to make changes to the norms.[12] As long as we can take the foundational norm for granted (which, of course, is one of the great points of debate for theories of legal positivism, but which I leave aside here), actors are assigned certain roles and institutions are created that together form vehicles for normative change. On the other hand, there is a clear sense of who is subject to the legal order: subjects are defined by it (think of legal personhood) or explicitly recognized as subjects or barred from being so. Territoriality is the most common principle of inclusion, but personal

[11] In addition to Kelsen, prominent examples include H. L. A. Hart, *The Concept of Law* (Oxford: Clarendon Press, 1961), and Joseph Raz, *The Authority of Law* (Oxford: Clarendon Press, 1979).

[12] There is thus a close relation between actors and norms in systemic order that is exemplified by Hart's notion of officials. Officials and secondary rules are mutually dependent in Hart's theory.

systems are also used. The essential point is that it is the legal order itself – the norms within it – that specifies its applicability.

In an interactional legal order, there is no such clear definition of the roles of actors: it is up to the actors themselves to determine the norms of the order. This is an intersubjective process: by taking part in the legal order, an actor subjects himself to the interactional norms of the order. A crucial aspect is therefore the identification with the practice and the group engaged in it. By identifying as a participant, you submit yourself to the expectations that are part of that practice, but depending on the circumstances, you may also help shape those expectations. This is not meant as an optimistic picture: because a tacit understanding of norms and relationships is a large factor in interactional legal orders, they may suppress in elusive ways. There may easily be a conservative streak in interactional legal order because of the weight of set expectations and norms. Once you participate in the practice, there will often seem to be no choice but to accept the norms that are in use. However, practices may also leave room for plurality and be open to change from within.

3 INTER-SYSTEMIC OR INTER-PRACTICAL: RELATING LEGAL ORDER TO INTER-LEGALITY

In this section, the aim is to discuss the implications of both views for the conceptualization of inter-legality. One of the attractive points of the idea of inter-legality is that it draws attention to the overlap and interconnectedness of legal orders. It makes sense of the possibility that legal orders may be combined, integrating norms of one order into another. In my understanding, inter-legality as such does not make a specific claim about the feasibility of welding together the norms of different orders: it leaves room for both integration and conflict. Here, I want to address these two consequences of the plurality of norms from different orders from both the systemic and the interactional perspectives.

As a preliminary step, it is useful to give a brief account of how each perspective deals with conflicting norms within one legal order. Systemic legal order works with conflict rules, the most important one being hierarchy: the higher norm sets aside the lower norm (well-known as the *lex superior* conflict rule). There are many other conflict rules, and what these have in common is their ex ante character: the rules purport to offer a solution for any conflict between norms that may arise in future. In addition, systemic legal order authorizes specific actors or institutions to deal with conflicting norms, primarily (but not exclusively) courts.

Interactional legal order is more reactive: the relationship between norms remains undefined, and there is no presumption that norms will conflict. If conflicts do arise, these are resolved on an ad hoc basis or, similarly to systemic order, by an actor who decides what to do with the conflict. The authority of the actor in question may be based on a variety of factors, such as tradition, power, or social standing. More importantly, in interactional legal order, not every conflict between norms needs to be resolved. If a conflict is not serious and does not threaten the functioning of the practice, there is not much need to address it. Alternatively, one can argue that conflict only needs resolution if the participants in the legal order feel it needs to be resolved.

This difference can then be extended to the relation to other legal orders: How do a systemic and an interactional view make sense of normative claims from different backgrounds? From the point of view of systemic legal order, the question can be posed in two ways: first, how a norm from one legal order can be internalized in another; and second, which legal order should have priority when two norms clash. The legal discussion on multilevel legal orders can be used to illustrate this.[13] A European national system, such as the Dutch or the German, is bound to incorporate the norms produced by the EU. Mostly, this means following the rules of the EU treaties, which define the competence of EU lawmakers. This relationship between EU and member states was solidified in the well-known cases of *Van Gend & Loos* and *Costa* v *ENEL*.[14] However, these (foundational) treaty rules do not always give clear answers when an EU rule and a national rule conflict. In those cases, the foundational norms of the EU system may be pitted against those of a member state, of which cases before the German Constitutional Court are good examples. On the one hand, there are nice sets of rules for negotiating the application of rules from a different legal order: in addition to deference to norms from a higher order, think also of international private law rules establishing a public order test, or jurisdiction rules based on territoriality. On the other hand, there will always be the underlying question of the ultimate priority on the level of foundational documents. The apparent paradox of the Dutch Constitution can serve as a case in point: it specifies that directly applicable international law has precedence over national law (article 94).[15] This is a general rule of deference

[13] On this point particularly, I owe much to discussions with Thomas Riesthuis, who is writing a dissertation theorizing on multilevel legal orders.

[14] Case 26/62, *Van Gend & Loos* v *Nederlandse Administratie der Belastingen*, ECLI:EU:C:1963:1, and case 6/64, *Costa* v *ENEL*, ECLI:EU:C:1964:66.

[15] The text of article 94 reads: "Statutory regulations in force within the Kingdom shall not be applicable if such application is in conflict with provisions of treaties or of resolutions by international institutions that are binding on all persons."

to international law as a higher order. But is the priority of international over Dutch law itself not determined by national law (i.e., is it not the Dutch Constitution that rules by establishing this priority)? Can a constitution relinquish its own place at the top of the hierarchy? It may also happen that neither of the two legal orders gives in, at which point the systemic view has no resources to resolve the conflict. In the worst case, there is a stalemate of two superiority claims and then political power takes over.

Inter-Legality in systemic legal order can thus be characterized as the attempt to fit parts of a legal order into another legal order, with the aim of smoothing out inconsistencies and preserving the integrity of the system. Systemic legal order has tools to achieve such reconfigurations of legal orders, but these tools may run out when there is a conflict at a foundational level.[16]

From the point of view of interactional legal order, the questions of different normative claims are rather different. The starting point here is the uses actors make of different norms in practice. A norm from a different legal order may be called upon to support a claim or interpretation if one of the actors involved in the conflict sees the relevance of that norm, and conflicts between norms become important when others call upon competing norms. Much anthropological work stresses the positive use certain groups in society make of the national legal order in their traditional customary or religious legal orders.[17] Norms that make sense in daily life are combined with each other to form a legal order that combines elements from different legal backgrounds. Although it may sound as if this is a matter of picking and choosing norms that a group likes, this is not a fair picture. In many situations, norms are presented because they are backed up by powerful actors or institutions. If the local police enforces state criminal law, it is to be expected that those criminal law norms would exert some influence in the local community. However, here the work of Sally Falk Moore and Robert Ellickson may be used to give a more nuanced picture. As Moore argues in her theory of semiautonomous social fields, norms from a different legal order that is perceived to be outside of the direct environment of the participants in a local legal order will be interpreted in a way that

[16] The prominent debate on the interplay of legal orders from a systemic point of view has been that on (global) legal pluralism, most notably in relation to the work of N. Krisch, *Beyond Constitutionalism: The Pluralist Structure of Postnational Law* (Oxford: Oxford University Press, 2010), and P. S. Berman, *Global Legal Pluralism: A Jurisprudence of Law Beyond Borders* (Cambridge: Cambridge University Press, 2012).

[17] M. Simon Thomas, *The Challenge of Legal Pluralism: Local Dispute Settlement and the Indian-State Relationship in Ecuador* (Abingdon: Routledge, 2017).

fits the local practice.[18] And as Ellickson shows, participants in a local practice can treat the norms of the national legal order as merely a background to their internal affairs, and only appeal to those norms when an outsider enters the practice.[19] Moreover, people may try to use particular norms instrumentally, and may try out various routes to further their own interests. A good example is provided by Julia Eckert, who describes how a divorce in a Mumbai slum unfolds.[20] The conflict over the return of the dowry is put before a caste council (*Jamaat*), which recommends reconciliation; Tara, the mother of the wife, turns to a local nongovernmental organization, which threatens to file a case of "dowry harassment" against the husband, and thereby to involve the police, and finally she claims additional maintenance on the basis of a rumor about a Supreme Court case. Eckert argues that the case exemplifies the transformation of legal understandings and claims in the process of trying to further one's interest. In this divorce case, various norms were appealed to that could be said to conflict, but were all accepted by Tara: customary marriage law, national legal divorce law, and women's rights. According to Eckert, all of these were combined by Tara on the basis of her feeling that the husband had treated her daughter unjustly. Eckert characterizes the case as an example of inter-legality and reinterprets inter-legality as "different norms and normative orders informing each other," resulting in new legal meanings.

At this point, an interactional conception of legal order may be said to reach its limits. One could argue that it leads to an unordered view of law because it reduces any legal ordering to its relevance to the interactional problem at hand and the interpretation given to that problem by particular actors.[21] One might say that plurality of both norms and expectations may exist as long as there is no visible – or felt – clash. Once a problem of conflicting expectations and opposing normative claims is experienced, normative resources need to be mobilized to resolve that conflict, either by finding common ground or compromise or by turning to a mechanism or actor to

[18] S. F. Moore, "Law and Social Change: The Semi-Autonomous Social Field As an Appropriate Subject of Study," (1973) 7 *Law and Society Review* 719.

[19] R. C. Ellickson, *Order without Law: How Neighbors Settle Disputes* (Cambridge, MA: Harvard University Press, 1991).

[20] J. Eckert, "What is the Context of 'Law in Context'?" in S. P. Dolan and L. Heckendorn Urscheler (eds.), *Concepts of Law: Comparative, Jurisprudential, and Social Science Perspectives* (Abingdon: Routledge, 2014), 225.

[21] S. Taekema, "Fragments and Continuities of Law and ICT: A Pragmatist Approach to Understanding Legal Pluralism," in W. de Been, P. Arora, and M. Hildebrandt (eds.), *Crossroads in New Media, Identity and Law: The Shape of Diversity to Come* (London: Palgrave Macmillan, 2015), 80.

decide. In an interactional conception, order is thus mainly invisible, making the boundaries of the ordered practice invisible too. From the point of view of some actors, like Tara, the notion of legal order has no meaning – they simply need resources to solve problems. However, this perspective cannot be generalized: a variety of actors take part in legal ordering, with different notions of what their particular legal orders mean.

Some examples: for some groups, a national legal order may come to be experienced as complementing a religious legal order, as Wibo van Rossum argues in relation to the Alevi minority in the Netherlands.[22] Some claims may be regarded as best treated by the Alevi *cem*, while others are seen as better suited to being brought before a state court. Others, especially those who work with a national legal order professionally, such as lawyers or judges, may identify with that legal order to such an extent that they hardly recognize other legal orders as relevant. This may be true of non-state legal orders such as religious or customary orders, as well as of supranational orders.[23]

Inter-Legality in interactional legal order therefore points to a variety of possible links between legal orders. Most importantly, inter-legality can become an integral part of an interactional process of transforming a legal order. The development of a legal order can take place in numerous different instances that give rise to a plurality of legal practices. However, since the key component in interactional legal order is the formation of reciprocal expectations, there is a limit to the pluralization of practice; ultimately, participants together determine what the legal order becomes.

4 THE VALUES OF ORDERS

So far, I have presented two extreme, ideal-typical conceptions of legal order, highlighting and even magnifying the differences between them. These views can be moderated by investigating how each may acknowledge the relevance of the other perspective on order. A systemic view may acknowledge the relevance of interactional practice for the formation or interpretation of norms. An interactional view may acknowledge the importance of ordered sets of norms in shaping interactional expectations. There will, however, be an asymmetry, prioritizing the primary viewpoint: for instance, the implicit or

22 W. van Rossum, "Religious Courts alongside Secular State Courts: The Case of the Turkish Alevis," (2008) 8 *Law, Social Justice & Global Development Journal* 1–17.

23 E.g., on the limited engagement with European law by Polish judges, see U. Jaremba, *National Judges As EU Law Judges: The Polish Civil Law System* (Leiden: Martinus Nijhoff, 2014).

tacit understanding of order in the interactional view is difficult to conceptualize in a systemic view. Vice versa, the mere existence of written rules has no purchase in an interactional view. This point – that there is not a perfect middle that combines the two in equal measure – may be contested. For instance, the argument made by Nicole Roughan about the relative authority of law focuses on the interactions between authorities, but uses a systemic account of legal order. She develops her account in response to Raz's idea of the supremacy claim of legal systems, working in plurality by replacing that idea with a relative authority claim.[24] Although relative authority can be interpreted as the introduction of an interactional element, the conceptual base is still a systemic concept of legal order.

In this section, I want to explore whether a focus on the legal values acknowledged in either view can help to forge connections between the systemic and the interactional view of legal order. My intuition here is that in both views values are important sources for explaining and justifying the character of legal order. My main focus will be on the value of coherence, the primary reason for this being that coherence is the legal value most closely connected to the notion of order. However, because the value of coherence is linked to other legal values (such as justice and legal certainty), an exclusive discussion of coherence makes little sense. Neil MacCormick even defines coherence as a matter of relating norms to "justifying and explanatory values"; it is the interconnection between values and principles that provides coherence in law.[25]

Coherence is mainly discussed in the context of legal (judicial) reasoning (i.e., when a particular decision or interpretation is made, it is required that it needs to cohere with the set of relevant other decisions, interpretations, or norms).[26] Coherence differs from consistency in its relationship to justification.[27] Whereas consistency between norms simply means that they do not contradict, coherence requires that the set of norms makes sense as a whole. Both in a systemic and in an interactional view of legal order, coherence seems to matter, but its value is more limited in an interactional view. In a systemic view, coherence has a closer link to consistency: for instance, conflict rules provide formal ways to smooth out inconsistencies. When the contents of a higher and lower rule conflict, the formal hierarchy dissolves the inconsistency. Coherence mainly comes in when the interrelations

[24] N. Roughan, *Authorities: Conflicts, Cooperation, and Transnational Legal Theory* (Oxford: Oxford University Press, 2013), at 154–157.

[25] N. MacCormick, *Legal Reasoning and Legal Theory* (Oxford: Oxford University Press, 1978), at 153.

[26] A. Amaya, "Legal Justification by Optimal Coherence," (2011) 24 *Ratio Juris* 304.

[27] J. Hage, "Law and Coherence," (2004) 17 *Ratio Juris* 87, 88.

between rules at higher levels or with principles need to be addressed. In an interactional view, coherence is primarily a matter of the experienced sense that participants make of the practice. There is a need to justify actions and interpretations in light of the point of the practice. This does not always require an extensive argument on the way an action relates to the practice as a whole; it may be enough that a plausible story can be told in light of the interactions that are going on.[28]

At this point, it is useful to reference the discussion on different forms of coherence. In the debate on coherence theory, a distinction is made between global coherence and local coherence. Global coherence requires coherence of the whole set of norms, while local coherence only requires coherence with the norms relevant for the decision. From the earlier discussion of systemic legal order, it is apparent that the global form of coherence fits this more closely, because it requires coherence down to the level of the basic norms. If we view legal order as an interactive practice, coherence is only needed to make sense of interactions and the resolution of particular conflicting normative claims. Then local coherence, in the form of a relatively small set of principles with which to cohere in the context of the problem at hand, seems sufficient. However, within a systemic view, it is also possible to argue that global coherence is too strong a requirement. Especially if the systemic character of a legal order is based on the formal attribution of the competence to make norms (as in a Kelsenian system), it is the non-contradiction of competences rather than the coherence of the substantive norms that matters. The distinction between global and local coherence therefore does not map the two ideal types neatly.

However, the distinction between global and local coherence is still helpful here because it can be used to explore with which other values coherence may be associated. In this light, global and local coherence still have a primary association with the systemic and the interactional views of legal order, respectively. Amalia Amaya explains the difference between global and local coherence as the difference between a commitment to holistic justification (i.e., in the light of the system of beliefs as a whole) and a commitment to contextual justification (i.e., adapting the standards of justification to the context of the decision).[29]

[28] Although he does not conceptualize his notion in terms of interaction or practice, Del Mar's discussion of "deep coherence" seems to fit here. He emphasizes the way understanding of rules is embedded in experience and its dependence on narrative images (based on the work of Bernard Jackson); see M. Del Mar, "System Values and Understanding Legal Language," (2008) 21 *Leiden Journal of International Law* 29, 45.

[29] A. Amaya, *The Tapestry of Reason: An Inquiry into the Nature of Coherence and Its Role in Legal Argument* (Oxford: Hart, 2015), at 473 and 526, respectively.

Thus, the link between systemic versus practice views of legal order and coherence can be made by distinguishing between holistic and contextualist coherence. This distinction also allows for clarifying the links between coherence and other values within conceptions of legal order. A first link is one to different conceptions of the value of justice. A main driver for holistic coherence is the value of formal equality (or "formal justice" in Radbruch's terms); requiring coherence supports equal application of norms. Treating like cases alike combines well with coherence of underlying principles. Contextualist coherence, on the other hand, is fueled by equity or justice in the individual case: the fair solution of the problem at hand is of primary importance.

However, in the different interpretations of justice we can also see the possible links between the systemic and the interactional views: local claims for justice are not just local, they may also have "global" overtones and inspirations. Whereas most legal claims are demands for a just solution to a conflict or problem, some claims extend to the broader principles of a legal order as such. Many human rights claims, for instance, are not simply problem-solving claims – they are demands for legal recognition of a principle or even an identity.

To illustrate: requiring Muslim girls to take part in coed swimming classes is not just a solution to a school's problem of organizing its curriculum, it is also the expression of a broad state policy of integration in education that has repercussions for religion-based claims in other policy areas.[30] This is an example that can also be framed as an inter-legality issue: claims based on religious order are brought into the state legal order, bringing up the question whether they can peacefully coexist. In Switzerland, the answer in this particular conflict is: no. From a systemic point of view, there is an establishment of the precedence of one legal order over the other, or simply the denial of the legal character of the religious claim: not every normative order equals a legal order.[31] From an interactional view, matters are different: the line between legal and nonlegal is blurred, and a group practice may treat certain religious rules as law. In that case, the story does not stop here: the process of inter-legality will continue, although one needs to be close to see it. Will the concessions made by the schools – allowing burkini swimsuits – be accepted, or will the parents turn their backs on public schools? In the interactional

[30] *Osmanoglu and Kocabas* v *Switzerland*, Application No. 29086/12, January 10, 2017.

[31] Under the latter interpretation, this is a case of normative pluralism rather than inter-legality; see J. Klabbers and T. Piiparinen (eds.), *Normative Pluralism and International Law: Exploring Global Governance* (Cambridge: Cambridge University Press, 2013).

view, the dynamics of the interactions in the local context will continue and may build up to a new conflict.

One way of explaining the turn to global coherence and formal justice is by recognizing the internal logic of a court such as the European Court of Human Rights as prioritizing a systemic view of legal order. Here, the demand for justice needs to take the specified form of a claim to recognition of religious freedom; other ways of framing the problem do not fit. The language of the court frames the problem as a foundational conflict between values of freedom and equality and highlights the role of the state to make policy choices between them. If there is a sound justification, the state is allowed to prescribe formal equality, and the court can thereby tell a coherent story of the system of human rights protection. Some attention is paid to the experience of the people involved (e.g., in the discussion of the possible accommodation of the parents' concerns), but this is limited.

To step back again from the context of this example, there is another way of understanding the pull of global or holistic coherence in relation to justice, which starts from an interactional view of order. One of the main theoretical sources of the interactional view is pragmatism, which is particularly relevant in this context.[32] A pragmatist view starts from problem-solving experience and highlights the role of values and principles in contributing to solving problems.[33] For Dewey, this meant seeing values as hypotheses, as proposed directions for problem-solving. A crucial corollary of this view is that the endorsement of particular values needs to be based on broad consequentialist reasoning: only if the overall consequences of adopting such values are justifiable should they be used as the basis for solving the problem. Although this consequentialist reasoning is done in the context of the particular problem at hand, and thus demands local coherence and fairness, there is no clear stopping place for consequential reasoning: all relevant consequences need to be taken on board. Therefore, the consequences for the larger practice and the direction it is pushed to by a proposed solution will often be part of the reasoning. Although the starting point and the action to be taken as the outcome of the inquiry are local and problem-based, the reasoning in the inquiry may take on board larger issues of formal justice and equality. In a view of legal order as interactional practice, specifically legal values may be recognized that tend toward a more holistic interpretation of coherence. In addition

[32] F. V. Kratochwil, "Making Sense of 'International Practices'," in Adler and Pouliot (eds.), *International Practices*, 36.

[33] J. Dewey, *The Quest for Certainty*, reproduced in J. Dewey, *The Later Works, 1925–1953, Volume 4* (Carbondale: Southern Illinois University Press, 2008, Boydston ed.).

to formal equality, legal certainty is important, as is the rule of law value of legality.[34] These values provide an opening to systemic considerations in an interactional view, to be balanced against typically interactional legal values such as responsiveness and fairness. A pragmatist interpretation of interactional legal order can thus bring in a dimension of systemic order without fully succumbing to a systemic mode of argumentation.

5 THE INTER-LEGALITIES BETWEEN INTERACTIONAL AND SYSTEMIC ORDER IN A TRANSNATIONAL CONTEXT

I ended the previous section with a brief discussion of pragmatist underpinnings of interactional legal order and the way this can bring in values associated with systemic legal order. In this section, I will pursue this line further by going into the ways in which a conceptualization of legal order from the interactional perspective may bring in aspects of the systemic view. The context of application is that of transnational legal phenomena,[35] because this is the legal context in which the idea of inter-legality seems to apply most clearly. This is of course without denying – as should be clear from the discussion above – that inter-legality may also be observed within a national context. The transnational legal context referred to includes both phenomena beyond national borders, of international law, and across borders, involving national as well as international law.

In the area of international law, a good starting point is the theory of Jutta Brunnée and Stephen Toope,[36] which is one of the very few theories that explicitly adopts the label of "interactional law." On the basis of Fuller's principles of legality, they present international law as primarily a practice of legality. They describe lawmaking as an activity that depends on shared understandings in practices that (come to) share principles of legality as criteria for legitimate legal norms. Positive law and legal rules are thus, on the one hand, the outcome of interactional processes and, on the other hand, "a step on the way to legality."[37] The crucial element in their theory is the development of shared legal understandings in practice, to which the creation

[34] At least in the senses endorsed by Selznick and Fuller. See, respectively, P. Selznick, "Sociology and Natural Law," (1961) 6 *Natural Law Forum* 84, and L. L. Fuller, *The Morality of Law*, 2nd edn. (New Haven, CT: Yale University Press, 1969).

[35] I use Jessup's broad definition of transnational law "to include all law that regulates actions or events that transcend national frontiers"; see P. C. Jessup, *Transnational Law* (New Haven, CT: Yale University Press, 1956), at 1.

[36] Brunnée and Toope, *Legitimacy and Legality*.

[37] Ibid., at 72.

of a formal legal norm contributes, but only marginally. Thus, we could describe their theory as an interactional view of legal order with a minor role for a systemic element in the form of formally valid legal norms. They apply this combination in their discussions of specific international legal regimes, such as the global climate change regime and the United Nations prohibition of torture. These regimes are analyzed in terms of the emergence of shared legal understandings based on principles of legality in a community of practice.

At this point, there is an ambiguity in their theory, which is important in the light of inter-legality. On the one hand, they see interactional law as a "particular type of community of practice, nourished by broader social practices, but distinct from them";[38] on the other hand, they emphasize the existence of "a plurality of communities of practice, often with overlapping priorities and memberships."[39] The latter is stated in the context of denying the existence of a "world community" of international law and arguing that communities of practice may be thin communities of mutual engagement rather than sharing values. However, it seems strange to speak of interactional law as a community of practice, as if it were a particular practice we could identify. Interactional law is a legal form (in Fuller's sense) that needs a particular context to take the shape of "a practice"; rather than being a (community of) practice, interactional law is a form of law that needs practices to sustain it.[40]

The emphasis on plural interactional practices is important because it enables discussion of practices as particular legal regimes. I would argue that there is no overarching practice of "interactional law" as such. This point does raise the question of identifying interactional legal practices that we already encountered in the discussion of interactional order at the end of Section 3: What marks the scope or boundary of the order or practice? Here, it seems that systemic legal order may also have a role to fulfill. Focusing on attempts to create legal norms, it becomes possible to identify interactional legal practices by looking at the system-based aim: What are they trying to create? And who is involved in this effort? In the international context, treaty-making may therefore be a natural focal point for identifying possible interactional legal practices.

[38] Ibid., at 69.
[39] Ibid., at 81.
[40] Hence Fuller's idea that schools, associations, churches, etc., form their own internal legal order, which can become formalized quite quickly, a development he describes as "creeping legalism"; see Fuller, *The Principles of Social Order*, at 78.

Here, the notion of a regime as a combination of an interactional legal order with a focus on system-building may be a way to conceptualize particular legal orders, at least in the transnational context. The legal order then appears as the interactional practice of those actors that engage with each other in the formation, support, and possibly the breakdown of a coherent set of norms. The legal nature of this practice is then by no means limited to, or even primarily exemplified by, these enacted norms: these are embedded in the interactional normative expectations. However, participants will probably see the production of these norms as providing meaning and focus to the practice. A good example consists of transnational regimes that are developed by non-state actors, such as certification bodies. A much-studied certification scheme is that of the Forest Stewardship Council, which develops certification standards and procedures for sustainable forestry.[41] The interactions of the various private actors involved are focused on regulating forestry through standard-setting and the ensuing certification process. The inter-legality aspects of such a scheme are various: on the input side of standard-setting, there is reference to other norms (e.g., global environmental law) that sustain the scheme's legitimacy[42]; on the output side (e.g., the use of certified wood), there is interaction with, for instance, government procurement law.[43] Inter-Legality then supports such a non-state transnational legal order by providing a connection to public legal norms.

Inter-Legality between interactional legal orders, or between regimes in this sense, may come in with the legal understandings that participants in the legal order bring with them. Regimes are formed by actors who have previous ideas and normative expectations about law, on which they will draw in the process of forming a new interactional practice. Inter-Legality may take the form of explicit proposals to bring in a cherished or useful element from another legal order, but it may also take the form of implicit legal understandings that come along in the process. Drawing on Fuller's distinction between interactional law and enacted law, we may see the implicit legal understandings of interactional order as being combined with the formal norms of making enacted law. In the transnational context, the combination of interactional and systemic order can be said to take the form of an interactional practice of (re-)creating legal norms in which

41 S. Bernstein and B. Cashore, "Can Non-State Global Governance Be Legitimate? An Analytical Framework," (2007) 1 *Regulation and Governance* 347, 350.

42 Ibid., at 352.

43 A. Latu, "Public Procurement and Private Certification: The Case of the UK TPP," *Comparative Research in Law & Political Economy. Research Paper* No. 53/2013, available at https://ssrn.com/abstract=2360264.

inter-legality means drawing on both different implicit ideas of law and various explicit appeals to legal norms from elsewhere.

What does this entail for more locally grounded legal orders, such as the religious orders discussed earlier? The main difference seems to be the "thickness" of the ties between the legal order and the social environment in which it is embedded. In many situations, some legal orders are more firmly connected to the social order than we see in the realm of transnational governance, mainly because, locally, the same groups of people are engaged in multiple practices together. Particularly when such groups sees various practices (religious, legal, political) as expressive of their community identity, their shared norms may be stronger too. Because people then easily draw on the same shared understandings, inter-legality may appear less abundant. However, if we return to some of the anthropological work discussed earlier, this seems an unwarranted conclusion: in almost any context, there are contacts with others outside of a core group. People work elsewhere, travel, and speak to others, which may all be sources for bringing in elements from other legal orders. Here, too, the formal norms of another legal order may be a source of inspiration to advocate change, in addition to the more implicit transformations through shifting expectations and ideas. A prime example of this role of norms from another legal order is the appeal of international human rights norms in various local contexts. An interesting development is the direct appeal of cities to international human rights in order to inform local policies.[44]

So far, I have investigated how elements of systemic order might be relevant to interactional order. Here, I should discuss one serious objection that may be advanced against prioritizing the interactional view. If legal practice in the traditional sense is taken as central (i.e., the work of legal practitioners), the systemic view of legal order seems to be much more prominent. One way of putting the point is in terms of the language of law: Can we speak of law without depending on systemic legal order? It is undoubtedly true that it is near impossible for jurists trained on the basis of formal law to resist a terminology in which norms, systems, fit, and validity are central. Moreover, the shape of law in our current orders is to a large extent enacted law, which is much easier to speak of in terms of the existence of a set of norms. However, this does not mean interaction is irrelevant, nor (I would argue) that interaction must be subordinate to system in a theory of legal order. There are three points that at least should be made.

[44] B. Oomen, M. F. Davis, and M. Grigolo, *Global Urban Justice: The Rise of Human Rights Cities* (Cambridge: Cambridge University Press, 2016).

First, enacted law cannot thrive on its own. If there are no interactional practices of accepting norms, of recognizing the authority of lawmakers, or of enforcing norms, then enacted law cannot survive.[45] Therefore, even if you start to build a view of legal order based on enacted norms, there comes a point at which interactional practice needs to be referred to in order to understand how these norms are sustained. Second, language is hard to separate from practices, and if we focus on language use rather than on the propositional content of that language, interactional practice already becomes more prominent.[46] Although the systemic aspects of legal order are highly visible in our legal language, they are by no means all: people also speak in terms of justice, of legal argument and interpretation, and of the meaning of law. Third, a connected but more wide-ranging point: language and the accompanying cultural aspects of law – of images, stories, and metaphors – are crucial for how people think about law and about themselves as legal actors or legal subjects. This dependence on language and culture has two sides: on the one hand, language and culture provide shared understanding; on the other hand, they are open to people's actions and changes, meaning that they also enable creativity. There are various metaphors and images that can be used, that can be contrasted and combined, and that can be renewed or replaced. The plurality of legal cultural life can (and should) be used to make the most of law. Telling alternative stories is an important part of the renewal of legal orders. The aspect of storytelling in law, so well presented by Cover,[47] is also a natural way of bringing coherence, both because the meaning of narratives depends on making sense of them as a whole and because narratives are told to others and enable the forming of shared understandings.[48] In an interactional view of legal order, the cultural embedding of law is easier to take on board. And this also provides a possibly richer understanding of inter-legality as the construction of meaning on the basis

[45] E.g., see Fuller, *The Principles of Social Order*; S. Taekema and W. Van der Burg, "Towards a Fruitful Cooperation between Legal Philosophy, Legal Sociology and Doctrinal Research: How Legal Interactionism May Bridge Unproductive Oppositions," in R. Nobles and D. Schiff (eds.), *Law, Society and Community. Socio-Legal Essays in Honour of Roger Cotterrell* (Farnham: Ashgate, 2014), 129.

[46] For a specific account of linguistic practice in international courts, see V. Willems, "International Courts and Tribunals and their Linguistic Practices: A Communities of Practice Approach," (2017) 30 *International Journal for the Semiotics of Law* 181.

[47] See R. Cover, "The Supreme Court 1982 Term. Foreword: Nomos and Narrative," (1983) 97 *Harvard Law Review* 4.

[48] Cover stresses the importance of myths as part of a legal tradition; ibid., at 9.

of different stories about law.[49] One way to put it, again taking a cue from Cover, is to see inter-legality as a way to create a world. If inter-legality is seen as a way in which people live with law, the various aspects of the legal world – norms, language, culture, thought, and actions – combine to create inter-legal order.

6 CONCLUDING REMARKS

By contrasting and combining two views of legal order – the systemic and the interactional – I hope to have provided a dynamic account of inter-legality. Whereas a systemic view of order implies aiming for a smooth combination of elements from different orders so as to do away with tensions, an interactional view tracks the actions of participants in legal order and the ways they use various aspects of different practices. By seeing inter-legality as part of a process of combining and recreating orders, it becomes a crucial part of understanding legal change. However, although I have argued for prioritizing interactional order, the more important (and possibly more generally acceptable) message of this chapter is that both views of legal order need to take some of the elements of the other view on board. From a systemic point of view, one should not forget the dependence of the system on international practice to underpin the working and change of legal orders. From an interactional point of view, attention should be on the role of systemic elements such as enacted norms as focal points for orderly practices. The purpose of both will be to give a sound and imaginative account of the world of law in which inter-legality is in play.

49 Here, the idea of intertextuality comes to mind. Intertextuality is relevant to understanding how meaning is constructed in narrative, but also in law; see M. Valverde, *Chronotopes of Law. Jurisdiction, Scale and Governance* (Abingdon: Routledge, 2015). Valverde's account of intertextuality is clearly interactional, and interestingly she points out the close affinity between Bakhtin's idea of intertextuality and de Sousa Santos's inter-legality.

PART II

Realities and Inter-Legality Questions

5

Why and What (State) Jurisdiction

Legal Plurality, Individual Equality and Territorial Legitimacy

SAMANTHA BESSON[1]

1 INTRODUCTION

In their invitation to contribute, the editors of this book have asked me to address two questions: first, 'Does inter-legality affect our concept of jurisdiction?' Second, and more specifically: 'What does it mean to speak of jurisdiction when several rules emanating from several legal orders can claim that they must be applied at the same time?'

The scope of this chapter precludes addressing what 'inter-legality'[2] amounts to, both sociologically and normatively.[3] There will be no discussion, as a result, of how one should relate inter-legality to current debates about 'legal pluralism'[4]

1 Many thanks to Jan Klabbers and Gianluigi Palombella for their invitation to contribute to this volume and to participate in a workshop at the Scuola Superiore Sant'Anna in Pisa on 17–18 February 2017. Thanks also to Tilmann Altwicker and Oliver Diggelmann for their invitation to present at the IVR Research Lunch series at the University of Zurich on 18 May 2017 and to Damian Cueni for his helpful comments. Thank you to Sanne Taekema, Christian Joerges, Yuval Shany, Lorenzo Gasbarri, Maria Varaki and Anna Petrig for their feedback on those occasions. Last but not least, special thanks to Alain Supiot for our discussions and to Lucien Hürlimann for his research and editorial assistance.

2 The term was first coined by legal anthropologists: see e.g., B. de Sousa Santos, *Toward a New Common Sense: Law, Science and Politics in the Paradigmatic Transition* (London: Routledge, 1995), at 473; J. Eckert, 'What is the Context of "Law in Context"?' in S. P. Dolan and L. Heckendorn Urscheler (eds.), *Concepts of Law: Comparative, Jurisprudential, and Social Science Perspectives* (London: Routledge, 2014), 225.

3 On the implications of 'inter-legality' for the concept of law itself, see Chapter 4 in this volume.

4 See, e.g., S. Besson, 'The Authority of International Law – Lifting the State Veil', (2009) 31 *Sydney Law Review* 343; S. Besson, 'European Legal Pluralism after Kadi', (2009) 5 *European Constitutional Law Review* 237; S. Besson, 'The Truth about Legal Pluralism, Review of Nico Krisch's Beyond Constitutionalism: The Pluralist Structure of Postnational Law', (2012) 8 *European Constitutional Law Review* 354; S. Besson, 'International Law's Relative Authority, Review of Nicole Roughan's Authorities. Conflicts, Cooperation and Transnational Legal Theory', (2015) 6 *Jurisprudence* 169.

in legal theory[5] and of whether analytical legal positivism can or cannot accommodate it.[6] The chapter assumes, instead, and for the sake of the argument, that inter-legality means what the second question refers to (i.e., some form of 'legal plurality').[7] In short, legal plurality is taken to describe and characterize the coexistence of several distinct legal systems or orders,[8] or perhaps legal subsystems or orders, within a single independent political community, like that of a state, albeit not exclusively, and, although it is not a necessary consequence, the potential risk of normative conflict this legal concurrence may give rise to.

The legal orders whose norms may be overlapping in the domestic legal order[9] may range from infranational orders (e.g., the law of federated

5 See e.g., S. E. Merry, 'Legal Pluralism', (1988) 22 *Law and Society Review* 869; S. Roberts, 'After Government? On Representing Law without the State', (2005) 68 *Modern Law Review* 1; P. S. Berman, 'Global Legal Pluralism', (2007) 80 *Southern California Law Review* 1155; W. Twining, *Globalisation and Legal Scholarship* (Nijmegen: Wolf Legal Publishers, 2009); K. Culver and M. Giudice, *Legality's Borders – An Essay in General Jurisprudence* (Oxford: Oxford University Press, 2010); N. Krisch, *Beyond Constitutionalism: The Pluralist Structure of Postnational Law* (Oxford: Oxford University Press, 2010); N. Roughan, *Authorities: Conflict, Cooperation, and Transnational Legal Theory* (Oxford: Oxford University Press, 2013), chapter 7; T. Schultz, *Transnational Legality: Stateless Law and International Arbitration* (Oxford: Oxford University Press, 2014); J. Griffiths, 'Legal Pluralism', in J. D. Wright (ed.), *International Encyclopedia of the Social & Behavioral Sciences*, 2nd edn, vol. 13 (Amsterdam: Elsevier, 2015), 757; R. Cotterell, 'Does Global Legal Pluralism Need a Concept of Law?' in U. Baxi, C. McCrudden and A. Paliwala (eds.), *Law's Ethical, Global and Theoretical Contexts. Essays in Honour of William Twining* (Cambridge: Cambridge University Press, 2015), 303; N. Roughan, 'Mind the Gaps: Authority and Legality in International Law', (2016) 27 *European Journal of International Law* 329; R. Michaels, 'Law and Recognition – Towards a Relational Concept of Law', in N. Roughan and A. Halpin (eds.), *In Pursuit of Pluralist Jurisprudence* (Cambridge: Cambridge University Press, 2017), 90.

6 See e.g., J. Dickson, 'Towards a Theory of European Union Legal Systems', in J. Dickson and P. Eleftheriadis (eds.), *Philosophical Foundations of European Union Law* (Oxford: Oxford University Press, 2012), 25; J. Waldron, 'Legal Pluralism and the Contrast between Hart's Jurisprudence and Fuller's', in P. Cane (ed.), *The Hart–Fuller Debate in the Twenty-First Century* (Oxford: Oxford University Press, 2010), 135; Schultz, *Transnational Legality*, chapter 4; Michaels, 'Law and Recognition'.

7 Of course, part of this chapter's argument about jurisdiction could also be made with respect to the other side of the question, i.e., the theoretical and normative qualifications of legal plurality (qua legal pluralism; see Besson, 'Review of Krisch', and Besson, 'Relative Authority'). Among the other meanings of inter-legality, besides the descriptive one based on legal plurality endorsed as a starting point in this chapter, one may also think, for example, of the reactive self-regulation *process* among legal orders on the one hand, or of one or many non–system-dependent moral or legal *principles* like the rule of law, legality itself or justice that may be invoked in every legal order to manage conflicts with other legal orders (see Chapter 1) on the other.

8 I am not distinguishing between legal 'systems' and 'orders' in this chapter. I am also assuming that all those legal orders are 'legal' in the relevant sense.

9 This mode of exposition (by reference to state or domestic law) has been questioned to the extent that it assumes that state law remains the legal order of reference and that the other legal

entities, indigenous law or religious law) to transnational orders (e.g., *lex mercatoria* or *lex electronica*), international orders (e.g., international criminal law, international trade law or United Nations [UN] law), supranational orders (e.g., European Union [EU] law) or even other foreign domestic orders (e.g., foreign tax, competition or environmental law). Each of those legal orders may also be considered more or less pluralistic in itself (e.g., due to the fragmentation of international law into self-contained or autonomous regimes or to the plurality of international courts),[10] thereby making each layer of legal plurality multilayered.

What has led to this overlap between norms stemming from various legal orders is the development of what one may refer to as the 'global' or 'transnational' circumstances of contemporary social and political life, be they related to the increasing mobility of state agents, people and/or things[11] or to the rise of shared or even common interests. Besides the usual tandem of domestic and international law,[12] the regulation of those new circumstances and interests has taken different non-territorialized forms following a plurality of other relations between the regulator and the people or the

orders should be conceived against that background. See e.g., Michaels, 'Law and Recognition'. The fact is – as I will explain and then argue in this chapter – that state law remains the legal order of reference in practice, for it is not only the most comprehensive legal order (see J. Raz, 'Why the State', [2014] 38 *King's College London Dickson Poon School of Law Legal Studies Research Paper Series*), but also the one in which most of the legal norms stemming from all other legal orders are adjudicated and enforced, and even, in some cases, developed further. See also Roberts, 'After Government?' at 17–18; S. Sassen, 'The State and Globalization', in R. B. Hall and T. J. Biersteker (eds.), *The Emergence of Private Authority in Global Governance* (Cambridge: Cambridge University Press, 2002), 91, 107; G. Handl, 'Extra-Territoriality and Transnational Legal Authority', in G. Handl, J. Zekoll and P. Zumbansen (eds.), *Beyond Territoriality – Transnational Legal Authority in an Age of Globalization* (Leiden: Brill, 2012), 3, 6; P. Zumbansen, 'The Regulatory Landscape of Global Governance and Transnational Legal Authority', in ibid., 551, 556–557. As a matter of fact, those legal orders are not usually concerned with (excluding or pre-empting) the law from other legal orders, and hence with the issue of legal plurality.

10 See e.g., J. E. Alvarez, 'Beware: Boundary Crossings', in T. Kahana and A. Scolnicov (eds.), *Boundaries of State, Boundaries of Rights: Human Rights, Private Actors, and Positive Obligations* (Cambridge: Cambridge University Press, 2016), 43.

11 On those transnational circumstances, see e.g., S. Besson, 'Human Rights as Transnational Constitutional Law', in A. Lang and A. Wiener (eds.), *Handbook on Global Constitutionalism* (Cheltenham: Edward Elgar, 2017), 234.

12 On the notion of 'common interests' in international law, see e.g., S. Besson, 'Community Interests in the Identification of International Law – With a Special Emphasis on Treaty Interpretation and Customary Law Identification', in E. Benvenisti and G. Nolte (eds.), *Community Obligations Across International Law* (Oxford: Oxford University Press, 2018), at 50; S. Besson, 'Community Interests in International Law – Whose Interests are They and How does One Identify Them?', in ibid., 36.

matters regulated.[13] This contemporary process of 'deterritorialization' of law[14] is actually dual: it has grown bottom-up with infranational law, but also top-down with transnational law.[15] It is accompanied by a third process that one may term the 'overterritorialization' of law across borders,[16] which takes place either laterally through the extraterritorial exercise of domestic jurisdiction or top-down through the development of larger legal ensembles like the EU.

Against this pluralistic legal background, it is common to identify a tension between legal plurality and the concept of jurisdiction, understood for now to mean the right or power to enact, enforce or adjudicate law. More specifically, the legal order whose jurisdiction can be questioned by legal plurality is presumably one that is comprehensive in scope or, at least, exclusive in its power to rule. If it were limited in its material scope, indeed, concurrence with other legal orders would not matter that much, but it would matter even less should that legal order not also claim to rule free from external legal constraints.[17] What this means is that the jurisdiction at stake in this alleged opposition to legal plurality, and in this chapter as a result, is state law's jurisdiction, and not the 'jurisdiction' of other legal orders, be they

[13] On the tension between territorial legal regulation and other forms of international, transnational or infranational legal regulation, see e.g., G. Teubner, *Global Law without a State* (Aldershot: Dartmouth, 1997); R. Michaels, 'Territorial Jurisdiction after Territoriality', in P. J. Slot and M. Bultermann (eds.), *Globalisation and Jurisdiction* (Leiden: Kluwer, 2004), pp. 105–130; N. Walker, 'Beyond Boundary Disputes and Basic Grids: Mapping the Global Disorder of Normative Orders', (2006) 8 *International Journal of Constitutional Law* 373; S. Sassen, *Territory, Authority, Rights: From Medieval to Global Assemblages* (Princeton, NJ: Princeton University Press, 2006); Handl, 'Extra-Territoriality'; G. Shaffer, 'International Law and Global Public Goods in a Legal Pluralist World', (2012) 12 *European Journal of International Law* 669; Krisch, 'Beyond Constitutionalism'; D. Bethlehem, 'The End of Geography: The Changing Nature of the International System and the Challenge to International Law', (2014) 25 *European Journal of International Law* 9, 15–17.

[14] On deterritorialization in international law, see e.g., C. Brölmann, 'Deterritorializing International Law: Moving Away from the Divide between National and International Law', in A. Nollkaemper and A. Nijman (eds.), *New Perspectives on the Divide between National and International Law* (Oxford: Oxford University Press, 2007), 84; T. Schultz, 'Carving Up the Internet: Jurisdiction, Legal Orders, and the Private/Public International Law Interface', (2008) 19 *European Journal of International Law* 799, 800–803; Shaffer, 'Global Public Goods'; A. Colangelo, 'Spatial Legality', (2012) 107 *Northwestern University Law Review* 69.

[15] On different similar moves away from and towards territoriality across legal history, see A. Supiot, 'L'inscription territoriale des lois', (2008) 11 *Esprit* 151, 160.

[16] See also Supiot, 'L'inscription territoriale', 153; K. Raustiala, 'Empire and Extraterritoriality in Twentieth Century America', (2011) 40 *Southwestern Law Review* 605.

[17] I am assuming therefore that 'inter-jurisdiction' or 'jurisdictional plurality' would be a contradiction in terms. In any case, it would make the question of this chapter entirely moot and boil down to a discussion of 'legal plurality'.

infranational, international or transnational or those of domestic or international courts.[18] This focus on state (law) jurisdiction is actually confirmed by the use of the term 'jurisdiction' in ordinary language or, more precisely, the absence thereof in other contexts than state law[19] – the only exception being its use in the context of a supranational and hence statelike organization: the EU.[20]

In response to what may be termed 'the challenge of legal plurality to (state law) jurisdiction', the aim of the present chapter is double: first, it purports to explain why jurisdiction has become a central institution in (domestic and international) law and, by extension, in domestic and international legal theory, and actually still is in the pervasive and persistent circumstances of legal plurality (why jurisdiction?); and, second, it aims to show how jurisdiction should best be conceived in its relation to infranational law, transnational law, foreign domestic law and international law whose norms apply concurrently to domestic ones, but whose respective impact on and relationship to domestic law should be approached differently in each case (what jurisdiction?). The proposed argument is both descriptive, when it assesses the sociological relevance of the legal rules on jurisdiction and the social reality underlying them, and normative, when it interprets the law so as to fit and justify the corresponding rules. It approaches law as a normative social

[18] Of course, one sometimes refers to infranational, transnational, international or supranational courts having 'jurisdiction'. This may be considered as a semantic extension from the vocabulary of state law and national courts' adjudicative jurisdiction, however, because international courts' (*ratione personae, materiae, temporis* or *loci*) jurisdiction amounts to an extension of the states that constitute them and give them jurisdiction. In any case, not all courts necessarily correspond to the legal orders they are speaking the law for, and especially not international ones, and should not therefore be considered as having 'jurisdiction' stricto sensu. For a discussion of international courts' jurisdiction and inter-legality, see Chapter 14. For a different take, see P. S. Berman, 'The Globalization of Jurisdiction', (2002) 151 *University of Pennsylvania Law Review* 311.

[19] Scope precludes developing a full jurisprudential argument about why and what state in international law: see Raz, 'Why the State'.

[20] On the 'competences' or 'functions' as opposed to the 'jurisdiction' and 'sovereignty' of other international organizations (IOs), see J. Klabbers, *International Law* (Cambridge: Cambridge University Press, 2013), at 90, 98–100. The justification for this difference, I will argue, has to do with the territorial and political dimension of state and domestic law (and, by extension, maybe of the EU and EU law) being the law of a people or political community on a given territory, but also with the characteristics of territorial jurisdiction (i.e., its comprehensiveness, exclusiveness and pre-emptiveness). When an IO exercises what may look like 'jurisdiction' (e.g., in the territories administered by the UN), it is merely because it functions by delegation of the jurisdiction of the state whose territory it is (and the same may also be argued, of course, of the EU).

practice that can change our social environment (provided it pertains to things that may be changed, and not all of them may be[21]), but is also responsive to it.[22]

Interestingly, (state law) jurisdiction has not yet attracted much attention in either domestic or international legal theory. In domestic legal theory, of course, related issues have been addressed by legal philosophers, albeit from the distinct perspective of other normative concepts like (legitimate) authority or sovereignty. Discussions of the latter only very tangentially mention the concept of jurisdiction, presumably due to the blind spot of self-legislation since domestic law constitutes and constrains its own jurisdiction.[23] Moreover, when jurisdiction is discussed, albeit indirectly, by those authors, it is usually in relation to international law only or, more generally, by reference to legal plurality as a whole, but then in a non-distinctive and un-nuanced fashion that assumes that legal plurality implies legal equality.[24] Filling this gap and providing a more refined account of both jurisdiction and the circumstances of legal plurality is therefore one of the contributions of this chapter to domestic jurisprudence.

At first, one may expect to find more advanced discussions in international legal theory to the extent that jurisdiction corresponds to a pivotal set of rules in international law. After all, international law constitutes each state's jurisdiction by making it equal to that of others and independent from them on the one hand, and constrains it both externally in its relation to others (e.g., in terms of delineation of borders or of the non-intervention principle) and internally in its domestic exercise (e.g., in terms of human rights or criminal law, and even arguably in terms of democratic standards) on the other. Again, however, among international lawyers and legal theorists, theoretical as opposed to doctrinal discussions of jurisdiction in circumstances of legal plurality not only tend to be quite rare and dated, but also have a limited

[21] On the resistance of territoriality despite the multiple regimes of legal relation to territory across legal history, see e.g., Supiot, 'L'inscription Territoriale', 154; Bethlehem, 'End of Geography', 15. Contra: D. S. Koller, 'The End of Geography: The Changing Nature of the International System and the Challenge to International Law: A Reply to Daniel Bethlehem', (2014) 25 *European Journal of International Law* 25.

[22] See also Raz, 'Why the State'.

[23] See e.g., Roughan, 'Mind the Gaps', 333–334.

[24] As I will argue, legal plurality does not imply legal equality: the kind of claims to authority made by those different kinds of law should not too quickly be identified with one another, and this in turn affects their different relationships, including their different relationships to each state of jurisdiction's legal order. Contra: Roughan, 'Authorities', chapters 7 and 8; Raz, 'Why the State'; Roughan, 'Mind the Gaps'. See, however, the ambitious introduction by Handl, 'Extra-Territoriality', at 8. See also Besson, 'Relative Authority', at 172–173.

regime-specific focus.[25] Most discussions have mapped the reasons for the current transnational and hence 'extraterritorial' circumstances of states' jurisdiction and for the increase or decrease of cases of concurrent or conflicting jurisdiction on the one hand, and discussed, albeit inconclusively, the different principles envisaged so far for their resolution on the other.[26] Curiously, however, very little has been written about the concept of jurisdiction itself, and especially its nature and scope.[27] Jurisdiction is still conceived as 'exclusive' and 'unlimited' by reference to the early 1930s case law of the Permanent Court of International Justice (PCIJ) or arbitral tribunals,[28] and referred to solely as a right or power of the state.

[25] See the critique by A. Bianchi, 'Reply to Professor Maier', in K. M. Meessen (ed.), *Extraterritorial Jurisdiction in Theory and Practice* (The Hague: Kluwer Law International, 1996), 74, at 89, 100.

[26] See e.g., C. Ryngaert, *Jurisdiction in International Law*, 2nd edn (Oxford: Oxford University Press, 2015); C. Staker, 'Jurisdiction', in M. D. Evans (ed.), *International Law*, 4th edn (Oxford: Oxford University Press, 2014), 309–335; R. Liivoja, 'Book Review of Jurisdiction in International Law by Cedric Ryngaert', (2008) 19 *Finnish Yearbook of International Law* 397; Berman, 'Globalization of Jurisdiction'; H. G. Maier, 'Jurisdictional Rules in Customary International Law', in Meessen (ed.), *Extraterritorial Jurisdiction*, 64; Bianchi, 'Reply'; M. Bos, 'Preliminary Report on the Extraterritorial Jurisdiction of States', (1993) 65 *Yearbook of the International Law Institute* 14; F. A. Mann, 'The Doctrine of International Jurisdiction Revisited after Twenty Years', (1984) 186 *Recueil des Cours* 1–116; M. Akehurst, 'Jurisdiction in International Law', (1972–1973) 46 *British Yearbook of International Law* 145; F. A. Mann, 'The Doctrine of Jurisdiction in International Law', (1964) 111 *Recueil des Cours* 1.

[27] Interestingly, private international law is an exception in this respect. This should not come as a surprise as it focuses solely on individuals, independently from their respective political communities and relevant territories, and resolving conflict of law in private matters has been its main concern from the beginning. See e.g., H. G. Maier, 'Extraterritorial Jurisdiction at a Crossroads: An Intersection between Public and Private International Law', (1982) 76 *American journal of International Law* 280; A. F. Lowenfeld, 'International Litigation and the Quest for Reasonableness: General Course on Private International Law', (1994) 245 *Recueil des Cours* 1; International Bar Association (IBA), *Report of the Task Force on Extraterritorial Jurisdiction* (2009); Michaels, 'Law and Recognition'. This almost exclusive focus on private international law in the literature on jurisdiction has had consequences for debates about jurisdiction in public international law given that questions of conflicts of law are essentially questions pertaining to private law on the one hand, and have been regarded as domestic ones and discussed almost exclusively in domestic fora, and especially domestic courts, on the other. For a discussion of this issue, see Bianchi, 'Reply', at 80–81; H. Buxbaum, 'Territory, Territoriality and the Resolution of Jurisdictional Conflict', (2009) 57 *American Journal of Comparative Law* 631; Ryngaert, *Jurisdiction in International Law*, at 16–22. For integrative efforts, however, see C. Joerges, P. F. Kjaer and T. Ralli, 'A New Type of Conflicts – Law as Constitutional Form in the Postnational Constellation', (2011) 2 *Transnational Legal Theory* 153; R. Rödl, 'Democratic Juridification without Statisation: Law of Conflict of Laws Instead of a World State', (2011) 2 *Transnational Legal Theory* 193.

[28] See e.g., *Island of Palmas (Netherlands v. USA)*, Arbitral Award of 4 April 1928, 2 *Reports of International Arbitral Awards* 829, at 838. See also *The Case of the S.S. 'Lotus' (France v. Turkey)*, [1927] Publ. PCIJ, Series A, No. 10.

This conceptual and theoretical neglect of jurisdiction in international legal theory is both surprising and unsurprising. On the one hand, it may seem surprising, as I have just explained, because the principle of states' jurisdiction is a structural principle of the international legal order and its customary law underpinnings have even been captured by some authors as the international 'law on laws'.[29] One may therefore expect that any lack of fit between the practice of states and those customary rules of jurisdiction would lead to their amendment or even extinction, and hence to lively discussions among international lawyers and legal theorists. As a matter of fact, this puzzlement about the resilience of state jurisdiction in circumstances of legal plurality (that would seem to have made it irrelevant in practice) is probably what lies behind the contemporary scholarly challenge to the comprehensive and exclusive conception of state authority and jurisdiction.[30] However, on the other hand, this theoretical neglect of jurisdiction could also be expected when one knows how most international legal principles pertaining to the main international lawmaker (i.e., the state, and its personhood, territory or sovereignty) belong to the blind spots of international law and lawyers and are difficult to question or change from within the practice and the theory of international law itself.

The claim of the chapter is that revisiting the concept of jurisdiction is key to reconciling domestic and international lawyers with what is sometimes regarded, at least under some conception of jurisdiction, as a problematic gap between domestic and international facts and norms. It is only by explaining the sociological and normative resilience of the concept and revisiting some of our current conceptions that we can change our level of expectation of what jurisdiction implies normatively. This way, jurisdiction can remain the significant principle it once was and, arguably, still is and should be in the contemporary transnational circumstances of domestic and international law, and not the anomalous Westphalian leftover some may consider it to be.[31] What is also at stake, beyond conceptual clarity, is, as I will argue, the protection of individual equality and political legitimacy, which underpin the justification of state jurisdiction, against the risks of imperialism, parochialism and individualism that come with legal plurality.[32]

29 See the editors' preface in Ryngaert, *Jurisdiction in International Law*; Maier, 'Customary International Law'.

30 See e.g., Roughan, 'Mind the Gaps', at 334, 338.

31 See e.g., Bethlehem, 'End of Geography', 17–18.

32 On the recent disenchantment regarding legal plurality, see e.g., Roberts, 'After Government?' at 17–18; Zumbansen, 'Global Governance', at 556–557.

In a nutshell, the chapter's argument is the following: it starts by observing that the state legal order remains the main source of legal rules in our political communities and argues that, as a result, its laws should be such that they can claim legitimate authority over a people in a given territory and in particular respect to our individual equality before the law. This can still best be achieved, the chapter argues, by reinforcing three features of state jurisdiction qua territorial jurisdiction: its comprehensive (or unlimited) material scope, exclusivity (or independence) and pre-emptiveness (or primacy). Thus, state jurisdiction does and should remain a central feature of law today despite and, actually, because of the plurality of laws overlapping the same people in a territory and the potential threat this constitutes to their equality before the law and the generality of law. Of course, and this is the first contribution of the chapter, jurisdiction is both a domestic and international legal construct and, as a result, is legally constrained from both sides. Those constraints, and especially the international ones, should not be conflated with external limits excluded by the concept of jurisdiction, but are the mark of an advanced form of legal ordering and relational legitimation in the increasingly transnational circumstances of human and social life. Secondly, jurisdiction amounts not only to a right, but also to a duty, and is therefore best captured arguably as a responsibility of state law. This is particularly important in the transnational circumstances that increasingly characterize our social and legal life today and the common interests they give rise to, because it accounts for why states should exercise their jurisdiction in order to address global problems together and through international law institutions and procedures, but also for why states should resist jurisdictionally certain moves of infranational, transnational or foreign displacement of their domestic law.

Accordingly, the structure of the argument proposed in this chapter is three-pronged. The chapter starts by presenting what 'jurisdiction' means, distinguishing different aspects or dimensions of jurisdiction and delineating that concept from related ones in domestic and international legal theory and especially authority, legitimacy and sovereignty (Section 2). The next section explores the continuing sociological relevance of state jurisdiction in domestic and international law despite legal plurality, and explains, from the perspective of domestic and international legal theory, why jurisdiction should actually matter precisely because of legal plurality (Section 3). In Section 4, the chapter turns to how jurisdiction should be reconceived in circumstances of legal plurality, and especially in its relationship to infranational law, transnational law and foreign domestic law.

Finally, a caveat about the scope of the chapter is in order. Its scope precludes addressing some issues that are related to state jurisdiction in circumstances of legal plurality but should not be conflated with it, and in particular the following three: the relations between different norms or regimes within international law itself;[33] the relations between different international courts;[34] and the relations between EU and international law or between EU law and the domestic law of non-member states, even though the latter are regularly framed as a case of concurrent and conflicting jurisdiction.[35] Moreover, in the interest of inclusion and universality in the conclusions reached about international law in the chapter, the region-specific question of the relationship of integration between the domestic law of EU member states and EU law and its implications in terms of state (and EU) (law) jurisdiction are not broached here either.[36]

2 JURISDICTION

Jurisdiction is a polysemic concept and has come to mean very different things both in domestic and in international law, whose construction it is – not to mention the conceptual diversity and contradictions that come with the many languages and cultures of domestic and international law.[37] The complexity of the concept of jurisdiction should not come as a surprise since it encapsulates the normative concept of law itself (literally *juris*-dictio). It actually works, furthermore, as a condition to or, at least, in close relationship with many other normative concepts related to law and legality, such as 'validity', 'authority', 'legitimacy' or 'sovereignty'. The law enacted, applied and adjudicated over by authorities that have jurisdiction is indeed valid law. It also has de facto authority, once jurisdiction is exercised, and that authority claims, as a result, to be justified or legitimate. Finally, jurisdiction amounts to a dimension of sovereignty to the extent that it is a condition of the independence of the state.

In short, jurisdiction may be defined as the right or power/competence of each state, under domestic and international law, to enact, enforce and adjudicate over valid domestic law. By extension, and although this is not

33 See e.g., Alvarez, 'Boundary Crossings'.

34 See e.g., Chapter 14.

35 See e.g., S. Francq, 'The Scope of Secondary Community Law in the Light of the Methods of Private International Law – Or the Other Way Around?' (2006) 8 *Yearbook of Private International Law* 333; J. Scott, 'The New EU "Extraterritoriality"', (2014) 51 *Common Market Law Review* 1343.

36 See Chapters 6 and 9. See also Besson, 'After Kadi'; Dickson, 'European Union Legal Systems' on the specificities of European legal pluralism.

37 In French, for instance, '*juridiction*' is only used to refer to the power or competence to adjudicate of a court, and by extension to the court itself. In German, '*Zuständigkeit*' (i.e., competence) is used for jurisdiction, but has no normative implications whatsoever.

how jurisdiction will be used in this chapter, it is sometimes also used with three further meanings. Thus, it is used to also refer to: when it is exercised, the de facto authority or effective *power* that jurisdiction grants to the law and, by extension, to the state whose jurisdiction it is[38]; the *legitimacy* or legitimate authority that jurisdiction can give rise to provided it is justified, to the extent that the exercise of jurisdiction and hence de facto authority implies a claim to legitimate authority[39]; and even the *territory* of the state or law whose jurisdiction it is, given that jurisdiction is primarily territorial.[40] Those extensions of the concept of jurisdiction qua normative power draw attention to the dual descriptive cum normative nature of the concept of jurisdiction: when it is exercised, it is both a power and a claim to have a right to exercise that power. This echoes similar features of the concepts of authority[41] and sovereignty.[42]

A few key dimensions of the concept of jurisdiction have to be emphasized, and in particular the nature, the subjects, the object, the content, the basis and the constraints of jurisdiction. Those common traits are reconstructed from the current general practice of state jurisdiction in domestic and international law.[43]

First of all, the *nature* of jurisdiction – it flows from the definition just given that jurisdiction is legally constituted and amounts therefore to a set of legal rules.[44] Those rules are both domestic and international. Domestically, rules of jurisdiction are usually of a constitutional nature. Importantly, the

38 On this conception of 'jurisdiction' in international human rights law qua effective control, see e.g., M. Milanovic, *Extraterritorial Application of Human Rights Treaties: Law, Principles, and Policy* (Oxford: Oxford University Press, 2011), 30 ff.; S. Besson, 'The Extraterritoriality of the European Convention on Human Rights. Why Human Rights Depend on Jurisdiction and What Jurisdiction Amounts To', (2012) 25 *Leiden Journal of International Law* 857, 862–866.

39 See e.g., Milanovic, *Extraterritorial Human Rights*, p. 23; V. Lowe, 'Jurisdiction', in M. D. Evans (ed.), *International Law*, 2nd edn (Oxford: Oxford University Press, 2006), 335. Because 'authority' itself may be used to mean legitimate authority as much as de facto power (see e.g., J. Raz, 'The Problem of Authority: Revisiting the Service Conception', [2006] 90 *Minnesota Law Review* 1003, 1005; Roughan, 'Mind the Gaps', 331–334), it is best, in order to avoid confusion, not to refer to jurisdiction qua authority.

40 On the ambivalence of the term 'jurisdiction', see Milanovic, *Extraterritorial Human Rights*, 39. Of course, as I explained before, 'jurisdiction' may also refer to the power or competence to adjudicate of a court, and by extension to the court itself, as it does in French.

41 Raz, 'Authority', 1005.

42 S. Besson, 'Sovereignty', in R. Wolfrum et al. (eds.), *Max Planck Encyclopedia of Public International Law*, Vol. 9 (Oxford: Oxford University Press, 2012), 366.

43 This chapter focuses on the general international law regime of jurisdiction and not on specific regimes thereof. Some comparisons are drawn with state jurisdiction under international human rights law, however (see Besson, 'Extraterritoriality').

44 On institutions and the corresponding interrelated set of rules, see Raz, 'Why the State'.

modern state's jurisdiction is not only set up by domestic rules, but also by international ones. There are two sets of rules stemming from two legal orders for one single jurisdiction. International law rules constitute each state's jurisdiction from the outside, as it were, by making it both equal to that of others and independent from them.[45] It would be wrong, therefore, to see international law as only setting constraints on state jurisdiction: it also constitutes it in the first place. Those rules of international law are mostly of a customary origin for they arise from state practice and have been referred to as the 'law on laws'.[46]

What one may conceive, in other words, as the 'dual legality' of jurisdiction is an important feature for understanding how state jurisdiction relates to international law.[47] To mention just one of its implications, changes in one set of rules of jurisdiction necessarily affect the other, but they are not identical and have distinct validity.[48] What this means is that jurisdiction is constructed legally so as to resist, and its international cum domestic dimension explains how resilient it has been over time.

Second, the *subjects* of jurisdiction – jurisdiction belongs to the state, but also by extension to its domestic law. Importantly, however, broadly speaking, jurisdiction is political and need not be reduced to its legal aspects. It is exercised actively by all political authorities, ranging from the legislature and the judiciary to the executive.

Moving to the passive side of jurisdiction, law binds people (or institutions constituted of people), and jurisdiction is exercised over people, therefore, and not over things,[49] activities or territory. Of course, the latter does provide, for the reasons that will be discussed, a basis for relating those people to the state and to the legal order of jurisdiction. It is indeed people's presence on a territory that relates them to the state whose jurisdiction may therefore be

45 For an indication of this mutuality, see the *Lotus* case, at 18.

46 See the editors' preface in Ryngaert, *Jurisdiction in International Law*; Maier, 'Customary International Law'. See also H. Kelsen, *Principles of International Law* (New York: Rinehart & Company Inc., 1952), at 94, on the limitation of the spheres of validity of domestic law as an essential function of international law.

47 On this duality of domestic and international law jurisdiction in the human rights context, see Besson, 'Extraterritoriality', at 862–866.

48 Bianchi, 'Reply', at 100.

49 There is a clear tendency in the practice and some of the literature, however, to elude this fact and its normative implications for the concept of jurisdiction. For instance, as we will see, the bases of jurisdiction are often reified and what is sought after is the strongest and hence 'reasonable' link or nexus to an object or an activity, and not to people (see e.g., Schultz, 'Carving Up the Internet', 816–819; Colangelo, 'Spatial Legality'; Bethlehem, 'End of Geography', 22–24; P. Stephan, 'Competing Sovereignty and Laws' Domains', [2018] 45 *Pepperdine Law Review* 239.

described as (primarily, albeit not only) territorial.[50] Interestingly, the passive subject of state jurisdiction is a group of people (i.e., a community[51] of people on a territory), and not distinct individuals as is the case under the international human rights law's concept of jurisdiction.[52] This is at least the case for its main basis (i.e., territory) and for the main kind of jurisdiction (i.e., territorial jurisdiction). The other bases of jurisdiction, as we will see, may extend state jurisdiction to regulate people and activities in a more individualized fashion. Jurisdiction amounts, in other words, to a normative relationship between the state's lawmaking institutions and people subjected to it.[53]

Third, the *objects* of jurisdiction – all state institutions may exercise jurisdiction and this, in turn, accounts for the breadth of the objects of jurisdiction.

50 Territorial jurisdiction may also match personal jurisdiction (i.e., jurisdiction over people who are related to a state by their nationality), to the extent that the acquisition of nationality often depends on being born or being present on the state's territory (see also Supiot, 'L'Inscription Territoriale', 156; for a critique of nationality's growing disconnection from the state's territory through its marketization, however, see K. Surak, 'Global Citizenship 2.0. The Growth of Citizenship by Investment Programs', (2016) 3 *Investment Migration Working Paper*). However, both kinds of jurisdiction need not match one another strictly: territorial jurisdiction is more inclusive and may apply to non-nationals, and personal jurisdiction extends to nationals outside the state territory.

51 As we will see, that community of people on a territory may also be described as a 'political community' or as a 'people', but at this stage of the presentation, the political dimension of that community is irrelevant. In any case, the question of the (territorial) boundaries of a political community, and by extension of democracy, is famously moot: see e.g., F. G. Whelan, 'Prologue: Democratic Theory and the Boundary Problem', in R. Pennock and J. Chapman (eds.), *Nomos XXV: Liberal Democracy* (1983), 13.

52 In short, state jurisdiction in international human rights law may be distinguished from state jurisdiction in general international law in at least four respects: (i) it is about control or de facto authority only, and not necessarily also about prescribing, enforcing or adjudicating law; (ii) it need not be legal or de jure and abide by the internal constraints of jurisdiction that stem from international law; (iii) it is primarily personal, and only occasionally spatial/territorial as well (by presumption on official state territory or on grounds of evidence of effective control outside of the territory); and (iv) it is individual, and not general or collective, to the extent that what matters is that it is exercised over a given right-holder in particular. Of course, both kinds of state jurisdiction are related: (i) if a state exercises jurisdiction under general international law, it is presumed to have jurisdiction under international human rights law, at least on its territory, and this could also be established in case there is evidence of effective control in the context of its exercise of extraterritorial jurisdiction within the constraints of international law; (ii) there is a general positive duty for states under international human rights law to exercise their jurisdiction under general international law, at least on their territory, and hence to regain it in case it is no longer effective. See Besson, 'Extraterritoriality'; S. Besson, 'Shared Responsibilities under the ECHR – Concurrent Jurisdictions, Duties and Responsibilities', in J. Motoc et al. (eds.), *The ECHR and General International Law* (Oxford: Oxford University Press, 2018), 155.

53 Besson, 'Extraterritoriality', 864–866.

Jurisdiction pertains indeed to the enactment (legislative authorities, prescriptive jurisdiction), the enforcement (executive authorities, executive jurisdiction) or the adjudication (judicial authorities, adjudicative jurisdiction) of domestic law, and by extension, as we will see, of international law (e.g., the domestic development of customary international law or general principles, or the domestic enforcement or adjudication of any other norm of international law).

The distinction between those objects of jurisdiction is of particular relevance in circumstances of extraterritorial jurisdiction, for it is used to set limits on the kind of jurisdiction that may be exercised by a state outside of its territory. However, it is largely moot in practice. It is often very difficult to know whether a domestic court exercises prescriptive or adjudicative jurisdiction. It is complex, for instance, to assess whether the universal criminal (adjudicative, and even executive) jurisdiction exercised by a domestic court does not also contribute to the development of international and domestic criminal law in the area.

Fourth, the *content* of jurisdiction – jurisdiction amounts to a right (to enact, enforce or adjudicate law), or, as it is also sometimes phrased, as a power or competence to do so.[54] This explains why jurisdiction is sometimes described as a corollary of sovereignty that amounts to the state's ensemble of rights or competences (of jurisdiction),[55] and is often referred to as 'independence'.[56]

Importantly, although it is not usually presented as such, jurisdiction also amounts to a duty to the extent that it sometimes has to be exercised. It may actually be best to refer to it, in a more encompassing and non-allocated and non-directed way, as a responsibility. It is the case under the domestic rules of jurisdiction as much as under those of international law. Thus, one may mention duties to exercise territorial jurisdiction under domestic and international human rights law,[57] for instance, but another example consists of states' duties under domestic and international criminal law. The latter

[54] See e.g., J. Crawford, *Brownlie's Principles of International Law*, 8th edn (Oxford: Oxford University Press, 2012), at 457 on 'jurisdictional competence'.

[55] Besson, 'Sovereignty'.

[56] *Island of Palmas*, at 838.

[57] See e.g., ECtHR, Grand Chamber, *Catan and Others v Moldova and Russia*, Application Nos. 43370/04, 8252/05 and 18454/06, Judgement of 19 October 2012; *Chiragov and Others v Armenia*, Application No. 13216/05, Judgement of 16 June 2015. See S. Besson, 'L'extraterritorialité des droits de l'homme internationaux: Juridictions concurrentes, obligations conjointes et responsabilités partagées', in P. d'Argent (ed.), *Droit des frontières internationales* (Paris: Pedone, 2016), 245.

explains in turn why universal jurisdiction in international human rights law or criminal law (e.g., under the international principle of prohibition of torture) may be considered a duty of states, and not just a right.[58] This right/responsibility duality of jurisdiction echoes the regime of sovereignty under international law that is increasingly approached both as an ensemble of rights and as a set of responsibilities.[59]

Fifth, the *bases*, grounds or titles of jurisdiction – as I explained before, jurisdiction is always personal to the extent that it amounts to a normative relationship between a state('s law) and the people subjected to those laws. The question is how to determine what relates a group of people to a given state and legal order in advance and in a collective or general fashion.[60] The bases or titles of jurisdiction do precisely that: they determine the personal relationship of jurisdiction between a state and its legal order on the one hand, and a group of people subject to its laws on the other. They do so by reference to a salient type of general connection or nexus between such a group of people and its institutions.

There are usually four types of basis of jurisdiction and, by extension, of jurisdiction. Jurisdiction applies primarily to people situated on a state's (official) territory ('territorial jurisdiction'; and not, by extension, on a territory the state controls effectively and regularly like a state would, but that is not its official territory) (i), but also outside of its territory,[61] and by extension of its territorial basis, jurisdiction also covers the enactment of law that pertains to its nationals ('personal jurisdiction') (ii), law that protects its (vital) interests ('protective jurisdiction') (iii) and, more universally, law that protects certain fundamental community interests or goods ('universal jurisdiction') (iv).[62] Those four bases of jurisdiction are equal and cannot be ranked in any given order. They may even overlap in certain cases. Importantly, the latter three depend on territorial jurisdiction, which they complement: not only did they

58 Klabbers, *International Law*, at 94–96. For a similar 'duty to exercise effective jurisdiction' in the law of the sea, see Chapter 8.

59 Besson, 'Sovereignty'.

60 To that extent, state jurisdiction in domestic and general international law is different from 'jurisdiction' in international (and domestic) human rights law that is individual (over the individual right-holder) and not collective or, at least, not necessarily. See Besson, 'Extraterritoriality', 868–870.

61 That kind of 'extraterritorial' albeit territorial or spatial jurisdiction, qua effective and regular normative control exercised (over people outside the official territory) may trigger human rights duties under international human rights law, however: see Besson, 'Extraterritoriality'.

62 Note that there is a difference between the 'extraterritorial' bases of jurisdiction that give the state a right to enact domestic laws that applies to subjects situated outside of its territory and the mere impact of those laws outside of its territory.

grow from it historically, but also they cannot exist without it. The three extraterritorial bases are best considered along a continuum of connection to states' interests, ranging from individual personal ones (e.g., nationality), over collective national ones (e.g., security) and all the way to collective universal ones (e.g., peace, life). Arguably, universal jurisdiction differs from the other three to the extent that states exercise it in the name of the international community of states, and not in their own.[63] This may explain why its contours remain contested and it is rarely applied in practice. In turn, the lack of general practice may affect its ability to be considered customary.[64]

Importantly, and as noted, the three bases of extraterritorial jurisdiction are defined by reference to territorial jurisdiction that amounts to the main connection between a state, or legal order, and its people. After all, people have always lived on a territory, and it is on that basis that the law organizes their lives and that lawmaking and politics work.[65] In turn, because many people live on earth and not one, to quote Arendt, those people inhabit different territories and different legal orders organize their lives.[66] This does not prevent those people from different territories, of course, from 'forming a world together',[67] to quote Arendt again. This is done through international law and the interstate regulation of common problems and of interjurisdictional issues that would otherwise fall into the interstices of many juxtaposed state jurisdictions.[68] Examples of such international lawmaking abound, and one may mention international criminal law, international immunities law or international environmental law as means of regulating matters of common interests and settling the jurisdictional issues that would arise otherwise.

Of course, it is precisely because borders are porous that 'extraterritorial' bases of (state) jurisdiction were identified from the very beginning alongside territorial jurisdiction in international law.[69] International law could not possibly cover all those transnational circumstances. No general international

63 To that extent, Klabbers, *International Law*, at 106, is right to claim that, in some cases, "the extraterritorial reach of State jurisdiction serves as the functional equivalent of global governance."

64 S. Yee, 'A Call for a More Rigorous Assessment of Universal Jurisdiction', (2013) 107 *Proceedings of the American Society of International Law* 242.

65 Supiot, 'L'inscription territoriale', at 160.

66 See Arendt, *On Revolution* (London: Penguin, 1963), at 175; Arendt, *Eichmann in Jerusalem: A Report on the Banality of Evil* (London: Penguin, 2006), at 21.

67 Arendt, *On Revolution*, at 175.

68 Klabbers, *International Law*, at 92.

69 C. Schmitt, *Der Nomos der Erde im Völkerrecht des Jus Publicum Europaeum* (Köln: Greven, 1950), on the 'Nomos der Erde' and the inherent limitations of the idea of states' territorial jurisdiction from the very beginning. See also Handl, 'Extra-Territoriality', at 4.

treaty could indeed be sufficiently encompassing to settle those issues. Of course, specific jurisdictional treaties could be negotiated ad hoc, but those would then tend to be unfair.[70] However, because those extraterritorial bases of jurisdiction necessarily lead to overlaps of jurisdiction between states and their respective legal orders, various general principles have developed in international law to manage that concurrence and the potential conflicts it may give rise to. One principle seems to be that extraterritorial jurisdiction may only be prescriptive, at the exclusion of executive and adjudicative jurisdiction that are primarily and exclusively territorial.[71] Of course, even prescriptive jurisdiction may be submitted to prohibitions (i.e., constraints) under international law.[72] When it is not, each state retains discretion about how best to use it.[73] Over time, that discretion has led states to adopt common practices on the matter and customary principles have arisen from domestic and/or public or private international law, such as comity, equity or reciprocity.[74] The fact is, however, that the distinction between the legal and illegal exercises of extraterritorial jurisdiction remains moot, and these exercises vary hugely from legal regime to legal regime and domestic jurisdiction to domestic jurisdiction. The tendency, however, is to privilege the bases of extraterritorial jurisdiction that come the closest to territory on the continuum presented before. This may be illustrated by the success of the 'effects doctrine', especially in Europe. Generally, consent is regarded as a circumstance precluding unlawfulness, and peaceful dispute settlement is required in case of open conflicts of jurisdiction. Other principles have been suggested by domestic legislatures[75] and courts and within doctrinal discussions,[76] but

[70] Bianchi, 'Reply', at 81–82. See also Ryngaert, *Jurisdiction in International Law*, at 197–208. As I will argue in Section 3.2, however, this should not prevent states from negotiating general treaties regulating those issues ex ante.

[71] Crawford, *Brownlie's Principles*, at 486.

[72] When it considers the extraterritorial application of foreign domestic law, this chapter focuses mostly on prescriptive jurisdiction to the extent that it focuses on the circumstances of legal plurality, and hence on uses of extraterritorial jurisdiction that are considered legal under international law.

[73] This corresponds to the regime set up by the PCIJ in *Lotus*, at 18–19. For extensive interpretations, see Ryngaert, *Jurisdiction in International Law*, chapter 2; Bianchi, 'Reply', at 83–85.

[74] For detailed discussions, see Ryngaert, *Jurisdiction in International Law*, chapter 6; Bianchi, 'Reply', at 85–89.

[75] See e.g., US Restatement (Third) of Foreign Relations Law, para. 403 (1987). For a discussion, see Ryngaert, *Jurisdiction in International Law*, chapter 5 and at 208–215.

[76] See e.g., Ryngaert, *Jurisdiction in International Law*, chapter 6; Bianchi, 'Reply', at 88–89 and 92–99.

without much echo in practice so far and certainly not enough generality and coherence to become customary as a result.

Finally, the *constraints* of jurisdiction – jurisdiction is inherently constrained. Jurisdiction is both rule-based and rule-constrained as a result. Domestic and international law both constitute (state) jurisdiction and constrain it at the same time. International law constraints work both externally in a state's jurisdiction's relation to others (e.g., through the non-intervention principle) and internally with respect to its domestic scope and exercise (e.g., through international human rights law). It is important to stress again how international rules of constraint, as much as international constitutive rules, pertain both to the internal functions of jurisdiction and to its external relations.[77] Thus, the idea of *domaine reservé* (i.e., the part of domestic jurisdiction that may not be limited by international law[78]) is itself determined by international law as a constraint of state jurisdiction. Those constraints should not be conflated with external limits, however (i.e., those limits that arise from other legal orders). As we will see, such limits are in principle excluded by jurisdiction: it is the point of jurisdiction indeed that it may be exercised independently and freely of external limits. Internal legal constraints are not considered contrary to that feature, however, because they may always be amended or lifted by the state and legal order of jurisdiction itself. This is true of domestic law, of course, but also of international law constraints that states contribute to establishing together through common international lawmaking and that impose themselves validly and with primacy over domestic law.

3 WHY JURISDICTION?

The concept of jurisdiction defined, it is time to turn to our first question: why jurisdiction? This section first determines, in a descriptive fashion, how (state) jurisdiction has become a central institution in (domestic and international) law and, by extension, in domestic and international legal theory (Section 3.1) and, second, whether it still is in the current pervasive and persistent circumstances of legal plurality (Section 3.2). In a third and more normative step, the next section identifies instrumental moral reasons that justify the centrality

[77] This is why it is wrong to oppose jurisdiction qua system of power to a system of justification: like 'authority', 'jurisdiction' combines both dimensions, as I explained above.

[78] On Article 2(7) of the UN Charter, see e.g., K. Ahmed, 'The Domestic Jurisdiction Clause in the UN Charter: A Historical View', (2006) 10 *Singapore Yearbook of International Law* 175.

of jurisdiction and argues for it not only despite, but because of legal plurality (Section 3.3).

A few remarks are in order about the test of centrality or relevance used here. What matters for the present discussion is that state jurisdiction may be considered important for the modern social and political organization of human life. Of course, qua legal institution and set of rules, jurisdiction is necessarily considered important by domestic and international law and by domestic and international lawyers themselves. However, it is not this internal legal perspective that matters for our purpose, but the social reality underlying those legal phenomena and one that may be subjected to an external empirical and sociological assessment, although this is a difficult distinction to draw in practice and to implement theoretically, not the least because large parts of the material are still in flux and the related developments speculative.

3.1 *The Original Relevance of Jurisdiction*

There are, I would like to claim, three characteristics of state jurisdiction in its current regime of domestic and international law that explain why it has gained central relevance in the social and political organization of human life: comprehensiveness, exclusiveness and pre-emptiveness. Interestingly, and unsurprisingly, those features match the internal perspective of state jurisdiction and the perception reflected in its rules under domestic and international law.[79] What makes them important for our purpose here, however, is not their legal underpinnings, for those may always be changed so as to make this true and are self-fulfilling to that extent, but their social and political relevance. Of course, some of those characteristics could be shared in part by other (non-state) legal orders and their respective set of competences or powers (as opposed to 'jurisdiction' sensu stricto). However, as will become clear in the course of the chapter, no other legal order, most probably for lack of a territorial basis, has come close to sharing all of them and to the same degree.[80] So, state jurisdiction has also been comparatively more significant in all three aspects.

Importantly, one should emphasize that none of those socially and politically relevant features are sufficient for a legal order to be considered a state's legal order.[81] Nor, conversely, are they necessary conditions for an order to be considered legal in the first place, or even for it to be conceived

[79] See e.g., *Island of Palmas*, at 838.

[80] See even Schultz, 'Transnational Legality', chapter 4.

[81] See also Raz, 'Why the State'.

in legal positivist terms.[82] In other words, the point of this section is not to question, in a comparative way, the legality of other legal orders in a context of legal plurality.

The first socially and politically significant feature of state jurisdiction is its *comprehensiveness* of scope. What matters is not the extent or size of the material scope of jurisdiction in itself, but how comprehensive jurisdiction is within that scope. In principle, the scope of state jurisdiction is open or unlimited.[83] What this means is that it is able to address any of the stakes shared by people on a given territory, whether it does so effectively or not.

What one may observe, at least in European and Western states, is that this has tended to be supported socially and politically ever since the seventeenth century and most clearly in the twentieth century, both internally in each state and externally in their international relations to other states. It is a feature that has also gone by the name of 'unlimited' or 'plenary' jurisdiction in international law.[84] Of course, there have been drawbacks and the process has been multi-speed. However, international law developments in the second part of the twentieth century such as positive duties of states under international human rights law to protect human rights in all dimensions of their jurisdiction in their territory[85] have heightened the social visibility and relevance of the comprehensiveness of their jurisdiction, and even of states' responsibility for it. As a result, social and political evidence supports this feature of state jurisdiction and the idea that it is or at least could be comprehensive or unlimited.

The second socially and politically significant feature of state jurisdiction is its *exclusiveness* in the matters it regulates. What this means is that domestic legal orders are not only comprehensive in their material scope, but also exclude the authority or right to rule of other legal orders in the matters regulated within this scope. No other legal order may set limits on domestic jurisdiction, unless those limits are internalized, of course, and become domestic or international law constraints, as I explained in Section 1. Examples of the latter would be infranational norms stemming from the legal orders of federated entities or UN Security Council resolutions.[86]

82 Contra: Schultz, 'Transnational Legality', chapter 4. On alternative accounts of (non-state) jurisdiction to be considered in international law, see e.g., S. Pahuja, 'Laws of Encounter: A Jurisdictional Account of International Law', (2013) 1 *London Review of International Law* 63.

83 Raz, 'Why the State'.

84 See e.g., *Island of Palmas*, at 838; *Lotus*, at 18–19.

85 Besson, 'Extraterritoriality'; Besson, 'Juridictions Concurrentes'.

86 See e.g., C. Warbrick, 'The Jurisdiction of the Security Council: Original Intention and New World Order(s)', in P. Capps, M. Evans and S. Konstadinidis (eds.), *Asserting Jurisdiction: International and European Perspectives* (Oxford: Hart, 2003), 127.

What one may observe, at least in European and Western states, is that the exclusiveness of jurisdiction has tended to be supported socially and politically ever since the seventeenth century and most clearly in the twentieth century, both internally in each state and externally in their international relations to other states. It is a feature that has gone by the name of 'independence' or freedom from external constraints in international law.[87] Of course, as I explained in Section 1, domestic jurisdiction was, from the very beginning, concurrent in the same territory for people, and things have always tended to move around, and those transnational or global dimensions of social life have only increased since. What matters, however, is that the extraterritorial jurisdiction of other states and other external limits induced by other transnational or infranational legal orders have mostly been considered as the exception to the rule and therefore as something to be resisted against. They have also actually been governed from within by domestic or international law principles, as I explained in Section 1. One may mention, for instance, other titles of jurisdiction under international law or residual principles of international law like consent or peaceful dispute settlement. What this means, then, is that social and political evidence supports the salience of this second feature of state jurisdiction as well.

The third and final socially and politically significant feature of state jurisdiction is its *pre-emptiveness* over conflicting legal norms stemming from other legal orders in its comprehensive scope of exclusive regulation. What this means is that, in cases where its norms are to encounter those of another legal order within its jurisdiction, the state's legal order's norms claim to pre-empt or exclude them and to provide exclusionary reasons for action. Indeed, it is the point of authority and, by extension, of legal authority to relate to other competing authorities over the same subjects and, in the absence of organized deference or coordination between them, to claim to exclude them.[88] To that extent, the authority of domestic law is necessarily relational. It is even more the case of the authority of international law that binds states that are themselves authorities or officials for their own subjects: international law necessarily relates in the very structure of its authority to that of domestic law over those same individual subjects.[89] Of course, preemptiveness is compatible with the possibility of conflicts of norms stemming

[87] *Customs Régime between Germany and Austria (Protocol of March 19th, 1931)*, [1931] Publ. PCIJ, Series A./B. No. 41, at 37–54, para. 12. See also Article 2(7) of the UN Charter.

[88] Raz, 'Authority', 1020–1021.

[89] See Besson, 'Relative Authority', 174–176; Besson, 'State Veil'. Contra: Roughan, 'Mind the Gaps', 336.

from the same legal order or from other legal orders in case those external norms have been internalized. Such conflicts between equally pre-emptive norms are usually solved by reference to internal rules of conflict (whether those are material or procedural as in adjudication) and, in their absence, by recourse to practical rationality and the maximization of reasons.[90]

What one may observe, at least in European and Western states, is that this feature of state jurisdiction has tended to be supported socially and politically ever since the seventeenth century and most clearly in the twentieth century, both internally in each state and externally in their international relations to other states. It is a feature that has gone by the name of 'supremacy' of jurisdiction in international law. Of course, because authority is relational, supremacy is usually claimed in circumstances where it is questioned by other authorities and where the exclusiveness of jurisdiction is potentially limited. The regular questioning of supremacy in practice should not be taken as evidence of its lack of social relevance, however. What matters, indeed, is that pre-emptiveness amounts to a claim that can be made: it need not be effective to matter socially. In conclusion, then, social and political evidence supports the salience of this third feature of state jurisdiction as well.

3.2 *The Resilience of Jurisdiction in the Face of Legal Plurality*

Not only has state jurisdiction been sociologically significant in practice, but, as I would like to claim in this section, it still is despite and, arguably, because of legal plurality. To make this argument, it is important to distinguish between the sociological evidence one may gather for the current significance of state jurisdiction from three distinct constellations of legal plurality (i.e., that of infranational law, transnational law and foreign domestic law) and their respective impacts on state jurisdiction (i.e., from below, from above and from aside).

International law is precluded from this section's discussion of those constellations of legal plurality because, as I explained in Section 1, its rules are constitutive of state jurisdiction and amount to internal constraints to jurisdiction. Jurisdiction only exists as equal and independent jurisdiction juxtaposed to that of other states by virtue of international law. The inherent legal duality of jurisdiction therefore prevents one from considering the concurrent application of international law norms within the domestic legal order as an external threat and limitation to that order's jurisdiction and its

[90] Raz, 'Authority', 1023–1025.

comprehensiveness, exclusiveness and pre-emptiveness.[91] On the contrary, state jurisdiction is more comprehensive, exclusive and pre-emptive as a result of the international legal constraints that enhance it socially,[92] and even turn it, in some cases, into a social responsibility. In other words, and contrary to what one may read, the concurrent application of international law in domestic law does not lead to legal plurality.

That conclusion is actually confirmed from the perspective of international lawmaking itself: if state jurisdiction is inherently constituted and constrained by international law, the reverse is also true. The duality of domestic and international law in constituting jurisdiction also works inside-out, as it were.

In terms of sources, first of all, international law is still mostly made by states and for states qua authors and (direct) subjects of its legal norms.[93] Of course, the sources of international law have become more complex institutionally, and states' implication is, as a result, sometimes only indirect, as exemplified by international lawmaking through and by international organizations (IOs) and their respective institutions. However, the usual counterexamples from contemporary international law invoked to sideline states' implication and control over international lawmaking either belong to the peripheral realm of soft law (e.g., OECD standards) or imply some indirect form of state consent (e.g., IOs' and international courts' law).[94] Of course, as is the case in domestic law, the equality of states and the fairness of international lawmaking procedures are not always respected, but this does not support the argument that states are no longer the collective makers of international law and no longer have the jurisdiction to do so. Finally, one should add that the domestic legal order is the legal order in which most international law norms are adjudicated and enforced, and even, in some cases, developed further (e.g., qua customary norms or general principles).

With respect to its subjects, secondly, international law remains states' law. On the one hand, individuals, of course, qua subjects to state

91 Contra: Raz, 'Why the State'; Roughan, 'Mind the Gaps', 334, 338.

92 See also T. Endicott, 'The Logic of Freedom and Power', in S. Besson and J. Tasioulas (eds.), *The Philosophy of International Law* (Oxford: Oxford University Press, 2010), 245, on an analogy between individual freedom under domestic law and state sovereignty under international law.

93 Besson, 'State Veil'.

94 S. Besson, 'State Consent and Disagreement in International Law-Making – Dissolving the Paradox', (2016) 29 *Leiden Journal of International Law* 289; S. Besson, 'Law Beyond the State: A Reply to Liam Murphy', (2017) *European Journal of International Law* 233, on state consent as an exception to the legitimate authority of international law and its persistence in international lawmaking. Contra: N. Krisch, 'The Decay of Consent: International Law in an Age of Global Public Goods', (2014) 108 *American Journal of International Law* 1.

jurisdiction, have always been the subjects of international law.[95] This has long occurred only indirectly through their own authorities and representatives (i.e., states) that are direct subjects of international law. They have gradually also become direct subjects in some areas of international law, albeit more as beneficiaries of rights than as bearers of duties. This confirms the importance of their jurisdictional relationship to their respective states when their duties under international law are in question, for those individual duties usually rely on domestic law to arise. There is a difference, therefore, between individuals being subjects to and hence of international law and the latter exercising jurisdiction over them. IOs, on the other hand, have also become subjects of international law since the end of the Second World War. In practice, however, and even if this may be regrettable,[96] they have largely remained institutional constructs of their member states, and their legal personalities amount to institutional extensions of those states' personalities, at least in the latter's own institutional relationships to their individual subjects. Evidence for this is that states remain the main duty-bearers and responsibility-bearers under international law, even in domains where IOs have been delegated some of their member states' powers and rights that form part of the latter's jurisdiction. The main international law duties of IOs are internal only and owed to their member states. An explanation for this state of affairs is that IOs lack, for the most part, a political community that would tie them directly to a people and a territory[97] and grant them the kind of jurisdiction such a political relationship would give rise to. State jurisdiction remains the rule in international law, in other words, and so do its comprehensiveness, exclusiveness and pre-emptiveness. Even when an IO comes close to being considered as a political community with statelike territorial jurisdiction over a people, like the EU may be said to,[98] states may always exit, thereby confirming their institutional control over the IOs they have constituted.

To that extent, it is wrong to look at international law in isolation, and especially to conceive of its right to rule as a form of independent 'jurisdiction'

95 Besson, 'State Veil'.

96 For a critique of functionalism, see J. Klabbers, 'The EJIL Foreword: The Transformation of International Organizations Law', (2015) 26 *European Journal of International Law* 9.

97 S. Besson, 'Individual and State Liability for an International Organization's Responsibility – The Challenge of Fairness Unveiled', (2017) 6 *Rivista di filosofia del diritto-Journal of Legal Philosophy* 51.

98 For a critique of the EU's political quality, however, see D. Kochenov, 'Neo-Mediaeval Permutations of Personhood in the European Union', (2016) 13 *European University Institute Working Paper*.

and authority that could be approached as an external limit to state jurisdiction and authority.[99] Domestic and international law share the same subjects and mould the same authority and jurisdiction: that of the state over its people. It would be a categorical mistake, therefore, to place the relationship between domestic and international law into the same bag as relations between domestic law and other legal orders in discussions of legal plurality.[100]

The time has come to turn to the discussion of the three constellations of legal plurality that have been regarded as a threat to state jurisdiction in recent times, and to the demonstration that they have not made state jurisdiction redundant socially and politically – quite the contrary.

First of all, state jurisdiction in the face of *infranational* law – the first kind of legal order whose scope of application competes increasingly with that of domestic law is infranational law. Examples thereof may be religious law or indigenous populations' law. I am not including the law of federated entities to the extent that their respective jurisdiction is an internal matter of state jurisdiction, as I explained before, and one whose constraints on state jurisdiction are regulated internally.[101]

There is no doubt that those forms of infranational law have developed steadily in the last few years, thereby confirming the social reality of legal plurality. However, the fact is that this has not diminished the social importance of state jurisdiction. While infranational law does affect the comprehensiveness of the scope of jurisdiction and its exclusiveness, it has also given rise to strong reassertions of supremacy in important domains of exclusive jurisdiction. This may be exemplified in the field of human rights protection, and especially of equality between men and women or child protection and their opposability to religious law or, at least, to religious autonomy.[102]

Secondly, state jurisdiction in the face of *transnational* law – the second kind of legal order whose scope of application competes increasingly with that

[99] Contra: Roughan, 'Mind the Gaps', 340, 347–348. See also Besson, 'State Veil'; Besson, 'Relative Authority', 174–176.

[100] Contra: Roughan, *Authorities*, chapters 7 and 8; Roughan, 'Mind the Gaps'. See also Besson, 'Relative Authority', 172–173.

[101] Federated entities' law may, however, raise similar questions to the former in some constellations of federalism, especially when neither the central nor the local jurisdictional agendas are open or comprehensive. For discussions, see R. A. Dahl, 'Federalism and the Democratic Process', in J. R. Pennock and J. W. Chapman (eds.), *Nomos XXV: Liberal Democracy* (1983) 95; S. Besson, 'Fédéralisme et Droits de l'Homme: Une Introduction Thématique', in S. Besson and E. M. Belser (eds.), *La Convention européenne des droits de l'homme et les cantons* (Zurich: Schulthess, 2014), 7.

[102] ECtHR, Grand Chamber, *SAS v France*, Application No. 43835/11, Judgement of 1 July 2014.

of domestic law is transnational law. Transnational law is difficult to define except by reference to the straddling of categories, and in particular of the distinctions between private/public law, national/international law and practice/theory of law.[103] Examples thereof may be the private or 'negotiated'[104] law developed by transnational corporations (with or without states) and around commercial exchanges (*lex mercatoria*[105]) or the private law developed by private actors (with or without states) to regulate the Internet (*lex electronica*[106]).

There is no doubt that those forms of transnational law have developed at a fast rate in the last few years, thereby confirming the social reality of legal plurality. However, the fact is that this has not diminished the social importance of state jurisdiction. While transnational law does affect the comprehensiveness of the scope of jurisdiction and its exclusiveness, it has also given rise to strong reassertions of supremacy in important domains of exclusive jurisdiction. This may be exemplified in the context of cyber-regulation where, on the one hand, state's jurisdiction has been reaffirmed in all matters of external regulation of the Internet pertaining to privacy, security or crime,[107] and where, on the other, the internal regulation of the Internet itself has actually been largely dominated by one or few states (and their respective jurisdictions) from the very beginning and despite structural changes over time.[108] Another example may be given in the context of transnational commercial law: state jurisdiction has been reaffirmed recently, especially by China and, to a lesser extent, by India and Turkey, in the global regulation of markets. In Western and European countries, domestic jurisdiction has also been exercised anew to regulate transnational business exchanges that had temporarily escaped state regulation due to the latter's territorial ambit. One may mention, for instance, the introduction into domestic private law of the principle of corporate groups' liability for violation of human rights' due diligence by their dependent companies abroad.

[103] On the many meanings of 'transnational law' and their lack of commonality but for the idea that it straddles other characterizations and that it is actually becoming more and more encompassing of any form of legality, see Besson, 'Transnational Constitutional Law'.
[104] For this term, see Roberts, 'After Government?' at 18.
[105] O. Toth, *The Lex Mercatoria in Theory and Practice* (Oxford: Oxford University Press, 2017).
[106] Schultz, 'Carving Up the Internet', at 802–803 and 828–837; J. Zekoll, 'Jurisdiction in Cyberspace', in G. Handl et al. (eds.), *Beyond Territoriality*, 341.
[107] See Schultz, 'Carving Up the Internet', 801.
[108] J. Goldsmith and T. Wu, *Who Controls the Internet? Illusions of a Borderless World* (Oxford: Oxford University Press, 2006); K. Raustiala, 'Governing the Internet', (2016) 110 *American Journal of International Law* 491.

Finally, state jurisdiction in the face of *foreign domestic law* – the third kind of legal order whose scope of application increasingly competes with that of domestic law is foreign domestic law. The domestic law of other states may indeed apply within the domestic legal order when its jurisdiction relies on an extraterritorial basis, such as personal, protective or universal titles of jurisdiction. Examples abound in the fields of environmental, competition, financial or tax law, and the main states and entities implicated are the United States and the EU.

There is no doubt that those forms of extraterritorial domestic law have developed quickly in the last few years, thereby confirming the social reality of legal plurality. However, the fact is that this has not diminished the social importance of state jurisdiction. Importantly, none of the domestic institutions involved have suggested dispensing altogether with territorial jurisdiction, and all of them try hard to justify their jurisdiction's extraterritorial extension by reference to it. Even those who have suggested new bases of jurisdiction that fit its extraterritorial scope have only rarely suggested giving up on territorial jurisdiction: the latter remains a negative reference point for the diverse proposals for 'deemed', 'functional' or 'reasonable' jurisdiction, emphasizing the strongest link or nexus to the regulated object.[109] Moreover, while the extraterritorial jurisdiction of foreign domestic law does affect the comprehensiveness of the scope of jurisdiction and its exclusiveness, it has also given rise to strong reassertions of supremacy in important domains of exclusive jurisdiction. This may be exemplified by the backlash experienced by universal jurisdiction in criminal law and the recentring of domestic criminal jurisdiction onto cases where there is a territorial nexus to the accused.[110] Another example is the reinvigoration of the presumption against extraterritoriality in recent US constitutional law.[111]

In short, while it is correct to say that state jurisdiction is changing through its reactions to legal plurality, it has not been displaced. It certainly has not been replaced in the important social functions fulfilled by its

[109] R. Mallay, J. Manax and C. Nix, 'Constructing the State Extraterritorially: Jurisdictional Discourse, the National Interest, and Transnational Norms', (1990) 103 *Harvard Law Review* 1273; Bianchi, 'Reply', at 92–99; Michaels, 'Territorial Jurisdiction'; Schultz, 'Carving Up the Internet', at 816–819; Zumbansen, 'Global Governance'; Bethlehem, 'End of Geography', 22.

[110] Yee, 'Universal Jurisdiction'.

[111] Ryngaert, *Jurisdiction in International Law*, at ix; J. H. Knox, 'A Presumption against Extrajurisdictionality', (2010) 104 *American Journal of International Law* 351. On the Alien Tort Claim Act in the US Supreme Court's case law, see e.g., *Kiobel v Royal Dutch Petroleum Co.*, 133 US 1659 (2013); *Morrison v National Australia Bank*, 561 US 247 (2010); *RJR Nabisco, Inc. v The European Community*, 579 US __ (2016).

comprehensiveness, exclusiveness and pre-emptiveness.[112] One may actually even emphasize its resilience in the face of legal plurality and the renewed importance it has gained in the circumstances of persistent and pervasive legal plurality. Even if jurisdiction has not been displaced, however, some of the changes it is experiencing should affect the way we approach it in practice. I will return to the impacts of those three constellations of legal plurality on our future conception of state jurisdiction in Section 4.

3.3 *The Justification of Jurisdiction for Political Legitimacy*

Not only has state jurisdiction been sociologically relevant and arguably still is, but it may also be considered as justified from a normative perspective. Of course, as I explained in Section 1, jurisdiction amounts to a set of legal rules. As such, therefore, it does not require a moral justification besides a justification for the authority of the valid law issued. Curiously, however, the legitimacy of jurisdiction is rarely discussed in the literature or, at least, not as such.[113] An explanation for this gap in the literature may be that jurisdiction has increasingly been reified to the extent that instead of being approached as a relationship between a state and people, it is considered as pertaining to things (e.g., cyber data,[114] taxable assets) or activities (e.g., business transactions, financial activities) entirely separate from people and then projected back onto them. Once jurisdiction and the law it enacts are cut off from the individual subjects they apply to, moral justification and, more generally, legitimacy no longer seem like relevant questions. Such a reifying approach misses the point of jurisdiction, however, which, as I explained in Section 1, amounts to a relationship between the state and people. It also ignores, more generally, what law itself amounts to, to the extent that law guides the action of people and should be justified morally to them. Jurisdiction should therefore be structured legally in such a way that the authority exercised over people on its basis is actually able to have the legitimacy it

[112] See also Raz, 'Why the State'.

[113] They do indeed come back in through the backdoor, as exemplified by the discussion of 'reasonableness' or 'subsidiarity' in Bianchi, 'Reply', at 74 (who conflates legality and legitimacy), or Ryngaert, *Jurisdiction in International Law*, chapter 6 (who focuses on the democratic legitimacy of extraterritorial jurisdiction, but without concern for its legality in the first place). Neither of them discusses the identity of the subjects to extraterritorial state jurisdiction and their link to that state, however.

[114] On the disconnection of data from people in the cyberspace, see e.g., M.-A. Frison-Roche, 'Penser le monde à partir de la notion de "donnée",' in M.-A. Frison-Roche (ed.), *Internet, espace d'interrégulation (Paris: Dalloz, 2016), at 7–16.*

claims on the one hand, and that the sovereignty it is a facet of can be exercised responsibly on the other. In other words, it is the connection between jurisdiction and legitimacy – but also between jurisdiction and sovereignty – that gives jurisdiction a normative dimension and requires that it be such that the authority and sovereignty it underpins be morally justifiable. In turn, this implies some form of instrumental moral justifiability of jurisdiction itself by reference to its contribution to political legitimacy.[115]

There are at least two ways of providing an instrumental justification of jurisdiction over a people in a given territory by reference to political legitimacy. Importantly, this justification should also extend to the three features of jurisdiction (i.e., its comprehensiveness, exclusiveness and pre-emptiveness). Based on the concept of jurisdiction presented in Section 1 and its territorial dimension, this implies primarily justifying territorial jurisdiction.

The first way to approach the instrumental justification of jurisdiction would be to establish – on the basis of an *anthropological* argument – that human beings are rooted territorially, especially as social and political groups, and that this has implications for their political and legal organization.[116] What seems clear, indeed, is that the territorial ties of human laws have only rarely been disrupted in human history, and that this applies all around the globe.[117] Those territorial ties have varied greatly, of course, and no one connection between the law and territory has been the same across culture and history, before and after the emergence of the state and its globalization through international law.[118] However, that link has remained a constant dimension of legality even when new threats to it have arisen every now and then and have had to be solved anew through a different kind of legal connection to that territory.[119]

[115] Of course, as we will see, political legitimacy or the justification of political authority is itself instrumental and relies on content-independent reasons. See also Raz, 'Authority'; Besson, 'State Veil'.

[116] See, for instance, Arendt's argument for what she calls the 'territorial principle': Arendt, *On Revolution*, at 175; Arendt, *Eichmann in Jerusalem*, at 21.

[117] For such an argument, see e.g., Supiot, 'L'inscription territoriale', at 154–156, referring to Montesquieu's '*esprit des lois*'. See also D. Liberski-Bagnoud, *Les Dieux du territoire – Penser autrement la généalogie* (Paris: Centre National de la Recherche Scientifique/Édition de la Maison des Sciences de l'Homme, 2002); P. Legendre, *Leçons X, Dogma: Instituer l'animal humain* (Paris: Fayard, 2017), at 35–36.

[118] P. J. Taylor, 'The State As Container: Territoriality in the Modern World-System', (1994) 18 *Progress in Human Geography* 151.

[119] A. Supiot, *Homo Juridicus – Essai sur la fonction anthropologique du Droit* (Paris: Points, 2005), at 163. For the resilience of territoriality in international law, see Bethlehem, 'End of Geography', 13–14.

What this means, therefore, is that the link between law and territory amounts clearly to more than a merely contingent marker of the relationship between the state (and its laws) and a given people, and hence between those people. It cannot simply be replaced by other (contingent) markers of sociability. The problem with the latter proposition, indeed, is that human life is not 'virtual', including in its social and political dimensions, and social bonds cannot be reduced to relations of communication as a result.[120] Such virtual ties may benefit or, in some cases, detract from physical and hence territorial social bonds, but it is difficult to see how they could replace them altogether. Of course, other social communities of interest or goals may develop beside, below or above political communities in each territory, but they should not be mistaken for the latter and regarded as interchangeable. What makes the social relationship between people on a given territory different is what those people do together on and with that territory, and not merely the fact that they live together (like cattle would) and have social ties of mere proximity.[121]

Importantly, nothing in this anthropological discussion of the territoriality of law implies any form of territorial property or ownership rights over portions of the territory,[122] whether individual (territorial property) or collective (territorial sovereignty) on the one hand, and whether alone or in conjunction with other individuals on the other. To that extent, it is distinct from Lockean or, more generally, liberal understandings of the territorial jurisdiction of states in domestic and international law.[123] The latter is just one of many examples in a long line of accounts of how state jurisdiction is intimately related to territory.

A second approach to the justification of state jurisdiction, and the one developed at length in this section, relies on a *moral* argument. It considers territorial jurisdiction as a necessary (albeit insufficient) requirement of political legitimacy. Of course, there may be other grounds for the legitimacy of law than grounds of political legitimacy. Thus, one may mention volitional, epistemic or coordinative grounds.[124] What I am interested in in this chapter,

[120] Contra: Schultz, 'Transnational Legality', chapter 4; Bethlehem, 'End of Geography', 22; Taylor, 'The State as Container'.

[121] Contra: Schultz, 'Transnational Legality', chapter 4.

[122] On the novelty and unicity in legal history of the recognition of individual and collective territorial rights in the seventeenth century, see Supiot, 'L'inscription territoriale', 157; J. G. Ruggie, 'Territoriality and Beyond: Problematizing Modernity in International Relations', (1993) 47 *International Organization* 139.

[123] D. Miller, 'Territorial Rights: Concept and Justification', (2012) 60 *Political Studies* 252.

[124] See e.g., Raz, 'Authority', 1012–1020; Besson, 'State Veil'.

however, is state jurisdiction qua political jurisdiction and its relationship to political legitimacy as a result, and more precisely to democratic legitimacy. True, there may be other kinds of political legitimacy than democratic legitimacy and other grounds thereof than equality, but this is the one I am interested in pursuing here.

The argument I propose goes as follows: territorial jurisdiction is instrumentally justified by reference to its contribution to democratic legitimacy, because the territoriality of law, and by extension its comprehensiveness, exclusiveness and pre-emptiveness on the territory, ensures the generality or general applicability of law to all members of the political community and hence enables the latter to respect individual equality before the law.[125] One of the conditions of public or political equality, and hence of democracy, is indeed that people share equal and interdependent stakes.[126] The decision-making process over those stakes and their legal regulation as a result should be such that it can respect that equality of stakes and their interdependence. This is what territorial jurisdiction contributes to securing, to the extent that people living on the same territory, and doing things together on that territory, are the most likely to share not only roughly equal, but also interdependent stakes across a broad range of issues in life.[127]

More specifically, the three characteristics of jurisdiction that have made it resilient over time in practice are also those that contribute to its instrumental justification by reference to political equality. The comprehensiveness of jurisdiction, first of all, ensures that the set of issues regulated over is sufficiently broad to reflect the interdependence of stakes underpinning them. Second, the exclusiveness of jurisdiction guarantees that those included in the lawmaking process are self-determining and deciding independently. Finally, the pre-emptiveness of jurisdiction ensures the equality between stakeholders by preventing other stakes than those that are shared equally from taking priority over the decision reached in respect of that public equality.

Of course, one may object to this argument by pushing it one step further and by arguing for *universal territoriality*. Arguably, indeed, the most justified kind of territorial jurisdiction from the perspective of public equality and democratic legitimacy would be universal. This is even more true today than it was in the past, especially in the light of the development of global common

[125] See also Waldron, 'Legal Pluralism'.

[126] T. Christiano, 'Democratic Legitimacy and International Institutions', in S. Besson and J. Tasioulas (eds.), *The Philosophy of International Law* (Oxford: Oxford University Press, 2010), 119, 130 ff; Dahl, 'Federalism'.

[127] See also T. Christiano, 'A Democratic Theory of Territory and Some Puzzles about Global Democracy', (2006) 37 *Journal of Social Philosophy* 81, 85–87, 98.

interests that require universal regulation and, more generally, of the development of interdependent stakes shared by people all over the globe.

The difficulty, however, was well flagged by Arendt when she referred to 'not man, but men' inhabiting the earth[128] and to the many peoples inhabiting different territories and having different laws[129] as a result. While we may share some stakes on a global plane and while some of them may be sufficiently interdependent, it is difficult to consider them equal. One may add – in line with the argument made in the previous sections – that it is only because there is more than one state's jurisdiction on earth that international law is needed, and even possible. Without international law, the legal duality of state jurisdiction would be lost. This would actually be problematic for political equality and democratic legitimacy themselves. International law amounts indeed to the source of the main constraints bearing on domestic jurisdiction, such as international human rights law and other international law rules that encapsulate and entrench the rules and principles constitutive of (domestic) democracy.[130]

At this stage, one may object that international law itself is not made democratically, and that it may be self-defeating to provide an instrumental justification of state jurisdiction based on democracy if state jurisdiction is itself constituted and internally constrained by international rules that are not democratic. As I have argued elsewhere, however, although there is no global political community and no universal territorial democracy backing the claim to authority of international law, there are ways to secure its democratic legitimacy.[131] One of those ways is democratic state consent.[132]

Conversely, another type of rejoinder may be to turn the proposed instrumental moral justification of state jurisdiction on its head and argue for *deterritorialized democracy*. Some authors, including myself in the past, have argued indeed that political legitimacy, and especially democracy, could themselves be (at least partly) deterritorialized following the main characteristic of transnational or global law,[133] thereby rendering this section's moral–political argument for territorial jurisdiction moot. This could happen, for instance,

[128] Arendt, *On Revolution*, at 175.

[129] Arendt, *Eichmann in Jerusalem*, at 21.

[130] See S. Besson, 'Human Rights and Democracy in a Global Context – Decoupling and Recoupling', (2011) 4 *Ethics and Global Politics* 19, on the 'decoupling' and 'recoupling' of human rights and democracy through international law.

[131] Besson, 'Lifting the State Veil'.

[132] Besson, 'Dissolving the Paradox'; Besson, 'Reply to Liam Murphy'.

[133] See e.g., S. Besson, 'Deliberative Demoi-cracy in the European Union. Towards the Deterritorialization of Democracy', in S. Besson and J. L. Marti (eds.), *Deliberative Democracy and Its Discontents* (Aldershot: Ashgate, 2006), 181; Brölmann, 'Deterritorializing'.

through the constitution of epistemic communities of deliberation that would include all those subjected to a given law into the deliberative process.

The difficulties with those arguments are immense, however, and it suffices to mention only a few here. One is that deliberation does not replace actual decision-making, and the latter remains largely territorial to date. Decision-making that does not include all those subjected to law and does not give them equal participation or representation may hardly be considered democratic as a result. Another difficulty is that such a deterritorialized political community, were it to stretch all the way to provide an effective inclusive decision-making procedure, would become dangerously diffuse and amorphous depending on the stakes, thereby giving rise to an egalitarian counter-critique. The sharing of equal and not only of interdependent stakes constitutes indeed one of the conditions of the right to political equality, and hence of democracy, and it would go amiss in this scenario. It is unlikely indeed that such a bundle of interdependent stakes could be shared equally by all people on earth.

A final remark is in order: nothing in the present argument should be read as reactionary. It is not the point of the argument, on the one hand, to hold on to a Westphalian order that has evolved gradually over time.[134] As I explained in Section 3.2, jurisdiction is resilient and has not been displaced, but this does not mean that it has not changed (precisely in order to remain so resilient) and that our conceptions should not be adapted. It will be the aim of the Section 4 to explain how.

Nor, on the other hand, is this argument about denying that, once upon a time in history, and a long time ago actually, laws were personal and the relationship between law and territory was organized differently. As I have argued, however, there is much to say in favour of the kind of political communities we have developed since, and especially in favour of the generality of law, individual equality and democratic legitimacy, all of them being principles protected and entrenched under the current system of international law. Reverting to a neo-medieval[135] personal status and hence to what was the rule in the pre-democratic age[136] is too high a price to pay for legal plurality.[137] This is true even if contemporary propositions for the return of the personal status are actually made, and quite paradoxically so, in the name of individual

[134] Contra: Bethlehem, 'End of Geography', 18; Koller, 'End of Geography', 28–29.

[135] On this term, see Kochenov, 'Personhood'.

[136] A. Wijffels, 'Bringing Peripheries into Focus', in d'Argent (ed.), *Droit des Frontières Internationales* 43.

[137] See also Roberts, 'After Government?' at 17–18, on the risk of legal representation without the state. For a discussion of inter-legality from the perspective of citizenship, see Chapter 6.

autonomy and sometimes even of cultural identity, and hence of domestic and international human rights law.[138] This is not to say that we may not do better than the current regime of territoriality of law and state jurisdiction to enhance the political and especially the democratic legitimacy of our laws, but it is important to understand what we have to lose in giving them up. As a matter of fact, we are not only entitled to compare options, but actually have a responsibility do so.

4 WHAT JURISDICTION?

Jurisdiction is a resilient concept despite and, I have also argued, because of legal plurality. This has been assessed from a sociological perspective, but its centrality was also justified instrumentally by reference to its contribution to the protection of political equality and hence to democratic legitimacy. Even if jurisdiction has not been displaced, its resilience has come as a reaction to legal plurality, and this should affect the way we approach it in practice.[139] Such a reconceptualization is even more important as territorial jurisdiction is morally justified and should work in such a way as to be able to resist the challenges of legal plurality.

It is from that perspective that the present section assesses the impact that the three constellations of legal plurality should have on our conceptions of state jurisdiction. Legal plurality does not necessarily imply legal equality between the different legal orders whose norms overlap within state jurisdiction.[140] It should not therefore be taken to mean that their relations should be the same across the board and they should all affect the concept of jurisdiction in the same way. The assessment will therefore distinguish between each of the three types of legal orders whose norms interact with domestic law and challenge its territorial jurisdiction in three different ways: from below (infranational law), from above (transnational law) or from aside (foreign domestic law).

[138] For a positive assessment of this 'personal empowerment' through deterritorialized international law, see Bethlehem, 'End of Geography', 19. For a counter-critique of those forms of 'global narcissism', see Supiot, 'L'Inscription Territoriale', 163.

[139] See also Bethlehem, 'End of Geography', 17.

[140] The equalization of all legal orders in circumstances of legal plurality may be explained by the anthropological origins of the discussion of legal plurality (and inter-legality) and (legal as well as other) anthropologists' tendency to reduce all forms of normativity, including legal normativity, into a single one. See D. Liberski-Bagnoud, 'Règne de la Loi, Régime des Interdits', in G. Longo (ed.), *Loi des Dieux, des hommes et de la nature* (Paris: Fayard, 2017), 39.

What infranational, transnational and foreign domestic law have in common is the threat they generate for the territoriality of law. They do so differently, however, and this affects their relationship to state jurisdiction and domestic law as a result. While infranational and transnational law imply some form of either personalized or even reified deterritorialization (Section 4.1), foreign domestic law brings in its wake a neo-imperialistic[141] project of overterritorialization (Section 4.2).[142]

4.1 *Reinforcing Jurisdiction in the Face of Legal Deterritorialization*

Whereas the deterritorialization through infranational law erodes territorial jurisdiction from within domestic law and bottom-up, the deterritorializing effect of transnational law is exercised from the outside and top-down.[143] Infranational and transnational law threaten to displace the territoriality of law by (re)personalizing jurisdiction or, worse, by depersonalizing it entirely. On the one hand, infranational law aims at replacing territoriality with new forms of personality of law and a neo-medieval personal status according to which each person is to be regulated differently by reference to personal characteristics (e.g., religion or culture). On the other hand, transnational law has gone further in deterritorializing and depersonalizing law, and has severed the law's claim to bind from any link to its individual subjects by referring only to objects or activities (e.g., data, business transactions, financial products) and then projecting those reified connections back onto individuals.[144]

This deterritorialization project common to infranational and transnational law, when the law stemming from those legal orders applies concurrently with domestic law in a given state's jurisdiction, is usually, albeit not exclusively,[145] justified by reference to the existence of universal, and hence by definition non-territorial, 'laws' in the broader sense of the term.[146] Those universal laws

[141] Raustalia, 'Empire and Extraterritoriality'. For a historical discussion of such imperialist exercises of extraterritorial jurisdiction in the nineteenth century, see T. Kayaoglu, 'The Extension of Westphalian Sovereignty: State Building and the Abolition of Extraterritoriality', (2007) 51 *International Studies Quarterly* 649.

[142] See also Supiot, 'L'inscription territoriale', at 154, 160.

[143] See, indirectly, ibid., at 160.

[144] This is actually a key tenet of most economic ideologies: projecting relations between things and people onto relationships between people. See e.g., L. Dumont, *Homo Aequalis I. Genèse et épanouissement de l'idéologie économique*, 2nd edn (Paris: Gallimard, 1985).

[145] This is not the case, for instance, with indigenous laws.

[146] On the common origins of the 'laws' of men, nature and religion in Western intellectual history, see Supiot, *Homo Juridicus*, chapter 2.

may be divine laws (e.g., in the case of infranational religious law) or the laws of economy and the market (e.g., in the case of transnational law like *lex mercatoria*), the laws of science and technology (e.g., in the case of transnational law like *lex electronica*) or even the laws of nature such as the laws of biology.[147] Famously, those laws know of no territory. Instead, they apply to 'space'[148] or 'domains',[149] terms that were once used only to refer to the sea, the air, the atmosphere or even the universe (i.e., spaces without territories and borders,[150] but also without people because they were deemed inhabitable). The increasing recourse to that terminology in the context of the recent discussions of infranational or transnational law and of their relationship to state jurisdiction should not come as a surprise, therefore. In the context of the extraterritorial exercise of state jurisdiction in particular, those terms come together with new 'technical', 'functional', 'rational' or 'scientific' jurisdictional nexi or ties[151] that are not only deterritorialized and depersonalized as a result, but also claim to be universal by reference to those other laws.

Such universal approaches to deterritorialization are not new in legal history,[152] but what is unprecedented in this case is their combination in current circumstances of legal plurality and the overlap of different deterritorialized legal orders at the same time. This overlap threatens to reduce the world to a 'flatland'[153] in which religious movements, powerful private actors, bureaucratic agents, governments and many others play indistinct parts. What this does, however, is take the law away from its many territories and hence from the many people that inhabit the earth, and deprive the relationship of jurisdiction from its egalitarian justification. Somehow, the innocent and

[147] Supiot, 'L'Inscription Territoriale', at 153.

[148] See e.g., Colangelo, 'Spatial Legality'; Zumbansen, 'Global Governance', at 551–553; Schultz, 'Transnational Legality', at 78; Mallay et al. 'State Extraterritoriality', at 1304. For a discussion of cyber 'space', see A. Zimmermann, 'International Law and "Cyber Space"', (2014) 3 *ESIL Reflections*.

[149] See e.g., Stephan, 'Competing Sovereignty'.

[150] Curiously, those are captured by the more encompassing notion of 'geography' in recent discussions among international lawyers: e.g., Bethlehem, 'End of Geography'; Koller, 'End of Geography'.

[151] See e.g., Mallay et al., 'Constructing the State Extraterritorially'; Bianchi, 'Reply', at 92–99; Michaels, 'Territorial Jurisdiction'; Schultz, 'Carving Up the Internet', 816–819; Zumbansen, 'Global Governance'; Bethlehem, 'End of Geography', 22.

[152] It suffices to think of the Catholic Church's roman-canonical laws that famously had no territory, but universal jurisdiction. See also Legendre, 'Dogma: Instituer l'Animal Humain', at 33–34.

[153] E. A. Abbott, *Flatland. A Romance of Many Dimensions* (London: Seeley and Co., 1884); T. L. Friedman, *The World Is Flat – The Globalized World in the Twenty-First Century* (New York: Penguin, 2006).

multicultural phenomena imagined by the early legal pluralists and anthropologists[154] do not appear very seductive anymore: they should be observed through the lenses of the kind of cultural exceptionalism or private imperialism they have engendered.[155]

What this means for the conception of state jurisdiction in the face of legal plurality is that the concurrence of infranational and transnational law should simply be rejected on grounds of individual equality[156] and democratic legitimacy. No conceptual adaptations of jurisdiction are required as a result of this kind of legal plurality.

Importantly, and despite an attractive prima facie correspondence between the jurisdictional invocation of those (non-human) universal laws and the universal scope of international law, deterritorialized legal universality should not be conflated with the universality of international law norms,[157] as exemplified by international human rights law or international criminal law.[158] Qua international law, the latter are part of the instruments developed to do what Arendt referred to aptly as 'forming a world' between the many people on earth and their many territorial laws. Those international legal norms rely on the keystone of state (territorial) jurisdiction for their development and implementation and should not be considered as competing with or threatening the former, as I explained in Section 1. Respect for universal standards in international law does not and should not have individual equality before the law and democracy as its price: they are meant to protect it from the outside.[159]

4.2 *Reconceiving Jurisdiction in the Face of Foreign Domestic Law*

Foreign domestic law applying extraterritorially, by contrast, displaces the territoriality of law but not completely: it adds a new layer of jurisdiction

[154] Merry, 'Legal Pluralism'; Griffiths, 'Legal Pluralism'; Cotterell, 'Global Legal Pluralism'.

[155] See also Roberts, 'After Government?' at 17–18.

[156] See also Waldron, 'Legal Pluralism', arguing against infranational law on grounds of equality before the law.

[157] This contrast is reminiscent of the one between universal justice and local legitimacy. See e.g., J. Waldron, 'Special Ties and Natural Justice', (1993) 22 *Philosophy and Public Affairs* 3. See also B. Pascal, *Thoughts*, Vol. 48 (New York: P.F. Collier and Son Company, 1909), at 294: "A strange *justice* that is bounded by a *river*! Truth on this side of the Pyrenees, error on the other side."

[158] Contra: Koller, 'End of Geography'.

[159] See Besson, 'Human Rights and Democracy' on democracy and international (human rights) law. For a critique of globalization from the perspective of democracy, see D. Rodrik, *The Globalization Paradox: Democracy and the Future of the World Economy* (New York: W.W. Norton, 2011).

that is not territorial from aside, while relying on another state's territorial jurisdiction to do so. To that extent, the states (e.g., the United States or the EU) whose extraterritorial jurisdiction is exercised overterritorialize in a neo-imperialistic way, but do so by reference to a non-territorial or deterritorialized nexus and again either by reference to shared personal characteristics or to reified ones.

The overlap between states' concurrent jurisdictions is more difficult to resist than deterritorialization through infranational or transnational law to the extent that it was part and parcel of the 'law on laws' or the domestic and international law of jurisdiction from the very beginning. There should be a way, therefore, for jurisdiction to be conceived in circumstances of legal plurality when that plurality stems from the overlap of distinct states' jurisdictions.

Different conceptions of state jurisdiction in circumstances of extraterritorial jurisdiction have been proposed in theory and practice. One should exclude from the outset conceptions inspired by the universal and hence deterritorialized laws of the economy or of science disparaged before (i.e., conceptions of jurisdiction reconceived as non-territorial domains or spaces and based on purely functional or technical nexi[160] on the one hand, and conceptions based on self-proclaimed rationalizations of a dominant state's interests based on the same types of nexi[161] on the other). This leaves us with one serious proposal for a new conception of jurisdiction to discuss, and that is Ryngaert's.[162]

In a nutshell, Ryngaert's reconceptualization of state jurisdiction is based on the principle of subsidiarity. It relies on the observation that each state bears a responsibility under international law to protect certain *common interests* (e.g., universal human rights or environmental law standards) and argues that when the state with *the most effective connection* to the activity regulated is *unable or unwilling to act*, other states are entitled to do so instead, provided the state of territorial jurisdiction does not explicitly oppose a veto.[163]

There are many difficulties with this argument, and only a few of them are mentioned here. The first one is that the proposed account relies on the principle of subsidiarity. Surprisingly, however, given how controversial that principle is, Ryngaert does not specify which ones of the many conceptions of

[160] See e.g., Colangelo, 'Spatial Legality'; Bethlehem, 'End of Geography', 22; Stephan, 'Competing Sovereignty'.
[161] See e.g., Bianchi, 'Reply', at 92–99; Lowenfeld, 'International Litigation'.
[162] Ryngaert, *Jurisdiction in International Law*, chapter 6.
[163] Ibid., 215 ff.

subsidiarity we know of it is based on, and especially what the justification for the latter could be.[164] This is important because it affects in turn the kind of subsidiarity test one should apply and the limits that bear on subsidiarity. We do not know, for instance, how the 'inability' is measured, and this merely begs the question of the standard of subsidiarity, just as we remain unsure about why the 'unwillingness' does not equate with the 'veto' that is mentioned as a limit to subsidiarity. What is clear, in any case, is that the egalitarian and democratic justification(s) of subsidiarity that apply in international human rights law[165] would not be applicable here in the absence of an encompassing global political community. As a matter of fact, most instances of the principle of subsidiarity we know of in contemporary law require a broader and encompassing unit or entity, and usually a political one, and both are absent in contemporary international law. Importantly, moreover, subsidiarity cannot itself work as ground for the attribution of competences rather than for their allocation or exercise. In most contexts in which the principle of subsidiarity is used, indeed, it allocates pre-existing competences or their exercise. The problem is that Ryngaert's argument is precisely meant to provide a ground for jurisdiction or competence and, instead of doing so, it passes the buck by invoking subsidiarity.

Second, the argument relies on an understanding of the basis of extraterritorial jurisdiction that comes dangerously close to the functional and technical ones disparaged before. In doing so, it endorses the return of the universal laws of economy, science or nature. There is no clear link made to people, for instance, in the proposed account of jurisdiction, and it is difficult to see how jurisdiction over people could be determined on the basis of the proposed notion of most effective 'connection' to an activity. As a matter of fact, meeting such an invocation of subsidiarity in combination with such jurisdiction grounds does not really come as a surprise when one knows how the principle of subsidiarity has been used to maximize efficiency by liberal economic doctrines in the past, including in EU and international law.[166]

Finally, the absence of a common procedure for deciding on the inability or unwillingness of a state to act and on the ability or willingness of one (or many) other state(s) to intervene makes it difficult to see how the proposed test in this revised conception of jurisdiction is so different from the reasonableness test used by other conceptions of extraterritorial protective

[164] Besson, 'Subsidiarity in International Human Rights'.
[165] Ibid.
[166] J. Barroche, *Etat, Libéralisme et Christianisme – Critique de la Subsidiarité Européenne* (Paris: Dalloz, 2012), at 563.

jurisdiction and their self-proclaimed justification. States are bound to disagree reasonably about those issues and an institutionalized procedure would therefore be needed to decide fairly. It is not because common interests are at stake that states will necessarily behave in a less self-interested fashion – the reverse is also true in any case.[167] There is no global political community yet, and the mere invocation of a 'global human community' by Ryngaert is not enough to justify the decisions that are unilaterally made in its name.[168] In short, the proposed conception looks like a compromise between many of the other conceptions put forward in the literature, but one that faces, as a result, all the problems the latter bring with them.[169]

Where does this leave us with respect to our revised conception of state jurisdiction in circumstances of extraterritorial jurisdiction? As I explained before, the tendency in state practice is to ground jurisdiction back into territory as much as possible, including when the aim is to protect vital interests by resorting to the 'effects doctrine' and identifying some territorial connection. Based on the instrumental egalitarian justification provided for territorial jurisdiction in Section 3.3, this recentring on territorial jurisdiction is justified. What this means for personal jurisdiction, then, is that it too should be exercised as closely as possible to a territorial nexus. It should also be used whenever possible to grant individual rights, and not to generate duties. Finally, universal jurisdiction, provided it is exercised outside of any territorial nexus – and this has become quite rare in recent practice – should be reserved for the enforcement and adjudication of international law, and hence to cases where states act in the name of international law in the absence of international institutions.

Of course, states have certain responsibilities to act under international law that may lead them to enact and enforce law outside of their territorial jurisdiction in some cases, such as in cases where there are common interests to protect. Examples may be drawn from international environmental law, international criminal law or international human rights law. As I explained in Section 1, indeed, state jurisdiction does not only amount to a right to regulate, but also a responsibility to do so. It follows from the social resilience of state jurisdiction and from its moral justification in terms of democratic legitimacy, however, that states should privilege joint action under

[167] See Besson, 'Community Interests – Special Emphasis'; Besson, 'Community Interests – Whose Interests?' for a critique of the idea that states are unable to defend common interests and necessarily behave in a self-interested fashion.

[168] Contra: Koller, 'End of Geography', 29.

[169] See also Liivoja, 'Book Review'.

international law to unilateral extensions of jurisdiction and, when needed, work at the creation of international institutions. The responsibility side of jurisdiction also requires states to resist more actively against foreign law's application within the scope of their territorial jurisdiction.

The idea that states may take international law into their own hands cannot be justified by the mere absence of global institutions.[170] What they should take into their own hands instead is the building of international institutions able to address those issues in the respect of individual and state equality.

5 CONCLUSION

Prima facie, state jurisdiction, as it stems from domestic and international law, and especially its comprehensiveness, exclusiveness and pre-emptiveness, would seems to be challenged by legal plurality. As this chapter has established, however, territorial jurisdiction has not only become a central institution in social and political practice since the seventeenth century, but it has proven resilient to the circumstances of pervasive and persistent legal plurality. It has not been displaced and is not about to be either, despite legal plurality, and actually, as I have argued, because of it. There are anthropological explanations to be found in the territoriality of law for the resilience of state jurisdiction, but this chapter has also advanced instrumental moral reasons such as the protection of individual equality and democratic legitimacy.

Those sociological and normative conclusions provide grounds to resist some of the deterritorializing dimensions of legal plurality, and in particular the development of infranational and transnational law and the erosion of territorial jurisdiction those new legalities have instilled from below and from above. The third constellation of legal plurality, however (i.e., the increasing extraterritoriality of other states' jurisdiction), amounts to the most challenging of the three: it takes the appearance of an overterritorialization of law, but contributes in fact to the erosion of territorial jurisdiction from aside. It calls for a reconceptualization of state jurisdiction, this chapter has argued, but not one that trades it for self-proclaimed assessments of what is in the common interest or, worse, universal scientific or economic rationalizations thereof.

What is needed instead of such forms of globalized law are international law and institutions in which state and, by extension, individual equality are respected in deciding on those controversial issues and forming a world together. As the chapter made clear, indeed, international law itself should

[170] Contra: Klabbers, *International Law*, at 103; Bianchi, 'Reply', at 84–85.

not be considered as an external limitation to state jurisdiction, but is, on the contrary, a constitutive part of the latter's dual legality with domestic law. It does not contribute, as a result, to the phenomenon of legal plurality, and strengthens rather than threatens state jurisdiction and, in return, is itself largely strengthened by state jurisdiction. As a matter of fact, exercising jurisdiction together is also an international responsibility of states. *Pace* Friedman, the world is far from being flat. The problems of humanity may be global, but our political communities are not. The question facing us now, however, is whether most individuals still remember what the latter are.

6

Inter-Legality – Citizenship – Inter-Citizenship

DIMITRY KOCHENOV[1]

1 INTRODUCTION

The spectacular short-sightedness of the perceived territorial limitations of authority and the starting point of absolute sovereign legality taken seriously – the key characteristic of the Westphalian approach this collective volume embarks on criticizing[2] – is nowhere better visible than in the complex world of citizenship law, where the stubborn reality has always been more a thorn in the side of the legal observer than an actual backbone of analysis.[3] Inter-Legality could be a useful starting point for the assessment of the complex realities of legal–political belonging, putting our understanding on more solid ground.

The claim of this chapter is very simple: the citizenship law field worldwide offers an excellent example of 'unavoidable interconnectedness of legalities',[4] as Palombella puts it. Citizenship is always yet never Westphalian (Section 2), even less so in the context of European Union (EU) Law (Section 3), thus offering a fascinating case study in inter-legality (Section 4). Moreover, the recent global rise of inter-citizenships – full extension of work and residence rights outside of the country granting citizenship nevertheless based on that status – infuses the claim in favour of the inter-legality perspective with even more empirical validity, as the territorial application of the most important rights citizenship brings – to work and to reside – and the sovereign territory of the states issuing the status have parted ways – in the EU and elsewhere (Section 5).

[1] I am much indebted to Gianluigi Palombella for his patience and generous engagement and would also like to thank Jacquelyn Veraldi and Bhavna Prashanth for their kind help.

[2] See Chapter 1.

[3] This chapter is inspired by and draws on the argument in my *Citizenship* (Cambridge, MA: MIT Press, forthcoming).

[4] See Chapter 16.

2 THE NATIONAL LEGAL NARRATIVE AND INTERNATIONAL LAW

Making a citizen is an ideology-inspired legal exercise, implying a choice among the available bodies who could be useful or not for the achievement of the goals of the authority at any given time, whatever these are. Those bodies that are less useful are simply excluded and do not exist in the eyes of the law, being proclaimed non-citizens. Exclusions can run along any lines: geography of origin, race, religion, education, language, time – you name it, and a legal–historical example will be found. The citizenship's capacity to exclude is its core function, which means that in the 'golden days' of citizenship – the mythical days of the concept's absolute just authority – the exclusion at the level of the *legal status* could only rarely be questioned: equality is *among* citizens, remember? As a consequence, working with citizens, the authority enjoys an almost universal carte blanche, as the story goes: you create ethnic electorates,[5] you assign those who are not white enough to your liking to the 'ancestral homelands' to proclaim them to be 'foreigners',[6] you declare those you send away as ideologically[7] or racially deficient as non-citizens.[8] The long history of fragrant discrimination is as rich and diverse as citizenship's constant effectiveness to justify it by muting any objections at the core: 'But she was not a citizen!' Under this paradigm, the core question before looking at rights, entitlements, duties and equality claims is: *who* is a citizen in this society? This is a question to which only the public authority in charge is entitled by its own law to give an answer. Those who are not citizens are per se entitled to nothing, and this is legally and politically right, we are told, even if frequently also morally unjust. Legalization and justification of essentially randomized discrimination is the core function of citizenship, after all.

What is crucial about citizenship is that, mostly due to its importance in relation to the legal status of every individual, it is generally viewed as a key element of state sovereignty. Indeed, citizenship law holds the key to one of the crucial elements of statehood: the population. As a consequence,

5 R. C. Visek, 'Creating Ethnic Electorate through Legal Restorationism: Citizenship Rights in Estonia', (1997) 38 *Harvard International Law Journal* 315.

6 J. Dugard, 'South Africa's Independent Homelands: An Exercise in Denationalization', (1980) 10 *Denver Journal of International Law and Policy* 11.

7 L. Chamberlain, *The Philosophy Steamer: Lenin and the Exile of the Intelligentsia* (London: Atlantic Books, 2006).

8 K. Rundle, 'The Impossibility of an Exterminatory Legality', (2009) 59 *University of Toronto Law Journal* 65.

international law allows states themselves to establish who their citizens are.[9] There is no sectoral citizenship regime at the international level. While states pretend to decide on citizenship alone, there is a constant interplay of legalities at hand, as we shall see. The 1930 Hague Convention on Certain Questions Relating to the Conflict of Nationality Laws is unequivocally clear on who is the boss: "it is for each state to determine under its own law who are its nationals."[10] Thus, nationality can only be conferred by national law – international law as it stands today can only hypothetically influence such state decisions.[11] It certainly cannot separately confer nationality on individuals. Even the famous dictum of the Permanent Court of International Justice (PCIJ) in the *Tunis and Morocco Nationality Decrees* case, where the PCIJ opined that in the future the role played by international law in the sphere of conferral of citizenship rights would increase,[12] did not alter the reality of national dominance in the citizenship domain. This chapter will challenge the beautiful idealism of this Westphalian reading of the law, offering inter-legality as a perspective that is better positioned to capture citizenship's complexity.

The picture becomes more complicated once the rules on the recognition of nationality under international law are taken into account. Following the International Court of Justice (ICJ) decision in the *Nottebohm* case, states are not obliged to recognise the nationality lawfully conferred on an individual by another state even if the said individual does not have any other. The approach to the framing of citizenship adopted in the international legal documents thus begs for an extremely cautious reading. While states are free to determine who their citizens are, this determination does not always work on the international plane and, as a consequence, can have a purely internal

9 A. Sironi, 'Nationality of Individuals in Public International Law', in S. Forlati and A. Annoni (eds.), *The Changing Role of Nationality in International Law* (Abingdon: Routledge, 2014), 54 (and the literature cited therein).

10 LN Doc. C 24 M. 13.1931.V., Art. 1. See also Art. 2 of the Convention: "Any question as to whether a person possesses the nationality of a particular State shall be determined in accordance with the law of that State." For a representative list of international documents regulating citizenship status and the obligations of citizens, see K. Rubinstein and D. Adler, 'International Citizenship: The Future of Nationality in a Globalized World', (2000) 7 *Indiana Journal of Global Legal Studies* 519, 525 and note 32.

11 In this regard, see *Proposed Amendments to the Naturalization Provisions of the Constitution of Costa Rica*, Advisory Opinion OC-4/84, Inter-American Court of Human Rights Series A No. 4 (19 January 1984).

12 *Nationality Decrees Issued in Tunis and Morocco* (Advisory Opinion) [1923] PCIJ Reports, Series B No. 4, 24.

effect and deprive people of any access to justice.[13] The European Union aside, which dismissed this absurd perspective as an excursion, in the words of Advocate General Tesauro, into the "romantic period of international law,"[14] and which will be discussed in the section that follows, at present all attempts to regulate citizenship issues at the international level have been far from successful. Even worse, international rules often created obstacles to effective regulation of citizenship as they attempted very hard – and unsuccessfully – to perfect the Westphalian model of absolute sovereignty, which cannot possibly work in this area, due to the basic historical approaches to how citizenships are granted, passed on and revoked.

The absolute majority of citizenships are distributed at birth based on *ius sanguinis* (bloodlines) and *ius soli* (place of birth) principles, or, which is more frequent, the combination of the two.[15] Directly from the principle of sovereignty flows that any state can only regulate what happens within its realm, so it takes another state's willingness to claim someone as a citizen and the neatness of the Westphalian presentation is gone. Anyone who tells you that the allocation of citizenships in the world is logical and clearly flows from the neat separation of the world into well-founded constitutional systems backing the legality of such allocations would thus not be telling the truth. Local birth is good for Uruguayans but irrelevant to Germans; a tenured professorship in a local university is irrelevant to Germans, but was a key to immediate citizenship in Austria until 2008; 'being active in the diaspora' is irrelevant to Austrians, but can make you a Pole; having a Lebanese mother is irrelevant to the Lebanese, but a Jewish mother, even without an Israeli citizenship, can make you an Israeli. The rules are truly diverse and the examples of this

[13] *Nottebohm* (Liechtenstein v Guatemala), [1955] ICJ Reports 4. The citizenship of Liechtenstein held by Mr Nottebohm was not recognised by Guatemala, the latter state treating Mr Nottebohm as a German citizen – a status he did not hold. The ICJ agreed with such a restrictive vision, ruling that nationality is a "legal bond having as its basis a social fact of attachment, a genuine connection of experience, interests and sentiments, together with the existence of reciprocal rights and duties." The ICJ failed to mention, however, that in the absence of any other nationality but that of Liechtenstein and with 'genuine connection' only to Guatemala, precisely the state aggressing him, Mr Nottebohm was deprived of any remedy as a result of the controversial decision, even if limited only to the recognition of nationality for the purposes of diplomatic protection. To see the incoherence of the judgement, see the Dissenting Opinion of Judge Klæstad and the dissenting opinion of Judge Read. For analysis, see the literature recommended in A. Bleckmann, 'The Personal Jurisdiction of the European Community', (1980) 17 *Common Market Law Review* 467, 477 and note 16.

[14] Case C-369/90 *Micheletti*, ECLI:EU:C:1992:295, para. 5.

[15] The best resource on this issue is the EUDO Citizenship Database of the European University Institute in Florence.

diversity are countless: what is taken for granted as best practice in one country can seem almost outrageous in another.

Such diversity of regulations creates challenges. Not knowing the rules can result in surprises and depends on the combination of the nationality rules in a child's country of birth and the countries of citizenship of the parents. A Moscow-born child of a Dane who himself was born outside of Denmark to a naturalized father and a Jordanian mother will be Russian, unable to reside with the parents in Denmark without a residence permit or even enter the country without a visa. Jordan does not allow for *ius sanguinis* transfer of citizenship via the mother, and Danish law limits to two generations the number of *ius sanguinis* citizenship transfers abroad. Consequently, the child, born stateless in this case, will receive Russian citizenship by birth, even though Russia does not recognise *ius soli* in general (unless the child is otherwise stateless, that is). Similar cases are more common than one would expect, illustrating the randomness of citizenship assignment. In other words, laws of many states, including but not limited to the state of birth of the child, the states of birth of the parents, states of the citizenship of the parents, state-custodians of the ethnic groups to which the parents belong, the religion of the parents and other factors will be at play at the moment of the grant of citizenship at birth. Any determination of birthright citizenship could thus be a case of inter-legality par excellence: while a state can decide for itself, several other states will have equally valid (legal, as long as legality is the only measure of validity) reasons to claim the same newborn.

Although 98 per cent of the world's population never undergoes a change of citizenship status once initially assigned, acquisition of citizenship by naturalization is usually more frequently in the spotlight. Importantly, the rules of naturalizations are no simpler or more intuitive than those for the acquisition of citizenship status by birth. Some are extremely complex: a special Act of Parliament is still required in Iceland to naturalize anyone. Some are relatively simple: buy a home of a particular value in the Caribbean or donate to one 'Sugar Cane Diversification Fund' or other and you are a citizen of an island of your choice, starting from USD 100,000 per family with a seasonal hurricane discount.[16] Some naturalization rules were even easier in the past. The German states of the Holy Roman Empire, in one example, used 'presumed naturalization', as Fahrmeir reported.[17] Residence in a new

[16] K. Surak, 'Global Citizenship 2.0 – The Growth of Investment Citizenship Programmes', (2016) IMC Working Papers No. 2016/03.

[17] A. F. Fahrmeir, 'Nineteenth-Century German Citizenships: A Reconsideration', (1997) 40 *Historical Journal* 721.

German state implied, for any foreign German, the acquisition of a new citizenship once the entry fees had been paid and a certain residence period had lapsed.

As already mentioned, the majority of the international legal instruments aimed at regulating citizenship issues engaged in ghost-hunting – instead of effectively addressing issues of vital importance, such as the imminent need of reduction of statelessness,[18] they concentrated on combating double nationality,[19] thus focusing on ensuring absolute sovereignty of states over their claimed populations as opposed to protecting human rights and equality. The rise of human rights and global migration,[20] coupled with the elimination of gender discrimination in the citizenship law in the majority of states doing well on the Human Development Index around the world - thus empowering women to pass on nationality and radically increasing the number of multinational children[21] - brought to an end the reign of the doctrine of insoluble allegiance assuming, in the words of Sir William Blackstone, "a debt of gratitude which cannot be forfeited, cancelled or altered by any change of time, place or circumstance,"[22] and thus making either acquiring a new nationality or changing the original nationality virtually impossible. Naturalisations and the change of nationality are both legally recognised reality.[23] Agreeing with Chan, at present, "there seems to be a general consensus that

[18] Among the instruments addressing this issue, see Protocol Relating to a Certain Case of Statelessness (adopted 12 April 1930, entered into force 1 July 1937) 179 LNTS 115; Special Protocol Concerning Statelessness (signed 12 April 1930), League of Nations Document C. 227. M.114.1930.V; Convention on the Reduction of Statelessness (adopted 30 August 1961, entered into force 13 December 1975) 989 UNTS 175. The document is only ratified by a handful of states. For analysis, see Chan (1991), 2 *et seq.*, who is critical of the international legal developments in this area.

[19] Council of Europe Convention on Reduction of Cases of Multiple Nationality (1963) ETS no. 43; Protocol to this Convention (1977) ETS no. 96.

[20] L. Bosniak, 'Citizenship Denationalized', (2000) 7 *Indiana Journal of Global Legal Studies* 447; C. Joppke, *Citizenship and Immigration* (Cambridge: Polity, 2010); C. Joppke, 'The Instrumental Turn of Citizenship', (2018) *Journal of Ethnic and Migration Studies* 1.

[21] C. L. Bredbenner, *A Nationality of Her Own* (Berkeley: University of California Press, 1998).

[22] Blackstone, as cited in Rubinstein and Adler, 'International Citizenship', 519, 530. See also P. Spiro, 'Dual Nationality and the Meaning of Citizenship', (1997) 46 *Emory Law Journal* 1411, 1419–1430.

[23] The legal attitudes towards dual nationality are becoming less hostile: see e.g., European Convention on Nationality (1997) ETS 166. In Art. 14, the Convention allows double nationality in some cases. In the United States, dual nationality became possible de jure after the Supreme Court ruling in *Afroyim v Rusk*, 387 US 253; 87 SCt 1660; 18 L, Ed, 2d 757; 1967. Cf.: P. Weil, *The Sovereign Citizen* (Philadelphia: University of Pennsylvania Press, 2012). Also in the EU, the majority of the member states do not prohibit double nationality: D. Kochenov, 'Dual Nationality in the EU: An Argument for Tolerance', (2011) 11 *European Law Journal* 323; D. A. J. G. de Groot, 'Free Movement of Dual EU Citizens', (2018) 3 (3) *European Papers*, 1075.

everyone is entitled to change his nationality."[24] The toleration of multiple nationalities, as wonderfully documented by Spiro, is *the* norm in current international relations.[25]

As a result of the global constitutional developments of the last decades, international law, while having no authority to come up with strict substantive rules on citizenship, also lost its battle to guarantee absolute freedom of one and one state only to claim each particular human being. As a consequence, the interpenetration of citizenship laws around the world is higher today than it has ever been. Beyond citizenship acquisition at birth, which is potentially governed, as we have seen, by a number of national legal systems, all of which view themselves as endowed with a legitimate claim of authority over the issue, naturalisations are equally governed by combinations of laws of a number of states, no matter what each individual state actually has on the books. This is because naturalisation rules usually differ depending on the citizenships that the applicant already holds – a Romanian naturalizes in Italy 60 per cent faster than an American, and a Phillipino 133 per cent faster in Spain than a Tunisian – but also on the citizenship rules of the state of original nationality. Morocco does not allow for its citizenship renunciation, in one example, which means that any Moroccan naturalizing in a country requiring such renunciation, such as the Russian Federation, will necessarily fall under an exception: there is no way for the Russian legal system to change Moroccan law. Since every single citizenship is a product of several legal systems, unlike what the Westphalian understanding of sovereignty in determining the 'people' would make us believe, any citizenship – and I repeat – every single citizenship granted anywhere in the world is a potential case study of inter-legality stretching to the core of the very essence of popular sovereignty: the core mechanism of legitimation of power in the world today.

European citizenship itself, in not replacing but complementing national citizenship as specified in the Treaties[26] and in the Danish Declaration appended to the Maastricht Treaty,[27] is also a definitive step in the direction of the legal affirmation of the reality of multiple legal approaches to the

[24] J. M. M. Chan, 'The Right to a Nationality As a Human Right: The Current Trend towards Recognition', (1991) 12 *Human Rights Law Journal* 1, 8.

[25] P. Spiro, *At Home in Two Countries* (New York: New York University Press, 2016).

[26] Arts 9 TEU and 20 TFEU. M. Szpunar and M. E. Blas López, 'Some Reflections on Member State Nationality: A Prerequisite of EU Citizenship and an Obstacle to Its Enjoyment', in D. Kochenov (ed.), *EU Citizenship and Federalism: The Role of Rights* (Cambridge: Cambridge University Press, 2017), 107.

[27] The Danish Declaration, Treaty on European Union [1992] OJ C348/01.

individual in the EU: all now claimed by at least two legal systems.[28] This is an affirmation of inter-legality: the building of reality based on numerous equally valid legal claims that could also contradict each other in the case of determining the core legal status of each and every European. Such anti-Westphalian reality brings about an unavoidable outcome of making citizenship less totalitarian and more aware of its own limitations in the global context where legalities compete and overlap.

3 EUROPEAN CITIZENSHIP AND INTER-LEGALITY

Although acquired via *ius tractum*, by derivation from national citizenships of the member states,[29] EU citizenship, besides supplying the holders with supranational rights beyond their states of origin, also alters the essence of the member state nationalities it is derived from,[30] including the rules of loss and acquisition of such nationalities,[31] as well as their mutual recognition by all the member states of the EU[32] and non-discrimination among the nationals

[28] Cf.: H.-U. Jessurun d'Oliveira, 'Europees Burgerschap: Dubbele Nationaliteit?' in W. F. W. Van Ballegooij (ed.), *Europees Burgerschap* (The Hague: T.M.C. Asser Press, 2004), 91.

[29] D. Kochenov, '*Ius Tractum* of Many Faces', (2009) 15 *Columbia Journal of European Law* 169. This position is also confirmed by the fact that the Court respects the Declarations made by the member states in clarifying the meaning of their nationalities in the context of EU law. See Case C-192/99 *Kaur*, ECLI:EU:C:2001:106; H. Toner, 'Annotation Case C-192/99 *Kaur* [2001]', (2002) 39 *Common Market Law Review* 881. *Kaur* thus continued the British African Indians' saga, analysed by A. Lester, 'Thirty Years On: The East African Case Revisited', (2002) 47 *Public Law* 52.

[30] Art. 9 of the Treaty on the EU (TEU); Art. 20 of the Treaty on the Functioning of the EU (TFEU) [2009] OJ C115/1. Szpunar and Blas López, 'Some Reflections'; D. Kochenov 'Rounding Up the Circle: The Mutation of Member States' Nationalities under Pressure from EU Citizenship', (2010) EUI RSCAS 2010/23.

[31] Case C-135/08 *Janko Rottman*, ECLI:EU:C:2010:104; for a brief selection in this sea of reactions, see e.g., S. Adam and P. Van Elsuwege, 'Citizenship Rights and the Federal Balance between the European Union and Its Member States', (2012) 37 *European Law Review* 176; A. Tryfonidou, 'Redefining the Outer Boundaries of EU Law', (2012) 18 *European Public Law* 493; A. Hinarejos, 'Extending Citizenship and the Scope of EU Law', (2011) 70 *Cambridge Law Journal* 309; L. J. Ankersmit and W. W. Geursen, '*Ruiz Zambrano*: De Interne Situatie Voorbij', (2011) 4 *Asiel en Migrantenrecht* 156; P. Van Elsuwege, 'Shifting Boundaries?' (2011) 38 *Legal Issues of Economic Integration* 263; D. Kochenov, 'Annotation of Case C-135/08, *Rottman*,' (2010) 47 *Common Market Law Review* 1831; G. R. de Groot, 'Overwegingen over de *Janko Rottman* – Beslissing van het Europese Hof van Justitie', (2010) 5/6 *Asiel en Migrantenrecht* 293; H.-U. Jessurun d'Oliveira, 'Ontkoppeling van Nationaliteit en Unieburgerschap?' (2010) *Nederlandsch Juristenblad* 785; S. Iglesias Sánchez, '¿Hacia una Nueva Relación entre la Nacionalidad Estatal y la Cuidadanía Europea?' (2010) 37 *Revista de Derecho Comunitario Europeo* 933.

[32] *Micheletti*, para. 10.

based on the mode of acquisition of their nationalities.[33] Simply put, although the acquisition and the loss of nationality are not among the issues which the EU is empowered to regulate,[34] the very existence of the internal market,[35] amplified by the notion of EU citizenship, makes the retention of the pre-existing modes of regulation of such de jure extra-*acquis* issues by the member states clearly unsustainable.

It goes without saying that the general duty of loyalty is at work in this field of law just as in any other[36]: the member states cannot, when acting within their sphere of competence, imperil the achievement of the goals of integration by undermining the nature and functioning of the EU citizenship status. This basic point is particularly clear following the decision of the Court of Justice of the European Union (CJEU) in *Rottman*.[37] The same considerations apply both to the status as such and to the enjoyment of the rights associated with the supranational status.[38] It is fundamental to realise in this regard that although the member states do enjoy the competence to regulate this issue, supranational law limits the way in which this competence can be exercised in practice to a significant degree, and this is not done in a pluralist fashion: the member states are simply not free to pretend that EU law obligations are of no relevance in this domain.[39]

Internal markets and EU citizenship work together to transform the nationality policies of the member states not by empowering the EU to act in the field of the conferral of nationalities by the member states, but simply by bringing a profound change to the whole meaning of the member states' nationalities in contemporary Europe. This evolution is the key to the

33 Case 136/78 *Ministère Public v Auer*, ECLI:EU:C:1979:34, para. 28.

34 See e.g., the opinion of AG Poiares Maduro in *Rottman*, ECLI:EU:C:2009:588, para. 17: "la détermination des conditions d'acquisition et de perte de la nationalité, – et donc de la citoyenneté de l'Union –, relève de la compétence exclusive des États membres" (also see the references cited therein). This notwithstanding the famous *obiter dictum* in *Micheletti* that a decision on nationality should be taken by the member states with "due regard of Community law": *Micheletti*, para. 10. In practice, the EU took part in the framing of state nationality laws on several occasions, all during the pre-accession process, when dealing with the member states-to-be. For analysis, see D. Kochenov, 'Pre-Accession, Naturalization, and "Due Regard to Community Law": The European Union's "Steering" of Citizenship Policies in Candidate Countries during the Fifth Enlargement', (2004) 4 *Romanian Journal of Political Science* 71.

35 Art. 26(2) TFEU.

36 Kochenov, '*Rottman* Annotation'.

37 *Rottmann*.

38 D. Kochenov, 'A Real European Citizenship: A New Jurisdiction Test', (2011) 18 *Columbia Journal of European Law* 55.

39 D. Kochenov and J. Lindeboom, 'Pluralism through Its Denial: The Success of EU Citizenship', in M. Avbelj and G. Davies (eds.), *Handbook on Legal Pluralism in the EU* (Cheltenham: Edward Elgar, 2018), 179.

understanding of the dynamic development of the legal essence of EU citizenship of the near future, as it affects access to supranational status as well as the delimitation of the scope of EU law. EU citizenship has emerged as a federal citizenship[40] endowed with a structural significance in the edifice of EU law. As EU citizenship plays a fundamentally important role in the shaping of EU federalism, the line that could be drawn between the legal concepts of member state nationality and EU citizenship is becoming ever more flexible and contested.

Already today several member states differentiate at a formal level between EU citizens and third-country nationals in their naturalisation procedures. These differences are not minor at all. In Italy, for example, the length of minimal legal residence in order to qualify for naturalisation is drastically different for the two categories in question: while EU citizens naturalise in four years, third-country nationals have to wait six years longer.[41] In the near future, the number of member states to introduce such differences, as well as the reach of the differences themselves, is likely to proliferate, reflecting the importance of EU law in providing EU citizens with virtually unlimited access to de facto unconditional residence and work in the territory of the EU, thus removing EU citizens who chose to reside outside of their member state of nationality from the category of simple 'foreigners'. Formal naturalisation simplifications thus come on top of the EU law guarantees, which infinitely simplify the meeting of *any* standard naturalisation requirements.[42] Ultimately, the establishment of diverging naturalisation requirements for EU citizens and third-country nationals means that a distinction is made between the acquisition of EU citizenship (necessarily coupled with a

[40] For the analyses of European citizenship from a federal perspective, see Kochenov, *EU Citizenship and Federalism*; C. Schönberger, 'European Citizenship as Federal Citizenship', (2007) 19 *European Review of Public Law* 63. See also G. L. Neuman, 'Fédéralisme et Citoyenneté aux Etats Unis et dans l'Union Européenne', (2003) 21 *Critique Internationale* 151; A. P. van der Mei, 'Freedom of Movement for Indigents', (2002) 19 *Arizona Journal of International and Comparative Law* 803; F. Strumia, 'Citizenship and Free Movement', (2006) 12 *Columbia Journal of European Law* 714; C. W. A. Timmermans, 'Lifting the Veil of Union Citizens' Rights', in N. Colneric et al. (eds.), *Festschrift für Gil Carlos Rodríguez Iglesias* (Berlin: Berliner Wissenschafts-Verlag, 2003), 195. For a truly magisterial analysis, see C. Schönberger, *Unionsbürger. Europas Föderales Bürgerrecht in Vergleichender Sicht* (Mohr: Siebeck, 2006).

[41] Legge N 91/1992; G. Zincone and M. Basili, 'Country Report: Italy', (2010) EUDO Citizenship Observatory RSCAS/EUDO-CIT-CR 2010/35, 13.

[42] Consequently, those member states' nationals who naturalise in their new member state of residence automatically fall within the scope of EU law, even when they lost their previous member state's nationality, since EU law permitted them to meet the necessary residence requirements: Opinion of AG Poiares Maduro in *Rottman*, paras 10–11.

member state's nationality) and the mere acquisition of another member state nationality by EU citizens. This is a fundamental development, bound to have far-reaching consequences for the legal essence of both legal statuses in question.

Naturalisation in the member state of residence is already less important by far for EU citizens than for the third-country nationals. This is so because a number of key rights formerly associated with state nationality are granted to EU citizens directly by the EU legal order. Among these are virtually unconditional rights of entry, residence, taking up employment and, crucially, non-discrimination on the basis of nationality.[43] An oft-cited phrase coined by Gareth Davies attributes to Article 18 TFEU – provocatively, but no doubt correctly – the abolition of the nationalities of the member states.[44] Currently, it is not member state nationality but EU citizenship that provides Europeans with the most considerable array of rights, so long as, by virtue of this status, rights in *all* EU member states instead of only one are extended and any discrimination on the basis of nationality is prohibited. Unquestionably, therefore, EU citizens not having the nationality of the member state where they reside are no longer simple 'foreigners' in the EU. Since *Lounes*, this applies also to those EU citizens who opted to naturalise in their member states of residence.[45]

This shift from foreigners to European citizens coupled with the tensions it brought about did not affect the core understanding of the federal compact in Europe, however: the creation of EU citizenship notwithstanding, as Ulrich Everling rightly put it, the member states "hold responsibility for their peoples,"[46] underscoring the crucial importance of their nationalities, to which they alone hold the key,[47] even if loyalty to EU law is required when

[43] For a critical analysis, see Kochenov '*Ius Tractum*', 206 (and the literature cited therein).

[44] G. T. Davies, '"Any Place I Hang My Hat?"' (2005) 11 *European Law Journal* 43; Evans put it slightly differently: "possession of the nationality of one Member State rather than that of another loses all real significance," see A. Evans 'Nationality Law and European Integration', (1991) 16 *European Law Review* 190, 195.

[45] Case C-165/16, *Toufik Lounes* ECLI:EU:C:2017:862; de Groot, 'Free Movement'.

[46] U. Everling, 'The European Union As a Federal Association of States and Citizens', in A. von Bogdandy and J. Bast (eds.), *Principles of European Constitutional Law* (Oxford: Hart, 2006), 677.

[47] See Art. 1 of the Convention Governing Certain Questions Relating to the Conflict of Nationalities, The Hague, 12 April 1930, entered into force 1 July 1937, 179 LNTS 89, 99. This position is also confirmed by the fact that the Court respects the Declarations made by the member states in clarifying the meaning of their nationalities in the context of EU law. See the *Kaur* case; cf.: Sironi, 'Nationality of Individuals'.

such a key is used.[48] As a consequence, EU citizenship, though a legal status that is '*autonome*'[49] – autonomous of the nationalities of the member states – does not exist without a nationality of a member state, numerous academic[50] and institutional[51] calls for such a development notwithstanding.

This being said, the EU tends not to notice *ex lege* and thus not to protect any of its most vulnerable citizens: the poor,[52] the uneducated,[53] the criminal,[54] the mothers of children with special needs.[55] The 'good' EU citizen, as the CJEU teaches us,[56] is thus the one – and only the one – who meets the expectations of the internal market: to exist in the eyes of EU law, it is indispensable to earn, to be relatively healthy and to be engaged across borders, real or imaginary (i.e., to be able to contribute to the internal market the EU is creating).[57] The plight of recognition of all those not falling within this image of the 'good' is interpreted away as having no connection to EU law.[58] In this sense, EU citizenship is definitely 'neo-medieval': it is the

[48] See also *Rottman*, para. 56; *Micheletti*, para. 10. For analyses, see Sánchez, '¿Hacia una Nueva Relación?'; Kochenov, 'A Real European Citizenship', at 77.

[49] Opinion of AG Poiares Maduro in *Rottman*, paras 11, 23: "Tel est le miracle de la citoyenneté de l'Union: elle renforce les liens qui nous unissent à nos États (dans la mesure où nous sommes à présent des citoyens européens précisément parce que nous sommes des nationaux de nos États) et, en même temps, elle nous en émancipe (dans la mesure où nous sommes à présent des citoyens au-delà de nos États)."

[50] D. Kostakopoulou, 'European Union Citizenship and Member State Nationality', in J. Shaw (ed.), *Has the European Court of Justice Challenged Member State Sovereignty in Nationality Law?* (2011) EUI Working Paper RSCAS 2011/5, 21; Jessurun d'Oliveira, 'Ontkoppeling'.

[51] See e.g., most recently, European Economic and Social Committee, 'Opinion on a More Inclusive Citizenship Open to Immigrants (Own-Initiative Opinion)' (Rapporteur P. Castaños, SOC/479, 16 October 2013): "The Committee proposes that, in future, when the EU undertakes a new report of the Treaty (TFEU), it amends Article 20 so that third-country nationals who have stable, long-term resident status can also become EU citizens" (para. 1.11).

[52] Case C-86/12, *Alokpa and Others v Ministre du Travail, de l'Emploi et de l'Immigration*, ECLI:EU:C:2013:645.

[53] Case C-333/13, *Dano* ECLIU:C:2014:2358; D. Schiek, 'Perspectives on Social Citizenship in the EU', in Kochenov (ed.), *EU Citizenship and Federalism*, 341.

[54] Case C-348/09 *PI v Oberbürgermeisterin der Stadt Remscheid* ECLI:EU:C:2012:300, and Case C-378/12 *Onuekwere v Secretary of State for the Home Department* ECLI:EU:C:2014:13; U. Belavusau and D. Kochenov, 'Kirchberg Dispensing the Punishment', (2016) 41 *European Law Review* 557.

[55] Case C-434/09, *McCarthy v Secretary of State for the Home Department*, ECLI:EU:C:2011:277.

[56] L. Azoulai, 'Transfiguring European Citizenship: From Member State Territory to Union Territory', in Kochenov (ed.), *EU Citizenship and Federalism*, 178.

[57] D. Kochenov, 'On Tiles and Pillars', in Kochenov (ed.), *EU Citizenship and Federalism*, 3; C. O'Brien, *Unity in Adversity* (Oxford: Hart, 2017).

[58] C. O'Brien, 'I Trade Therefore I Am', (2013) 50 *Common Market Law Review* 1643; P. C. de Sousa, 'Quest for the Holy Grail', (2014) 20 *European Law Journal* 499; D. Kochenov, 'Citizenship of Personal Circumstances in Europe', in D. Thym (ed.), *Reinventing European Citizenship* (Oxford: Hart, 2017), 37.

personal circumstances of the holder, not the formal legal status as such, that play the crucial role in determining whether EU law – the law that has extended the status – would actually apply to the situation of the concrete individual or not.[59]

Notwithstanding the slowed down progress towards a formal legal status of equal citizens in the EU, it is clear that the successful development of the internal market is bound to diminish the legal effects of particular member states' nationalities even further, no matter what the formal and official delimitation of competences between the EU and its member states is likely to be. Inter-Legality is at work here, just like with international law on citizenship considered in the previous section of this chapter, and there are three main consequences. The first is the widening of the gap between EU citizens and third-country nationals in the EU even further. The second is the obvious need to adapt the member states' nationalities to the new reality, constructing legal statuses more aware of their limitations. The diminution in the importance of the nationalities of the member states as legally meaningful statuses naturally reaffirms the rise of EU citizenship to the most prominent position in regulating the rights of EU citizens. Thirdly, and most crucially, the rules of determination of the scope of EU law need to prevent the EU from failing its most vulnerable citizens in a situation when the national-level protections are bound to weaken as indicated above. To come back to inter-legality, it is unquestionable that the member states are fully dependent on each other, on international law rules and also on the law of the EU in their framing of nationality. There is no unlimited sovereign competence in this field anymore, if such a competence was ever there.

4 GLOBAL CITIZENSHIP LAW AS AN IDEAL CASE STUDY OF INTER-LEGALITY

All our textbooks on citizenship glorify several light-hearted assumptions that have never and will never be true: that citizenship forms a political community which is value-based; that exclusion based on citizenship is just and makes sense because it protects such values; that the proclamation of equality based on legal status alone, which is distributed with no regard to the individual characteristics, abilities and desires of any person, makes sense and is defensible in the context of modern constitutionalism, which values the value-based approach to the individual and despises randomness

[59] D. Kochenov, 'Neo-Mediaeval Permutations of Personhood in Europe', in L. Azoulai et al. (eds.), *Ideas of the Person and Personhood in European Union Law* (Oxford: Hart, 2016), 133.

and neo-feudal status ascriptions.[60] Virtually all the key theorists who touched upon citizenship take it as a status of full belonging to a community of equals existing, more or less, in a vacuum – the foreigners and the aliens are so irrelevant for the academic seekers of justice in the citizenship field that they simply disappear, from T. H. Marshall[61] to Dworkin and Rawls. The picture that states all over the world paint in their law, mimicked by the majority of theorists – with important exceptions of the likes of Joppke, Carens and Spiro,[62] to name just a few – is that sovereign states, having power to decide in whose interests they will purport to act, make citizens and treat them equally in a delicate tango of proclaimed non-discriminating love and absolute exclusion. The in-betweens – colonials, women, dissenters, foreigners and those who are 'bad' citizens, who do not fit the officially proclaimed worthy portrait of a citizens (for the lack of Aryan blood, presence of an Arabic accent of, like in Liberia, a non-'Negro' ancestor[63]) – do not enter this picture at all: in the eyes of the state, they are irrelevant[64] – they do not exist. The state alone, we are told, makes those whom it recognises and agrees to see into citizens by an act of its uniquely empowering will.

Yet, it is obvious, of course, as has been shown above, that no state can do this cleanly and neatly by itself: the world is crowded – not Marshall's vacuum. Even worse, no state can make citizens without overstepping the moral and ethical imperative of our time: the treatment of individuals equally as a result of their belonging to humanity, endowed with free will, as Carens has wonderfully explained.[65] Citizenship, a result of the ascription of legal statuses that is ultimately not rationalisable beyond the needs of particular states in particular times, is thus in an inherent conflict with the mantras of modern constitutionalism and cannot be reconciled with it.[66]

60 L. Bosniak, 'Persons and Citizens in Constitutional Thought', (2010) 8 *International Journal of Constitutional Law* 9; A. Shachar, *The Birthright Lottery* (Cambridge, MA: Harvard University Press, 2009).

61 T. H. Marshall, *Class, Citizenship, and Social Development* (Chicago: University of Chicago Press, 1977).

62 Joppke, *Citizenship and Immigration*; J. Carens, *The Ethics of Immigration* (Oxford: Oxford University Press, 2013); J. Carens, 'Aliens and Citizens: The Case for Open Borders', (1987) 49 *Review of Politics* 251; Spiro, *At Home in Two Countries*.

63 Art. 27(b) of the Liberian constitution lists birth and naturalisation citizenship as "restricted to the negroes."

64 J. Scott, *Seeing Like a State* (New Haven, CT: Yale University Press, 1998).

65 Carens, 'Aliens and Citizens', 251. For a wonderful survey of key attempts at such rationalisations, see M. Gibney, 'The Rights of Non-Citizens to Membership', in C. Sawyer and B. K. Blitz (eds.), *Statelessness in the European Union* (Cambridge: Cambridge University Press, 2011), 41.

66 Kochenov, *Citizenship*.

Moreover, states only decide on this to a certain degree: international obligations, other states claiming the same bodies – frequently long dead, as is the case with Genghis Khan, claimed by a handful of states, and Marquis de Lafayette[67] – as their citizens and supranational/subnational legal statuses and rights connected therewith are constantly a part of the picture. In fact, states are in a constant struggle to align their approaches to citizenship to make it 'work' both through international law and practice[68] and informally through conflicts for which no reliable choice of law rules would be available. When the United States makes Americans and Austria makes Austrians and endow them with rights, there is much more at play than simply US or Austrian law. Interestingly, this is of course not a case of any kind of a flexible navigation between the legal orders by an enlightened judge. This is the reason why pluralism never solved this problem.[69] Each of the participating public authorities claiming the same person has its own legality on its side, leaving no place to balancing, rationalisation and negotiation.

An American journalist with an Iranian father critical of Iran will die in an Iranian jail on the first visit to the country he did not know he was legally connected to. He will not die an American and no American consular workers will be in the position to help. A nationalist Italian minister unwilling to let Muslim immigrants settle in their country would obviously have nothing to say against a move of an Austrian son of Chechen refugees from Vienna to Rome: EU citizenship protects this person whatever Italians think.[70] Even more subtly though – when Italy makes a million Italians in Latin America,[71] when a birth-tourist is heading to Canada[72] and when a

[67] Lafayette was naturalised by President Obama long after his death: D. Rennie, 'Lafayette to Be Given American Citizenship', *The Telegraph* (Washington, 19 July 2002), www.telegraph.co.uk/news/worldnews/northamerica/usa/1401930/Lafayette-to-be-given-American-citizenship.html (accessed 26 June 2018).

[68] Cf.: Sironi, 'Nationality of Individuals'.

[69] R. D. Kelemen, 'The Dangers of Constitutional Pluralism', in Avbelj and Davies (eds.), *Legal Pluralism*, 392; G. Letsas, 'Harmonic Law: The Case against Legal Pluralism', in J. Dickson and P. Eleftheriadis (eds.), *Philosophical Foundations of European Union Law* (Oxford: Oxford University Press, 2012), 77. For the application of legal pluralism to the citizenship law field, see Kochenov and Lindeboom, 'Pluralism through Its Denial'.

[70] G. T. Davies, 'The Humiliation of the State as a Constitutional Tactic', in F. Amtenbrink and P. van den Berg (eds.), *The Constitutional Integrity of the European Union* (The Hague: T.M.C. Asser Press, 2010), 147.

[71] For more similar examples, see G. R. de Groot, 'Towards a European Nationality Law', (2004) 8 *Electronic Journal of Comparative Law*.

[72] Y. Harpaz, 'Compensatory Citizenship: Dual Nationality As a Strategy of Global Upward Mobility', (2018) 36 *Journal of Ethnic and Migration Studies*.

Serb learns basic Hungarian to claim pre-Trianon 'heritage'[73] – legal orders constantly fight for human beings. Once again, since states use legality and violence to produce the truths governing and shaping reality and creating rights and obligations for the individuals endowed (or not) with the citizenship status, there is no place here for enlightened deliberations and pluralist balancing. This fight is constantly ongoing, and each particular sovereign's law only regulates it to a very limited degree. As a result, it sometimes takes the law of several polities, besides international and frequently supranational law, to help establish the actual citizenships map of the world. The law of one state, however all-encompassing its usual claim to the 'general ends' of regulation and legitimacy, would never be enough. In a situation where pluralism does not help pierce through the legal problems that arise in this important context, inter-legality could be a suitable theoretical framework to deploy.

Sometimes the fight for bodies leads to mutually exclusive citizenship claims and is a zero-sum game, like when Hungarian-speaking Slovaks are outlawed at home, losing citizenship for accepting Hungarian nationality.[74] But frequently the story is more interesting: multiple citizenship toleration is on the rise, and we are gradually discovering that the self-proclaimed 'value' communities of citizens are not immune to choice, making any claims of value-based citizenships absurd with the sole exception, probably, of Vatican City citizenship. Citizenships as valueless legal statuses are also superimposed very significantly in the contemporary world, making the mapping of legal statuses of belonging to states a much more interesting exercise than what textbooks and ideological works written to restate the political expediency of neo-feudal random ascription of rights and obligations would seem to suggest.[75]

If all the citizenships were roughly the same in terms of the actual rights and obligations they entail for their holders, there would be reasons to agree with T. H. Marshall's and others' abstractions and to stop emphasising the multiplicity of legal statuses outside of each particular state with its particular citizenship. Research shows, however, that contemporary citizenships, which have overwhelmingly far-reaching implications for the lives lived by their

[73] J.-M. Arraiza, 'Good Neighbourliness as a Limit to Extraterritorial Citizenship: The Case of Hungary and Slovakia', in D. Kochenov and E. Basheska (eds.), *Good Neighbourliness in the European Legal Context* (Leiden: Martinus Nijhoff, 2015), 114.

[74] Ibid.

[75] R. Baubock et al., *Democratic Inclusion* (Manchester: Manchester University Press, 2017). See especially Peter Spiro's contribution to the volume: P. Spiro, 'Stakeholder Theory Won't Save Citizenship'.

owners, are so diverse that drawing parallels is sometimes difficult.[76] The first regular attempt to compare citizenships as legal statuses of attachment to states as opposed to the states themselves reveals that the absolute majority of the world's citizenship statuses is of much lower quality than the ones conferred by a handful of Western European, North American and other highly developed nations.[77] This basic and predictable finding has far-reaching implications for the profiling of citizenship as a "right to have rights," *pace* Arendt: numerous citizenships in the world are so bad that the only possible talk could be of liabilities, not rights. This finding is in tune with economics inequality research: life chances and prosperity are distributed unequally around the world more in special than in class terms. The correlation with citizenships is clear: the absolute majority of the holders of the liability statuses ascribed by birth are in the world's gutter, thus being deprived of any rights and opportunities even remotely comparable to those enjoyed in the global North, as Milanovic successfully demonstrates.[78] Citizenship is unquestionably the tool to keep them there. Indeed, it has turned into one of the crucial tools to ensure the preservation of spacial inequalities in the world, since *all* the borders all around the world are always locked for the holders of liability-level legal statuses, while remaining open for the holders of the elite citizenships of North America and Western Europe.

This diversity and interpenetration going side by side with the proud place of citizenship at the core of the political legitimation of state power and thus one of the crucial legalities in the inter-legality package makes citizenship law a particularly interesting case study of inter-legality and the limitations of the sovereigntist Westphalian mantras, alongside other examples provided in this volume.[79] Palombella is right: the "holistic character of the law"[80] has to be reflected much better than it is now in the mainstream literature, which gives inter-legality a particular boost. Looking at the citizenship law of the EU, as has been done in the previous section of this chapter, makes this point particularly clear.

It is important to purge the world of multiple legalities of the dreams of subjectivity. Through legalistic affirmations and violence, the law's task is to

[76] D. Kochenov and J. Lindeboom, 'Empirical Assessment of the Quality of Nationalities', (2017) 4 *European Journal of Comparative Law and Governance* 314.

[77] D. Kochenov and J. Lindeboom (eds.), *Kalin and Kochenov's Quality of Nationality Index*, 4th ed. (Oxford: Hart Publishing, 2019). For a visualisation of the data for all the world's citizenships since 2013, please visit www.nationalityindex.org.

[78] B. Milanovic, *Global Inequality* (Cambridge, MA: Harvard University Press, 2016).

[79] See e.g., Chapters 3 and 12.

[80] See Chapter 16.

shape the truth. What individual members of any society think is only relevant as far as it could potentially undermine the effectiveness of governance – and usually, it cannot boast such far-reaching effects. This is why citizenship is never about perceptions, cultures and identities at the point where the border between those who are in and those who are out is drawn, following Brubacker, who provided the most iconic definition of the concept of citizenship: as an object and instrument of closure.[81] Once you are out by law, it is of no relevance what you think about your citizenship and what your culture is, as long as you cannot make a legalistic claim to be included based on the contours of the legal truth the state professes. Bourdieu is right that the law is very effective in pre-empting the recognition of what lies outwith the realm of the reality it has mandated and created,[82] branding as non-existent any fact of social reality not overlapping with the legal truth,[83] however harsh is the world shaped by the latter.[84] No matter how European you feel and how much you protest, thereby engaging in the 'acts of citizenship',[85] if you do not have the right papers, you are a foreigner.

In the world of citizenship regulation, states always deeply depended on each other's law as well as common international and supranational approaches, resulting in a vision of legal sovereignty that is particularly richly footnoted with crucially important disclaimers. Even more so, in the world of global citizenship law today we clearly and unquestionably witness an intensification of the interpenetration of legalities governing each concrete situation. Never before, not even in the times of the colonial empires ignored in the textbooks, was the Westphalian view of the law further removed from reality than now: with the mutual extension of core citizenship rights based on each other's citizenship statuses, a huge number of the world's states has decoupled the most significant citizenship rights, including the rights of work, residence and often non-discrimination on the basis of being a foreigner, from the territory of the state issuing the legal status of citizenship in the first place. Following a long-forgotten proposal by the great A. V. Dicey, I call this phenomenon the rise of 'inter-citizenships'.

81 R. Brubacker, *Citizenship and Nationhood in France and Germany* (Cambridge, MA: Harvard University Press, 1992), 18.

82 P. Bourdieu, 'The Force of Law: Toward a Sociology of the Juridical Field', (1987) 38 *Hastings Law Journal* 814.

83 J. M. Balkin, 'The Proliferation of Legal Truth', (2003) 26 *Harvard Journal of Law and Public Policy* 9.

84 J. M. Balkin, 'Agreements with Hell and Other Objects of Our Faith', (1997) 65 *Fordham Law Review* 1703.

85 E. Isin and G. Nielsen (eds.), *Acts of Citizenship* (New York: ZED Books, 2008).

5 INTER-CITIZENSHIPS AND INTER-LEGALITY

Any classical citizenship presumes a correlation between the legal status created and enforced by the authority – say, a Sri Lankan citizenship – and the territory of rights, in particular political rights and the right to reside and work, corresponding to the territory of the issuing state – thus, the Sri Lankan territory.[86] Research shows that this correlation does not any more hold true in the twenty-first century for the majority of jurisdictions around the world.[87] This core finding is the starting point of this section. While Sri Lankan citizenship, similarly to a Mongolian one, still comes with a package of rights usable uniquely in Sri Lanka or Mongolia, respectively, the citizenship status issued by more than half of the nations around the world is no longer limited to the territory controlled by the issuing authority. The majority of the citizenships of the most highly developed nations are passports to full inclusion in dozens of states, rather than to one state only. This alters a crucial aspect of citizenship's story: its scope.

Indeed, the hitherto unquestioned correlation between citizenship rights and sovereign territory is changing in many places: more and more citizenships around the world secure access to key citizenship rights, including residence, work and also not infrequently political rights,[88] outside the confines of the sovereign territory whose authority is behind the grant of the legal status of citizenship in the first place. Importantly, this does not only concern the (quasi-)citizenship of the (formerly) subordinated colonies that, through some version of a 'compact of free association'[89] with what used to be the 'mother country', would extend the rights in the colonial centre to the former colonial subjects: think of the Micronesians in the United States[90] or – if I am not stretching it – Belarussians in Russia.[91] The logic of opening up the sovereign territory and thus, potentially, the access to citizenship status as

[86] For a story of citizenship rights that does not fetishise the political entitlements, see Kochenov, *Citizenship*.

[87] Kochenov and Lindeboom, 'Empirical Assessment'.

[88] F. Fabbrini, 'The Political Side of EU Citizenship in the Context of EU Federalism', in Kochenov (ed.), *EU Citizenship and Federalism*, 271.

[89] C. Keitner and W. M. Reisman, 'Free Association: The United States Experience', (2003) 39 *Texas International Law Journal* 1.

[90] T. Lam Dang, 'Relation Associative: Les États Fédérés de Micronésie: Les Spécificités de l'Association', in J. Faberon et al. (eds.), *Destins des Collectivités Politiques d'Océanie*, Vol. 1 (Marseille: Presses Universitaires d'Aix-Marseille, 2011), 373.

[91] N. A. Voronina, 'Sojuznoje Hosudarstvo Rossija – Belarus: Opyt Pravovogo Regulirovanija', (2013) 3 *NB: Mezhdunarodnoje Parvo* 52.

such for each other's citizens, first proposed by A. V. Dicey at the end of the nineteenth century,[92] while only destined to find cold reception then, came to work well around the world today. From the Gulf Cooperation Council,[93] to Latin America[94], West Africa (at least on paper),[95] the Nordic countries[96] and, more broadly, the EU,[97] the dislocation of the citizenship–sovereign territory correlation has turned into a fundamentally important trend in contemporary citizenship evolution, what one might brand as the rise of inter-citizenships penetrating two or more jurisdictions via the same legal status enhanced through the binding requirement of mutual recognition.

Sri Lanka, Mongolia, Madagascar and the likes are now exceptions, while the correlation between citizenship, the national territory, and the scope of the rights citizenship grants, which these statuses espouse, used to be the norm 100 years ago. Almost half the nations around the world today issue citizenship statuses recognised by other nations, in terms of often virtually unconditional access to the national territory for work and settlement. So, a Bahraini is welcome to work and reside in the other five Gulf Cooperation Council states, a Norwegian in 41 European nations and an Armenian in Belarus, Georgia, Kazakhstan, Kyrgyzstan and the Russian Federation. From ECOWAS in Western Africa and MERCOSUR in Latin America to the New Zealand–Australia arrangement and the core rights granted to Indians in Nepal and Bhutan, as well as the full access to the US territory and labour market granted to Nauru, Palau and Federated States of Micronesia citizens, the decoupling of the territory where the core non-political rights of citizenship are enjoyed and the territory of the state granting citizenship is now a universal phenomenon.

92 L. Dyer, 'Anglo-Saxon Citizenship: A Proposition by Professor Dicey Looking to This End', (1897) 3 *The Barrister* 107. The new status was to be inaugurated on 1 January 1901, but the proposal did not generate enough following for this plan to become a reality.

93 Z. Babar, 'Free Mobility within the Gulf Cooperation Council', (2011) Center for International and Regional Studies Occasional Paper No. 8.

94 D. Acosta Arcarazo, 'Turning the Immigration Policy Paradox Upside Down? Populist Liberalism and Discursive Gaps in South America', (2015) 49 *International Migration Review* 659. See also D. Acosta Arcarazo and A. Geddes, 'Transnational Diffusion or Different Models? Regional Approaches to Migration Governance in the European Union and MERCOSUR', (2014) 16 *European Journal of Migration Law* 13.

95 A. Adepoju, 'Fostering Free Movement of Persons in West Africa: Achievements, Constraints, and Prospects for Intraregional Migration', (2002) 40 *International Migration* 3; A. Adepoju, 'Migration Management in West Africa within the Context of ECOWAS Protocol on Free Movement of Persons and the Common Approach on Migration', in OECD (ed.), *Regional Challenges of West African Migration* (Paris: OECD Publishing, 2009), 17.

96 M. Kuisma, 'Nordic Models of Citizenship: Lessons from Social History for Theorising Policy Change in the "Age of Globalisation"', (2007) 12 *New Political Economy* 87.

97 Kochenov (ed.), *EU Citizenship and Federalism*.

The global phenomenon of citizenship interpenetration at the level of work and residence rights has overwhelming significance for the conceptualisation of sovereignty, citizenship and territory. More and more states issue legal statuses today that entitle the holders to citizenship rights outside of the sovereign realm of the issuing country. The implication of the palette of rights associated with each particular legal status of this kind is that states de facto do nothing less than issue multiple citizenships: France – full access for work and residence to 41 countries and territories, Armenia – to six, India – to three, etc. To acquire reliable information on this phenomenon and test it empirically, the Quality of Nationality Index (QNI), which I edit every year (the 2017 edition together with Justin Lindeboom) relies on International Air Transport Association database searches for long-term visa-free stays (up to a year), and then checking all the nationalities/countries of permitted long-term visa-free stays against the law of the destination country in question to get to know the rules of access to the labour market. The results of this exercise, covering all the nationalities of the world and all the countries and territories with their own border controls, are presented in Figure 6.1.[98] Taking the settlement abroad criterion when analysing the rights of each of the world's nationalities is indispensable of course, since a microstate nationality – say, that of Liechtenstein or Malta – can grant residence and work rights in dozens of other states, thus boosting the rights value of the citizenship in question. And vice versa, a nationality of a larger country, such as China, can provide access to zero foreign destinations for visa-free work and long-term residence.

This part of the QNI illustrates very vividly the global shift from a mono-correlation between state territory, citizenship status and rights towards a new reality of the enjoyment of citizenship rights in numerous states based on one citizenship status fully recognised as a generator of rights also by a number of states outside of the territory of the issuing country. The extremes emerging on the spectrum of rights–territory interconnections replacing the mono-correlation vary from citizenships granting per se no residence and work rights in any territory at all, like the British Overseas Territories citizenship (which is only valid for access to the territory of the issuing entity with a special endorsement unrelated to the holding of the status as such) to the citizenships of the countries endowing their nationals with no access to the right to settle and work in the territory of foreign states, like Mongolia and Sri Lanka mentioned above, finally to the leaders of the new trend, all of which are

[98] Source: author's original research, also used in the QNI: www.nationalityindex.org.

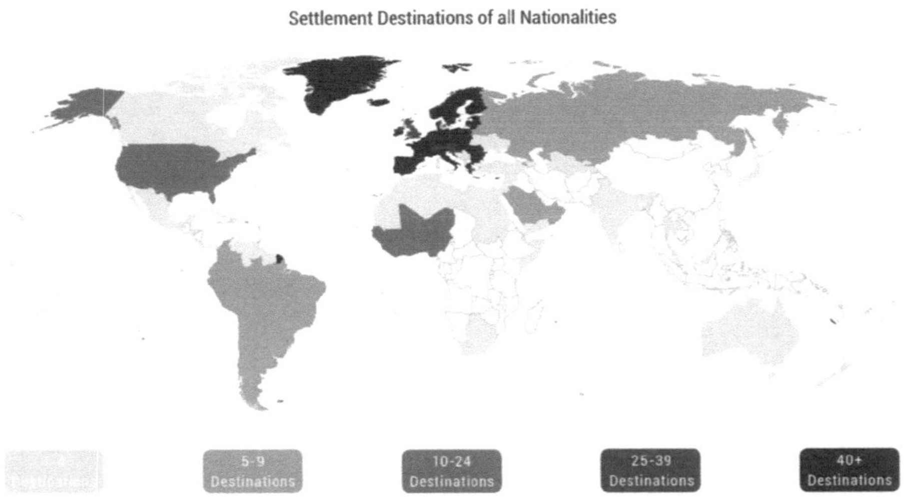

FIGURE 6.1 Inter-citizenships of the world

European nations. Such leaders emerging based on the number of foreign states and territories allowing settlement and work are France, Denmark and the Netherlands, whose citizens can settle – no questions asked – in the largest numbers of states and territories abroad, thus turning these citizenships in the legal entitlements of access to more than 40 state territories and labour markets without any pre-authorisations.

Once this new crucial trend in citizenship law and policy is visualised, the map of the world changes to a great degree. In Figure 6.1, you find the representation of this new trend where the shade of the country is darker depending on the number of foreign states allowing the holders of its citizenship to settle and work in their territories without visas and permits, thus de facto extending the nation's territory for the holders of those particular citizenships: this is the map of the inter-citizenships of the world.

A vivid illustration of inter-legality at play, this map allows us profoundly to rethink the political maps of the world: some of the borders on it are necessarily illusory from the practical work and residence perspective, which boosts the rights of individual citizens and obviously questions the current approaches to the understanding of the demoi in all the countries involved. If the notion of the people – the body politic – endowed with political rights is to correlate with the territory where the laws are made and enforced, it is on the face of it problematic to exclude from political life all those who enjoy full access to the territory of the state for life and work by virtue of their foreign citizenship. To inform a Colombian – who has a right to be present without any pre-authorisations (subject to a clean criminal record alone) and work in Argentina, Brazil and a number of other Latin American nations[99] – that no political rights could ever extend to her since she is a foreigner is both counterintuitive and problematic: once a single working–living space has been created between countries and the right to be part of a society other than the one to which you legally belong by virtue of your citizenship is extended based on the same citizenship status, what is at stake, it seems, is more than merely inter-legality at play in the context of the framing of citizenship. Rather, we are witnessing the redefinition of the meaning of the people through inter-legality.

The emerging picture is quite different from the majority of the textbook-friendly assumptions. The inter-citizenship interpenetration of territorial rights was anticipated by the legendary English constitutionalist, A. V. Dicey, as long ago as in 1897. Addressing the Fellows of All Souls at Oxford, Dicey put

[99] D. Acosta Arcarazo, *National versus the Foreigner in South America* (Cambridge: Cambridge University Press, 2018).

forward a proposal for Anglo-Saxon 'inter-citizenship': full mutual recognition of citizenships between the British Empire and the United States, to mark the coming of the twentieth century.[100]

Although not taken seriously at that time, Dicey actually predicted the future: whether we like it or not, the separation of the world into states and of the people of the world into citizens is arbitrary. States with similar cultures and close ties between populations were bound to experience migration and a need to correct or ameliorate the steep exclusions created by the legal proclamation of foreignness affecting their populations. The inter-citizenships proposed by Dicey are thus one of the core elements of the citizenship landscape in the twenty-first century world, shaping the rights enjoyed by hundreds of millions of individuals around the globe. To map territories of rights correlating with every citizenship following the new trend is a very useful exercise to show what the geography of work and settlement freedom actually is like for the holders of each particular nationality in a situation where the correlation between citizenship and territory is no more. None of the modern inter-citizenships is as expansive in scope as what Dicey originally proposed, but the trend is much more widespread than what even the most courageous minds at the end of the nineteenth century could have anticipated.

This change can be explained by both the emergence of regional integration blocks (EU, MERCOSUR, ECOWAS) and the gradual deterioration of the former empires – continuing postcolonial ties, as is attested to by the gradually waning inter-citizenships of the former Soviet space and between some parts of the former British Empire (India and its satellites, Australia–New Zealand), as well as the US empire (states in free association, such as Micronesia). An intermediary option is also possible, as demonstrated by the Latin American countries enjoying historical colonial ties as well as revamped integration in the sphere of migration. Global trends in citizenship development around the world allow the conclusion that the strict correlation between the state territory issuing citizenship and the geographical scope of the key rights of such citizenship have perished for good, opening up a number of crucial questions for legal theorists and practitioners to address.

The global rise of inter-citizenships is the arch-example of inter-legality at play, since it amounts to allowing the law of foreign nations to determine the potential contours of the peoples and citizenship of the nations participating in inter-citizenship arrangements. The EU, discussed in detail above, is a great

[100] Dyer, 'Anglo-Saxon Citizenship', 107.

but – as the map in Figure 6.1 demonstrates – not a unique example worldwide of such an approach to co-framing belonging among several states.

6 CONCLUSION

The story this chapter retold demonstrates that it is more correct than ever that "we need a point of view that does not start from the *systems, the closed orders*, but indeed from the enmeshing circumstances in which legality appears a composite chance, not already the outcome of a top-down grand design of the world (as one, two, or many legal orders)."[101] Citizenship law is one of those fields that inherently depends on a simultaneous operation of a number of legalities in a situation where international law plays more a symbolic than a proactive role. Although any state perspective tends to downplay the resulting complexities, mono-systemic perspectives are absolutely incapable of switching off alternative legalities at play. Even more crucially, inter-legality sheds light on a much messier picture of citizenship–territoriality correlations compared with what political maps in any schoolbook offer. As territory and crucial rights of citizenship parted ways, the narratives of peoplehood and Westphalian sovereignty legitimation need to be adapted to fit the reality of a world more complex than the one described by sovereigntist constitutionalism and legal pluralism – more complex, and less open to dialogue, as legalities clash and shape, each often mutually exclusive truth.

[101] See Chapter 16.

7

Trade and Inter-Legality

ANTONELLO TANCREDI

1 INTRODUCTION

One of the core issues raised by the descriptive part of the inter-legality project is whether international, supranational or national interpreters adopt a self-referential stance when faced with the overlapping of legal regimes arising from their interconnectedness, or, alternatively, they take into consideration elements impinging on the case from other legal systems. In other words, this relates to whether they are geared towards a project centred on the primacy/autonomy (or dominion) of the legal system within which they operate or choose to focus on the pursuit of the common good, an ideal of justice that also invites critical scrutiny from the other legal orders simultaneously (inter-)connected with the same set of concrete circumstances.

When these questions refer to the multilateral system regulating of international trade based on World Trade Organization (WTO) agreements, they immediately bring to mind some of the most hotly debated issues concerning its functioning and its relationship with the external normative environment, such as the question of the (absence) of direct effect, fragmentation and defragmentation, the issue of self-contained regimes, the balance between the liberalization of trade and the right to regulate, trade/non-trade concerns, etc.

The WTO has been accused of being a means of imposing a worldwide neo-liberal agenda since its very creation, and the series of protests and riots surrounding the 1999 WTO Ministerial Conference in Seattle made the WTO a target for the antiglobalization movement. The WTO was depicted as an undemocratic institution jeopardizing social justice, human rights and environmental protection – a symbol of neo-liberal ideology – and many feared that its Appellate Body would become the 'executive wing' of this grand design, guided by its deep-seated liberalization telos.

Have such fears proven to be justified? After almost 25 years since the entry into force of the WTO Marrakech Agreements, the picture is a mixed one, but – as has been pointed out by Howse[1] – it would certainly be an exaggeration to affirm that the WTO institutions, and primarily the dispute-settlement bodies, have behaved as the ultimate enforcers of a neo-liberal agenda or in such a way as to represent the ultimate guardian of some grand design of 'deep liberalization' by 'constitutionalizing'[2] a one-sided project of economic globalization, ensuring its enforcement and implementation.

As far as issues of inter-legality are concerned, a similar conclusion can be substantiated through a two-step analysis, since the study of the relationship between the multilateral trade system and the external legal orders involve at least two different dimensions. A first dimension – which could be defined as 'exogenous' to the multilateral trade system – concerns the relationship between the WTO legal rules and the domestic legal orders of its contracting parties (i.e., the effects that the WTO rules are allowed to produce at the domestic level). On the other hand, a second – endogenous (to international law) – dimension concerns the relationship between WTO law and the norms established by other general or conventional sources of international law.

In the following paragraphs, the exogenous aspects (the lack of direct effect and the ongoing recognition of a domestic right to regulate) of the issue of trade and inter-legality will be addressed first (Sections 2–4), while the endogenous elements of this relationship (i.e., the interaction between WTO law and 'external' international law, seen from the perspective of the multilateral trade system) will be examined later (Sections 6 and 7). Section 5 will briefly examine the potentialities deriving from recourse to a political process in order to strike a fairer balance between trade and non-trade issues. The conclusions will highlight some of the contributions the trade sector can make to the inter-legality project.

2 DENIAL OF A DIRECT EFFECT OF WTO LAW AS AN ACT OF 'RESISTANCE' IN THE PURSUIT OF THE COMMON GOOD

As mentioned above, the first dimension to examine is the relationships between WTO norms and the internal legal systems of its contracting parties.

[1] R. Howse, 'The World Trade Organization 20 Years On: Global Governance by Judiciary', (2016) 27 *European Journal of International Law* 9.

[2] See E.-U. Petersmann, 'Human Rights and International Economic Law in the 21st Century. The Need to Clarify Their Interrelationships', (2001) 4 *Journal of International Economic Law* 3; E.-U. Petersmann, 'Human Rights, International Economic Law and "Constitutional Justice"', (2008) 19 *European Journal of International Law* 769.

In this regard, a key point is that fear of the superimposition of an external agenda in the trade sphere was so widespread that the major trading partners (the United States, the European Union [EU], Australia, Canada, India, Japan and later China),[3] accounting for the vast majority of world trade, blocked the direct effect of WTO law in their own legal orders. It was a clear signal that they were preparing themselves for resistance, civil disobedience, and "intense social contestation about the locus of authority and the right for decision-making"[4] on matters concerning, inter alia, food safety, environmental and animal protection, health security etc. This act of resistance, however, was not necessarily a one-sided affirmation of the primacy of domestic concerns, interests and values. Indeed, it was based also (if not primarily) on the analysis of the substantial reciprocity underlying most WTO obligations and the functioning of the WTO dispute settlement system. In *Portugal*, the European Court of Justice in particular recalled that any contracting Party, even if finding itself in a situation of non-compliance with WTO obligations, still enjoyed significant 'scope for manoeuvre' in order to negotiate a solution on the implementation of the dispute settlement bodies' rulings.[5] Denial of direct effect was thus justified by also taking into account the inherent features of the treaty-based system at issue and thus the will of its contracting parties as expressed in the relevant WTO treaties.

3 As for the United States, see Section 102 (a) (1) ("No provision of any of the Uruguay Round Agreements... that is inconsistent with any law of the United States shall have effect"), and Section 102 (c) (1) (B) ("No person other than the United States may challenge, in any action brought under any provision of law, any action or inaction by any department, agency, or other instrumentality of the United States, any State, or any political subdivision of a State on the ground that such action or inaction is inconsistent with such agreement") of the Uruguay Round Agreements Act passed by the US Congress on 1 December 1994, Public Law 103-465 [H.R. 5110]. On the position of the Unites States, see J. H. Jackson, 'The Great 1994 Sovereignty Debate: United States Acceptance and Implementation of the Uruguay Round Results', in J. H. Jackson, *The Jurisprudence of GATT and the WTO* (Cambridge: Cambridge University Press, 2000), 367; and D. Leebron, 'Implementation of the Uruguay Round Results in the United States', in J. H. Jackson and A. O. Sykes (eds.), *Implementing the Uruguay Round* (Oxford: Oxford University Press, 1997), 175. On Japan, see Y. Iwasawa, 'Constitutional Problems Involved in Implementing the Uruguay Round in Japan', in ibid., 137. Regarding Canada, see D. P. Steger, 'Canadian Interpretation of the Agreement Establishing the World Trade Organization', in ibid., 243. On China, see X. Zhang, *Implementation of the WTO Agreements in China* (London: Wildy, Simmons & Hill Publishing, 2005), 89.

4 N. Krisch, *Beyond Constitutionalism: the Pluralist Structure of Postnational Law* (Oxford, Oxford University Press, 2010), 206.

5 Case C-149/96, *Portuguese Republic v Council of the European Union*, ECLI:EU:C:1999:574, paras 42–47.

It is important to note that this stance met with the substantial agreement of the WTO dispute settlement organs. In fact, soon after the European Court of Justice (ECJ) ruling in *Portugal*, a WTO panel observed that "[n]either the GATT nor the WTO has so far been interpreted by GATT/WTO institutions as a legal order producing direct effect. Following this approach the GATT/WTO did not create a new legal order the subjects of which comprise both Contracting Parties or Members and nationals."[6] The echo, by contrast, of *Van Gend & Loos* – where the ECJ had argued that "the Community constitutes a new legal order of international law . . . the subjects of which comprise not only Member States but also their nationals"[7] – came across loud and clear.

On the other hand, the will to ensure that all interests were represented for the sake of pursuing the general interest also played a pivotal role in the ECJ's relevant case law. To clarify this, an explanatory detour is in order. The attitude of judicial self-restraint adopted by the Luxembourg judges in their WTO case law is, in fact, a cloth woven from many strands. Some of these strands – as we have mentioned – call for an examination of the legal nature of the WTO dispute-settlement system, and indeed the very nature of the obligations arising from the system. Others, however, pose the question of what legal significance may be attributed to reciprocity as a guiding principle in the interpretation and implementation of treaty obligations at the international level. Others, finally, involve sensitive institutional aspects of EU law, starting from the value and content of the principle of institutional balance, considered a key principle in EU constitutional structure.

The principle of institutional balance is not explicitly set out in the Treaties establishing the EU, so to identify its meaning and content, we have to look to the case law of the EU courts, as it is here that the principle was recognized. In this regard, some scholars make a distinction between the *legal* and the *political* content of the principle. The former is essentially linked to Art. 7.1 of the EC Treaty (after Lisbon, Art. 13.2 TEU) and elaborations on it in the jurisprudence of the EC courts. Viewed from this perspective,[8] the principle would essentially require individual organs – to quote former Art. 7 EC Treaty (current Art. 13 TEU) – to "act within the limits of the powers conferred on it in the Treaties," as they are subject to the control of the courts. It would therefore be a *static* or *negative* notion, essentially a reflection and a result of

6 *United States – Sections 301–310 of the Trade Act of 1974 – Report of the Panel* (22 December 1999) WT/DS152/R, para. 7.72.

7 Case 26-62, *NV Algemene Transport – En Expeditie Onderneming van Gend & Loos v Netherlands Inland Revenue Administration*, ECLI:EU:C:1963:1, at 12.

8 See, for instance, L. A. J. Senden, 'Soft Law and Its Implications for Institutional Balance in the EC', (2005) 1 *Utrecht Law Review* 79, 86.

the principle of attributed competences.[9] This legal concept should be kept distinct from the *political* principle. This, on the other hand, is a *dynamic/positive* concept of a normative nature, no longer based on a formal distribution of competences unable to grasp constantly evolving institutional realities, but focused on joint participation in the political and legislative decision-making process. In this capacity, the function of the principle is to ensure that *all interests are represented* in the shaping of political decisions. This political notion of institutional balancing – which appears to primarily reflect the classical theory of representative democracy[10] – has also been linked with the deliberative democracy model.[11] According to Lenaerts and Verhoeven, for instance, "a proper understanding of institutional balance can contribute to more democracy since it focuses on issues of interest representation and fair procedure,"[12] a remark also made by Advocate General Geelhoed.[13] More precisely, the principle in question "requires the makers of the European constitution to shape institutions and the interactions between them in such a manner that each interest and constituency present in the Union is duly represented and co-operates with others in the frame of an institutionalized debate towards the formulation of the common good."[14] The functional link between democracy, institutional balancing and the pursuit of the public good is also emphasized by Craig, who suggests that the roots of this democratic model are in the tradition of the republican

[9] B. Driessen, 'Interinstitutional Conventions and Institutional Balance', (2008) 33 *European Law Review* 550, 562.

[10] See S. Ninatti, *How Do Our Judges Conceive of Democracy? The Democratic Nature of the Community Decision-Making Process under Scrutiny of the European Court of Justice*, Jean Monnet Working Paper 10/03, 11. On the other hand, M. Zuleeg, 'Demokratie und Wirtschaftsverfassung in der Rechtsprechung des Europäischen Gerichtshofs', (1982) 16 *Europarecht* 21, 24, maintained that the idea of democracy hidden in the institutional framework of the EC, and alluded to in the *Isoglucose* judgements, is participatory, rather than representative. One of the reasons leading to this conclusion is that the European Parliament does not represent a single people, but the *peoples* of Europe.

[11] K. Lenaerts and A. Verhoeven, 'Institutional Balance as a Guarantee for Democracy in EU Governance', in C. Joerges and R. Dehousse (eds.), *Good Governance in Europe's Integrated Market* (Oxford: Oxford University Press, 2002), 35, 43, note 35 (where it is also specified that institutional balancing does not "address other issues that are also of importance in the deliberative–democratic model, such as, for instance, the quality of informal processes of will-formation [that must inform institutional levels of decision-making]").

[12] Ibid.

[13] According to whom, by adopting the co-decision procedure, "account may be taken of as many interests as possible" (see the Opinion of AG Geelhoed, Case C-491/01, *Imperial Tobacco Limited v Secretary of State for Health*, ECLI:EU:C:2002:476, para. 180).

[14] Lenaerts and Verhoeven, 'Institutional Balance', at 47.

conception of democratic ordering.[15] The definition of institutional balance in terms of the fair representation of interests has also been suggested by Curtin[16] and Joerges and Neyer.[17] The common argument is that each institution represents a different interest or constituency. Indeed, pursuant to Art. 10 TEU, "Citizens are directly represented at Union level in the European Parliament. Member States are represented in the European Council by their Heads of State or Government and in the Council by their governments," while Art. 17 TEU states that "the Commission shall promote the general interest of the Union." Consequently, it is argued that only the interaction between the institutions alone ensures fair representation of interests and deliberation aimed at the attainment of the common good.

At first glance, in the WTO-related case law of the EC courts, there are more echoes of the legal version of the principle at issue here than the political. The problem, in essence, was not to invade the deliberative space that the court considered to belong to the political bodies. Indeed, this is essentially the kind of argument raised by the court in *Van Parys* and *FIAMM* where, in referring to the developments in the WTO dispute on *Bananas*, the ECJ claimed that the denial of direct effect was meant to preserve the possibility "to reconcile EC obligations under the WTO agreements with those in respect of the ACP States, and with the requirements inherent in the implementation of the common agricultural policy."[18] Accordingly, the EC concluded two memoranda of understanding on implementation with the United States and Ecuador in April 2001[19] and the WTO Ministerial Conference at Doha later granted two waivers pursuant to Art. IX (3) and (4) of the WTO Agreement in November 2001.[20]

[15] P. Craig, 'The Nature of the Community: Integration, Democracy, and Legitimacy', in P. Craig and G. De Búrca (eds.), *The Evolution of EU Law* (Oxford: Oxford University Press, 1999), 3, 37–38.

[16] D. Curtin, 'Civil Society and the European Union: Opening Spaces for Deliberative Democracy', (1999) *Collected Courses of the Academy of European Law* 185.

[17] C. Joerges and J. Neyer, 'From Intergovernmental Bargaining to Deliberative Political Processes: The Constitutionalization of Comitology', (1997) 3 *European Law Journal* 273.

[18] Paras 49–59 of the *Van Parys* judgement (Case C-377/02, *Van Parys NV v Belgisch Interventie – En Restitutiebureau*, ECLI:EU:C:2005:121) and para. 118 of the *FIAMM* judgement (Joined Cases C-120/06 and C-121/06, *Fabbrica Italiana Accumulatori Motocarri Montecchio SpA (FIAMM) v Council and Commission, Giorgio Fedon & Figli SpA v Council and Commission*, ECLI:EU:C:2008:476).

[19] *Understanding on Bananas between the European Communities and the United States of 11 April 2001* (WT/DS27/58 of 2 July 2001) and *Understanding on Bananas between the European Communities and Ecuador of 30 April 2001* (*ibidem*).

[20] For the text, see www.wto.org/english/thewto_e/minist_e/min01_e/mindecl_acp_ec_agre_e.htm (accessed 27 June 2018).

This, however, does not mean that the second, more political, perspective opened by the Court in its jurisprudence on the principle of institutional balance is completely irrelevant in the case of the WTO – quite the opposite, and for two reasons. Firstly, the principle may be evoked to heal the legitimacy gap of which WTO case law has always been accused. Where, in fact, institutional and legislative practice proves that the denial of direct effect has ended up having a positive impact on the democratic quality of decisions on trade issues, ensuring greater representation of the interests at stake through, for example, a higher level of parliamentary involvement, the principle in question could provide a constitutional justification for the position held by the Luxembourg judges. Or, at least, it would show that any assessment on the 'constitutionality' of this case law would be incomplete without taking into account the interaction between this principle, in both its versions, and the constitutional values enshrined in the Treaty.

Secondly, it is not entirely true that the WTO case law contains absolutely no reference to issues in some way linked to the 'political' notion of institutional balance. In the *FIAMM* judgement, for instance, the ECJ justified its decision to reject the possibility of private companies seeking damages following the EU's protracted non-compliance with the WTO's DSB rulings in the *Bananas* case, recalling that "the prospect of actions for damages is liable to hinder the exercise of the powers of the legislative authority whenever it has occasion to adopt, in the public interest, legislative measures which may adversely affect the interests of individuals."[21] In this passage, the court seems to imply that its decision also aims to preserve a space for public debate and political confrontation in which decisions for the common good may be taken. Such a space would not exist if EU courts decided to automatically apply the regulatory model established at the international level, especially as WTO rules – unlike other international agreements – touch on a large number of non-trade issues traditionally governed by domestic law.[22]

In this regard, some authors have argued that the denial of direct effect could be seen as a possible consequence of the 'pervasiveness' (or perhaps intrusiveness) of WTO agreements "touching upon all of the Community competences and policies in relation with practically the entire world."[23]

[21] FIAMM judgement, para. 121.

[22] For this reading, see A. Tancredi, 'On the Absence of Direct Effect of the WTO Dispute Settlement Body's Decisions in the EU Legal Order', in E. Cannizzaro, P. Palchetti and R. A. Wessel (eds.), *International Law as Law of the European Union* (Leiden: Martinus Nijhoff, 2012), 249, 262–264.

[23] P. Mengozzi, 'Private International Law and the WTO Law', (2001) 292 *Recueil des Cours* 249, 316.

Thus, it has been noted that GATT "fail[s] to reconcile the tension between trade liberalization and other social interests," since the "deregulatory impetus inherent in the current GATT privileges free trade 'over all', depicting it as an end in itself rather than as a means of achieving goals recognized by the international community."[24] According to this line of thought,[25] the ability of the EU and the United States to be selectively compliant would allow them to achieve a better balance between trade liberalization on the one hand and protecting the environment, health, consumers, workers, etc., on the other.

This does not mean simply aligning with the general criticisms of the constraints on democracy imposed with an iron fist by the WTO.[26] The WTO system has its safety valves – even if they are designed to operate as exceptions – as it is true that some of its rules can in turn make a valuable contribution to improving the deliberative quality of decision-making at the domestic level.[27] However, the fact remains that the WTO constitutes an additional layer of regulation that is likely to interfere with political decisions concerning interests, values and principles that, for good or ill, are perceived as essential within a given polity in a given moment. Whatever the final decision (i.e., whether these principles, etc., are sacrificed in the name of compliance with trade obligations or not), the mere fact of opening a space for public debate, aimed at striking a reasonable balance between trade and non-trade issues, could justify the position taken by the EC courts on the absence of a direct effect of WTO rules.[28] Viewed in this perspective, the

[24] J. Scott, 'The GATT and Community Law: Rethinking the "Regulatory Gap"', in J. Shaw and G. More (eds.), *New Legal Dynamics of European Union* (Oxford: Clarendon Press, 1995), 147, 164; D. C. Esty, 'The World Trade Organization's Legitimacy Crisis', (2002) 1 *World Trade Review* 7.

[25] See also A. Arcuri and S. Poli, *What Price for the Community Enforcement of WTO Law?* EUI Working Papers, Law 2010/1, at 32, according to whom "... in a system where other values are at stake (e.g., health and safety, political equilibria among Members with a difficult history, protection of intellectual property, etc.), leaving to the Members a safety valve for non-compliance in cases that are politically sensitive appears to be a good compromise."

[26] But on this, see J. Trachtman, 'Bananas, Direct Effect and Compliance', (1999) 10 *European Journal of International Law* 660 ("... if a standard of 'perfectionism' in compliance is established, the WTO legal system will come up embarrassingly short. The point is that there are important values that contend with compliance, not least of which is democratic legitimacy").

[27] As has been observed by R. Howse, 'Democracy, Science and Free Trade: Risk Regulation on Trial at the World Trade Organization', (2000) 98 *Michigan Law Review* 2329, with reference to the provisions of the SPS Agreement requiring a scientific assessment in order to justify the implementation of health regulations more stringent than those agreed on internationally.

[28] Which runs contrary to the opinion expressed by T. Cottier, 'International Trade Law: The Impact of Justiciability and Separations of Powers in EC Law', (2009) 5 *European Constitutional Law Review* 307, 320, whereby "the denial of direct effect of WTO law ... fails

pursuance of public interest is also in harmony with the constitutional pillars on which the EU legal structure is predicated, since it sets the conditions for respecting institutional balancing and the rule of law seen from the institutional perspective.

Finally, the fact that WTO norms are denied direct effect does not mean that they are deprived of every legal effect. The WTO case law, in fact, illustrates that the ECJ has found more subtle ways to give *indirect* effect to WTO agreements. Examples are the duty to interpret EU law consistently with WTO law and dispute settlement bodies' adopted reports (a technique that reduces the risk that breaches of WTO obligations might occur and preserves the autonomy of the EU legal order),[29] muted dialogue with WTO adjudicators and transformation of international rules into EU legal principles.[30]

to contribute to the institutional balance within the EC, as the political branches enjoy virtually unlimited discretion in shaping the rights and obligations of economic operators in foreign relations."

[29] As for WTO agreements, the principle of consistent interpretation was affirmed by the ECJ for the Anti-Dumping Agreement, the Anti-Subsidy Agreement and the TRIPs. See, for instance, Case C-61/94, *Commission v Germany*, ECLI:EU:C:1996:313, para. 52; Case C-286/02, *Bellio F. lli Srl v Prefettura di Treviso*, ECLI:EU:C:2004:212, para. 33; Case C-49/02, *Heidelberger Bauchemie GmbH*, ECLI:EU:C:2004:384, para. 20; Case C-76/00 P, *Petrotub SA and Republica SA v Council*, ECLI:EU:C:2003:4, para. 76; Case C-53/96, *Hermès International v FHT Marketing Choice*, ECLI:EU:C:1998:292, para. 28; Case C-431/05, *Merck Genéricos-Produtos Farmacêuticos Lda v Merck & Co. Inc. and Merck Sharp & Dohme Lda, ECLI:EU:* C:2007:496, para. 35 ("... if it should be found that there are Community rules in the sphere in question, Community law will apply, which will mean that it is necessary, as far as may be possible, to supply an interpretation in keeping with the TRIPs Agreement ... although no direct effect may be given to the provision of that agreement at issue"). Also Dispute Settlement Bodies' adopted decisions have been used as a parameter to interpret EC law; see, for instance, Case T-35/01, *Shanghai Teraoka Electronic Co. Ltd, Established v Council*, 2004, ECLI:EU:T:2004:317, paras 140–141 and 165; Case T-274/02, *Ritek and Prodisc Technology v Council*, ECLI:EU:T:2006:332, paras 97 and 103–108; Case T-45/06, *Reliance Industries Ltd. V. Council*, ECLI:EU:T:2008:398, para. 109; Case T-409/06, *Sun Sang Kong Yuen Shoes Factory (Hui Yang) Corp. Ltd. V. Council*, ECLI:EU:T:2010:69, paras 103–104; Case C-245/02, *Anheuser Busch Inc. v Budějovický Budvar, národní podnik*, ECLI:EU:C:2004:717, paras 55, 67 and 91; Case C-260/08, *Bundesfinanzdirektion West v HEKO Industrieerzeugnisse GmbH*, ECLI:EU:C:2009:768, para. 22. In the legal scholarship, see G. Gattinara, 'Consistent Interpretation of WTO Rulings in the EU Legal Order', in E. Cannizzaro, P. Palchetti and R. A. Wessel (eds.), *International Law*, 269.

[30] On this, see M. Bronckers, 'From "Direct Effect" to "Muted Dialogue": Recent Developments in the European Courts' Case Law on the WTO and Beyond', (2008) 11 *Journal of International Economic Law* 885.

3 BALANCING TRADE CONCERNS AND NATIONAL REGULATORY AUTONOMY

After examining the prompt response of some national legal systems to the fear of having a trade agenda superimposed by an external actor, we must now ask ourselves (admittedly, with the benefit of hindsight) whether this fear was actually justified. As we have already seen, it has often been argued that WTO law embodies a deep liberalization agenda that would unduly restrain states' prerogatives and in particular their capacity to honour their responsibilities in areas such as the protection of the environment, health, human rights and other social values.

In its submissions in the *Biotech* case, for instance, the EU raised the question of "whether the WTO is the appropriate international forum for resolving all the GMO issues,"[31] and stated that "it cannot be right that the Complainants should be allowed to impose their approach on the European Communities, or indeed on any other countries, and to do so through the WTO. Even less so at a time when the countries around the world are still trying to clarify the balance between risks and benefits."[32]

A number of complaints questioning the regulatory autonomy of the respondent state have been filed before the GATT 1947 and the WTO. Once it had been established that the measure being challenged was GATT/WTO-inconsistent (being incompatible with the obligations concerning, for instance, market access or national treatment), the issue of interpreting and defining the scope of the exception clauses was raised. Under GATT Art. XX, in particular, the analysis first focused on the 'relationship' of the trade-restrictive measure to the fulfilment of the interests enlisted and its 'necessity'. Then it comes the turn of the chapeau of Art. XX (i.e., whether a discriminatory or protectionist intent could be deemed to exist). With the entry into force of the WTO Agreements, similar claims have also been raised in the context of the General Agreement on Trade in Services (GATS) and thus in the field of the trade in services.

A second wave of disputes has been settled more recently. These have arisen from the inclusion within the new Agreements on Technical Barriers (TBT) and on Sanitary and Phytosanitary Measures (SPS) of new provisions that have

[31] *First Written Submission by the European Communities*, in *EC-Measures Affecting the Approval and Marketing of Biotech Products*, WT/DS/292, WT/DS/293, WT/DS/294, 17 May 2004, para. 10, at http://trade.ec.europa.eu/doclib/docs/2004/june/tradoc_117687.pdf (accessed 27 June 2018).

[32] Ibid., para. 2.

been interpreted by the WTO dispute settlement bodies as recognizing that members have a certain margin of regulatory autonomy giving them leeway to protect non-trade objectives.

On the first wave of cases concerning Art. XX of the GATT, already in *US – Shrimp*, the Appellate Body established that Members are permitted to discriminate against imports to conserve exhaustible natural resources. In order to satisfy the conditions of Art. XX's chapeau, the United States was required to meet flexibility and cooperation requirements.[33] In the subsequent Art. 21.5 case,[34] the Appellate Body ratified the US decision to ban Malaysian shrimp imports not meeting US fishing standards for conservation of sea turtles, based on its satisfaction of the environmental exception contained in GATT Art. XX (g) and its chapeau. A Member may thus discriminate against a product based on how the product is produced. The Appellate Body's ruling in *US – Shrimp* exposes the idea that the WTO bargain reflects a balance between an inherent and sovereign power to regulate and the prohibition to abuse this power for protectionist aims.

Panels and the Appellate Body have also accepted a very broad interpretation of the 'public morals' exception enshrined in GATT Art. XX(a). In *US – Gambling*, for instance, the Panel and the Appellate Body examined the meaning of the term 'public morals' as used in Art. XIV(a) of GATS, which is the GATS provision corresponding to GATT Art. XX(a). On that occasion, the Panel affirmed that "there may be sensitivities associated with the interpretation of the terms 'public morals' and 'public order' in the context of article XIV," and that "the content of these concepts for Members can vary in time and space, depending upon a range of factors, including prevailing social, cultural, ethical and religious values."[35] It added that "the Appellate Body has stated on several occasions that Members, in applying similar societal concepts, have the right to determine the level of protection that they consider appropriate." Accordingly, "the term 'public morals' denotes standards of right and wrong conduct maintained by or on behalf of a community or nation."[36]

Subsequently, in the *China – Publications* case, it became clear that the Appellate Body considered this equilibrium as the core of the WTO legal system seen as a whole. In this case, in fact, China sought to invoke the Art. XX

33 *United States – Import Prohibition of Certain Shrimp and Shrimp Products – Report of the Appellate Body* (12 October 1998) WT/DS58/AB/R, paras 172 and 177.

34 *United States – Import Prohibition of Certain Shrimp and Shrimp Products – Recourse to Article 21.5 of the DSU by Malaysia* (22 October 2001) WT/DS58/AB/RW, para. 152.

35 *United States – Measures Affecting the Cross-Border Supply of Gambling and Betting Services – Report of the Panel* (10 November 2014) WT/DS285/R, para. 6.461.

36 Ibid., para. 6.465.

exception as a defence with respect to obligations in its protocol of accession, even though Art. XX is not explicitly incorporated into the protocol. China argued that Art. XX was implicitly incorporated through the expression 'right to regulate' in the protocol. The Panel also took an expansive view of what constitutes public morals adopting the Panel's finding in *US – Gambling* within the context of GATT Art. XX(a).[37] As for the Appellate Body, it claimed to "... see the 'right to regulate', in the abstract, as an inherent power enjoyed by a Member's government, rather than a right bestowed by international treaties such as the WTO Agreement. With respect to trade, the WTO Agreement and its Annexes instead operate to, among other things, discipline the exercise of each Member's inherent power to regulate by requiring WTO members to comply with the obligations that they have assumed thereunder ... We observe, in this regard, that WTO Members' regulatory requirements may be WTO-consistent in one of the two ways. First, they may simply not contravene any WTO obligation. Secondly, even if they contravene a WTO obligation, they may be justified under an applicable exception."[38]

In other words, as has been observed, "WTO Members have not subordinated their inherent right to regulate to the telos of deep or even deepening integration but, rather, have agreed to limit the inherent right to regulate through specific legal disciplines."[39] Apart from this, there is no general relativization of sovereignty to a higher normative order held together by a neo-liberal telos or a particular vision of right or good. The only community telos is to avoid 'beggar thy neighbour' protective discrimination.

This approach has been further confirmed by the Appellate Body in *EC – Seals*.[40] In its ruling, in fact, the Appellate Body adopted a broad reading of the 'protection of public morals' clause enshrined in Art. XX(a) GATT by admitting that it also captures societal concerns regarding animal welfare.[41] Today, then, the public morals exception covers any measure deemed by a

[37] *China – Measures Affecting Trading Rights and Distribution Services for Certain Publications and Audiovisual Entertainment Products – Report of the Panel* (12 August 2009) WT/DS363/R, paras 7.759 and 7.788.

[38] *China – Measures Affecting Trading Rights and Distribution Services for Certain Publications and Audiovisual Entertainment Products – Report of the Appellate Body* (21 December 2009) WT/DS363/AB/R, paras 222–223.

[39] Howse, 'The World Trade Organization', 44–45.

[40] *European Communities – Measures Prohibiting the Importation and Marketing of Seal Products – Report of the Appellate Body* (22 May 2014) WT/DS400/AB/R, WT/DS401/AB/R, paras 5.289–5.290.

[41] For comments, see R. Howse, J. Langille and K. Sykes, 'Pluralism in Practice: Moral Legislation and the Law of the WTO after *Seal Products*', (2015) 48 *George Washington International Law Review* 81.

given society to be derived from the fundamental beliefs or values of that society, a sort of catch-all clause that also justifies measures for meeting objectives not explicitly stated in other exceptions of Art. XX. Consequently, it has been pointed out that if trade measures designed to protect animal welfare concerns fall under the public morality exception, then "so must trade measures addressed at serious international law violations, such as violations of core labour standards, human rights norms and international law including, perhaps eventually, carbon emitted in the production of a product beyond certain agreed limits."[42]

It must also be highlighted that Panels and the Appellate Body have interpreted the notion of 'necessity' of the trade-limiting measure in Art. XX(a) and (b) GATT more flexibly. This notion, in fact, is now easier to satisfy, having evolved from the strictly 'indispensable' or 'least restrictive trade measure test' to a continuum approach whereby the Appellate Body tends to examine whether a measure is 'apt to produce a material contribution'[43] to the protection of the objectives enlisted. This implies a 'weighing and balancing'[44] of a series of factors, including the importance of the common values and interests of different national societies. In *EC – Asbestos*, the Appellate Body recalled that "'the more vital or important [t]he common interests or values' pursued, the easier it would be to accept as 'necessary' measures designed to achieve those ends."[45] From a normative vantage point, then, it has been submitted that this reading of the requirement of 'necessity' also opens up to the possibility of considering other 'external' international agreements where non-trade values are protected.[46] Furthermore, when the protection of the values/interests at stake is recognized as imperative not by a single national

[42] A. A. Appleton, 'PIL and IEL: Will Seal Deaths Resurrect the Dream of International Legal Coherence?' (2014) *Questions of International Law, Zoom-in* 9, 15.

[43] *Brazil – Measures Affecting Imports of Retreated Tyres – Report of the Appellate Body* (3 December 2007) WT/DS332/AB/R, para. 151; *China – Publications and Audiovisual Products – Report of the Appellate Body*, para. 253.

[44] *Korea – Measures Affecting Imports of Fresh, Chilled and Frozen Beef – Report of the Appellate Body* (11 December 2000) WT/DS161/AB/R, WT/DS169/AB/R, para. 164 ("In sum, determination of whether a measure, which is not 'indispensable', may nevertheless be 'necessary' within the contemplation of Article XX(d), involves in every case a process of weighing and balancing a series of factors which prominently include the contribution made by the compliance measure to the enforcement of the law or regulation at issue, the importance of the common interests or values protected by that law or regulation . . ."); *Brazil – Retreated Tyres – Report of the Appellate Body*, para. 182; *China – Publications and Audiovisual Products – Report of the Appellate Body*, para. 242.

[45] *European Communities – Measures Affecting Asbestos and Asbestos-Containing Products – Report of the Appellate Body* (12 March 2001) WT/DS135/AB/R, para. 172.

[46] G. Adinolfi, 'Il Diritto non Scritto nel Sistema OMC', in P. Palchetti (ed.), *L'Incidenza del Diritto non Scritto sul Diritto Internazionale ed Europeo* (Naples: Editoriale Scientifica, 2016), 75, 103–104.

society but by the whole international community, as witnessed by the fact that they are protected by peremptory norms of general international law (*jus cogens*), their role in this balancing exercise should be strongly enhanced.

In a nutshell, the WTO dispute settlement bodies have consolidated a deferential rationality review approach to a member's overall policy interventions akin to the margin of appreciation doctrine employed by international human rights courts.[47]

4 SEQUITUR: 'POST-DISCRIMINATORY' WTO AGREEMENTS (TBT AND SPS) AND NATIONAL REGULATORY AUTONOMY

The TBT and SPS Agreements are traditionally considered as moving beyond the non-discrimination principles (national treatment and most favoured nation clause) of the GATT, thus representing a vehicle for global regulatory harmonization through the application of international standards. This is typically the case with Art. 3.1 and 3.2 SPS Agreement, which encourage members to adopt international standards in developing domestic measures and thus creating a rebuttable presumption of WTO consistency with the relevant provisions of the SPS Agreement and of GATT 1994. Under Art. 3.3 of the SPS Agreement, deviation from international standards in order to meet a higher level of protection must be justified with scientific evidence. Pursuant to Art. 5.1, this involves carrying out a new risk assessment that compels members to "take into account available scientific evidence" (Art. 5.2). Thus, the question regarding SPS measures is mostly one of whether and to what extent a WTO Member has produced scientific evidence to justify the need for a higher level of protection than is already afforded by international standards. In this regard, in *EC – Hormones*, the Appellate Body recognized that

> ... the risk that is to be evaluated in a risk assessment under Article 5.1 is not only risk ascertainable in a science laboratory ... but also risk in human societies as they actually exist, in other words, the actual potential for adverse effects on human health in the real world where people live and work and die.[48]

Accordingly, the EU was found to have violated the SPS Agreement also because it failed to produce any study showing the presence of real-world risk

[47] See M. Ioannidis, 'Deference Criteria in WTO Law and the Case for a Procedural Approach', in L. Gruszczynski and W. Werner (eds.), *Deference in International Courts and Tribunals: Standard of Review and Margin of Appreciation* (Oxford: Oxford University Press, 2014), 91.

[48] *European Communities – EC Measures Concerning Meat and Meat Products (Hormones) – Report of the Appellate Body* (16 January 1998) WT/DS26/AB/R, WT/DS48/AB/R, para. 187.

to human health. However, the idea that the SPS Agreement has a 'post-discriminatory' objective (i.e., it is meant to translate a neo-liberal 'deep integration' design into practice) was denied by the Appellate Body, pointing out that:

> The ultimate goal of the harmonization of SPS measures is to prevent the use of such measures for arbitrary or unjustifiable discrimination between Members or as a disguised restriction on international trade, without preventing Members from adopting or enforcing measures which are both 'necessary to protect' human life or health and 'based on scientific principles', and without requiring them to change their appropriate level of protection.[49]

Thus, harmonization is essentially a means of avoiding discrimination or disguised restrictions on trade, and not to abruptly impose a 'post-discriminatory', neo-liberal agenda. In any case, as the Appellate Body states, the "object and purpose of Article 3 is to promote the harmonization of the SPS measures . . . *on as wide a basis as possible*, while recognizing and safeguarding, at the same time, the right and duty of members to protect the life and health of their people" (emphasis added). This seems to imply that the obligation according to which members 'shall' base their sanitary and phytosanitary measures on international standards has a progressive, programmatic and conditional character.[50]

Furthermore, again in *EC – Hormones*, the Appellate Body, on the one hand, insisted on the sovereign right of any WTO Member to choose its own level of protection[51] and, on the other, despite not being persuaded that there is a precautionary principle in international law capable of overriding SPS treaty provisions, nevertheless stated that

> . . . a panel charged with determining, for instance, whether 'sufficient scientific evidence' exists to warrant the maintenance by a Member of a particular SPS measure may, of course, and should, bear in mind that responsible, representative governments commonly act from perspectives of prudence and precaution where risks of irreversible, e.g., life-terminating, damage to human health are concerned.[52]

This passage, containing guidance on interpretation for panels, implies that WTO members do have a degree of regulatory space,[53] though it cannot be

49 Ibid., para. 177.

50 Howse, 'The World Trade Organization', 57, speaks of "an aspirational, soft law, character."

51 *European Communities – EC Measures Concerning Meat and Meat Products (Hormones) – Report of the Appellate Body*, para. 172.

52 Ibid., para. 124.

53 Thus, M. Wagner, 'Regulatory Space in International Trade Law and International Investment Law', (2015) 36 *University of Pennsylvania Journal of International Law* 57.

considered unlimited, as Art. 5.7 of the SPS Agreement (a provision often deemed to reflect the precautionary principle operating as an exception to other provisions of the SPS Agreement) may only be invoked when "the body of available scientific evidence does not allow, in quantitative or qualitative terms, the performance of an adequate assessment of risks as required under Article 5.1."[54]

We turn now to the second wave of cases, this time concerning the TBT Agreement, recalling that under this agreement no provision expressly counterbalances the national treatment and most favoured nation obligations contained in its Art. 2.1, with general exceptions, as found in Art. XX of GATT. However, the sixth recital to the preamble of the TBT Agreement acknowledges that members may take measures necessary "for the protection of human health, or plant life or health, of the environment . . . subject to the requirement that they are not applied in a manner that would constitute a means of arbitrary or unjustifiable discrimination . . . or a disguised restriction on international trade." Art. 2.2, on the other hand, stipulates that "technical regulations shall not be more trade-restrictive than necessary" to fulfil a non-exhaustive list of legitimate objectives.

In 2012, the Appellate Body issued three separate reports (*US – Clove Cigarettes*, *US – Tuna II*, *US – COOL*) concerning, in particular, the interpretation of Art. 2.1 TBT. Each of these cases contributed to the understanding and limitation of the national treatment obligation by introducing and interpreting the concept of 'legitimate regulatory distinction' as a necessary step in the determination of a violation under Art. 2.1 TBT. In *US – Clove Cigarettes*, for instance, the Appellate Body affirmed that:

> . . . the object and purpose of the TBT Agreement is to strike a balance between, on the one hand, the objective of trade liberalization and, on the other hand, Members' right to regulate. This object and purpose therefore suggests that Article 2.1 should not be interpreted as prohibiting any detrimental impact on competitive opportunities for imports in cases where such detrimental impact stems exclusively from legitimate regulatory distinctions.[55]

In determining whether the detrimental impact stems exclusively from a legitimate regulatory distinction rather than reflecting discrimination against imported products, "a panel must carefully scrutinize . . . in particular,

[54] *Japan – Measures Affecting the Importation of Apples – Report of the Appellate Body* (26 November 2003) WT/DS245/AB/R, para. 179

[55] *United States – Measures Affecting the Production and Sale of Clove Cigarettes – Report of the Appellate Body* (4 April 2012) WT/DS406/AB/R, para. 174.

whether that technical regulation is even-handed."[56] In the case at issue, however, the differential treatment of clove cigarettes imported from Indonesia did not stem exclusively from a legitimate regulatory distinction, since the domestically produced menthol cigarettes exempted from the ban on flavoured cigarettes had the same product characteristics as imported clove cigarettes, making them equally appealing to young people. This was a contradiction of the stated objective pursued by the US legislation to reduce youth smoking.[57]

In *US – Tuna II (Mexico)*,[58] the Appellate Body reaffirmed that a less favourable treatment can stem from a legitimate regulatory distinction, provided it is applied in an even-handed manner (which was not the case in this dispute, since the US measure, meant to regulate the eligibility of tuna products for the 'dolphin-safe' label, pursued the protection of dolphins from certain techniques and in certain areas, but failed to address other fishing practices and other equally important areas). However, the *US – Tuna* ruling supports product labelling for environmental and conservation purposes, and, here again, if "products can be labelled to reflect dolphin safety, there is no reason why labels cannot be applied to reflect whether the manufacture of a product complies with human rights norms, international labour agreements, or other norms derived from public international law."[59]

Finally, *US – COOL* represents the dispute concerning the US statutory provisions and implementing regulations setting out the United States' mandatory country of origin labelling regime for beef and pork ('COOL measure'). The United States declared that the objective of this regime was to provide consumer information about the origins of certain meat products.[60] The Appellate Body agreed with the Panel that the COOL measure had a detrimental impact on imported livestock because its record-keeping and verification requirements created an incentive for processors to use exclusively domestic livestock and a disincentive against using like imported livestock. However, it also found that the Panel's analysis was incomplete because it did not go on to consider whether this de facto detrimental impact on imports stemmed exclusively from a legitimate regulatory distinction, in which case – according to the Appellate Body's rulings in *US – Clove*

[56] Ibid., para. 182.
[57] *Ibid.*, paras 225 and 236.
[58] *United States – Measures Concerning the Importation, Marketing and Sale of Tuna and Tuna Products – Report of the Appellate Body* (16 May 2012) WT/DS381/AB/R, paras 215–216.
[59] Appleton, 'PIL and IEL', 17.
[60] *United States – Certain Country of Origin Labelling (COOL) Requirements – Report of the Panel* (18 November 2011) WT/DS384/R, WT/DS386/R, para. 7.581.

Cigarettes and *US – Tuna II* – it would not have been inconsistent with Art. 2.1.[61] In its own analysis, the Appellate Body found that the COOL measure lacked even-handedness because its requirements imposed a disproportionate burden on upstream producers and processors of livestock in relation to the information conveyed to consumers through the mandatory labelling requirements for meat sold at the retail level.[62]

On the other hand, regarding Art. 2.2 of the TBT Agreement, in overturning the violations found by the panels in *US – Clove Cigarettes* and *Tuna – Dolphin II*, the Appellate Body indicated that this provision involves the same kind of weighing and balancing exercise as GATT Art. XX, which in this case also implies "a considerable margin of appreciation in examining possible alternative measures that a Member might take that are less restrictive."[63]

Overall, the Appellate Body has showed respect, if not deference, for the goals or objectives pursued by WTO Members' national regulations, abiding by its statements made in *EC – Hormones* that each member has the 'autonomous right'[64] to determine its own level of protection against a given harm (which, in principle, implies that it could also seek to achieve a zero risk), and in *US – Shrimp* that it will not make a judgement on the preferences of a specific society.[65] In *EC – Asbestos*, the same body considered it 'undisputed' that "WTO Members have the right to determine the level of protection of health that they consider appropriate in a given situation."[66] The Appellate Body thus ordinarily limits itself to assessing whether there are reasonable motives behind policy choices, given the obligation to avoid unnecessary trade restrictions.

5 BALANCING TRADE AND NON-TRADE INTERESTS THROUGH POLITICAL PROCESS: THE FIRST AMENDMENT TO A WTO RULE

One of the few instances where political process has been able to reverse the results of the Uruguay Round Agreements was the amendment introduced

61 *United States – Certain Country of Origin Labelling (COOL) Requirements – Report of the Appellate Body* (29 June 2012) WT/DS384/AB/R, WT/DS386/AB/R, paras 271 and 293.

62 Ibid., para. 349.

63 Howse, 'The World Trade Organization', 55.

64 *European Communities – EC Measures Concerning Meat and Meat Products (Hormones) – Report of the Appellate Body*, para. 172.

65 "We have *not* decided that the sovereign nations that are Members of the WTO cannot adopt effective measures to protect endangered species, such as sea turtles. Clearly, they can and should" (*United States – Import Prohibition of Certain Shrimp and Shrimp Products- Report of the Appellate Body* [12 October 1998] WT/DS58/AB/R, para. 185).

66 *European Communities – Measures Affecting Asbestos and Asbestos-Containing Products – Report of the Appellate Body* (12 March 2001) WT/DS135/AB/R, para. 168.

in 2005[67] to Art. 31 of the TRIPs Agreement in order to legalize the possibility for less developed countries with no autonomous manufacturing capacity to import generic medicines produced under systems of compulsory licenses from rich countries at low costs. The Protocol amending Art. 31 of TRIPs came into force on 23 January 2017. Before this Protocol, most medicines produced under compulsory licenses could only enter the domestic market in the country where they were produced. This amendment allows exporting countries to grant compulsory licenses to generic suppliers exclusively for the purpose of manufacturing and exporting needed medicines to countries lacking production capacity. By doing so, it helps the most vulnerable gain access to the drugs, helping to contain diseases such as HIV/AIDS, tuberculosis or malaria, as well as other epidemics. This amendment stabilizes the effects of a waiver adopted in 2003 in order to remove the limitations imposed in the TRIPs Agreement in order to supply the domestic market above all.

6 THE RELATIONSHIP BETWEEN WTO LAW AND THE 'EXTERNAL' INTERNATIONAL LAW

Let us now turn to the second dimension to be considered here, 'endogenous' to the international legal order. It concerns the relationship between WTO law and other international norms. Under the 'old' GATT 1947, some contracting parties appeared to treat the multilateral trade system as a self-contained regime. In a now famous passage of the first Appellate Body ruling adopted in the *US – Gasoline* case, however, it was held that the WTO Agreement could not be interpreted in 'clinical isolation' from public international law. This statement runs parallel to Art. 3.2 of the Dispute Settlement Understanding (DSU), which states that the dispute settlement system serves, inter alia, to clarify the existing provisions of the WTO-covered agreements "in accordance with customary rules of interpretation of public international law."

Accordingly, it may be said that, from the outset, the WTO legal system has been considered a branch of the greater tree of public international law. As a prominent member of the Appellate Body, Georges Abi-Saab has observed "... aucun traité ne peut exister dans le vide, 'cliniquement isolé' du droit international general ... Comment pourrait-il exister en effet hors de son

[67] The text of the Protocol amending the TRIPs Agreement and its Annex are attached to the Decision of the WTO General Council of 6 December 2005, WT/L/641, at www.wto.org/english/tratop_e/trips_e/wtl641_e.htm (accessed 27 June 2018).

environnement juridique?"[68] This same opinion was reaffirmed in 2006 by WTO Director General Lamy: "I agree with Professor Abi-Saab, from our Appellate Body, that in using general principles of public international law in its interpretation of the WTO provisions, the Appellate Body confirmed that the WTO is operating within the compound of international legal order."[69]

A well-known example of how the WTO dispute settlement bodies have opened up to the consideration of other international *treaty* norms and used them to interpret the relevant provisions of the WTO-covered agreements is the *US – Shrimp* dispute. Here, in fact, the Appellate Body employed a two-pronged strategy to enlarge the scope of the exception relating to the 'conservation of exhaustible natural resources' enshrined in Art. XX(g) of GATT and to overcome the idea that protected resources were only nonliving resources such as petroleum or iron ore. First, by resorting to an evolutive interpretation of the notion of 'exhaustible natural resources', it affirmed that these words "must be read by a treaty interpreter in the light of contemporary concerns of the community of nations about the protection and conservation of the environment."[70] Thus, the notion at issue was "not 'static' in its content but 'by definition evolutionary',"[71] citing in support the *Namibia* Advisory Opinion rendered by the International Court of Justice in 1971.[72] Consequently, it took into consideration modern international conventions and declarations, making frequent references to natural resources as embracing both living and nonliving resources, such as Art. 61 and 62 of the 1982 United Nations Convention on the Law of the Sea, the 1992 Rio de Janeiro Convention on Biological Diversity and Agenda 21 adopted by the 1992 United Nations Conference on Environment and Development. Significantly, it did so even if the respondent in the dispute (i.e., the United States) had not signed the UNCLOS and had not ratified the UN Convention on Biological Diversity. In this case, evolutionary interpretation was not predicated on the agreement of the parties, but on the perception that it was "too late in the day to suppose that Article XX(g) of the GATT 1994 may be read as referring only to the

[68] G. Abi-Saab, 'Le Règlement des Différends à l'OMC et le Droit International Général', in R. Yerxa and B. Wilson (eds.), *Questions Clés dans le Domaine du Règlement des Différends de l'OMC. Les Dix Premières Années* (Geneva: Secrétariat de l'OMC, 2007), 7, 11.

[69] P. Lamy, 'The Place of the WTO and Its Law in the International Legal Order', (2007) 17 *European Journal of International Law* 981.

[70] *United States – Import Prohibition of Certain Shrimp and Shrimp Products – Report of the Appellate Body*, para. 129.

[71] Ibid., para. 130.

[72] *Legal Consequences for States of the Continued Presence of South Africa in Namibia (South West Africa) Notwithstanding Security Council Resolution 276 (1970)*, [1971] ICJ Reports 31.

conservation of exhaustible mineral or other non-living resources."[73] The second move was to apply a teleological interpretation, emphasizing the importance of the reference to the 'objective of sustainable development' contained in the preamble of the Agreement establishing the WTO, in order to pilot the interpretation of the term 'exhaustible natural resources'.[74]

A very similar approach was later adopted the *China – Rare Earths* case, where the panel employed the same interpretative tools, namely an evolutive interpretation bringing into the picture some resolutions adopted by the UN General Assembly and the 1992 Rio Declaration on environment and development[75] and the objective of sustainable development, together with the principle of permanent sovereignty over natural resources in order to extend the scope of the notion of 'conservation' of exhaustible natural resources under Art. XX (g) of the GATT. As a result, "WTO members are entitled to design conservation policies that meet their development needs, determine how much of a resource should be exploited today and how much should be preserved for the future, including for use by future generations, in a manner consistent with their sustainable development needs and their international obligations."[76] In other words, WTO members are entitled to design conservation policies suitable for fulfilling their sustainable development objectives, even if this concept is not provided for in the treaty text.

In this regard, it has been submitted[77] that the tools of evolutive and teleological interpretation applied to the notion of 'sustainable development' could be employed not only to interpret the general exceptions of Art. XX, but also the principle of non-discrimination, one of the overarching principles of the WTO system as a whole. Following the example of *EC – Asbestos*[78] in fact, the notion of national treatment could also be read in the light of the principle of sustainable development. Accordingly, the concept of

[73] *United States – Import Prohibition of Certain Shrimp and Shrimp Products – Report of the Appellate Body*, para. 131.

[74] Ibid., para. 153.

[75] *China – Measures Related to the Exportation of Rare Earths, Tungsten, and Molybdenum – Report of the Panel* (26 March 2014) WT/DS431/R, WT/DS432/R, WT/DS433/R, paras 7.262–7.264.

[76] *China – Publications and Audiovisual Products – Report of the Appellate Body*, para. 7.267.

[77] V. Guèvremont, 'Traités Multilatéraux: Nouvelles Perspectives Relatives à l'Articulation', in V. Tomkievicz (ed.), *Les Sources et les Normes dans le Droit de l'OMC* (Paris: Pedone, 2012), 27.

[78] Where the Appellate Body highlighted that "'consumers' tastes tastes and habits regarding *fibres* ... are very likely to be shaped by the health risks associated with a product which is known to be highly carcinogenic" (*European Communities – Measures Affecting Asbestos and Asbestos-Containing Products – Report of the Appellate Body*, para. 122).

concurrence between products could then be read also in the light of non-trade values such as health. Furthermore, the fact that the assessment of likeness between products for the purposes of non-discrimination also involves processes and not only products could open the possibility of taking into consideration international rules on environment, health, culture and labour, which regulate these processes. Respect for labour rules or cultural diversity may thus create a distinction between products with similar physical characteristics, and consequently induce the dispute settlement bodies to consider apparently 'like' products to be non-substitutable. This, in turn, could help strike a better balance between trade and non-trade interests, and thus the trade objectives of the WTO regime and the legitimate regulatory claims of member states.

Turning now to the relationship between WTO law and *general* international law, Art. 3.2 of the DSU, as we have said, directs the dispute settlement bodies to employ international customary rules on interpretation, but does not resolve the issue of the applicable law. Are WTO dispute settlement bodies authorized to use non-WTO law in order to resolve the dispute brought before them? The silence of the DSU on the issue of the applicable law has been interpreted in various ways. For some, it excludes the possibility of turning to international general norms other than the rules on interpretation.[79] However, this is not the position of the Panel in the *Korea – Procurement* case, where it deemed that "customary international law . . . applies to the extent that the WTO treaty agreements do not contract out from it."[80] Customary rules and general principles of international law –

[79] See, for instance, G. Marceau, 'A Call for Coherence in International Law: Praises for the Prohibition against "Clinical Isolation" in WTO Dispute Settlement', (1999) 33 *Journal of World Trade* 87; G. Marceau, 'Conflict of Norms and Conflict of Jurisdictions: The Relationship between the WTO Agreement and the MEAs and Other Treaties', (2001) 35 *Journal of World Trade* 1081; J. P. Trachtman, 'The Domain of WTO Dispute Settlement Resolution', (1999) 40 *Harvard International Law Journal* 333; J. O. McGinnis, 'The Appropriate Hierarchy of Global Multilateralism and Customary International Law. The Example of the WTO', (2003) 42 *Virginia Journal of International Law* 229.

[80] *Korea – Measures Affecting Government Procurement – Report of the Panel* (1 May 2000) WT/DS163/R, para. 7.96. In the report of the Study Group of the International Law Commission finalized by Martti Koskenniemi on the *Fragmentation of International Law: Difficulties Arising from the Diversification and Expansion of International Law*, UN Doc. A/CN.4/L.682 (13 April 2006), para. 169, it is stated, citing explicitly the *Korea – Procurement* precedent, that "There seems, thus, little reason of principle to depart from the view that general international law supplements WTO law unless it has been specifically excluded and that so do other treaties which should, preferably, be read in harmony with the WTO covered treaties." In *Korea – Procurement*, the panel took a position consonant with the award rendered by the *Commission de Réclamations Franco-Mexicaine* on 19 October 1928, in the *George Pinson* case, where it was held that "[t]oute convention international doit être reputée s'en référer tacitement au droit

insofar as they have not been contracted out by the WTO treaties – may thus be used both to interpret WTO rules and to fill the gaps left open by them.[81]

Regarding interpretation, the potentialities implied in the systemic integration tool codified in Art. 31.3.(c) of the Vienna Convention on the Law of Treaties[82] as a means of integrating international treaty obligations into the WTO system have only apparently been downplayed by the position of the Panel in *EC – Biotech*.[83] In this ruling, the Panel held that "every relevant rule applicable in the relationship between the parties means all the parties to the treaty and not to the dispute." If all WTO members must be parties to an external treaty in order to use it as an interpretative tool in a given dispute between some of them, then not one treaty currently in force could be employed to this end.[84] Secondly, in order to be 'relevant', a rule must concern the same subject as the treaty terms being interpreted, and not every rule pertaining to the language being interpreted. Apparently, these statements rule out a substantial part of the wider 'normative environment' in the interpretation of WTO law. However, the importance of the external normative environment was subsequently emphasized by the Appellate Body in *EC – Large Aircraft*. In this case, the EC argued that the SCM Agreement should have been interpreted in the light of a 1992 bilateral agreement between the two parties to the dispute (itself and the United States). Relying on the *EC – Biotech* panel, on the other hand, the United States argued that only agreements to which all WTO members are parties should have been considered. The Appellate Body ruled that the bilateral agreement invoked by the EC was not a 'relevant rule' to take into account. On the other hand, it decided to comment on the correct interpretation of Art. 31(3)(c) by recognizing that:

international commun, pour toutes les questions qu'elle ne résout pas elle-même en termes exprès et d'une façon différente" (*George Pinson [FRANCE] v United Mexican States*, 5 *United Nations Reports of International Arbitral Awards* 422).

81 "The rules of customary law may be useful in order to fill in possible lacunae of the Treaty, to ascertain the meaning of undefined terms in its text or, more generally, to aid interpretation and implementation of its provisions" (*Amoco International Finance Corporation v Iran*, [1987/II] 15 *Iran–US Claims Tribunal Reports*, para. 112).

82 In the relevant passage, the provision provides: "There shall be taken into account, together with the context . . . (c) any relevant rules of international law applicable in the relations between the parties."

83 WTO, *European Communities – Measures Affecting the Approval and Marketing of Biotech Products – Report of the Panel* (21 November 2006) WT/DS291/R, WT/DS292/R, WT/DS293/R, paras 7.67–7.70.

84 C. Henckels, 'GMOs in the WTO: A Critique of the Panel's Legal Reasoning in *EC – Biotech*', (2006) 12 *Melbourne Journal of International Law* 278.

> ... a proper interpretation of the term 'the parties' must also take account of the fact that Article 31(3)(c) of the Vienna Convention is considered an expression of the 'principle of systemic integration' which, in the words of the ILC, seeks to ensure that 'international obligations are interpreted by reference to their normative environment' in a manner that gives 'coherence and meaningfulness' to the process of legal interpretation. In a multilateral context such as the WTO, when recourse is had to a non-WTO rule for the purposes of interpreting provisions of the WTO agreements, a delicate balance must be struck between, on the one hand, taking due account of an individual WTO Member's international obligations and, on the other hand, ensuring a consistent and harmonious approach to the interpretation of WTO law among all WTO Members.[85]

According to the Appellate Body, therefore, a non-WTO rule would be considered applicable only insofar as it reflects the 'common intention of the parties', one that does not require unanimity. This pronouncement leaves some room for Panels and the Appellate Body to use Art. 31(3)(c) to consider international treaty commitments entered into by the members from other international legal fora. Systemic integration may thus still represent a way of achieving coherence between WTO law and other subsystems under public international law.

Regarding the *application* of other international law rules by the WTO dispute settlement bodies, general international law has indeed been applied in order to fill the gaps left by WTO treaties, rather than to resolve substantive aspects of trade disputes. Thus, practice shows that WTO bodies can essentially turn to three types of general international rules: those concerning the law of treaties,[86]

[85] *European Communities and Certain Member States – Measures Affecting Trade in Large Civil Aircraft – Report of the Appellate Body* (18 May 2011) WT/DS316/AB/R, para. 845.

[86] See, for instance, *United States – Sections 301–310 of the Trade Act of 1974 – Report of the Panel* (22 December 1999) WT/DS152/R, para. 7.80 (invoking Art. 27 of the Vienna Convention on the Law of Treaties to recall that "[U]nder traditional public international law a State cannot rely on its domestic law as a justification for non-performance"); *Korea – Measures Affecting Government Procurement – Report of the Panel*, para. 7.123 (invoking Art. 48 of the Vienna Convention as a reminder that "error can be a ground for invalidating (part) of a treaty"); *Brazil – Measures Affecting Desiccated Coconut – Report of the Appellate Body* (21 February 1997) WT/DS22/AB/R, 15 ("Article 28 of the Vienna Convention contains a general principle of international law concerning the non-retroactivity of treaties"); *European Communities – Measures Concerning Meat and Meat Products (Hormones) – Recourse to Arbitration by the European Communities under Article 22.6 of the DSU – Decision by the Arbitrators* (12 July 1999) WT/DS26/ARB, para. 51 ("... the EC schedule, in accordance with Article 30 of the Vienna Convention on the Law of Treaties, has superseded and prevails over the bilateral agreements").

those on the responsibility of states[87] and procedural rules (mostly on evidence).[88] In this regard, recourse to general international law is justified essentially for functional reasons: it allows the system to perform its functions.[89]

The question remains however: what happens in the case of a conflict between a WTO rule and another rule of international law? The DSU does not feature a rule akin to Art. 103 of the UN Charter expressly providing for the primacy of WTO norms. However, some affirm that, in practice, Art. 3.2 DSU ("Recommendations and rulings of the DSB *cannot add to or diminish* the rights and obligations provided in the covered agreements" [emphasis added]) and Art. 19.2 ("In accordance with paragraph 2 of Article 3, in their findings and recommendations, the panel and Appellate Body cannot add to or diminish the rights and obligations provided in the covered agreements")

[87] WTO adjudicators have invoked (a) the rules on the subjective element of the international wrongful act: *Turkey – Restrictions on Imports of Textile and Clothing Products – Report of the Panel* (31 May 1999) WT/DS34/R, para. 8.3 ("... we also examine the rules of state responsibility in public international law ... and find that in the absence of a specific treaty provision individual states remain responsible for any wrongful act committed by their common organ"); *Canada – Measures Affecting the Importation of Milk and the Exportation of Dairy Products – Report of the Panel* (17 May 1999) WT/DS103/R, WT/DS113/R, para. 7.77, footnote 427 (referring to Article 7:2 of the Draft Articles on State Responsibility of the International Law Commission "which might be considered as reflecting customary international law"); (b) the rules on the objective element of the international wrongful act: *United States – Sections 301–310 of the Trade Act of 1974 – Report of the Panel*, paras 7.80–7.83 ("... under traditional public international law, legislation under which an eventual violation could, or even would, subsequently take place, does not normally in and of itself engage State responsibility ... State responsibility is incurred only when an actual violation takes place"); (c) the principle of proportionality of countermeasures: *European Communities – Regime for the Importation, Sale and Distribution of Bananas – Recourse to Arbitration by the European Communities under Article 22.6 of the DSU – Decision by the Arbitrators* (9 April 1999) WT/DS27/ARB, para. 6.16.

[88] *European Communities – Regime for the Importation, Sale and Distribution of Bananas – Report of the Appellate Body* (9 September 1997) WT/DS27/AB/R, para. 10 (nothing "prevents a WTO Member from determining the composition of its delegation in Appellate Body proceedings"); *United States – Anti-Dumping Act of 1916 – Report of the Appellate Body* (28 August 2000) WT/DS136/AB/R, WT/DS162/AB/R, para. 54, footnote 30 ("We note that it is a widely accepted rule that an international tribunal is entitled to consider the issue of its own jurisdiction on its own initiative, and to satisfy itself that it has jurisdiction in any case that comes before it"); *United States – Measures Affecting Imports of Woven Wool Shirts and Blouses from India – Report of the Appellate Body* (25 April 1997) WT/DS33/AB/R, 14 ("... the party who asserts a fact, whether the claimant or the respondent, is responsible for providing proof thereof"); *Indonesia – Certain Measures Affecting the Automobile Industry – Report of the Panel* (2 July 1998) WT/DS54/R, WT/DS55/R, WT/DS59/R, WT/DS64/R, para. 4.31 ("Principles of international law ... support Indonesia's position to have counsel of its choice to represent its interests during the WTO proceedings").

[89] On this, see A. Tancredi, 'OMC et Coutume(s)', in Tomkievicz (ed.), *Les Sources set les Normes*, 81.

would produce the same result of a rule of conflict establishing the primacy of WTO law.[90] In this regard, it is noteworthy that in *EC – Hormones*, the Appellate Body held that even assuming the existence under general international law of a general principle of precaution, this could not prevail over the rules contained in the SPS Agreement.[91] Subsequently, the primacy as *lex specialis* of Art. 5 of the SCM Agreement on the customary rule codified in Art. 14(1) of the International Law Commission Articles on state responsibility was recognized by the Appellate Body in *EC – Large Aircraft*.[92] More recently, in *Peru – Agricultural Products*,[93] it has been held that WTO rules on contracting out, suspending and limiting WTO obligations (including rules on waivers and Art. XXIV GATT) trump Art. 41 of the Vienna Convention on the Law of Treaties on inter se agreements.

7 THE RELATIONSHIP BETWEEN WTO DISPUTE SETTLEMENT BODIES AND OTHER INTERNATIONAL COURTS OR DISPUTE SETTLEMENT FORA

Finally, regarding the relationship between WTO Panels, the Appellate Body and other international tribunals, the approach is twofold. On the one hand, the Appellate Body has often cited the case law of the International Court of Justice (ICJ), recognizing its leading role in the development of principles whose status is vague or ambiguous. This was the case, for instance, with respect to the precautionary principle in *EC – Hormones*, where the decision not to take a position on the legal status of this principle was also justified by referring to the same stance taken by the ICJ in the *Gabcikovo–Nagymaros* judgement.[94] In *US – Shrimp*, instead – as already mentioned – the definition of the 'evolutionary principle' was borrowed from the ICJ's *Namibia* Advisory Opinion. In *US – Wool Shirts and Blouses*,[95] the invocation of the ICJ case

[90] See L. Bartels, 'Applicable Law in WTO Dispute Settlement Proceedings', (2001) 35 *Journal of World Trade* 499, 507.

[91] *European Communities – EC Measures Concerning Meat and Meat Products (Hormones) – Report of the Appellate Body*, para. 125.

[92] *European Communities and Certain Member States – Measures Affecting Trade in Large Civil Aircraft – Report of the Appellate Body*, para. 685.

[93] *Peru – Additional Duty on Imports of Certain Agricultural Products – Report of the Appellate Body* (31 July 2015) WT/DS457/AB/R, para. 5.112.

[94] *European Communities – EC Measures Concerning Meat and Meat Products (Hormones) – Report of the Appellate Body*, para. 123, footnote 93.

[95] *United States – Measure Affecting Imports of Woven Wool Shirts and Blouses from India – Report of the Appellate Body*, 14.

law was instrumental in proving the existence of a general principle according to which *ei qui affirmat, non ei qui negat, incumbit probatio*.

On the other hand, the Appellate Body has been unwilling to engage in meaningful dialogue or to accept a posture of complementarity vis-à-vis other international fora for the settlement of trade disputes, especially those established under Regional Trade Agreements or Free Trade Areas whose creation is authorized by Art. XXIV of the GATT and Art. V of the GATS under specific conditions. In this regard, the preservation of the integrity of the WTO dispute settlement mechanism was the main concern of the WTO adjudicators.[96]

By way of premise, it must be recalled that according to Art. 23 DSU (entitled 'Strengthening of the Multilateral System'), the WTO dispute settlement body is to be the *exclusive forum* for determining violations of the WTO-covered agreements.[97] This was decided in order to limit aggressive unilateralism (i.e., resorting to means of self-help through sanctions or economic threats against non-complying GATT/WTO Members). But Art. 23 DSU also implies that WTO Members must refrain from 'forum-shopping': they cannot migrate their disputes to a non-WTO forum. Given the compulsory nature of the WTO dispute settlement system, the Appellate Body has regularly rejected requests for the exercise of 'restraint' or 'deference' by WTO adjudicators in favour of other dispute settlement fora.

In *Mexico – Soft Drinks*,[98] for instance, the panel rejected Mexico's request that it refrain from exercising jurisdiction in view of the existence of a broader dispute involving NAFTA obligations. On appeal, the Appellate Body confirmed that panels may not decline jurisdiction, even when faced with claims that a dispute could find a more appropriate forum elsewhere. Indeed, the "decision by a panel to decline to exercise validly established jurisdiction would seem to 'diminish' the right of a complaining Member,"[99] thus violating the obligation of WTO adjudicators under DSU Art. 3(2) and 19(2).

In *Argentina – Poultry*, Argentina claimed that estoppel prevented Brazil from requesting before the WTO dispute settlement bodies the condemnation

[96] See G. Marceau, 'The Primacy of the WTO Dispute Settlement System', (2015) *Questions of International Law, Zoom-in* 23, 3. See also L. Zoppo, *La Soluzione delle Controversie Commerciali tra Stati tra Multilateralismo e Regionalismo* (Naples: Jovene, 2013), 337.

[97] "1. When Members seek the redress of a violation of obligations or other nullification or impairment of benefits under the covered agreements or an impediment to the attainment of any objective of the covered agreements, they shall have recourse to, and abide by, the rules and procedures of this Understanding."

[98] *Mexico – Tax Measures on Soft Drinks and Other Beverages – Report of the Panel* (7 October 2005) WT/DS308/R, para. 9.1.

[99] *Mexico – Tax Measures on Soft Drinks and Other Beverages – Report of the Appellate Body* (6 March 2006) WT/DS308/AB/R, para. 53.

of a measure it had unsuccessfully challenged before a MERCOSUR arbitral tribunal. The WTO panel held that a MERCOSUR ruling would in any case not be binding on WTO dispute settlement organs,[100] thus confirming that restrictions on the jurisdiction or on the legal findings of WTO adjudicating bodies may not derive from regional fora for dispute settlement.

In this connection, the Appellate Body has never shown any inclination to facilitate compliance by WTO members with obligations arising simultaneously under the WTO and Regional Trade Agreements. In other words, WTO Members' other international obligations do not constitute exceptions to the regular application of WTO law. In the *Brazil – Retreated Tyres* case, for instance, Brazil argued that a MERCOSUR arbitral award obliged it to refrain from applying a ban on the import of retreated tyres to the MERCOSUR Members. Whereas the panel deemed that the MERCOSUR arbitral award was such that the discrimination in Brazil's measure was not 'arbitrary or unjustifiable' and thus permissible under the chapeau of GATT Art. XX,[101] the Appellate Body rejected the possibility of the MERCOSUR ruling interfering with Brazil's WTO obligations, stating that "the ruling issued by the MERCOSUR arbitral tribunal is not an acceptable rationale for the discrimination, because it bears no relationship to the legitimate objective pursued by the Import Ban that falls within the purview of Article XX(b)."[102] Accordingly, Brazil was condemned as its behaviour was considered tantamount to unjustified discrimination, thus failing the chapeau of Art. XX GATT. As has been pointed out elsewhere,[103] there is actually no indication in Art. XX GATT that the justification must pertain to the 'purposes of the domestic scheme'. The Appellate Body could have found that the Brazilian discrimination was not unjustifiable, having regard to Art. XXIV.4 GATT where the contracting parties recognize "the desirability of increasing freedom of trade by the development, through voluntary agreements, of closer integration between the economies of the countries parties to such agreements," and thus also the desirability of the creation of regional trade areas like the MERCOSUR if their purpose is "to facilitate trade between the constituent territories and not to raise barriers to the trade of other contracting parties with such territories." Contrariwise, in order to maintain its environment-friendly measure and to comply with the WTO ruling, Brazil was forced to contravene the

[100] *Argentina – Definitive Anti-Dumping Duties on Poultry from Brazil – Report of the Panel* (22 April 2003) WT/DS241/R, para. 7.38.
[101] *Brazil – Retreated Tyres – Report of the Panel* (12 June 2007) WT/DS332/R, para. 7.271.
[102] *Brazil – Retreated Tyres – Report of the Appellate Body*, para. 228.
[103] Howse, 'The World Trade Organization', 73–74.

MERCOSUR arbitral award. In *Mexico – Soft Drinks*, furthermore, it was held that the reference contained in Art. XX (d) GATT to measures necessary to enforce 'laws, regulations and requirements' refers only to domestic law and thus could not include international agreements such as NAFTA.

Lastly, it must be remembered that pursuant to Art. 1.1 DSU, the jurisdiction of the WTO dispute settlement bodies is limited to disputes concerning the rights and obligations arising under WTO-covered agreements: Panels and the Appellate Body cannot become the adjudicators of non-WTO disputes. Consequently, again in *Mexico – Soft Drinks*, the Appellate Body rejected the idea that:

> ... in order to resolve the case, WTO panels and the Appellate Body would have to assume that there is a violation of the relevant international agreement (such as the NAFTA) by the complaining party, or they would have to assess whether the relevant international agreements has been violated. WTO panels and the Appellate Body would thus become adjudicators of non-WTO disputes ... This is not the function of panels and the Appellate Body as intended by the DSU.[104]

8 CONCLUSIONS

To sum up, one could trenchantly say that reports of a self-referential or even dominant posture on the part of the WTO vis-à-vis other (national or international) circuits of legality are greatly exaggerated. The idea that the multilateral trading system and its institutional bodies (especially the judicial branch) have developed a single-sided idea of what is good and would attempt to impose a deep-rooted liberalization agenda on the rest of the world is hardly corroborated by our analysis. Quite the contrary, recourse to a series of legal techniques has made it possible to leave open a space for reciprocal understanding, debate and comparison. The 'scope for manoeuvre' doctrine elaborated by the ECJ has guaranteed a space for democratic debate, civil disobedience and protection of non-trade societal values. The same has happened when the WTO dispute settlement bodies have recognized the existence of a fairly broad space to exercise domestic regulatory autonomy and public policy choices by member states – naturally within the limits of the prohibition of protectionist practices. Recourse to political process has helped to redefine the initial results of the Uruguay Round and to strike a fairer balance between the protection of intellectual property and health. Evolutive

[104] *Mexico – Tax Measures on Soft Drinks and Other Beverages – Report of the Appellate Body* (6 March 2006) WT/DS308/AB/R, para. 76.

and teleological interpretation have ensured a strong and productive link with the 'external normative space'. Furthermore, the 'no clinical isolation' mantra has generally kept alive the attention – and sometimes the deference – towards international law and the jurisprudence of other international courts, albeit limited to the reaffirmation of the self, vis-à-vis the challenges posed by the diffusion and the strengthening of trade regionalism. Consistent interpretation, muted dialogue and transformation of international rules into domestic legal principles have also represented softer techniques to avoid violations of international obligations while preserving the autonomy of legal systems.

Beyond (and behind) these remarks, one should always bear in mind that, according to another well-known mantra, the WTO remains a 'member-driven' organization, more exposed than other legal subsystems (e.g., human rights treaties) to the direct influence and decisional power of its member states.

8

Inter-Legality and the Protection of Marine Ecosystems

LAURA PINESCHI

1 INTRODUCTION

In a perfect world, environmental protection and conservation of natural resources should be governed, at the global level, according to a comprehensive and integrated approach. It can hardly be said, however, that the international legal order may be considered as the most suitable to meet this need. Being a decentralized legal system, it has very limited tools to ensure a coherent approach to the governance of natural ecosystems in general and, in particular, of the marine ecosystems beyond any national jurisdiction. Notably, conflicts can arise from the collision between obligations deriving from different legal regimes regulating legitimate – but competing – interests between environmental concerns and human activities (fishing, navigation, mineral exploration and exploitation, international trade, military operations, etc.). Clashes and intersections can also arise between treaty regimes aimed at protecting the environment or conserving natural resources, but from different perspectives (global, regional, local; general, sectoral, etc.) or according to different approaches. Current practice shows indeed objective difficulties in the application of a number of multilateral environmental agreements (MEAs) due to the overlapping of their scope and area of application. Conflict clauses have been included in some instruments; however, their vague and ambiguous formulation or problematic interpretation make these provisions of limited value in creating positive synergies and interactions with other regimes.[1]

[1] In this sense, see R. Caddell, "'Only Connect'? Regime Interaction and Global Biodiversity Conservation," in M. Bowman, P. Davies, and E. Goodwin (eds.), *Research Handbook on Biodiversity and Law* (Cheltenham: Edward Elgar, 2016), 443.

Conscious of the detrimental effects that the fragmentation into a plurality of legal orders, regimes, and regulatory authorities can produce on sound environmental governance, the United Nations (UN) has encouraged the development of formal cooperative arrangements or other institutional links between MEAs and their respective treaty bodies.[2] Some concrete results have been brought, but systematic institutional integration and compliance with environmental commitments[3] are far from certain.

The UN has also promoted intergovernmental cooperation for the negotiation of a new binding instrument aimed at strengthening the conservation and sustainable use of marine biodiversity beyond areas of national jurisdiction. Nevertheless, this process is very slow.[4] Even assuming that a

[2] For a general survey, see R. Wolfrum and N. Matz, *Conflicts in International Environmental Law* (Berlin: Springer, 2003), at 119 ff. In particular, on treaty conflicts and possible solutions to foster regime interactions, see *Fragmentation of International Law: Difficulties Arising from the Diversification and Expansion of International Law. Report of the Study Group of the International Law Commission Finalized by Martti Koskenniemi*, UN Doc. A/CN.4/L.682 of April 13, 2006; N. Matz-Lück, "Harmonization, Systemic Integration and 'Mutual Supportiveness' as Conflict-Solution Techniques: Different Modes of Interpretation as a Challenge to Negative Effects of Fragmentation?" (2006) 17 *Finnish Yearbook of International Law* 39; R. Pavoni, "Mutual Supportiveness as a Principle of Interpretation and Law-Making: A Watershed for the 'WTO-and-Competing-Regimes' Debate?" (2010) 21 *European Journal of International Law*, 649; J. Klabbers, "Beyond the Vienna Convention: Conflicting Treaty Provisions," in E. Cannizzaro (ed.), *The Law of Treaties beyond the Vienna Convention* (Oxford: Oxford University Press, 2011), 192; N. Matz-Lück, "Norm Interpretation across International Regimes: Competences and Legitimacy," in M. A. Young (ed.), *Regime Interaction in International Law. Facing Fragmentation* (Cambridge: Cambridge University Press, 2012), 201; J. Finke, *Regime-Collisions: Tensions between Treaties (and How to Solve them)*, in C. Tams, A. Tzanakopoulos, and A. Zimmerman (eds.), *Research Handbook on the Law of Treaties* (Cheltenham: Edward Elgar, 2014), 415; M. Andenas and E. Bjorge (eds.), *A Farewell to Fragmentation. Reassertion and Convergence in International Law* (Cambridge: Cambridge University Press, 2015); D. Russo, "Addressing the Relation between Treaties by Means of 'Saving Clauses'," (2015) 85 *British Yearbook of International Law* 133; V. Jeutner, *Irresolvable Norm Conflicts in International Law. The Concept of a Legal Dilemma* (Oxford: Oxford University Press, 2017).

[3] See e.g., K. Scott, "International Environmental Governance: Managing Fragmentation through Institutional Connection," (2011) 12 *Melbourne Journal of International Law* 1. On institutional interaction in the context of non-compliance mechanisms, see C. Pitea, "Multiplication and Overlap of Non-Compliance Procedures and Mechanisms: Towards Better Coordination?" in T. Treves et al. (eds.), *Non-Compliance Procedures and Mechanisms and the Effectiveness of International Environmental Agreements* (The Hague: T.M.C. Asser Press, 2009), 439.

[4] The intergovernmental Conference for the negotiation of an internationally binding instrument on conservation and sustainable use of marine biodiversity beyond national jurisdiction held its first session in September 2018; its final outcome is not expected before 2020; see UN Doc. A/71/733, February 27, 2017, para. 62 ff. For further information, see C. Payne, "Biodiversity in High Seas Areas: An Integrated Legal Approach," *ASIL Insights*,

new convention will sooner or later enter into force, it is unlikely that it will definitely solve – or make obsolete – all problems of coherence and coordination among different regimes concerning the conservation of marine natural resources and the protection of their environment.

Likewise, international judges – as well as experts operating under compliance mechanisms established under MEAs – are aware of the complexity of the situation and of the important role they can play when addressing global environmental problems in a fragmented legal order. General rules on treaty interpretation and general principles of international environmental law can be useful instruments in their hands to foster the unity of the system. Nevertheless, doubt remains as to whether domestic courts, international tribunals, and MEA treaty bodies have always used all available means to enhance complementarities between different legal regimes[5] and the protection of marine ecosystems.

The objective of the present chapter is to explore the notion of inter-legality with specific reference to the protection of marine ecosystems in areas beyond any national jurisdiction. Starting from the assumption that systemic integration – as a basic principle of international environmental law and a fundamental component of the general rule of treaty interpretation – is one of the most useful means for the coordination of conflicting legal regimes applicable to the same maritime areas (Section 2), attention will be focused on the practical application of this method to cases that have been recently scrutinized by international jurisdictions. Due to space constraints, special consideration will be given to the case of *Whaling in the Antarctic*.[6] Notably, the dispute settled by the International Court of Justice (ICJ) in 2014 will be the occasion to reflect on challenges posed by subordination clauses aimed at preserving ambiguity rather than fostering positive synergies for the harmony of the international legal system (Section 3). Some tentative conclusions will follow in the closing section.

September 1, 2017. Aspirations concerning the development of an international instrument in this area had already been expressed in *The Future We Want*, UN Doc. A/RES/66/288, September 11, 2012, para. 162.

[5] For an illustration of conflicting case law, see e.g., A.-S. Tabau and S. Maljean-Dubois, "Non-Compliance Mechanisms: Interaction between the Kyoto Protocol System and the European Union," (2010) 21 *European Journal of International Law* 749; A. Cardesa-Salzmann, "Constitutionalizing Secondary Rules in Global Environmental Regimes: Non-Compliance Procedures and the Enforcement of Multilateral Environmental Agreements," (2012) 24 *Journal of Environmental Law*, 103, 126 ff.

[6] *Whaling in the Antarctic* (*Australia* v *Japan*: *New Zealand Intervening*), [2014] ICJ Reports 226.

2 TOWARD A COMPREHENSIVE APPROACH TO THE PROTECTION OF MARINE ECOSYSTEMS: THE PRINCIPLE OF INTEGRATION

Both Agenda 21, adopted by the UN Rio Conference on Environment and Development of 1992,[7] and *The Future We Want*, the outcome document of the UN Conference on Sustainable Development of 2012,[8] characterize the ecosystem approach as the most appropriate tool for implementing the obligations of the UN Convention on the Law of the Sea (hereinafter: LOS Convention). In particular, in *The Future We Want*, states recognize that "oceans, seas and coastal areas form an integrated and essential component of the Earth's ecosystem and are critical to sustaining it." As a result, they commit themselves:

> ... to protect, and restore, the health, productivity and resilience of oceans and marine ecosystems, and to maintain their biodiversity, enabling their conservation and sustainable use for present and future generations, and *to effectively apply an ecosystem approach* and the precautionary approach in the management, in accordance with international law, of activities having an impact on the marine environment, to deliver on all three dimensions of sustainable development.[9]

Various international instruments contain a definition of "ecosystem approach";[10] none of them, however, is fully satisfactory[11] or may be considered

[7] Available at https://sustainabledevelopment.un.org/outcomedocuments/agenda21.

[8] See UN Doc. A/RES/66/288, para. 17.1: "The marine environment – including the oceans and all seas and adjacent coastal areas – *forms an integrated whole that is an essential component of the global life-support system* and a positive asset that presents opportunities for sustainable development. International law, as reflected in the provisions of the United Nations Convention on the Law of the Sea ... sets forth rights and obligations of States and provides the international basis upon which to pursue the protection and sustainable development of the marine and coastal environment and its resources. This requires new approaches to marine and coastal area management and development, at the national, subregional, regional and global levels, *approaches that are integrated in content and are precautionary and anticipatory in ambit*" (emphasis added).

[9] *The Future We Want*, para. 158. On the key elements of the ecosystem approach that make it a landmark strategy for a coherent and integrated management of land, water, and living resources, see E. Morgera, "The Ecosystem Approach and the Precautionary Principle," in E. Morgera and J. Razzaque (eds.), *Biodiversity and Nature Protection Law* (Cheltenham: Edward Elgar, 2017), 70 (emphasis added).

[10] See e.g., Decision VII/11, adopted by the Conference of the Parties under the Convention on Biological Diversity in 2004 (*Ecosystem Approach*, Doc. UNEP/CBD/COP/DEC/VII/11, April 13, 2004, Annex I) and the Regulation (EU) No. 1380/2013 of December 11, 2013, on the Common Fisheries Policy, *Official Journal of the European Union* L 354/22, December 28, 2013, article 4.

[11] It has been observed, for instance, that some definitions are mainly focused on different aspects of the ecosystem approach or correspond to a reductive notion of this concept (substantially coinciding with the concept of sustainable management of natural resources). In other cases, the purpose of this strategy risks being confused with its means of implementation. For further

the expression of a general agreement.[12] Whatever its correct definition may be,[13] this concept presupposes a holistic approach that is not easy to implement.[14] If, in fact, the LOS Convention is generally recognized to provide an overall framework for the application of this approach to global oceans governance,[15] it can hardly be denied that, as a framework convention, it mostly lays down general obligations and guiding principles for its State Parties, while some norms are vague or ambiguous in their formulation. In its Preamble, the Parties recognize that "the problems of ocean space are closely interrelated and need to be considered as a whole," but nowhere is the expression "ecosystem approach" mentioned.[16] In addition, the LOS Convention provisions do not exhaust every aspect of the protection of the marine environment. Various rules concerning the conservation and sustainable development of ocean resources are contained in a number of multilateral treaties that have been stipulated before and after the LOS Convention at the global and regional level. Problems of coordination may thus arise in the application of various conventional rules in addition to those that usually emerge in the case of international standards and national provisions providing for different levels of environmental protection.

In principle, the solution of conflicts between legal systems is quite simple if they are addressed by explicit provisions (i.e., saving clauses that allow State Parties to conclude bilateral or multilateral agreements or to adopt domestic

considerations, see E. Kirk, "The Ecosystem Approach and the Search for an Objective and Content for the Concept of Holistic Ocean Governance," (2015) 46 *Ocean Development and International Law* 33.

12 See L. van Hoof, "Fisheries Management, the Ecosystem Approach, Regionalisation and the Elephants in the Room," (2015) 60 *Marine Policy* 37.

13 In the following analysis, "ecosystem approach" will be understood as a policy aimed at managing spaces – whose borders are based on natural, not political elements – according to an integrated approach in decision-making, that takes into account the interdependence between the components of the habitats of the ecosystem concerned, all human activities affecting the conservation and sustainable development of the spaces in question, and the knowledge and uncertainties related to the same ecosystem.

14 On the challenges arising from the implementation of an ecosystem approach in environmental governance, see F. M. Platjouw, *Environmental Law and the Ecosystem Approach: Maintaining Ecological Integrity through Consistency in Law* (London: Routledge, 2016).

15 See e.g., the Preamble of the LOS Convention, according to which the State Parties declare to be conscious that "the problems of ocean space are closely interrelated and need to be considered as a whole" (recital 3).

16 The Convention is based on a strict sectoral approach that divides the sea into spaces, measured according to different distances from the coast (territorial sea, exclusive economic zone, high seas), which is the exact opposite of the ecosystem approach.

measures supplementing or strengthening their treaty's obligations with a higher level of protection). This practice is rather common in the protection of the environment. Several MEAs indeed authorize State Parties to enact domestic measures additional to (or more stringent than) those agreed at the intergovernmental level.[17]

A similar result can be achieved when a multilateral treaty stipulates that protective measures adopted at the international level constitute "a minimum standard of stringency." Therefore, State Parties cannot take measures that are less environmentally sound than the international ones. By way of example, under article 209, para. 2 of the LOS Convention, domestic laws and regulations that states enact to prevent, reduce, and control pollution of the marine environment from activities in the area "undertaken by vessels, installations, structures and other devices flying their flag or of their registry or operating under their authority . . . shall be no less effective than the international rules, regulations and procedures" established in accordance with the Convention.

Absent, however, any express saving clause, can it be assumed that, in case of a different level of protection, the norm that best protects the general interest in the preservation of the global environmental balance should always be applied? In other words, does a stricter obligation always prevail over national and international provisions providing for a lower standard of environmental protection? And if so, what arguments could be invoked in support of this assumption?

To answer this question, the resort to the criterion of the hierarchical relationship between international norms is of little use in the area under discussion. Nothing precludes, on the abstract level, the possibility to invoke the non-application of a treaty rule, except in case of a peremptory rule for the protection of the environment or the conservation of natural resources. The rules prohibiting the massive pollution of the atmosphere or oceans and the destruction of essential elements for the conservation of the global environment, as climate or the ozone layer, could be assumed by way of example.[18] Lacking, however, any consistent state practice, these assertions remain confined to a merely abstract level.

[17] See e.g., the Convention on the Conservation of European Wildlife and Natural Habitats (1979), article 12: "The Contracting Parties may adopt stricter measures for the conservation of wild flora and fauna and their natural habitats than those provided under this Convention." The Convention entered into force on June 1, 1982; text available at www.coe.int/en/web/conventions/full-list/-/conventions/rms/0900001680078af.

[18] For a discussion on the possible emergence of peremptory environmental norms, see L. J. Kotzé, "Constitutional Conversations in the Anthropocene: In Search of Environmental *Jus Cogens* Norms," (2015) 46 *Netherlands Yearbook of International Law* 241.

The application of article 103 of the UN Charter is also of limited usefulness for our discussion. According to this provision, in case of a conflict between the obligations assumed by UN member states under the Charter and any other international agreement, the obligations of the former shall prevail over the latter. It is, however, unlikely that the priority of the most stringent obligations for the protection of the environment under MEAs over other international obligations can be invoked on the basis of the alleged purpose of the former to maintain international peace and security.[19]

Finally, it could be argued that stricter obligations should always prevail over lower standards of behavior if, by so doing, the general interest of the international community as a whole should be better warranted. Such a solution should in fact be consistent with the general due diligence obligation that requires states to use all the best available means to ensure the protection of the environment of other states and of areas beyond any national jurisdiction.[20] It might be wondered, however, if the same argument could be invoked if a conflict clause provided for the prevalence of an older convention on a subsequent and more stringent treaty. Notably, could such a clause lawfully be ignored if the interest of the international community as a whole would be better protected?

In light of the foregoing, the interpretative approach seems to be preferred, and not only because it allows us to manage situations of real or apparent conflict on a case-by-case basis. The application of general interpretative principles (i.e., evolutive interpretation, systemic interpretation, treaty effectiveness) is in fact one of the most useful means of complying with a principle of crucial importance for the achievement of sustainable development: the principle of integration.

According to its formulation under the Rio Declaration on Environment and Development, a careful balance between economic, environmental, and social factors is required in every decision-making process to meet sustainable development:

[19] On the possibility of invoking article 103 of the UN Charter according to an extensive interpretation of the notion of maintenance of international peace and security (i.e., maintenance of global environmental security), see F. Francioni, "Il rapporto tra protezione dell'ambiente, libertà del commercio e disciplina degli investimenti," in A. Fodella and L. Pineschi (eds.), *La protezione dell'ambiente nel diritto internazionale* (Torino: Giappichelli, 2009), 173.

[20] Rio Declaration on Environment and Development, *Report of the United Nations Conference on Environment and Development (Rio de Janeiro, 3–14 June 1992)*, Annex I, UN Doc. A/CONF.151/26 (Vol. I), August 12, 1992, Principle 2.

> In order to achieve sustainable development, environmental protection shall constitute an integral part of the development process and cannot be considered in isolation from it.[21]

It would be reductive, however, to limit the scope of this principle to the reconciliation between economic development and environmental protection. Among the different ways it may be construed, the *integration as a judicial reasoning tool* deserves particular consideration for the purposes of our discussion.

As the International Law Association (ILA) Committee on the International Law on Sustainable Development highlighted in its Second Report (Toronto, 2006),[22] judges (and treaty interpreters, *lato sensu*)[23] may use various integrative tools in their legal reasoning to ensure better connections between rules or legal regimes. Conflicts may be first reconciled utilizing all techniques of the treaty interpretation process. The Report suggests, for instance, "less literal forms of treaty interpretation" and a greater reliance on a treaty's object and purpose; temporal barriers may be transcended through evolutionary interpretation; and the principle of systemic integration, as expressed by article 31, para. 3(c), of the 1969 Vienna Convention on the Law of Treaties (VCLT) should also be widely utilized.[24] General principles of international environmental law are also particularly useful for achieving the same purpose. As a result:

[21] Ibid., Principle 4. On the principle of integration as a general rule of international law, see A. J. Hernández, "El principio de integración de los aspectos económicos, sociales y medioambientales del desarrollo sostenibile," (2012) 64 *Revista Española de Derecho Internacional* 153, and V. Barral and P.M. Dupuy, "Sustainable Development through Integration," in J. Vinuales (ed.), *The Rio Declaration on Environment and Development: A Commentary* (Oxford: Oxford University Press, 2015), at 168 ff. On the exact meaning and purpose of "integration," see in particular C. Voigt, "The Principle of Sustainable Development. Integration and Ecological Integrity," in C. Voigt (ed.), *Rule of Law for Nature. New Dimensions and Ideas in Environmental Law* (Cambridge: Cambridge University Press, 2013), 146.

[22] ILA, *Report of the Seventy-Second Conference (Toronto 4–8 June 2006)* (London: ILA, 2006), 467. The Report focused on the principle of integration as a fundamental component of sustainable development; a special section regarded "legal integration" (which "is usually lost within general discussion" – at 483), which includes normative interrelationships and judicial reasoning.

[23] As the Committee pointed out, "though such reasoning techniques are most likely to be seen in such obvious tribunals as the International Court, the International Tribunal for the Law of the Sea (ITLOS) and the WTO Appellate Body, they may also be evident, in one form or another, in a more diverse array of forums, including human rights courts and supervisory bodies, domestic and regional courts, as well as possibly international organizations and other treaty bodies, such as sessions of Conferences of the Parties, whenever they are acting in a quasi-interpretative capacity." See *ILA Report*, at 493.

[24] Ibid., at 492.

> Promoting the development of *integration as a judicial reasoning tool* should allow a judicial body to act in a more integrated manner than is currently the case. Perhaps ... courts and tribunals, rather than developing a reductionist approach to problems through the judicial application of some kind of formula or methodology in which rules are modified and misshaped, should instead recognise the complexity of the system of which they form part and seek to use the law sensibly and rationally to provide a coordinated answer; not so much integration for its own sake, but rather using integration as a lens through which synergies are found and then built upon.[25]

If, then, courts and tribunals may play a decisive role in ensuring sustainable development when guided by the principle of integration, it cannot be overlooked that, according to the same Report, "Integration by means of judicial reasoning is ... presently at a very early stage of evolution; neither fully understood nor accepted."[26]

Despite a dramatic development of the international case law on environmental matters during the last decade, a certain elusive approach continues to be shown by international courts and tribunals with respect to the application of this principle. Against this background, the advisory opinion rendered by the Seabed Disputes Chamber of ITLOS (hereinafter: the Chamber) on *Responsibilities and obligations of States sponsoring persons and entities with respect to activities in the Area* in 2011[27] represents a rare exception. The principles of integration and sustainable development are never explicitly mentioned. However, through the integration of general obligations and principles of international environmental law within its legal reasoning, the Chamber has adopted a comprehensive approach, with beneficial results for the protection of the marine ecosystems and for the internal coherence and effectiveness of the international legal regime.

The Chamber made a genuine effort at harmonization, using all available means to establish connections and to fill the interstices left by the conventional regime[28] to prevent conflicts or unilateral determinations by single states. The respect of the common interest of humankind, which transcends the individual interest of any state, is safeguarded through the indication of detailed obligations incumbent upon sponsoring states when the global

[25] Ibid., at 496 (emphasis added).

[26] Ibid., at 492.

[27] Advisory opinion No. 17, *Responsibilities and obligations of States sponsoring persons and entities with respect to activities in the Area* [2011] *ITLOS Reports* 10.

[28] In this sense, see S. Robert-Cuendet, "Responsabilités et obligations des etats qui patronnent des personnes et des entités dans le cadre des activités menées dans la zone (avis consultative 1er Février 2011)," (2011) 57 *Annuaire Français de Droit International* 464.

interest of the international community as a whole is at stake.[29] In addition, the method of systemic integration, coupled with the principle of effectiveness, allowed the Chamber to emphasize the role – *de lege lata* and *de lege ferenda* – that the institutional machinery established by the LOS Convention can play in ensuring the effective protection of the interest of the international community as a whole.[30]

The advisory opinion will not be analyzed in this chapter,[31] for the questions the Chamber was requested to answer did not involve the solution of actual conflicts between colliding obligations arising from different legal regimes. Suffice it here to recall that the accurate reconstruction in the opinion of the due diligence obligations expressed in very vague wording by the LOS Convention[32] represents a valuable contribution by the Chamber to preventing possible conflicts between national and international obligations in the future. Accordingly, the opinion may be also considered as a useful point

[29] In particular, see ITLOS, *Responsibilities and obligations of States*, para. 230 ff. For further considerations, see P. Gautier, "Les vertus pratiques des obligations générales relatives à l'environnement dans la Convention des Nations Unies sur le Droit de la Mer," in N. Boschiero et al. (eds.), *International Courts and the Development of International Law: Essays in Honour of Tullio Treves* (Dordrecht: Springer, 2013), 365, 374 ff. On the challenges posed to a correct ecosystem approach by a too wide margin of appreciation left to national decision-makers, see F. M. Platjouw, "The Need to Recognize a Coherent Legal System As an Important Element of the Ecosystem Approach," in Voigt (ed.), *Rule of Law*, 164.

[30] Suffice it to mention the emphasis given by the Chamber to its own power of review when it argues that "[a]ny failure on the part of the sponsoring State to act reasonably may be challenged before this Chamber under article 187 (b) (i) of the Convention"; "Reasonableness and non-arbitrariness must remain the hallmarks of any action taken by the sponsoring State," ITLOS, *Responsibilities and obligations of States*, para. 230. A similar approach is also adopted to emphasize the role that the Authority – as an expression of collective interests – can play to ensure an effective remedy: ibid., para. 180.

[31] For comments, see D. Freestone, "Responsibilities and Obligations of States Sponsoring Persons and Entities with Respect to Activities in the Area," (2011) 105 *American Journal of International Law* 755; D. French, "From the Depths: Rich Pickings of Principles of Sustainable Development and General International Law on the Ocean Floor – The Seabed Disputes Chamber's 2011 Advisory Opinion," (2011) 26 *International Journal of Marine and Coastal Law* 525; G. Handl, "Responsibilities and Obligations of States Sponsoring Persons and Entities with Respect to Activities in the Area: The International Tribunal of the Law of the Sea's Recent Contribution to International Environmental Law," (2011) 20 *Review of European, Comparative and International Environmental Law* 208; S. Maljean-Dubois, "L'Enjeu de protection de l'environnement dans l'exploration et l'exploitation de la zone: l'apport de l'avis de la chambre du Tribunal international du droit de la mer du 1er février 2011," (2011) 57 *Annuaire du Droit de la Mer*, 367; S. Robert-Cuendet, "Responsabilités et Obligations"; L. Pineschi, "The Duty of Environmental Impact Assessment in the First ITLOS Chamber's Advisory Opinion: Toward the Supremacy of the General Rule to Protect and Preserve the Marine Environment as a Common Value?" in Boschiero et al. (eds.), *Liber Treves*, 425.

[32] See article 139, para. 1, and Annex III, article 4, para. 4 ("responsibility to ensure").

of reference for the correct implementation of article 209, paragraph 2, of the LOS Convention.[33]

3 THE ICJ JUDGMENT OF 2014 ON *WHALING IN THE ANTARCTIC*: AN UNFINISHED SCORE?

The ICJ judgment in the case on *Whaling in the Antarctic* of March 31, 2014 (*Australia* v *Japan, New Zealand intervening*), is in many respects a landmark decision.[34] However, the narrow interpretative approach, deliberately adopted by the Court in its legal reasoning, leaves room to some considerations from the perspective of inter-legality and the protection of marine ecosystems. The dispute concerned the interpretation of article VIII, para. 1 of the International Convention for the Regulation of Whaling (ICRW).[35] According to this article, State Parties are conferred a discretionary power to release special permits to capture, kill, or treat whales, if requested for scientific purposes.[36]

33 As noted above, laws and regulations that State Parties to the LOS Convention adopt to prevent, reduce, and control pollution of the marine environment from activities in the area "shall be no less effective than the international rules, regulations and procedures" established in accordance with Part XI of the same Convention.

34 For comments, see, among others, J. Arato, "Subsequent Practice in the Whaling Case and What the ICJ Implies about Treaty Interpretation in International Organizations," *EJIL Talk!* March 31, 2014; E. Cannizzaro, "Margin of Appreciation and Reasonableness in the ICJ's Decision in the Whaling Case," in B. Bonafé et al. (eds.), *Les limites du droit international. Essais en l'honneur de Joe Verhoeven* (Brussels: Bruylant, 2014), 449; M. Fitzmaurice and D. Tamada (eds.), *Whaling in the Antarctic. Significance and Implications of the ICJ Judgment* (Leiden: Martinus Nijhoff, 2014); C. Ragni, "Interpretazione dei Trattati e standard of review nella giurisprudenza della Corte internazionale di giustizia: riflessioni sull'affare della caccia alla balena nell'antartico," (2014) 97 *Rivista di Diritto Internazionale* 725; P. Martin-Bidou, "L'Affaire de la Chasse à la Balaine dans l'Antarctique: Droit des Traités ou Protection des Espèces?" (2015) 119 *Revue Générale de Droit International Public* 403; J. D'Aspremont, "The International Court of Justice, the Whales and the Blurring of the Lines between Sources and Interpretation," (2016) 27 *European Journal of International Law* 1027; B. Gogarty and P. Lawrence, "The ICJ Whaling Case: Missed Opportunity to Advance the Rule of Law in Resolving Science-Related Disputes in Global Commons?" (2017) 77 *Zeitschrift für auslandisches öffentliches Recht und Völkerrecht* 161.

35 Washington, December 2, 1946, entered into force on November 10, 1948. Text available at https://iwc.int/convention. On the ICRW, see in particular P. Birnie, *International Regulation of Whaling: From Conservation of Whaling to Conservation of Whales and Regulation of Whale Watching* (New York: Oceana Publications, 1985); M. Fitzmaurice, *Whaling and International Law* (Cambridge: Cambridge University Press, 2015).

36 According to article VIII, para. 1: "Notwithstanding anything contained in this Convention any Contracting Government may grant to any of its nationals a special permit authorizing that national to kill, take and treat whales for purposes of scientific research subject to such restrictions as to number and subject to such other conditions as the Contracting Government thinks fit, and the killing, taking, and treating of whales in accordance with the provisions of

Australia challenged before the Court the legitimacy of JARPA II,[37] a scientific program undertaken by Japan in the Southern Ocean since 2005 that included the use of lethal methods for hunting and treating various whale species.

The Court held that the special permits issued by Japan under JARPA II were not consistent with article VIII, para. 1, ICRW and that the excessive number of lethal captures appeared unreasonable for the purposes of scientific research.[38] While admitting that State Parties to the ICRW have a certain discretion in applying article VIII, para. 1, ICRW, the Court excluded that subjective assessment of State Parties may be so broad as to justify the adoption of unilateral decisions.[39] Accordingly, Japan was ordered to revoke any existing authorization, permit, or license and to refrain from granting any further permits under JARPA II.[40]

It should be noted, though, that the scrutiny of the Court was restricted to the scientific purpose of the Japanese programs.[41] In addition, the principle of systemic integration has not been invoked by the parties with the specific intent of "remedying any perceived fragmentation, but rather in relation to strengthening the argument of the development over time of the object and purpose of the ICRW."[42] Accordingly, doubts remain as to whether further considerations could have been developed through a systemic integration of ICRW with international obligations arising from other international legal regimes applicable to the area covered by JARPA II.

This kind of approach would have first highlighted the broader context in which whaling authorized by Japan was to be placed. These activities have been mainly carried out in Antarctic waters.[43] Accordingly, it should not be

this article shall be exempt from the operation of this Convention. Each Contracting Government shall report at once to the Commission all such authorizations which it has granted. Each Contracting Government may at any time revoke any such special permit which it has granted."

37 Second Phase of the Japanese Whale Research Program under Special Permit in the Antarctic.

38 *Whaling in the Antarctic*, paras. 209–212 and 227.

39 Ibid., para. 61.

40 Ibid., para. 245.

41 Ibid., paras 67–69.

42 Fitzmaurice, *Whaling and International Law*, at 225. For a thorough analysis of the issues of dynamic interpretation of treaties and the principle of systemic integration with regard to the ICRW in the pleadings, judgment, and judges' opinion in the *Whaling* case, see: M. Fitzmaurice, "The Whaling Convention and Thorny Issues of Interpretation," in M. Fitzmaurice and Tamada D. (eds.), *Whaling in the Antarctic*, at 99–106.

43 The JARPA II Research Plan operated within the Southern Ocean Sanctuary, established by the ICRW Schedule, para. 7.b). On the exact area covered by JARPA II, see the *Plan for the Second Phase of the Japanese Whale Research Program under Special Permit in the Antarctic*

overlooked – as the international jurisprudence repeatedly stressed – that the conservation of living resources is an essential element for the protection and preservation of the marine environment.[44] It is equally important to point out that Antarctica is an area characterized by a particularly vulnerable ecosystem, with a significant influence on the global environmental balance. These considerations would have also allowed the clarification of the relationship between two legal regimes – the so-called Antarctic Treaty System (ATS) and the ICRW – as provided for by a saving clause contained in the Madrid Protocol to the Antarctic Treaty (Madrid, October 4, 1991; hereinafter: PEPAT)[45] and in other binding instruments of the ATS.[46] Annex II to PEPAT, concerning the conservation of Antarctic fauna and flora, contains a subordination clause, according to which nothing in the Annex "shall derogate from the rights and obligations of Parties under the International Convention for the Regulation of Whaling" (article 7); article 4, para. 2 of PEPAT indirectly produces similar effects.[47]

Apparently, however, neither the interaction between whales and the ecosystem in which they live[48] nor the relationship between the ICRW and other treaties providing for the environmental protection and conservation of the Southern Ocean have been taken into account. With regard to the first point, the impact that the killing of a considerable number of whales can produce both on the Antarctic ecosystem and on its dependent and associated ecosystems cannot be underestimated. By way of example, the inevitable reduction of nutrients in the surrounding marine environment should be mentioned:

> The role of whales and other marine mammals in recycling nutrients has largely been ignored. Researchers demonstrated that whale faeces increase

(JARPA II) – Monitoring of the Antarctic Ecosystem and Development of New Management Objectives for Whales Resources, submitted by Japan to the ICRW Scientific Committee in 2005, Doc. SC/57/01, www.icrwhale.org/pdf/SC57O1.pdf, at 12–13.

44 See e.g., ITLOS, *Request for an Advisory Opinion Submitted by the Sub-Regional Fisheries Commission (SRFC)*, Advisory Opinion No. 19, [2015] ITLOS Reports, para. 216, and Permanent Court of Arbitration, Case No. 2013-19, *South China Sea Arbitration (Philippines v China)*, award of July 12, 2016, paras. 939–959.

45 Text available at www.ats.aq/e/ep.htm; PEPAT entered into force on January 14, 1998.

46 See e.g., Convention on the Conservation of Antarctic Marine Living Resources (1980; hereinafter: CCAMLR), article 7. CCAMLR entered into force on May 20, 1980; text available at www.ccamlr.org/en/organisation/camlr-convention-text.

47 See also article 6 CCAMLR.

48 "Clearly the ICRW is about whales and whaling, hence, the relevant knowledge must be about the subject matter of the treaty, namely that knowledge pursued must relate to whales and/or their interaction with the physical or natural world"; see Gogarty and Lawrence, "The ICJ Whaling Case," at 189.

> primary production, and in turn secondary production (resulting in bigger fisheries), wherever whales occur in high densities. In carrying nutrients such as nitrogen from deeper waters where whales feed to the surface, they function as an "upward biological pump," reversing previous assumptions about the role of whales in nutrient cycling. Recovering whale populations are expected to play an ever more important role in increasing nutrients, helping fisheries and improving the health of marine ecosystems.[49]

No less important is the connection between whale conservation and the prevention of climatic changes:

> Whales store oceanic carbon, and indeed, because of their large size, store more carbon than smaller marine species of an equivalent total biomass. Researchers estimating the amount of carbon storage in living baleen whales calculated that the decline in large whales due to commercial whaling has reduced the carbon sink by 9 million tonnes, equivalent to 110 000 hectares of forest. The authors argue that "rebuilding populations of fish and whales would be comparable to other carbon management schemes." Their calculations "suggest that conserving larger species and largest individuals within species should be a top conservation priority" because of their potential as an oceanic carbon store.[50]

Some further considerations might also be added if article VIII of the ICRW was interpreted according to the principle of systemic integration (i.e., taking into account "any relevant rules of international law applicable in the relations between the parties"[51] to the multilateral treaties applicable to the Antarctic Treaty area[52]). As already mentioned, JARPA II was developed in an area partially covered by PEPAT (South to 60° South Latitude). State Parties to the Madrid Protocol (including Japan) have committed themselves to the comprehensive protection of the Antarctic environment and dependent and associated ecosystems in the interest of humankind as a whole.[53] To this end,

[49] *State of the Cetacean Environment Report* (SOCER 201 – SC/63/E1), available at https://iwc.int/soccer, at 7.

[50] Ibid., at 13.

[51] VCLT, article 31, para. 3.(c).

[52] Unfortunately, this legal issue has attracted scant consideration by legal scholars. Among the few exceptions, see R. Baird, "The Antarctic Treaty System and Japan's Scientific Whaling in the Southern Ocean – Is There an Obligation to Protect the Antarctic Marine Ecosystem?" (2008) 11 *Asia Pacific Journal of Environmental Law* 193; D. Rothwell and T. Stephens, *The Regulation of Southern Ocean Whaling: What Role for the Antarctic Treaty System?*, Sydney Law School Research Paper, No. 09/20, April 2009.

[53] PEPAT, Preamble, recital 8 and article 2. It should also not be overlooked that the UN General Assembly endorsed PEPAT with resolution 49/80 of December 15, 1994, where, inter alia, "it welcome[d] the designation, in the Protocol, of Antarctica, as a natural reserve devoted

Antarctica and its adjacent waters have been designated as a natural reserve.[54] Accordingly, human activities in Antarctica "shall be planned and conducted so as to limit adverse impacts on the Antarctic environment and dependent and associated ecosystems."[55] Nonetheless, under a textual interpretation of the subordination clause contained in PEPAT and its Annex II mentioned above, in case of conflict between PEPAT and ICRW, the obligations of the ICRW prevail, in derogation to the general rule *lex posterior derogat priori*.[56]

It can hardly be argued, however, that this clause can be invoked to legitimize a behavior in total disregard of the object and purpose of PEPAT. First, the obligations of the ICRW are saved by PEPAT, provided that (it might be added) the former are properly applied. Any unilateral decision in violation of the provisions of the ICRW[57] or adopted without giving due regard to the duty of cooperation with the International Whaling Commission (IWC) and Scientific Committee,[58] as the ICJ found in the case of the Japanese research program, is not covered by the saving clause.

Second, pursuant to PEPAT, article 13, State Parties are expected to exercise "appropriate efforts" to the end that no one (therefore including states that are not bound to this instrument) engages in activities contrary to the Protocol. Accordingly, it would be unreasonable at least that State Parties to this instrument would disregard its object and scope whenever they engage in activities covered by the ICRW.

Third, even assuming that insurmountable conflicts arise between the two binding instruments, it is reasonable to believe that State Parties to PEPAT and ICRW, when issuing permits relating to activities carried out in the Antarctic Treaty area (South to 60° South Latitude), take (and prove to have taken) into account the peculiarity of this vulnerable ecosystem. To this end, the actions undertaken should be consistent with the object and purpose of PEPAT, along with the general environmental principles therein enshrined, as expressed by article 3:

> The protection of the Antarctic environment and dependent and associated ecosystems and the intrinsic value of Antarctica, including its wilderness and aesthetic values and its value as an area for the conduct of scientific research,

to peace and science and the procedures contained in the Protocol regarding the protection of the Antarctic environment and dependent and associated ecosystems in the planning and conduct of all activities in Antarctica," UN Doc. A/RES/49/80, Preamble, recital 10.

54 PEPAT, Preamble, recital 2 and article 2.

55 Article 3, para. 2.(a).

56 VCLT, article 30, para. 2.

57 See ICJ, *Whaling in the Antarctic*, paras. 46 and 61.

58 Ibid., paras. 83 and 137.

> in particular research essential to understanding the global environment, shall be fundamental considerations in the planning and conduct of all activities in the Antarctic Treaty area.[59]

Neither Australia nor New Zealand raised the issue of an alleged conflict between Japan's whaling program and the purpose of the Antarctic Treaty regime before the ICJ.[60] It has also been observed that before the submission of the *Whaling in the Antarctic* case to the court, the issue had been "ignored within the ATS including from some of Japan's fiercest anti-whaling critics such as Australia, New Zealand, the United Kingdom and the United States."[61] Finally, no concrete steps have ever been taken within the ICRW or the ATS to foster a constructive dialogue or concrete forms of cooperation between the two legal systems.[62]

The reluctance of the ATPs to bring the whaling debate within the ATS can hardly be explained unless the true rationale of the aforementioned conflict clauses (i.e., to avert any detrimental impact of controversial issues upon the harmony of the ATS) is duly taken into account:

> The point is that the stakes are already too high for any one State to risk destabilizing the framework upon which the Antarctic Treaty System is premised. The treaty works, by and large, because it creates enough ambiguity for all Parties to put issues of territoriality to one side. It works well because there is no ongoing conflict between the Parties. The intractable issue of whaling has mired the meetings of the IWC, with Japan threatening to withdraw from the Commission. Whilst some States have dismissed Japan's threats as mere theatrics, the alternatives to the IWC are less than clear and fraught with uncertainty. It is very much a case of better the devil you know.[63]

If, therefore, the purpose of these clauses is not to bring into connection two different regimes, but to preserve the separation between two parallel worlds, a distinction is to be made. At the political level, this solution can be considered as a good diplomatic compromise to ensure the stability of international relations with regard to an entire continent. At the legal level, however, different conclusions can be drawn if the subordination clause is interpreted

59 PEPAT, article 3, para. 1.

60 "The international judges hardly venture into matters that have not been raised by the parties. It should be noted, though, that the principle *ne ultra petita* does not apply to the legal arguments of the parties (*jura novit curia*);" see e.g., R. Kolb, "General Principles of Procedural Law," in A. Zimmermann, C. Tomuschat, and K. Oellers-Frahm (eds.), *The Statute of the International Court of Justice* (Oxford: Oxford University Press, 2006), at 811–812.

61 Rothwell and Stephens, *The Regulation*, at 11.

62 Ibid., at 8 ff.

63 Baird, "The Antarctic Treaty System," at 199.

according to the principle of effectiveness. Conflict clauses such as those provided by PEPAT in favor of the ICRW are static rather than dynamic and respond to a logic of development of international environmental law based upon a sectorial approach.[64] Nevertheless, general rules on interpretation, as codified by the VCLT, continue to be applied and should play a significant role in ensuring the internal coherence of the international legal order and, above all, the respect of the international community's interest in the protection of a common good.

4 CONCLUDING REMARKS

If the main purpose of the inter-legality approach is to cope with the interconnectedness and complexity of reality by a legal approach capable of recollecting the relevant legal 'fragments' (as suggested in Chapter 1 through 16 of this volume), integration as a judicial tool is a valuable instrument for ensuring positive synergies and interconnections between different legal regimes when the protection of marine ecosystems, as a global common good, is at stake. In addition, the adoption of a comprehensive approach allows the interpreter to build bridges and establish connections between conventional regimes not only to avert conflicts, but also to prevent unilateral determinations inconsistent with the general interest of humankind.

A certain reluctance of courts and tribunals to approach cases with implications for the sound management of the environmental balance of the oceans through the lens of the principle of integration can be explained in various ways. The situation is, however, more complex than it looks. The ecosystem approach to the management of the oceans pursues an overarching goal: the overall balance of marine ecosystems. The judiciary and monitoring treaty bodies can play a crucial role in achieving this final objective, but the adoption of an integrated approach in their legal reasoning is not sufficient. A further step is necessary, notably a shift from the traditional synallagmatic conception of international obligations to a modern approach that enhances and duly takes into account rights and duties pertaining to the international community as a whole.

In addition, the activity of judicial and nonjudicial bodies should be supported by the consistent action of states. First, governments should adopt

[64] Wolfrum and Matz, *Conflicts*, at 128, who also observe that "it would have been much more effective to apply the ecosystem approach of the Protocol for Environmental Protection of the Antarctic Treaty to whales, as opposed to exempting whaling in its totality from the applicability of this Protocol."

a more effective, integrated approach in the lawmaking process through a genuine "attempt to recognize and build upon the linkages that exist between different rules and, at a higher level of conception, different grouping of rules."[65] Second, states should actually perform the obligations incumbent upon them under judgments rendered by international courts and tribunals;[66] recommendations adopted by treaty bodies under compliance procedures should also be taken in due regard. Third, an integrated approach should be adopted by states and international organizations when planning their national and international policies and programs. Finally, systemic cooperation between treaty bodies could foster a shift from a sectoral approach to a modern vision of a comprehensive and coherent approach to the governance of global ecosystems. Is this a mere utopia? Definitely, it is something very similar to a perfect world. A lot could be done, nevertheless, to make the present world somehow less imperfect.

65 ILA, *Report*. 485. See also Platjouw, *Environmental Law*, at 206–207: ". . . we do not necessarily require complex and difficult legal systems to protect ecosystems effectively. . . . When law is designed as a system, predictability and consistency increase while complexity and discretion decrease."

66 In November 2015, Japan announced its resumption of whaling activities in the Antarctic under a New Special Permit Program (NEWREP-A); for further details, see M. Johnson, "Whaling in the Antarctic – The ICJ Decision and its Consequences for future Special Permit Whaling," (2014) 32 *Australian Yearbook of International Law* 87.

9

Managing Inter-Legality

Conceptualizing the European Union's Interactions with International Investment Law

PANOS KOUTRAKOS

1 INTRODUCTION

In few areas does inter-legality present legal and policy challenges as starkly as in the interplay between international investment law and European Union (EU) law. Consider the facts of the ongoing *Micula* saga: prior to acceding to the EU, the Romanian authorities withdrew incentives for new foreign investments on the ground of incompatibility with EU state aid law. The investors brought proceedings before an International Centre for Settlement of Investment Disputes (ICSID) Arbitral Tribunal against Romania, arguing that the withdrawal of such incentives amounted to a violation of the 2002 Bilateral Investment Treaty (BIT) between Romania and Sweden. Once awarded $250 million in damages, they brought a successful action before the Bucharest Tribunal seeking to enforce the award. In the meantime, Romania appealed unsuccessfully against the award before an ICSID ad hoc Committee.[1] The European Commission decided that the payment of the compensation awarded by the Arbitral Tribunal would be illegal under EU law as it would constitute state aid pursuant to Article 107(1) TFEU, and that Romania should recover any compensation it had already paid to the claimants in implementation of the award.[2] The investors challenged this decision before the General Court of the European Union[3] and have also brought actions before courts of a number of member states (Belgium,

[1] *Ioan Micula, Viorel Micula, S.C. European Food S.A, S.C. Starmill S.R.L. and S.C. Multipack S.R.L. v Romania*, ICSID Case No. ARB/05/20 – Decision on annulment.

[2] Commission Decision 2015/1470 on State Aid SA. (2014/C) (ex 2014/NN) implemented by Romania – Arbitral award Micula v Romania of 11 December 2013 [2015] OJ L 232/43.

[3] Case T-694/15 and Case T-704/15 (pending).

Luxembourg, the United Kingdom[4] and France), as well as the United States,[5] in order to enforce the arbitral award.

The above overview illustrates how the interactions between international investment law and EU law give rise to legal disputes that emerge in a variety of procedural settings and in an ever-wider canvas, involving national and transnational courts and arbitral tribunals, as well as courts in third states. The *Micula* case is but one illustration of the specific legal challenges that inter-legality raises in the context of international investment and EU law.

There are at least three reasons that render this area worth exploring from the vantage point of inter-legality and its management. First, it touches upon the most fundamental characteristics of the EU legal order, including the primacy of its law, the exclusive jurisdiction of the Court of Justice of the European Union (CJEU), the central role of domestic courts in the application of EU law and the principle of non-discrimination.

Second, the above issues raised by inter-legality in this area have recently been brought to sharp relief in a range of legal contexts. In a public enforcement context, and in response to the short shrift that most member states have given the Commission's long-standing objection to intra-EU BITs,[6] the Commission initiated proceedings in June 2015 against five member states and has requested information from the remaining 21. Another context relates to the interactions between the Court of Justice and domestic courts: in response to a reference by the German Federal Court of Justice (*Bundesgerichtshof*), the Court of Justice held in *Achmea* that the provision of investor–state settlement dispute (ISDS) in the BIT between Czechoslovakia and the Netherlands was contrary to EU primary law.[7] Finally, there is also the context of the interactions between member state governments and the Court of Justice: Belgium requested an Opinion pursuant to Article 218(11) TFEU on the compatibility of the arbitration procedure laid down in the Comprehensive Economic and Trade Agreement between Canada and the EU and its member states (CETA) with EU primary law.[8]

Third, the above disputes and the fundamental questions they raise have emerged with increasing intensity and in a politically charged environment

[4] [2017] EWHC 31 (Comm) (www.italaw.com/sites/default/files/case-documents/italaw8133_6.pdf).

[5] See the recent decision of the US Court of Appeal (2nd Cir) www.italaw.com/sites/default/files/case-documents/italaw94011.pdf.

[6] With the exception of Italy and Ireland, which have terminated their intra-EU BITs.

[7] Case C-284/16, *Slovak Republic v Achmea BV* EU:C:2018:158.

[8] Opinion 1/17 (pending).

where investment arbitration is viewed with distinct scepticism, if not outright hostility, by the wider public.[9]

The way, therefore, with which these issues have been dealt is not yet settled. This is an open debate, and seeking to provide answers, let alone to predict what the official institutional and judicial response would be, is to give a hostage to fortune. This chapter, instead, will draw on the existing practice of the EU's institutions, including its courts, in order to conceptualize different approaches to the management of inter-legality in the area. It will articulate three such approaches, ranging from conflict to integration to harmonious coexistence.

2 EXPANSION AND CONFLICT: SEEKING PRECEDENCE FOR EU LAW

Over the years, the European Commission has argued – quite forcefully – that EU law has rendered intra-EU BITs inapplicable. To that effect, it has intervened in a number of proceedings before arbitral tribunals, putting forward various arguments, including the automatic termination of the relevant agreements following accession to the EU by both its parties. The consistency with which this argument has been made varies. In *Eastern Sugar*, for instance, whilst the Czech Republic raised it, the European Commission put forward submissions that were viewed by the Arbitral Tribunal "for the most part diplomatic and ambiguous" and that suggested that automatic termination was not advocated.[10] In the more recent *Micula* case, however, the Commission argued that "the E.U. Treaties superseded the Sweden–Romania BIT as a result of Romania's accession to the European

[9] This hostility was expressed most vociferously in the context of the now moribund Transatlantic Trade and Investment Partnership (TTIP). It was in response to it that the Commission has put forward its proposal for an investment court (European Commission, Concept Paper: Investment in TTIP and beyond – the path for reform: Enhancing the right to regulate and moving from current ad hoc arbitration towards an Investment Court). The debate about the problems of the arbitration system in international investment has given rise to voluminous literature. See, amongst others, J. Maupin, 'Transparency in International Investment Law: The Good, the Bad, and the Murky', in A. Bianchi and A. Peters (eds.), *Transparency in International Law* (Cambridge: Cambridge University Press, 2013), 142; J. E. Kalicki and A. Joubin-Bret (eds.), *Reshaping the Investor–State Dispute Settlement System – Journeys for the 21st Century* (Leiden: Martinus Nijhoff, 2015); M. Waibel et al. (eds.), *The Backlash against Investment Arbitration: Perceptions and Reality* (The Hague: Kluwer, 2010).

[10] *Eastern Sugar B.V. (Netherlands) v The Czech Republic*, SCC Case No. 088/2004, Partial Award, para. 119 (the quote is from para. 120).

Union, terminating the latter, or, at the very least, rendering Articles 7 and 10 of that BIT inapplicable."[11]

As a matter of principle, this objection[12] is not surprising. In normative terms, it draws on the principle of autonomy of EU law that, in the light of the recent case law of the Court of Justice (e.g., in Opinion 1/09[13] and Opinion 2/13,[14] let alone the judgement in *Achmea* itself, which will be examined below) has been construed in increasingly broad terms.[15] It is also about the competence of the Union to carry out an investment policy, not least pursuant to the amendments introduced by the Lisbon Treaty.[16] In policy terms, the EU has been seeking to define its investment policy in its negotiations with third countries, including the CETA and the Agreements with Singapore and Vietnam, the negotiation of investment chapters in agreements with India, Malaysia, Egypt, Jordan, Morocco and Tunisia and the negotiation of standalone agreements with China and Myanmar. This gradually emerging policy would be buttressed by comprehensive claims about the invalidity of existing intra-EU BITs.

There is, however, a whiff of maximalism about the argument of automatic termination of intra-EU BITs. It marginalizes the significance of the termination procedures in BITs. By disregarding the international law nature of the rules that it deems to be contrary to EU law, the Commission's argument does not sit comfortably with the approach that the Court of Justice has adopted in a similar context. It is recalled that, in its effort to reconcile the pre-existing international obligations of member states with EU law pursuant to Article 351 TFEU, the Court places considerable emphasis on full compliance with the international rules on the termination of the relevant treaty concluded by the member state.[17] In doing so, the Court of Justice takes the rule laid down in

[11] *Ioan Micula, Viorel Micula, S.C. European Food S.A, S.C. Starmill S.R.L. and S.C. Multipack S.R.L. v Romania*, ICSID Case No. ARB/05/20 – Decision on annulment, para. 330 (referring to para. 92 of the Commission's submission). See also Commission Decision 2015/1470 [2015] OJ L 232/43 at para. 102. In another recent case, Poland did not make this argument: Partial Award in PCA Case No. 2013-01 *Enkev Beheer B.V. v Poland*.

[12] See the discussion in A. Reinisch, 'Articles 30 and 59 of the Vienna Convention on the Law of Treaties in Action: The Decisions on Jurisdiction in the *Eastern Sugar* and *Eureko* Investment Arbitrations', (2012) 39 *Legal Issues of Economic Integration* 157.

[13] ECLI:EU:C:2011:123.

[14] ECLI:EU:C:2014:2454.

[15] For an analysis of the principle in the context of investment law, see S. Hindelang, 'The Autonomy of the European Legal Order – EU Constitutional Limits to Investor–State Arbitration on the Basis of Future EU Investment-Related Agreements', (2013) 4 *European Yearbook of International Economic Law* 187.

[16] See P. Koutrakos, *EU International Relations Law*, 2nd edn (Oxford: Hart, 2015), at 30 ff.

[17] See, for instance, Case C-478/07 *Budvar*, ECLI:EU:C:2009:521.

Article 65 of the Vienna Convention on the Law of Treaties seriously. Viewed from this angle, the decision of the Commission to tackle the question of the compatibility of intra-EU BITs directly by bringing enforcement actions against certain member states is, in normative terms, preferable.[18]

The automatic termination argument is also at odds with the Court's own approach to succession of treaties as a matter of EU law. It is recalled that only in relation to GATT 1947 did the Court accept – back in the early 1970s – that the member states had passed on to the European Economic Community (as it then was) the rights and obligations they had assumed pursuant to GATT 1947.[19] Admittedly, the two cases are not entirely similar, as the latter case was about whether the Community was bound by an agreement concluded by its member states. There is, however, an analogy between the two legal contexts insofar as they tell us how the EU deals with the legal effects of successive international treaties of potentially overlapping scope. Put differently, at the core of both legal contexts, the main issue is whether an agreement concluded by the member states has been subsumed by EU law (in the case of intra-EU BITs rendering them invalid, whereas in the context of other agreements binding the EU itself).

It is recalled that, in dealing with the principle of treaty succession, the Court of Justice has adopted an extremely narrow approach.[20]

It is only where the EU has assumed "all the powers previously exercised by the Member States that fall within the convention in question" that the Union has succeeded the member states.[21] This case law suggests that the powers and obligations laid down in a treaty concluded by the member states would be subsumed by the Union pursuant to the EU Treaties only if there was a complete overlap between their provisions.

Is there such an overlap between the intra-EU BITs and the EU Treaties so as to suggest that the former are rendered invalid by the latter? In his Opinion in

18 The Commission initiated proceedings against Austria, the Netherlands, Romania, Slovakia and Sweden in June 2015 whilst it requested information from the remaining 21 member states (Ireland and Italy have terminated their intra-EU BITs).

19 Joined cases 21–24/72, *International Fruit Company*, ECLI:EU:C:1972:115.

20 See the analysis in Koutrakos, *EU International Relations Law*, 212–219, and R. Schütze, 'The "Succession Doctrine" and the European Union', in A. Arnull et al. (eds.), *A Constitutional Order of States? Essays in Honour of Alan Dashwood* (Oxford: Hart, 2011), 459.

21 Case C-366/10 *Air Transport Association of America (ATAA)*, ECLI:EU:C:2011:864, para. 63 regarding the Convention on International Civil Aviation. See also C-301/09 *Bogiatzi*, ECLI: EU:C:2010:756 about the Convention for the Unification of Certain Rules Relating to International Carriage by Air; Case C-379/92 *Peralta*, ECLI:EU:C:1994:296, para. 16 and Case C-308/06 *Intertanko*, ECLI:EU:C:2008:312, para. 48, about the International Convention for the Prevention of Pollution from Ships of 1973, as supplemented by the Protocol of 17 February 1978; Case C-481/13 *Qurbani*, ECLI:EU:C:2014:2101 about Geneva Convention of 28 July 1951 and the Protocol of 31 January 1967 relating to the status of refugees.

Achmea, Advocate General Wathelet argued forcefully and convincingly that the answer was negative.[22] And the Court of Justice in Opinion 2/15 on the conclusion of the EU–Singapore Free Trade Agreement held that Title IV, Chapter 4 TFEU on free movement of capital does not confer on the EU exclusive competence in relation to portfolio investment.[23] The invalidity objection raised in relation to intra-EU BITs is not, therefore, fully substantiated.

There is also a broader problem with the invalidity objection: it appears to conflate the issue of competence with that of compatibility. It does not follow that the existence or emergence of EU competence would necessarily and automatically render other rules binding on member states invalid.[24] This confusion between competence and compatibility with EU law in cases where EU law interacts with other international legal regimes is also apparent in other areas. For instance, the line of reasoning in the judgement of the Court of Justice in *Mox Plant*[25] is based on the same misguided premise. The judgement engages in an esoteric and convoluted analysis of what the conclusion of the United Nations Convention on the Law of the Sea (UNCLOS) signified for the exercise of the Union's competence, even though the wide scope of the duty of cooperation had already been established.[26]

The above overview illustrates a somewhat maximalist approach to the interactions between EU law and international investment law that seeks to establish the precedence of the former on the basis of an exceedingly broad construction of the Union's competence. This approach does not engage with the subtleties of the specific context within which the Court of Justice has articulated the unique features of the EU legal order, neither does it explore any alternatives that would introduce greater tolerance of other international legal regimes.

We find this approach in the recent *Achmea* judgement that the Court rendered in March 2018. This is the first case where the Court of Justice has been asked directly to rule on the compatibility of intra-EU BITs with EU law. The case arose from a reference from the *Bundesgerichtshof*, before which an annulment action had been brought against the final award by an arbitral tribunal constituted under the BIT between the Netherlands and

[22] Case C-284/16, *Achmea*, ECLI:EU:C:2017:699, paras 179–228. In its judgement, the Court of Justice did not deal with the issue.

[23] ECLI:EU:C:2017:376.

[24] See also P. Strik, *Shaping the Single European Market in the Field of Foreign Direct Investment* (Oxford: Hart, 2014), 217.

[25] Case C-459/03, *Commission v Ireland*, ECLI:EU:C:2006:345.

[26] See the criticism in Koutrakos, *EU International Relations Law*, 185–186.

Czechoslovakia. This case is not about a substantive incompatibility between the intra-EU BIT in question and EU law. In fact, no such argument was put forward. This case raises, instead, a broader question of a constitutional nature: does the ISDS mechanism provided for in the Agreement[27] and pursuant to which the arbitral tribunal rendered its award violate three of the main tenets of EU law, namely the principle of non-discrimination (Article 18 TEU), the preliminary reference procedure (Article 267 TFEU) and the exclusive jurisdiction of the Court of Justice (Article 344 TFEU)?

In its judgement, the Court held that the arbitration procedure laid down in the intra-BIT was contrary both to the preliminary reference procedure and the exclusive jurisdiction of the Court of Justice (it did not examine its compatibility with the principle of non-discrimination). This conclusion was reached on the basis of three main considerations. Firstly, as arbitral tribunals take account of domestic law and international treaties between the contracting parties and given that EU law forms part of both of these sets of rules, arbitral tribunals may be called on to interpret or apply EU law (including provisions on the freedom of establishment and free movement of capital). Secondly, arbitral tribunals may not refer questions about the interpretation and application of EU law to the Court of Justice because they do not constitute parts of the judicial system of the contracting member states. Their decisions, therefore, are not subject to the mechanisms that ensure the full effectiveness of EU law. Thirdly, the decisions of arbitral tribunals are not subject to full judicial review by domestic courts, which may not, therefore, refer EU law issues pertaining to such decisions to the Court of Justice.

The language in *Achmea* is couched at a high level of abstraction and the central thread that underlies the judgement is the principle of autonomy. Introduced in the early constitutionalizing case law in order to safeguard the normative features of the then-nascent legal order from challenges from domestic law,[28] autonomy has become prominent in later case law as a shield from interferences from international law.[29] It is on that later case law that the judgement draws, and in particular the much criticized Opinion 2/13,[30]

[27] Art. 8 of the BIT between the Netherlands and Czechoslovakia.

[28] See J. W. van Rossem, 'The Autonomy of EU Law: More Is Less?' in R. A. Wessel and S. Blockmans (eds.), *Between Autonomy and Dependence – The EU Legal Order under the Influence of International Organisations* (Dordrecht: Springer, 2013), 13.

[29] See the overview in J. Odermatt, 'The Principle of Autonomy: An Adolescent Disease of EU External Relations Law?' in M. Cremona (ed.), *Structural Principles in EU External Relations Law* (Oxford: Hart, 2018), 291.

[30] Opinion 2/13 (*ECHR*), ECLI:EU:C:2014:2454. See, amongst others, B. De Witte and Š. Imamovic, 'Opinion 2/13 on Accession to the ECHR: Defending the EU Legal Order against a

where the Court concluded that the draft agreement on the Union's accession to the European Convention on Human Rights (ECHR) was contrary to the principle of autonomy.

In its construction of the principle, the judgement in *Achmea* illustrates a most orthodox reading of the orthodoxy of EU law. This is characterized by a degree of formalism. Take, for instance, the argument that arbitral tribunals may rule on the interpretation or application of EU law. This may well be the case, however in practice the jurisdiction of arbitral tribunals is confined to the interpretation and application of the BITs pursuant to which a dispute has been brought before them, and their approach to EU law matters may not bind either the EU or the Member States as a matter of EU law. The judgement in *Achmea* may appear to suggest that every time an EU law issue pertains to a dispute before any international tribunal, the autonomy of the EU legal order would be at stake and the Court's exclusive jurisdiction would need to be triggered. The implications of such a maximalist position would be striking, especially in light of the nuanced approach of the Arbitral Tribunal itself in *Achmea*, which had pointed out that "[w]hat the ECJ has is a monopoly on the final and authoritative interpretation of EU law."[31]

It follows from the above that the criterion we find in the judgement for ascertaining consistency with EU law (May an EU law issue related to the dispute be brought before an arbitral tribunal?) is too broad. As such, it enables the Court to construe the reach of the EU legal order in similarly broad terms and to articulate an antagonistic relationship with international investment law. A narrower criterion (May an arbitral award bind a member state to a given interpretation of EU law?) would provide a more nuanced picture of the interactions between EU, international and national law. It would also lead to a different approach to inter-legality: rather than conflict, it would be about managing the coexistence of EU and international investment law. Such an alternative approach is at least arguable. It was suggested by Advocate General Wathelet in his Opinion in *Achmea* (ignored completely by the Court) and will be examined in Section 4 below. It is also suggested by the Commission and the Council themselves, albeit in an extra-EU BIT: CETA includes a domestic law clause that makes it clear that the Investment

Foreign Human Rights Court', (2015) 40 *European Law Review* 683; S. Peers, 'The EU's Accession to the ECHR: The Dream Becomes a Nightmare', (2015) 16 *German Law Journal* 213; and E. Spaventa, 'A Very Fearful Court? The Protection of Fundamental Rights in the European Union after Opinion 2/13', (2015) 22 *Maastricht Journal of European and Comparative Law* 35.

[31] PCA Case No 2008-13, *Eureko B.V v Slovak Republic*, Award on Jurisdiction, Arbitrability and Suspension (26 October 2010), para. 282.

Tribunal established under its provisions would not bind the parties to any meaning it may give to domestic law.[32] The consistency of this clause with EU law is the subject matter of the pending request for an Opinion pursuant to Article 288(11) TFEU.

There is a thread, therefore, that brings together the Commission's approach to intra-EU BITs and the judgement in *Achmea*: it views inter-legality as a space for conflict between EU and international investment law, as a threat that EU law may only address on the basis of an expansive reading of what the Court understands the principle of autonomy to be about. The context within which this approach has been adopted – namely in treaty relations between member states – is quite specific: it highlights any potential conflict with EU law more starkly, given the constitutionalized setting within which relations between member states are regulated. In *Achmea*, for instance, we find references to the principle of mutual trust to which the intra-EU BIT provision for arbitration runs counter,[33] as well as an effort in the final paragraphs of the judgement to distinguish between intra-EU and extra-EU agreements.[34] The judgement, however, is couched in such abstract terms that it invites its own misreading. Be that as it may, the following sections will examine alternative approaches to inter-legality, where conflict may give way to pragmatism.

3 PRAGMATISM AND INTEGRATION: MANAGING THE INTERNATIONAL OBLIGATIONS OF THE MEMBER STATES

If we stepped beyond the intra-EU setting examined in the above section, we find another context within which the clash between international investment and EU law emerges in BITs concluded by member states with third countries (extra-BITs). The legal position of these agreements became controversial after the Treaty of Lisbon had entered into force. This was because investment had been included for the first time within the scope of the Common

[32] [2017] OJ L 11/23, Art. 8.31(2) CETA: "The Tribunal shall not have jurisdiction to determine the legality of a measure, alleged to constitute a breach of this Agreement, under the domestic law of the disputing Party. For greater certainty, in determining the consistency of a measure with this Agreement, the Tribunal may consider, as appropriate, the domestic law of the disputing Party as a matter of fact. In doing so, the Tribunal shall follow the prevailing interpretation given to the domestic law by the courts or authorities of that Party and any meaning given to domestic law by the Tribunal shall not be binding upon the courts or the authorities of that Party."

[33] Case C-284/16 *Achmea*, paras 34 and 58.

[34] Ibid., para. 58,

Commercial Policy pursuant to Article 207 TFEU. As the EU had been endowed with express external competence in the area, and given the exclusive nature of this competence,[35] the power of the member states to retain investment agreements appeared to be incompatible with EU law. This was not an insignificant matter, given that approximately 1,400 agreements concluded by member states were in force.

And yet the EU did not demand that such agreements be revoked. Instead, it introduced a set of transitional arrangements that brought the management and amendment of the BITs that the member states had concluded within the scope of EU law. Adopted in 2012, Regulation 1219/2012 (the 'Grandfathering Regulation') provides for the maintenance in force and amendment of existing as well as the negotiation and conclusion of new BITs under certain conditions.[36] It establishes a procedural framework at the centre of which is the Commission itself. On the one hand, existing agreements are authorized by the Commission following their notification by all the member states. Such authorization may be granted notwithstanding the Union's competence in the area[37] and without prejudice to other EU law obligations of the member states.[38] The Commission reviews the notified agreements in order to assess whether they are compatible with EU law, they overlap with an agreement that the Union negotiates or they constitute an obstacle to the development and implementation of the Union's investment policies. These would also constitute grounds for withdrawal of an authorization by the Commission.

On the other hand, the amendment of an existing BIT or the conclusion of a new BIT is also subject to authorization following a notification by the member state concerned. Such notification[39] should be submitted at least five months prior to the commencement of the negotiations. This information is then disseminated to the other member states, and, within three months, the Commission ascertains whether to authorize the opening of formal negotiations. Such an assessment would depend on whether the opening of negotiations would be in conflict with EU law, whether it would be superfluous in the light of imminent negotiations of an EU agreement, whether it is inconsistent with the EU's principles and objectives for external action or whether it

[35] Art. 3(1)(e) TFEU.
[36] Reg. 1219/2012 establishing transitional arrangements for bilateral investment agreements between member states and third countries, [2012] OJ L 351/40.
[37] See Preamble 3 and Art. 1 of Reg. 1219/2012.
[38] Ibid., Art. 3.
[39] The notification should cover the provisions to be addressed in the negotiations, the objectives of the negotiations and any other relevant information.

constitutes a serious obstacle to the negotiation or conclusion of BITs with third countries by the EU. All BITs notified to the Commission are published annually.[40]

The Grandfathering Regulation is but an example of member states being empowered to exercise powers that primary law is deemed to have conferred on the Union. In fact, the notion of authorizing member states to act in areas of EU-exclusive competence is intrinsically linked to the notion of exclusivity. When the Court of Justice held – 33 years prior to the entry into force of the Lisbon Treaty – that the Union's competence in Common Commercial Policy was exclusive, it also held that member states could act autonomously "only ... by virtue of specific authorisation by the Community."[41] Viewed from this angle, the approach illustrated by the Grandfathering Regulation is not novel. If we stepped back even farther, we would also find other contexts where, whilst acting autonomously under international law, member states act on behalf of the EU. This may be the case in the context of an international organization that covers an area that falls, even partly, within the Union's competence, but whose membership is not open to other international organizations.[42] In such instances, whilst the EU may not become a member under international law, it relies on its member states that are members and are bound to pursue the Union's interests in the context of the organization in question. In doing so, they are subject to rigorous duties that stem from the duty of cooperation and have been interpreted by the Court in exceedingly broad terms.[43]

What the Grandfathering Regulation does is lay down a set of rules and procedures of considerable scope and intensity in order to manage the interactions between member states and the Commission. It refers not only to the opening of negotiations and the signature and conclusion of BITs, but also to the application of such agreements. In the process of the negotiation of a BIT, for instance, the Commission may require that a member state include any appropriate clauses and may request to participate in the negotiations. As for the application of the agreement, the Commission must be kept informed without undue delay of all meetings under existing BITs and is entitled to

[40] For the more recent list, see [2018] OJ C 149/1.

[41] Case 41/76, *Donckerwolcke*, ECLI:EU:C:1976:182, para. 33.

[42] See, for instance, the International Labour Organisation.

[43] See Case C-45/07, *Commission v Greece (IMO)*, ECLI:EU:C:2009:81 and Opinion 1/13 (Hague Convention on the Civil Aspects of the International Child Abduction), ECLI:EU:C:2014:2303. See M. Cremona, 'Member States As Trustees of the Union Interest: Participating in International Agreements on Behalf of the European Union', in Arnull et al. (eds.), *Essays in Honour of Alan Dashwood*, 435, and Koutrakos, *EU International Relations Law*, 196–200.

require that the member state concerned take a particular position. Similarly, any dispute that may arise about the application of a BIT must be notified to the Commission, which may even require that it participate in any settlement procedure. Its agreement is also required prior to the activation of any dispute settlement mechanisms included in the BIT by the member state concerned.

In other words, the Grandfathering Regulation does not reserve for the Commission the role of a distant and neutral assessor. Instead, it enables the Union's executive to be quite intrusive in all phases of the negotiation, conclusion and application of BITs concluded by member states. This role is viewed as flowing directly from the overall function of the Commission as the guardian of the EU Treaties. The degree of intensity that characterizes the regime governing the management of international treaties concluded by member states illustrates the strong integrating dimension of these rules. This model of integration does not amount to substituting international rules binding on member states with EU rules. Instead, it is about managing the application of international rules within an EU framework on the basis of an intensely proceduralized set of rules. In essence, therefore, integration in this case is about the coexistence of international rules that bind the member states, but not the EU, with EU law. Put differently, the Grandfathering Regulation is about managing inter-legality in a manner that would preserve the integrity of the EU legal order without interfering with the formal existence and application of international law.

There are two main factors that explain the emergence of this model of managing inter-legality. The first is legal and is about the extension of the Union's Common Commercial Policy (CCP) to cover investment at Lisbon. Article 207 TFEU refers to foreign direct investment, which is about the maintenance of lasting and direct links, and does not cover, therefore, portfolio investment, which is about the movement of private equity for personal gain and without the element of lasting influence. When the Treaty of Lisbon entered into force, however, the scope of the Union's exclusive competence to conclude international agreements in the area of investment was shrouded in uncertainty. On the one hand, the scope of foreign direct investment itself (which was covered by Article 207 TFEU) was not clear. For instance, would it cover only the admission of foreign investment and the establishment of investors, or would it also extend to the post-admission treatment of foreign investors, including the principle of fair and equitable treatment?[44] On the

[44] See A. Dimopoulos, *EU Foreign Investment Law* (Oxford: Oxford University Press, 2011), 47–61. For a restrictive approach, see M. Krajewski, 'The Reform of the Common Commercial Policy', in A. Biondi, P. Eeckhout and S. Ripley (eds.), *EU Law After Lisbon*

other hand, the Commission was arguing that the Union's competence in the area of foreign investment had already become exclusive, as the EU rules on the free movement of capital, which applied to movement from and to a third country too, had given rise to implied exclusivity.[45] It follows from the above that the scope of what the Union could do post-Lisbon on the international scene in the area of investment was contested. This state of uncertainty had implications for the member states, as it would strengthen their determination to retain and exercise their power to apply their investment treaties.

The second factor that explains the integration model illustrated by the Grandfathering Regulation follows from the above, and is practical: the determination of investment policy may not come about on the basis of a single policy measure. It requires a careful weighing of various economic, policy and political considerations and entails a long and complex process that involves a range of different actors. In other words, the entry into force of the Lisbon Treaty on 1 December 2009 and the endowment of the Union with exclusive competence in certain areas of foreign investment by no means gave rise to a Union investment policy. Practical exigencies, therefore, would have rendered the possibility of a member state revoking parts of its BITs in the light of the Union's exclusive competence and in anticipation of a Union approach inconceivable. Investors could not possibly be left in a vacuum, as legal uncertainty would undermine investor confidence.

The significance of the above practical considerations was acknowledged by the Commission. In a communication it adopted in July 2010, it suggested that the determination of the Union's investment policy is a 'gradual and targeted' process that requires time and needs to take a number of factors into account:[46] "While it is the Union's responsibility to promote the European model and the single market as a destination for foreign investors, . . . it seems neither feasible nor desirable to replace the investment promotion efforts of Member States, as long as they fit with the common commercial policy and remain consistent with EU law."[47]

This practical factor suggests that pragmatism was paramount for dealing with the interactions between the international obligations of the member states on the one hand, and the emerging policy of the Union on the other

(Oxford: Oxford University Press, 2012), 292, at 303–304. For a broad approach, see P. Eeckhout, *EU External Relations Law*, 2nd edn (Oxford: Oxford University Press, 2011), 64–65.

45 COM (2010) 343 fin *Towards a Comprehensive European International Investment Policy* (Brussels, 7 July 2010), at 8.

46 Ibid., at 2.

47 Ibid., at 6.

hand. The central role of pragmatism in the area also emerges clearly in relation to the legal factor outlined above. This becomes apparent in the aftermath of Opinion 2/15 on the signing and conclusion of the Free Trade Agreement between the EU and Singapore.[48] In this ruling, the Court of Justice interpreted the scope of foreign direct investment under Article 207 TFEU broadly, whereas it held that the TFEU provisions on movement of capital did not give rise to implied exclusive competence in the area of portfolio investment.

It is noteworthy that the main question that this division of powers has raised for policy-makers is in relation to future agreements that the EU negotiates: should these be concluded as mixed agreements (given that, in addition to portfolio investment, the Court held in Opinion 2/15 that provisions on ISDS fall beyond the Union's exclusive competence)? Or should the investment provisions be removed from free trade agreements in order to enable the EU to conclude the latter without the participation of the member states?[49] The emphasis of the post-Opinion 2/15 debate is not on the implications of the ruling for the international obligations that the member states have already assumed. These are deemed to have been dealt with satisfactorily pursuant to the model of integration illustrated by the Grandfathering Regulation. In other words, the clarification of the legal landscape has not done away with the pragmatic function of the transitional arrangements already agreed upon in relation to member states' extra-EU BITs.

The analysis of the model of integration discussed in this section raises a further question: does the term 'integration' sit comfortably with the maintenance of both the existing agreements and the power of the member states to amend them? Put differently, does the approach adopted in the Grandfathering Regulation not question the extent to which the management of the international obligations of the member states have been Europeanized? The answer to this question is negative on two grounds. First, the intensity of the procedural duties that the Regulation imposes on national authorities and the direct involvement of the Commission in the process of application, amendment and negotiation of the relevant BITs suggest a rigorous legal context within which international investment law and EU law interact. Second, the agreements dealt with by the Grandfathering Regulation are viewed by the Union's institutions as fully within the EU's emerging

48 ECLI:EU:C:2017:376.

49 After the writing of this chapter was completed, the agreement with Singapore was split into two: a trade agreement to which only the EU is a party and an investment protection agreement that is mixed.

investment policy. This is illustrated by the Commission's proposal for the negotiation of a Convention establishing a multilateral court for the settlement of investment disputes that refers to the above agreements expressly.[50]

4 ACCEPTANCE AND COEXISTENCE: ENSURING THE HARMONIOUS INTERACTIONS BETWEEN EU LAW AND INTRA-EU BITS

The analysis has explored two different approaches to the management of inter-legality in the area of international investment and EU law that emerge in different contexts. In the context of intra-EU BITs, we find an understanding of inter-legality in conflictual terms, which is underpinned by a strong concern for the autonomy of the EU legal order. In the context of extra-EU BITs, a pragmatic understanding of the limits of EU action prevails and is translated in a set of rigorous substantive and procedural rules that govern the coexistence of international and EU law.

It is not, however, context that necessarily dictates the Union's response. In fact, a more harmonious construction of inter-legality is possible even in the context of intra-EU agreements. This was illustrated by the Opinion of Advocate General Wathelet in *Achmea*.[51] While ignored by the Court, this Opinion is worth examining, as it articulates a thoughtful understanding of managing inter-legality in the area. It suggests that the right of investors to rely upon arbitral tribunals in order to enforce intra-EU BITs is in full compliance with EU law. The main thrust of his argument is threefold. First, the principle of non-discrimination is not violated, as intra-EU BITs are similar to double taxation treaties, which have been viewed by the Court as consistent with EU law.[52] Second, arbitral tribunals established by an intra-EU BIT meet all the requirements necessary for them to be considered courts or tribunals in the meaning of Article 267 TFEU[53] and, as they are common to the two member states that are parties to the treaty in question,[54] they are

[50] COM (2017) 493 fin *Recommendation for a Council Decision Authorising the Opening of Negotiations for a Convention Establishing a Multilateral Court for the Settlement of Investment Disputes* (Brussels, 13 September 2017).

[51] Case C-284/16, *Achmea*, ECLI:EU:C:2017:699.

[52] Case C-376/03, *D*, ECLI:EU:C:2005:424. This was a point that was not examined by the Court.

[53] The requirements are set out in Case C-54/96, *Dorsch Consult*, ECLI:EU:C:1997:413, para. 23, and have been reaffirmed ever since (e.g., Case C-394/11, *Belov*, ECLI:EU:C:2013:48, para. 38).

[54] See Case C-337/95, *Parfums Christian Dior*, ECLI:EU:C:1997:517, para. 21, where a court established under an international treaty concluded between the BENELUX countries was deemed to be in the same position as courts of tribunals in the meaning of Art. 267 TFEU. Advocate General Wathelet had expressed this view briefly in his Opinion in CJEU, Case C-567/14, *Genentech*, ECLI:EU:C:2016:177, footnote 34 (considering arbitral tribunals as

bound by this provision as far as the application and interpretation of EU law is concerned. Third, the role of arbitral tribunals pursuant to intra-EU BITs does not violate the Court's exclusive jurisdiction under Article 344 TFEU, as they are required to respect the principles of EU law, failing which the member states would be liable in damages[55] and subject to enforcement actions by the Commission and other member states.[56]

The Opinion was viewed at the time as "shockingly firm"[57] and "a remarkable defence of ISDS."[58] From the point of view of inter-legality, the approach adopted by Advocate General Wathelet illustrates a symbiotic relationship between intra-BITs and EU law. It understands them as two distinct legal spheres, the interactions of which need not threaten the functioning of either. In developing this approach, his line of reasoning is characterized by two main features. The first is a strong realist streak that anchors the Opinion on the practice of arbitral tribunals set up under intra-EU BITs. This is apparent in different contexts. Advocate General Wathelet points out that "the systemic risk which, according to the Commission, intra-EU BITs represent to the uniformity and effectiveness of EI law is greatly exaggerated"[59]; he refers to United Nations Conference on Trade and Development's (UNCTAD) statistics, according to which investors have been successful in only 16.1 per cent of intra-EU BIT arbitral proceedings over several decades,[60] and he points out that in none of these cases were arbitral tribunals required to review the validity of EU measures or the compatibility of domestic measures with EU law.[61] Furthermore, he refers to *Micula* as the single case where an arbitral award is viewed as contrary to EU law (and even that case he views as irrelevant as EU law was not applicable, given that Romania had not acceded to the EU when the arbitration commenced).[62]

The second feature of the analysis in the Opinion is the avoidance of grand teleological arguments. This is in stark contrast to the judgement of the Court

courts common to a number of member states for the purposes of Art. 267 TFEU "could help to ensure the correct and effective implementation of EU law").

55 Case C-224/01, *Köbler*, ECLI:EU:C:2003:513.

56 Arts 258 and 259 TFEU.

57 I. Dimitrov, 'Digesting the AG Wathelet Opinion in Case C-284/16 *Slowakische Republik v Achmea BV*. Is It a Trap?' Available at http://arbitrationblog.kluwerarbitration.com/2017/10/07/digesting-ag-wathelet-opinion-case-c-28416-slowakische-republik-v-achmea-bv-trap.

58 A. Carta and L. Ankersmit, 'AG Wathelet in C-284/16 Achmea: Savind ISDS?' Available at https://europeanlawblog.eu/tag/ag-wathelet-in-c-28416-achmea.

59 Para. 44 of the Opinion, and again in para. 45.

60 Para. 44 of the Opinion.

61 Para. 45 of the Opinion.

62 Para. 45 and n49 of the Opinion.

and the high level of abstraction in which it is couched. Whilst setting out an open approach to the coexistence of intra-BITs and EU law, the Advocate General puts forward arguments that are based on the strict and textual wording of the law. For instance, he argues that Article 344 TFEU does not support the exclusive jurisdiction argument because it refers to member states only, and therefore does not cover actions brought by individuals (a point that was ignored by the Court in its judgement).[63] In a similar vein, his construction of the intra-EU BITs as being in a symbiotic relationship with EU law draws upon the limited purview of the jurisdiction of arbitral tribunals that does not cover the validity of EU measures under EU law. It is also based on the capacity of EU law to deal with any threats to autonomy that may emerge, as the structures and principles laid down in the Treaties are sufficient to absorb any tensions that may arise, such as in the context of the preliminary reference procedure (Article 267 TFEU) and the principle of state liability.

There is a thread that brings together the approach outlined above and the position that the Court of Justice took in the *Kadi* litigation regarding the application of EU law human rights standards to EU measures adopted pursuant to United Nations Security Council (UNSC) resolutions.[64] It is recalled that this line of case law is based on the assumption that the Court of Justice lacks jurisdiction to review the lawfulness of a UNSC resolution, even on grounds of compliance with *jus cogens*, and that therefore:

> … any judgment given by the Community judicature deciding that a Community measure intended to give effect to such a resolution is contrary to a higher rule of law in the Community legal order would not entail any challenge to the primacy of that resolution in international law.[65]

The approach set out in *Kadi* was criticized as 'inward-looking' and at odds with "the self-presentation of the EU as an organization which maintains particular fidelity to international law and institutions."[66] And yet, the logic of this approach is based on the premise that the special status of the Treaties establishing the EU and the autonomy of the EU legal order would not be

63 See also his narrow reading of Opinion 2/13, which had found a violation of Article 344 TFEU in relation to actions brought between member states or by member states against the EU, but not by individuals: paras 151–152 of the Opinion (with reference to paras 201–214 of Opinion 2/13).

64 Joined Cases C-402/05 P and C-415/05 P, *Kadi and Al Barakaat International Foundations*, ECLI:EU:C:2008:461.

65 Ibid., para. 288.

66 G. de Búrca, 'The ECJ and the International Legal Order: A Re-Evaluation', in G. de Búrca and J. H. H. Weiler (eds.), *The Worlds of European Constitutionalism* (Cambridge: Cambridge University Press, 2012), 105, at 140.

seen as a threat to the principle of international law and the hierarchies that this has introduced.[67] Put differently, the latter may coexist with the EU legal order without diluting the unique features of either, especially given the context within which this approach was adopted and the widely contested nature of the UN listing rules in question.[68] This understanding of the interactions between public international law and EU law, which underpins the entire body of the Court's case law on smart sanctions,[69] is also borne out by the practical implications of *Kadi* insofar as at no point during the long saga was the EU forced to ignore the UN measures requiring that member states freeze the relevant assets.[70] The pronouncement of the illegality of the EU implementing regulations did not, therefore, entail a violation of international law by the member states.

It is this notion of coexistence that we see in the Opinion in *Achmea* on the interactions of international investment law and EU law. The approach adopted by Advocate General Wathelet may appear somewhat paradoxical: whilst he acknowledges the dispute settlement regime laid down in intra-EU BITs as autonomous from and in compliance with the EU legal order, this is so because the latter is viewed as powerful enough to impose its discipline on arbitral tribunals. After all, the possibility of state liability for a violation of EU law is about bringing the conduct of arbitral tribunals into the purview of the EU legal order. Does this not condition the coexistence that the learned Advocate General appears to sanction by subjugating one legal regime to the other?

The answer to this question is negative. After all, we see a similar approach to the coexistence of intra-EU BITs with EU law in arbitral Tribunals. In *Euram*, for instance,[71] whilst the Tribunal rejected all the jurisdictional objections put forward by both the Commission and Slovakia about the application of the BIT to Austrian investors, it made it clear that it had no

67 See also the analysis in G. Pavlakos and J. Pauwelyn, 'Principled Monism and the Normative Conception of Coercion under International Law', in M. Evans and P. Koutrakos (eds.), *Beyond the Established Legal Orders: Policy Interconnections between the EU and the Rest of the World* (Oxford: Hart, 2011), 317.

68 This point is analysed in Koutrakos, *EU International Relations Law*, 223–226.

69 See Case C-548/09 P, *Bank Melli Iran v Council*, ECLI:EU:C:2011:735, para. 105, and Joined Cases C-584/10 P, C-593/10 P and C-595/10 P, *Kadi II*, ECLI:EU:C:2013:518, para. 67.

70 The point is made in J. Larik, 'EU Counter-Terrorism and the "Strict Observance" of International Law: Sewing the Seamless Coat of Compliance', in E. Herlin-Karnell and C. Matera (eds.), *External Dimension of the EU Counter-Terrorism Policy* (2014) CLEER Working Paper 2014/2 33.

71 *European American Investment Bank AG v Slovakia*, PCA Case No. 2010-17, Award on Jurisdiction (22 October 2012), at para. 263.

power to determine the validity of an act of an EU institution. It also pointed out that "if a Member State were minded to enforce an arbitral award that would violate EU law, tools remain in the hands of the EU institutions – and particularly the ECJ – to ensure a proper application of EU law."[72] We find this approach in *Achmea* too, where the Arbitral Tribunal refers to its "clear and fixed limitation on [its] jurisdiction," which does not extend the power to rule on alleged breaches of EU law.[73] It is this line of reasoning that we see in the Advocate General's Opinion in *Achmea* too.

In any case, whilst understood as two separate legal regimes, ISDSs under intra-EU BITs and EU law are connected by a factor that they have in common and is essential to their functioning, namely domestic courts. In his Opinion, Advocate General Wathelet stresses the role of domestic courts in the enforcement of arbitral awards and therefore in ensuring that no incompatibility with EU law would arise. As for their contribution to EU law, it is not for nothing that they have been described as 'the powerhouse' of the EU legal order.[74] After all, the Court of Justice itself refers to them as "guardians of th[e EU] legal order and the judicial system of the European Union."[75] Their position in the management of inter-legality will be examined in the following section.

5 THE ROLE OF DOMESTIC COURTS

The role of domestic courts emerges as a significant component of managing the symbiotic relationship between international investment protection and EU law. It is recalled, for instance, that the case in *Achmea* arose from a preliminary reference by the German *Bundesgerichtshof*. After all, it is domestic courts that are often caught in the middle when it comes to the parallel application of these two legal regimes.

The role of domestic courts is illustrated with striking clarity in the *Achmea* case, albeit from two contrasting perspectives. In the judgement, it emerges as the main reason for rejecting the legality of intra-EU BITs under EU law. It is their jurisdiction to interpret and apply EU law under Article 19 TEU that the Court claims to protect, as the binding nature of arbitral awards is deemed to prevent them from exercising unlimited judicial review and

72 Ibid., para. 264.

73 PCA Case No. 2008-13, *Achmea*, Award on Jurisdiction, Arbitrability and Suspension (26 October 2010), para. 290.

74 D. Edward, 'National Courts – The Powerhouse of Community Law', (2002–2003) 5 *Cambridge Yearbook of European Legal Studies* 1.

75 Opinion 1/09 (*European and Community Patents Courts*), ECLI:EU:C:2011:123, para. 66.

making a reference under Article 267 TFEU.[76] There is delicious irony in the Court's concern that ISDSs would deprive domestic courts of their jurisdiction to refer, given that the *Achmea* judgement itself was in response to a reference by the *Bundesgerichtshof*. This is not the first time that the Court of Justice has stressed the rights of domestic courts in order to substantiate its own strong reading of autonomy of EU law. In fact, this is a thread that underpins the more recent rulings on the interactions between EU and international law. A case in point is Opinion 1/09 where a draft agreement on a unified patent litigation system was found to impinge on the rights of domestic courts to refer issues of EU law to the Court of Justice under Article 267 TFEU.[77] There is no analysis of Article 344 TFEU in the *Achmea* judgement. Instead, the Court appears to be a zealous guardian of the jurisdiction of domestic courts.

At the other end of the spectrum, Advocate General Wathelet suggests that the existing rules enable domestic courts to play a central role in the management of inter-legality. After all, it is they that enforce arbitral awards and, in the process, may be faced with difficult questions about the relationship between international investment and EU law. And it is they that may control the enforcement of such awards on the basis of their compatibility with public policy.[78] In other words, the role with which international investment law endows domestic courts enables the latter to rely upon EU law and act as EU law courts, hence safeguarding the autonomy of the EU legal order.

There is a recent case that illustrates quite how domestic courts may assume this constructive role. This has arisen in the context of the *Micula* litigation (which makes it all the more interesting given that, according to Advocate General Wathelet, *Micula* is the only case so far suggesting that the enforcement of an arbitral award pursuant to an intra-EU BIT might give rise to a substantive incompatibility with EU law). Having obtained an arbitral award in their favour, the claimants sought to enforce it before, amongst others, English courts. The award was registered in the High Court by means of an

[76] See *Achmea*, paras 36, 50 and 55.

[77] Opinion 1/09; see P. Koutrakos, 'The Court of Justice as the Guardian of National Courts – Or Not?' (2011) 36 *European Law Review* 319.

[78] In Case C-126/97, *Eco Swiss*, ECLI:EU:C:1999:269, it was held that a domestic court could refuse to enforce an arbitral award on public policy grounds, including compliance with the EU's competition and state aid rules. This public policy exception is allowed under international rules governing investment arbitration (Art. V (2)(b) of the 1958 Convention for the Recognition and Enforcement of Foreign Arbitral Awards), but not all of them (Art. 53(1) International Centre for Settlement of Investment Disputes Convention).

Order pursuant to the domestic law implementing the International Centre for the Settlement of Investment Disputes (ICSID) Convention in the United Kingdom.[79] The Order was challenged by the Romanian Government, supported by the Commission, on EU law grounds.

In January 2017, the High Court rejected the Romanian appeal, but granted a stay of enforcement proceedings pending the resolution by the General Court (the first-instance court of the EU) of the annulment action against the Commission's Decision that had found the enforcement of the award to constitute payment of unlawful state aid.[80] This decision was based on a distinction between registration and enforcement of the arbitral award: while necessary under domestic law implementing ICSID, registration did not amount to enforcement and could not, therefore, give rise to the risk of a conflict between decisions of domestic and EU institutions. This was not the case with the enforcement of the award, as it hinged on the determination of issues pending before the EU courts. Mr Justice Blair equated the award, following its registration under English law, to a final domestic judgement. As domestic courts are bound by EU law and the duty of cooperation, the High Court

> ... cannot therefore proceed to enforce the judgment consequent on registration of the Award in circumstances in which the Commission has prohibited Romania from making any payment under the Award to the claimants because in doing so, the court would, in effect, be acting unlawfully. This does not (in the court's view) create a conflict with the international obligations of the UK as contained in the 1966 Arbitration Act implementing the ICSID Convention in UK law, because a purely domestic judgment would be subject to the same limitation.[81]

This is an elegant and deeply pragmatic approach: on the one hand, it seeks to comply with EU law and take seriously the obligations under which domestic courts function; on the other hand, it is faithful to the letter of the international commitments assumed by the United Kingdom in the context of ICSID. This is by no means the only example of a domestic court seeking to reconcile the obligations that result from different supranational legal regimes, neither is international investment protection and EU law the only case where domestic courts are called upon to engage in this at times delicate exercise. Another case in point is the position of domestic courts in the area of asylum

79 Arbitration (International Investment Disputes) Act 1966.

80 After the writing of this chapter was completed, the Court of Appeal upheld the judgement ([2018] EWCA Civ 1801) and found its conclusion "pragmatic" and "principled" (para. 249).

81 Ibid., para. 132.

protection and in the light of the ECHR and EU law.[82] This is an area where two at first sight irreconcilable strands of case law have emerged. On the one hand, the Court of Justice has interpreted the principle of mutual confidence, which is the very foundation of the Dublin Regulation that governs asylum applications,[83] broadly and would only allow deviations in the light of systemic deficiencies, a term that it has construed narrowly.[84] On the other hand, the European Court of Human Rights (ECtHR) appeared to prescribe a considerably lower threshold, as it required "a thorough and individualized examination of the situation of the person concerned" in the context of transfers under the Dublin Regulation.[85] In doing so, the ECtHR did not refer to the strict approach to exceptions from the principle of mutual trust adopted by the Court of Justice in Case C-394/12, *Abdullahi*. How is this circle to be squared? English courts have been trying to square this circle by reading both lines of case law narrowly and within their specific factual and legal contexts.[86] In doing so, they show acute awareness of the need to comply with the international obligations assumed by the state whilst bringing any differences that emerge from parallel developments of international case law under different legal regimes.

The examples mentioned above illustrate the comity that domestic courts may show in order to manage compliance with international obligations that may appear to be, at first sight, irreconcilable. Whilst comity by international and transnational tribunals is essential for the tensions between different legal regimes to be managed effectively without compromising the integrity of the respective sets of rules,[87] it is also necessary for the function of domestic courts. After all, had the *Bundesgerichtshof* declined to refer in *Achmea* and had the High Court refused to stay proceedings in *Micula*, the challenges of the

[82] On the challenges of inter-legality and human rights protection, see Chapter 14.

[83] Regulation 343/2003 [2003] OJ L 50/1.

[84] See Case C-411/10, *NS*, ECLI:EU:C:2011:865, paras 80–86; Case C-4/11, *Puid*, ECLI:EU:C:2013:740, para. 30, and *Abdullahi*, para 60.

[85] *Tarakhel v Switzerland*, Application No. 29217/12, 4 November 2014, para. 104.

[86] See *MS, NA, SG v The Secretary of State for the Home Department* [2015] EWHC 1095 (Admin) paras 137–138, and *R (Yosief Weldegaber) v Secretary of State for the Home Department* [2015] UKUT 70(IAC), para. 15. See also the Supreme Court's judgement in *EM (Eritrea)* [2014] UKSC 12, where the CJEU's judgement in *Abdullahi* is not taken into account, even though it had been rendered two months earlier.

[87] See P. Koutrakos, 'The Relevance of EU Law for Arbitral Tribunals: (Not) Managing the Lingering Tension', (2016) 17 *Journal of World Investment and Trade* 873. For comity in relation to the role of the Court of Justice, see A. Skordas, 'Völkerrechtsfreundlichkeit as Comity and the Disquiet of Neoformalism: A Response to Jan Klabbers', in P. Koutrakos (ed.), *European Foreign Policy: Legal and Political Perspectives* (Cheltenham: Edward Elgar, 2011), 115.

symbiosis between intra-EU BITs and EU law would have been felt more acutely. Similarly, had the English courts become more creative and selective in ensuring compliance with ECHR and EU obligations, the application of the Dublin Regulation would have been undermined and the ECtHR and the Court of Justice would have been put in a difficult position. This is, after all, yet another practical reason that underlines the role of domestic courts in the functioning of inter-legality: they give the transnational courts both the opportunity and space to shape the interactions between their respective legal orders.

6 CONCLUSION

This chapter examined an area that is still evolving. The interactions between international investment law and EU law give rise to challenges that are yet to be dealt with fully and are currently under review by both domestic courts and the courts of the EU. Drawing on recent policy and judicial practice, the analysis here conceptualized three possible approaches to the interactions between these areas of law. Ranging from conflict to integration to harmonious coexistence, these approaches emerge in different contexts and are still under development.

Their analysis raises three main points. First, there are no hard and fast rules as to what inter-legality entails in different areas of interacting legal regimes. In the field covered in this chapter, different facets of these interactions give rise to different challenges, and their management depends on, amongst others, the legal, political and policy circumstances that may prevail at the time and therefore give rise to context-specific answers. There is, in other words, a certain fluidity that characterizes what inter-legality means in practice, and this has consequences for our effort to articulate general rules about how best to deal with it.

Second, the management of inter-legality may entail reliance upon strikingly contrasting approaches. Principled objection and pragmatic coexistence may offer different – albeit parallel – ways of tackling the challenges of inter-legality. The well-documented quest by certain EU institutions for broadening the Union's competence both in law and in fact does not rule out a more conciliatory approach to the ways in which EU law interacts with international investment law on the basis of political constraints and practical considerations.

Third, while this chapter suggested subtler ways of achieving coexistence between the two sets of rules on the basis of mechanisms of mutual accommodation that would not undermine the fundamental features of either, to strive for harmonious coexistence is to make a leap of faith. It is to assume that the main actors in each legal regime would show comity and avoid tensions that would challenge the limits of each other's authority. In his approach in *Achmea*, for instance, Advocate General Wathelet assumes that arbitral tribunals would be willing to play the role that he envisages for them in the context of the application of Article 267 TFEU. He also assumes that, just because there has not been a major substantive clash between intra-EU BITs and EU law, there would not be one in the future. No such leap of faith was envisaged by the Court of Justice, where even the theoretical possibility of a clash would render the coexistence of the jurisdiction of arbitral tribunals and EU law mechanisms intolerable. Put differently, the notion of harmonious coexistence requires a shared understanding of how best to manage interacting sets of rules. And this may not always be taken for granted.

10

The Perils of Complacency

The European Human Rights Backlash

ANDRÁS SAJÓ AND SERGIO GIULIANO

1 INTRODUCTION

A sad duty calls us to discuss the challenges posed by today's legal landscape: the existence of multiple and overlapping normative[1] arrangements, as we thought to know it, is openly challenged. In many instances, there is no ordering left to deal with these competing systems or bodies of law. In this entropy, supranational constitutionalism – and human rights protection in particular – seems to fall back into the hands of sovereign states.

Law, as a closed normative system that exists at the level of the sovereign state, seems to be an imperfect model in the globalized world. As a practical consequence, the same set of factual circumstances usually correlates to different norms that originate in different yet intertwined legal systems. This causes redundancy and contradiction between legal norms to be the rule as opposed to the exception. This is not only the nightmare of an analytical philosopher of law – it is the daily staple of national and international courts.

The label intended in this volume to describe this phenomenon is that of "inter-legality." The term has been used to cover different notions in several disciplines of law. In legal anthropology, it has been defined in a procedural and substantial way as "*process of adoption of elements of a dominant legal order, both national and international, and of the frames of meaning that constitute these orders, into the practices of a local legal order* ... or as the outcome of such process, a hybrid new legal order."[2]

[1] Throughout this chapter, "normative" is used both in its philosophical and legal meaning. No further specifications are made, since the context of their use make their meaning self-evident.

[2] A. Hoekema, "European Legal Encounters between Minority and Majority Culture: Cases of Interlegality," (2005) 51 *Journal of Legal Pluralism and Unofficial Law* 1, at 11 (emphasis in original).

In sociology of law, arguably where the term was first used, inter-legality is conceived within the purview of phenomenological sociology.[3] According to De Sousa Santos, it is legal plurality, again not as legal pluralism, but as "different legal spaces superimposed, interpenetrated and mixed in our minds, as much as in our actions."[4] For him, "We live in a time of porous legality or of legal porosity, multiple networks of legal orders forcing us to constant transitions and trespassing."[5]

These are conceptually different approaches: legal anthropology derives from cultural diversity or interculturality, while sociology is interested in inter-legality in a broader, globalized fashion. However, both share the same intent to separate inter-legality from legal pluralism. The idea of inter-legality as a concept is to capture the relational facet among overlapping normative arrangements, whereas legal pluralism assumes a plurality of normative arrangements operating in parallel (coordinated or not).[6] That is, inter-legality focuses on both the ways the legal systems are intertwined as well as the fact that they mutually influence each other. The rapport is such that it makes it impossible to describe one without referring to the other(s).

But what about inter-legality from a pragmatic perspective, specifically through the lens of adjudication? For the enterprise of adjudication, inter-legality is a problem, not a solution. The relation between these legal systems is far from clear, but it must be determined, at least temporarily, when the judge or the administrator has to decide a case.[7] Yet there is no established hierarchy (there could not be). There is a plethora of binding norms that are not enforced and "soft-law" legal norms that have various degrees of normative force (if not legally, at least factually); and both actors and decisions have the capacity to impact realities far beyond their normal scope of action.[8]

From the perspective of the judge, this means choosing which system to apply where there are no applicable conflict of law rules (and where conflict

[3] B. de Sousa Santos, "Law: A Map of Misreading. Toward a Postmodern Conception of Law," (1987) 14 *Journal of Law and Society* 279, 288.

[4] B. de Sousa Santos, *Toward a New Legal Common Sense: Legal, Globalization, and Emancipation* (New York: Routledge, 1995), at 472–473.

[5] Ibid. Several legal scholars have adopted de Sousa Santos's conception to describe different fields of law, particularly private law. See M. Amstutz, "In-Between Worlds: *Marleasing* and the Emergence of Interlegality in Legal Reasoning," (2005) 11 *European Law Journal* 766; and M. Kenny, "Globalization, Interlegality and Europeanized Contract Law," (2002) 21 *Penn State International Law Review* 569.

[6] See de Sousa Santos, *Toward a New Legal Common Sense*, at 472.

[7] However, if the solution is ad hoc, it will contribute to the threatening chaos.

[8] See A. Sajó and R. Uitz, *The Constitution of Freedom* (Oxford: Oxford University Press, 2017), chapter 12.

of law regimes do not govern the fuzzy relations of inter-legality). Perhaps the judge shall attempt to harmonize these interlocked systems, but there is no authoritative theory, methodology, or doctrine for such optimization. Or the judge may refuse to frame the problem as one of competing regimes, handling the matter on jurisdictional grounds.[9] This approach is also part of the inter-legality conundrum: isolating systems means also managing their relationship. Of course, it is common in a national system too that the judge chooses between different sets of norms, creating a certain interconnectedness or balance. For example, a legal relationship of a manager may qualify as a labor law matter or one governed by the rules of mandate in private law or governed by corporate law. But the level of uncertainty including that of jurisdiction is higher in situations discussed under the heading of inter-legality.

In this sense, judging in cases where competing legal regimes may be more or less equally applicable represents a particular aspect of inter-legality. On the one hand, it freezes inter-legal relations in the decision, selecting one or another aspect of the connections. The judgment becomes a new fact of inter-legality. But in the fuzziness of inter-legality, there is no finality. The competition and cooperation in the inter-legality space continues, and the new fact of the decision is added to the network, bringing a change into a system that is itself in constant change.

From the perspective of an international human rights judgment (the topic of this chapter), the judgment requires execution and expects precedential value and expressive force (i.e., a certain substantive position will be transposed in other jurisdictions). But these "conclusions" are to be drawn in other legal regimes. The judgment may not be executed within its jurisdiction or may not be followed in other cases with overlapping jurisdictions.[10] This is exactly the peculiarity of inter-legality.

[9] This was the judicial position of one of the authors of this chapter in a partially dissenting opinion in *Al-Dulimi and Montana Management Inc. v Switzerland*, Application no. 5809/08, November 26, 2013. The case concerned the freezing of assets in Switzerland of an Iraqi national and a company registered in Panama (of which the first was managing director) in accordance with a United Nations Security Council Resolution, which provided for sanctions against the former Iraqi regime. The partially dissenting opinion, while agreeing with the finding of a violation of Article 6 of the Convention, considered the case inadmissible *ratione personae*. The majority judgment was upheld in its entirety by a majority of the Grand Chamber in its Judgment of June 21, 2016.

[10] *Burmych v Ukraine* [GC], Applications nos. 46852/13 et al., October 12, 2017, is a case in point. The European Court of Human Rights (ECtHR) found Ukraine to be in violation of the Convention for the non-execution of domestic judgments and indicated that structural changes were needed to remedy the situation. When Ukraine failed to carry out the reforms, the ECtHR declared that it would not deal with these cases, as the supervision of the execution of the judgments of the Court are a matter for the Committee of Ministers. The Secretariat of the

Of course, the attempt of the scholar to understand inter-legality differs from that of the judge, yet both will view the legal system not as fragmented with parallel components, but as relations among the normative arrangements that make or form part of it. The difficulty for the practitioner is that there is no clear metatheory applicable to arrange the fragments. As the example of judicially enforced international human rights law indicates, this makes international human rights law particularly malleable.

In this chapter, we will focus on the inter-legality of constitutionalism with special reference to human rights law as a source of fundamental rights (we consider this as a species to the genus inter-legality). Within this context, we will first briefly describe the development of multilayered constitutionalism and its foundational inconsistencies. We will later discuss the normative implications of the literature that has analyzed this phenomenon and the reality of practices it has justified or criticized. As legal theory is a substantial part of inter-legality, where the description became performative, it is of importance to understand how, in certain instances, the emerging description contributes to the destruction of the very picture it describes. We will argue that in light of a series of institutional responses to the unraveling of domestic forces, the literature shall not function as a legitimizing force of setbacks to the fulfillment of the promises of the enterprise of human rights.

The uncritical acceptance (even celebration) of theories and practices of deferentialism as tools for creating the "proper" balancing in the name of realism (doctrines of margin of appreciation, constitutional identity, etc.) is often the revenge of nationalism and sovereignty adulation. As far as international courts are concerned, subsidiarity and other theories of deferentialism (including domestic theories of sovereignty) should be treated in a more critical manner. A legal regime (be it the European Union [EU] system that opens itself up to national and constitutional identity or the ECtHR that brings into its own legal dogmatics the approval for the disregard of its own principles in the name of subsidiarity and "nation states know better how to

Committee declared that from then on all complaints were to be addressed to the Ukrainian Ministry of Justice. Likewise, the Court of Justice of the European Union (CJEU) and the ECtHR ruled that the UN system of freezing assets did not satisfy the rule of law (fair trial); see *Kadi v. Council of the EU* (2008) C-402 and 415/05, ECLI:EU:C:2008:461, and *Al-Dulimi*, respectively. This had no direct effect on the UN system. As to effects on nation states, they are uneven and unclear. Prior to the requirements of these courts, the EU Council Framework Decision 2003/577/JHA required judicial control (within the EU). The 2008 *Kadi* judgment seems to have influenced the applicable legal regimes in the EU with Directive 2014/42/EU of the European Parliament and of the Council of April 3, 2014. But the UN Security Council system represents a normative system that does not necessarily reflect the one that was followed by the CJEU, and there is no preset rule that would coordinate these two systems.

realize human rights") gives up its claim to follow its own aims within a relatively closed legality. By denying the legitimacy of its own standards, favoring margin of appreciation instead of its own all-European standards, it gives up the battle without a fight. The problem is that by advocating for some form of inter-legality, such as multilayered constitutionalism (a descriptively accurate concept), and praising its uncertainties, this will provide an opportunity to dilute one's own legal system (in this case, lowering human rights standards by letting states determine their content entirely).

2 THE ADVENT AND REALITY OF MULTILAYERED CONSTITUTIONALISM

It is hard (and even unnecessary for present purposes) to point out the moment that could mark the unraveling of multilayered constitutionalism or international human rights.[11] In any case, during the second half of the twentieth century – and with the hopes of establishing international principles and mechanisms to avoid the recurrence of the worst chapter of human history – there was an outburst of international documents and institutions. Both treaties and treaty bodies (whose decisions or recommendations have more or less binding power and create international responsibility), populated the international arena and set the groundwork for the advent of multilayered constitutions.[12]

After the fall of authoritarian regimes – during the rise of Second and particularly Third Wave Democracies[13] – countries saw this international groundwork as a solid foundation for their constitutions' democratic identities and international credibility. Within this context, by the end of the century, international norms and standards (including the decisions of their interpretive bodies) became internalized in domestic constitutions and legal systems. Domestic and transnational actors believed sovereign power could be limited from the top by imposing constitutional standards of rule of law, institutionalism, and human rights.

In parallel, the rapid growth of globalization due to distance-shrinking technologies and market-opening government policies made it easier (and in some cases necessary) for other noninstitutional networks to appear (such as

[11] For one account on human rights, see S. Moyn, *The Last Utopia* (Cambridge, MA: Harvard University Press, 2010).

[12] Sajó and Uitz, *The Constitution of Freedom*, at 449 ff.

[13] S. Huntington, *The Third Wave: Democratization in the Late Twentieth Century* (Norman: University of Oklahoma Press, 1991).

transnational horizontal professional networks) and for domestic actors to have transnational impact. From the perspective of constitutionalism, professional networks serve the purpose of constitutional cross-fertilization.[14] At the same time, domestic actors, in a reality where different normative layers overlap and influence each other, can affect the outcomes of decisions that do not directly involve their state of origin. They can achieve this either by participating as third parties or by cooperating with their counterparts in other states to bring similar claims before different bodies to create a substantial, favorable supranational jurisprudence. In principle, their interaction can generate common standards and norms. But while the democratic spillover seems to have bypassed national boundaries, it is not without resistance and not without keeping the forces of such resistance ready to mobilize for a *reconquista*.

Much of today's inter-legality is caused by the mere fact that distances have shrunk. What happens in one corner of the world is heard and impacts the other in a matter of seconds. But much of it is also due to an attempt to found global networks that establish the ground rules of what certain more or less affiliated actors (described today, with scorn, as cosmopolitan elites) morally found to be the correct (or at least best) way for human beings to develop: democracy and the rule of law as the basis for the lexical priority and advancement of individual freedom.

Be that as it may, at this point, international law, domestic constitutions, and transnational norms and networks have merged in such a way that it is clear that traditional national sovereignty-based constitutional arrangements do not capture the realities of contemporary supranational interdependencies. In fact, international courts were established as part of the top-down effort to, among other things, coordinate these interactions. This is what multilayered constitutionalism consists of – or at least, it can be argued that this was a reality in the making.

Traditional constitutionalism meant the limiting of absolute power particularly by its allocation, both vertical and horizontal, as well as the ability of mutual checking and balancing at a national level, within the boundaries of national borders and the territoriality of constitutions. It was hoped that a multilayered constitutional system would contribute to this project of checking concentrations of power. This hope was not fully unreasonable. However, multilayered constitutionalism with its many supranational dimensions of

[14] See A.-M. Slaughter, "Judicial Globalization," (1999–2000) 40 *Virginia Journal of International Law* 1103, 1120–1123, explaining how judges meeting face-to-face in intra- and inter-regional meetings fostered judicial comity, cooperation, and constitutional cross-fertilization.

power, within undefined and blurred normative arrangements, resulted in an increase of unchecked domestic government power. That is, with the diffusion of the locus of power came the diffusion of accountability, especially democratic accountability. Legal norms are now developed without parliamentary control (i.e., the production of global law without states),[15] and domestic executives can claim powerlessness regarding international decisions where, in reality, they mobilize those decisions for their executive advantage. To put it bluntly: while multilayered constitutionalism promised an additional layer of control over government power, it became in many instances a tool of executive self-aggrandizement. In other instances, nongovernmental special interest groups use the power vacuum of inter-legality for their own interests.

The hope during this process of internationalization of constitutionalism and rule of law was that committed actors (both domestic and supranational) would form a community in an emerging global order. With the rise of democracies and globalization, the playing field of constitutional law became much bigger. There was an attempt to define common rules for the extended field, but those who were developing these rules were without the ability to execute them. But the existence of a global order as such rested and rests on the will of the very subjects it purports to limit: domestic states. A legal argument (like all arguments) makes sense only in an interpretative community, even if that community is an open one and some of its members are part of a transnational network. There are national and international judges who deny that foreign judges sitting at an international bench will ever understand national law when they apply supranational law.[16] While it is argued that "judges from different legal systems share common beliefs, values and a self-perception and understanding of their role in the legal system and in society,"[17] the empirical evidence supporting it is limited, and it is more part of the vulnerable narrative of politeness that keeps their inter-legality together, until challenged by local realities. Hence the difficulty of operating a supranational quasi-sovereign state (both regarding power and legitimacy) over existing domestic sovereign states. This is the case even if the entities beyond the

[15] G. Teubner, "Global Bukowina: Legal Pluralism in World Society," in G. Teubner (ed.), *Global Law without a State* (Dartmouth: Ashgate, 1997), 3.

[16] Lord Hoffmann, "The Universality of Human Rights," Judicial Studies Board Annual Lecture, March 19, 2009, available at www.brandeis.edu/ethics/pdfs/internationaljustice/biij/BIIJ2013/hoffmann.pdf ("human rights are universal in abstraction but national in application," at 11).

[17] M. Claes and M. de Visser, "Are You Networked Yet? On Dialogues in European Judicial Networks," (2012) 8 *Utrecht Law Review* 100. Of course, national epistemic communities vary: some of them are more open, less developed, etc.

nation-state do not have the threatening elements of sovereign superior power and even if domestic sovereignty has been subject to a process of dilution.

Thus, constitutions shaped by diverse supranational documents and actors with overlapping and blurred scopes of action were the inevitable result of the inability of supranational decisions to be binding not only de jure but also de facto. A system that purports to establish a binding set of rules but constantly depends on the will of its players takes, like trust, decades to build and seconds to collapse.

This state of affairs now develops in a rapidly changing global context fertile for the destruction of trust. The stories of backlash against internationalizing forces and globalization (fueled by nationalistic populisms, the advent of global economic crises, and/or the rise of transnational terror networks) went from prophecy to reality, especially when American scholarship and politics joined the backlash movement[18] and the outliers became the mainstream.

The combination of a malleable system and a hostile environment seriously curtailed this supra-constitutional aspiration, and more particularly that of an effective international human rights regime. Even though many constitutions were amended to automatically incorporate international treaties (or did so by virtue of apex courts' decisions),[19] there is now a tendency of either open defiance to the recognition of the binding effect of supranational case law,[20] constant threats to withdraw from supranational arrangements (or actual action – as in the cases of Venezuela and Burundi), or just plain de facto noncompliance through time.[21]

[18] E. A. Posner, "Liberal Internationalism and the Populist Backlash," in *University of Chicago Public Law Working Paper No. 606*, January 11, 2017.

[19] For example, Art. 120 of the Constitution of the Netherlands and many Latin American constitutions that directly incorporated international human rights treaties. See E. M. Gongora-Mera, *Inter-American Judicial Constitutionalism: On the Constitutional Rank of Human Rights Treaties in Latin America through National and Inter-American Adjudication* (San José: Inter-American Institute of Human Rights, 2011). The Hungarian Constitutional Court recognized the relevance of supranational principles and norms in the unalterable core of Hungary's Constitution: see Decision 61/2011 (VII. 13.) AB of the Constitutional Court of the Republic of Hungary, ABH 2011, 290, 321.

[20] See Section 3 for a small survey on the cases of Italy, Russia, and the United Kingdom.

[21] F. Basch et al., "La Efectividad del Sistema Interamericano de Protección de Derechos Humanos: Un Enfoque Cuantitativo Sobre su Funcionamiento y Sobre el Cumplimento de sus Decisiones," (2010) 7 *SUR* 12. In the European system of human rights, it suffices to say that there is a continued increase in cases pending before the Committee of Ministers for more than five years. While in 2011 these cases accounted for some 20 percent of the total, by the end of 2015 they rose to 55 percent. In total, nearly 11,000 cases have not been fully implemented by domestic authorities. See Council of Europe, "Ninth Annual Report of the Committee of Ministers," *Supervision of the Execution of Judgements and Decisions of the European Court of Human Rights* (2015), at 10.

For its part, however, the literature tried to perform with words what actions could not. It tried to cover the gaps created by the shortcomings of interlegality. But the gaps could not be covered, only hidden in plain sight by wishful theory. Committed to the ideals of a linear path to more democratization, rule of law, and human rights (perhaps confusing the path and fate of economic globalization with that of legal globalization), many international scholars insisted on the idea of continuous and inevitable global constitutional convergence and thus dangerously downplayed the – then dormant and now roused – defiance and scornful domestic dissent.

Furthermore, a new development was taking place at the national level. The rise of judicial review (and its overestimated internationalization) saw the parallel birth of a tradition of mistrust against courts and an overconfident rhetoric regarding the ability of the political powers (particularly the legislative) to protect human rights.[22] Although this tradition was genuinely democratic in its intentions, it set the intellectual groundwork for the populist countermovement against globalization. The growing nationalist rhetoric saw in this tradition the potential to frame the outsider: if domestic courts were not to be trusted, neither could be international institutions and networks (let alone supranational courts). The populist claim therefore incorporated a transnational dimension. It demanded not only the locus of power to be placed back in the sovereign states à la Bodin, but to return to a parliamentary sovereignty à la Dicey (although in many cases of new democracies and others that rely heavily on the separation of powers, it is not – it cannot be – a "return").

Of course, by definition, populism relies on a majoritarian (formalistic and procedural) understanding of democracy. It is therefore intolerant to the idea that certain values should preclude the people's will. As we have said elsewhere:

> Sovereigntists are naturally against constitutionalism's aspirations of constraining absolute power and protecting minorities. Consequently, their parallel domestic rise throughout the world in the past years puts the adjudicative supra-national bodies twice in jeopardy: first, in terms of their aspirations of supranational integration (both regional and global); second, in their constitutional, sovereign-limiting and counter-majoritarian aspirations. Both aspects are the reverse of the same coin: as supranational bodies, they

[22] M. Tushnet, *Taking the Constitution Away from the Courts* (Princeton, NJ: Princeton University Press, 1999); R. M. Unger, *What Should Legal Analysis Become?* (London: Verso, 1996); R. Bellamy, *Political Constitutionalism. A Republican Defence of the Constitutionality of Democracy* (Cambridge: Cambridge University Press, 2007); and J. Waldron, "The Core Case against Judicial Review," (2006) 115 *Yale Law Journal* 1346.

suffer the so-called democratic deficit; as adjudicative bodies, their only asset is legitimacy, for they hold neither the power of the purse nor the power of the sword.[23]

3 THE REACTION TO THE REACTION: LEVELING DOWN

The theorem of supranational adjudication holds that the more complex the implementation measure needed and the more it departs from domestic constitutional self-understanding, the more unlikely it is for a government to spend political capital on its implementation. But long gone are the days when governments, even in democratic states, needed external validation for the legitimacy of their acts. This means that with backlash on the rise, supranational adjudication becomes even more troublesome. *Noncompliance* with international norms is now the common currency of states to find mutually reinforcing strength. While in the context of globalization defiance was a way of losing legitimacy and political capital, within the context of backlash, defiance has instead become (particularly in places where the unbound national sovereign state is free of foreign interests) a way of gaining both legitimacy and political capital.

The dilemma of actors with a supranational scope (whether domestic or international) is whether to stand their ground or compromise. In both cases, legitimacy is lost (which is exactly what makes it a dilemma – hopefully, a false one). In the first case, they lose efficacy and, consequently, authority. In the second case, it means leveling down (i.e., the acceptance of the watering down of the very system that gave them legitimacy in the first place). While it seeks self-preservation, it destroys its very foundations. Supranational courts that face this dilemma should decide, then, between "letting human rights violations go de facto unpunished (. . .) but at least de jure condemned, or by enduring human rights violations and thus deciding to run away to live to fight another day."[24]

In the European context, some examples within the case law of the ECtHR are illustrative of this tension. The United Kingdom's refusal to revise the blanket ban on prisoners voting rights has become the paradigmatic example of a state publicly defying the Court and it being used as a political platform.[25]

23 A. Sajó and S. Giuliano, "Is the Decline of Globalization the End of Human Rights (As We Believe to Know Them)?" (2017) 8 *Annuario di Diritto Comparato e di Studi Legislativi*.

24 Ibid.

25 T. Whitehead, "Cameron Vows to Defy Europe on Prisoner Voting," *The Telegraph*, May 24, 2012, available at www.telegraph.co.uk/news/politics/9285408/Cameron-vows-to-defy-Europe-on-prisoner-voting.html (accessed January 14, 2018).

Even though the judgment in *Hirst*[26] could have been construed as giving little margin of action to the state, the Court later clarified, in similar cases involving other states, that the boundaries for reform were wide and permissible.[27] Yet the United Kingdom's position has not changed on the matter (of course, neither has the pertinent statute), and the Court still receives the same cases and hands down the same resolution.[28] Moreover, empowered by the United Kingdom's self-congratulatory defiance, Russia has denied to comply with a similar case against it.[29] In fact, the Russian Constitutional Court, after the Duma passed a statute broadening its jurisdiction and competence, stated that it can decide whether or not a ECtHR judgment can be disregarded by the Russian Government, if the Russian Constitutional Court deems such ruling to be against the Russian Constitution.[30]

A similar fate was avoided regarding the displaying of crucifixes in public school classrooms. In *Lautsi v Italy*,[31] a Chamber ruling decided such display violated Article 2 of Protocol No. 1 taken together with Article 9 of the Convention.[32] The Italian Government showed a clear unwillingness to comply with the original decision of the Court[33] and requested the referral to the Grand Chamber, where another 20 parties were allowed as third-party interveners in the proceedings (ten of whom were member states from the Council of Europe who opposed the Chamber ruling). Furthermore, during this time, the Italian Constitutional Court issued two rulings (unrelated to *Lautsi*) where it held that Italy would not be bound by decisions by an international court where they were considered to be illegitimate for being opposed to the Italian Constitution.[34] The Grand Chamber of the Court finally overruled the Chamber's decision and ruled in favor of Italy.[35]

26 *Hirst v United Kingdom*, [GC] Application No. 74025/01, October 6, 2005.

27 *Scoppola v Italy (No. 3)*, Application Nos. 60041708 and 60054/08, November 23, 2010, para. 83; and *Soyler v Turkey*, Application No. 29411/07, September 17, 2013, para. 33.

28 See *Millibank and Others v United Kingdom*, Application No. 44473/14, June 30, 2016.

29 *Anchugov & Gladkov v. Russia*, Applications Nos. 11157/04 and 15162/05, July 4, 2013.

30 See *Postanovlenie Konstitutsionnogo Suda RF* [Ruling of the Russian Federation Constitutional Court of July 14, 2015], *Rossiiskaia Gazeta*, July 27, 2015.

31 See *Lautsi v Italy*, Application no. 30814/06, November 3, 2009.

32 It did so by relying on the principles established by previous case law in *Folgerø and Others v Norway*, Application no. 15472/02, June 29, 2007.

33 After the Chamber decision, a Bill was introduced in the Italian Senate making it mandatory for public schools to display crucifixes, and mayors of several municipalities throughout Italy ordered schools and public offices to display them under penalty of fines.

34 *Corte Constituzionale*, decisions of November 26, 2009, No. 311, and December 4, 2009, No. 317.

35 *Lautsi v Italy* [GC], Application no. 30814/06, March 18, 2011.

Within this context of defiance and inter-legality, it was not long before the Court began lowering human rights standards previously established by its own case law.[36] However, this occurred within first extending the jurisdiction of the Court, creating new overlaps with other normative orders. In the last decade or so, the Court had been progressively expanding its jurisdiction to extraterritorial violations of human rights with the doctrine of "effective control." This doctrine began in *Bankovic*,[37] where it was used to reject jurisdiction on NATO military bombings during the Kosovo crisis. Yet the Court began expanding the concept of effective control and therefore its jurisdiction under Article 1 of the European Convention. First, it recognized the possibility for states to exercise some temporary or other kind of degree of extraterritorial effective control.[38] Then, it asserted that this effective control could be established by the extraterritorial activity of state agents operating "whether lawfully or unlawfully."[39] Finally, the Court expanded the concept to include the mere "exercise of physical power and control over the person in question."[40] These were all cases where the Court faced the intersection of international human rights law with the law of war (both in terms of *jus ad bellum* and *jus in bello*), and avoided any analysis, specifically since respondent states in these cases had not derogated from the Convention through Article 15.

It was not long until the domestic backlash presented itself, specifically in the United Kingdom regarding the Iraqi cases. In *Hassan*, the Court reaffirmed the extraterritorial jurisdiction of the Convention, regardless of the existence of an international conflict and the lack of derogation through Article 15.[41] However, this time it held that compliance with humanitarian law provisions in the Third and Fourth Geneva Conventions amounted to compliance with Article 5 of the Convention in times of international conflict.[42] This was the first time the Court allowed a somewhat implicit derogation from the Convention. The case therefore shows an instance where inter-legality provided the opportunity, in the face of backlash, of lowering of international

[36] In other areas, however, the Court tried to extend potential protection of fundamental rights, or at least the applicability of the Convention.
[37] *Bankovic and Others v Belgium and 16 Other Contracting States*, Application no. 52207/99, December 19, 2001.
[38] *Issa and Others v Turkey*, Application no. 31821/96, November 16, 2004, para. 74. Although in this case, for lack of evidence, the Court found no basis for jurisdiction.
[39] *Pad and Others v Turkey*, Application no. 60167/00, June 28, 2007, para. 53.
[40] *Al-Skeini and Others v United Kingdom*, Application no. 55721/07, July 7, 2011, para. 136.
[41] *Hassan v United Kingdom*, Application no. 29750/09, September 16, 2014, para. 80.
[42] Ibid., paras. 107–111.

human rights law standards through the application of a different body of law (or the reinterpretation of the intersection of two overlapping legal systems).

Other cases regarding freedom of expression have shared a similar fate. In a case regarding the refusal to broadcast a nongovernmental organization (NGO) commercial against pig farming methods, the Court found a violation of Article 10 (the refusal was based on a Swiss statute that prohibited political advertising outside elections).[43] A similar case involved Norway and was ruled in the same terms by the Court, thus consolidating the case law.[44] Furthermore, the Court had to rule on the first case again due to the refusal by local authorities to reopen the domestic case and air the commercial.[45] Even though the first judgment of the Court did not contain a specific remedy, the second judgment saw the not broadcasting of the commercial (due to the refusal to reopen domestic proceedings in lieu of internal laws) as a violation of the Convention and the Chamber Judgment. According to these cases, states have little margin to limit freedom of expression, which is even narrower in terms of political speech and questions of public interest (and even more so in cases of prior restraint). Both in Norway and in Switzerland (as well as other states), the laws and practices were amended to soften the blanket bans on political advertising in order to comply with the Court's standard.[46]

But the Court walked back on this standard, handing down an opposite ruling in an almost identical case against the United Kingdom, which made the Norwegian and Swiss legislators look overzealous in applying the Court's case law. The case *Animal Defenders*[47] concerned the refusal to air a commercial by an NGO opposing the keeping and exhibition of primates in zoos under a similar law to that of Switzerland (a blanket ban of political advertising outside election periods). What had been considered disproportionate and unnecessary in a democratic society in *VgT and Tv Vest As* became proportionate and necessary in a democratic society in *Animal Defenders*. The reason was that the general ban was carefully debated in parliament and unanimously

43 *VgT Verein Gegen Tierfabriken v Switzerland*, Application no. 24699/94, June 28, 2001.
44 *Tv Vest As & Rogaland Pensjonistparti v Norway*, Application no. 21132/05, December 11, 2008.
45 *Verein Gegen Tierfabriken Schweiz (Vgt) v Switzerland (No. 2)*, Application no. 32772/02, June 30, 2009.
46 In the Norwegian case, although the main statute was kept in place, the Statute of the National Public Broadcaster (NRK) was changed to include an obligation to provide broad and balanced coverage of political elections and editorial coverage to smaller parties; see *TV Vest As and Rogaland Pensjonistparti*, Application no. 21132/05, Final Resolution CM/ResDH (2011), 234.
47 *Animal Defenders International v United Kingdom*, Application no. 48876/08, April 22, 2013.

passed (even though specialists who presented in special committees alerted of the potential unconformity of the bill to the Convention in view of the existing case law).[48] According to the majority:

> The quality of the parliamentary and judicial review of the necessity of the measure is of particular importance in this respect, including to the operation of the relevant margin of appreciation.[49]

Yet nowhere in the then-existing case law of the Court were states granted more margin of appreciation for the alleged democratic legitimacy of the legislation. The idea that a more profoundly debated law should allow states to depart from established case law has not only no good principle behind it, but also can easily be manipulated by domestic authorities. In fact, although it was mentioned briefly in the text of the Judgment, it is now being increasingly used by defendants (and accepted by the Court) to argue in favor of granting a wider margin of appreciation.[50] This line of argumentation only makes the eventual adverse decision by the Court more politically costly for the local authorities to implement, and therefore more likely for them not to comply with such a decision. But while this might explain the ruling by the Court, in no way does it justify it. *Animal Defenders* is thus the paradigmatic example of the Court backtracking on its own footsteps after having generated expectations of human rights standards and compliance, setting a dangerous precedent for human rights protection across Europe. In terms of the dilemma posed at the beginning of this section, it is hard to see how such a decision does anything to improve the legitimacy of the Court.

The Court has also retracted on previous case law without specific reasons in a case regarding prison conditions and their relation to inhuman and degrading treatment.[51] In *Muršić*, the Court decided that there was no violation of Article 3 of the Convention, even though the applicant had spent several weeks in confinement with less than four square meters of personal space (including

[48] See ibid., para. 9 of the first dissent opinion and paras. 35–64 of the majority ruling.

[49] Ibid., para. 108.

[50] See *Baka v Hungary* [GC], Application no. 20261/12, June 23, 2016, para. 161; A.-M.V. *v Finland*, Application no. 53251/13, March 23, 2017, para. 82; *Orlovskaya Iskra v Russia*, Application no. 42911/08, February 21, 2017, para. 113; *Novikova and Others v Russia*, Applications nos. 25501/07, 57569/11, 80153/12, 5790/13, and 35015/13, April 26, 2016, para. 194; and *Garib v The Netherlands*, Application no. 43494/09, February 23, 2016, para. 113, pending referral before the Grand Chamber – to name a few.

[51] For another case of the Court backtracking from its own standards, see *Ibrahim and Others v the United Kingdom*, Application nos. 50541/08, 50571/08, 50573/08, and 40351/09, September 13, 2016.

nonconsecutive periods of less than three square meters).[52] This position clearly contradicted that of the international network of national specialists (the Council of Europe's Committee for the Prevention of Torture and Inhuman or Degrading Treatment or Punishment [CPT]). Yet the Court chose not to follow the CPT standards of four square meters of personal space and of previous case law, creating different levels of presumption against the state (one below three square meters and another one between three and four square meters).

Instead of looking to its own standards, the Court acted as if its mission were to legitimize domestic decisions. Certain expressions are telling: "cumulative effects,"[53] "comprehensive approach,"[54] "overall assessment,"[55] "the assessment of the minimum level ... is, in the nature of things, relative,"[56] "will depend on all the circumstances of the case,"[57] to name a few.[58]

The "holistic review" discourse, which gives any circumstance the capacity to change the fate of human rights compliance, is accompanied by a strong rhetoric on democratic legitimacy and domestic sovereignty. A dissenting opinion in a recent case on the right to access information as part of the right to freedom of speech is illustrative in this sense:

> The principle requiring a practical and effective interpretation of the Convention, by reference to its object and purpose, is not an open invitation for the judges of this Court to elevate any positive development in the member states to the level of a binding international norm, thus limiting the states' sovereign and democratic rights.[59]

And:

> Today's judgment thus severely limits the significance of the 2009 Convention [on Access to Information], and in fact deprives the member States of the power to decide for themselves, based on their own sovereign and democratic

[52] *Muršić v Croatia*, Application no. 7334/13, October 20, 2016. It did find, however, a violation in a consecutive period of 26 days in which the applicant disposed of less than three square meters.

[53] Ibid., para. 121.

[54] Ibid., para. 123.

[55] Ibid., para. 124.

[56] Ibid., para. 122.

[57] Ibid., para. 122.

[58] *Ibrahim* follows this same path: "proceedings as a whole," "overall fairness," and "holistic assessment"; see *Ibrahim v UK*, paras. 252, 257, and 260, respectively.

[59] *Magyar Helsinki Bizottság v Hungary*, Application no. 18030/11, November 8, 2016, dissenting opinion of Judge Spano, joined by Judge Kjølbro, para. 16.

will, whether they wish to be bound by obligations in this area at the international level.[60]

In short, in the European context, the ECtHR has, against the Preamble of the Convention, backed down from both the maintenance and the further realization of human rights. On their part, scholars have – in accordance with the momentum of trying to cover up the gaps in the system – come up with elegant labels to disguise this.[61]

The "dialogue" literature, for example, is copious,[62] and usually holds a rather narrow (if not empty) vision of dialogue. Part of the judicial dialogue literature has labeled and praised unprincipled compromise as dialogue. *Animal Defenders*, for example, has been referred to as a "successful dialogue with Strasbourg."[63] If at all, however, the case would be not an example of dialogue, but of appeasement of one of the most relentless and powerful defiers of the Court. Dialogue seen this way is nothing but noncommittal.

Judicial dialogue (in certain versions) used to be the polite way to avoid conflict. In this logic, subsidiarity is mistaken with deference, and cooperation with concession. Of course, it can be useful to listen informally to domestic judicial positions and explanations, but such informality is troubling where law is about formalism. As long as it was not challenged by domestic interests expressed as sovereignty and identity, judicial dialogue was believed to be a *modus vivendi* of inter-legality, capable of making a transition to multilayered constitutionalism, "given its insistence on moving away from final authority (and the combative relationship this entails) to a more non-hierarchical

60 Ibid., para. 33.

61 "Subsidiarity" and "dialogue" are some of these labels. For the second, see the references in the following note; for the first, see A. Mowbray, "Subsidiarity and the European Convention on Human Rights," (2015) 15 *Human Rights Law Review* 313; M. Hunter-Henin, "Living Together in an Age of Religious Diversity: Lessons from *Baby Loup* and *SAS*," (2015) 4 *Oxford Journal of Law and Religion* 94 (discussing a balanced and nuanced reasoning by the Court); S. Besson, "Subsidiarity in International Human Rights Law – What Is Subsidiary about Human Rights?" (2016) 61 *American Journal of Jurisprudence* 69 (discussing the democratic and epistemic justifications of subsidiarity and its so-called procedural, substantive, and remedial aspects).

62 For literature on the "dialogic" interactions between the ECtHR and domestic courts, see G. Martinico and O. Pollicino, *The Interaction between Europe's Legal Systems: Judicial Dialogue and the Creation of Supranational Laws* (Cheltenham: Edward Elgar, 2012); G. Repetto (ed.), *The Constitutional Relevance of the ECHR in Domestic and European Law: An Italian Perspective* (Antwerp: Intersentia, 2013); P. W. Hogg and A. A. Bushell, "The Charter Dialogue between Courts and Legislatures (Or Perhaps the Charter of Rights Isn't Such a Bad Thing After All)," (1997) 35 *Osgoode Hall Law Journal* 75.

63 See Lady Hale, "What's the Point of Human Rights?" Warwick Law Lecture 2013, November 28, 2013, at 9.

(and cooperative) approach."[64] But it was a *modus vivendi* based on silence. The moment of truth came when national courts realized that they could live in peace with international courts in respectful disregard. As far as the ECtHR and some of the national identity-respecting judgments of the CJEU are concerned, the problem is that these international courts seem to tolerate if not endorse the backlash into sovereignty. Of course, given the indeterminacy by spontaneous design of inter-legality, this is not the only trend, but this one seems to be different and destructive, where the others are perhaps simply maintaining indeterminacy.

While the early literature prepared the terrain for the unraveling of backlash, the current literature, moving for example from criticism of margin of appreciation to respect for the doctrine[65] under the momentum of complacency, is legitimizing both the backlash and its response. Where we describe a tendency to lower standards, others see an "age of subsidiarity," a phase that will be manifested by the Court's engagement with empowering the member states to truly "bring rights home."[66] Judge Spano, writing extrajudicially, has argued that "the Convention is not an instrument of human rights unification … but only lays down minimum standards."[67] Regardless of the questionable assertion of "minimum standards," it can be easily said that the aforementioned cases show that this alleged "age of subsidiarity" is a euphemism for the fact that the Court is slowly leveling down. Similarly, setting minimum standards is nothing but lowering standards to the minimum our legalist rhetoric allows. It is celebrated as providing an opportunity for national courts to follow it by not being stringent. It is clearly a language that can bring down the intricate web of inter-legality that assumes that discussing the interconnectedness of legal systems is destructive (and not in the sense of the emperor's clothes). Moreover, in the context of human rights, this is not moving toward a higher level of protection on the basis of the supremacy of international law. On the contrary, it goes back to the national, where the shortcomings of domestic solutions are justified by this being a sovereign

64 Claes and de Visser, "Are You Networked Yet?" at 113.

65 For instance, O. M. Arnardóttir, in a Court supremacy-friendly article, wrote that the margin of appreciation as used by the Court in recent case law "allows for a deeper and more timely penetration of the Court's case law into the national legal systems than the precedential value of the Court's judgments in the traditional sense does": see "*Res Interpretata, Erga Omnes* Effect and the Role of the Margin of Appreciation in Giving Domestic Effect to the Judgments of the European Court of Human Rights," (2017) 28 *European Journal of International Law* 819, 843.

66 R. Spano, "Universality or Diversity of Human Rights? Strasbourg in the Age of Subsidiarity," (2014) 14 *Human Rights Law Review* 487, 491.

67 Ibid., at 493.

national solution with better knowledge of what human rights locally are. As the Court itself has said, "The national authorities have direct democratic legitimation and are . . . in principle better placed than an international court to evaluate local needs and conditions."[68]

This trend shows the ultimate dangers of inter-legality as peaceful coexistence. The celebrated "proceduralization of human rights law" means that the "supervisory" role of the international court will limit itself to ensuring that its considerations are *mentioned*. Whether the substantive requirements are satisfied is not its business, especially if a domestic judge has the skills and time to write lengthy and detailed reasoning with sufficient reference to case law.[69] In our view, however, the scholarship, in the spirit of appeasement and complacency, should not mirror the supranational actors who, baffled by the levels of defiance, retrench and run away to live to fight another day.

4 NOT AN EPILOGUE

In the multilayered, intertwined, and interdependent arrangement that the European human rights system is, it is certainly not an easy task to maintain the "control [of their] limited areas, immunized from external objectives."[70] Just as a constitutional narrative is constructed over time, with the participation of different actors that cannot write further chapters without being true to the previous ones,[71] the multilayered constitutional narrative demands actors to be aware of their interdependence and of the need for them to work on the creation of that narrative; to give it unity, certainty, and coherence.

We said that one of the characteristics of the multilayered system is that actors – both domestic and supranational – have the capacity of having transnational impact, since globalization broadened their scope of action and influence. Judges are by no means the exception, and whether domestic or international, they should be aware of their transnational impact (even symbolic) and of their role in this construction. Needless to say, this capacity entails the responsibility of acting accordingly.

Inter-Legality calls our attention to these interrelations, and rightly so. It is likely that the contemporary system of multilayered constitutionalism seems to be a plurality of autonomous but interrelated systems. Given the delicate

68 S.A.S. v *France* [GC], Application no. 43835/11, July 1, 2014, para. 129.
69 Of course, this is also part of inter-legality.
70 G. Palombella, chapter 16, infra, 368.
71 R. Dworkin, *Law's Empire* (London: Fontana, 1986).

balance, it was a condition of maintaining that balance not to expressly grant an absolute hierarchical priority to any of the participants in the interaction. Nico Krisch argued that "pluralism favors pragmatic, incremental processes of mutual accommodation and potential convergence, without overstretching the authority of the norms and institutions that form the regime."[72] But the strategic normative conclusion based on the avoidance of hierarchy, namely that "for the creation and consolidation of European and global political and legal institutions, this may be more beneficial than the existence of an overarching framework which will often antagonize actors and fail to match its social environment,"[73] seems to suggest a judicial strategy that, while allowing the survival of human rights, runs the risk of turning human rights into a legality of little practical importance.

The cases described above show a rereading by the ECtHR of its previous case law to allow exceptions where there should be none. In this sense, they fail to fit into the greater frame that captures all of the legal arrangements at play. Playing strategic games comes at a price. The legitimacy of the judgments will suffer. The recent leading cases of the ECtHR are alarming examples of internal inconsistency where the Court both retracts its own case law and relinquishes a level of human rights protection already granted. This goes against the "further realization of human rights" as set out in the Preamble of the Convention; it cannot "whittle down an existing right or create a new 'exception' or 'justification' which is not expressly recognized in the Convention."[74]

The carving of small, unprincipled exceptions in human rights standards makes the ECtHR look like a court that decides on equity rather than on law, thus leaving the door open for future ad hocery. The cases are perfect examples of the Court using "holistic" or "overall" approaches as legal guises for leveling down. The ECtHR cannot be a court that decides on a case-by-case basis. This only adds to the entropy of multilayered constitutionalism. Human rights standards cannot be ad hoc – they must be principled. And human rights-committed academia should not guise these developments with legitimizing rhetoric of dialogue, democratic legitimacy, and subsidiarity, thus appeasing the domestic demand for sovereignty not as a legitimate form of self-rule but as an illegitimate form of unaccountability.

[72] N. Krisch, "Who Is Afraid of Radical Pluralism? Legal Order and Political Stability in the Postnational Space," (2011) 24 *Ratio Juris* 386, 407.

[73] Ibid.

[74] *Austin v United Kingdom*, Applications nos. 39692/09, 40713/09, and 41008/09, March 15, 2012, para. 53.

Just as dialogue need not be deference, accommodating the challenges of inter-legality should in no way mean leveling down. Liberal constitutionalism has a normative moral claim that justifies the lexical priority of freedom[75] – anything that compromises beyond that renounces its foundations. Elevating the aspirations of liberal constitutionalism to the transnational level, and maintaining them there, requires the same vigilant actors that domestic constitutionalism does, from citizens to scholars and judges.

75 A. Sajó, "Liberty and Its Competitors," in R. Uitz (ed.), *Freedom and Its Enemies: The Tragedy of Liberty* (The Hague: Eleven International Publishing, 2015), 1.

11

Inter-Legality and Criminal Law

ALBERTO DI MARTINO

1 A PREMISE IN A "LEGITIMACY TO PARTICIPATE" DEBATE

It may appear unusual, even intrepid, to host a contribution from the bulwark of general criminal law within the framework of a theoretical endeavor to conceptualize inter-legality. Criminal law is a body of law seemingly obsessed with legality – and not *inter*-legality – issues, both at domestic and international levels.[1] The principle of *nullum crimen, nulla poena sine lege* is traditionally conceived as a domestic, refractory rule of hierarchy rooted in the exclusiveness of state sovereignty in exerting coercive powers on anyone staying within the borders of the state's territory, as well as on everyone causing whatever harm to its nationals or interests. More specifically, criminalization authority[2] is mainly[3] reserved to the legislature as the most democratic branch

[1] A useful overview on (similarities and differences in the meaning, scope and shape of) the legality principle in criminal law is provided in the sections devoted to legality and sources of criminal law, in relation to 16 selected countries and the Statute of the International Criminal Court, in K. J. Heller and M. Dubber (eds.), *The Handbook of Comparative Criminal Law* (Stanford, CA: Stanford University Press, 2011). See also G. Hallevy, *A Modern Treatise on the Principle of Legality in Criminal Law* (Berlin-Heidelberg, Springer, 2010).

[2] Criminalization is meant here basically as the power to decide whether to create new offence definitions or to extend existing ones. From a sociological point of view, it may be differently defined: for instance, "at the level of *phenomenon* itself" as "the use of traditional criminal tactics and styles in various forms of political marginality. At the level of *categorization* (social reaction) . . . means the re-allocation of political acts into criminal categories (for example, through terminology such as 'gangs', 'thugs', 'bandits', 'hooligans' or 'crazies')": S. Cohen, "Crime and Politics: Spot the Difference," (1996) 47 *British Journal of Sociology* 1, 4 (emphasis in original).

[3] In some jurisdictions, especially in common law jurisdictions that have not adopted a comprehensive criminal code, a trend towards the improvement of the legality principle as defined here is noticed; for example, in Australia, in spite of the absence of "an entrenched national bill of rights," the bulk of offences are statutory, there is a common law presumption against the retrospective application of penal laws and the executive has no power to declare

of government:[4] democratic legitimacy as a fair balance between political majority and minorities cannot be equally claimed either by the judiciary or by the executive, while likewise at the international level no international organization can claim such a political legitimacy. On the contrary, inter-legality is regarded as a porous category aiming at depicting the interconnectedness of overlapping legal regimes and orders, whereby, it is suggested, either the norm to be applied in a specific case derives from a different context and from a different regime of legality, or the norm to be applied results from a concurring or competing legal order.[5]

The above-sketched and so often underscored parochial attitude of criminal law may explain the long-lasting absence – but for authoritative but limited exceptions – of criminal "doctrine" from international debates on comparison in legal disciplines. Scholars of comparative law mainly ignore in their treatises the specific domain of criminal law and its substantive principles. Criminal justice is rarely a guest figure in legal frescos on fundamental methodological issues of legal comparison; criminal scholars who have "founded" and/or broadened comparison in criminal justice, at least (but not uniquely) in continental Europe, are not even cited.[6] An interest in procedural systems in civil law countries is sometimes traceable, occupying a handful of pages in leading US works such as Rudolf Schlesinger's.[7] That

conduct unlawful: S. Bronitt, "Australia," in Heller and Dubber (eds.), *Handbook*, 49, 52–54 (quoted at 52); in Canada, the Supreme Court (1950) "refused to rely on common-law offences on the basis that they 'would introduce great uncertainty into the administration of the Criminal Law'," and a few years later all common law offences but for one were abolished by a parliamentary law. In other common law jurisdictions such as the United Kingdom, a traditional "shadowy engagement" with the principle has been, since the enactment of the Human Rights Act (1998), flanked by an increasing awareness of the principle: A. J. Ashworth, "United Kingdom," in Heller and Dubber (eds.), *Handbook*, 532. In some jurisdictions, courts are not allowed to create criminal offences, but they are entitled to create criminal defenses – see I. Kugler, "Israel," in Heller and Dubber (eds.), *Handbook*, 353.

4 Recently, e.g., P. H. Robinson, "Four Distinctions that Glanville Williams Did Not Make: The Practical Benefits of Examining the Interrelation among Criminal Law Doctrines," in D. J. Baker and J. Horder (eds.), *The Sanctity of Life and the Criminal Law: The Legacy of Glanville Williams* (Cambridge: Cambridge University Press, 2013), 122.

5 See e.g., Chapter 1.

6 I am referring, for example, to Hans-Heinrich Jescheck and Albin Eser (founder and successor in the direction of the otherwise well-known German "Max-Planck-Institut für ausländisches und Internationales Strafrecht" in Freiburg im Breisgau). Neither of them are even mentioned in the name index compiled by B. Markesinis and J. Fedke, *Judicial Recourse to Foreign Law* (Abingdon: Routledge, 2006); for more detail, see B. Markesinis and J. Fedke, *Engaging with Foreign Law* (Oxford: Hart, 2009), 86.

7 R. Schlesinger, *Schlesinger's Comparative Law: Cases, Text, Materials*, 4th edn. (Mineola, NY: Foundation Press, 1980).

interest appears to be driven, at least from a didactical point of view, by practical reasons (e.g., US military personnel serving abroad as well as civilian personnel of missions are often subjected to the criminal jurisdiction of host states according to Status of Forces Agreements, facing the daily reality of investigations and court hearings in civil law countries). Hence, it appears relevant to know which principles and possibly what operational attitudes govern trials and the criminal process as a whole. Apart from this, until very recently, it has been hard to find signs of real dialogue among scholars, not to mention the "sound of silence" between Anglo-American and continental criminal law cultures, but for very few exceptions.[8] Since criminal law is or has for a long time been thought to be the branch of law most strictly related to national sovereignty, it might have appeared of low interest for comparison and less susceptible to internationalization. In fact, the reason that this body of law is by its nature mainly domestic, territorial, and "parochial" is twofold. First, sovereignty means to legitimately exert coercive powers on individuals *over and within* a territory, defined by legal or factual boundaries, however broadly they may be drawn. Second, coercive powers exerted *on* individuals' bodies *exist* naturally on a territory (individuals could be on the move, of course, possibly attracting many jurisdictional pretenses, though they do not move anymore if apprehended and sent to a lockup, thus being subjected to the plenary power of the detaining authority, be it a state or not). The very specific, unique feature of criminal law is that of disposing of lives: it is law governing a bio-power.

Therefore, it is commonly stated as a matter of principle that criminal law is territorial in its scope.[9] Of course, territoriality as a rule has its exceptions, though they are derogations from what is still considered as a general principle. Consequently, national judges apply only domestic criminal law, not foreign law[10]; the latter is not (nor should it be) directly enforceable abroad

[8] See G. Fletcher, *Basic Concepts of Criminal Law* (Oxford: Oxford University Press, 1998). A further partial testimony of a dialogue is the book edited by A. P. Simester, A. Du Bois-Pedain, and U. Neumann, *Liberal Criminal Theory: Essays for Andreas von Hirsch* (Oxford: Hart, 2014). Some studies offer not a single reference to continental literature; an example is P. H. Robinson, S. P. Garvey, and K. Kessler Ferzan (eds.), *Criminal Law Conversations* (Oxford: Oxford University Press, 2009). For a tentative dialogue, see A. Eser, *Comparative Criminal Law: Development, Aims, Methods* (Munich: Beck, 2017); however, it seems that comparative criminal law is "on the rise, at least in terms of standing on its own feet": A. Eser, "Book Review: Comparative Concepts of Criminal Law," (2016) 23 *Maastricht Journal of European and Comparative Law* 375.

[9] Territoriality is sometimes considered to be the only "principle" of criminal jurisdiction recognized by customary international law. For a legal–philosophical approach, see A. Chehtman, *Philosophical Foundations of Extraterritorial Punishment* (Oxford: Oxford University Press, 2010), esp. 56–59.

[10] Foreign law can be at most "taken into consideration" (*pris en compte*).

by enforcement agencies without the consent of the territorial state, due to comity reasons: only (police and judicial) cooperation is admissible and practicable,[11] and with due respect for individuals' rights.[12] Approximation of criminal laws possibly pursued at the regional level (within the framework of international organizations such as the European Union (EU) or the Council of Europe) aims at smoothing that cooperation rather than enforcing common values protected by criminal law provisions. And even there, where common values are enforced,[13] this happens only through the mediation of domestic legislation.

2 LEGALITY IN CRIMINAL LAW AS A MULTIFACETED PRINCIPLE

Against this background, one might be tempted to sum up: legality and not *inter*-legality is the key word in criminal law. An autonomous category of inter-legality would be to no avail for this branch of law. However, I wish to maintain that contrasting legality and inter-legality is a flawed approach.

To begin with, "legality" in criminal law is not simply – at least no longer – a domestic rule of hierarchy in a mere formal sense; that is, a procedural "guarantee of power's non arbitrariness" and therefore a "jurisdiction-related conception, mainly turning upon *obedience* and *conformity* with the law."[14] More substantially, "in its modern form it means that criminal liability and punishment can be based only on a prior legislative enactment of liability rules expressed with adequate precision and clarity."[15] Its content is therefore multifaceted, along with the functions it aims at performing in relation to individual liberty.

It has to be seen as a principle, all the more so in present times when it has not only a domestic dimension, but also is internationally recognized as a

[11] See esp. A. Eser, O. Lagodny, and C. L. Blakesley (eds.), *The Individual As Subject of International Cooperation in Criminal Matters* (Baden-Baden: Nomos, 2002).

[12] For example, abductions by CIA officials from a third country (Italy) to another country (Egypt) where torture may be perpetrated have been declared illegal by the European Court of Human Rights: *Nasr and Ghali v Italy*, Application no. 44883/09, February 23, 2016.

[13] Through duties to criminalize set forth by international conventions or directly applicable legislation (e.g., enacted on the basis of Art. 83 TFEU); see Section 4.2. On the limits of symbolic EU criminal law, notwithstanding the acknowledgment that European criminal law "should also be seen as a statement of values" and "not limited to instrumental reasons," see T. Elholm and R. Colson, "The Symbolic Purpose of EU Criminal Law," in R. Colson and S. Field (eds.), *EU Criminal Justice and the Challenges of Diversity: Legal Cultures in the Area of Freedom, Security and Justice* (Cambridge: Cambridge University Press, 2016), 56, 59–63.

[14] G. Palombella, "The Rule of Law at Home and Abroad," (2016) 8 *Hague Journal of the Rule of Law* 1, 7 (emphasis added).

[15] P. H. Robinson, "United States," in Heller and Dubber (eds.), *Handbook*, 566.

general principle of law or "customary international human rights law."[16] It is a principle not *because* it is nowadays widely recognized at the national and international level, but more deeply because it incorporates and expresses the very function of criminal law as a body of *law*.

In particular, whereas the actual source of institutional force is the bare governmental power of apprehending bodies (police power),[17] criminal law is there to set both the foundations and the legal boundaries to that use. Legality has been consequently conceived first and foremost as "domestic legal base" for any governmental use of force, primarily for creating crimes and extending their offense definition, be it the statutory law or the common law. The legislative monopoly of defining crime is therefore to be seen in that function of setting restraints on policy-making in criminal matters.[18] This approach, despite its having been articulated in the era of *Nationalstaaten*, is nevertheless the more convincing and binding as democratic states are concerned. "In a democracy the legislature – the most representative branch of government – is generally thought to be the proper body to exercise the criminalization decision."[19] Today, the expression "state monopoly" carries the meaning of democratic, parliamentary monopoly of criminalization choices.[20]

Hence, legality in criminal law is different from legality as a concept concerned formally with the hierarchy of norms. From a formal point of view, it singles out the only legitimate source(s) of criminal norms: mostly the legislature, sometimes the judiciary – as it predominantly was throughout history and partly still is in common law countries – provided that institutional arrangements entrust the latter with similar political legitimacy.[21] No source without democratic legitimacy is admitted, or if admitted in some legal orders, it is limited to secondary tasks (contracts are never a source of criminal provisions; regulations are limited to minor offences and

16 K. Gallant, *The Principle of Legality in International and Comparative Criminal Law* (Cambridge: Cambridge University Press, 2009), 9.

17 K. J. Heller and M. D. Dubber, "Introduction: Comparative Criminal Law," in Heller and Dubber (eds.), *Handbook*, 2, rightly label the police power "as essentially discretionary, and defined by its very indefinability," and therefore "incompatible with principled critique."

18 F. von Liszt, "Gutachten für die internationale kriminalistische Vereinigung," reprinted in F. von Liszt, *Strafrechtliche Aufsätze und Vorträge: Band II* (Berlin: De Gruyter, 1905), 80.

19 Robinson, "United States," 567.

20 On legislative supremacy, see R. Ekins, "Judicial Supremacy and the Rule of Law," (2003) 119 *Law Quarterly Review* 127, 147.

21 N. Lacey, *In Search of Criminal Responsibility: Ideas, Interests and Institutions* (Oxford: Oxford University Press, 2016), underlines this aspect: "it is not so much the development of the political values underlying legality as the institutional preconditions for realizing them, which underpin the changing contours of the concept" (198); "emerging ideas of legality, particularly in the context of public law, are closely connected to the changing structure of power" (201).

may be enacted only under control of a different constitutional body, as in France, or are limited to regulatory offences within the framework legislation, as in Canada; the judiciary may create or broaden defenses but not offence definitions, as in Israel).

What is important at this stage is to ask for the rationale behind that selection of sources. The answer lies in its function of hindering institutional arbitrariness. From a substantial point of view, the content of legality as a principle is defined in modern democracies and in particular in constitutional democracies by its "oppositional stance," namely its function of protecting the individual against bare coercive power: an all-round, full-fledged safeguard *against* the legislature (non-retroactivity), *against* the executive branch (parliamentary law), and *against* the judiciary (no application by analogy). From this functional point of view, the legality principle in criminal law is far more than one-sided legality; on the contrary, as a multifaceted promise of protection against institutional power, it expresses both formal instances and substantial safeguards, especially the control over the power exerted by the same legislature and by any other public body entrusted with authority of criminalization decisions. It therefore incorporates "rule of law" instances.

In a transnational context, where disparate sources of limitation of individual liberty operate, the need for protection and for even more rigorous legal restraints upon executive powers is indisputable. The proper function of the legality principle remains unfettered and reveals itself, perhaps paradoxically, as independent from the system in which it is called to display its protective attitude. What might change are the ways in which it concretely operates.

It seems from the above that, through the specificity of its legality principle as a "system-independent" principle, criminal law reveals its peculiar stance behind appearances when inter-legality issues are raised. In the following, I aim to show that the contemporary broad internationalization and globalization of criminal law is at the same time paradoxical (Section 3) and paradigmatic (Section 4) for inter-legality issues. And, more deeply, inter-legality raises a preliminary question about the very nature of criminal law when states' boundaries are blurred and the former monopoly of states' "legitimate violence" leaves room for transnational extension.[22]

[22] R. Cotterrell, "The Concept of Crime and Transnational Networks of Community," in V. Mitsilegas, P. Alldridge, and L. Cheliotis (eds.), *Globalisation, Criminal Law and Criminal Justice* (Oxford: Hart, 2015), 11.

3 PARADOXICAL FEATURE

As explained above, since criminal law has been historically conceived as related to the very highest degree to a state's sovereignty on a given territory, the very concept of inter-legality might appear at first glance incompatible with the intrinsic feature of this branch of law: penal laws are bound to a given territory, enforcement authorities can legitimately act within domestic borders, and judges must adjudicate according domestic law.

However, this picture is no longer reflecting the reality of criminal law. Transnational criminality (organized or not) has shown that "crime control is beyond the state,"[23] and over time, this has resulted in progressively strengthened police and judicial cooperation at both the regional and global level in order to avoid loopholes in the net cast against it.[24] Cooperation has further suggested harmonization of substantial criminal law and criminal procedures through various international and supranational instruments. The distinctiveness of criminal law in comparison with other branches of law seems, therefore, to fade.

As recently asserted at the level of the EU:

> Today, a judgement in civil and commercial matters of a national court must be automatically recognized and enforced in another Member State and a European Arrest Warrant against an alleged criminal issued in one Member State must be executed in another Member State. Those are clear examples of why all Member States need to be concerned if the rule of law principle is not fully respected in one Member State. This is why the EU has strong interest in safeguarding and strengthening the rule of law threats across the Union.[25]

Frankly, contrasting the execution of a judgment in civil and commercial matters to the transnational circulation of a judicial arrest warrant sounds a bit shattering. Be this as it may, the extract is quoted here with the aim of showing that multilevel regulations and their operational consequences have run into the bulwark of criminal law as well; in the example above, the circulation of the arrest warrant is the consequence of a Framework Decision of the EU. Well, the circulation of domestic decisions might be deemed to be a typical

[23] Cohen, "Crime and Politics."

[24] However, I would like to mention a critical assessment of "questionable assertions about the size, nature and novelty of this 'new' transnational threat" provided by the political scientist P. Andreas, "Illicit Globalisation Myths and Misconceptions," in Mitsilegas et al. (eds.), *Globalisation*, esp. 51 ff (quotation at 63).

[25] A *New EU Framework to Strengthen the Rule of Law* (11.3.2014), COM (2014) 158 final, p. 5.

inter-legality issue. If we define inter-legality as "unavoidable interconnectedness of legalities," the European arrest warrant is nothing else than the means of connection from at least two domestic legalities (that of the emitting judge and that of the executing one) and the supranational legal order of the EU. Through such an interplay, legal orders become connected as to their "criminal limb." This happens, as regards the arrest warrant and other similar European regulations, by virtue of a (highly criticized) ideological presumption: the mutual trust at the European level. Behind the very idea of trust and mutual recognition is, on the one hand, the difference and the separateness of legalities, and on the other hand, the practical necessity to "manage national legal diversity" through a reinterpretation of certain legal concepts in an autonomous, uniform manner under EU law.[26] Within the EU legal order, mutual recognition appears, therefore, as the conceptual switch from domestic legality to inter-legality.

4 PARADIGM

The paradigmatic feature comes along with the paradoxical one, both historically and in present times. Criminal law in action has always been – and nowadays certainly is – an area of law typically concerned with inter-legality issues. Historically, a well-known attitude of domestic legal systems since the late medieval era is that of "getting a glimpse" of the outside: this metaphor depicts the fact that states unilaterally retain jurisdiction to prescribe (i.e., the freedom [*Kompetenz-Kompetenz*] to unilaterally establish extraterritorial jurisdiction and/or to take into account [*prise en compte*] the *lex loci*, mainly the more lenient territorial law in case of extraterritorial jurisdiction based on the so-called "active personality principle"). By contrast, criminal law does not "throw its hands" beyond national boundaries:[27] states do not have unilateral jurisdiction to extraterritorially enforce domestic provisions. Retaining exclusive competence to define the boundaries of jurisdiction does not mean that conflicts of jurisdiction cannot arise whenever many states claim jurisdiction over a crime according to different "links" (territoriality, nationality of the agent or the victim, etc.). Conflicts of jurisdiction, for whose solution no binding instrument is in force internationally, cannot be considered as such to be inter-legality issues. However, I wish to underline that in spite of

[26] V. Mitsilegas, "Managing Legal Diversity in Europe's Area of Criminal Justice: The Role of Autonomous Concepts," in Colson and Field (eds.), *Challenges of Diversity*, 125.

[27] As the renowned Italian scholar Francesco Carrara put it: "Delitti commessi all'estero," in F. Carrara, *Opuscoli di Diritto Criminale*, 2nd edn. (Lucca: Giusti, 1870).

the unilaterality of the *Kompetenz-Kompetenz*, a typical inter-legality issue may nonetheless arise. It may happen that a state claiming extraterritorial criminal jurisdiction takes into consideration the *lex loci*; that is, the fact that the behavior satisfies the elements of a crime according to the law of the territorial state, which, for example, decides not to hand over the case for trial. For instance, this may happen whenever a state claims jurisdiction according to the so-called "representation" principle or representational jurisdiction.[28] The judge faces here thorny questions as to whether justifications, excuses, statutes of limitation, etc., provided for in the legal order of the state of commission must be taken into consideration in adjudicating the case at stake.[29]

Another aspect of overcoming the domestic separateness of criminal law in the international arena is worth adding. At least since the mid-1960s, explicit duties to penalize started to spread at the international and supranational level (differences as to the scope and reach of them are not relevant here), sparked by transnational forms of criminality. Consequently, a fabric of multiple obligations for nation-states is woven, to be considered in both its horizontal and vertical dimensions: respectively, interstate relations and as the supranational as well as international level. In the following, I will sketch how domestic criminal law might be affected by inter-legality issues in both the horizontal (Section 4.1) and vertical dimensions (Section 4.2).

4.1 *A Glimpse of the Outside (Inter-Legality in the Horizontal Dimension)*

The general rule of the territorial ambit of criminal law was already formulated in the seventeenth century: "*extra territorium iusdicenti impune non paretur.*"[30] However, horizontal conflicts in interstate relationships have always arisen in connection with extraterritorial jurisdiction (i.e., through the extension either of the ambit of substantial criminal law or of the domestic jurisdiction to alleged crimes committed abroad according to a "substantial link" or "principle" [be it the active personality principle, the passive personality principle, the flag principle, the representation principle, or the universal

[28] On representational or vicarious jurisdiction (*stellvertretende Strafrechtspflege*), see, in English, Chehtman, *Philosophical Foundations*, 76 ff, and its definition text accompanying footnote 87 ("this principle provides an extraterritorial state").

[29] I do not go here into further details. Cf. especially A. Eser, "Grundlagen und Grenzen 'stellvertretender Strafrechtspflege' (§ 7 Abs. 2 Nr. 2 StGB) – Zur Problematik der 'identischer Tatnorm' bei Auslandstaten, insbesondere bei Amnestierung am Tatort," (1993) *Juristenzeitung* 875.

[30] Burgundus, *Tractatus ad Consuetudines Flandriae* (1621) (no duty of obedience in front of an authority acting beyond the limits of its jurisdiction).

principle]). Besides, the very concept of territoriality urges relativization even in those legal orders (such as those of the United Kingdom and United States) traditionally most committed to self-restraint in affirming extraterritorial jurisdiction,[31] unless an explicit statutory provision provides for "clear evidence of congressional intent." Conceptual tools for expanding the concept of territory are those of "subjective" and "objective" territoriality. To put it in the words of Justice Holmes: "Acts done outside a jurisdiction, but *intended to* produce *and producing* detrimental effects within it, justify a state in punishing the cause of the harm as if he had been present at the effect, if the state should succeed in getting him within his power."[32] As is well-known, competing jurisdictions spark off jurisdictional conflicts, for which to date no definitive criterion for resolution according to a given hierarchy has been internationally accepted.

4.2 *Duties to Penalize (Inter-Legality in the Vertical Dimension)*

Since the mid-1960s, a new phenomenon has arisen: that of the penetration of national criminal law by international and supranational law. Explicit duties to penalize emerge at the international and supranational level (differences as to the reach of them are not of significance here) – currently a deeply rooted attitude of international bodies. Most recently, this *vertical dimension* of inter-legality is portrayed by overlapping, variously interacting and mutually reinforcing universal and regional instruments of governing crime through different tools of governance.[33] Consequently, a fabric of multiple obligations for nation-states is woven. What lies behind this evolution is the shift of the political (and sometimes legal) authority of criminalization decisions from the territorial state to other entities, with different status in international law.

This vertical dimension of inter-legality reveals itself as the most problematic, intriguing, and risky for the traditional concepts of criminal law. It is therefore appropriate to sketch the historical evolution of the progressive erosion of national sovereignty in allocating fundamental criminalization choices.

At the outset of this evolution, international conventions timidly advocated extraterritorial jurisdiction over certain types of offences in order to avoid impunity. For example, according to the Convention on Offences and

[31] "(A)part from exceptional cases in which specific provisions is made in regard to acts committed abroad, the whole body of the criminal law of England deals only with acts committed in England": Viscount Simons, in *Cox v Army Council*, 1963, LR-AC 48, 67.

[32] 221 U.S. 285 (1911) (emphasis added).

[33] V. Mitsilegas, "The European Union and the Global Governance of Crime," in Mitsilegas et al. (eds.), *Globalisation*, 1.

Certain Other Acts Committed on Board Aircraft (1963), the state of registration of the aircraft is competent to exercise jurisdiction over offences and acts committed on board; each contracting state shall take such measures as may be necessary to establish its jurisdiction as the state of registration over offences committed on board aircraft registered in such a state. The Convention does not exclude any criminal jurisdiction exercised in accordance to national law.

From then onwards, international conventions have provided for more explicit duties to penalize accompanied by a detailed drafting of the offence definition and – later on – a more complex system of provisions encompassing substantive and procedural law: from the Convention for the Suppression of Unlawful Seizure of Aircraft (1970) to the International Convention for the Suppression of the Financing of Terrorism (1999), and the United Nations Convention against Corruption (2003), to mention only very few examples. This trend is noticeable at both the universal and the regional level (for the regional level, see, e.g., the conventions of the Council of Europe in criminal matters).

In more recent times, international organizations and bodies that, until now, have been deprived of direct competence in criminal law due to their lack of proper democratic legitimacy have been vested – or have claimed to be entrusted – with the power to exercise the criminalization decision. Think, for instance, of the EU after Lisbon (Art. 82 ff TFUE) and the Security Council resolutions after 9/11 in particular as regard the phenomenon of foreign fighters.[34]

[34] UN SC Res. 2178/2014, 24.9.2014, operational part, n. 5 and 65. Decides that Member States shall, consistent with international human rights law, international refugee law, and international humanitarian law, prevent and suppress the recruiting, organizing, transporting or equipping of individuals who travel to a State other than their States of residence or nationality for the purpose of the perpetration, planning, or preparation of, or participation in, terrorist acts or the providing or receiving of terrorist training, and the financing of their travel and of their activities.

6. . . . all Member States shall ensure that any person who participates in the financing, planning, preparation or perpetration of terrorist acts or in supporting terrorist acts is brought to justice, and decides that all States shall ensure that their domestic laws and regulations establish serious criminal offenses sufficient to provide the ability to prosecute and to penalize in a manner duly reflecting the seriousness of the offense:

(a) their nationals who travel or attempt to travel to a State other than their States of residence or nationality, and other individuals who travel or attempt to travel from their territories to a State other than their States of residence or nationality, for the purpose of the perpetration, planning, or preparation of, or participation in, terrorist acts, or the providing or receiving of terrorist training;

(b) the wilful provision or collection, by any means, directly or indirectly, of funds by their nationals or in their territories with the intention that the funds should be used, or in the

The reason that this evolution is important, even though not homogenous in terms of its nature and "ripeness," is twofold. On the one hand, it seems to mark an irreversible shift as regards the political remit of criminalization decisions. Domestic legislatures are often entrusted with the task of merely technically implementing penalization decisions made by different authorities and at a different level (see the EU practice of setting through directives standard minimum rules for offence provisions and penalties). Here, the adjudication process may easily face inter-legality issues. For instance, if the national government does not implement international/supranational obligations, but the domestic constitution provides for mechanisms for safeguarding that internal rules are in line with international law, the judge will activate those mechanisms in order for incompatible domestic provisions to be annulled (e.g., through constitutional review) or declared non-applicable.

On the other hand, if globalization means proliferation of the levels of governing of complex phenomena also through criminalization (from narcotic drugs to economic crimes, from environmental offences to corruption and terrorism), then the interplay of the horizontal and vertical dimensions of (inter-)legality becomes even more twisted. States are at least seemingly "subjected" to different and often contradictory obligations. Some of them are binding, some others are not; some are binding only as to the achievements, some others as to the means; they are possibly different as to the content and not necessarily coherent, nor always compatible either with human rights standards or with fundamental principles of domestic legal order.

The masterly analytical overview provided, for instance, by Valsamis Mitsilegas sheds insightful light on "the emergence of global standards and norms in the governance of crime ... accompanied by international mechanisms aimed at targeting not states, but individuals."[35] I only wish to add here two reflections. First, the circulation of models – the synergy and

knowledge that they are to be used, in order to finance the travel of individuals who travel to a State other than their States of residence or nationality for the purpose of the perpetration, planning, or preparation of, or participation in, terrorist acts or the providing or receiving of terrorist training; and,

(c) the wilful organization, or other facilitation, including acts of recruitment, by their nationals or in their territories, of the travel of individuals who travel to a State other than their States of residence or nationality for the purpose of the perpetration, planning, or preparation of, or participation in, terrorist acts or the providing or receiving of terrorist training.

[35] Mitsilegas, "Managing Legal Diversity," 153. The author focuses on the role of the EU at four levels of global governance: via global multilateral treatises, via regional multilateral treatises, via the emergence of "soft law," and via the emergence of "global administrative law."

cross-fertilization between international law, soft law, and Community/union law[36] – does not exclude an active role for domestic experiences (possibly carried by state negotiators). For instance, the offence definition of money laundering has existed in Italy since 1978 and provided a path for a handful of supranational legal (criminal and administrative) instruments to counter this type of illicit behavior. Similarly, and perhaps more evidently, the definition of organized crime (*rectius*, group) and further substantive provisions drafted by the Palermo Convention against Transnational Organized Crime, along with other preventive countermeasures, echo the Italian experience in fighting against the Mafia as a criminal organization with specific features – being always on the move.[37] Second, describing the cross-fertilization and synergy among legal orders even in criminal matters, as well as highlighting some inconsistencies[38] as to the specific content of legal instruments, should not lead to obliterating the functional/operational difference between offence definitions at the international/supranational level and offence provisions within a domestic legal order.

The first ones (international definitions) aim at directing the state action of implementing international rules and standards through harmonization, when needed in order to facilitate cooperation against transnational crimes of a (mainly) grave nature. Offence definitions drafted by domestic implementing legislation direct the conduct not primarily of states, but of individuals – this is done by precisely and prospectively showing the border and straddling the line between what is prohibited and what is not, in accordance with the fundamental principle of legality with all its corollaries or multifaceted rationales, if one prefers that term.[39]

By pointing out the different aims of the offence definition within different legal orders (domestic, international, supranational), I would underline that the very moment when international definitions are transposed into domestic legal order, thus directly (even though only potentially) affecting individuals, is not a merely operational step. Not only rules come into play at this stage, but also principles: at this stage, it is up to the domestic legislature to implement

[36] Whose major step Mitsilegas sees in the conclusion of the 1988 Vienna Convention against Illicit Trafficking in Narcotic Drugs (UN level) followed at the regional (European) level by the first Money Laundering Directive of 1991.

[37] F. Varese, *Mafias on the Move. How Organized Crime Conquers New Territories* (Princeton, NJ: Princeton University Press, 2011).

[38] E.g., unlike the Palermo Convention, the EU Framework Decision on Terrorism does not mention the "direction" of an organized criminal group: see Mitsilegas, "Managing Legal Diversity," 163.

[39] E.g., Robinson, "Four Distinctions," 123.

its own fundamental principles of criminal liability, such as proportionality, culpability, etc. For example, in a legal order where the harm principle is taken in a strictly objective way, causing harm could not be legitimately punished with the same penalty as merely attempting to cause it; gravity issues must be addressed in setting penalties or at least in sentencing; a fortiori, a course of conduct that does not satisfy the constituent elements of a criminal offence could not be punished even if the agent is convinced that (s)he is committing a crime.

By the way, this jurisdiction-dependent feature of liability principles is that which legal philosophers often underestimate or even deny,[40] deluding themselves that legal reasoning on issues of morality and (in) law may be resolved without any reference to the various and discrete fundamental attitudes of domestic law.

Another instance of interference between international instruments of a regulatory nature and criminal law is the field of effectual enforcement of international binding policies. Where measures that restrict freedom of individuals are adopted, the problem arises as to whether criminal law safeguards are applicable irrespective of the formal administrative nature of the relevant provisions. The issue at stake is a very multifaceted one. As the instance of "listing" for antiterrorist purposes shows, it sometimes proves difficult to precisely canvass the multilevel relationships among legal orders of different natures. From a rather practical point of view, in addition, it would not be meaningful and feasible to delegate the protection of fundamental human rights to the domestic judicial review of international instruments.

Here, we might be able to admit that political choices to restrict personal freedoms can be taken outside traditional democratic processes, since the fundamental choices on criminalization are not directly involved. Nevertheless, the very feature of criminal law is at stake here. Are administrative measures curbing personal liberty sanctions of a substantially criminal nature? If the answer sounds positive, then the functional safeguards of criminal law

[40] E.g., take the question raised by D. Husak, "The Philosophy of Criminal Law: Extending the Debates," (2013) 7 *Criminal Law and Philosophy* 353: an individual has sexual intercourse with a deaf–mute quadriplegic who was (maybe) consenting to sex, but the defendant "could not have known the woman was consenting ... he is probably guilty of committing the *wrong* of rape ... Does the law have reason to treat the defendant *as if* he is a rapist, even if he is not? Is the defendant guilty of attempted rape?" (emphasis in original). The answer is inevitably jurisdiction-dependent, since an objective-oriented criminal system will answer differently (no crime if you engage in a behavior that does not amount to a crime, even if you think it is a crime: see the Italian concept of "*reato putativo*" and the German concept of *Wahndelikt*) compared to subjective-oriented ones (bad intentions can be punished).

must be in place.[41] But even assuming that the principle of legality (conceived as above) cannot play a sensible role, the issue of "political legitimacy" is crucial in decentralized international lawmaking.[42] The problem here is that the domestic level is involved only randomly (targeted individuals may be living in one territory rather than in another) and conflicts of obligations arise: there is a need for equality of protection that cannot be afforded by municipal law. Therefore, one dares to imagine that the protection tools should be "near" the source, rather than near the place where the effects are produced. As Judge Pinto de Albuquerque of the European Court of Human Rights (ECtHR) puts it, "the risk of a cacophony of multiple regional constitutional orders … can only be prevented once a World Human Rights Court comes into being."[43]

The consequence would be that the place where political decisions not only involving states but also reverberating against individuals are taken should also be the place where (i.e., the level at which) the system of protection shall be developed and operating in practice. This will need far-reaching changes of institutional frameworks (e.g., the setting up of a specialized section for judicial review of UN monitoring bodies, or of the International Court of Justice; see e.g., the setting up by the African Union, through the so-called Malabo Protocol, of a new section for international crimes of the African Court on Human and Peoples' Rights).[44]

A final (but important) well-known level of inter-legality involving criminal matters is that of the international judiciary: think of the ECtHR and the Court of Justice of the EU. Let us consider, for instance, the case law of the ECtHR requiring positive obligations for states to protect human rights through proper criminalization of harmful actions (commonly mentioned is the ruling on the rape exemption and the prohibition of torture).

I want to briefly argue here that there is a fundamental distinction between this kind of obligation and that arising from other international covenants

[41] On that point, see the powerful concurring opinion of Judge Pinto de Albuquerque as to the judgment of the European Court of Human Rights (GC), *Al Dulimi and Montana Management Inc. v Switzerland*, Application no. 5809/08, June 21, 2016, paras. 26, 37: if one type of confiscation imposed on the suspect is punitive in nature (para. 26), then "the Convention criteria for triggering the procedural guarantees of the criminal limb of Article 6, and in particular the presumption of innocence" (para. 37).

[42] Ibid., para. 71.

[43] Ibid.

[44] Statute of the African Court of Justice and Human and Peoples' Rights (Statute of the African Court), annex to the Protocol on Amendments to the Protocol on the Statute of the African Court of Justice and Human Rights (Protocol on Amendments), adopted on June 27, 2014, arts. 28A–28M. Fifteen ratifications are required for the Protocol to enter into force.

setting forth duties of criminalization. According to the latter, it is an obligation to draft the abstract offence definition; the former are the result of judicial review on the domestic system in action, conducted under "the duty to take into account all relevant circumstances of a particular case."[45] The Court is not essentially concerned with setting abstract standards of conduct for individuals; rather, it ascertains whether a fundamental right is actually and effectively protected in the concrete life of a legal order. Consequently, the very concept of "law" – the legality principle, art. 7 ECHR – is here to be explained as requiring the existence of an actual legal source according to which the liberty has been sacrificed – be it a legislative provision, unwritten law, or case law (effectual evaluation). This is the actual and not sufficiently fathomed reason why "legality could only in a general sense require laws to have a democratic origin."[46]

A problem arises here, nevertheless, because the question of *legitimacy* of that source in the municipal legal order remains open: the Court is not a Court of fourth instance – it must base upon the domestic legal rules and their interpretation (we may define that starting point as the *offered legality, legalità offerta*: abstract legality is not sufficient but is necessary to satisfy the protection of the right to liberty in criminal matters).

On the one hand, "quality requirements" should satisfy the Court as a general principle (effectual perspective: we can define it as the *obtained legality, legalità raggiunta*).[47] On the other hand, this substantial view should come up alongside the formal requirement in order to enhance, not diminish the level of protection. That proposition can be directly deduced from the general principle enshrined in Article 53 of the Convention: the text cannot be interpreted as if it is allowed to limit or derogate from rights recognized by other sources in national or international law. The consequence is that whenever a domestic legal order requires written parliamentary law for offence definition, the Court should start the review by assessing – possibly ex officio – whether that basic requirement exists. The Court should be more proactive in the field of Article 7 than it is in the case when other conventional

[45] Recently, see ECtHR (GC), *Muršić v Croatia*, Application no. 7334/13, October 20, 2016, para. 112. Among the extensive scholarly literature, see G. Lautenbach, *The Concept of the Rule of Law and the European Court of Human Rights* (Oxford: Oxford University Press, 2013), esp. 83–86, 185–192, 202 ff.

[46] Ibid., 204: given wide divergences among national legal systems, the "Convention legality standard cannot aim at the same level of sophistication." This is not false, but this is a description and not a proper explanation. I argue differently in the text.

[47] T. Padovani, "Il Crepuscolo della Legalità nel Processo Penale. Riflessioni Antistoriche sulle Dimensioni Processuali della Legalità Penale," (1999) *L'Indice Penale* 527.

rights are concerned, precisely on the assumption that "(t)he power of review in such cases must be greater than normal because it is the law itself, and its application by national courts, that is the essence of the right in question."[48] Far from being *une formule rituelle* – as it has been sometimes defined – that hardly has any practical significance, Article 53 appears as a key provision within the framework of a complex system of legalities.

5 SOME FINAL REMARKS

Intertwinement among orders and accumulation of layers of legalities are realities of the criminal justice system. The concept of inter-legality may therefore appear useful for empirically describing the modern situation of criminal law, at least from the mid-1960s when the trend to set obligations to criminalize became firmly established in international relations and in the practice of competent international organizations. Its virtue is primarily to aptly denote the different levels at which political decisions of creating crimes or extending existing ones are taken.

However, more than its descriptive ability, to be praised is its prescriptive potential ("normative" in the philosophical sense of the word); that is, however many levels of political choice there may be, they must all conform to the fundamental aim of the legality principle as a general principle of law.[49] This aim is to set boundaries on institutional (legislative, administrative, judicial) power to dispose of citizens' personal liberty. Recalling this rationale does not mean harking back to old-fashioned categories; rather, it recommends cautiousness in evaluating the destiny of classical legal notions, concepts, and doctrines elaborated over time as safeguards of personal liberty (which would be the more at risk, by the way, if the sovereign authority subcontracted out the policing function to private or uncontrolled powerful public interests). Far from being a formal rule of hierarchy, in contemporary democracies, legality essentially requires *internal* control mechanisms and accepts *external* control – here inter-legality issues arise – over both abstract and concrete criminalization decisions.[50] Due to what we have labeled as the "oppositional stance" of the principle above, control over power is an integral part of institutional arrangements required by legality-based, modern democratic criminal law.

48 W. Schabas, *The European Convention on Human Rights: A Commentary* (Oxford: Oxford University Press, 2015), 338.

49 Gallant, *The Principle of Legality*, 66.

50 Abstract decisions involve, in particular, creating or not creating new crimes. Concrete decisions involve imposing criminal sanctions in the absence of a legal basis or not punishing contrary to duties to do so.

In contemporary constitutional legal orders, external as well as domestic judicial control upon the concrete features of every legal order in action needs to be carried out according to an "effectual perspective" (i.e., in order to effectively protect liberty and human rights). Here, rule of law issues are at stake: preference should be given to the legal construction – combining different layers of legal orders – that provides the broadest safeguards "in action" in unison with the (inter-)legality rationale: this is the only way to safeguard political legitimacy to the entire system.

In the *Melloni* case, for instance,[51] the Court of Justice of the EU expressed the opinion that individual procedural rights of (only) domestic constitutional rank have no precedence over judicial cooperation imposed by an EU instrument based on mutual trust (the European Arrest Warrant). I want to maintain that such an abstract point of view is flawed. The same result of triggering smooth cooperation in criminal matters could have been reached under more stringent theoretical premises; in fact, the presence of the accused at trial is not as such a safeguard to his or her rights and liberties. The protective nature of this *right to be present* depends on the personal choice of the individual person. It might happen that the legal order in which the freedom of choice of whether to stand trial or not is safeguarded is to be considered as the most "liberal" one; thus, no hurdle against cooperation through the European Arrest Warrant should have been provided by the domestic court of the executing state against the issuing authority. That is why a proper interpretation of provisions such as Article 53 ECHR or Article 53 of the EU Charter of Fundamental Rights is of paramount importance in inter-legality issues involving criminal law. A successful accomplishment of the protection system presupposes an "inter-legal" perspective.

[51] Case C-399/11, *Melloni v Ministerio Fiscal*, ECLI:EU:C:2013:107, esp. paras 55 ff: "where an EU legal act calls for national implementing measures, national authorities and courts remain free to apply national standards of protection of fundamental rights, provided that the level of protection provided for by the Charter, as interpreted by the Court, and the primacy, unity and effectiveness of EU law are not thereby compromised" (para 60).

PART III

Shaping Inter-Legality

12

Shaping Inter-Legality

The Role of Administrative Law Techniques and Their Implications

EDOARDO CHITI

1 INTER-LEGALITY AS RECOGNITION? PARAMETERS AND RESEARCH QUESTIONS

This chapter is based on four main premises. To begin with, it assumes that the world community is now dominated by a multitude of legal orders, each of them responsible for one specific sector. This is certainly true for the various international and transnational regimes established since the last two decades of the twentieth century. Each of these regulatory systems works in a specific area where global issues arise (e.g., security, environmental protection, financial supervision), has developed its own 'legality' and carries out a sector-based responsibility.[1] As for the states, they remain 'general ends' entities. But they nevertheless tend to lose their capacity to work as unitary centres of responsibility and face an ever-stronger process of sectoral fragmentation of their action and legality.[2] Indeed, this is at the same time

[1] The proliferation of functionally specialized regulatory systems beyond the state is openly recognized by various strands of research on the transformations of the world community in the last two decades, irrespective of the overall perspective and core concepts of each of them (international law, international relations, legal globalization, global administrative law, etc.): for all, see S. Cassese, *The Global Polity: Global Dimensions of Democracy and the Rule of Law* (Seville: Global Law Press, 2012), 22 ff; for a historical account of the long-term intellectual processes that have contributed to the establishment of the current structure of the world community, see M. Mazower, *Governing the World: The History of an Idea, 1815 to the Present* (London: Penguin, 2013). What is peculiar to the project of the present book is its reference to 'legality': the ongoing process of proliferation of non-national regulatory systems by sector has implied a particularization of legality as it existed in the states into a plurality of 'legalities' distinct by sector.

[2] This is a much less noticed process. While it is almost a truism to say that the growth of specialized organizations beyond the state has led to functional fragmentation and diversification in the world community, the states are still largely understood as 'general ends' polities, capable of balancing competing interests and values. There are, however, exceptions: in particular, see S. Cassese, 'Nel Labirinto delle Globalizzazioni', (2007) 57 *Rivista*

a cause and an effect of the proliferation of international and transnational regimes operating in specific sectors.

Moreover, this huge amount of national and non-national legal orders and regimes interact systematically between themselves. By using the term 'interaction', we broadly refer to a relationship that is at the same time material, institutional and legal and does not necessarily imply a coordinated effort or a joint enterprise. Indeed, the interaction between the various legal orders is often due to the inevitable interconnections of the substantive objectives of each legal order (e.g., the interconnection between different objectives of social regulation, such as food security, health security and environmental protection). On other occasions, however, it takes the form of a clash or a latent competition between conflicting objectives (e.g., neo-liberal projects of economic integration carried out by international or transnational regimes may clash with welfare policies carried out by social-democratic states).[3]

In addition to this, the systematic interaction among the various orders and regimes operating in the world community implies that none of them understands itself or works as a self-contained legal regime. Rather, each of them accepts, implicitly or explicitly, in its establishing legal framework and concrete functioning, the validity of the legality of the other legal orders and regimes. The recognition of the validity of other orders' legality and of the existing legal connections between different orders is not imposed by any superior authority or overarching legal principle, but it depends on the initiative of the relevant orders. It responds to the functional and normative exigency to address issues that lay at the intersection between legal orders. Most importantly, it implies that such issues have to be solved by identifying and applying a composite law made up of an open set of norms rooted in different orders and jointly capable of ensuring a fair and effective treatment of the case. This overall process of recognition, together with the effects that it determines, is the legal situation that we can conceptualize as 'inter-legality'.[4]

Trimestrale di Diritto Pubblico 921, pointing to the functional 'disaggregation' of the states and to the gradual weakening of their capacity to operate as sites in which all relevant interests, although potentially conflicting, may be appropriately reconciled.

3 All strands of legal research on the changing structure and functioning of the world community recognize in one way or another that segmentation is accompanied by the inevitable interaction among the legal orders operating in the world community: for all, see E. Benvenisti, *The Law of Global Governance* (The Hague: Hague Academy of International Law, 2014). Each field of research, however, has its own way of describing the forms and mechanisms of the interactions between the relevant actors and understanding their general implications.

4 This is – of course – the core idea of this book and what distinguishes it from other research projects on the transformation of the world community: see Chapter 1 by the editors.

Finally, as a process of recognition, inter-legality may operate in a variety of different situations. It may involve different types of relations, such as the horizontal relationships between two or more regulatory systems beyond the state (e.g., the Food and Agriculture Organization [FAO] and the World Health Organization [WHO]), the vertical relationships between non-national and national legal orders (e.g., the World Trade Organization [WTO] and its member states) and the triangular relationships between a regulatory system beyond the state, a supranational organization and the states that are members of both of them (e.g., the Aarhus Convention Compliance Committee, the states that are parties to the Aarhus Convention and the European Union [EU]). Moreover, inter-legality may occur both within one single sector (e.g., environmental protection) in which sets of partially overlapping institutions governing a particular issue area operate as a 'regime complex'[5] and across distinct policy fields (e.g., trade and health protection). In the latter case, it is likely to imply a balancing between competing public interests. In the former case, it rather implies a management of the intra-sector variation in the ways in which the relevant sectoral interest is interpreted by all involved legal orders.

Using these assumptions as starting points, this chapter aims to discuss how administrative law techniques can sustain and structure inter-legality. As a process of recognition, inter-legality is shaped by a number of specific techniques capable of affecting its features and internal dynamics. Such techniques, deployed by the orders at stake, include the administrative law instruments that are used by each legal order by sector to govern the interactions between the processes of administrative implementation of its own first-level measures and the implementing processes of other contiguous legal orders (the establishment of joint administrative proceedings and joint administrations, the search for functional equivalence of parallel regulations, the provision of mechanisms for the balancing of different public interests, etc.). What are the administrative law techniques that are

[5] The notion has been coined by K. Raustiala and D. G. Victor, 'The Regime Complex of Plant Genetic Resources', (2004) 58 *International Organization* 277. See also R. O. Keohane and D. G. Victor, *The Regime Complex for Climate Change*, Harvard Kennedy School, Discussion Paper 10-33, available at www.belfercenter.org/sites/default/files/legacy/files/Keohane_Victor_Final_2.pdf, where "regime complexes" are defined as arrangements located between two extremes, one characterized by "fully integrated institutions that impose regulation through comprehensive, hierarchical rules" and another characterized by "highly fragmented collections of institutions with no identifiable core and weak or nonexistent linkages between regime elements": in the case of regime complexes, "there are connections between the specific and relatively narrow regimes, but no overall architecture that structures the whole set" (at 4).

used by the legal orders at stake to govern inter-legality? How do they shape and structure inter-legality? And how does inter-legality – as shaped by such techniques – contribute to the characterization of the legal space in which it operates?

The structure of the chapter reflects this set of research questions. The chapter first identifies and discusses the different types of administrative law techniques that are used to govern inter-legality (Sections 2 and 3). It then points to the circumstance that such techniques do not promote one single notion of inter-legality, but many (Section 4). Finally, it presents some reflections on the way in which inter-legality affects and shapes the legal space in which it operates (Section 5).

2 INTER-LEGALITY THROUGH ADMINISTRATIVE LAW

As a process of recognition, inter-legality does not just happen. The single national and non-national legal orders operating in the world community do not meet their interlocutors because of some metaphysical force at work. Of course, there are several reasons – functional, economic, and political – that drive towards the mutual recognition of the orders' legality. But inter-legality – as a process of recognition – is triggered and sustained through specific legal and institutional arrangements laid down by the relevant legal orders. It is through these arrangements that inter-legality actually takes place. Moreover, these arrangements are not neutral technologies. They actively contribute to shaping the contents and functions of inter-legality.

The instruments through which inter-legality is operationalized are of different types. One fundamental set of instruments is that of the principles and rules governing the relations between the legal sources of the systems involved in the process of mutual recognition. The way in which a legal order recognizes the validity of another legal order is defined – before any other thing – by the doctrines that regulate the interactions between its legal sources and those of the other. The typical interplay is that between norms and measures adopted by the sectoral regulatory systems beyond the state and the norms of the participating national orders (e.g., the operationalization in the domestic orders of the standards applicable to national administrations adopted in the WTO system). But the interplay may involve two or more regulatory systems beyond the state, such as in cases in which a private actor invokes before a judicial or quasi-judicial body of a regulatory system a norm rooted in a different legal order. The doctrines governing the interplay between norms may structure the contact between legal orders in many different ways. For example, they may insulate a legal order from any possible influence of the law of other legal orders, but they can also promote the full opening of a system by recognizing the supremacy and the direct effect of external norms. As a halfway house between these two extremes, they may – and they actually do – operate through variable aperture settings, allowing relative closure or relative openness, depending on the case. This is a fundamental layer of analysis in an enquiry devoted to reconstruct the 'mechanics' of inter-legality. Indeed, it is the set of doctrines governing the interplay between norms that establishes the basic conditions for the identification of the norms applicable to issues raised by the overlapping of two or more legal orders.

This chapter, however, aims at focusing on a different set of instruments through which inter-legality is operationalized. Instead of taking into consideration the principles and rules structuring the relations between legal sources of different systems, it discusses the administrative law instruments that are used by each legal order by sector to govern the interactions between the processes of administrative implementation of its own first-level measures and the implementing processes of other legal orders. I therefore assume that each legal order has its own administrative machinery, responsible for the implementation of first-level measures, and I ask how the existing organizational and procedural arrangements are designed to take into account other orders' legality and to trigger the process of recognition that is the heart of inter-legality.

The argument developed in the following pages may be summarized as follows: the administrative law techniques used in each legal order do not sustain and structure one single type of inter-legality, but many. While virtually all legal orders accept their reciprocal validity, the administrative law techniques used to govern the interactions between their implementing processes promote different types of recognition. I would like to suggest that there are three main groups of hypotheses: (i) one in which the implementation processes of the various relevant legal orders are regulated in such a way to support the joint administrative execution of political decisions jointly elaborated by two or more legal orders, (ii) a second group in which the implementation processes promote indirect convergence, rather than joint administrative execution, (iii) a number of cases in which the implementation processes of the legal orders at stake protect their regulatory policies and sustain their open or latent competition. These three situations will be considered in turn with a view to reconstructing their distinguishing features. Once we recognize this diversity of situations, we can better understand inter-legality as a changing legal situation.

3 THREE LEGAL SITUATIONS

3.1 *Joint Responsibility*

The implementation process is on many occasions regulated in such a way as to support the joint administrative execution of political decisions that have been jointly elaborated or at least shared by two or more legal orders. In this kind of situation, the reciprocal recognition between legal orders is an overt and explicit purpose of the principles and rules governing the administrative implementation in each of the legal orders at stake. Moreover, it is specifically meant as a coordinated administrative action implying a joint responsibility – either trans-sectoral or infra-sectoral – of two or more legal orders.

3.1.1 Basic Pattern

The reality of institutional interactions in the world community provides a growing number of examples of joint responsibility. Joint responsibility takes place in highly sensitive fields, ranging from military security – where a 'complex' made up of the UN, NATO, EU and their member states is at work – to financial stability – in which the Financial Stability Board operates as a coordinator of several converging regulatory regimes (and social regulation; see, e.g., the Inter-Organization Programme for the Sound Management of Chemicals, called to increase the effectiveness of the international chemical safety programmes). Sometimes, it does not occur within a single sector, but it involves contiguous policy areas, as is shown by the Codex Alimentarius Commission and other 'international agencies'.

We will consider some of these examples in the following pages. Before doing so, though, it is important to clarify the basic pattern of the legal situation that we have qualified as joint responsibility. Three aspects of such a pattern are significant. First, joint administrative execution takes place where there has been a process of interconnection between two or more legal orders at the level of their political decision-making. A plurality of different regimes, in other words, have come to an agreement on a specific policy objective falling within their respective spheres of competence. This may occur in several ways. For example, the interconnection at the level of political decision-making may result from the relationships existing between the founding norms of the relevant legal orders, as in the cases in which one of the regimes must develop policies compatible with the principles and rules of another. But it may also stem from the establishment of joint working groups made up of representatives of all legal orders involved and responsible for the coordination of the decision-making processes internal to the various regimes.

While joint political decision-making may take a diversity of forms, it always implies a balancing between different and competing interests when it takes place through legal orders operating in different fields, such as security and human rights protection. When it is internal to one particular issue area, such as environmental protection, it rather involves a reconciliation of the specific views, values and orientations of all regimes involved.

Second, the structure and contents of the implementing arrangements promoting joint administrative execution between two or more political orders vary from case to case. It is not possible to establish a taxonomy of the multiple ways in which the joint execution of political decisions elaborated by a plurality of legal orders is structured and arranged. This is due to the structural complexity of the world community and to the very limited development of empirical research on this specific issue. We can nevertheless identify two basic instruments for joint execution: one organizational and the other procedural. Indeed, the arrangements for joint execution make large use of composite or mixed bodies; that is, of bodies made up of representatives at the administrative level (e.g., the secretariats) of all the regimes involved and usually responsible for the coordination of all the actors involved in the implementation process. In addition to this, the administrative procedures through which the implementation process in the involved legal orders take place are reciprocally coordinated and interrelated in a variety of ways, ranging from functional interdependence of formally autonomous proceedings to the establishment of composite administrative procedures; that is, administrative procedures that involve administrations of different legal orders and are subject to rules produced by the legal orders to which the involved administrations belong. The overall result is that the administrations of the relevant regimes are called upon to operate as components of wider 'common administrative systems', meant as forms of composition of national and non-national bodies jointly responsible for the implementation of measures and policies jointly adopted by a plurality of regimes. The existence of administrative arrangements functionally orientated to joint execution does not imply, of course, that the implementation process is smooth and unproblematic. On the contrary, joint execution may be characterized by contestation, opposition and resistance by some of the administrations involved in the process, particularly national administrations (e.g., because they oppose the substantive policies that they are supposed to implement or have difficulties in adapting them to local problems and contexts).[6]

[6] On the general sources of opposition by national administrations in the implementation of supranational policies, see R. B. Stewart, 'Global Standards for National Societies', in

Third, what the various arrangements for joint administrative execution have in common is their functional orientation: in spite of all their possible variations, they are always instrumental to inter-legality. By establishing such arrangements, the involved legal orders recognize that they are not self-referential systems, operating as distinct and autonomous organizations, but rather are interlinked orders, reciprocally accepting their validity. Moreover, they explicitly aim at structuring their interrelations and at establishing a joint responsibility for the overall management of a shared political programme. The process of mutual recognition is not imposed by any superior authority or overarching legal principle, but is triggered by the free initiative of the legal orders involved and implies the establishment of a common regulatory framework made up of a plurality of norms rooted in all the involved orders, as well as of norms common to all of them. This type of inter-legality, based on joint responsibility, does not necessarily assume that the relevant regimes share a number of values. But it nevertheless aims at committing the actors to identifying the potential value conflicts, searching for a convergence on some key elements of the relevant policy field and promoting some form of solidarity between them.

3.1.2 Infra-Sectoral Joint Responsibility: The Example of Global Security

One example of joint responsibility is provided by the management of 'global security'. It illustrates the situation in which the inter-legality process takes place within one single policy field and involves several organizations beyond the state as well as the states that are members of those organizations. Over the last two decades, there has been a clear process of functional convergence between a plurality of international regimes responsible in the field of military security. Such a process of convergence stems from a complex game of forces: the ever-closer 'horizontal' integration between the functional disciplines and policies of regional bodies operating in the area of security, such as the EU and NATO[7];

S. Cassese (ed.), *Research Handbook on Global Administrative Law* (Cheltenham: Edward Elgar, 2015), 175, 183 ff.

7 For example, the Treaty on the European Union (TEU) provides that the EU policy must be compatible with the common security and defence policy adopted in the context of the North-Atlantic Treaty (Article 42/2), while NATO's current 'strategic concept', adopted in 2010, highlights the compatibility of the EU common foreign and security policy with the North-Atlantic Alliance's activities and the commitment to "play complementary and mutually reinforcing roles in supporting international peace and security" (see *Active Engagement, Modern Defence. Strategic Concept for the Defence and Security of the Members of the North Atlantic Treaty Organization*, 2010, available at www.nato.int/cps/en/natohq/topics_82705.htm).

the 'vertical' framing of regional disciplines by UN law[8]; and the unifying capacity of certain global institutions, such as the G8 and the Organization for Security and Co-operation in Europe (OSCE), which tend to develop strategies for global security within the UN framework.[9] As a result of the interactions between these forces, a number of different non-national regimes tend to operate in a functionally coordinated manner, with a view to the achievement of a common policy objective. Such a policy objective is set, in overall terms, by UN law and consists in the security of the world community, broadly meant as the maintenance of the integrity of the global order and covering not only the interruption of hostilities between fighting parties, but also the restoration of international legality and the protection of fundamental rights in interstate conflicts and in domestic crises within an individual state.[10]

Unsurprisingly, the process of functional convergence between a plurality of non-national regimes has been accompanied by a process of organizational interconnection, both at the level of political decision-making and at the level of administrative implementation. As for administrative implementation, a plurality of UN, regional and national administrations may be said to be jointly responsible for carrying out the military operations and other coercive actions required to implement the adopted political decisions.

8 The functional supremacy of the UN is clearly recognized both by the EU and NATO: as for the former, see e.g., Articles 21 and 42 of the TEU, as well as the 'global strategy' elaborated in 2016 by the High Representative of the Union for Foreign Affairs and Security Policy, *Shared Vision, Common Action: A Stronger Europe. A Global Strategy for the European Union's Foreign and Security Policy*, available at https://eeas.europa.eu/archives/docs/top_stories/pdf/eugs_review_web.pdf; as for NATO, see *Active Engagement, Modern Defence*, paras 2, 18, and 31.

9 For this perspective, emphasizing the horizontal and vertical connections between the functional disciplines and policies of several organizations beyond the state, see E. Chiti, *L'Amministrazione Militare* (Milan: Giuffrè, 2007), p. 88 ff; in the same vein, but paying specific attention to the role of the EU, see the contributions collected in part II of B. van Vooren, S. Blockmans and J. Wouters (eds.), *The EU's Role in Global Governance* (Oxford: Oxford University Press, 2013), and particularly P. Koutrakos, 'The European Union in the Global Security Architecture', in van Vooren et al. (eds.), *The EU's Role in Global Governance*, 81, at 82–85.

10 Such a broad understanding of global security, which goes beyond the traditional interpretation of the UN Charter, has been developed since the mid-1990s by the General Assembly and the Security Council, which have interpreted the notions of 'threat to the peace', 'breach of the peace' and 'act of aggression' in such a way to include cases of severe violations of human rights. This has implied a shift from a merely negative approach, focused on responding to specific crises, to a conception of security as an emerging public policy characterized by an active promotion of fundamental rights and protection of individuals within state borders and against any possible opposition by states. On the tensions inherent in this definition of global security, see E. Chiti, 'The European Security and Defense Administration within the Context of the Global Legal Space', (2007) *NYU School of Law Jean Monnet Working Paper* 7/07, 10 ff.

In the implementation process, the Security Council is given a position of functional prominence over the national administrations, as well as over the regional organizations (the EU and NATO). Moreover, the latter cooperate horizontally in many ways, including joint bodies such as the so-called 'NATO–EU Ad Hoc Working Groups', meeting since mid-2000 and aimed at discussing security issues, modalities for EU access to NATO facilities and the operating capabilities of both organizations.[11] In this way, each administration – either national or non-national – operates as a component of a wider administration, which is polycentric but functionally unitary and relies on a number of mechanisms of cooperation and integration among the different agencies involved.

By promoting and sustaining such a process of administrative interconnection, the UN, NATO, the EU and the other orders involved not only reciprocally recognize their validity, but also structure their relationships in such a way as to establish a joint responsibility for the implementation of a number of shared political decisions on global security. The process of mutual recognition leads to the emergence of a composite administrative law. Indeed, the functioning of the polycentric but functionally unitary administration responsible for global security is governed by a regulatory framework that results from the interconnection of different legal sources, rooted in the various orders involved in the implementation process. This law disciplines the material execution of military operations and other enforcement measures implying the use of military means.[12] As for its functional rationale, it may be characterized as a law of administrative integration by sector, as it aims to allow, by means of administrative tools, the joint action of a plurality of different administrations, both national and non-national, in a specific policy field. Finally, the process of inter-legality implies in this context a high degree of cohesion, value sharing and commitment to solidarity between all the regimes involved.

[11] See *NATO Handbook*, NATO Office of Information and Press, 2001, 103, available at https://blackboard.angelo.edu/bbcswebdav/institution/LFA/CSS/.../NATO_handbook.pdf.

[12] For example, in the case of a Security Council authorization of the use of coercive force by states or regional organizations, the overall regulatory framework of the envisaged military operation is laid down by UN norms, while the definition of all the necessary details is left to national or regional law. This corresponds to the division of labour between the UN and the coalition of states or regional organizations: while the political responsibility of the military operation is usually attributed to the former (through the Security Council, sometimes assisted by the Secretary-General), the strategic, operational and tactical responsibilities are conferred to the latter, which autonomously proceed to the punctual definition of the competent authorities and autonomously regulate their ways of functioning.

3.1.3 Trans-Sectoral Joint Responsibility: The Example of 'International Agencies'

A second interesting example of joint responsibility is provided by the proliferation of international agencies. This is a well-established phenomenon in the world community, consisting in the setting up of bodies by two or more regulatory systems beyond the state in areas where the problems they face go beyond their individual competences. While these bodies may be established on the basis of a treaty concluded between international organizations (as was the case with the Joint Vienna Institute, created in 1992 by the Bank for International Settlements, the European Bank for Reconstruction and Development, the International Bank for Reconstruction and Development, the International Monetary Fund and the Organization for Economic Cooperation and Development, later joined by the WTO), more frequently they are the result of decisions taken by the respective organizations. It is not even exceptional for the above-mentioned 'subsidiary organs' to act as a 'parent organization' for the newly created bodies. Thus, in 1994, the United Nations International Children's Emergency Fund (UNICEF), the United Nations Development Programme (UNDP), the United Nations Population Fund (UNFPA), the United Nations Educational, Scientific and Cultural Organization (UNESCO), the WHO and the World Bank together instituted UNAIDS (the Joint United Nations Programme on HIV/AIDS); earlier examples include the World Food Programme (WFP; created by the FAO and the WHO in 1961), the Codex Alimentarius Commission (CAC; a 1962 FAO and WHO initiative), the International Trade Centre (created by the WTO and the United Nations Conference on Trade and Development [UNCTAD] in 1968), the Intergovernmental Panel on Climate Change (created by the World Meteorological Organization [WMO] and the United Nations Environment Programme [UNEP] in 1998), the Joint Group of Experts in the Scientific Aspects of Marine Environmental Protection (GESAMP; created by the International Maritime Organization, FAO, UNESCO and WMO in 1969) and the Global Environmental Facility (GEF; created by the World Bank in 1991 and joined by the UNDP and UNEP).[13]

[13] C. Martini, 'States' Control over New International Organization', (2006) 6 *Global Jurist*; E. Chiti and R. A. Wessel, 'The Emergence of International Agencies in the Global Administrative Space', in R. Collins and N. D. White (eds.), *International Organizations and the Idea of Autonomy* (London: Routledge, 2011), 143.

International agencies illustrate the situation in which inter-legality as joint responsibility takes place across distinct although contiguous policy fields involving two or more organizations beyond the state as well as their member states. Indeed, they are usually responsible for the administrative implementation of programmes jointly agreed by two or more international organizations and implying a balancing between potentially competing interests, or at least a reconciliation between different interpretations of the same interest at stake. For example, since 1963, the CAC has been responsible for implementing the Joint FAO/WHO Food Standards Programme, the basic purpose of which is to combine the protection of the health of consumers with the establishment of fair practices in the food trade. The CAC is called to balance these two diverging interests by promoting the coordination of all food standards work undertaken by international governmental and non-governmental organizations and by adopting non-binding standards and publishing them in a Codex Alimentarius.[14]

Moreover, international agencies are designed as institutions functionally orientated to foster 'horizontal' and 'vertical' administrative integration between the parent organizations and their member states. They certainly are a highly institutionalized type of mixed administrative organization. Their membership is usually linked to that of the establishing organizations and therefore open to all member states and other members of the parent organization. Their internal structure reflects the architecture of the parent organizations and is centred on a number of bodies made up of representatives of all members (in the case of plenary collegiate bodies) or of a limited number of members (as for the executive committee and the subsidiary bodies). Their technical expertise allows international agencies to operate at a certain distance from their parent organizations, but the parent organizations usually exercise rather strict control over the agencies' actions, and the participation of the member states in their internal bodies limits their operational autonomy.

This specific arrangement for joint administrative execution is certainly instrumental to promoting inter-legality, which may be said to be the fundamental functional rationale for the establishment of international agencies. International agencies are institutionally called to operationalize at the administrative level the joint responsibility of two or more parent organizations that have reciprocally recognized their validity and have acknowledged the necessity to operate as coordinated and complementary institutions in the steering

[14] See Article 1 of the Statutes of the Codex Alimentarius Commission, available at www.fao.org/docrep/005/Y2200E/y2200e02.htm. For an informative account, see FAO/WHO, *Understanding Codex Alimentarius Commission*, available at www.fao.org/3/a-i5667e.pdf.

and implementation of a shared programme. Such an implementing activity is subject to a regulatory framework that is common to the involved orders. Moreover, it implies the adoption of standards aimed at balancing the potentially diverging interests pursued by the establishing regimes. At the core of this type of inter-legality therefore lies a commitment towards balancing interests and reconciliation between two or more international regimes.

3.2 *Coordination of Different Responsibilities*

Inter-Legality may be operationalized not only through administrative instruments supporting the joint execution of political decisions shared by two or more legal orders, but also through instruments capable of triggering processes of indirect convergence between a number of legal orders in the implementation of parallel and autonomous political decisions. In this type of situation, the reciprocal recognition between legal orders is an implicit purpose of the implementing arrangements at work in the relevant legal orders. Moreover, inter-legality does not imply a joint responsibility of two or more legal orders, but rather consists in a more relaxed coordination of different trans- or infra-sectoral responsibilities.

3.2.1 Distinguishing Features

Coordination of different responsibilities takes place in many different contexts. A simple example is that of the 'liaison groups' called to foster administrative cooperation between different organizations operating in the same policy field: this is the case, for example, of the Biodiversity Liaison Group, established in 2004 with the mandate to maximize effectiveness in the implementation processes of each biodiversity-related convention. Other examples include the institutional relationships between EU administrations and international regimes (e.g., Europol and Interpol) and the coordination promoted within the 'United Nations system' by the Chief Executives Board for Coordination (CEB), which brings together the heads of 31 specialized international organizations with the purpose of promoting global policy coherence in a variety of fields.

In Section 3.2.2, the example of administrative cooperation between European agencies and international bodies will be discussed. In order to understand the legal situation that we have qualified as 'coordination of different responsibilities', however, it is first of all necessary to point to its fundamental structure. It is characterized by three distinguishing elements. To begin with, it is not required that the relevant legal orders have functionally or organizationally coordinated their political decision-making processes. On the contrary, each legal order autonomously carries out its political decision-making process according to its own founding norms and political procedures. The typical situation is therefore one involving two or more regulatory organizations beyond the state, rather than a number of sectoral regimes beyond the state and their constituencies; that is, their member states. Indeed, the vertical relationship between sectoral regimes beyond the state and their constituencies always implies a coordination of their respective political decision-making processes, usually through the definition of the relationships between their norms and measures. Differently from joint execution, indirect convergence does not imply any balancing between conflicting interests or reconciliation of different values at the level of political decision-making.

Second, the implementing arrangements do not aim at allowing a joint administrative execution by the involved legal orders. Instead, the administrative bodies of each legal order operate in parallel, internally to their own systems. Powers of implementation are thus retained by each individual order, rather than shared or reciprocally coordinated within a wider framework. However, the administrative bodies of the various relevant legal orders operate on the basis of rules that are functionally orientated to ensure some operational convergence between themselves. One example is provided by the 'borrowing regimes' technique, as happens in the case of the endorsement by the WTO of the Codex Alimentarius standards through the Agreement on the Application of Sanitary and Phytosanitary Measures.

Finally, the implementing arrangements for indirect convergence are instrumental to the operationalization of inter-legality. Although they rarely set the explicit purpose of reciprocal recognition, they are based on the basic idea that the organizations beyond the state are not self-sufficient regimes, but rather legal orders inevitably called to interact for material and institutional reasons. Moreover, inter-legality does not necessarily assume or promote a joint, trans- or infra-sectoral responsibility of two or more legal orders. More modestly, it implies a coordination of a plurality of tasks and responsibilities that remain distinct from each other but are carried out by each legal order at the administrative level in such a way as to avoid or minimize unreasonable outcomes with respect to issues being raised at their intersections. Such rather relaxed coordination of different responsibilities may nevertheless imply the establishment of a common regulatory framework; for example, administrative cooperation between European agencies and international regimes, which will be discussed in the next section, is usually operationalized either through non-binding memoranda of understanding or binding administrative agreements laying down reciprocal obligations and duties. As for its overall rationale, inter-legality does not imply, in this context, any commitment of the various actors to identify and solve the potential value conflicts. Rather, it aims at allowing a harmonious coexistence between a number of legal orders through the minimization of the possible inconsistencies, overlaps and tensions that may arise between them at the operational level and in the management of issues determined by their overlaps.

3.2.2 The Example of Administrative Cooperation between European Agencies and International Bodies

The coordination of different responsibilities may be illustrated through the example of administrative cooperation between European agencies and international regimes. Such cooperation takes place within the context of single sectors, rather than across different policy fields. It involves, on the one hand, a specific type of EU administration, namely the so-called European agencies, and on the other hand, institutions or bodies of international regimes, from formal international organizations to the international regimes that have emerged and proliferated in the last decade, such as transnational networks, exemplified by arrangements such as the Basel Committee, the International Organization of Securities Commissions (IOSCO) and the Financial and Stability Board (FSB). While international regimes usually operate in one specific policy field, European agencies are part of a legal order (that of the EU), competent in a variety of sectors and called upon to find a balance between its multiple and competing policy objectives. Nevertheless, they can be represented as single-mission administrations capable of developing, within a composite and fragmented EU administrative system made up of a plurality of parallel sectoral administrations, their own preferences and practices.[15]

Individual European agencies and international regimes cooperate outside any form of coordination of their decision-making processes. Moreover, each of the two parties retains its own powers of implementation. In spite of this, they develop different types of arrangements aimed at ensuring some operational convergence between themselves in the exercise of their individual administrative actions and leading to the coordination of their individual responsibilities.

[15] For an overall account of the 'agencification' process in the EU, see E. Chiti, 'Decentralized Implementation: European Agencies', in R. Schütze and T. Tridimas (eds.), *Oxford Principles of European Union Law: Volume I: The European Union Legal Order* (Oxford: Oxford University Press, 2018), 748.

European agencies and international regimes may first of all cooperate through a wide variety of non-binding or 'soft law' arrangements, both formal and informal. Formal arrangements mainly consist of memoranda of understanding, which are not technically binding. Informal arrangements include exchanges of 'best practices' and de facto working relations, such as exchanges of information or reciprocal participation in the absence of a formalized instrument of cooperation. These measures of informal cooperation leave both the relevant European agency and international body with much room for manoeuvre. When 'soft law' arrangements are used, European agencies and international bodies remain free to comply or not with the soft law instruments that have been arranged, although there are several reasons for compliance, including reputational considerations.

The most important instrument of administrative cooperation, however, is that of agreements concluded by a European agency and an international regime or one of its internal bodies. European agencies have acted either on the basis of an express provision in the establishing regulation or relying on provisions providing them with generic international cooperation tasks instrumental to their core mandate. Europol has, for example, relied on Article 23 of the Europol Decision[16] to sign 'operational' and 'strategic' agreements with Interpol, the World Customs Organization and the United Nations Office on Drugs and Crime, while the European Monitoring Centre for Drugs and Drug Addiction (EMCDDA) has concluded a cooperation agreement with Interpol without explicit empowerment in the establishing Regulation that loosely envisages that EMCDDA's international cooperation is to be based on 'working arrangements'.[17] As acts binding on the contracting parties only (international regimes and individual European agencies, rather than the EU as a whole), agreements must be complied with and implemented by the European agencies and international bodies that have concluded them. This reflects their nature as 'administrative agreements', concluded directly by a European and an international administrative body through a simplified procedure and with the purpose of addressing issues of low political salience. This type of agreement does not usually need implementing acts. European agencies have to exercise their powers in observance of the agreements that they have concluded and to develop administrative practices consistent with their provisions. The breach of agreements by European agencies can be

[16] Article 23 of Council Decision 2009/371/JHA [2009] OJ L121/3. Article 23 requires Council approval for Europol international agreements after consultation with the Management Board and, where exchange of personal data is concerned, after the opinion of the Joint Supervisory Body obtained via the Management Board.

[17] Article 20 of Regulation 1920/2006 (recast) [2006] OJ L376/1.

challenged by the relevant international body in ways often envisaged by the agreements themselves.

One example is provided by the Agreement between Interpol and Europol that establishes several cooperation duties, such as reciprocal consultation on matters of common interest, as well as a detailed procedure for the transmission and processing of information.[18] By laying down such cooperation duties, the Agreement does not envisage a joint responsibility between Interpol and Europol, but rather aims at coordinating the individual responsibilities of each of the two organizations in such a way as to enhance the effectiveness of their parallel administrative actions. It also provides a common regulatory framework made up of norms agreed by both parties. Such a common regulatory framework is rather detailed and also envisages a number of dispute resolutions mechanisms. Indeed, the Agreement provides that disputes between the two parties concerning the interpretation or application of the agreement must be settled amicably between the Director of Europol and the Secretary General of Interpol; if this proves impossible, the dispute may be referred for advice to an ad hoc Committee composed of no more than three Europol and three Interpol representatives and called upon to submit an advice to the Director of Europol and the Secretary General of Interpol. Breach of an agreement might also be challenged before the Court of Justice of the EU (CJEU), especially where the breach concerns a provision granting third parties a right. Fully in line with the rationale of inter-legality, which is before any other things a process orientated to address issues arising at the intersections of different systems, the Interpol/Europol Agreement grants third parties the right to have access to data transmitted by the two parties on the conditions envisaged by the Agreement. Violation might allow agency conduct to be challenged before the CJEU as a breach of a self-assumed obligation vis-à-vis third parties.

3.3 *Conflict of Responsibilities*

In a third group of situations, the implementation processes of the various legal orders are regulated in such a way as to reciprocally protect their regulatory policies and choices. This happens when two or more legal orders operate in a position of latent or open competition (either because they promote different policies in the same policy field, such as environmental

[18] Agreement between Interpol and Europol (5.11.2001) and memorandum of understanding on the establishment of a secure communication line between Europol and Interpol (11.10.2011), available on the Europol website.

protection, or because they promote conflicting goals, such as market integration and social protection). In this kind of situation, the principles and rules governing their implementation processes recognize the validity of the other legal orders in a non-cooperative sense; that is, to defend a single legal order and to protect and expand its own responsibility by sector. Inter-Legality therefore implies a conflict between different responsibilities.

3.3.1 General Framework

The clash between norms from different legal orders is often considered as the paradigmatic situation of regime interaction, leading to diversification and fragmentation in the 'bureaucratic haze'[19] now dominating the world community. While this statement may overemphasize the tensions and collisions between organizations beyond the state,[20] the existing legal and institutional reality provides many examples of administrative instruments supporting the conflict of responsibilities, rather than their coordination or joint exercise. One may refer to the friction between regimes pursuing conflicting purposes, such as the WTO and the Cartagena Protocol on Biosafety, or asserting different values, such as the UN and the EU in their counterterrorism activities. Tensions may also exist between organizations beyond the state pursuing apparently homogeneous interests, as is shown by inconsistencies between universal and regional organizations promoting human rights protection[21] and by potential conflicts between WTO rules, UNESCO's Cultural Diversity Convention and human rights.[22]

Before illustrating some examples of the situation of a conflict of responsibilities, it is appropriate to describe its basic pattern, which presents three distinguishing features. First, the relevant legal orders protect the autonomy of

[19] Mazower, *Governing the World*, at xvii.

[20] See e.g., J. L. Dunoff, 'A New Approach to Regime Interaction', in M. A. Young (ed.), *Regime Interaction in International Law: Facing Fragmentation* (Cambridge: Cambridge University Press, 2012), 136. For a radically constructivist position, see A. Peters, 'The Refinement of International Law: From Fragmentation to Regime Interaction and Politicization', (2017) 15 *International Journal of Constitutional Law* 627, arguing that "the fragmentation-episode has now given way to an era of 'harmonisation'": but this position almost denies the existence of conflicts of responsibilities within 'international law' and exaggerates the constitutional relevance of the integration efforts and techniques deployed by international courts and tribunals.

[21] See e.g., E. Voeten, 'Competition and Complementarity between Global and Regional Human Rights Institutions', (2017) 8 *Global Policy* 119.

[22] D. Pulkowski, *The Law and Politics of International Regime Conflict* (Oxford: Oxford University Press, 2014), in particular chapter 4.

their individual political decision-making processes. From this point of view, this group of cases replicate and further develop the rationale of the situation that has been previously characterized as coordination of different responsibilities. Each legal order autonomously elaborates its own political agenda and carries out its own mission and sectoral policy. The search for political autonomy is indeed a political choice, sometimes facilitated by the founding norms, but often adopted in the absence of any formal closure requirement. This implies that the political institutions of the involved legal orders do not engage in any balancing between the different interests pursued by each regime or attempt to reconcile their different interpretations of one individual interest. As in the case of coordination of different responsibilities, therefore, the typical situation in which competition takes place is that of the horizontal relations between two or more regulatory organizations beyond the state, as the vertical or triangular relations between the sectoral regimes beyond the state and their member states normally imply a coordination of their political decision-making processes.

Moreover, in the implementing arrangements promoting competition between the legal orders at stake, administrative powers are not only retained by each individual system, but are also exercised on the basis of rules that are functionally orientated to exclude any form of operational convergence between the different systems. The relevant legal orders therefore operate both at the political and the administrative levels as rival and competing regimes. This happens, for example, when the rules of a specific legal order contain incentives to induce private actors to join and comply with its own requirements instead of other existing legal regimes. Another example is that of the rules opposing the possible influence exercised in a specific legal order by the substantive policies embodied in the decisions taken by other legal orders, such as because such decisions concern different interests or because they are considered incompatible with the values of the relevant regime. This game of 'relative closure' can thus be played with positive as well as negative regulatory norms, mainly of a substantive rather than procedural nature.

Finally, although non-cooperative in nature, the implementing arrangements promoting competition between rival regimes are nevertheless instrumental to the operationalization of inter-legality. As with the arrangements at work in the legal situations examined in the previous pages, those promoting competition also imply a recognition of the validity of the other competing legal regimes. They support, however, a specific type of inter-legality: one that implies neither the establishment of a joint responsibility between two or more legal orders nor a coordination of their individual responsibilities. When competition is at stake, inter-legality implies that the involved regimes aim to minimize the unreasonable outcomes of issues being raised at their intersections by defending or expanding their own individual responsibilities. This also has consequence for the relevant legal discipline applied by the administrations of the competing orders, which is typically made up only of norms rooted in the order in which each administration operates, but nevertheless is designed in such a way as to take into account the discipline applicable in the competing regimes. As for its rationale, inter-legality does not bring with itself any commitment of the various actors involved either to solve the potential value conflicts or at least to lay down the operational conditions for a harmonious coexistence. In this context, inter-legality rather implies that major value conflicts should be accepted, as they reflect different policy choices that each legal order wants to defend and articulate. Inconsistencies, frictions and conflicts are therefore taken for granted, and none of the involved legal orders is committed to minimizing them. What the involved legal orders can do is simply to structure and formalize the regulatory competition resulting from the clash between their legal systems, such as by openly recognizing the existence of a conflict between norms and by explaining the underlying normative and functional reasons that justify the set of rules applicable by each of them.

3.3.2 The Example of EU and International Environmental Management Systems

During the 1990s, the EU developed an Eco-Management and Audit Scheme (EMAS). EMAS is a voluntary management tool for organizations aimed at improving their environmental and financial performance and at communicating their environmental achievements to stakeholders and society in general.[23] It is part of the EU strategy on sustainable growth based on a more resource-efficient, greener and more competitive economy. It reflects the attempts of EU institutions to reach such objectives through instruments based on collaboration and partnership with enterprises rather than on legislative requirements.[24] EMAS was established in 1995 and originally restricted to

[23] Regulation (EC) No. 1221/2009 of the European Parliament and of the Council of 25 November 2009 on the voluntary participation by organizations in a Community eco-management and audit scheme (EMAS), repealing Regulation (EC) No. 761/2001 and Commission Decisions 2001/681/EC and 2006/193/EC, OJEU 2009 L 342. See also the Commission Regulation (EU) 2017/1505 of 28 August 2017, amending Annexes I, II and III to Regulation No. 1221/2009.

[24] An account of the EMAS is provided by J. Clausen, M. Keil and M. Jungwirth, 'The State of EMAS in the EU. Eco-Management as a Tool for Sustainable Development', Literature Study (for EMAS II Conference, 26–27 June 2002, Brussels, Belgium); and M. S. Wenk, *The European Union's Eco-Management and Audit Scheme (EMAS)* (Heidelberg: Springer, 2005).

companies in industrial sectors. Since 2001, it has been open to all organizations, including public bodies.[25] Reasons to seek EMAS registration include the wish to enhance production efficiency, internal management culture, reputation, transparency with stakeholders and legislative compliance. The implementation of EMAS involves a plurality of actors, including the Commission, a number of EU composite bodies, national authorities and bodies designated by the member states. EMAS, however, is not the only example of an environmental management system beyond the state. It operates next to many other environmental management systems that are rapidly spreading in the world community.[26] One remarkable example is provided by EN ISO 14001, a certifiable standard adopted by the International Organization for Standardization (ISO). It provides the most important requirements for an environmental management system and it is used worldwide by public and private organizations.

Interestingly enough, the relationships between EMAS and EN ISO 14001 are not at all smooth. They rather illustrate the situation in which two or more legal orders – in this case, the EU and the ISO – reciprocally recognize their validity in a non-cooperative sense. EMAS and EN ISO 14001 share the same objective: to provide good environmental management. Moreover, environmental protection is certainly one of the sectors in which the EU and international regimes tend to mutually reinforce each other through cross-implementations and integrated administrations. However, the relations between EMAS and other environmental management systems developed by non-EU actors, such as EN ISO 14001, are competitive instead of cooperative. EMAS and EN ISO 14001 do not operate as two functionally complementary schemes, serving the same purposes through equivalent regulatory frameworks. On the contrary, the EU is developing its own political strategy towards sustainable growth, for which EMAS is instrumental.

[25] To receive EMAS registration, an organization has to take several steps. First, it has to conduct an environmental review considering all environmental aspects of its activities. Second, it has to develop an environmental programme focusing on specific environmental objectives and targets. Third, it has to establish an effective environmental management system (EMS) aimed at achieving the organization's environmental policy. Fourth, it has to carry out an environmental audit assessing in particular the management system in place. Finally, it has to provide a statement of its environmental performance that lays down the results achieved. The environmental review, EMS, audit procedure and environmental statement must be approved by 'environmental verifiers' accredited by national independent 'accreditation bodies'. Validated statements are then sent for registration to the EMAS Competent Bodies designated by the member states. Registered organizations can use the EMAS logo.

[26] See S. Schaltegger, M. Bennett, R. L. Burritt and C. Jasch (eds.), *Environmental Management Accounting for Cleaner Production* (Heidelberg: Springer, 2008).

EMAS's implementing arrangement, moreover, is designed in such a way as to induce private actors to join and comply with EMAS's requirements as an alternative to other existing legal regimes. Indeed, the current EU legal framework for EMAS explicitly aims at strengthening EMAS's outreach, such as by making EMAS certification possible for organizations and sites located outside the EU. In addition to this, EU institutions consider EMAS more advanced than EN ISO 14001 and encourage EU and non-EU organizations that are already EN ISO 14001 certified to 'step up' to EMAS. EMAS is considered more rigorous because the environmental performance of the organization is continuously being improved, legal compliance is required and checked throughout the whole process before and after registration and strict internal environmental auditing is carried out. As for the move from EN ISO 14001 to EMAS, the Commission has issued a number of guidelines to facilitate organizations in taking all the necessary additional steps.

The overall dynamic of the relationships between EMAS and EN ISO 14001 promotes the type of inter-legality that may be described as a conflict of responsibilities. The EU implementing arrangement certainly implies a recognition by the EU of the validity of the ISO legal regime, although such recognition takes place through a non-cooperative framework. Moreover, the promotion of competition between EMAS and EN ISO 14001 aims to respond to an issue being raised at the intersections between the EU and ISO: the attempt to increase EMAS registrations is indeed based on the EU institutions' conviction that choosing EN ISO 14001 may lower the quality of environmental management in the world community and negatively affect the advancement of the EU policy for environmental protection. Whether regulatory competition is a sound policy choice for the EU, however, remains to be seen: recent figures show that numbers of EN ISO 14001 registrations are constantly increasing, while EMAS registrations are going through a process of stagnation.[27]

3.3.3 The Example of the UN and EU Fight against Terrorism

The relationship between UN and EU counterterrorism actions provides a second and more nuanced example of conflict between different responsibilities.

[27] On the phenomenon of EMAS dropouts and their underlying motivations, see R. Merli, M. C. Lucchetti, M. Preziosi and G. Arcese, 'Motivations Behind the EMAS Stagnation and Enabling Measures to Stimulate New Registrations: Characterization of Public Administrations and Private-Owned Organizations', May 2017, available at www.advancesincleanerproduction.net/sixth/files/sessoes/6B/8/merli_r_et_al_academic.pdf. See also *NATO Handbook*, NATO Office of Information and Press, 2006, 248 ff, available at www.nato.int/docu/handbook/2006/hb-en-2006.pdf.

Both the UN and the EU have been increasingly engaged in the last 15 years in the fight against terrorism. The policies gradually developed respectively by the UN and the EU are certainly interconnected. Indeed, where the UN policy is carried out through international measures that are (practically speaking) binding on the EU, exemplified by the 'smart sanctions' and asset-freezing decisions taken by the UN Security Council and its subcommittees, such measures must be complied with by EU institutions and bodies. More precisely, EU political institutions and administrative bodies are required to implement international measures through EU legislation or executive rulemaking or, where the relevant international measures do not require implementing acts, to exercise their powers in observance of those measures and to comply fully with their commitments in the context of international regimes. However, EU political institutions and administrations must implement international measures in such a way as to respect the rule of law as established and protected in the EU legal order. Their obligation to comply with international measures, in other words, has a remarkable limit: EU institutions and administrations cannot implement international measures in a way that does not respect the EU rule of law, a principle that represents at one and the same time the basic foundation of the EU as an autonomous legal order, of EU administrative law and indeed of judicial review generally.

This is one of the main implications of the European Court of Justice's (ECJ) *Kadi* judgement, where the implementation within the EU of a number of resolutions concerning asset-freezing adopted by the Security Council under Chapter VII of the UN Charter was at stake.[28] As the ECJ famously put it, the EU is an autonomous legal system based on the rule of law, from which a number of constitutional guarantees stem, including the principle of effective procedural and judicial protection, which cannot be prejudiced by an international agreement. This implies that EU and national political institutions and administrative bodies have to respect the set of subprinciples and rights falling within the rule of law when implementing international measures such as the resolutions adopted by the UN Security Council in its fight against terrorism. Moreover, EU courts must ensure the review of the lawfulness of EU regulatory and administrative acts designed to give effect to international measures in the light of the fundamental rights forming an integral part of the EU legal order. The outcome in *Kadi* and later cases was the application of the EU law principle of the rights of the defence to persons affected by asset-stripping measures. In *Kadi*, the listing procedure

[28] See Joined Cases C-402/05 P and C-415/05 P *Yassin Abdullah Kadi and Al Barakaat International Foundation v Council and Commission* [2008] ECR I-6351.

was held invalid, since no guarantee was given as to the communication of the inculpatory evidence against the appellants or as to their being heard in that connection.

Admittedly, the relationship between UN and EU counterterrorism actions – as shaped by the ECJ in *Kadi* – can be read in different ways. It might appear to some as the typical situation of what we have labelled as 'joint responsibility', for the EU and the UN are interconnected at the level of their political decision-making. Others might argue that the relationship between UN and EU actions does not fall within the scope of inter-legality, as the ECJ, by introducing a sharp distinction between the UN and the EU legal systems, has represented its review of the validity of an EU measure as a decision purely internal to the EU legal order. There are good reasons, however, to consider the relationship as a case of inter-legality, and more precisely as a case of inter-legality of the kind that we have qualified as 'conflicts between different responsibilities'. Indeed, the construction presented by the ECJ implies a recognition of the validity of the UN legal system, insofar as the ECJ explicitly recognizes the substantial link between the resolutions adopted by the Security Council and the contested EU Regulation, which is designed to give effect to and implement the former. Moreover, the ECJ aims to minimize the unreasonable outcomes of an issue being raised at the intersections between the UN and the EU legal systems, as is typical of the inter-legality rationale. Again, it does so by defending the individual responsibility of the EU legal order. While the doctrine laid down by the ECJ (now CJEU) implies that the EU recognizes the validity of the international measures adopted by the UN Security Council and its subcommittees, it also defends one major component of the EU legal order: namely, the set of rights and principles derived from the overarching principle of the rule of law, which is safeguarded from any possible restrictions imposed by international regimes. When international measures clash with this component of EU law, the autonomy of the EU legal order is to be protected and the conflict of values has to be accepted rather than solved through bargaining or coordination, as the EU openly asserts the prominence of its specific ethos over that promoted by the UN Security Council. The only possible way to manage the conflict is to make it explicit, to explain its underlying legal reasons and to clarify its scope, which is what the Court actually does in the *Kadi* case law. By asserting the overarching principle of the rule of law, however, the Court is not simply defending the responsibility of the EU legal order. It also proves ready to expand the EU influence beyond the boundaries of its jurisdiction. Indeed, the closure of the EU legal order in cases in which the implementation of international measures breaches the rule of law may promote the EU understanding of due process and good governance as universal values not only within the EU, but also at the international level. This is demonstrated by the fact that the *Kadi* case law indirectly induced the UN Security Council to introduce a first set of administrative guarantees and to establish a general delisting procedure that individuals may activate through a national government, although it remains disputed as to whether the new legal framework is sufficient to afford effective protection to the individuals and organizations listed at the UN level.

4 INTER-LEGALITY AS A CHANGING LEGAL SITUATION

The previous pages have reconstructed the administrative law avenues and techniques sustaining inter-legality as a process of recognition. Inter-Legality, it has been pointed out, is shaped by many factors, including the organizational and procedural arrangements that are used by each legal order to govern the implementation of its own first-level measures.

Admittedly, the implementing arrangements at work in the various legal orders do not sustain one single notion of inter-legality, but many. This chapter has identified three main groups of implementation processes: implementation processes supporting the joint administrative execution of political decisions jointly elaborated by two or more legal orders; implementation processes promoting indirect convergence rather than joint administrative execution; and implementation processes encouraging the open or latent competition between legal orders. In all these cases, the implementing arrangements contribute to shaping inter-legality as a rule and process of recognition. But each type promotes a specific type of inter-legality. The arrangements for joint administrative execution explicitly aim at establishing a joint responsibility between the legal orders at stake, which implies a shared commitment of all involved actors to identifying the potential value conflicts and to searching for convergence on some key elements of the relevant policy field. Instead, the implementing arrangements for indirect convergence are instrumental to the operationalization of a different kind of inter-legality, one that does not promote a joint responsibility of two or more legal orders, but rather consists in a more relaxed coordination of different trans- or infra-sectoral responsibilities, with the purpose of minimizing the possible inconsistencies and tensions that may arise between two or more legal orders at the operational level. As for the implementing arrangements driving to competition between rival regimes, they support a type of inter-legality implying a conflict between the individual responsibilities of two or more legal orders, each of which aims at minimizing the unreasonable outcomes of issues being raised at their intersections by defending or expanding its own responsibility.

We therefore face a diversity of situations. Once we recognize this, we can better understand inter-legality as a changing notion, ranging from (i) joint responsibility to (ii) coordination of different responsibilities and (iii) conflict of responsibilities. We can also recognize the variety of problems that the operation of inter-legality may raise. For example, the first two types of inter-legality largely depend on the capacity of states and legal orders beyond the state to develop effective and workable implementing processes and practices. Inter-Legality as a conflict of responsibilities instead raises concerns about forum shopping and the ability to deliver public goods: while each of the involved legal orders may rationalize the conflict with the other regimes by making it explicit, by explaining its underlying normative and functional reasons and by clarifying its scope, the precise effects of this rationalizing action depend on many different variables, including private actors' behaviours, and they are to be assessed on a case-by-case basis.

While the further exploration of the plural and changing notion of inter-legality is to be left to future research, it is appropriate to conclude this chapter with some reflections on the ways in which inter-legality affects and shapes the legal space in which it operates. Inter-Legality, indeed, is not at all neutral. It contributes to constructing the legal space where it works both as a rule and as a process.

5 THE IMPLICATIONS OF INTER-LEGALITY: RETHINKING THE LEGAL SPACE

5.1 *An Alternative to the International Law Paradigm*

To begin with, inter-legality – as shaped by administrative law techniques – cannot be easily accommodated within the traditional representation of the world community as a legal system articulated in two separated sets of legal orders: the 'international legal order', dominated by interstate relations and governed by international law, and the plurality of national legal orders, regulated by domestic law.

Inter-Legality rejects such a representation in two ways. First, it breaks down the dichotomy between the international and the national legal orders. Indeed, while preserving the formal relevance of states in the world community, inter-legality through administrative law instruments attenuates the states' powers of intermediation, especially in cases of joint administrative execution. Moreover, it establishes a number of relations not only between states, as assumed by dualism, but also among regulatory organizations beyond the state – individuals, firms, non-governmental organizations (NGOs) and other social and economic actors called to reciprocally interact in a great variety of ways. Second, inter-legality is based on an understanding of the nature of non-national regimes that is not coherent with the conventional public international law model. In such a model, the various types of regulatory organizations beyond the state are to be considered alternatively as 'subjects' of the international legal order, provided that they present the necessary requirements, starting with the fundamental requirement of legal personality, or bodies purely instrumental to the subjects of the international legal order, primarily states and international organizations. Inter-Legality is based on the radically alternative assumption that the flourishing variety of systems beyond the state are not subjects of any wider legal order, but simply legal orders by themselves, reciprocally interacting in a plurality of ways. From this point of view, inter-legality may be considered as a direct challenge to the conventional paradigm of international law. It substitutes the consolidated image of two sets of parallel legal orders – the international legal order and the national ones – with a representation of the world community as a legal space in which a multitude of national and non-national legal orders coexist one next to the others and systematically interact between themselves.

5.2 *An Alternative to Legal Globalism*

Inter-Legality is an alternative not only to the conventional paradigm of public international law, but also to the main understandings elaborated by the 'global administrative law' scholarship. Let us first consider the notion of 'global administrative space' proposed by Kingsbury, Krisch and Stewart in their seminal and influential article on the emergence of global administrative law.[29] The concept of global administrative space refers to a legal reality that breaks down the traditional dichotomy between international space and national polities. In the new global administrative space, a growing number of international and transnational regulatory regimes exercise genuine administrative functions, such as rulemaking and adjudication. Moreover, not only states but also individuals, firms, NGOs and other social and economic actors interact in a great variety of ways. The legal space of interstate relations, traditionally dominated by international law, and the

[29] B. Kingsbury, N. Krisch and R. B. Stewart, 'The Emergence of Global Administrative Law', (2005) 68 *Law and Contemporary Problems* 15.

legal space of domestic polities, regulated by national law, are not swept aside, but instead are reshaped within the context of a wider and more complex global administrative space. According to Kingsbury, Krisch and Stewart, moreover, the global administrative space is mainly governed by global administrative law, a plural and fragmented body of law bringing together different components, such as the administrative law of international organizations, national regulation of the domestic effects of a foreign state's administrative acts, the new area of regulations governing the structure and functioning of global administrations and a number of general principles and mechanisms of accountability.

Inter-Legality might appear to be in principle compatible with the notion of global administrative space that refers to a non-unitary, highly differentiated and plural legal context in which a great variety of interactions between different regimes systematically occur, as is assumed by inter-legality. Such a perspective, however, would be misleading. There are two reasons why inter-legality can be considered as an alternative to the concept of global administrative space rather than as a compatible analytical tool. First, while inter-legality does not deny the existence of a 'global administrative law', it certainly does not promote it as a fundamental instrument for the stabilization and legitimization of the world community, as it is instead assumed by the concept of global administrative space. Second, and most importantly, inter-legality presupposes the existence of a plurality of different legal orders and is an attempt to conceptualize their interactions, while the notion of global administrative space qualifies the regulatory organizations beyond the state as 'administrations' or 'institutions', thus referring to a unitary – though internally plural and fragmented – legal order in which the various systems operate as institutions. The radically plural understanding of the world community that founds the notion of inter-legality is therefore qualitatively different from the representation of the global administrative space, where the key notions for describing and trying to explain the relationships between different systems are those of 'networking' and 'linkage',[30] rather than inter-legality.

A similar line of reasoning may be developed in relation to another representation of the world community elaborated by the global administrative law

[30] Unsurprisingly, the 'global administrative law' scholarship has extensively explored the instruments and processes of 'global networking'. For an account of this line of research, see M. Savino, 'Linkages between Global Regimes and Interactions with Civil Society', in Cassese (ed.), *Research Handbook*, 131; and P. Craig, 'Global Networks and Shared Administration', ibid., 153.

scholarship: that of 'global polity', whose emergence has been argued by Sabino Cassese.[31] The notions of global polity and global administrative space share a number of similarities. They both refer to a legal reality that breaks down the traditional dichotomy between international space and national polities. They both emphasize the pluralism inherent in this new reality. Moreover, they are not mutually exclusive, at least in the sense that the global polity might imply the existence of a global administrative space. The notion of global polity, however, expressly refers to a political component of this new reality. The global polity is 'a global political organization' resulting from the process of globalization and from the proliferation of global regulatory regimes. It is not a unitary legal order, and not even a plurality of legal orders provided with some hierarchical structure; rather, it is "a mosaic of legal systems, with different layers (local, national, regional, global) and a plurality of sectorial regulatory regimes."[32] The reference to a global political organization also seems to imply a reference to a societal structure, one that is of course plural and multilayered.

The types of inter-legality that have been reconstructed in this chapter might be considered as some of the instruments through which the plurality of legal regimes populating the global polity interact between themselves in order to address issues that lay at their intersection. On the contrary, however, they provide a conceptual alternative to the global polity, as they explain the dynamics between the responsibilities of different regimes and legal orders, rather than discussing their capacity to exercise authority. The perspective of inter-legality might even question the concept of global polity per se by pointing to the ambiguities of a representation of the world community that aims at bringing together pluralism on the one hand and command and compliance on the other.

Finally, inter-legality is also an alternative to a third major representation of the world community sometimes proposed by the global administrative law scholarship: the one pointing to the existence of a global legal order. Such a representation has been elaborated by a number of authors pointing to the circumstance that the world community possesses the three typical elements of a legal order: a multiplicity of subjects (mainly states and individuals), an organizational structure (international organizations, global regulatory regimes, national administrations, etc.) and increasingly complex regulation

[31] Cassese, *The Global Polity*.

[32] Ibid., at 175.

(derived from various sources of law, not only conventional in nature).[33] The notion of a global legal order should not be considered as strongly monist. While it assumes that an overall legal order exists, it does not imply that it is organized as a global polity. Moreover, its essential structure and ways of functioning acknowledge the pluralism of global governance.

Inter-Legality, however, does not easily fit in this construction. Joint responsibility, coordinated responsibilities and conflicts of responsibilities are three types of inter-legality through administrative instruments that structure the interactions between different legal systems with a view to addressing issues arising at their intersections. The notion of a global legal order instead suggests that some of the functions exercised by regulatory organizations beyond the state – such as military security or environmental protection – are rooted in the global legal order itself. Administrative functions can be said to be rooted in the global legal order when the relevant global administrations pursue goals and interests affecting all the subjects of the world community, rather than single entities in the global legal space. This point is extraneous to the perspective of inter-legality. Even when it takes the specific form of joint responsibility, inter-legality does not imply that the administrative function that is exercised by the involved regimes is rooted in a wider legal order. That function is rather grounded in the various legal orders involved who become jointly responsible for its exercise.

5.3 *Looking Ahead*

Admittedly, inter-legality is not at all a one-size-fits-all concept. On the contrary, it is a rather inflexible concept. As a notion pointing to a process of recognition shaped by administrative law techniques, it rejects the representation of the world community provided by the traditional public international law model. Moreover, it is an alternative to the main understandings elaborated by global administrative law scholarship. Inter-Legality is based on plurality and in turn promotes plurality. Once we recognize this, we not only understand why inter-legality is not at ease with the representations of the world community that have been recalled in the previous pages, we also

[33] The existence of a global legal order has first been argued by Sabino Cassese in his 'Lo Spazio Giuridico Globale', (2002) 52 *Rivista Trimestrale di Diritto Pubblico* 323. See also S. Battini, *Amministrazioni senza Stato. Profili di Diritto Amministrativo Internazionale* (Milan: Giuffrè, 2003), 197 ff, although the emergence of global administrative law and its grounding in the global legal order are presented in this book as ongoing rather than fully accomplished processes; and Chiti, *L'Amministrazione Militare*, using the notion of global order within the context of an enquiry into the emerging global administrative law of military security.

identify a new set of questions that this chapter had to leave open. What shall be the precise features of the pluralist space that inter-legality is promoting? Shall it be a 'controlled', legally domesticated pluralism, as the enquiry carried out in this chapter might suggest? Or shall it be a more conflictual pluralism based on systemic tensions between the various orders, not mediated by law? And what are the legal principles and instruments that shall operate next to inter-legality to structure the interactions within a radically plural world community?

13

Global Law As Inter-Contextuality and As Inter-Legality

POUL F. KJAER

1 INTRODUCTION

Since the 1990s, the effect of globalization on law and legal developments has been a central topic of scholarly debate.[1] To date, however, the debate has been marked by three substantial deficiencies that this chapter seeks to remedy through a reconceptualization of global law as a law of inter-contextuality expressed through inter-legality and materialized through a particular body of legal norms that can be characterized as connectivity norms.

The first deficiency is a historical and empirical one. Both critics as well as advocates of 'non-state law' share the assumption that 'law beyond the state' and related legal norms have gained in centrality when compared with previous historical times.[2] While global law, including both public and private global governance law as well as regional occurrences such as European Union (EU) law, has undergone profound transformations since the structural transformations that followed the de-colonialization processes of the mid-twentieth century, we do not have more global law relative to other types of law today than in previous historical times.

The second deficiency is a methodological one. The vast majority of scholarship on global law is either of an analytical nature, drawing on insights

[1] See e.g., M. Shapiro, 'The Globalization of Law', (1993) 1 *Indiana Journal of Global Legal Studies* 37.

[2] For the critics, see e.g., D. Grimm, *Constitutionalism: Past, Present, and Future* (Oxford: Oxford University Press, 2016); M. Loughlin, 'The Misconceived Search for Global Law', (2017) 8 *Transnational Legal Theory* 353. For the advocates, see e.g., P. S. Berman, *Global Legal Pluralism: A Jurisprudence of Law beyond Borders* (Cambridge: Cambridge University Press, 2012); G. Teubner, 'Global Bukowina: Legal Pluralism in the World Society', in G. *Teubner* (ed.), *Global Law without a State* (Brookfield: Dartmouth, 1997), 3.

from philosophy,[3] or empirically observes the existence of global law and the degree of compliance with global legal norms at a given moment in time.[4] While both approaches bring something to the table, they remain static approaches incapable of explaining and evaluating the transformation of global law over time.[5]

The third deficiency is a conceptual–theoretical one. In most instances, global law is understood as a unitary law producing singular legal norms with a planetary reach[6] or, alternatively, a radical pluralist perspective is adopted, dismissing the existence of singular global norms.[7] Both of these approaches, however, misapprehend the structural characteristics, functions and societal effects of global law. Instead, a third positon between unitary and radical pluralist perspectives can be adopted through an understanding of global law and its related legal norms as a decentred kind of inter-contextual law characterized by inter-legality.[8]

Global law can be defined as a legal phenomenon that, *in principle*, is unlimited in reach (i.e., as claiming validity without reference or limitation to a specific territory or population, albeit for practical reasons, it will be limited in most cases).[9] This makes global law distinct from national, international,

[3] See e.g., T. Pogge, 'Fighting Global Poverty', (2017) 13 *International Journal of Law in Context* 512.

[4] See e.g., G. Shaffer and T. Ginsburg, 'The Empirical Turn in International Legal Scholarship', (2012) 106 *American Journal of International Law* 1; M. Zürn, 'Introduction: Law and Compliance at Different Levels', in M. Zürn and C. Joerges (eds.), *Law and Governance in Postnational Europe: Compliance beyond the Nation-State* (Cambridge: Cambridge University Press, 2005), 1.

[5] H. Brunkhorst, *Critical Theory of Legal Revolutions: Evolutionary Perspectives* (London: Bloomsbury, 2014).

[6] See e.g., J. Habermas, 'The Constitutionalization of International Law and the Legitimation Problems of a Constitution for World Society', (2008) 15 *Constellations* 444.

[7] N. Krisch, *Beyond Constitutionalism: The Pluralist Structure of Postnational Law* (Oxford: Oxford University Press, 2010).

[8] M. Amstutz and V. Karavas, 'Weltrecht: Ein Derridasches Monster', in G.-P. Calliess, A. Fischer-Lescano, D. Wielsch and P. Zumbansen (eds.), *Soziologische Jurisprudenz. Festschrift für Gunther Teubner zum 65. Geburtstag* (Berlin: Walter de Gruyter, 2009), 645; T. Duve, 'Was Ist "Multinormativität?" – Einführende Bemerkungen', (2017) 25 *Rechtsgeschichte – Legal History* 88.

[9] S. Cassese, *Il Diritto Globale. Giustizia e Democrazia Oltre lo Stato* (Turin: Einaudi, 2009); B. Frydman, 'Comment Penser le Droit Global?' in J.-Y. Chérot and B. Frydman (eds.), *La Science du Droit dans la Globalisation* (Brussels: Bruylant, 2012), 17; P. Le Golf, 'Global Law: A Legal Phenomenon Emerging from the Process of Globalization', (2007) 14 *Indiana Journal of Global Legal Studies* 119; G. Lhuilier, *Le Droit Transnational* (Paris: Dalloz, 2016); H. Lindahl, *Fault Lines of Globalization: Legal Order and the Politics of A-Legality* (Oxford: Oxford University Press, 2013); G. Palombella, *È Possibile una Legalità Globale? Il Rule of Law e la Governance del Mondo* (Bologna: Il Mulino, 2012), G. Palombella, 'Global Law and the

transnational and community-based living law as defined in the following manner: national law, the law of nation-states as derived from the concept of sovereignty; international law, the law between nation-states; transnational law, any law that, in terms of jurisdiction, source or effect, crosses national boundaries, thereby producing negative or positive externalities while continuing to rely on national legal sources and instruments[10]; and living law, social norms fulfilling lawlike functions within a community.[11] These four types of law might therefore potentially act as sources of inter-legal global law to the extent that they are deployed in an inter-contextual manner.

Reflecting its inter-legal structure, the substantial normative content of global law is furthermore characterized by a relative structural predominance of connectivity norms. Connectivity norms are orientated towards the facilitation of transplantations (i.e., the extraction, transmission and incorporation of components of meaning) from one legally structured context to another (e.g., as is the case within international trade and investment law, internal market law or legally sanctioned missionary activities within religious law).[12] The concept of connectivity norms thereby differs from the classical understanding of norms as coherency norms aimed at establishing coherency *within* a collectivity on the basis of prescriptions of actions that limit the scope of possible future actions and the invoking of sanctions in the case of non-compliance.[13] It also differs from a progressive understanding of norms as possibility norms, implying the articulation of possible futures on the basis of a distinction between the factual and the counterfactual (i.e., through a distance

Law on the Globe', (2012) 4 *Italian Journal of Public Law* 53; N. Walker, *Intimations of Global Law* (Cambridge: Cambridge University Press, 2015); M. Xifaras, 'The Global Turn in Legal Theory', (2016) 29 *Canadian Journal of Law and Jurisprudence* 215.

[10] P. C. Jessup, *Transnational Law* (New Haven, CT: Yale University Press, 1956); Walker, *Intimations of Global Law*; G.-P. Calliess and P. Zumbansen, *Rough Consensus and Running Code: A Theory of Transnational Private Law* (Oxford: Hart Publishing, 2010).

[11] R. Cotterrell, *Living Law: Studies in Legal and Social Theory* (Farnham: Ashgate Publishing, 2008); E. Ehrlich, *Grundlegung der Soziologie des Rechts*, 4th edn (Berlin: Duncker & Humblot, 1989 [1913]).

[12] E.g., for trade law, see D. Trubek and P. Cottrell, 'Robert Hudec and the Theory of International Economic Law: The Law of Global Space in Developing Countries', in C. Thomas and J. Trachtman (eds.), *Developing Countries in the WTO Legal System* (Oxford: Oxford University Press, 2009), 129.

[13] E.g., J. Blake and D. Kingsley, 'Norms, Values, and Sanctions', in R. Faris (ed.), *Handbook of Modern Sociology* (Chicago: Rand-McNally, 1964), 456; H. J. Morgenthau, *La Réalité des Normes: En Particulier Normes du Droit International. Fondement d'une Théorie des Norms* (Paris: Félix Alcan, 1934); T. Parsons, *The Structure of Social Action: A Study in Social Theory with Special Reference to a Group of Recent European Writers* (New York: Free Press, 1968 [1937]).

to the factual world, with the objective of accentuating the openness of the future).[14] Connectivity norms are, in other words, a third type of norm located in-between coherency and possibility norms.

2 THE HISTORICITY OF GLOBAL LAW

Global law can also be understood as boundary-less or universalizing law historically manifested in imperial and religious (e.g., Christian, Jewish and Islamic law). The duality of imperial and religious law not only preceded nation-state and international law, but also remained the dominant form of law until recent historical times. For religious law, the ongoing clashes between secularized 'Western law' and Islamic law and the Holy See's continued insistence on formal supremacy vis-à-vis all worldly and temporal powers testifies that this battle is not over yet.[15] The globality of imperial law was manifested in its claim to universal supremacy or a *primus inter pares* position vis-à-vis all other worldly powers as found, for example, in both Roman law and in the legal conceptuality of Chinese, Japanese and Persian imperial law until the twentieth century. Classical imperial law was based on a built-in asymmetry in favour of the imperial power vis-à-vis other powers, as expressed, for example, through the Chinese tributary system formally only acknowledging other states as tributary states, as well as through the concept of 'suzerain' (i.e., upper-sovereign), originally used to describe the asymmetric relations between the Ottoman Empire and surrounding powers.[16] In the European context, imperial law remained the paradigmatic form of law until the implosion of the Austro-Hungarian, German, Ottoman and Russian empires in 1917/1918, as all of the European empires formally claimed (albeit the claim was increasingly diluted as time progressed) successor status to either the West or East Roman Empires and thereby a transcendent status as universal powers.

From the late fifteenth century until the mid-twentieth century, social processes with a factual global reach were, however, predominantly structured

[14] R. M. Cover, 'The Supreme Court 1982 Term Foreword: Nomos and Narrative', (1983) 97 *Harvard Law Review* 4; N. Luhmann, *Rechtssystem und Rechtsdogmatik* (Stuttgart: Kohlhammer, 1974); C. Möllers, *Die Möglichkeit der Normen. Über eine Praxis jenseits von Moralität und Kausalität* (Berlin: Suhrkamp Verlag, 2015).

[15] P. F. Kjaer, 'Claim-Making and Parallel Universes: The Legal Pluralism of Church, State and Empire in Europe', in G. Davies and M. Avbelj (eds.), *Handbook on EU Legal Pluralism* (Cheltenham: Edward Elgar Publishing, 2018), 11.

[16] For China, see S. Nianshen, '"Tributary" from a Multilateral and Multilayered Perspective', (2012) 5 *Chinese Journal of International Politics* 155.

through the colonial variant of imperial law. Colonial law is a specific subspecies of law with particular characteristics. This does not imply an understanding of colonial law as a unified law with a coherent doctrinal basis. Colonial law is instead to be conceived of as a collage of partly overlapping and partly contradictory legal principles and practices derived from a range of jurisdictions and sources producing a variety of different effects.[17]

In its various forms, colonial law shares three overarching characteristics:

Globality: A common denominator of colonial law is that it can be deployed in a nonspecified number of geographical locations, thereby gaining a specific non-territorial trait. This is, for example, expressed in the concept of terra nullius and legal principles concerning the right to exploration, passage and settlement.

Asymmetry: Just as classical imperial law was based on a built-in bias in favour of the imperial power vis-à-vis other powers, the norms of colonial law are derived from asymmetric distinctions, such as Christians/non-Christians and civilized/non-civilized, thereby allowing for the use of 'unequal treaties' between colonial powers and legal entities subject to colonialization or colonial interference.[18]

A *materiality/norm nexus*: Colonial law implied a two-way street between the legal facilitation of the extraction of values of a predominantly economic nature and the imposition of values and social praxes of a principally religious and moral nature, as expressed, for example, through missionary and civilizing activities.

In practice, colonial law thereby came to act as hybrid law, structuring relations between *different* European legal orders and the rest of the world. This is reflected in a tension between the existence of singular *ius publicum europaeum* and the anchoring of colonial law within different European (i.e., Belgian, British, Danish, Dutch, French, German, Italian, Portuguese, Russian and Spanish) legal orders.[19] More fundamentally, it is reflected in

[17] A. Fitzmaurice, *Sovereignty, Property and Empire, 1500–2000* (Cambridge: Cambridge University Press, 2014); O. Grandmaison, 'The Exception and the Rule: On French Colonial Law', (2006) 53 *Diogenes* 34; M. Koskenniemi, 'Colonial Laws: Sources, Strategies and Lessons?' (2016) 18 *Journal of the History of International Law* 248; J. Osterhammel, *Colonialism: A Theoretical Overview*, 2nd edn (Princeton, NJ: Princeton University Press, 2005).

[18] For China, see e.g., D. Wang, 'The Discourse of Unequal Treaties in Modern China', (2003) 76 *Pacific Affairs* 399.

[19] C. Schmitt, *Der Nomos der Erde. Im Völkerrecht des Jus Publicum Europaeum* (Berlin: Duncker & Humblot, 1950).

the way colonial law, based on a fundamental asymmetry in favour of the colonial powers, establishes material interconnectedness through its location in-between the (inter-)national legal orders of the colonial powers and local (pre-existing) legal orders and the customary living law of societies subject to colonialization.[20] Colonial law can thereby be understood as a law of in-betweenness and inter-contextuality or as an 'in-between world's law'[21] – a type of in-betweenness that furthermore served a constitutive function insofar as both the legal conglomerate of rather diverse elements making up the *ius publicum europaeum* and the living law of colonized societies were constituted in this process. Rather than being 'pure', 'natural' or 'indigenous', the living law of colonial society often emerged in the meeting with Europeans as a part of a strategy aimed at handling the intrusion,[22] just as the constitutive distinction of the *ius publicum europaeum* was the distinction between Europeans and non-Europeans. Meeting within the form of asymmetric colonial law was, in other words, the relational interaction embedded in the material interconnectedness between colonizers and the colonized, which constituted both. Colonial law took the form of assemblages combining elements from focal social processes (i.e., economic and religious processes), from indigenous law and social practices as well as from the legal and social orders of the colonizing powers, effectively creating a third space characterized by norms of connectivity and interconnectedness that was part of neither the world of colonizers nor the colonized.

3 GLOBAL GOVERNANCE LAW AS POST-IMPERIAL LAW

Today, few remnants of colonialism exist, with the United Nations currently listing 17 territories as having colonial status.[23] The structural transformation brought about by decolonization and the concordant breakdown of the Eurocentric world is, however, still not sufficiently understood, with the actual effects of this transformation only starting to become visible with the ongoing breakdown of the Western-centric (i.e., United States–centric) world that

[20] M. Chanock, *Law, Custom, and Social Order: The Colonial Experience in Malawi and Zambia* (Cambridge: Cambridge University Press, 1985).

[21] M. Amstutz, 'In-Between Worlds: *Marleasing* and the Emergence of Interlegality in Legal Reasoning', (2005) 11 *European Law Journal* 766.

[22] L. Benton, *Law and Colonial Cultures: Legal Regimes in World History, 1400–1900* (Cambridge: Cambridge University Press, 2002); S. E. Merry, 'From Law and Colonialism to Law and Globalization', (2003) 28 *Law and Social Inquiry* 569.

[23] www.un.org/en/decolonization/nonselfgovterritories.shtml (accessed 14 March 2018).

succeeded the Eurocentric world.[24] Decolonization, however, implied a dual and simultaneous structural transformation of legal ordering. First, there was a globalization of statehood through the massive multiplication of the number of states in the wake of decolonization, thereby indicating that the widespread narrative concerning the withering away of the state is empirically unfounded. On the contrary, since 1945, the largest expansion of statehood to date has occurred. Until the mid-twentieth century, statehood remained a limited phenomenon, and it is only in very recent historical times that statehood became globalized. Second, there was the restructuring of global law from centre/periphery-based asymmetric colonial law to the type of functional regimes or, as is the case with the EU, conglomerates of functional regimes, which is the central characteristic of contemporary global governance.[25] Statehood and extensive forms of global law are therefore not structured in a zero-sum relation where more of one implies less of the other. On the contrary, they are mutually constitutive, with more of one implying more of the other. The formation and consolidation of modern territorial states in Western Europe was closely linked to the emergence of increasingly vast colonial empires and vice versa. The progressive transformation of territorial states into nation-states was, in a similar vein, intimately linked to the emergence of contemporary global governance. From the establishment of the first modern public international organization, *La Commission centrale pour la navigation du Rhin*, initiated at the Congress of Vienna in 1815, to the explosion in the number of global governance sites in the latter half of the twentieth century, the evolution of modern global governance has gone hand in hand with the concordant expansion and deepening of statehood.[26]

The law of the continental empires of Eurasia, stretching from Europe to China, and the colonial empires of the westernmost European states had considerable differences in their legal structuring while in principle sharing a boundary-less and asymmetric approach to the world. In a similar vein, contemporary global governance law comes in two species: a predominantly

[24] P. F. Kjaer, *Constitutionalism in the Global Realm – A Sociological Approach* (Abingdon: Routledge, 2014).

[25] A. Fischer-Lescano and G. Teubner, 'Regime-Collisions: The Vain Search for Legal Unity in the Fragmentation of Global Law', (2004) 25 *Michigan Journal of International Law* 999; A. Fischer-Lescano and G. Teubner, *Regime-Kollisionen: Zur Fragmentierung des globalen Rechts* (Frankfurt am Main: Suhrkamp Verlag, 2006); M. Koskenniemi and P. Leino, 'Fragmentation of International Law? Postmodern Anxieties', (2002) 15 *Leiden Journal of International Law* 553–559. For the EU, see P. F. Kjaer, *Between Governing and Governance: On the Emergence, Function and Form of Europe's Post-National Constellation* (Oxford: Hart Publishing, 2010).

[26] Kjaer, *Constitutionalism in the Global Realm.*

private law (i.e., contract law) structuring of global connectivity mainly orientated towards economic exchanges and a public law structuring of, in principle, boundary-less political power, as particularly manifested in EU law. The relationship between the pre-existing imperial legal formations and contemporary global governance is at the same time one of perfect continuity and fundamental discontinuity. Just like modern territorially delineated European nation-states emerged from *within* pre-existing feudal forms of legal ordering while still obtaining a fundamentally different form and normative outlook, both species of contemporary global governance emerged from *within* the pre-existing imperial forms while being substantially transformed in the process of emergence, leading to a reliance on different organizational principles and normative objectives.[27] Contemporary global law can therefore be understood as functional, but not as normative, equivalents to imperial and colonial law. Functionally, global law in its imperial as well as contemporary governance forms can be understood as being aimed at facilitating transplantations of components of meaning from one legally structured context to another and can, as such, be understood as a decentred phenomenon manifested in inter-contextuality and inter-legality.[28] In terms of the normative foundation, the essential outlook and guiding principles have, however, changed from asymmetric distinctions to a formal reliance on symmetric articulations of fundamental equality as most notably expressed in the formal adherence to global human rights.[29]

The connectivity orientation is clearly observable in relation to the private law organization of global value chains serving as a central infrastructure of the global economy.[30] A global value chain can be defined as a contract-based network stretching from suppliers to customers and capital owners that, just as in colonial law, is engaged in the transplantation (i.e., extraction, transmission and incorporation) of condensed components of meaning with economic value (i.e., capital, products and persons) from one legally structured societal context to another, with such transplantations being either upstream or downstream or a combination thereof, and implying boundary crossings. The legal norms guiding, stabilizing and enabling global value chains are therefore to be

27 For European nation-states, see N. Elias. *Über den Prozeß der Zivilisation, Band 2* (Frankfurt am Main: Suhrkamp Verlag, 1976 [1938]).

28 M. Amstutz and V. Karavas, 'Weltrecht: Ein Derridasches Monster'; B. de Sousa Santos, *Toward a New Legal Common Sense* (Cambridge: Cambridge University Press, 2002).

29 P. F. Kjaer, 'Constitutionalizing Connectivity: The Constitutional Grid of World Society', *Journal of Law and Society*, Vol 45, Issue S1, 114–34.

30 G. Baars et al., 'The Role of Law in Global Value Chains: A Research Manifesto', (2016) 4 *London Review of International Law* 57.

thought of as connectivity norms (i.e., norms orientated towards a facilitation of material transplantations across contextual boundaries), which are intrinsically linked to issues of inter-contextuality and inter-legality.

In contrast to the common understanding of global value chains as a recent phenomenon, a near to evident relation exists between colonial law and contemporary global value chain law. The post–World War II emergence of global value chains was largely a reinvention, as legally structured transplantations have been a constitutive element of commerce from day one, just as value chains with a global reach have been running since the emergence of European colonialism in the late fifteenth century. The slave trade, for example, coming out of Africa for the Arabic world as well as the Americas, also implied complex value chains and elaborated legal framings.[31] Similarly to colonial law, as a collage of partly overlapping and partly contradictory legal principles and practices, a global value chain law is a collage of legal, managerial and other social praxes, techniques and principles that tend to establish internal normative orders acting as third spaces between the various sites connected through value chains[32] – normative orders that are reflected in self-descriptions and articulations of justifications for the processes they facilitate and stabilize.[33] In addition, a contemporary global value chain law is characterized by the same kind of mixture between public and private as colonial setups were. As argued by Martti Koskenniemi, colonialism was from the outset predominantly a private law–based endeavour,[34] and only gradually did public law gain a larger role on the basis of an increased switch from the maintenance of trading posts to direct territorial conquest and control. Colonial law is therefore not easily categorized as either private or public law. In a

[31] P. Manning, 'The Slave Trade: "The Formal Demographics of a Global System"', in J. E. Inikori and S. L. Engerman (eds.), *The Atlantic Slave Trade: Effects on Economies, Societies and Peoples in Africa, the Americas, and Europe* (Durham, NC: Duke University Press, 1992), 117.

[32] L. C. Backer, 'Economic Globalization and the Rise of Efficient Systems of Global Private Lawmaking: Wal-Mart as Global Legislator', (2007) 39 *University of Connecticut Law Review* 1739; L. C. Backer, 'Are Supply Chains Transnational Legal Orders? What We Can Learn from the Rana Plaza Factory Building Collapse', (2016) 1 *UC Irvine Journal of International, Transnational and Comparative Law* 11; L. C. Backer, 'Theorizing Regulatory Governance within its Ecology: The Structure of Management in an Age of Globalization', (2018) 24(5) *Contemporary Politics* (607–630); K. H. Eller, 'Private Governance of Global Value Chains from Within: Lessons From and For Transnational Law', (2017) 8 *Transnational Legal Theory* 296.

[33] P. F. Kjaer, 'Why Justification? The Structure of Public Power in Transnational Contexts', (2017) 8 *Transnational Legal Theory* 8.

[34] M. Koskenniemi, 'Empire and International Law: The Real Spanish Contribution', (2011) 61 *University of Toronto Law Journal* 1.

similar vein, global value chain law is characterized by a structural predominance of private law, while hybrid constellations have emerged with (inter-) national public law institutions ranging from the EU, OECD and the UN (e.g., the UN Global Compact), as well as nation-state initiatives, and a corresponding focus on issues such as corporate social responsibility, human rights, labour and environmental regulation and anti-corruption initiatives.[35]

In a similar vein, the EU legal order – the most mature and manifest non-state public law legal order – grew out of the European continental empires. In spite of the resilience of 'Westphalian semantics', freestanding and sovereign nation-states have never existed in the European context. Modern Germany and Italy emerged and operated as Prussia and Piedmont-Sardinia within the pre-existing imperial frame of the Holy Roman Empire until 1806, as well as its various succeeding formations. The same is the case with the nation-states of Central and Eastern Europe. From the implosion of the Central and Eastern European empires to 1945 in the case of Western Europe and until the fall of the Soviet Union in 1991 for Eastern Europe, the totalitarian version of imperialism, transcending nation-state categories, maintained dominance. A development that in the interwar period was complemented with a transnational cartelization of the economy in relation to its dominant sectors, such as aluminium, steel, coal and rubber, effectively – and in complementarity with colonialism – established a private law–based transnational ordering of the global economy.[36]

It was first the dual and simultaneous reconstitution of Western European nation-states and the establishment of a public law–based, transnational law–based order for Western Europe in the immediate post–World War II years that established the outright supremacy of legally constituted public power in Western Europe. All continental Western European states obtained new constitutions or substantially revised their constitutions in this period while launching far-reaching socio-economic reforms. Simultaneously, the transnational order of Western Europe was reconstructed via the allied occupation regime in

35 See e.g., EU Directive on Non-Financial and Diversity Information (Directive 2014/95/EU); ISO 26000 Standard on Social Responsibility; OECD Guidelines for Multinational Enterprises. See also K. Buhmann, 'Business and Human Rights: Understanding the UN Guiding Principles from the Perspective of Transnational Business Governance Interactions', (2015) 6 *Transnational Legal Theory* 399; S. Deva and D. Bilchitz (eds.), *Human Rights Obligations of Business: Beyond the Corporate Responsibility to Respect?* (Cambridge: Cambridge University Press, 2013).

36 P. F. Kjaer, 'The Transnational Constitution of Europe's Social Market Economies. A Question of Constitutional Imbalances?' *Journal of Common Market Studies*, Vol 57, Issue 1, 143–58.

Germany from 1945–1955, the Marshall Plan from 1947 to 1951 and the processes initiated with the Schuman Declaration of 1950 leading to the establishment of the European Coal and Steel Community of 1952 and subsequently the Treaty of Rome and the European Economic Community in 1957.[37]

The EU legal order that grew out of these initiatives is in several aspects to be understood as a post-imperial legal order. It is a legal order that runs in parallel to the legal orders of the member states. As such, the EU legal order is not to be understood as representing the sum of member state legal orders, but rather as an autonomous legal order running side by side with member state legal orders, with none of them factually enjoying supremacy in spite of the internal claims of both member states and the EU represented by the Court of Justice of the EU to supremacy.[38] Just like the earth and the underworld are linked by the River Styx in Greek mythology, the EU and the member state legal orders are materially interconnected through Comitology Committees and other in-between governance arrangements allowing for the transfer of legal texts, political decisions, knowledge, personnel and other components of meaning between them. As a result of this structural setup, both the EU and the member state legal orders thereby obtain spaces where they can maintain their internal conceptuality of autonomy while being structurally dependent on each other within an inter-legal arrangement.[39]

A second trait is that EU law, as especially embodied in the principles of the single market concerning free non-discriminatory flow of goods, capital, services and labour, is primarily structured on the basis of connectivity norms (i.e., norms aimed at enabling the separation, transmission and incorporation of components of meaning) from one legally structured context to another. As such, the legal structure and principles of the EU and the effects they produce are of a fundamentally different kind from those engrained in the constitutional orders of nation-states. While nation-states also aim to facilitate interconnectedness, this is predominantly expressed through and subordinate to principles of unity aimed at establishing collectivity through coherency norms. This is particularly clear within constitutional law as, for example, expressed through reference to states or nations as indissoluble unities.[40]

[37] Brunkhorst, *Critical Theory of Legal Revolutions*; J. E. Fossum and A. J. Menéndez, *The Constitution's Gift: A Constitutional Theory for a Democratic European Union* (Lanham, MD: Rowman & Littlefield, 2011).

[38] Kjaer, 'Claim-making and Parallel Universes'.

[39] Kjaer, *Between Governing and Governance*.

[40] For example, the indissoluble unity of the Spanish Nation as stated in Section 2 of the Preamble of the Spanish Constitution, available at www.congreso.es/portal/page/portal/Congreso/Congreso/Hist_Normas/Norm/const_espa_texto_ingles_0.pdf.

The EU is therefore neither a functional nor a normative equivalent to its member states, but a complementary structure standing in an orthogonal relationship to its members.

A third characteristic of the EU is it boundarylessness. The only material criterion for enlargement is that the applicant state is a 'European state', with no definition or delineation given in geographical, cultural or political terms.[41] As the concept of Europe has always been in flux – at different times in history referring to the Mediterranean basin, including North Africa and parts of the contemporary Middle East; the Christian world; or the part of the world subscribing to the Western Church as well as periodically excluding or including Russia – it remains a factually springy delineation. Also, due to its self-description as an "area of freedom, security and justice" and as an "economic area" rather than as a territorial entity, the EU gains the trait of being, in principle, a boundary-less entity that has no prescribed territorial limits. As such, the EU is a boundary-less structure operating in the dimension of space rather than territory.[42] The EU is an entity that, furthermore, has been structurally driven forward not only by the implosion of the continental empires, but also by the reconfiguration of Europe's relations to the rest of the world, as the implosion of the overseas colonial empires provided the functional need for substituting colonial market access with increased European integration – a need most visible in relation to the accession of the United Kingdom to the European Community in the face of the implosion of its empire. Also in the case of the United Kingdom, the idea of a sovereign nation unbound by global structures, as currently envisaged by advocates of Brexit, has never had factual reality. The United Kingdom emerged and became institutionally stabilized as a state in a process that went hand in hand with the expansion of the empire, and as such the United Kingdom was always embedded in a legal structure that was larger than itself. In the moment of decolonization, the imperial form of global integration was merely substituted with integration into the European construct, with this alteration, however, implying a switch from a reliance on the asymmetric norms of colonialism to the symmetric norms of equality formally guiding relations between EU member states. While serving as a functional equivalent to empire, emerging as a response to the implosion of both the continental and the colonial empires of Europe, the EU is formally committed to the 'respect for human

[41] https://web.archive.org/web/20060321034825/http://www.europarl.eu.int/enlargement/briefings/23a2_en.htm.

[42] A. Supiot, 'The Territorial Inscription of Laws', in G.-P. Calliess et al. (eds.), *Festschrift Teubner*, 375.

dignity and human rights, freedom, democracy, equality and the rule of law',[43] and this makes its normative articulations fundamentally different from those engrained in imperial law.[44]

As we will return to in the following section, the emergence and evolution of the EU legal order can thus be considered part of a fundamental transformation away from the asymmetric norms characterizing imperial law and towards a new foundation in symmetric norms, as is most clearly visible in the turn to human rights, acting as an inherent part of contemporary global governance law. However, one important difference can be observed in this regard. While the EU is emphasizing the equality of its member states, it is factually acting as suzerain (i.e., upper-sovereign) in relation to its immediate neighbours. Belarus remains the only state in the region with which the EU does not have a structured legal relationship. The members of the European Economic Area (Iceland, Liechtenstein and Norway), as well as states such as Switzerland and Turkey, are all subject to 'unequal treaties' factually admitting the EU as the central source of law and the Court of Justice of the EU as the final arbiter and authority when it comes to the relations between these states and the EU. The EU is currently seeking to replicate this approach in its relationship with the United Kingdom as part of the ongoing Brexit process. This is visible, for example, through the initial EU demand concerning indefinite extraterritorial jurisdiction for the Court of Justice of the EU when it comes to EU citizens residing in the United Kingdom and a call for the Court to act as the final authority in future legal disputes. So while one motive behind Brexit might be a longing for the asymmetric form of globality inherent to empire, the pursuit of Brexit is likely to lead to a new form of asymmetric relationship between the United Kingdom and the EU, with the United Kingdom in the subordinate position.

4 FROM ASYMMETRIC TO SYMMETRIC INTER-LEGALITY?

Contemporary global governance law from EU law to global supply chain law is, like its imperial predecessors, primarily orientated towards the facilitation of transplantations (i.e., the extraction, transmission and incorporation of components of meaning from one legally structured context to another). Imperial law in both its continental and in its colonial form relied on fundamentally asymmetric relations between centre and periphery on the basis of legally

[43] http://europarlamentti.info/en/values-and-objectives/values/.

[44] Although the norms of equality were severely impacted by the Euro crisis and the subsequent bailouts. See J. White. 'Authority after Emergency Rule', (2015) 78 *Modern Law Review* 585.

entrenched normative distinctions between Christians/non-Christians, civilized/non-civilized and upper and lower sovereigns. The issue of the EU's legal relations to its immediate neighbours apart, this is fundamentally different in contemporary global governance law, which to a large extent derives its normativity from human rights.

The abounding human rights literature essentially circles around three perspectives. The first perspective relates to continuity approaches emphasizing linear connections between, on the one hand, the Atlantic (i.e., American, French and Haitian) revolutions of the late eighteenth century and the abolition movement in relation to slave trade and slavery, and, on the other hand, the contemporary global human rights regime.[45] The second perspective relates to approaches taking a middle way between continuity and discontinuity by emphasizing the Holocaust, such as the UN Declaration of Human Rights of 1948 and the European Convention on Human Rights from 1953 providing central impetus to the evolution of human rights.[46] The third perspective relates to discontinuity approaches, emphasizing decolonization and other political developments in the 1960s and 1970s as the central vehicles for the emergence of global human rights.[47]

Common to these three approaches, however, is a strong emphasis on the normative value of human rights and comparatively little emphasis on the actual structure, location and effects of human rights norms in world society and the differences between human rights and earlier articulations of normativity as found in imperial law. When contextualized within the broader context of global law, three core characteristics of human rights can, however, be observed, which enable an understanding of them as falling within the category of global law. First, human rights are characterized by globality and boundarylessness insofar as they act as a universal public good that can be deployed and drawn upon in an infinite number of legal and social contexts and, as such, transcend territorial boundaries. Second, the normative foundation of human rights is bound up in a notion of fundamental equality of all humans, thereby giving them an explicit symmetric foundation that

[45] S. Buck-Morss, *Hegel, Haiti, and Universal History* (Pittsburgh, PA: University of Pittsburgh Press, 2009); L. Hunt. *Inventing Human Rights: A History* (New York: W.W. Norton & Company, 2007); J. S. Martinez, *The Slave Trade and the Origins of International Human Rights Law* (Oxford: Oxford University Press, 2014).

[46] P. Alston. 'Does the Past Matter? On the Origins of Human Rights', (2013) 126 *Harvard Law Review* 2043; S.-L. Hoffmann, 'Human Rights and History', (2016) 232 *Past and Present* 279.

[47] S. Jensen. *The Making of International Human Rights: The 1960s, Decolonization, and the Reconstruction of Global Values* (Cambridge: Cambridge University Press, 2016); S. Moyn, *The Last Utopia: Human Rights in History* (Cambridge, MA: Harvard University Press, 2010).

differs from the asymmetric distinctions of imperial law. Third, there is a drive to universalization, in the sense that institutionalized human rights settings are characterized by expansionist internal dynamics materializing in quests for 'complete inclusion' (i.e., the counterfactual proposition that all of humanity – both formally and factually – should be subject to human rights protection).[48]

While imperial law as well as contemporary global governance law in their external effects are orientated towards the facilitation of non-legal transplantations (i.e., the extraction, transmission and incorporation of meaning components with, for example, economic, moral, political or religious value from one legally structured context to another), human rights have historically served as a vehicle for the transplantation of law itself. From a sociological jurisprudence perspective, emphasizing the actual external effect of law, human rights act as a vehicle for the self-transplantations of law – most notably legal norms, but also a broader range of legal instruments and institutions – from one contextual setting to another. As reflected in the continuity/discontinuity debate on human rights, existing genealogies tend to be not only Western-centric, but also Anglo-American–centric, focusing on the historical experiences of the United Kingdom and its empire and the United States and its global engagements.[49] In particular, in German scholarship, an understanding of global human rights as possessing the potential to establish coherence on a global scale has emerged through an understanding of global human rights as a self-constituting framework introducing a hierarchy of norms within global law settings.[50] From both the Anglo-American and the German perspectives, human rights thereby come to appear as a singular and coherent set of norms. Such perspectives, however, cover up the paradox that the quest for symmetric global norms to date has been based on a profoundly asymmetric relationship, with the advocates of symmetry largely being located in a part of the world enjoying an asymmetrical structural position vis-à-vis the rest of the world. The ongoing decentring of the Western-centric world is, however, likely to challenge the singular perspective. Rather than conceiving of global human rights as a singular set of norms, it might be considered a common resource of symmetric normative

[48] K. P. Japp, 'Zur Funktion der Menschenrechte in der Weltgesellschaft', in B. Heintz and B. Leisering (eds.), *Menschenrechte in der Weltgesellschaft. Deutungswandel und Wirkungsweise eines globalen Leitwerts* (Frankfurt am Main: Campus Verlag, 2015), 65.

[49] For an exception in relation to France, see Grandmaison, 'The Exception and the Rule'.

[50] H. Brunkhorst, 'Dialectical Snares: Human Rights and Democracy in the World Society', (2009) 2 *Ethics and Global Politics* 219.

articulations with a conglomerate character from where legal actors located at different sites of the local, national or transnational levels of world society can derive norms enabling them to address concrete legal problems.[51] The actual manifestation of human rights might therefore be relationally decided in the concrete societal and legal contexts in which they are transplanted and not least in the third spaces located in-between the multitude of community-based, state-based and transnational legal orders making up the global legal landscape.

5 CONCLUSION: THE INTER-LEGALITY FUNCTION OF GLOBAL LAW

Global law is an inter-legal and inter-contextual phenomenon characterized by boundarylessness and universalization. While global law has undergone profound structural transformations as expressed in the transformations from imperial and colonial law to contemporary global governance law, the core functional nucleus of global law remains. Global law settings are characterized by a structural pre-eminence of connectivity norms, as opposed to coherence or possibility norms, and an external orientation towards the facilitation of transplantations (i.e., the extraction, transmission and incorporation of components of meaning from one legally structured context to another). It is a law that constitutes a third space between sites of extraction and sites of incorporation, establishing material interconnectedness while belonging to neither the extraction nor the incorporation site.

Global law has undergone a profound transformation in its internal conceptuality and structural composition as part of the switch from imperial and colonial law to contemporary global governance law. This transformation is most clearly expressed in the reconstruction of connectivity norms as symmetric norms aimed at ensuring fundamental equality, as opposed to the asymmetric foundation of imperial law as expressed in imperial distinctions such as Christians/non-Christians and civilized/non-civilized and the concept of suzerain (i.e., upper-sovereign). The symmetric conceptuality inherent to contemporary global governance law is most explicitly found in the adherence to global human rights. To date, global human rights have, however, served as vehicles of transplantations of legal norms with a European and Western imprint to the rest of the world, thereby acting as a vehicle for the self-transplantation of law. In the post–Western-centric world, global

[51] A. Supiot, *Homo Juridicus. Essai sur la Fonction Anthropologique du Droit* (Paris: Édition du Seuil, 2005).

human rights might, however, be considered a common resource of normative articulations with a conglomerate character from where legal actors located at different sites of the local, national or transnational levels of world society can derive norms enabling them to address concrete legal problems. Such a perspective is in tune with the actual function, evolution and location of global law as a decentred 'in-between worlds' phenomenon characterized by inter-contextuality and inter-legality.

14

International Courts As Inter-Legality Hubs

YUVAL SHANY

1 INTRODUCTION

This volume deals with the relations between distinct regulatory frameworks (i.e., semi-closed international legal orders built around a functional logic, specialized institutions, and particular bodies of expertise and epistemology). Its underlying normative premise is that in complex social systems composed of multiple regulatory frameworks, one set of "legalities" must be cognizant of other sets of "legalities," notwithstanding the stance taken by any specific legal order toward the way in which specific normative conflicts should be reconciled (e.g., monism, dualism, or pluralism). This means that some form of cross-regulation – *inter-legality* – is essential, even if at a "second-order" level; that is, between the institutions interpreting and applying the competing regulatory frameworks.

The present chapter applies the volume's overarching theoretical construct to the work of international courts and tribunals. Such courts and tribunals serve as inter-legality hubs since they increasingly experience jurisdictional competition, which confronts them with some of the practical difficulties of inter-legality and the need to consider, in connection with their law interpretation and law application activities, developing an understanding of situations of inter-legality and their normative implications. Note that international courts are typically embedded in specific legal orders, such as the World Trade Organization (WTO) or European Union (EU), and their jurisdiction is often tied to the interpretation and application of a specific legal instrument, such as the Rome Statute or the European Convention on Human Rights (ECHR). Reconciling situations of inter-legality requires them to construct normative and institutional "bridges" across different regulatory frameworks – in other words, to engage at different levels with external legal orders and external institutions.

The two claims I develop in this chapter are as follows: (1) up until now, the engagement of international courts and tribunals with the concept of inter-legality has often been superficial. Although courts found pragmatic ways to circumvent most of the practical challenges posed by inter-legality (e.g., by foregrounding or backgrounding the jurisdictional and substantive aspects of specific regulatory frameworks), they have not fully come to terms with the deep implications of inter-legality for the rule of law in international life and (2) the institutional configuration of international courts exacerbates some of the normative and practical challenges of inter-legality. This is because international courts adhere to an idiosyncratic set of interests that further complicate the relations between the competing regulatory frameworks. For example, international courts typically have an interest in maintaining their own judicial power, legitimacy, and effectiveness, and this interest often translates into claims of authority across legal regimes and across the national/international divide, which induce them to prioritize certain legal frameworks over others. Courts also sometime "pull" the jurisdictional and substantive norms they apply toward their professional comfort zones, thereby affecting their choices regarding the regulation of situations of inter-legality. The relative power and institutional agendas of international courts therefore influence their engagement with the concept of inter-legality and complicate our ability to isolate principled normative considerations about how to bridge multiple regulatory frameworks from institutional considerations.

The first part of this chapter (Section 2) discusses my first claim concerning international courts' ability to avoid overt jurisdictional clashes and inconsistent rulings through a variety of legal interpretation techniques, which might nonetheless fail to seize the inter-legality "bull" by its "horns." For example, conflict-avoidance techniques resorted to by international courts and tribunals leave in place much of the tensions and inconsistencies attendant to the competing regulatory frameworks. The second part of the chapter (Section 3) illustrates the ways in which the particular institutional and ideological agendas of international courts might influence the manner in which they deal with situations of inter-legality, using case studies from the field of international human rights law involving interaction with other bodies of law. Section 4 concludes.

2 NAVIGATING BETWEEN COMPETING REGULATORY FRAMEWORKS

The discourse surrounding the competing jurisdictions of international courts, which reached its heyday in the late 1990s and early 2000s, focused to a large extent on the procedural implications of jurisdictional overlap.

Several research works explored the application of "hard" coordination principles such as *lis alibi pendens* and *res judicata*, which aim to prevent multiple proceedings,[1] and "soft" coordination principles, such as comity and *abus de droit*, which aim to offer discretionary principles for prioritizing the jurisdiction of one judicial forum over the other.[2] Another body of literature dealt with the problem of the fragmentation of international law resulting from inconsistent interpretation and application of legal norms by different judicial institutions.[3]

Interest in this type of question has receded in recent years, however. Although incompatible decisions by international courts and tribunals still abound, more or less stable practical modalities have emerged to manage jurisdictional and normative conflicts in ways that refute the dire predictions about judicial anarchy and high levels of legal uncertainty the proliferation of international courts and tribunals.[4] Still, I maintain that the deep implications of inter-legality for the rule of law in international life have remained under-addressed in international judicial decisions. At times, such implications were ignored altogether, and at other times they were treated only at a superficial level.

The decision of the Court of Justice of the EU (CJEU) in *Kadi v Council*, which involved an attempt by a regional court to regulate the relations between two international legal orders, may illustrate this point.[5] As is well-known, the Court nullified in its judgment EC Regulation 881/

[1] See e.g., K. Oellers-Frahm, "Multiplication of International Courts and Tribunals and Conflicting Jurisdictions – Problems and Possible Solutions," (2001) 5 *Max Planck Yearbook of United Nations Law* 67; C. McLachlan, *Lis Pendens in International Litigation* (The Hague: Hague Academy of International Law, 2009); Y. Shany, *The Competing Jurisdictions of International Courts and Tribunals* (Oxford: Oxford University Press, 2004).

[2] See e.g., N. Lavranos, "The Solange-Method as a Tool for Regulating Competing Jurisdictions among International Courts and Tribunals," (2008) 30 *Loyola LA International and Comparative Law Review* 275; W. Worster, "Competition and Comity in the Fragmentation of International Law," (2009) 34 *Brooklyn Journal of International Law* 119; A. D. Mitchell, "Good Faith in WTO Dispute Settlement," (2006) 7 *Melbourne Journal of International Law* 339.

[3] See e.g., P. Webb, *International Judicial Integration and Fragmentation* (Oxford: Oxford University Press, 2013); A. Reinisch, "The Proliferation of International Dispute Settlement Mechanisms: The Threat of Fragmentation vs. the Promise of a More Effective System," in I. Buffard et al. (eds.), *International Law between Universalism and Fragmentation: Festschrift in Honor of Gerhard Hafner* (Leiden: Martinus Nijhoff, 2008), 107; J. Pauwelyn, *Conflict of Norms in Public International Law: How WTO Law Relates to other Rules of International Law* (Cambridge: Cambridge University Press, 2003).

[4] See L. Boisson de Chazournes, "Plurality in the Fabric of International Courts and Tribunals: The Threads of a Managerial Approach," (2017) 28 *European Journal of International Law* 13.

[5] Joined Cases C-402/05 P and C-415/05 P, *Kadi v Council*, ECLI:EU:C:2008:461.

2002, implementing the sanction regime introduced in Security Council Resolution 1390 (2002) against persons and entities associated with Bin Laden, Al Qaeda, and the Taliban, due to a breach of general principles of EU law. This holding resulted in a direct clash between the two principal regulatory frameworks implicated in the case – EU law and UN law. But instead of confronting directly the challenge posed by this manifestation of inter-legality (i.e., the need to somehow manage the relations between the separate legal orders to which EU/UN member states are concurrently subject), the CJEU chose to adopt a "tunnel vision"-like policy of ignoring the impact of the decision rendered within one legal order on the other legal order:

> In this regard, it must be emphasized that, in circumstances such as those of these cases, the review of lawfulness thus to be ensured by the Community judicature applies to the Community act intended to give effect to the international agreement at issue, *and not to the latter as such.*[6] (emphasis added)

And that:

> [I]t is not a consequence of the principles governing the international legal order under the United Nations that any judicial review of the internal lawfulness of the contested regulation in the light of fundamental freedoms is excluded by virtue of the fact that the measure is intended to give effect to a resolution of the Security Council adopted under Chapter VII of the Charter of the United Nations.[7]

Put differently, the Court exercised review only of the implementing EU measure, and such review was allegedly not influenced by the legality or illegality of the Security Council Resolution under general international law.

This dualist position, effectively entailing regime selection (or review of legality using "tunnel vision"), does not deal directly with the real challenges of inter-legality – EU/UN member states are still subject to conflicting regulation – and of the ensuing need to find ways to mediate the conflict stemming from their participation in two separate and at times incompatible legal orders. Note, however, that although Security Council Resolution 1390 remains legally unaffected by the decision of the CJEU in *Kadi*, the obstacles to its implementation presented by the nullification of Regulation 881/2002 have led the UN Security Council to strengthen some rule of law

6 Ibid., para. 286.
7 Ibid., para. 299.

safeguards attendant to the sanctions regime.[8] Hence, at least on the UN side, some cognizance has been taken of the situation of inter-legality.

The *Kadi* approach of embracing a sharp rule of selection between competing regulatory frameworks, typically in favor of the legal order in which the deciding court is embedded, can also be found in judicial decisions addressing jurisdictional competition between different international courts, or between national and international courts. Unfortunately, here too states were left to deal through other means with the full normative and institutional implications of inter-legality.

One example of a similar "tunnel vision" approach, applied to jurisdictional competition, is the CJEU advisory opinion on the *EU Accession to the ECHR*. In this case, the CJEU rejected an attempt to merge two regulatory frameworks, EU law and the ECHR – a solution that would constitute an important step in the direction of comprehensively addressing an inter-legality situation.[9] In its decision, the Court opined that accession to the ECHR, and the attendant acceptance of the compulsory jurisdiction of the European Court of Human Rights (ECtHR) over the EU and EU legal instruments would interfere with specific EU procedural and substantive principles, including the "mutual trust" principle allowing member states to rely on the implementation of EU law by other member states, the exclusive jurisdiction of the CJEU over EU-related legal disputes, and the limits set on review of measures undertaken under the Common Foreign and Security Policy. It would also require in cases submitted against the EU and its member states a review by an external body – the ECtHR – of the precise division of labor between them (as corespondents), thereby disrupting the functioning of the EU. As a result of these considerations, the CJEU was of the opinion that the systemic welfare of the EU would not be well-served by accession under the terms of the draft accession agreement.

Like with *Kadi*, however, the advisory opinion does little to mitigate the difficulties encountered by member states as a result of their need to comply with two separate regulatory frameworks that espouse different procedural and substantive approaches to similar issues. In fact, the decision by the Court that explains the differences between the two systems of protection accentuates the inter-legality challenge confronting states participating in both regulatory

8 See e.g., E. de Wet, "Judicial Challenges to the Security Council's Use of Sanctions," in J. Farrall and H. Charlesworth (eds.), *Strengthening the Rule of Law Through the UN Security Council* (Abingdon: Routledge, 2016), 193.

9 Opinion 2/13 (*ECHR*), ECLI:EU:C:2014:2454.

frameworks. It is precisely this challenge that had led them to opt for accession and that the CJEU's decision has left unresolved for the time being.[10]

Another example of a jurisdictional conflict resulting in a binary regime selection can be found in the face-off between the Italian court system and the International Court of Justice (ICJ) over the question of jurisdictional immunities. Following the *Ferrini* litigation, in which civil courts in Italy – all the way up to the Court of Cassation – refused to afford Germany immunity from tort litigation pertaining to World War II-era atrocities,[11] Germany was able to obtain in 2012 an ICJ judgment pronouncing the illegality under international law of the domestic judicial decisions, ordering Italy to provide it with restitution:

> The decisions and measures infringing Germany's jurisdictional immunities which are still in force must cease to have effect, and the effects which have already been produced by those decisions and measures must be reversed, in such a way that the situation which existed before the wrongful acts were committed is re-established. It has not been alleged or demonstrated that restitution would be materially impossible in this case, or that it would involve a burden for Italy out of all proportion to the benefit deriving from it. In particular, the fact that some of the violations may have been committed by judicial organs, and some of the legal decisions in question have become final in Italian domestic law, does not lift the obligation incumbent upon Italy to make restitution. On the other hand, the Respondent has the right to choose the means it considers best suited to achieve the required result.[12]

In reaffirming Italy's right to choose those measures that are best suited for implementing its restitution obligation under international law, the ICJ acknowledged Italy's domestic legal constraints and, by implication, the inter-legal attributes of the situation. Still, the practical and conceptual problems confronting the Italian state due to it being subject to two incompatible legal orders remained in place. These difficulties were exacerbated following the 2014 judgment of the Italian Constitutional Court that offered a mirror image of the ICJ's decision, requiring Italy to follow its constitutional

[10] European Parliament Think Tank, *EU Accession to the European Convention on Human Rights* (July 2017), available at www.europarl.europa.eu/thinktank/en/document.html?reference=EPRS_BRI%282017%29607298.

[11] See Case 5044/04, *Ferrini v Federal Republic of Germany*, Judgment of the Italian Court of Cassation of March 11, 2004, available at www.asser.nl/upload/documents/DomCLIC/Docs/NLP/Italy/Ferrini_Cassazione_6-11-2003.pdf.

[12] *Jurisdictional Immunities of the State* (Germany v Italy), [2012] ICJ Reports 99, 153–154.

"effective remedy" norm notwithstanding its international law obligation to recognize sovereign immunity and comply with ICJ judgments:

> In the present case, the impossibility of effective judicial protection of fundamental rights, acknowledged by the ICJ and confirmed before that Court by the [Federal Republic of Germany], makes apparent the contrast between international law, as defined by the ICJ, and Articles 2 and 24 of the Constitution. This contrast, insofar as the international law of immunity of States from the civil jurisdiction of other States includes acts considered *jure imperii* that violated international law and fundamental human rights, obliges this Court to declare that, to the extent that international law extends immunity to actions for damages caused by such serious violations, the referral of Article 10, para. 1 of the Constitution does not operate. Consequently, insofar as the law of immunity from jurisdiction of States conflicts with the aforementioned fundamental principles [of the Constitution], it has not entered the Italian legal order and, therefore, does not have any effect therein.[13]

The upshot is that judicial decisions purporting to regulate jurisdictional conflicts or conflicts between competing regulatory frameworks do not necessarily address the situations of inter-legality underlying the conflicts referred to adjudication. Consequently, states may find themselves, on an ongoing basis, bound by disjointed, incompatible, yet simultaneously applicable legal orders. The existence of legal hierarchies – such as the paramount status of the constitution in domestic law or *jus cogens* under international law – may further exacerbate the inadequacy of the response to situations of inter-legality, as it reinforces a tendency to apply one body of law to the exclusion of others, without attempting to give some effect to the interplay between them.

Even international courts that strive to address the fragmentation of international law through the construction of "bridges" across applicable regulatory frameworks may struggle to fully come to terms with the notion of inter-legality that underlies fragmentation. For example, the ICJ case law on the parallel application of international humanitarian law (IHL) and international human rights law (IHRL) offers two principal approaches to such situations of inter-legality: *lex specialis* and *cumulative application*. Under the *lex specialis* approach, introduced in the 1996 ICJ *Nuclear Weapons* advisory opinion, the general provisions of IHRL ought to be construed according to the more specific provisions of IHL.[14] At first sight, this appears to be a promising

[13] Judgment no. 238/2014 of the Italian Constitutional Court of October 22, 2014, para. 3.5.

[14] *Legality of the Threat or Use of Nuclear Weapons*, [1996] ICJ Reports 226, 240 ("The Court observes that the protection of the International Covenant on Civil and Political Rights does

approach that strives to give simultaneous yet coordinated effect to all applicable legal bodies. Still, the full impact of inter-legality has not been appreciated by the advisory opinion. Although it was held that IHRL should be construed in light of IHL, the opinion does not explain whether IHRL also influences the contents of IHL (and if so, under what conditions). Nor does it fully acknowledge the complementary and at times mutually supporting role of the two legal frameworks (e.g., with respect to remedies and the involvement of legal institutions embedded in different legal regimes).

The cumulative approach takes a different position, underscoring the complementary role of IHRL and IHL, but largely ignoring the interpretative interplay between the competing regulatory frameworks – in particular, the contextual assumptions that invite the application of IHL and arguably should also shape the manner of application of IHRL. Hence, for example, the holding of the ICJ in the 2004 *Wall* advisory opinion that IHL and essentially all IHRL treaties apply in the Palestinian Territories occupied by Israel effectively in a rule prioritizing the application IHRL, since it generally affords higher protection standards that go beyond those found in IHL.[15] While this approach is attractive from the perspective of individual right-holders, it does

not cease in times of war, except by operation of Article 4 of the Covenant whereby certain provisions may be derogated from in a time of national emergency. Respect for the right to life is not, however, such a provision. In principle, the right not arbitrarily to be deprived of one's life applies also in hostilities. The test of what is an arbitrary deprivation of life, however, then falls to be determined by the applicable *lex specialis*, namely, the law applicable in armed conflict which is designed to regulate the conduct of hostilities. Thus, whether a particular loss of life, through the use of a certain weapon in warfare, is to be considered an arbitrary deprivation of life contrary to Article 6 of the Covenant, can only be decided by reference to the law applicable in armed conflict and not deduced from the terms of the Covenant itself").

[15] *Legal Consequences of the Construction of a Wall in the Occupied Palestinian Territory*, [2004] ICJ Reports 136, 178 ("More generally, the Court considers that the protection offered by human rights conventions does not cease in case of armed conflict, save through the effect of provisions for derogation of the kind to be found in Article 4 of the International Covenant on Civil and Political Rights. As regards the relationship between international humanitarian law and human rights law, there are thus three possible situations: some rights may be exclusively matters of international humanitarian law; others may be exclusively matters of human rights law; yet others may be matters of both these branches of international law. In order to answer the question put to it, the Court will have to take into consideration both these branches of international law, namely human rights law and, as *lex specialis*, international humanitarian law"). See also *Armed Activities on the Territory of the Congo* (Democratic Republic of the Congo v. Uganda), [2005] ICJ Reports 168, 179 ("The Court, having concluded that Uganda was an occupying Power in Ituri at the relevant time, finds that Uganda's responsibility is engaged both for any acts of its military that violated its international obligations and for any lack of vigilance in preventing violations of human rights and international humanitarian law by other actors present in the occupied territory, including rebel groups acting on their own account").

disrupt the internal balance and logic of IHL, which is arguably a more closely tailored regulatory framework (i.e., *lex specialis*) in situations of conflict and belligerent occupation than IHRL, which regulates all exercises of governmental power in both peacetime and wartime.[16]

In sum, international court decisions appear to confront the challenge posed by situations of inter-legality through three principal approaches: (1) application of "tunnel vision" or prioritization of one legal regime over all other; (2) attempts to merge legal orders; and (3) efforts to accumulate legal orders. The first approach, exemplified in the CJEU's *Kadi* and *Accession to the ECHR* cases and in the *Jurisdictional Immunities* litigation, typically involves approaching inter-legality situations exclusively from the perspective of the legal order in which the court is embedded. This approach is particularly dominant among international courts that are authorized to apply a specific treaty, thus excluding all other regulatory frameworks that apply to the relevant states.[17] It is also used by such courts for resolving problems of competing jurisdictions, which constitute the institutional manifestation of situations of inter-legality – states subject to multiple overlapping legal orders that provide different adjudicatory processes for authoritative determination of their legal obligations.[18]

As indicated above, a "tunnel vision" approach may be effective in disposing of a specific dispute, but avoids dealing with the root causes of the legal difficulty – the existence of multiple legal orders exerting normative and institutional pulls in different directions on the same states. In fact, the "tunnel vision" approach resorted to by specific courts creates conditions for conflicting judgments by different international and national courts (as illustrated by the face-off between the ICJ and the Italian Constitutional Court). This might

[16] This out-of-context application of IHRL instruments, without the necessary interpretative adjustments, has been regarded by Judge Higgins as strange. See *Wall*, Separate Opinion of Judge Higgins, at 213 ("So far as the International Covenant on Economic, Social and Cultural Rights is concerned, the situation is even stranger, given the programmatic requirements for the fulfilment of this category of right").

[17] Cf., Report of the Study Group of the International Law Commission (finalized by M. Koskenniemi), *Fragmentation of International Law: Difficulties Arising from the Diversification and Expansion of International Law*, UN Doc. A/CN.4/L.682 (2006), at 247 ("At an institutional level, the proliferation of implementation organs – often courts and tribunals – for specific treaty-regimes has given rise to a concern over deviating jurisprudence and forum-shopping. The rights and obligations of legal subjects may depend on which body is seized to recognize them").

[18] For a discussion, see Y. Shany, *The Competing Jurisdictions of International Courts and Tribunals* (Oxford: Oxford University Press, 2003), 26.

result in adjudication not even succeeding in resolving the particular dispute referred to it.

The other approaches, which the ICJ experimented with in its case law on the interplay between IHL and IHRL, seem to represent more promising avenues, as they offer two models for specifically acknowledging situations of inter-legality – merging regulatory frameworks or applying them cumulatively. Yet, as indicated above, both approaches as applied by the ICJ have not fully grasped the complexity of the interpretive and institutional interplay between different legal orders in situations of inter-legality.

The next section presents two additional sets of jurisdictional conflicts that give rise to further attempts to construct interpretative "bridges" between different regulatory frameworks in ways that go beyond the rather crude methods applied by the ICJ in the IHL/IHRL cases. Still, a new complication arises. It appears as if the institutional interests and perspectives of the involved courts influence their interpretive choices in the discussed cases. Arguably, such idiosyncratic interests and perspectives further confound the regulation of inter-legality situations.

3 SKEWED BRIDGES ACROSS LEGAL ORDERS?

There is a rich literature describing the manner in which judicial decisions issued by international courts and tribunals are influenced by their institutional agendas and priorities.[19] It is well established that over and beyond sociological explanations for specific normative preferences (or biases),[20] international courts and tribunals also have institutional interests in maintaining or enhancing their judicial power, legitimacy, and effectiveness, and these interests often translate into claims of authority across legal regimes and across the national/international divide. Their agendas and priorities also manifest themselves in the interpretations of the law they apply, which brings them within comfort zones or "cocoons" in which they can exercise their special expertise and promote their normative preferences.

[19] See e.g., S. Dothan, "How International Courts Enhance their Legitimacy," (2013) 14 *Theoretical Inquiries in Law* 455; K. Alter, "Agents or Trustees? International Courts in Their Political Context," (2008) 14 *European Journal of International Relations* 33; Y. Shany, *Assessing the Effectiveness of International Courts* (Oxford: Oxford University Press, 2014), 24–25.

[20] See, generally, M. R. Madsen, "Sociological Approaches to International Courts," in C. P. R. Romano, K. Alter, and Y. Shany (eds.), *The Oxford Handbook of International Adjudication* (Oxford: Oxford University Press, 2013), 388.

The involvement of different international courts possessing their own sets of interests in situations of inter-legality creates a potentially distorting prism through which the relationship between competing regulatory frameworks is regarded, and their involvement may create new problems of normative coordination and institutional alignment. For example, differences between the legal powers exercised by international courts and differences in their political clout may shape the approach of relevant states to the overlapping legal orders to a greater extent than an abstract normative analysis of the interrelations between the said legal orders.[21] So, situations of inter-legality appear to invite the application of a complex, dialectical-like interplay between normative tensions, jurisdictional competition, and institutional power struggles.

I will try to demonstrate the dynamics of the aforementioned interplay through a review of two sets of cases involving the intra-European division of labor in processing asylum applications (the so-called "Dublin cases") and the complicated relationship between Security Council Resolutions on Iraq and Afghanistan and the background norms of IHL and IHRL against which they apply. Arguably, the identity of the law-appliers – national courts or international courts, human rights courts, or regional integrations bodies – has been a critical factor in shaping the respective legal arrangements and outcomes of adjudication, as well as the manner in which situations of inter-legality were addressed.

The "Dublin cases" involve a series of ECtHR, CJEU and UN Human Rights Committee (HRC) decisions on return of asylum seekers to the state of first entry into the EU/Schengen area in which they applied or should have applied for asylum. These states of first entry are typically Southern or Eastern European countries like Greece, Italy, or Bulgaria. According to the Dublin II/III Procedure,[22] asylum applications should be processed in the state of first entry in order to avoid "asylum-shopping." This rule creates an easy-to-apply division of labor principle (whose fairness to "frontier countries" has been

[21] See e.g., literature addressing the "gravitational pull" of the WTO dispute settlement procedures: R. Uruena, "Temporariness and Change in Global Governance," (2014) 45 *Netherlands Yearbook of International Law* 19, 30; M. Varella, *Internationalization of Law: Globalization, International Law and Complexity* (Dordrecht: Springer, 2014), 156.

[22] Regulation (EU) no. 604/2013 of the European Parliament and of the Council of June 26, 2013, establishing the criteria and mechanisms for determining the member state responsible for examining an application for international protection lodged in one of the member states by a third-country national or a stateless person, 2013 OJ L 180/31; Council Regulation (EC) no. 343/2003 of February 18, 2003, establishing the criteria and mechanisms for determining the member state responsible for examining an asylum application lodged in one of the member states by a third-country national (no longer in force), 2003 OJ 50/1.

nonetheless questioned),[23] which emanates from the notion that the EU operates as a single legal area with comparable asylum standards, rendering all countries equally competent to vet entry and to afford comparable protections to asylum seekers.

Yet, in a number of cases, the leading of which is *MSS v Greece and Belgium*,[24] the ECtHR has rejected attempts to execute Dublin transfers, where the conditions in the state of first entry, including immigration detention conditions and asylum procedures, fell below the standards of Article 3 of the ECHR, implying thereby that IHRL norms – especially those reflecting absolute *jus cogens* norms such as the prohibition against torture and ill treatment – override EU law[25] and domestic immigration law. Such substandard conditions may be caused by a systematic failure in the state of first entry, the particular circumstances of the asylum seeker in question, or a combination of both. A similar approach has been taken by the UN HRC in certain "Dublin cases" involving transfers to Italy and Bulgaria.[26] By contrast, the CJEU has embraced in its case law a more stringent standard, holding that only systemic deficiencies in asylum procedures or reception conditions that create a real risk of exposure to inhuman or degrading treatment would deny the transferring state the right to return the asylum seeker to the state of first entry.[27]

Formally speaking, the aforementioned Dublin cases do not generate normative conflicts under international law. Since the Dublin Regulation allows but does not require states to transfer individuals back to the state of first entry, transferring states can follow the more protective standards under IHRL without violating their obligations under EU law. Still, the policy assumptions underlying the Dublin Procedure – that asylum applications should be submitted at the state of first entry (a principle designed to organize and stabilize asylum procedures in the Schengen area) and that asylum procedures and

23 See e.g., E. Küçük, "The Principle of Solidarity and Fairness in Sharing Responsibility: More than Window Dressing?" (2016) 22 *European Law Journal* 448.

24 *MSS v Greece and Belgium*, Application no. 30696/09, January 21, 2011. See also *Sharifi v Italy and Greece*, Application no. 16643/09, October 21, 2014; *Tarakhel v Switzerland*, Application no. 29217/12, November 4, 2014.

25 Another EU regulation implicated in the Dublin cases is the Reception Directive – Directive 2013/33/EU of the European Parliament and of the Council of June 26, 2013, laying down standards for the reception of applicants for international protection, 2013 OJ L 180/96.

26 See e.g., *Jasin v Denmark*, Comm. no. 2360/2014, Views of the UN HRC of July 22, 2015; *R.A.A. and Z.M. v Denmark*, Comm. no. 2608/2015, Views of the UN HRC of October 28, 2016; *Hashi v Denmark*, Comm. no. 2470/2014, Views of the UN HRC of July 28, 2017.

27 Cases C-411/10 and 493/10, *N.S. v Secretary of State for the Home Department*, ECLI:EU:C:2011:865; C-394/12, *Abdullahi v Bundesasylamt*, ECLI:EU:C:2013:813.

reception conditions across the different EU members should be regarded as meeting the same minimal human rights standards (and that, as a result, states can mutually trust one another in dealing with asylum seekers) – are undermined by the state-by-state human rights compliance analysis undertaken by the ECtHR and the UN HRC.

The situation confronting the different courts exercising jurisdiction over "Dublin cases" is thus a situation of inter-legality, involving the co-applicability of different regulatory frameworks with distinct legal rationales and policy imperatives. Arguably, the different outcomes can be explained, inter alia, through reference to differences in judicial policy and judicial sensibility: human rights courts approach the question of Dublin transfers from a victim-oriented point of view, whereas the CJEU approaches it from a European integration perspective. Hence, in case of doubt as to whether country conditions are suitable for specific vulnerable individuals, the human rights courts tend to err on the side of caution and require the transferring state to obtain individual assurances from the receiving state. The sensibility of the CJEU, on the other hand, appears to direct it to heavily rely on the principle of "mutual trust" in the applicability of European standards to all individuals across the Schengen areas. This important principle can only be ignored if it is shown that a particular member state experiences a systemic failure in its asylum reception policies. So it may be the identity of the court applying the law that determines the foregrounding or backgrounding of the relevant legal norms, depending on the norms and the court's political and ideological commitments and on the goals of the specific legal regime it which it is embedded.

It is quite possible that differences in the judicial approach to the relative weight to be assigned to the principle of "mutual trust" are part of the explanation for the collapse of the EU accession process to the ECHR. This is because it may have been difficult for the CJEU to accept subjecting the application of EU norms to another judicial institution that does not share the normative priorities of the EU. Indeed, the CJEU advisory opinion on *EU Accession to the ECHR* explains that:

> [I]t should be noted that the principle of mutual trust between the Member States is of fundamental importance in EU law, given that it allows an area without internal borders to be created and maintained. That principle requires, particularly with regard to the area of freedom, security and justice, each of those States, save in exceptional circumstances, to consider all the other Member States to be complying with EU law and particularly with the fundamental rights recognized by EU law . . . Thus, when implementing EU law, the Member States may, under EU law, be required to presume that

> fundamental rights have been observed by the other Member States, so that not only may they not demand a higher level of national protection of fundamental rights from another Member State than that provided by EU law, but, save in exceptional cases, they may not check whether that other Member State has actually, in a specific case, observed the fundamental rights guaranteed by the EU … In so far as the ECHR would, in requiring the EU and the Member States to be considered Contracting Parties not only in their relations with Contracting Parties which are not Member States of the EU but also in their relations with each other, including where such relations are governed by EU law, require a Member State to check that another Member State has observed fundamental rights, even though EU law imposes an obligation of mutual trust between those Member States, accession is liable to upset the underlying balance of the EU and undermine the autonomy of EU law.[28]

Put differently, the authorization of the ECtHR to invoke EU law without guarantees that it would adopt the same judicial approach of the CJEU would disrupt the internal balance of EU law. Hence, retaining the self-contained nature of EU law, as applied by the EU institutions, is better from the CJEU's perspective than allowing external courts to engage with it in situations of inter-legality.

Another example of the existence of jurisdictional competition and its attendant competing judicial policies as a complicating factor in situations of inter-legality can be found in the string of litigation on the interplay between IHRL, IHL, and Security Council Resolutions allegedly authorizing security measures taken by the United Kingdom in Iraq and Afghanistan. Several decisions issued by UK courts and the ECtHR illustrate differences in the degree of willingness of different courts to assume that Security Council Resolutions or IHL may justify deviation from IHRL norms with or without explicit textual authorization.

In *Al-Jedda*, the House of Lords was confronted with the question of whether UK forces in Iraq could place in security detention a UK citizen suspected of supplying rebels with arms, notwithstanding the fact that the ECHR does not list such grounds of detention as a permissible exception to the right to liberty. The ECHR was not the only applicable legal framework in the case, however. Since the United Kingdom was also authorized by Security Council Resolution 1546 to take "all necessary measures to

[28] Opinion 2/13 (*ECHR*), paras. 191–194.

contribute to the maintenance of security and stability in Iraq,"[29] it arguably had the authority to resort to security detention if necessary to implement the Resolution.

According to the House of Lords, the Security Council Resolution won out by virtue of Article 103 of the UN Charter, notwithstanding the permissive language used in the authorizing part of the Resolution. This outcome was supported by a purposeful interpretation of the authorizing language in light of the importance of the Council's peace and security mandate and the absence of a legal duty for the United Kingdom to send troops to implement the Resolution (which explains the choice of permissive language). Still, as Lord Bingham wrote, the United Kingdom should try to apply the authority under Resolution 1546 in a way that would minimize the deviation from Article 5 of the ECHR:

> Thus there is a clash between on the one hand a power or duty to detain exercisable on the express authority of the Security Council and, on the other, a fundamental human right which the UK has undertaken to secure to those (like the appellant) within its jurisdiction. How are these to be reconciled? There is in my opinion only one way in which they can be reconciled: by ruling that the UK may lawfully, where it is necessary for imperative reasons of security, exercise the power to detain authorized by UNSCR 1546 and successive resolutions, but must ensure that the detainee's rights under article 5 are not infringed to any greater extent than is inherent in such detention. I would resolve the second issue in this sense.[30]

This is an interesting acknowledgment of a situation of inter-legality, representing an attempt to prioritize a superior norm (Security Council Resolution) while complying as much as possible with the other relevant regulatory frameworks. In its review of the same case, the ECtHR, however, took another approach, prioritizing Article 5 of the ECHR over the Security Council Resolution through insisting on the position that only an explicit deviation from Article 5 by the Resolution could lead to the invocation of Article 103 of the Charter:

> In the event of any ambiguity in the terms of a United Nations Security Council resolution, the Court must therefore choose the interpretation which is most in harmony with the requirements of the Convention and which avoids any conflict of obligations. In the light of the United

[29] Security Council Res. 1546, UN Doc. S/RES/1546 (2004).
[30] *R (on the application of Al-Jedda) v Secretary of State for Defence*, [2007] UKHL 58, para. 39 (per Bingham LJ).

> Nations' important role in promoting and encouraging respect for human rights, it is to be expected that clear and explicit language would be used were the Security Council to intend States to take particular measures which would conflict with their obligations under international human rights law.[31]

Since the Resolution did not explicitly require states to deviate from their obligations under IHRL, including the ECHR, the Court held that the United Kingdom could not invoke it to justify engaging in security detention without trial.

The difference in approach between the House of Lords and the ECHR to addressing the same situation of inter-legality, assigning "right of way" to different norms, can be explained in part by the respective courts' embeddedness within distinct normative frameworks. It is perhaps not surprising that the House of Lords – the highest judicial instance of a permanent member of the Security Council – opted for an interpretation of inter-legality that prioritized the effectiveness of Security Council Resolution 1546, whereas the ECtHR minimized its legal significance, creating an interpretative presumption in favor of the application of its core treaty – the ECHR. These different legal constructions may also be reflective of differences in legal sensibilities regarding the balance to be struck between human rights on the one hand and international peace and security and the operational needs of military forces in Iraq on the other. It is interesting to note in this regard that the ECtHR emphasized in its decision the inclusion of respect for human rights in the core principles of the UN Charter, suggesting that the Resolution's peace and security objective ought to be balanced against human rights norms internally due to constraints imposed by the UN Charter, and externally due to the interpretative dominance of the mandatory language of the ECHR. Arguably, this represents an attempt by the ECtHR to influence the legal discourse beyond its core instrument – the ECHR.

The next major decision by the ECtHR relating to questions of security detention in Iraq and the multiple legal frameworks purporting to regulate it is found in *Hassan v UK*, where the Court went beyond the *Al-Jedda* judgment by effectively reading new grounds of detention into Article 5 of the ECHR: the application of powers of detention under IHL in situations of international armed conflict.[32] Put differently, the Court addressed a

[31] *Al-Jedda v UK*, Application no. 27021/08, July 7, 2011, para. 102.
[32] *Hassan v UK*, Application no. 29750/09, September 16, 2014, paras. 102–103.

situation of inter-legality confronting it that appeared to produce clearly incompatible legal outcomes (impermissibility of security detention under the ECHR vs. permissibility of security detention under the Third and Fourth Geneva Conventions) through a creative interpretative construction that read the permissive IHL norm as a new exception to the restrictive ECHR rule. In taking this approach, the ECtHR followed, to some extent, the footsteps of the House of Lords in *Al-Jedda*. This is because the Court's holding that the procedural guarantees of Article 5 continue to apply to detentions sanctioned under IHL implied that the new exception brought about only a minimal deviation from the protections afforded by Article 5.

One possible explanation for the Court's willingness to expand the list of grounds for detention in times of international armed conflict is the understanding that, unlike in the case of Security Council Resolutions, states do not have a realistic option of changing the language of the Geneva Conventions (which were formulated before the ECHR was concluded) or the ECHR, and thus cannot address the normative challenge attendant to the situation of inter-legality in any manner other than through engaging in creative interpretation of existing legal instruments. Furthermore, an ECtHR judgment that would have upheld the restrictive ECHR norm over permissive IHL norms might have put states involved in armed conflicts in a difficult legal position, denying their ability to apply battlefield detention powers. This would have resulted most likely in such states derogating from the ECHR – a counterproductive outcome, potentially doing away with most ECHR safeguards and transforming the situation from one of inter-legality to a situation governed almost exclusively by IHL.[33]

The amalgamated normative framework created in the *Hassan* judgments failed, however, to clarify which body of law should obtain the "right of way" – that is, under what conditions one regulatory framework should be read as effectively amending the other. This uncertainty manifested itself directly in the 2017 *Al-Waheed* judgment of the UK Supreme Court.[34] The case involved security detentions in Iraq and Afghanistan pursuant to Security Council Resolutions in circumstances resembling those reviewed in *Al-Jedda*. Since the ECtHR rejected in the latter case the possibility of invoking Security Council Resolutions to override the ECHR (i.e., the approach previously taken in *Al-Jedda* by the House of Lords), the UK Supreme Court did not

[33] Ibid., para. 90.
[34] *Al-Waheed v Ministry of Defence*, [2017] UKSC 2.

rely this time on Article 103 of the UN Charter. Instead, it followed the *Hassan* approach by maintaining that Article 5 does not preclude conflict-related detention that is authorized by another international law instrument. Whereas in *Hassan* the ECtHR relied on IHL for reading such an exception into Article 5, the Supreme Court held that Security Council Resolutions may also create an exception to Article 5 even in situations not qualifying as international armed conflicts.

The upshot of the judgment is that whereas the ECtHR read Resolution 1546 in light of the ECHR as not including security detention power, the Supreme Court read the ECHR in light of Security Council Resolutions 1546 (and its follow-up resolutions)[35] and 1510 (and its follow-up resolutions)[36] as including the power to authorize security detentions that the Resolutions implicitly recognized (according to the Court, the Resolutions aimed to extend the powers possessed by occupying forces beyond the end of occupation, suggesting an intention to reauthorize the same security detention policies available in situations of occupation in connection with an armed conflict).[37]

This reasoning is, however, circular in nature, as suggested by one of the minority judges on the Supreme Court.[38] It assumes that in the situation of inter-legality confronting the Court, it should interpret the ECHR according to the relevant Security Council Resolutions, and not – as was done by the ECtHR in *Al-Jedda* – to construe the latter in light of the former. This circularity underscores the space left for the realization of institutional agendas and ideological preferences in applying international law in situations of inter-legality. The national court opted, without directly contradicting the regional court, for a legal construction downplaying the human rights constraints imposed on its government and beefing up the status of the Security Council Resolutions it supported, whereas the regional court prioritized the regional human rights instrument over the needs of collective security. Different philosophies about the application of human rights law to overseas military operations and the subjection of the Security Council to human rights standards may also explain the propensity to either foreground or background the ECHR.

35 See e.g., Security Council Resolution 1723, UN Doc. S/RES/1723 (2006).

36 Security Council Resolution 1510, UN Doc. S/RES/1510 (2003); Security Council Resolution 1890, UN Doc. S/RES/1890 (2009).

37 *Al-Waheed*, para. 30 (per Lord Sumption).

38 *Al-Waheed*, para. 297 (per Lord Reed).

4 CONCLUSIONS

International courts have been quite active in confronting specific jurisdictional and normative conflicts deriving from situations of inter-legality, serving in effect as hubs of inter-legality. The *Kadi* case, the *Jurisdictional Immunities* litigation before the ICJ and the Italian Constitutional Court, and the ECtHR's *Al-Jedda* case are paradigmatic examples of prioritizing one regulatory framework over another through establishing a normative hierarchy or applying interpretative presumptions that accord "right of way" to a particular legal order. Still, the resolution of a specific dispute – often through "tunnel vision" employed by a particular court – does not fully address the challenges of inter-legality. States remain bound even after the specific dispute has been resolved by a multiplicity of bodies of law, which pull them in different directions and exert on them unique normative influences and institutional pressures.

It is against this background that efforts aimed at merging regulatory frameworks or reading them cumulatively should be evaluated. Here, too, some attempts have been more successful than others in capturing the complexity of situations of inter-legality. Good examples of merging decisions are the ICJ advisory opinion on the *Legality of Nuclear Weapons*, which read IHL into the concept of "arbitrary deprivation of life" (Article 6 of the ICCPR), and the ECtHR judgment in *Hassan*, which effectively integrated security detention under the Geneva Conventions into the ECHR in ways that resulted in the application of both bodies of law in an adjusted and approximated manner. At the same time, the ECtHR's *Al-Jedda* judgment and the ICJ's *Wall* advisory opinion, which cumulatively applied different legal sources, prioritized in effect the more protective body of law (IHRL) in ways that appear to only nominally acknowledge the influence of inter-legality on the interpretation and application of the body of law.

The inconsistent approach to addressing situations of inter-legality may also be attributed to gaps between the different courts' legal authorities and their expertise in the relevant subject matter. Arguably, once removed from the "cocoon" of a specialized regime, international courts face difficulties in asserting their authority and expertise and in enforcing their decisions. Thus, the ECtHR may hesitate to apply bodies of law that exceed its core competence, such as Security Council Resolutions to situations of armed conflict or EU law or refugee law to "Dublin transfers," and opts at times to disengage from situations of inter-legality by prioritizing the ECHR. At the same time, remaining in the specialized "cocoon" confines the reach and impact of international courts, rendering them increasingly irrelevant. At times, this leads to them trying to engage with a multiplicity of regulatory frameworks, and struggles ensue over the de facto and de jure hierarchy between them.

Finally, the engagement of international courts and tribunals with situations of inter-legality cannot be divorced from their own institutional agendas and policy preferences. Hence, the manner in which they confront situations of inter-legality is simultaneously influenced by normative tensions, jurisdictional competition, and institutional power struggles. This explains the standoffs between different courts, the creation of "skewed" normative "bridges," and the inconsistent application of models of normative and institutional interaction.

15

Judging Inter-Legality

JAN KLABBERS

1 INTRODUCTION

During the 1920s, one of the most notorious criminal trials in the history of the United States took place. Two young men of Italian descent, capable of speaking only broken English and going by the names Nicola Sacco and Bartolomeo Vanzetti, were found guilty of murder in the first degree. Subsequent investigations suggested that not all evidence had been equally credible, and proceedings were organized with a view to possibly reopening the case. The judge in these proceedings, however, a gentleman named Thayer, found no problem with the initial decision and dismissed the case. Felix Frankfurter, then a young law professor at Harvard on his way to becoming an influential Supreme Court Justice, wrote a scathing commentary, concentrating in large part on the role of Judge Thayer.

Some of Frankfurter's words are worth quoting in full, and all focus on, one might say, Judge Thayer's epistemic virtues – or rather, lack thereof:

> By what is left out and by what is put in, the uninformed reader of Judge Thayer's opinion would be wholly misled as to the real facts of the case … I assert with deep regret but without the slightest fear of disproof, that certainly in modern times Judge Thayer's opinion stands unmatched, happily, for discrepancies between what the record discloses and what the opinion conveys. His 25,000 word document cannot accurately be described otherwise than as a farrago of misquotations, misrepresentations, suppressions and mutilations … The opinion is literally honeycombed with demonstrable errors, and infused by a spirit alien to judicial utterance.[1]

[1] F. Frankfurter, *The Case of Sacco and Vanzetti: A Critical Analysis for Lawyers and Laymen* (New York: Little, Brown & Co., 1961 [1927]), at 104.

And if this were not bad enough, Frankfurter goes on to quote an editorial in the (to his mind) conservative *Boston Herald*, suggesting that Judge Thayer's opinion "carries the tone of the advocate rather than the arbitrator."[2]

The performance of Judge Thayer reminds us that judges are human – all too human, perhaps – and that their humanity (or the absence thereof) affects their reasoning and their decisions. Indeed, judges have to be human; there is too much at stake for the individuals who find themselves in court to let their fate be decided on the basis of an algorithm or by some electronic device, and the popularity of jurimetrics as a decision-making device proved happily short-lived. But with human performance come human fallibilities, and uncertainty enters the picture on a deep, fundamental level. This has always been recognized, of course: Justice Cardozo could conclude his lectures on the nature of the judicial process almost a century ago by suggesting that the judge must "balance all his [sic] ingredients, his philosophy, his logic, his analogies, his histories, his customs, his sense of right, and all the rest, and adding a little here and taking out a little there, must determine, as wisely as he can, which weight shall tip the scales."[3] And Ronald Dworkin famously devised a judge of "superhuman skill, learning, patience and acumen,"[4] "an imaginary judge of superhuman intellectual power and patience," and christened him (again, him) Hercules.[5] The point to note, of course, is that Dworkin's Hercules is supposed to be no mere ordinary mortal, but is rather imagined to be superhuman.

Regardless of the setting, it appears to be commonly accepted that judges are usually constrained by the political environment in which they work. Richard Posner, himself a judge for many decades, suggests that judges tend to realize that they should not go "too far" in their politics, for fear of retaliation or at least a response by the political branches of government.[6] And Sir Hersch Lauterpacht, in the rather different setting of a still-developing international law, in the 1930s acknowledged that international judges should exercise circumspection and restraint, lest governments would turn away from judicial dispute settlement altogether.[7]

2 Ibid., at 104–105.

3 B. N. Cardozo, *The Nature of the Judicial Process* (New Haven, CT: Yale University Press, 1991 [1921]), at 162.

4 R. Dworkin, *Taking Rights Seriously* (Cambridge, MA: Harvard University Press, 1978), at 105.

5 R. Dworkin, *Law's Empire* (London: Fontana, 1986), at 239.

6 R. A. Posner, *How Judges Think* (Cambridge, MA: Harvard University Press, 2008), at 375.

7 H. Lauterpacht, *The Function of Law in the International Community* (Oxford: Oxford University Press, 2011 [1933]), at 112.

But if it is generally accepted that there is more to judging than technical competence alone, it is by no means clear what this "more" is and how it can be conceptualized. In addition, if inter-legality is taken seriously, it is not even clear anymore (assuming it ever was) what technical competence stands for: if the hallmark of inter-legality is the overlapping of distinct legal orders that can each plausibly claim applicability, then it would seem that technical competence in only one of these overlapping legal orders is no longer sufficient. And this, in turn, may well come to be accompanied by practical problems: many law schools, for example, prove unable or unwilling to properly distinguish between foreign law and international law, typically suggesting that questions of, say, American law or Chinese law will be handled by the international law section. Sadly, this is not limited to law schools alone: during his confirmation hearings, US Supreme Court Justice Neil Gorsuch displayed that he suffered from the same lack of understanding.[8]

In other words, inter-legality will demand a broader type of skill set from judges than what has hitherto been the standard. Judges will need to be competent not only in the legal system in which they have been predominantly trained and socialized, but also in applying legal rules and principles stemming from other legal systems – at least if they want to do justice in individual cases.[9] The remainder of this chapter will discuss the sorts of qualities judges will need generally, eventually zooming in on the specific demands stemming from inter-legality. It will do so from a largely virtue ethical perspective, recently heralded by Luban and Wendell as a promising avenue for further thinking in legal ethics, even if only as a complement to more rule-based or situationist ethics: "... any account of legal ethics that leaves out the actor and the judgments we pass on the actor misses something crucial ..."[10]

Even so, one probably does not need to be a virtue ethicist to acknowledge that judging is not just a matter of mechanistically applying a given set of rules to a given set of facts. Indeed, such a mechanistic perspective falls into the

8 A. Roberts, "Pledging American Exceptionalism? US Supreme Court Justice Gorsuch on International Law," available at http://opiniojuris.org/2017/05/23/33125 (accessed December 12, 2017).

9 While there is not all that much literature on inter-legality just yet, what there is tends to be confined to sketching normative conflicts or conflicts between regimes without specifically addressing the role of the judiciary. Still, what follows is consistent with this literature; see e.g., A. Fischer-Lescano and G. Teubner, *Regime-Kollisionen: Zur Fragmentierung des globalen Rechts* (Frankfurt am Main: Surhkamp, 2006), 34–40.

10 D. Luban and W. B. Wendell, "Philosophical Legal Ethics: An Affectionate History," (2017) 30 *Georgetown Journal of Legal Ethics* 337, at 364.

familiar vicious circle: to figure out what the relevant facts are, one needs to have an inkling about the relevant rule; but to figure out what the relevant rule is, one needs to have an inkling about the relevant facts. Hence, judging requires something additional, and this has been acknowledged by even die-hard "law and economics" scholars, socialized into thinking about individuals mostly in the aggregate and trained in assuming behavioral patterns. If even rationalists such as Eric Posner and Adrian Vermeule can acknowledge that judging may involve a degree of "epistemic humility" (a version of one of the virtues), then it would seem that there is some room to explore the virtues.[11]

One final remark: this chapter is limited to discussing the qualities necessary or desirable for rendering judgment in cases reaching the bench and on the assumption that the judge need not make up his or her mind about the broader setting in which he or she operates. These are, however, not the only questions with an ethical component reaching judges. Thus, some judges may want to ask themselves to what extent their work is helping to prop up an unlawful regime; some may feel they have to join a majority opinion to send a strong political message, even though privately they would have thought of dissenting or concurring; some may need to reflect on whether their earlier or their extrajudicial activities may affect their judgment;[12] some may worry about the compatibility (vel non) of rules stemming from two distinct yet overlapping legal orders;[13] and others may have to come to terms with finding themselves on the bench on what are essentially show trials.[14] Such situations raise profound ethical issues, but this is not the place to address these.

[11] E. Posner and A. Vermeule, "The Votes of Other Judges," (2016) 105 *Georgetown Law Journal* 159, e.g., at 163.

[12] One of the judges at the Special Court for Sierra Leone, for example, had written rather strong words about acts he was later expected to adjudicate, and this caused some understandable havoc. Given the judge's refusal to recuse himself, his colleagues had to disqualify him from the proceedings. The episode is recorded in D. Terris, C. Romano, and L. Swigart, *The International Judge: An Introduction to the Men and Women Who Decide the World's Cases* (Oxford: Oxford University Press, 2007), at 198–199. For a more in-depth discussion, see F. Mégrét, "International Judges and Experts' Impartiality and the Problem of Past Declarations," (2011) 10 *Law and Practice of International Courts and Tribunals* 31.

[13] A possible example may involve the 1989 *Rainbow Warrior* arbitration between New Zealand and France, which could have resulted in the confinement of two French secret service agents possibly in violation of habeas corpus or fair trial rights under the European Convention of Human Rights.

[14] See e.g., J. Klabbers, "Principled Pragmatist? Bert Röling and the Emergence of International Criminal Law," in F. Mégrét and I. Tallgren (eds.), *The Dawn of a New Discipline* (forthcoming).

2 THE SETTING: INTER-LEGALITY

Much of the literature on the ethics of judging (or lawyering more broadly), for all its merits, remains a little abstract. One basic distinction is that between civil and criminal cases, and it is generally assumed that these come with different demands. The lawyer in a criminal trial, it is often claimed, is subject to different ethical demands than those that inform or should inform the company lawyer or the lawyer in civil cases, partly because in the criminal case there is no equality of arms between the parties. When the lawyer's client is pitted against the almighty power of the prosecuting state, as in criminal proceedings, the lawyer may be allowed to engage in practices and tactics that would otherwise not be acceptable. Where, on the other hand, there is equality of arms to begin with (as is presumed to be the case in civil proceedings), the ethical standards might be a little stricter.[15]

But beyond this basic distinction between criminal and civil proceedings, much of the literature takes a one-size-fits-all approach, in which lawyers and judges are expected or supposed to behave in certain ways regardless of the circumstances. It is supposed not to matter much whether the dispute is about child custody or an inheritance or an unfriendly corporate takeover. It is supposed not to matter a great deal whether the dispute involves individual citizens or large multinational companies, or whether it concerns the interpretation of an obscure municipal regulation or a country's constitution. And it is supposed not to matter all that much in which jurisdiction the matter comes before court. In other words, much of the literature abstracts from concrete circumstances and posits an ideal type of reasoning.

There is, one should hasten to add, nothing particularly wrong or surprising about this. Much moral philosophy assumes a similar approach: reasoning from first principles set in an abstract universe so as to provide possible guidelines for concrete action in concrete circumstances. This is useful in that it can provide considerable clarification. The one problem, however, is that the concrete circumstances rarely match the abstract universe in which the guidelines were first formulated. As Ignatieff puts it with admirable economy: "We are always in a particular situation, a context, a moment – a

[15] See e.g., D. Luban, *Lawyers and Justice: An Ethical Study* (Princeton, NJ: Princeton University Press, 1988); A. I. Applbaum, *Ethics for Adversaries: The Morality of Roles in Public and Professional Life* (Princeton, NJ: Princeton University Press, 1999).

place in space and time – and we are always with others, with people whose opinion shapes us and whose views we wish to shape."[16]

With this in mind, it is no good just to adopt the main insights derived from virtue jurisprudence and boldly proclaim that these also apply in the inter-legality setting. Instead, it might be useful first to set out what types of legal issues judges may be confronted with under conditions of inter-legality. This is not to show how widespread (or not) inter-legality is. What should be appreciated though is that inter-legality comes with its own sets of demands, above and beyond those we regularly associate with judging. In what follows, I will outline two different but complicated scenarios, derived from real-life situations (if a little stylized so as not to overcomplicate things[17]).

One caveat is in order. What follows will not specifically discuss the familiar trope of how judges should address judgments of foreign courts. This is a related but distinct issue. The question of how to handle foreign judgments may play a role in inter-legality settings in that those judgments may form part of the corpus of law to be applied. Inter-Legality is distinct though in suggesting that the application of foreign law is not limited to following foreign judgments as if they were precedents, or drawing inspiration from them.

The first scenario is a familiar one, derived from the well-known plight of Mr. Kadi.[18] Mr. Kadi, a Saudi businessman, found much to his dismay that on the instigation of the Security Council, his European bank account had been frozen, on the suspicion that he was involved in the financing of terrorism. Needless to say, he was not particularly pleased with this development. The source of his displeasure was a European Union (EU) regulation, implementing verbatim the relevant Security Council decision. This decision, so he suggested, did not respect several of his recognized human rights (the right to property, as well as the rights to access to justice and a fair trial) and thus should be null and void, and he went to the courts of the EU in order to achieve justice.

The case pits two different jurisdictions against each other. On the one hand, there is the Security Council of the United Nations (UN), and it is uncontested that, for member states of the UN, decisions of the Security

[16] M. Ignatieff, *The Ordinary Virtues: Moral Order in a Divided World* (Cambridge, MA: Harvard University Press, 2017), at 209.

[17] What matters here, after all, is not descriptive accuracy, but gaining a heuristic understanding.

[18] See especially Case C-402/05 P, *Kadi and Al Barakaat* v *Council and Commission*, ECLI:EU:C:2008:461. Commentary is by now voluminous; see e.g., C. Eckes, *EU Counter-Terrorist Policies and Fundamental Rights: The Case of Individual Sanctions* (Oxford: Oxford University Press, 2009).

Council prevail over other relevant considerations and, indeed, prevail over conflicting obligations resting on those member states. This does not solve all issues, of course: one could argue, albeit not without problems,[19] that the Security Council ought to respect or at least consider human rights in its decision-making, and that when it takes decisions that do not do so, these shall be void. On such a reading, the case would be a simple one: the decision would legally be nonexistent, and thus there would be no need, let alone an obligation, to implement it. Hence, his bank accounts should be opened again and perhaps, if he suffered damage, the UN could be held liable for such damage.[20]

The Court of Justice of the EU (CJEU) took a different approach. The EU legislator is bound to respect human rights. This is considered to be among the constitutional values of the EU, and it was on this basis that the CJEU eventually reached its decision. It held that the implementing regulation was an EU legislative instrument that, accordingly, should meet the EU's constitutional criteria. Seeing that it violated Mr. Kadi's human rights, the CJEU held that the EU regulation was void. Mr. Kadi should be taken off the blacklist and his accounts unfrozen.

The decision was widely welcomed and heralded as a victory for human rights, but it is important to realize that it was not self-evident that this ought to have been the obvious legal outcome. The Court's judgment proved possible only upon assuming that the facts of the case took place within the closed universe of the EU; it proved possible only upon the assumption that the EU regulation at issue was a self-standing instrument rather than, in reality, implementing a Security Council decision. One may expect in the EU that EU decisions live up to human rights standards, but this places the member states of the EU in a bind when the EU aims to implement instruments emanating from elsewhere. Under the UN Charter, they are expected to give effect to Security Council decisions, and therewith keep Mr. Kadi's accounts frozen; under EU law, by contrast, they are asked to ignore the EU regulation implementing the Security Council decision, as it must be considered invalid.

[19] The main problem here is that the UN Charter does not unequivocally instruct the Security Council to respect human rights in its decision-making, and it is not immediately clear where a legal obligation to respect human rights would stem from. See more generally J. Klabbers, "The Sources of International Organizations' Law: Reflections on Accountability," in S. Besson and J. d'Aspremont (eds.), *The Oxford Handbook of the Sources of International Law* (Oxford: Oxford University Press, 2017), 987.

[20] This presumes a lot, though. It would seem more than likely that the UN would invoke its well-nigh absolute immunity against any suit for damages in this scenario.

Hence, the UN expects them to do X, but the EU expects those same states to do non-X.[21]

What the case makes clear is that matters cannot be convincingly reduced to a single jurisdiction or a single body of expertise. A case such as *Kadi* involves questions concerning the relationship between international law and EU law, a topic on which legislative guidance is largely missing and, indeed, could hardly be present: the EU could, hypothetically, close itself off from any effect of UN law, but even then, it is by no means certain why such a closing off would need to be respected by UN law – there is no meta-rule in existence on the relations between legal orders, nor could there be such a meta-rule in all likelihood. To make things more complicated still, the first EU judicial decision, taken by its lower-level court, actually suggested that the EU courts have a limited right of judicial review of UN regulations. This would apply to the extent that these are alleged to violate what are known as *jus cogens* rules: peremptory norms from which no derogation is permitted.[22]

What is important to appreciate is that, as a technical matter, the case could easily have had a different outcome. The CJEU could have decided (unlikely as this may sound in light of its earlier jurisprudence[23]) to respect the supremacy of UN law. This would not have been too difficult to substantiate. While UN law does not, as such, bind the EU as an actor in its own right (the EU not being a member of the UN itself), nonetheless all its member states are bound by the Charter, and the Charter itself proclaims supremacy, something that is confirmed in other instruments.[24] It is, moreover, not all that eccentric to herald the main purpose of the UN (to achieve peace and security) as one of the supreme values of the international community. On such a line of reasoning, the global war on terror and the need to secure peace and security would trump the protection of the individual rights to property and access to justice of a wealthy businessman.

On the other hand, the Court's actual outcome is also clearly defensible: opting to have human rights prevail over the global war on terror (and, in the

[21] A recent monograph on normative conflict is V. Jeutner, *Irresolvable Norm Conflicts in International Law: The Concept of a Legal Dilemma* (Oxford: Oxford University Press, 2017).

[22] Case T-315/01, *Kadi v Council and Commission*, ECLI:EU:T:2005:332. The Court of First Instance found, *in casu*, that no such rules were involved, and that accordingly there was nothing wrong with the Security Council decision and thus not with the EU regulation either. In other words, it tested the legality of the relevant instruments against what it held to be general international law, but not against the EU's constitutional provisions.

[23] J. Klabbers, "The Reception of International Law in the EU Legal Order," in R. Schütze and T. Tridimas (eds.), *Oxford Principles of European Union Law. Volume I: The European Union Legal Order* (Oxford: Oxford University Press, 2018), 1208.

[24] See Article 30 of the Vienna Convention on the Law of Treaties.

process, solidifying the European integration project a little more). The Court, in other words, had a genuine choice between two options, both of them technically justifiable and both of them intuitively morally plausible as well. The Court was required to exercise some discretion, and needed to display an understanding of both EU law and public international law. Indeed, it is at least arguable that this is where the first instance case faltered: the Court of First Instance (now the EU's General Court), by implying that Security Council decisions can be tested against *jus cogens*, seemed to suggest that *jus cogens* norms are not merely substantively peremptory, but also grant jurisdiction to each and every court willing to look at them – and this is a construction that would strike most international lawyers as implausible, perhaps even simply incorrect.[25]

The second example is different, and stems from the United States. It regularly happens that foreign nationals have been suspected of crimes and are prosecuted for those crimes. Under international law, those foreign nationals must be offered the possibility of consular assistance (at least if both states concerned are parties to the Vienna Convention on Consular Relations[26]), but in the rough-and-tumble world of crime and punishment, this does not always happen – local police officers and sheriffs may not always be aware of the obligation, or they may not be aware that a suspect is actually a foreign national, and more sinister reasons for not informing arrested individuals of their right to consular assistance cannot categorically be excluded.[27]

This raises several possible (and sometimes actual) issues. One of these is that sometimes the International Court of Justice (ICJ) gets involved, with the home state of the foreign national asking the ICJ to order the United States (to stick to the example) to stay the execution of criminals found guilty and sentenced to death, so as to allow for possible reconsideration of their cases. This, in turn, raises issues about the relationships between courts: Should US courts follow orders issued by the ICJ? The US Supreme Court has been very reluctant to acknowledge as much, sometimes suggesting orders of the ICJ are mere recommendations, and more recently suggesting that while the United States might be bound by a treaty's terms, it need not immediately accept the interpretation thereof by an international court as authoritative.[28]

[25] And perhaps this helps explain why, in a later decision, the International Court of Justice made a sharp distinction between substantive rules (including *jus cogens*) and procedural rules: see *Jurisdictional Immunities of the State* (Germany v Italy; Greece Intervening), [2012] ICJ Reports 99.

[26] Article 36 of the Convention is relevant here. The chance that both states involved are bound by the terms of the convention is large: it has 179 parties as of December 2017.

[27] See e.g., *Avena and Other Mexican Nationals* (Mexico v USA), [2004] ICJ Reports 12.

[28] See *José Ernesto Medellín v Texas*, US Supreme Court, 552 US 1 (2008).

What adds a further complication is that, in cases such as this, it is not merely several substantive sets of rules demanding attention, but there are also procedural rules involved, and those rules may come to have an impact on the final decision. That such a scenario is not entirely impossible is illustrated by the "procedural default" rule applicable in US criminal law. The rule, in a nutshell, prohibits criminal defendants from raising on appeal issues that were not raised at the first instance. This may work well in normal events and clearly serves the goal of trial economy, but creates problems in cases where foreign nationals have stood trial without having been informed of their right to consular assistance. Having been convicted in the first instance without assistance, they cannot on appeal invoke the wrongful absence of consular assistance, even if it is precisely the absence of consular assistance that may have contributed to a guilty verdict or a strict sentence.[29]

These examples may suffice to sketch the sort of issues that may be at stake: the interplay of rules emanating from different jurisdictions or legal systems but relating to the same conduct, the complexities involved in having sufficient knowledge and competence in a variety of legal systems, and the interplay between law and justice that may accompany the application of procedural rules. In other words, inter-legality places heavy demands on judges, both in terms of their competence and in terms of their attitude.

3 ON VIRTUE JURISPRUDENCE

While people have been discussing what makes a good or decent judge for many decades, it has been over the last decade or two that virtue jurisprudence has made some waves. Virtue jurisprudence derives, as the label suggests, from virtue ethics (or virtue theory, as it is sometimes referred to), a distinct branch of ethics often traced back to the writings of Aristotle in the West and the not all that dissimilar writings of Confucius in the East. The idea behind virtue ethics is that one should not so much evaluate the ethical nature (vel non) of specific acts, but rather concentrate on the ethical qualities of the actor. This allows not just for assessing events, but also inquiring into why they happened. After all, sometimes it is difficult or awkward to assess an act without looking into the context: getting an abortion after being raped is rather different from

[29] The example is derived from criminal proceedings against Mr. Breard, as this came before the ICJ in the late 1990s. See *Case Concerning the Vienna Convention on Consular Relations* (Paraguay v USA); Request for Indication of Provisional Measures, [1998] ICJ Reports 248; for comments and references, see, briefly, J. Klabbers, "Executing Mr Breard," (1998) 67 *Nordic Journal of International Law* 357.

getting an abortion in order to make money on a reality television show. Even those who are "pro-choice" might, while accepting the former, be opposed to the latter, yet regular deontological or consequentialist accounts might not offer the tools to make the differentiation. Virtue ethics, however, does: a virtuous person, one might suppose, however "virtuous" is precisely defined, is unlikely to have an abortion (or endorse one) for financial gain.

For Aristotle, who was far more explicit on the virtues than Confucius, the virtues played a role in a teleological existence. The purpose of life, briefly put, resides in achieving excellence, happiness, or flourishing (*eudaimonia*). The virtues, then, are character traits – developed from a young age and inculcated through education, experience, and imitation – that make for a happy, flourishing life. These include honesty and humility, courage and magnanimity, temperance and patience.[30] Some of the virtues Aristotle listed are no longer generally accepted as such: wittiness, for example, is not generally considered particularly virtuous anymore, although in some professions it may nonetheless be highly desired (e.g., stand-up comedy can hardly do without it). Other virtues have been added by later thinkers: most notably, faith, hope, and charity were considered by Aquinas to have some use for a religious life, and perhaps beyond as well.[31]

It seems well accepted that even if the virtues may be of universal application (this is debated, although sometimes on false premises[32]), there is nonetheless an argument to be made that different professional or social roles come with different virtues or – more accurately perhaps – that the same virtue plays out in specific ways in specific roles.[33] One concrete example may be this: typically, one would expect one's doctors to be honest (although the degree of honesty can be subject to local variations), but even where a doctor is generally expected to be honest, he or she should not be so bluntly honest

30 Aristotle set this out predominantly in his *Ethics*. I have used the version as published by Penguin in 1976, translated by J. A. K. Thomson and with an introduction by J. Barnes. Confucius' best-known teachings are known as *The Analects* (London: Penguin, 1979, D. C. Lau transl.).

31 Aquinas, *Treatise on the Virtues* (Notre Dame, IN: University of Notre Dame Press, 1984, J. Oesterle transl.).

32 Often, in everyday parlance, virtues and values are conflated. While the relationship between the two is a complicated one, the universality of values may legitimately be doubted. Whether virtues are by definition parochial seems less certain – it is hard to think, for example, of cultures where honesty or courage or humility would not be appreciated. On the former, see e.g., E. M. Meade, "The Commodification of Values," in L. May and J. Kohn (eds.), *Hannah Arendt: Twenty Years Later* (Cambridge, MA: MIT Press, 1997), 107.

33 J. Oakley and D. Cocking, *Virtue Ethics and Professional Roles* (Cambridge: Cambridge University Press, 2001); R. S. Downie, *Roles and Values: An Introduction to Social Ethics* (London: Methuen and Co., 1971).

as to tell a terminally ill child that she will be dead within a week. One can construe this as a particular form honesty should take, or perhaps as the necessity to combine honesty with empathy, or some related construction.

By contrast, the accountant is expected to be brutally honest at all times, at least in his or her professional capacity. An accountant who does not provide insight into his or her client's finances with great transparency is not doing his or her job properly, and an accountant who aims to hide an unpleasant truth behind opaque representations (let alone one who "cooks the books") is eventually doing his or her client a disservice. Thus, it seems, specific professional roles can come with specific versions of the virtues. Honesty demands different demeanor from a doctor than from an accountant. It is not the case, one may presume, that people's character changes when they take on different roles: Cohen has persuasively suggested that the individual as teacher is not essentially different from the same individual as parent.[34] But it is plausible to suggest that different roles come with different responsibilities that, in turn, make different demands on the character of the individuals occupying such roles. The roles, in turn, may be professional roles, but not exclusively so: social roles, too, constructed by social expectations, may come with ideas about virtues. Thus, a "good parent" is often distinguished from a "bad parent," even though the law might not make a distinction[35] and there are no formal job descriptions available as to what makes for a "good parent."[36]

On this line of thinking, it is not eccentric to propose that judges, too, can be expected to possess certain characteristics, and it is this thought that has been picked up in a set of writings loosely referred to as "virtue jurisprudence." The underlying premise is the idea that the judge, too, is not just a cog in the machine of justice (or administration), but is also a moral actor and, what is more, has a moral obligation toward his or her role, or as Powell once put it, the "obligation to remain within the role is itself a moral obligation."[37] There can be little doubt that part of this obligation is an obligation to uphold the law – this can be cast, it seems, as an obligation equally strong in both law and

34 G. A. Cohen, "Beliefs and Rôles," (1966–1967) 67 *Proceedings of the Aristotelian Society* 17.

35 The law typically does not distinguish between good and bad parenting, but may make punishable specific acts that, in turn, may be associated with bad parenting. Surely, though, the parent who would only do the bare minimum – what is legally required – is unlikely to be considered a good parent.

36 M. Smiley, *Moral Responsibility and the Boundaries of Community* (Chicago: University of Chicago Press, 1992). There are unofficial descriptions available of course: see e.g., B. Bettelheim, *A Good Enough Parent* (New York: Vintage, 1988).

37 H. J. Powell, *Constitutional Conscience: The Moral Dimension of Judicial Decision* (Chicago: University of Chicago Press, 2008), at 41.

morals. Burton puts the matter in plain terms: "We simply cannot conceive of a legal system that did not hold its judges to such a duty."[38]

But surely, to posit a duty to uphold the law is only the starting point of any analysis – it cannot be its final conclusion. The interesting point is not merely *that* the judge should uphold the law; it is also a question of *how* best to do so, and whether this applies *in all circumstances*. On the latter point, opinions vary widely and deeply, with some positing that the duty is an absolute one and others suggesting that if the law is deeply flawed from a moral point of view, the judge may set it aside. This is a debate of long-standing pedigree, and need not detain us here;[39] it is usually taught under the label of "the Hart–Fuller debate,"[40] with Hart standing for the proposition that law demands absolute fidelity regardless of contents and Fuller standing for the proposition that the law should reveal a minimal moral content if it is to demand fidelity.[41]

Different authors provide different though largely overlapping depictions of the judicial virtues, and non-philosophers, too, seem to grasp intuitively that character traits are of relevance. As Terris, Romano, and Swigart write in a throwaway remark, such traits as "wisdom, common sense, and empathy" are "essential to good judgment."[42] Perhaps the most authoritative list is the one provided by Farrelly and Solum.[43] They note, for instance, that there is widespread agreement that judges should be *incorruptible* – corruption undermines the rule of law and whatever values the legal order aims to represent and protect, and does so even if the outcome of a corrupted decision would itself be acceptable or indistinguishable from one arrived at honestly. Similarly, they suggest that judicial *sobriety* is a virtue: the judge who is easily

38 See S. Burton, *Judging in Good Faith* (Cambridge: Cambridge University Press, 1992), at 219. Burton grounds the duty in the oath judges take when sworn in, in conjunction with the entrustment of the judicial task by the public at large (at 218).

39 There is a point to be made, though: the judge looking to go beyond the law should do so only if well-endowed with judicial integrity and judicial wisdom. See L. B. Solum, "A Virtue-Centered Account of Equity and the Rule of Law," in C. Farrelly and L. B. Solum (eds.), *Virtue Jurisprudence* (New York: Palgrave MacMillan, 2008), 142, at 157–158.

40 H. L. A. Hart, "Positivism and the Separation of Law and Morals," (1958) 71 *Harvard Law Review* 593; L. L. Fuller, "Positivism and Fidelity to Law – A Reply to Professor Hart," (1958) 71 *Harvard Law Review* 630.

41 Usually, Radbruch is placed in the same box as Fuller. For Radbruch, however, it seemed that the matter was rather one of balancing: the positivist value of legal certainty (itself an ethical concern) could be outweighed if the legal certainty this ensured would be manifestly unjust. See G. Radbruch, *Einführung in die Rechtswissenschaft*, 13th edn. (Stuttgart: Koehler Verlag, 1980, Zweigert ed.), at 14.

42 See Terris et al., *The International Judge*, at 193.

43 What follows draws on C. Farrelly and L. B. Solum, "An Introduction to Aretaic Theories of Law," in Farrelly and Solum (eds.), *Virtue Jurisprudence* 1.

swayed by drink or drugs, or generally by a desire for the finer things in life, might not be fully focused on the task at hand. Here, perhaps, MacIntyre's distinction between goods internal to a practice and goods external to a practice proved inspirational:[44] the individual who becomes a judge only in order to achieve fame and glory or to earn a good salary misses an important dimension of what it means to be a judge.

Farrelly and Solum also nominate judicial *courage* as a judicial virtue, and explain that this may come in two forms. On the one hand, there is *physical courage*: the judge who is easily intimidated by physical violence may not be very suitable, although some settings might be more prone to threats of such violence than others. In organized crime trials[45] or family court (where emotions can run deep), physical threats may play a greater role than in traffic court. On the other hand, there is *civic courage*: a judge deciding a controversial case must be ready to be socially ostracized or face public opprobrium, and "not be tempted to sacrifice justice on the altar of public opinion."[46]

Judicial temperament and *impartiality* are next on Farrelly and Solum's list. Judges should not let themselves be guided by anger; they should keep their temper in check, if only to prevent them from becoming partisan. Anger at the crimes of a suspect may easily morph into partiality, clouding judgment. An absence of anger, on the other hand, might not be all that conducive either: to some extent, a judge may need to tap into his or her sense of right and wrong – though without it rendering his or her approach partial. Aristotle aimed to formulate some such approach by positing his "doctrine of the mean": too much of any virtue would not be good, but neither would too little. Too much courage becomes recklessness; too little courage equals cowardice. Likewise, too little anger spells cold-bloodedness and a lack of compassion or empathy,[47] whereas too much anger may create a red mist.[48] Be that as it may, if there is

44 A. MacIntyre, *After Virtue: A Study in Moral Theory*, 2nd edn. (London: Duckworth, 1985).

45 Former International Criminal Tribunal for the former Yugoslavia (ICTY) Prosecutor Carla del Ponte could picture herself as a courageous prosecutor partly under reference to her role in fighting organized crime while a prosecutor in Switzerland. See C. del Ponte with C. Sudetic, *Mevrouw de Aanklager* (Amsterdam: Bezige Bij, 2008, Van der Waa transl.)

46 Farrelly and Solum, "An Introduction," at 10.

47 Farrelly and Solum do not explicitly list compassion or empathy, though it would appear that the absence thereof can have dire consequences for judging. Elsewhere, I discuss the example of the *Perincek* cases of the European Court of Human Rights (coming very close to genocide denial) in such terms in J. Klabbers, "Doing Justice? Bureaucracy, the Rule of Law and Virtue Ethics," (2017) 6 *Rivista di Filosofia del Diritto* 27.

48 Not everyone is convinced by the philosophical underpinnings of the doctrine of the mean: see e.g., B. Williams, *Ethics and the Limits of Philosophy* (Cambridge, MA: Harvard University Press, 1985).

universal or near-universal agreement on one judicial virtue it regards impartiality, mentioned in well-nigh all codes of ethics for the judiciary as indispensable.[49]

Judicial *diligence* is a virtue of a different nature, but a virtue nonetheless. Judging can be hard work, and judges may be tempted to cut corners, not read all the briefs equally carefully, refer to familiar case law from memory, recommend settlements so as to reduce their workload, or rely disproportionately on their clerks. Closely related, dixit Farrelly and Solum, is *carefulness*: judges ought to ensure that their work is careful and meticulous, carefully drafted and written, well-researched, etc. Needless to say (but here we are entering the level of technical competence), judges should possess and display judicial intelligence and learning, as well as craft and skill.

Farrelly and Solum's list is not carved in stone, but provides a useful starting point. Others have been more economical. Burton, for example, writing in the early 1990s, aimed to capture most of the above under the heading of good faith: a judge acting in good faith would be a virtuous judge.[50] Powell, writing 15 years after Burton and limiting himself to the specific setting of the US Supreme Court, was more expansive and spelled out a handful of judicial virtues, largely overlapping with Farrelly and Solum's list. For Powell, it seems the most relevant virtues include faith (in the intelligibility of the Constitution), integrity and candor, humility, and acquiescence (i.e., the willingness to accept the premises underlying binding precedent even if and when convinced those premises are mistaken).[51]

More recently, the notion of friendship (which itself can be seen as having Aristotelian overtones, relating to his idea of *philia*) has assumed some prominence in two distinct ways. The first of these suggests – without explicit reference to the virtues – that judges can learn from those who are their methodological friends: originalists, for example, might take notice if fellow originalists reach a different conclusion in a particular case, more so than when a different conclusion is reached or endorsed by colleagues with whom they have little methodological affinity. While it remains a little unclear whether the authors aim to describe or rather to endorse (or both perhaps) methodological friendship, nonetheless the underlying idea taps into judicial humility: when confronted with methodological friends reaching different

49 See also Mégrét, "International Judges and Experts' Impartiality."
50 Burton, *Judging in Good Faith*.
51 See Powell, *Constitutional Conscience*, esp. 85–99.

conclusions, the judge would be well-advised to take notice and perhaps adjust his or her opinion in the light of that of his or her colleagues.[52]

If this idea of friendship taps into a predominantly American discussion, concerned with such questions as to what explains the voting behavior of judges, the second notion of friendship is more interesting, and was developed recently by Iris van Domselaar, inspired in part, it seems, by the work of Martha Nussbaum.[53] To van Domselaar's mind, judges should display what she calls a "six-pack of judicial virtues," largely overlapping with the list provided by Farrelly and Solum: judicial perception, judicial courage, judicial temperance, judicial justice, judicial impartiality, and judicial independency are the six elements of her six-pack. These, however, on their own are not sufficient, she suggests, as they do not yet meet a demand that is "crucial for the legitimacy of the exercise of state power: the demand of equal respect."[54]

The argument goes as follows: it is one thing for judges to be virtuous and for courts to reach their decisions virtuously. This implies, however, that different judges or courts can reach different conclusions concerning the same cases – an appeal to the virtues, it seems, weakens the authority of the law, which becomes less certain, predictable, and stable. This creates a legitimacy deficit: Why would a disaffected individual have to accept an outcome that is negative for him or her if the outcome might just as well have been positive and the only difference between outcomes resides in the character of the judge? van Domselaar proposes to fill the gap under reference to Aristotle's notion of friendship, characterized as it is by "mutual well-wishing"[55] and therewith furthering mutual trust. Both judges and citizens involved in legal proceedings should foster a civic friendship attitude. With respect to citizens, this would express their support for the common good, even in the face of an adverse decision; for the judge, it implies empathy for

52 W. Baude and R. D. Doerfler, "Arguing with Friends," available at https://papers.ssrn.com/sol3/papers.cfm?abstract_id=2985032 (accessed December 27, 2017).

53 I. van Domselaar, "Moral Quality in Adjudication: On Judicial Virtues and Civic Friendship," (2015) 44 *Netherlands Journal of Legal Philosophy* 24. van Domselaar's broader work clearly has Nussbaumian overtones: see e.g., I. van Domselaar, *The Fragility of Rightness: Adjudication and the Primacy of Practice* (doctoral thesis, University of Amsterdam, 2014).

54 van Domselaar, "Moral Quality," at 40. Elsewhere, she explains in greater detail why the regular model of judging as an exercise in applied moral theory is insufficient: see I. van Domselaar, "A Neo-Aristotelian Notion of Reciprocity: About Civic Friendship and (the Troublesome Character of) Right Judicial Decision," in L. Huppes-Cluysenaer and N. M. M. S. Coelho (eds.), *Aristotle and the Philosophy of Law: Theory, Practice and Justice* (Dordrecht: Springer, 2013), 223.

55 van Domselaar, "Moral Quality," at 41.

the situations of all parties involved, and thus reassuring citizens that their interests are taken seriously.

van Domselaar's approach raises a few questions. She takes her cues from private law settings (civil cases), and it seems plausible enough that here the judge can operate as a friend to both parties. One wonders, though, whether the same can or even should happen also in criminal proceedings. Defendants in criminal trials may be most strongly in need of a friendly attitude from the bench, but may be the least likely to receive it, and if there is something to the insight that friendship must be earned, then it is indeed precisely in criminal proceedings that *philia* might end up lacking.[56]

Another question is how van Domselaar's civic friendship model relates to other models where a strict and mechanistic reliance on the law is replaced by something closer to wisdom, whether it concerns the *kadi* justice discussed by Max Weber a century ago or the more modern incarnations in the form of commissions of wise (and often white) men, or the powers of courts to occasionally decide *ex aequo et bono*.[57] In other words, is there anything that remains specifically *legal* about the work of judges exercising civic friendship?

Be that as it may, the great merit of van Domselaar's approach is that she realizes that judicial decision-making is an exercise of state power and thus, like all exercises of state power, is in need of justification. Her model explicitly links judicial virtues to political theory[58] in ways that Aristotle would probably have appreciated but have often gone missing.[59] A similar disposition is displayed by Powell, for whom constitutional virtue is placed against the background of – or correlates with – three (what he calls) "substantive commitments."[60] The first of these is the priority of the political: the US Constitution (this, after all, is the context in which he writes) channels political struggle, but cannot and should not displace it. Second, constitutional orthodoxy is to be avoided: the Constitution might facilitate decision-making, but does not carve into stone values that need to be accepted by all;

[56] Elsewhere, she rather briefly suggests that civic friendship also applies to criminal proceedings, as committing a serious wrong does not need to spell the end of friendship. See van Domselaar, "A Neo-Aristotelian Notion," at 242–244.

[57] See Article 38(2) Statute ICJ.

[58] It is a little more common to link citizen virtue to political theory, in particular republicanism. Fine examples include P. Pettit, *Republicanism: A Theory of Freedom and Government* (Oxford: Oxford University Press, 1997) and I. Honohan, *Civic Republicanism* (London: Routledge, 2002).

[59] Farrelly and Solum, for example, for all their merits, in "Aretaic Theories" largely discuss virtue jurisprudence in isolation from political theory.

[60] Powell, *Constitutional Conscience*, at 110.

instead, it recognizes the "legitimacy of disagreement."[61] Third, the Constitution is thought to be all-inclusive, which is a different way of saying that no one can legitimately be excluded from the political community.

In their different ways, then, both Powell and van Domselaar point to the political setting in which judicial decision-making takes place, and while this is not a particularly novel insight, it is useful to be reminded of it every now and then, precisely because much work on judging portrays judging as a nonpolitical activity. But if there is a political context to reckon with, then one of the hallmarks of inter-legality is that this context is undergoing change – and this cannot but affect the judicial virtues.

4 INTER-LEGALITY AND THE JUDICIAL VIRTUES

Inter-Legality, as noted before, involves the overlapping of legal spaces to such an extent that it is conceivable that behavior illegal in one of these spaces might be perfectly legal in another relevant space, or that behavior conducted in one of the relevant spaces might be affected by legal considerations in another one. Needless to say, this rules out the simple situation where, say, one would argue against the death penalty in the United States on the grounds that it is prohibited in the Netherlands. Inter-Legality might come to play a role, though, if the individual on trial is a US citizen suspected of committing a crime on Dutch soil. An early and highly intriguing example is the *Short* case, concerning the murder of a civilian committed by a US soldier based in the Netherlands on Dutch soil. The Dutch refused to extradite, precisely because of death penalty concerns, and eventually the US authorities agreed to drop the possibility of the death penalty in the case at hand, therewith facilitating the extradition of Mr. Short to the United States.[62]

Some of the virtues will retain their familiar contours and contents (if that is a proper word to use), regardless of whether the setting can be described as involving inter-legality. Thus, *sobriety* as a virtue is unlikely to be affected, and if judicial *incorruptibility* is a virtue, as Farrelly and Solum sensibly contend, its contents are unlikely to be affected by inter-legality, except in the largely hypothetical setting where one of the legal spaces involved would place a premium on corruption in ways the other(s) would not. More likely is, perhaps, the setting where different conceptions of corruption or

[61] Ibid., at 112.

[62] See *Short v The Netherlands* (Hoge Raad, 1990), reproduced in (1990) 29 *International Legal Materials* 1378; for a brief discussion, see R. Liivoja, *Criminal Jurisdiction Over Armed Forces Abroad* (Cambridge: Cambridge University Press, 2017), at 4.

incorruptibility may be at stake. A judge from a jurisdiction where, for example, nepotism is regarded as innocent or even as praiseworthy might have to adapt this position when confronted with different incorruptibility standards elsewhere. Even this, though, seems rather unlikely, partly because disapproval of the most rampant forms of corruption is widely shared (even if not always honored[63]) and partly because issues involving nepotism may be unlikely to involve several distinct legal spaces.[64]

With other judicial virtues, however, inter-legality might affect how judges act. Largely epistemological virtues such as *craft*, *skill*, *learning*, and *intelligence* will need to be expanded: craft, skill, and learning will need to encompass the craft, skill, and learning to work across legal spaces. It is hypothetically possible that a judge who is very good in his or her own jurisdiction might lack the necessary skill or craft to accommodate a multitude of legal spaces.[65] This will, in practice, owe something to language skills, but other factors may also come to the fore. For instance, the interaction between civil and common law systems might introduce elements of unfamiliarity, as might differences relating to doctrines such a monism and dualism. All this will demand a certain judicial intelligence and application, although it is difficult to say whether demands on intelligence per se will be affected. *Diligence* and *carefulness* will need to be expanded, no doubt, in settings of inter-legality, but as with intelligence, this may entail a difference of degree rather than of kind.

Inter-Legality is more likely to affect the virtues of *courage* and *impartiality*, as influenced by *temperament*. The highly nationalist judge, who regards his own legal system as the best invention since sliced bread, might quickly be offended by even the slightest hint at an inter-legality aspect, and this might affect his impartiality: his tendency to uphold his national legal order may prompt him not to look any further and ignore the possible inter-legality aspects of the case before him. If so, this affects his impartiality. If nationalism is a matter of temperament, then the temper and the partiality may end up

63 Clever administrators, moreover, can manipulate corruption to look innocent and the result of following proper procedure. Decision-making bodies can be stacked with allies, for example, rendering it unnecessary to engage in visible forms of bribery and the like.

64 Unlikely, but not excluded: the hiring of her dentist and a lawyer acquaintance as policy advisors by Edith Cresson, at the time a member of the EU Commission, raised quite a few eyebrows outside France, while inside France few seemed to be surprised. See Case C-432/04, *Commission v Edith Cresson*, ECLI:EU:C:2006:455.

65 The possibility is more than merely hypothetical, though: the lawyers occupying the CJEU, brilliant in their handling of EU law, often apply international law in ways that international lawyers might consider flawed, either applying customary international law in an unexpected manner or making categorical mistakes in applying institutions from the law of treaties. Some examples are listed in Klabbers, "The Reception of International Law."

going hand in hand in directions not easily reconcilable with any conception of judicial virtue.

Moreover, it is here that the legitimacy aspect comes in. Being an exercise of state power, judgments need to be justified in terms recognizable within the relevant political community, as both Powell and van Domselaar intimate.[66] But the hallmark of inter-legality is that it changes the contours of the relevant political community: this can no longer be defined solely in terms of territory and national boundaries (and the accompanying jurisdictional apparatus), but will need to consider the question of how a judgment can be justified also in terms recognizable (and preferably acceptable) to other jurisdictions involved. It is here that the aforementioned *Kadi* decision of the CJEU generated the greatest doubt: the CJEU reached its decision by sweeping the relevant international law under the rug, by conjuring up a world where no international law existed, and as a result, the decision will always remain vulnerable to criticism from that angle.[67]

But perhaps the most obviously affected (or affectable) of the judicial virtues is the virtue of *courage*. Decisions involving inter-legality may be expected (more so than ordinary, single–legal space decisions) to involve national sentiments and affinities, therewith stimulating the sort of jingoism that judges may fear. If domestic decisions can raise the emotions so much that individuals involved may have to fear for their lives (think of the risks run by doctors who are known to have performed abortions[68]), then situations with an inter-legality element may involve even greater risks. Hence, a judge's *physical courage* may be severely tested.

More severely tested, though, will be his or her *civic courage*: if civic courage is all about withstanding social disapproval and ostracism, about resisting peer pressure in various forms (including pressure from those whose peer status merely derives from being a fellow national), inter-legality scenarios may potentially add explosive elements to the mix. How is one to withstand demonstrations, nasty press comments or comments on social media, the pressure from fellow judges and pundits, etc.? If a British Member of Parliament sees fit to enquire after the identity of law professors teaching

66 See the discussion in the previous section.

67 It nonetheless has a fair amount of defenders. Among the more sophisticated defenses of the CJEU's position, even in light of international law, is A. Tzanakopoulos, *Disobeying the Security Council: Countermeasures against Wrongful Sanctions* (Oxford: Oxford University Press, 2011).

68 https://splinternews.com/these-are-the-11-americans-who-have-been-murdered-by-an-1793853233 (accessed November 7, 2017).

EU law in the United Kingdom[69] and US Presidents (well, one of them) can dismiss members of the judiciary as "so-called judges,"[70] then surely serious pressure can also be exercised on judges involved in inter-legality cases, outlandish as this might (and does) sound.

5 INCULCATING THE VIRTUES

Aristotle realized that the virtues were mostly obtained through education, whether in the family or at school, although he reserved a place for legislating the virtues as well – something followed by others, and often in such a way as to impose a particular version of the virtues on society.[71] In this line of thought, there might be some merit in fine-tuning codes of judicial ethics with inter-legality in mind, but not too much should be expected, for the familiar reason that deontological rules (of which codes of ethics are a species) can never apply themselves; they would still need to be read and interpreted with the very virtues they demand, including practical wisdom – and practical wisdom is not something one can be told to engage in, in much the same way that one cannot be ordered to be spontaneous.

To the extent that the judicial virtues rely on regular everyday virtue, one can only hope that future judges will be taught from their early days onwards to be sufficiently courageous, honest, etc. Here, there is little that can be done to prepare judges specifically for inter-legality. Things may be different, though, with the intellectual or epistemological virtues: since judges will by definition be trained in the law, legal training can enhance the sort of (technical) competence required for judging in conditions of inter-legality. That is not to say that lawyers can or even should be trained in the details of two or more legal orders, but it is to say that legal training can focus more on understanding and less on comprehensive knowledge than is currently often the case.

In a hilarious essay, Lon Fuller once suggested that legal education in the United States was overly concentrated on isolated and decontextualized legal problems – lawyers would be too much trained in litigation and too little in

69 www.theguardian.com/education/2017/oct/24/universities-mccarthyism-mp-demands-list-brexit-chris-heaton-harris (accessed November 8, 2017).

70 www.washingtonpost.com/news/the-fix/wp/2017/02/04/trump-lashes-out-at-federal-judge-who-temporarily-blocked-travel-ban/ (accessed November 8, 2017).

71 Among the more sophisticated examples is R. P. George, *Making Men Moral: Civil Liberties and Public Morality* (Oxford: Clarendon Press, 1993).

thinking through the problems of social and economic order, never mind justice.[72] In continental Europe, the problem is often of a different nature: legal studies are too much geared toward mastering knowledge of the rules, without much interest in the why and how of those rules, or even in how to apply them. Grossly generalizing: if in the United States law is taught as abstract problem-solving, in continental Europe it is often taught as a game of memory. Neither method is bound to be particularly helpful in conditions of inter-legality.

Inter-Legality demands an understanding of rules rather than a comprehensive knowledge of what they say, and it demands this across jurisdictions. Since it is impossible or impracticable to memorize the details of a variety of legal systems, even in a narrow domain (say, consumer protection or corporate governance), the focus will need to come to rest on understanding the law, and understanding that law always exists in context – various contexts, in fact. Europe's policy-makers may have grasped this when stimulating student exchanges within Europe from the 1990s onwards:[73] the Finnish law student specializing in corporate governance may learn much from how corporate governance is regulated in France or Portugal; the German law student specializing in consumer protection may learn much from studying consumer protection law in Greece or Ireland. In reality, however, it rarely works this way: students on exchange tend to follow those courses that they can use to replace courses they should otherwise have taken at their home universities, such as public international law, EU law, or legal theory, but rarely take courses that present them with a mirror that could help them to understand their own legal systems better through an encounter with other systems.

That said, the great heuristic value of studying public international law resides in the circumstance that, as a single domain, it is so broad that a focus on studying it through its rules is literally impossible.[74] Public international law encompasses most domains familiar from domestic law (ranging from contract and property to administration and criminal matters), but usually these are taught in a single course by a single professor in a limited amount of

[72] L. L. Fuller, "On Legal Education," reproduced in K. I. Winston (ed.), *The Principles of Social Order: Selected Essays of Lon L. Fuller* (Oxford: Hart, 2001), 293.

[73] In fact, it is more likely that student exchanges were created for other reasons, not least of them the creation of a supranational sense of European identity and solidarity.

[74] See also J. Klabbers, "Legal Education in the Balance: Accommodating Flexibility," (2006) 56 *Journal of Legal Education* 196.

time; the result is that any such course must by definition concentrate on basic principles and on inculcating an understanding as to why the system is what it is.[75]

If inter-legality demands the flexibility of mind to work across jurisdictions and with a view to doing justice in individual cases, then it would seem to follow that judges need to be trained, at least to some extent, along those lines. A familiarity with the main legal systems may be useful, suggesting that there is a bigger place in the curriculum for substantive comparative law than is usually granted.[76] An understanding of the different conceptions of justice and the disagreements surrounding it may be useful, which suggests perhaps a greater place for justice-oriented legal philosophy in the curriculum than is often the case, and perhaps integrated in other domains as well. One example might be to study private law in part by concentrating on how it strives to contribute to justice and what concept of justice may underpin it.[77]

Finally, an underappreciated method of learning is imitation. On some level, this is perhaps the most effective method. As Michael Oakeshott once remarked, "practical knowledge can neither be taught nor learned, but only imparted and acquired . . . and the only way to acquire it is by apprenticeship to a master . . . because it can be acquired only by continuous contact with one who is perpetually practicing it."[78] In later writings, this is sometimes referred to as learning from exemplars, or *exempla* – role models widely admired and appreciated for being good (both technically and in terms of virtue) at what they do and serving as sources of inspiration.[79]

[75] If there is a law school with separate chairs in international organizations law, international human rights law, international environmental law, international criminal law, international economic law, and international humanitarian law, as well as general international law (which could address general issues, diplomatic law, adjudication, law of treaties, etc.), I am not aware of its existence.

[76] Typically, comparative law courses focus on method rather than substance, and are considered of marginal relevance at most law schools at any rate.

[77] What I have in mind is something along the lines of E. J. Weinrib, *The Idea of Private Law*, rev. edn. (Oxford: Oxford University Press, 2012), while realizing that his approach draws on libertarian philosophies that may not be universally shared.

[78] M. Oakeshott, "Rationalism in Politics," reproduced in M. Oakeshott, *Rationalism in Politics and Other Essays* (London: Methuen and Co., 1962), 1, at 11. Elsewhere in the same piece, he suggests that morality learned by memorizing moral precepts is to reduce it to a technique, not worthy of the name (at 35).

[79] For a lucid discussion, see A. Amaya, "Exemplarism and Judicial Virtue," (2013) 25 *Law & Literature* 428. I have elsewhere discussed novelist and essayist Albert Camus as an exemplar of virtue; see J. Klabbers, "The Passion and the Spirit: Albert Camus as Moral Politician," (2016) 1 *European Papers* 13.

6 FINAL REMARKS

Dworkin's Hercules had it relatively easy: he was never asked to engage with more than one jurisdiction at the time, and to the limited extent that his reconstructed version of international law envisaged a judicial organ, this court was mostly involved in judicial review rather than in the settlement of disputes.[80] The discussion above lists a number of the judicial virtues that may be implicated in inter-legality. If inter-legality involves the attempt to do justice in individual cases across overlapping legal spaces, however, it would seem that other virtues too may meaningfully be discussed. Thus, it would seem that *practical wisdom* remains of great relevance, regardless of the number of legal spaces involved: judges must retain a sense of which rules to apply in relation to which facts. Thus put, however, inter-legality may complicate the puzzle, but not alter it fundamentally.

More likely to be affected is the virtue of *justice*, but if so, then with a twist. Curiously, none of the lists of judicial virtues discussed earlier singles out justice as a judicial virtue, and Aristotle himself seemed to treat justice as something of an overarching virtue, presenting the proverb that "[i]n justice is summed up the whole of virtue."[81] And yet, he also suggested that "the object of the judge is to be a sort of personified Justice."[82] Perhaps there is merit in the suggestion made by Bernard Williams some time ago that injustice can flow from neglect of the other virtues[83]: the judge who is lazy or ill-tempered may end up with an unjust judgment, not unlike the judge at work in the Sacco and Vanzetti proceedings.

In the end, there is a lot to be said for Hutchinson's claim that "[t]he test of good judging might well be less about getting it right than about doing it well."[84] This applies to ordinary, single-jurisdiction cases, but would also have an application in the inter-legality setting. Where various outcomes may be equally compelling, at the very least the judge addressing inter-legality should make sure that no legal interest is left unaddressed. Where several outcomes are equally compelling and persuasive from the perspectives of their own legal orders, one can only hope for a virtuous judge.

80 R. Dworkin, "A New Philosophy for International Law," (2013) 41 *Philosophy and Public Affairs* 2, esp. at 28.

81 Aristotle, *Ethics*, book V, at 173.

82 Ibid., at 181.

83 B. Williams, "Justice As a Virtue," in A. Oksenberg Rorty (ed.), *Essays on Aristotle's Ethics* (Berkeley: University of California Press, 1980), 189.

84 A. C. Hutchinson, *Laughing at the Gods: Great Judges and How They Made the Common Law* (Cambridge: Cambridge University Press, 2012), at 268.

16

Theory, Realities, and Promises of Inter-Legality
A Manifesto

GIANLUIGI PALOMBELLA

1 PREMISES

As is widely acknowledged, the administration and regulation of the world[1] have been increasingly changing the state-based setting of a Westphalian and Hobbesian order. Such a transformation is never complete,[2] however, and the law and multiple legalities around the globe are doomed to comprise diverse, overlapping, and interconnecting layers. The "suspended," incomplete nature of the transformation means, among other things,[3] that on the one hand states have safeguarded their hold on many issues, even those addressed in the regional or global areas through intergovernmental agreements, and have maintained the national role in making them possible and effective. Of course, the fundamental responsibilities of contemporary states continue to include the provision of political goods, and they are called upon to cover security, health care, education, law and order, overall economic welfare, and the general protection of citizens. In the midst of the recent economic crisis, the state response to the drawbacks of economic financial globalization has triggered the perception of a resilient role of the state, all in all a "return of the state," or the suspicion that the state had never withdrawn despite the beliefs of

[1] Interesting insights on such transformations can be found in J. L. Dunoff and J. P. Trachtman (eds.), *Ruling the World? Constitutionalism, International Law, and Global Governance* (Cambridge: Cambridge University Press, 2009).

[2] I have more extensively examined the global arena as the formation of a kind of "Penelope's public" ever in-between an accomplished frame of public law and its de-structuration in G. Palombella, "The (Re-)Constitution of the Public in a Global Arena," in C. MacAmlaigh, C. Michelon, and N. Walker (eds.), *After Public Law* (Oxford: Oxford University Press, 2013).

[3] On which see the important work by N. Walker, *Intimations of Global Law* (Cambridge: Cambridge University Press, 2014). Walker elaborates precisely on what he defines as the "intimated" quality of the global order; that is, something clearly emerging but unfulfilled, and yet "inexorable."

neoliberal theories.[4] José Alvarez has written that "the Westphalian system may be a blink of an eye in the scope of human history but we are living in its time. No one unfortunate enough to be outside Koskenniemi's 'wonderful artificiality' of statehood believes that it is a myth. Ask a Palestinian. As Michael Walzer put it in a recent lecture, only those lucky enough to live in a functioning state can afford to suggest that it is 'withering away'."[5]

On the other hand, states have reduced their control precisely because of the trans-boundary nature of the issues in an array of fields of emerging relevance, from security to climate and environment, health, trade, human rights, cultural heritage, and so forth. Moreover, the hold of nation-states on treaty-based law has to coexist with the intrusive development of a large part of international law itself, affecting not just external independence, but also internal autonomy of states, developing common public goods[6] irreducible to the pursuit of national interests alone. Notably, the bewildering proliferation of extra-state regimes and international organizations, often including jurisdictional or para-jurisdictional conflict-treating bodies,[7] has loosened the chain of states' control, in many respects. The autonomy and the independence of international organizations are improving, partly in order to legitimize their outputs, partly in view of fostering a consistent decision-making process: one that claims to be endowed with apolitical problem-solving qualities, serving the ambition to avoid realist approaches of self-interested bargaining among relevant parties (the Hobbesian paradigm).[8]

These are attempts at crossing the line between disorder and order, between private or unilateral and "public" or multilateral. The World Trade Organization (WTO), the European Union (EU), the United Nations Convention on the Law of the Sea (UNCLOS), the European Convention on Human Rights (ECHR), the Codex Alimentarius Commission, the World

4 J. Delwaide, "The Return of the State?" (2011) 19 *European Review* 69.

5 J. Alvarez, "The Return of the State," (2011) 20 *Minnesota Journal of International Law* 263.

6 In general, see N. Krisch, "The Decay of Consent: International Law in an Age of Public Goods," (2014) 108 *American Journal of International Law* 1; A. Nollkaemper, "International Adjudication of Global Public Goods: The Intersection of Substance and Procedure," (2012) 23 *European Journal of International Law* 769.

7 See e.g., R. Howse and R. Teitel, "Cross-Judging: Tribunalization in a Fragmented but Interconnected Global Order," (2009) 41 *NYU Journal of International Law and Politics* 959.

8 On the question of independence and its effectivity, limits, and prospects, see T. Johnson, *Organizational Progeny: Why Governments Are Losing Control over the Proliferating Structures of Global Governance* (Oxford: Oxford University Press, 2014). With reference to the regulatory governance then emerging in the European communities and their capacity to avoid hindrance from political negotiations, see the classic works by G. Majone, *Regulating Europe* (London: Routledge, 1996) and *The European Community As a Regulatory State* (The Hague: Martinus Nijhoff, 1995).

Intellectual Property Organization (WIPO), and the International Organization for Standardization (ISO; and the impressive number of equivalent entities of diverse nature and status) all draw our attention away from the traditional realist view of international political relations and beyond the frame of the restricted "public" of states. Most of this endeavor, then, hardly resembles the features of the institutional structures of the state (and mere interstate accommodation).

Furthermore, their significance is based on the fact that they spread specialized knowledge that enhances the need for administrative decision-making through functional fields both within and beyond the state. Thus, "the rise of information and of knowledge as the main resource and frame of reference for decision-making" defines functional borders; that is, it generates multilayered relationships both within and beyond the state at the transnational level.[9] Accordingly, with respect to the social dimensions of the practices, collective interactions are expected to develop that not only are de facto or de jure independent of national borders and established states, but cross-cut demoslike allegiances in transnational forms.[10] This was also viewed as a "deliberative representative" space[11] and, at least with respect to the EU, capable of affording deliberative experimental forms.[12] All in all, from such viewpoints, the functional division is called upon to replace or overlap with territorial separation.[13] These and other premises are factors whose diverse nature is mirrored in a mixed and interwoven setting of regimes and orders endowed with distinct and often self-referential normative structures.[14]

9 K.-H. Ladeur, "The Emergence of Global Administrative Law and Transnational Regulation," *NYU Institute for International Law and Justice Working Paper* 2011/1.

10 They gather stakeholders, interested groups, public or private regulators, experts, judges, arbitrators, and economic actors as much as fluid social movements, nongovernmental organizations, advocates, or pressure groups. On their role in constructing the global space and stabilizing normative expectations, see R. O. Keohane, "Social Norms and Agency in Global Politics," *NYU Straus Institute Working Paper*, 07/2010.

11 J. S. Dryzek and S. Niemeyer, "Discursive Representation," (2008) 102 *American Political Science Review* 481.

12 C. F. Sabel and J. Zeitlin (eds.), *Experimentalist Governance in the European Union: Towards a New Architecture* (Oxford: Oxford University Press, 2010).

13 Although, in the specific domain of the EU, it is more properly seen as a hybrid system, where governmental – or governing – and governance structures play complementary roles. See P. Kjaer, *Between Governing and Governance* (Oxford: Hart, 2010).

14 However, the state of the art is unresolved. As Walker rightly puts it, the *intimations* of global law hint at inexorability, but confronting reasons and counter-factors flourish and display multiple sources and grounds: Walker, *Intimations*, 159–180. At the same time, the stable character of such a setting is its "double normativity," insofar as law "should in some respects apply equally to all global contexts, while in other respects these various contexts continue to exhibit diversity. What is more, there is a shared sense that these two strains do not operate

The evocation of "inter-legality" in such a setting should not be meant as a vague shortcut for a diversity of confusing phenomena. In truth, nor should it be used simply to capture the plural coexistence among legalities as they create parallel worlds of normativity (that of global trade, of world health, of state welfare, of regional security, and so forth) running on their own. Inter-legality is to be recommended in order to focus on a different aspect: the unavoidable interconnectedness of legalities.

2 APPROACHING LEGALITIES: MATERIAL AND LEGAL, FRAGMENTS AND THE WHOLE

Such a claim is not, however, mirroring the ways orders and legalities are in fact presently conceived and organized. They are instead artificial constructions whose rationale is precisely meant to disentangle material interconnectedness and to separate spheres of legality. Different clusters, orders, regimes of law, administrations, and regulations are devised in order to master, govern, and rationalize[15] on a transnational scale the huge material complexity of reality; a functional differentiation has arisen (either accidentally or by *divide et impera* design) based on a separation of fields related to the goods and objectives of different character and content: to such sector-specific authorities, governing bodies, entities, and rule-generators we have allocated limited *ends* in single thematic orders devoted only to their specialized objectives (which do not embrace the totality of possible interests of an entire collectivity, as we knew them in the statist format). Therefore, while the scope and width of the ends pursued are so discrete and reduced, the potential addressees and the regulatory reach instead widen: territorially detached and regionally or globally extended, they serve (or target) a virtually global horizon of "affected" stakeholders, constituencies, interlocutors, actors, etc.

By contrast, the notion of norm-generation in the state context could be described precisely in opposite terms: territorial limitation on the one hand and the all-embracing substance of the respective order on the other, taking care of a totality of possible needs and ends – the pursuit of one of them

independently but are closely intertwined. Global law does not stand apart from more particular laws. Rather, where global law is at issue it is always in close connection with the operation of more particular strains of law" (ibid., at 24).

15 It is a matter of different rationales and rationalities that makes for the diversity of regimes and supports their final irreducible plurality: see A. Fischer-Lescano and G. Teubner, *Regime-Kollisionen: Zur Fragmentierung des globalen Rechts* (Frankfurt am Main: Suhrkamp, 2006); G. Teubner, "Global Bukowina: Legal Pluralism in the World Society," in G. Teubner (ed.), *Global Law without a State* (Dartmouth: Ashgate, 1997), 3.

cannot be seriously isolated from the pursuit of any other. Law as such connects to a circumscribed jurisdiction,[16] and within the latter it revolves around the very idea of (modern-style) legislation as general and de-individualized, capable of coping with the whole horizon of matters covering the *full circle* of human activities.

On the contrary, the relatively new forms of global regulation have to end up downplaying that venerable profile by changing and forfeiting the *holistic character of law*, which represented the state and the public interest as a whole under political control. Nonetheless, and despite clear-cut functional differentiation, the legal and organizational cleavages among diverse spheres of sector-specific legality, regimes, and orders, despite their useful coordinating and ordering functions, cannot perform their operation up to the point of concealing the underlying state of things. What they fruitfully conceptualize as parallel worlds are ultimately and inevitably impinging over each other.

Firstly, inter-legality is meant to account for the fact that practically none of the legalities or regimes, active on different levels, work effectively on their own. Their functional isolation is a myth. Not only from a material angle of content-dependent connectedness, but also from a legal point of view, these legalities are all in and of themselves insufficient or inefficient, and their functions remain "suspended" until they meet their interlocutors; and among those interlocutors are, indeed, other legalities. Not even the EU can do anything by itself: it needs to make its member states do things. The ECHR may well be conceived of as a kind of constitutional legality,[17] but its ordering strength depends on the ways "other" legal systems accept and implement its normative clauses.

On the other hand, as Koskenniemi aptly wrote years ago, among the consequences of the fragmentation of international law is that "particular regimes" are pitted against each other:

> . . . trade against environment, human rights against humanitarian law, law of the sea against European Community law. Whether some issue is qualified as a "trade" or "health" problem . . . or whether its dominant concerns are

[16] In contrast, with reference to the diffusion of global legislation, Kingsbury noted that the "real question might be whether it is possible to identify a determinate public at all," and thus, if the law is intended as speaking "in the name of the whole society," here it is often unpredictable "how far the whole society extends." See B. Kingsbury, "From Bilateralism to Publicness in International Law," in U. Fastenrath et al. (eds.), *From Bilateralism to Community Interest: Essays in Honour of Bruno Simma* (Oxford: Oxford University Press, 2011), 85.

[17] W. Sadurski, "Partnering with Strasbourg: Constitutionalisation of the European Court of Human Rights, the Accession of Central and East European States to the Council of Europe, and the Idea of Pilot Judgments," (2009) 9 *Human Rights Law Review* 397.

> those of "human rights" or "security," involves struggle for competence to decide. A fisheries issue may be seen in terms of the protection of natural resources or freedom of trade and contextualised either as part of a universal (WTO or Law of the Sea) or regional (European Union) regime. Each classification points to a different authority that will decide, with preferences and practices deviating from those of competing bodies.[18]

Be it a horizontal relation among supranational or international bodies or between them and the state, the issue reflects the limited capacity and relative failure of the conception of self-closed legality. It is not necessary here to indulge further in such a descriptive analysis. As I submit, more than once a realistic picture of the composite functioning of legality should better view it as inter-legality.

Thus, one should acknowledge the very fact that given inevitable complexity, many questions to be legally treated are only artificially (i.e., fictitiously) an insulated matter of sector law and regulation, and might most probably bear multiple concurring or competing rationales. Accordingly, inter-legality should register and mirror on the legal plane, when appropriate, the resilience of the material interconnections among functional fields and the reflexivity of such interconnectedness into the self-referential coherence of each order.

Material interconnectedness overflows and imbues the law – it trespasses the fault lines and the legal closure of discrete orders. It cannot easily be tamed or – even less so – ignored, and it comes to affect the nature and functioning of legality, despite the fact that different regimes were born to control limited areas, *immunized from external objectives*. Inter-Legality should better name the overlapping among regimes and orders as a consequence of interconnectedness. The most obvious example is that of the UN Security Council (UNSC) pursuing security and confronting human rights–related duties. This may happen as a matter of different legalities (UNSC and, say, ECHR) being involved. Here, the relevant issue is not whether legalities shall interface, but rather to observe that they are *already* interwoven.

Again, the experience of the state has already taught us about this matter. At the state level, we are used to fully reflecting on the legal plane such an interweaving: public health cannot be addressed through "health" policies unrelated to economic and financial budgetary resources; the economy affects social structures and should balance with rights. A state cannot be successful (whatever that may mean) if it fares well in one "field" by ruining everything

[18] M. Koskenniemi, "Global Legal Pluralism: Multiple Regimes and Multiple Modes of Thought," Lecture delivered at Harvard University, March 5, 2005, available at www.helsinki.fi/eci/Publications/Koskenniemi.

else. A state is a "general ends" entity, and its job is to be *responsible for the whole*, without aiming to execute one particular function at the expense of others. Fragments, in a nutshell, are the consequence of epistemic (and possibly ideological) perspectives, not vice versa. The comprehensive attitude is, of course, an impossible metaphysics beyond the state: but the difference does not reside in the nature of the problems and objects. Instead, it is due to their dimensions and the consequent impossibility of bringing matters, when beyond the state, under one unitary center of responsibility.

While such an interconnectedness flourishes, our ideas about legality are rather static and can hardly accommodate the state of affairs through legal means. If we look at such things from the perspective of Mr. Kadi,[19] the most famous among alleged Al Qaeda supporters according to the Sanctions Committee of the Security Council, it appears rather irrelevant to him whether his right is coherent within the limits of EU law, UN law, human rights law, or international law generally. Those different legalities are ultimately independent, and in doctrinal terms can be mutually contrasting and happily coexistent, eventually making Mr. Kadi's search for justice never-ending and unfinished. If conditional upon one particular legality, only in part governing the normative factors at stake, justice shall always remain a lame verdict.

3 THEORIZING INTER-LEGALITY: ON MODELS OF LEGALITY

Inter-Legality – in a novel concept meaning – can prompt our awareness and make some difference. The choice between monism and dualism that has divided theories concerning the relations between international and municipal law is traditionally a field of contestation. While it is true that, for the sake of international law, monist attitudes seem to spread, and states' courts "such as the German *Bundesverfassungsgericht*, are assuming a role in the '*dédoublement fonctionnel*' of their domestic and international functions, regarding themselves as guardians not only of domestic, but also of international law within their jurisdiction,"[20] nonetheless - as Andreas Paulus notes – they use not international, but domestic law as their normative system of reference. International law features only in their jurisprudence if and to the extent permitted by their domestic law.[21] If domestic courts therefore

[19] See the decision of the ECJ (now CJEU) in Joined Cases C-402/05 P, *Yassin Abdullah Kadi and Al Barakaat International Foundation v Council and Commission*, ECLI:EU:C:2008:461.

[20] A. Paulus, "National Courts and the International Rule of Law (Remarks on the book by André Nollkaemper)," (2012) 4 *Jerusalem Review of Legal Studies* 5, 8–9.

[21] Ibid.

"apply international law or implement international decisions, they do so because domestic law requires it, not because they are organs of the international community." Eventually, the situation is made harder for monists: international law "contains within itself several distinct legal orders, from the UN Charter to international criminal law, from human rights to investment law," in the absence of hierarchy and "where such hierarchy exists, as in Article 103 of the UN Charter, it appears increasingly problematic . . ."[22]

Alternatively, when holding to the other venerable notion, dualism, we assume that orders other than ours survive in their own right (think of state system and international law), but they are seen as *sheer facts* from an external point of view: their *normative* strength is null until it is incorporated or reauthorized and converted into "our" internal imperatives. But this would imply first that legalities are cycles[23] running in parallel and separately, and second that we have the option of whether to engage with other legalities or not. However, and bearing in mind what was already noted above, it is common knowledge that most often such an option is in fact unavailable. As Nollkaemper recalls cautiously, it is common understanding today that between domestic and international law, "While the fundamental distinction in terms of sources has remained (even though the traditional sources doctrine has been transformed in a much more complex system of validation), in principle, substance and subjects have come to overlap with domestic legal systems. This might open the door for at least a limited acceptance of a less dualistic relationship between international and national law."[24]

One can easily describe with the very idea of inter-legality that when diverse normative actors are involved, and they are de facto concurring or competing, it is rather abstract to assume that other legalities are to us only sheer "facts." It is not truly in our whim and hands to consider or exclude the *normative* character of other orders' sourced normativity. Although the state is often depicted as endowed with a double face, under the assumption that what it does "in the international order" is unrelated to the state "in national law". of course, in the easiest case, a claim from the European Court of Human Rights (ECtHR) has a normative strength at least for the parties to the Convention, as much as the Security Council has for the members of the UN, and it is rather abstract to assume that this has no relevance in the domestic legal order.

[22] Ibid.

[23] H. Triepel, *Völkerrecht und Landesrecht* (Leipzig: Verlag C. L. Hirschfeld, 1899), at 111.

[24] A. Nollkaemper, "Inside or Out: Two Types of International Legal Pluralism," in J. Klabbers and T. Piiparinen (eds.), *Normative Pluralism and International Law: Exploring Global Governance* (Cambridge: Cambridge University Press, 2013), 94.

Be advised, however, that compliance (or acceptance) is a different matter. The peril perhaps hidden in theorizing other orders as sheer facts is that we mistakenly conflate two different things: that is, the understanding of something as a normative claim and the application (or acceptance) of it into our universe. Normative claims can be comprehended and taken seriously even without granting them by necessity any transitive unconditional application (compliance) in our context. In general, as Habermas taught, if this "application" can be suspended, none of the parties is vested with an unconditionally superior authority, while the conflation between understanding and application can only happen under conditions of unbalanced weight of the parties, allegedly provided by faiths or supported by power.[25] On the other hand, it is precisely the fact that normativities are substantively interwoven in each instance that requires a full consideration of *them all*. Finally, factual circumstances (e.g., of political or economic power) often prevent some parties from having a free choice as to compliance or acceptance. It is rather common to admit that the factual scope of global regimes, from the ISO to the Internet Corporation for Assigned Names and Numbers (ICANN) and so forth, includes peoples and states, directly or indirectly affected, for many of whom exit or entry is not an option. Inter-Legality bears a conceptual emancipatory strength in this state of affairs insofar as it allows for scrutiny – not necessarily for unconditional acceptance – of normative claims, and its perspective refers to the legal assessment of countervailing reasons on a different stage of rightness other than sheer power.

[25] However, a normative claim can be seen as other than a fact and worthy of consideration as such, yet its acceptance in our own sphere can be *suspended* until its rightness or justification (value) is recognized and shared by the interlocutor. The claim and its suspension are studied by Habermas, such as in his criticism of Gadamer's hermeneutics that conflates the understanding of others' claims (of normative nature, of truth, etc.) with the *acceptance* of their meaning or value (as truth, as a norm for us, etc.) in our own context: H. G. Gadamer, *Truth and Method*, 2nd edn. (New York: Continuum, 1988), writes that as happens in the work of a judge, understanding of the text is only possible by granting to its meanings *application* into our context. ("Application does not mean first understanding a given universal in itself and then afterward applying it to a concrete case. It is the very understanding of the universal – the text – itself. Understanding proves to be a kind of effect and knows itself as such," at 341). Habermas discussed this model. When committed to comprehension, the "interpreter cannot understand the semantic content of a text if he is not in a position to present to himself the reasons that the author might have been able to adduce in defence of his utterances under suitable conditions." But these reasons cannot be taken to be "sound" unless the interpreter takes a "negative or positive position on them" (J. Habermas, *A Theory of Communicative Action, Volume 1* [Boston, MA: Beacon Press, 1981, McCarthy trans.], 132). Accordingly, Habermas pointed to "understanding" as requiring a "suspension" of any "applications" of someone else's claims into our horizon.

The above-mentioned, and most acclaimed, alternative to dualism – that is, monism[26] – in principle makes it impossible for the "inter" in "inter-legality" to ultimately surface at all. At the same time, the plural variety of legalities disappear, simply because their standing is deprived of ultimate autonomy, being made to depend on some higher comprehensive frame of normative reference or delegation. Monism from an international point of view would consider anything as part of one, unique order, with potential undermining of those legalities that would run contrary to the coherence of a world unity of law. In such a world legality, a legal *monarchy* would require a global material convergence and shared visions that are unavailable contingently. Interconnectedness depends in fact on large variety (not on unity), on which pluralism instead has insisted for a long time.

And once we account for a *pluralist* understanding of legal orders, be it soft or radical,[27] institutional or systemic,[28] the useful tool pluralism provides refers to the overcoming of the perspective of the "one" or of the "two," since it opens up the possibility of looking at the world as a wide "enmeshing" variety:[29] it is, however, rather difficult for its paradigms to allow for a *legal* account of interconnectedness, something we shall return to later. On the other hand, it is rather fair to say that inter-legality would relocate pluralism without rejecting some of its main findings.

[26] On the monism/dualism couple, see in general J. Polakiewicz, "International Law and Domestic (Municipal) Law, Law and Decisions of International Organizations and Courts," in R. Wolfrum (ed.), *Max Planck Encyclopedia of Public International Law* (Oxford: Oxford University Press, 2011).

[27] Exemplary is the reference to Neil McCormick's masterful discussion of legal pluralism, in that the author arrives at a softer form of *pluralism under international law,* although he started from subscribing to a form of "radical" pluralism recognizing the fact of the existence of different orders endowed with their own rules of recognition. N. McCormick, "Risking Constitutional Collision in Europe?" (1998) 18 *Oxford Journal of Legal Studies* 517; N. McCormick, "Beyond the Sovereign State," (1993) 56 *Modern Law Review,* 1; N. McCormick, "The Maastricht-Urteil: Sovereignty Now," (1995) 1 *European Law Journal* 259; N. McCormick, *Questioning Sovereignty: Law, State, and Nation in the European Commonwealth* (Oxford: Oxford University Press, 1999).

[28] This terminology is adopted by N. Krisch, *Beyond Constitutionalism: The Pluralist Structure of Postnational Law* (Oxford: Oxford University Press, 2010). Krisch writes that "the 'institutionalist' variant of pluralism represents less an alternative to than a continuation of constitutionalist themes" because it refers to a "common, constitutional framework" that "systemic pluralism" rejects "in favour of a decentred management of diversity." Eventually, systemic pluralism differs from dualism because it does not subscribe to the scheme that separates *two* legal orders: "the domestic order applied inside the State whereas the international order regulated States in their mutual interactions" (at 77).

[29] The extensive treatment and tenets of it are proposed in N. Krisch, *Beyond Constitutionalism.*

We have to focus on a specific aspect of a plurality of orders in order to account for the very fact that several times *either the norm to be applied in a specific case, and controlling it, derives from a different context and from a different regime of legality, or the norm to be applied results from a concurring/competing legality*. In either case, this very fact can be seen as such before we apply to it the lenses of a monist, dualist, or even pluralist scheme. Refraining from applying, since the outset, their ordering qualifications equates to abstaining from the adoption of their common interpretive scheme that revolves roughly around the *system* logics; accordingly, we need a point of view that does not start from the *systems, the closed orders*, but indeed from the enmeshing circumstances in which legality appears as a composite chance, not already the outcome of a top-down grand design of the world (as one, two, or many legal orders).

In order to explain the epistemic attitude involved here, one can resort to a governmental metaphor. Aristotle defined the forms of government through paradigms in terms of the one, or the few, or the many governing with a view to the common interest. But the prevailing of selfish interests, such as building wealth or power for only one or certain individuals or groups, would in any case make for despotic constitutions, regardless of the governing formula. "The perversions are as follows: of royalty, tyranny; of aristocracy, oligarchy; of constitutional government, democracy. For tyranny is a kind of monarchy which has in view the interest of the monarch only; oligarchy has in view the interest of the wealthy; democracy, of the needy: none of them the common good of all."[30] At the end, what makes the difference, in a nutshell, is not the "number-based" governing paradigmatic formula, but the pursuit of the common interest.

What Aristotle wrote might be interpreted, loosely, in a sense that requires pride of place for the epistemic perspective: what really counts is to abandon the perspective of the governors' interests, be they of the monarch, the aristocracy/oligarchy, or the "many," and take in all cases that from the common good that is the ultimate parameter of value (not structurally built into them). Similarly, if we want to reflect the variety and the interconnectedness as a fact characterizing legal orders and regimes, which surfaces in so many cases, the perspective from the systems (one, two, or many), as decisive as it is, is misleading, and might foreclose our understanding.

[30] Aristotle, *Politics* (Oxford: Clarendon Press, Jowett trans.), book III, part VII.

In this sense, inter-legality should better lead to changing the epistemic standpoint. As I submit, it is taking directly another perspective: the perspective of law.

4 ON THE PERSPECTIVE OF LAW

I assume that inter-legality does not take the systems standpoint. It takes instead the perspective of law. The latter does not have to necessarily start from system(s). Systems connect to the issue of validity, an issue that is not in itself under question here: all in all, validity is brought about by a fact or a norm concerning the accreditation of other (candidate) norms with reference to a given system. But I doubt that the systemic perspective – one, two, or many – can really and ultimately exhaust the legality problem and cover the subject that we wish to consider. In order to clarify this point, some preliminary considerations are in order, which should stress the difference on the one hand vis-à-vis a sociological understanding of inter-legality, and on the other vis-à-vis the achievements of the pluralist conception of legal orders.

de Sousa Santos refers to inter-legality as "legal porosity" and "multiple networks of legal orders forcing us to constant transitions and trespassing. Our legal life is constituted by an intersection of different legal orders, that is, by interlegality."[31] Thus, here the term points to how "we" are contemporarily involved in many circles of concurring legalities/orders. Accordingly, "we" avail of concurring or competing chances: given the somehow objective existence of orders, the socio-legal aspect emphasizes how legalities might appear, on the subjects' side, as an opportunity for popular control from below, a kind of counter-instrumentalization, and also allowing the use of their interstices and different orders against each other.[32] While centered around the actors' use of the contradictions of law's clusters as an instrument of power, such a perspective is more dependent upon contrasting law by pitting different instrumentalities one against the other than on enhancing how the structures of law provide for some paths of resilient fairness.

It is necessary to shift to some more determinate direction, allowing us to focus less upon a *sociological* profile and the perspective of subjects than upon

[31] B. de Sousa Santos, "Law: A Map of Misreading," in B. de Sousa Santos (ed.), *Toward a New Common Sense: Law, Science and Politics in the Paradigmatic Transition* (London: Routledge, 1995), 473.

[32] See also B. de Sousa Santos, "Beyond Neoliberal Governance: The World Social Forum As Subaltern Cosmopolitan Politics and Legality," in B. de Sousa Santos and C. A. Rodríguez-Garavito (eds.), *Law and Globalization from Below* (Cambridge: Cambridge University Press, 2005), 29.

the (legal) scope and meaning of legality. Inter-Legality, on a different level than de Sousa Santos's conception, starts from the fact that interconnections make up for a kind of *composite law*, one that results from the contents of separate sources in a number of recurrent situations.

It is useful to contrast the perspective from inter-legality against the paradigm of pluralism in order to differentiate the systems' perspective from that of law and inter-legality as such. While recognizing the autonomy and distinctiveness of diverse systems of law or self-closed legalities, the most genuine conception of legal pluralism – the radical one – avoids relapse into monist or dualist views and rejects the idea that pluralism has to be finally contained within a wider overarching principle of coherence, of conflict-solving, or hosted either under constitutional or international law (as in the McCormick proposal after his internationalist turn).[33] In the radical pluralist view, the common fact of systems' interference or conflict, to the extent that it is not legally domesticated in one way or the other, is to be left to some negotiation inter partes. The absence of pre-fixed criteria of confrontation allows for open and incremental solutions, interlocutions mainly on political premises, bringing the claims and ideologies pertaining to the interacting "systems" between, say, the neoliberal bias and the democratic interests of local governments, and so forth.

As a consequence, the alternatives run between suffering the instability and uncertainty of a brave radical systemic pluralism or converting the theory into a controlled pluralism (under the legal authority of common constitutional rules of reasonableness or under international law as a common order of reference). In the first case, legalities' disputes are channeled through mainly *political* avenues; in the second case, they are settled outside the pure or radical form of pluralism because the relevant legalities subordinate themselves to a wider *legal* order.[34]

While allowing for a pure plurality of autonomous systems, none of them is prior or privileged, as Krisch maintains:

> ... pluralism favors pragmatic, incremental processes of mutual accommodation and potential convergence, without overstretching the authority

[33] McCormick, *Questioning Sovereignty*.

[34] In truth, the two might even conflate; that is, it is not only that orders must subordinate to international law but, given the insufficient determinative capacity of international law alone, political negotiations are resorted to as well: think of the pronouncement of the ICJ in the 2012 dispute about the immunity of the German State. The ICJ concluded that, despite the availability of an international law answer to the question (provided by the customary rule of state immunity), nonetheless the legal and moral standing of the counterpart's claims needed to be addressed differently and maintained their normative justification. As a consequence, the Court recommended further "political negotiations." See *Jurisdictional Immunities of the State* (Germany v Italy: Greece Intervening), [2012] ICJ Reports 99.

> of the norms and institutions that form the regime. Because it allows the different layers of law to maintain their own fundamental, supreme norms, it also allows for meaningful signals about the limits of cooperation, thus anticipating political challenges. For the creation and consolidation of European and global political and legal institutions, this may be more beneficial than the existence of an overarching framework which will often antagonize actors and fail to match its social environment.[35]

However, pluralism in the most challenging form takes itself a kind of systemic view. Of course, starting from "many" revolutionizes, in and of itself, the "*appropriative*" bias affecting in diverse ways monism or dualism. Pluralism does not absorb or appropriate legalities in those senses, since it leaves them to their self-standing exclusive authority, without attempting to colonize them under the label of one, nor simply conceding that "others" can normatively communicate with us under an "incorporation" or appropriation free choice. The general point, through pluralist lenses, is that multiple systems have to learn from each other and more pragmatically discover incremental lines of understanding. But they are not under a legal obligation to do so, nor do they have any route available to actually do so through legal terms.

As submitted in this section, the notion of inter-legality leads to the "perspective of law." The pattern of the system bears many qualities and properties, and especially its potential exclusivity, completeness, and authority. Kelsen taught that the idea of *objective (meaning of law) legality*[36] to which he subscribes cannot be disentangled from the requirement of the *systemic validity* and *closure* that it requires. The Kelsenian view was admittedly shifting from state to law, and placing the state at the level of a consequential order authorised by the non-statist, wider international legal order, so that the systemic sphere moved beyond the state. Otherwise, the state paradigm traditionally hovered above the scope of law itself. According to one of the European masters of legal thought in the first half of the last century, "the compulsory nature of the rules in force, whatever their remote origin may be, appears henceforth as the effect of th[at] centralizing will . . . a true and proper subject . . . the State," granting

[35] N. Krisch, "Who is Afraid of Radical Pluralism? Legal Order and Political Stability in the Postnational Space," (2011) 24 *Ratio Juris* 386, 407.

[36] H. Kelsen, *Pure Theory of Law* (Berkeley: University of California Press, 1970, trans. Knight), e.g., at 201 ff.

for itself "exclusiveness rendered necessary in order to assure the unity of the system."[37]

Although mainly construed upon the state,[38] the system pattern is undoubted today as also encompassing international law, given the fact that it has acquired its rules of recognition.[39] However, such a world from one set of looking glasses covers realities only up to a certain point. An example can be derived by considering Benedict Kingsbury's argument about the concept of law in the extra-state environment: enquiring upon the *legality* of the array of concurring and competing regulations issued from an indefinite number of public, private, or hybrid regional and global authorities, Kingsbury suggests to fix requirements and criteria of recognition, be they referring to the nature of the sources and/or to the their content (oriented to requirements of publicness: respecting rationality, proportionality, basic human rights, the principle of legality, and the rule of law).[40] The legality question is thereby answered as a matter of criteria of *validity*. The global administrative law idea of legality, at which Kingsbury was hinting, was rightly referred to as non-matching and wider than international law as a single order. However, the solution looks imperfect because it asks for one global set of rules of recognition, one that is said to be still absent and its creation still to come. Although this outcome is somewhat ambiguous, it shows that we are used to solving the problem of legality by means of recognizing validity – and that is not always a perfect and conducive route.

While we recognize what makes something law in any given system (according to its own requirements of validity), we equally acknowledge –

37 G. del Vecchio, "On the Statuality of Law," (1937) 19 *Journal of Comparative Legislation and International Law* 1, 8–9.

38 That is among the reasons why Hart was at pains to recognize international law as a mature legal order: see H. L. A. Hart, *The Concept of Law*, 2nd edn. (Oxford: Oxford University Press, 1997), chapter X.

39 S. Besson, "Theorizing the Sources of International Law," in S. Besson and J. Tasioulas (eds.), *The Philosophy of International Law* (Oxford: Oxford University Press, 2010), 164; J. Waldron, "International Law: 'A Relatively Small and Unimportant' Part of Jurisprudence?" (2013) 427 *NYU Public Law and Legal Theory Working Papers* 209. Mehrdad Payandeh wrote that international law can be described as a system because it copes with "the problems of uncertainty, of the static character of the social rules, and of the inefficiency of the system in enforcing the rules"; in other words, it can "perform the three functions which Hart deems necessary for the existence of a legal system." See M. Payandeh, "The Concept of International Law in the Jurisprudence of H. L. A. Hart," (2010) 21 *European Journal of International Law* 967, 981.

40 B. Kingsbury, "The Concept of 'Law' in Global Administrative Law," (2009) 20 *European Journal of International Law* 12.

also through pioneering analyses of pluralist contexts – that legality overflows requirements of validity related to a specific order. Although pluralists would acknowledge many sources, practices, and also systems of validity (e.g., spontaneous, transnational, private self-ordering), nonetheless they can less clearly make the most of the fact of *interconnectedness*. Aptly taking an external viewpoint focusing on the indeed legitimate plurality of systemic views and allowing for a more realist, open-ended scenario, pluralist insight into law remains systemic, in the sense of Hartian or Kelsenian premises, and legality lives as a discrete segmental property. The systemic bias implies that legality flourishes inside the borders of each order. Accordingly, pluralism arrives at the recognition of multiple legalities, but beyond that threshold the *legal* perspective is mute or impossible to be taken at all. The "legal" stops with each discrete legalities' claim: their crossroads or interconnectedness is a fact that has no *legal* nature or appearance. But from the perspective of inter-legality, *interconnectedness* is itself *a legal* situation.

5 THE COMPREHENSIVE DRIVE OF INTER-LEGALITY

As I shall explain in what follows, inter-legality should be phrased as the proper dimension where the "law" cannot be made to depend on just one among the single normative orders that might be relevant in concrete circumstances. While *legality* and *validity* decouple, *inter-legality* construes a kind of *continuum* – it captures the legal compound.

As I recalled, it is true what de Sousa Santos wrote: we live "in between." But inter-legality is not just a state of things we can exploit and profit from in terms of the contradictions and divergences among separate and mutually irrelevant normative orders. Not as a *subjective* sociological notion but as an *objective legal* notion, inter-legality would allow us to consider the law as something different; we should pretend to avail of inter-legality in a different sense.

It would be less useful running after forum shopping if the fora were to consider the law – beyond one's own system legality – in some more comprehensive sense. By changing the perspective from systemic validity to legality, inter-legality concentrates on the law as wide as it happens to be relevant from the vantage point of the issues under consideration. In that very sense, for instance, one should acknowledge that in the flagship *Kadi* case, the relevant law is not just the EU law and its fundamental rights, but at the same time the law governing the Security Council and issued by it; and eventually, not just the rules empowering the Council to maintain security, but also the law of the UN Charter defending international human rights.[41]

In some aspects, even in medieval times, when multiple legalities were flourishing, the possible tussle might have been solved as a sheer matter of power or counter-power. But the common law guarding the delivering of justice was deemed to emerge from *things themselves*. Such a reference somehow deviated from the focus on the authoritative power toward the rationale emerging from the *res* itself. In that sense, the logics of *aequitas*, building on the case at issue, points to a normative layer that could overstep the diversity of claims rooted in different orders. Such a crosscutting level of legality, traditionally open and surfacing from the controversy concerning "justice," was later cancelled by exclusionary requirements of validity through the developing of law as an ordered system connected to the appearance of the modern state. In a sense, *validity overruled legality*.

What inter-legality – in its normative meaning – should do is to disrobe or undress norms of their systemic clothes (that grant them exclusionary strength) and uphold the normative claims raised by their interaction and interconnection. In a determined venue, the law surfaces as the composite legal nature of the issue under scrutiny. Such an operation is not possible on the level of an a priori, global, monist (or otherwise articulated), constitutional order, firstly because such an order does not really exist, secondly because, by contrast, the plurality of orders convenes different rationales and represents separate and discrete raisons d'être, thirdly because there is no premade solution under common global principles to the fragmented functions of legal regimes, and fourthly because adjudication does not – or should not – obey the logics of a (metaphysical) global system (i.e., looking at an abstract heaven), but should look instead to the potential *justice-related* function that belongs to things: what in medieval times – not by chance – was called *convenientia rerum*.

Beyond some loose medieval analogy, however, the point is to take into account (instead of ignoring or disregarding) the overlapping of normative ordering as in need of a measure of justice, one that is to be found through the appraisal of concrete cases. Once more, such an objective inheres in the scope and meaning of legality, while it has scarce affinity with systemic dilemmas. When normative orders interact, the legal "true proposition of law" cannot result out of unilateral and one-sided sources, but has to be spelled out within the enmeshing of *normative* circumstances. The effect of ordering the case at

[41] Otherwise, the race to simplification would address the complexity of the matter by seeking refuge in one or the other of the available system-related legal logics.

stake amounts to the ultimate recognition of what "the law is." As the Austin–Hartian tradition in legal thought reveals, positivist lenses are ill-equipped to face and address the ultra-systemic nature of legality. The rule of recognition solves questions of legal propositions in one system, but seems unsuited to treat issues where the solution is precisely "beyond"; that is, they are to be answered only in supra-systemic or inter-systemic terms. This requires an attitude driven by inter-legality, one that seeks to reach the layer controlling the case in its deepest fundus (i.e., the place where, one would say with Wittgenstein, "I have reached bedrock, and my spade is turned").[42] To be required to think of law in terms of interconnectedness, among many normativities' "ins," prevents our search for law from being stuck in one of them or in the other; that is, the "*aut . . . aut*" between "being in" and nothing. Legality again surfaces through the cases as a *continuum*, underlying discrete and separate bodies of law. I shall approximate this point in what follows.

6 THE JUDICIAL DRIVE TO JUSTICE AND COURTS' TASKS: INTERPRETING THE INTERPRETERS

6.1.

The exclusive nature of a legal order is most often conceptualized in consequence of the exclusive nature of sovereignty. But this picture, as we have seen, is insufficiently telling in the present scenarios. There are recursive features of legality that have been discussed in recent decades, precisely in order to cope with the multi-ordered character of the legal universe.

The recent discussion of the common layer of *jus gentium* stemmed from the need to open state legislation to the application or adoption of foreign law, and it was described as a matter of reason *and* consensus, in uncertain proportion.[43] By contrast, Hugo Grotius has been revisited as the author recognizing the plurality of legalities: Grotius identified *jus gentium* as widespread practice

[42] L. Wittgenstein, *Philosophical Investigations* (Oxford: Blackwell, 1953, Anscombe trans.), para. 217: "If I have exhausted the justifications I have reached bedrock, and my spade is turned. Then I am inclined to say: 'This is simply what I do'." The same sentence is recalled by E. Scoditti, "Corti e Carte dei Diritti," (2013) 2 *Rivista di Filosofia del Diritto* 379, aiming to explain how the case provides for the only and ultimate rule of recognition. An analogous observation, assuming that the center of gravity of a legal system is not in its apex but in the practice determining the scale of priorities through factual situations, is in G. Palombella, *E' Possibile una Legalità Globale? Il Rule of Law e la Governance del Mondo* (Bologna: Il Mulino, 2012), at 104–105.

[43] See Chapter 2 (especially discussing Waldron).

sustained through *consensus* (that is, on a voluntary basis), while the law of nature was mainly ascertainable as a matter of *reason*. As Kingsbury writes:

> This was an important distinction. Grotius's concept of *jus gentium* places it simply as part of the human voluntary law. It subsists alongside the *jus civile* (the law of a single nation), and the law that is the command of a paterfamilias to family members or of a master to a slave. These multiple legal orders are not necessarily in strictly hierarchical relationship one with the other, nor need they be strictly horizontal. Grotius thus has little difficulty accommodating a plurality of normative orders. Grotius was able to keep this pluralism morally and socially coherent through reference to the more fundamental normative systems of divine voluntary law and natural law. To give a doctrinal illustration, Grotius viewed slavery that results from capture in war as a legal structure of the jus gentium, but not of natural law.[44]

As interesting as it is, the point of solving such issues on the basis of a common overarching frame endures in many threads of scholarship. As Neil Walker noted, universalists stress the potential of law as reason, while pluralists stress law as *voluntas*: while to the former law is a point of departure, to the latter it is the arrival point of a vision of law instrumental to the creative political will.[45] But the plurality of legalities oversteps even such a division, insofar as it encompasses both the self-generative autonomy of reason in law and its interweaving with instrumental functions. The deeper distinction might be seen more in law conveying different *rationales* than in law being sourced on, say, generalized convention of spontaneous nature *or* political sovereign will. One might be reminded of Aristotle's reasoning on governmental forms, where the main difference is related to substance rather than to the features of the authority in place: whether the governor's objective refers to the interests of some or to those of the generality.

But of course, in our field, it is nonetheless fundamental – both for the orientation of law to the interests of all to be credible and with regard to the preservation of liberty – that reference also be made to the sources. The plurality of legalities is ensured if law is not monopolized by one single hand and if it stems from a variety of those capable of triggering the generation of law. Accordingly, rulers (be they sovereign states or omnipotent global regulators) should be respectful to a law that is not their own, if the rule of law, not of men, has to thrive.[46] Such premises, then, suggest that the plurality of sources

[44] B. Kingsbury, "Global Regulation and the New *Jus Gentium*," draft paper, p. 15, available at www.iilj.org/wp-content/uploads/2016/11/Kingsbury-A-New-Jus-Gentium-2006.pdf.

[45] Walker, *Intimations*, at 195–205.

[46] I have extensively dealt with this issue in G. Palombella, "The Rule of Law at Home and Abroad," (2016) 8 *Hague Journal on the Rule of Law* 1, and G. Palombella, "The Rule of Law as

(and, one might add, in a wider ultra-state setting, *legalities*) qualifies, in principle, as a legal precondition of non-domination through law and of liberty. Thus, what ultimately counts is the tension that translates into an equilibrium between them. Even in the "global" world that we are facing, the legal domination, be it by powerful nation-states or by regional or supra-national authorities, is a permanent risk, although in the contradictions between them one can find, as de Sousa Santos thought in his own terms, potential counterpoises. In such a situation, the pluralized structures of sources, legalities, and available normativities (including *jus gentium*, international law, natural law principles positivized in international law or in state constitutions, and so forth) contribute a multiple setting that makes for the composite *layers* as well as *contents* of law. The two things are equally essential. Accordingly, it is part of the mission of preserving a justified balance of fairness between *rationales*, sources, authorities, and legalities that the interpretation of law does not ignore such a diversity and accounts for it.

This places judges in a privileged and delicate position. They should of course apply the law that belongs to their jurisdiction. But in such cases where at stake is the very problem of interfering legalities, regimes, orders, jurisdictions, common goods of different kinds, or rights of states themselves, should we still expect them to take a sheer self-referential stance and forget about what is passing by in the real substance of the case in-between multiple legalities' settings? Is it still possible for us to think that no one has the responsibility for an outcome that consider the opposite vectors in play?

As to the scope of this chapter, what matters more to inter-legality is that it replaces the idea of purely insulated and self-referential legality without giving into the mainstream temptation of drawing global principles and rules and offering their dis-embedded constitutional promise. Inter-Legality is not an a priori construct but an empirical (so to speak) reconnaissance, in both senses of the term (exploration as well as recognition). Consequently, it exposes the interrelatedness of things, as relevant in legal terms, within the delimited sphere of justice-delivering function as a matter that, in principle, is case-related. Here, it provides a different attitude, according to which states, orders, and courts should be entrusted with the task of accounting for the whole extent of the wider legality (legalities) and question at stake, unhampered by the narrow perspective of source or jurisdiction and the division of labor that they implement and respond to.

Here, behind the interpretation of law and its findings, there are some moves that would shift our attention from the rule valid in our jurisdiction to the law

an Institutional Ideal," in L. Morlino and G. Palombella (eds.), *Rule of Law and Democracy: Internal and External Issues* (Leiden: Brill, 2010), 1.

relevant in the case and governing it. Although there is no space here for a more extensive treatment of the point, most of the legal reasoning premises to such a move are less dramatic than one can think. The point is to address the divergence among pre-fixed norms, overcoming their abstractness that might lead to a partial or one-sided determination of law. It is increasingly acknowledged that judicial decision-making in composite contexts of conflicting principles – even in constitutional orders – is not simply confirming the mythology of rule-based predictions. The interpretive outcome results less from the application of a valid rule than from a more open and nuanced itinerarium, where the reconstruction of the facts at hand is the occasion for the interpreter to arbitrate different rationales and countervailing principles on the basis of the investigation of the legality imbuing the issues and the features of the case.

Beyond systemic completeness and self-sufficiency, realities abound that do not occur in single places, being at the intersection between them, *in the absence of a third party authority and adjudicator*. Although a paramount "integrity" of the supranational context is a matter of "legislative" construction, and a kind of organic global legal system certainly seems out of sight, nonetheless a court's role in such an environment requires it to make the most of the different normative perspectives that converge into the subject under debate in order to identify the contribution to positive justice that convening different normative angles can offer. Contrary to the pursuit of a full-fledged ideal of justice that would correspond in legal terms to an enlightened constitutional architecture of the world, borrowing from Amartya Sen, the quest for justice – even in our legal sense – should avoid something like the Rawlsian "transcendental" notion of what justice is and implies once for all, and would better avail of "critical scrutiny from the perspective of others":[47] its true objective is best seen as *avoiding injustice*. Again, as an alternative to the Rawlsian faith in what perfect "institutions" can do, Sen complements the relevance of just institutions with the sense of responsibility for overall outcomes and social realizations.[48] Should that be absent, clear-cut institutions would possibly be unjust. Justice is (also) a matter of "responsibility," which requires gathering diverse sensitivities and reaching a kind of more comprehensive view by dissolving one-sidedness and ensuring the perspectives of others are heard. In this very sense, especially the highest courts or supranational courts shall have to judge in a double function (i.e., also in the view of showing how their institutional

[47] A. Sen, *The Idea of Justice* (Cambridge, MA: Harvard University Press, 2009), at 197.

[48] See, among various passages, Sen, *Idea of Justice*, at 21. From this point of view, the attitude to inter-legality and the underlying sense of the pursuit of just outcomes resembles the need for *virtue* in the practice of law, not only the precondition of just institutions; see Chapter 15.

allegiance does not ignore what comes to the case, as legally reasoned claims, from "other" normative orders).

6.2.

In 2008, Germany brought a case before the ICJ claiming that Italy had breached the rule of state immunity by allowing civil suits before the Italian courts for compensation to victims of Second World War crimes. The ICJ[49] ascertained that a customary rule exists granting state immunity for *acta jure imperii*, to which cases of grave war crimes are no exception. Such an immunity rule formulated by the Court is said to be strictly endowed with procedural primacy, which prevents the further appraisal of the merits. Accordingly, the violation of *jus cogens* norms by Germany does not displace its right to immunity, regardless of whether victims are thereby deprived of any means of redress.

The weakness of this pronouncement by the ICJ is at the root of subsequent judicial issues raised before the Italian Constitutional Court. As I have remarked elsewhere,[50] the ICJ still understands its role in a narrow way, a way that has prevented it from fully taking into account the real complexity of the case and the countervailing peremptory norms against international crimes and protecting human rights. So, it is a one-sided interpretation that not only overlooks the question of domestic protection of fundamental rights, but at the same time disregards important provisions belonging to international law. Sticking to the sheer *existence* of a customary rule is anything but a neutral stance. Moreover, the Court recognizes the insufficiency of its verdict: lacking a legal remedy to victims of war crimes, it suggests the reopening of further political negotiations, thus confessing self-inflicted impotence.[51] That is, based on the current self-understanding of the highest international court[52] as unable to convey the entire normative strength of the

[49] *Jurisdictional Immunities of the State*.

[50] G. Palombella, "German War Crimes and the Rule of International Law," (2016) 14 *Journal of International Criminal Justice* 607.

[51] See *Jurisdictional Immunities of the State*, para. 104: "... the Court is not unaware that the immunity from jurisdiction of Germany in accordance with international law may preclude judicial redress for the Italian nationals concerned. It considers however that the claims arising from the treatment of the Italian military internees ... together with other claims of Italian nationals which have allegedly not been settled – and which formed the basis for the Italian proceedings – could be the subject of further negotiation involving the two States concerned, with a view to resolving the issue."

[52] In general, on the attitudes of the ICJ, see G. I. Hernandez, "A Reluctant Guardian: The International Court of Justice and the Concept of International Community," (2013) 83 *British Yearbook of International Law* 13.

existing international legal order, it confines itself to a sheer arbiter between the arguments raised by the parties. Such a mind-set runs counter to the possibility that international law be interpreted in its integrity, and as a whole, as all courts have to do with regard to their own legal orders. This reflects the lack of a culture of justification, one that does not ignore the material and normative relations between different concurring sub-domains of international law. Such a culture of justification does not necessarily require that the Court plays some creative role,[53] but requires at least that it works through making the most of the legal order as *complete*[54] – all the more so since the point was not, in the present case, the absence of explicit words and norms, a gap that a judge should bridge by interpretation, but on the contrary, the point was the relevance of positive law that a judge should not be entitled to neglect or simply downplay to the status of mere moral recommendation. However, what is even more relevant to our inter-legality issue is the answer by the Italian Constitutional Court,[55] which reestablishes the importance of respecting human rights and access to justice and is considered by several commentators as self-regarding or dualist.[56] However, the Italian Court is not simply working as a gatekeeper – with reference to supreme principles.[57] Moreover, it is not deciding about the constitutionality of an internal, domestic rule, regardless of international law (a typical dualist attitude taken, for instance,

[53] See *Legality of the Threat or Use of Nuclear Weapons* (Advisory Opinion), [1996] ICJ Reports 226, Dissenting Opinion of Judge Higgins, esp. at 590–591.

[54] H. Lauterpacht, *The Function of Law in the International Community* (Oxford: Clarendon Press, 1933), at 66–67.

[55] Italian Constitutional Court, Judgment no. 238 of October 22, 2014, available at www.cortecostituzionale.it/documenti/download/doc/recent_judgments/S238_2013_en.pdf (hereinafter, "Judgment no. 238").

[56] R. Kolb, "The Relationship between the International and the Municipal Legal Order: Reflections on the Decision no 238/2014 of the Italian Constitutional Court," (2014) *Questions of International Law*, wrote: "The gist of decision no. 238/2014 is a separatist treatment of the two legal orders involved. It is a high peak of a new form of robust dualism. Dualism is here not limited to explain the penetration of international legal norms into the national legal order. It ventures further, extending to a denial of any constructive 'dialogue' with international law and the judgment of the ICJ." See also A. Peters, "Let Not Triepel Triumph – How to Make the Best out of Sentenza no. 238 of the Italian Constitutional Court for a Global Legal Order," available at https://verfassungsblog.de/let-not-triepel-triumph-make-best-sentenza-no-238-italian-constitutional-court-global-legal-order-2.

[57] A recent Note, "Constitutional Courts and International Law: Revisiting the Transatlantic Divide," (2016) 129 *Harvard Law Review* 1362, challenged the perception that the EU's *Kadi* judgment, and the decision of the Italian Constitutional Court no. 238/2014 (on state immunity) might be evidence of some American-style exceptionalism and a self-referential posture, and maintains that their resistance to international law obligations as "gatekeepers" is only exceptional, and is justified by the special nature of *some* internal principles – those deemed to be *supreme*.

by the ECJ in the 2008 *Kadi* decision), but about an international rule as interpreted by the ICJ and its compatibility with the Italian legal order (to allow for the incorporation required by Article 10 of the Italian Constitution). In truth, the Court works directly in-between the two legal orders, and has to consider and balance their respective normative claims in the case at hand. It manages to show that formal subjection to the pronouncements of the ICJ should be replaced by a consideration of the normative interactions at play.[58] Thinking otherwise would make the Court's judgment something like a lame verdict, neglecting the case's complexity.

In many ways, reasoning on such issues leads us to further and diverse questions involving our views of jurisdiction. I would offer two examples. One is the *Tadic* case at the Yugoslavia Tribunal (ICTY) and its pronouncement on jurisdiction;[59] the other is the reasoning of the ECtHR in *Al-Dulimi*.[60] Most of the discussions of the *Tadic* case use the famous sentence on the *self-contained* nature of international tribunals mainly as a reminder of the fragmented nature of extra-state law. As a consequence, the opinion can also be taken as the tenet that the many courts and regimes of law are in fact self-referential. That is not the only significance of the opinion, since more is said about the extent of a court's jurisdiction. I am inclined to draw from it the lesson that a court, as a matter of its judicial function properly meant, cannot be prevented from taking into account and even scrutinizing the wider spectrum of extra-state law if it comes as an essential, connected step for its due assessment.

The context of reference of the opinion concerns the question *of the lawfulness of the establishment of the International Tribunal – the issue of its "validity."* Unlike the Trial chamber, which assumed that the question of the validity of its own establishment exceeded the jurisdiction of the Tribunal because it concerned scrutiny of an act issued by the Security Council, the reasoning of the Appeals Chamber considers the question of *jurisdiction* as involving the issue of validity (or *lawful establishment*). President Antonio Cassese maintains that "jurisdiction" is to be intended as a "legal power to state the law." Contrary to what might happen in domestic orders (here comes the famous passage):

58 For greater depth on this, see G. Palombella, "*Senza Identità*. Dal Diritto Internazionale alla Corte Costituzionale tra Consuetudine, *Jus Cogens* e Principi 'Supremi'," (2015) 35 *Quaderni Costituzionali* 815.

59 *Prosecutor v Tadic*, Case no. IT-94-1-I, Decision on Defense Motion for Interlocutory Appeal on Jurisdiction, para. 11 (October 2, 1995).

60 *Al-Dulimi v Switzerland*, Application no. 5809/08, November 26, 2013.

> International law, because it lacks a centralized structure, does not provide for an integrated judicial system operating an orderly division of labour among a number of tribunals, where certain aspects or components of jurisdiction as a power could be centralized or vested in one of them but not the others. In international law, every tribunal is a self-contained system (unless otherwise provided).[61]

Accordingly, in the absence of an ordered structure of hierarchically defined assignments, every tribunal might have to take care of "certain aspects or components" that in a system of division of labor might be vested in other tribunals. If a general hierarchy does not exist, then a tribunal might extend its answer to aspects or components that would otherwise be placed in other tribunals. Thus, the sentence is not a plea to dismiss certain legal issues exceeding the narrow sphere of the fragment of international law to which the tribunal belongs, but actually a recommendation to the contrary.

President Cassese maintained that to think as the Trial Chamber had thought would be "totally ignoring any residual powers which may derive from the requirements of the 'judicial function' itself."[62] Moreover, assuming that the jurisdiction of a Tribunal is limited by the intention of the Security Council when establishing it would make the International Tribunal a mere "subsidiary organ" of the Council, under its power.[63]

As I see the issue, the point is not to transform every tribunal into a constitutional court assessing the legality of the acts by other international powers, including the Security Council, but to accept the right to exercise its jurisdiction by extending it to all the "incidental" questions that need to be addressed if the Tribunal has to decide and determine *the law* in the case before it, in view of its substantive or primary competence. To argue differently would prevent the Tribunal from exercising fully and properly its "judicial function."

Questions that are involved in the determination of law in the case before a court can present themselves in diverse semblances. One should be reminded of the reasoning of the EU Court of First Instance (now its

[61] *Tadic*, para. 11.

[62] Ibid., para. 14.

[63] According to the Appeals Chamber, such a view was to be opposed. It held that the power of *Kompetenz-Kompetenz* (i.e., the power to decide on its own jurisdiction) is inherent in the jurisdiction of a Tribunal itself, also according to the words of the ICJ: "[T]his principle, which is accepted by the general international law in the matter of arbitration, assumes particular force when the international tribunal is no longer an arbitral tribunal ... but is an institution which has been pre-established by an international instrument defining its jurisdiction and regulating its operation," and referred to in the *Nottebohm* case (Liechtenstein v. Guatemala), [1953] ICJ Reports 7, 119. See *Tadic*, para. 18.

General Court) in the 2005 decision in *Kadi*. The Court excluded the legality of resolutions of the Security Council from its jurisdiction. Unfortunately, such a question had instead to be considered a necessary premise to the legality of the EU regulation implementing it. Nonetheless, in its reasoning, the Court was not coherent enough to uphold completely its own view of the *hierarchy* under international law: surprisingly, it admitted its competence to scrutinize the acts of the Security Council in cases where rules of *jus cogens* are infringed. The milestone *Kadi* case offered a telling example of circumstances in which the interconnectedness of different orders and regimes is puzzling and cannot be addressed in a satisfactory manner by upholding a systemic view of some consistency without falling into unilateral and one-sided verdicts.

On the other hand, the subsequent decision of the ECJ also denied the interconnectedness of *orders* by assuming that, in a dualist sense, what the Court was entitled to do boils down to adjudicating rights in its own system and scrutinizing EU regulations by its own internal criteria, and such a scrutiny could not imply anything as to the legality of UNSC resolutions, nor any extension to that, in the separate "cycle" of the international order. Again, such reasoning adopts a formal reading of the case and ends up denying that the normative rationale of UNSC resolutions materially affects the issue at stake (and the case itself could never originate without them). In plain words, in the end, it made an argument for EU primary law to prevail over the obligations stemming from international law (thereby disregarding Article 103 UN). Beyond the virtuous defense of fundamental rights in the EU, the ECJ reasoning amounted to a dissimulated pronouncement about the primacy between two legal orders instead of a question of disagreement, an assessment about the infringement of fundamental rights in a supranational sphere where the two are interrelated. The two things are not compatible.

Courts are called upon to settle some cases that by their nature would not be generated unless two different legalities concur or are allegedly in conflict. Recent decades have shown that courts bear a higher responsibility in these circumstances, one that should exceed the limited view of "their own" legal system, although admittedly it would be technically preposterous to ask for them to judge from a standpoint that is not theirs.

An important example is the reasoning of the ECtHR in *Al-Dulimi*. Since Switzerland[64] had rejected Al-Dulimi's complaints and resolved to confiscate

[64] The Swiss Federal Tribunal (BGE 2A.783/784/785/2006, all of January 23, 2008) had maintained that it was not entitled to revise the legality of UNSC resolutions except in the event of violation of a *jus cogens* rule (as in the reasoning of the Court of First Instance of the

his assets, the Court decided that violation of Article 6 ECHR (access to justice) had taken place on behalf of the state, and that consequent responsibility fell on the state as a party to the Convention, regardless of the duty to implement sanctions from the Security Council, and even in the absence of any discretionary power on the part of the state. In the reasoning of the Court, judicial review was not granted either at the UN or in the domestic procedure. Denial of access to justice, even in pursuing the legitimate ends of peace and security, is deemed *disproportionate* to achieving those objectives.

The Court, in the same vein as earlier in *Al-Jedda*,[65] does not take a merely external attitude toward the normative corpus of the UN; instead, it assumes that it should be taken into consideration qua *normative* in its scope, meaning, and aims. Accordingly, its reasoning is not shielded in self-referential closure, but pursues a comprehensive assessment beyond the normative fabric of the European Convention alone. It states that apparently conflicting obligations from the UN Charter and the ECHR must be at their best harmonized and reconciled (Article 31(3)(c) of the Vienna Convention on the Law of Treaties).[66] But in fact, even beyond that, it transcended its *conventional* jurisdiction, designed under the legal positivist criteria of one's own rule of recognition. Admittedly, such a reasoning might have been facilitated (or this might be claimed by monist interpreters) by the fact that the ECtHR and the European Convention are themselves part of the international legal order as a whole, although as Paulus reminds us,[67] this is not any longer decisive, given the autonomy of many supranational bodies, their possible divergence, and the increasing "acoustic separation" among them.

The Court engages in a *proportionality* judgment; that is, a contextual evaluation between two divergent rules–principles (belonging in different domains), one that might exceed the strict limits of its own jurisdiction (such a judgment implies a revision of the legality of the Security Council resolution that other Courts being placed in the EU had considered themselves not competent to carry). Not far from such an attitude, even the reasoning of the Italian Constitutional Court in the case concerning the right of victims of war crimes to be allowed access to justice considers its responsibility as

EU in *Kadi*). After allowing Al-Dulimi more time for a further appeal to the Sanctions Committee (which was unsuccessful), the Tribunal concluded that Switzerland's behavior was legitimate and did not violate either domestic constitutional norms or Articles 6 and 13 of the ECHR.

65 ECtHR, *Al-Jedda v The United Kingdom*, Application no. 27021/08, July 7, 2011.

66 *Al-Dulimi*, para. 112.

67 Paulus, "National Courts."

justice-related, taking account of the normative weight brought about by the overall legality surfacing in its own case.

To conclude, bridging the gap that separates two or more orders requires deeper self-understanding and further insight into the purposes and meaning concerning the "grounds" of those laws, the mutual relation between institutions, and the founding ideals of the diverse orders in their relations. To tell the issue in Sen's words, the whole of composite outcomes is meant to be part of the Court's assessment – at least insofar as that is what is required within the remit of the issue to be solved.

One possible argument to justify this latter move – that is, a kind of "jurisdiction overstepping" – is that in such inter-legality circumstances, if courts have to live up to their judicial function and have to account for their justice-delivering task, they have to be *accountable* as regards their legal order, but they are *responsible* courts only in shouldering the entire normative complexity that affects the fate of the people in the issue before their authority.

Bibliography

Abbott, Edwin, *Flatland: A Romance of Many Dimensions* (London: Seeley and Co., 1884).

Abi-Saab, Georges, "Le règlement des différends à l'OMC et le droit international général," in Rufus Yerxa and Bruce Wilson (eds.), *Questions Clès dans le Domaine du Règlement des Différends de l'OMC: Les Dix Premières Années* (Geneva: Secrétariat de l'OMC, 2007), 7–11.

Acosta Arcarazo, Diego, *National versus the Foreigner in South America* (Cambridge: Cambridge University Press, 2018).

"Turning the Immigration Policy Paradox Upside Down? Populist Liberalism and Discursive Gaps in South America," (2015) 49 *International Migration Review* 659–696.

Acosta Arcarazo, Diego and Andrew Geddes, "Transnational Diffusion or Different Models? Regional Approaches to Migration Governance in the European Union and MERCOSUR," (2014) 16 *European Journal of Migration and Law* 19–44.

Adam, Stanislas and Peter Van Elsuwege, "Citizenship Rights and the Federal Balance between the European Union and Its Member States," (2012) 37 *European Law Review* 176–190.

Adepoju, Aderanti, "Fostering Free Movement of Persons in West Africa: Achievements, Constraints, and Prospects for Intraregional Migration," (2002) 40 *International Migration* 3–28.

"Migration Management in West Africa within the Context of ECOWAS Protocol on Free Movement of Persons and the Common Approach on Migration," in OECD (ed.), *Regional Challenges of West African Migration* (Paris: OECD Publishing, 2009), 17–47.

Adinolfi, Giovanna, "Il diritto non scritto nel sistema OMC," in Paolo Palchetti (ed.), *L'Incidenza del Diritto non Scritto sul Diritto Internazionale ed Europeo* (Naples: Editoriale Scientifica, 2016), 75–113.

Adler, Emanuel and Vincent Pouliot (eds.), *International Practices* (Cambridge: Cambridge University Press, 2011).

Akehurst, Michael, "Jurisdiction in International Law," (1972–1973) 46 *British Yearbook of International Law* 145–257.

Alston, Philip, "Does the Past Matter? On the Origins of Human Rights," (2013) 126 *Harvard Law Review* 2043–2081.

Alter, Karen J., "Agents or Trustees? International Courts in Their Political Context," (2008) 14 *European Journal of International Relations* 33–63.

Alvarez, José, "Beware: Boundary Crossings," in Tsvi Kahana and Anat Scolnicov (eds.), *Boundaries of State, Boundaries of Rights: Human Rights, Private Actors, and Positive Obligations* (Cambridge: Cambridge University Press, 2016), 43–93.

"The Return of the State," (2011) 20 *Minnesota Journal of International Law* 223–264.

Amaya, Amalia, "Exemplarism and Judicial Virtue," (2013) 25 *Law and Literature* 428–445.

"Legal Justification by Optimal Coherence," (2011) 24 *Ratio Juris* 304–329.

The Tapestry of Reason: An Inquiry into the Nature of Coherence and Its Role in Legal Argument (Oxford: Hart, 2015).

Amstutz, Marc, "In-Between Worlds: *Marleasing* and the Emergence of Interlegality in Legal Reasoning" (2005) 11 *European Law Journal* 766–784.

Amstutz, Marc and Vagios Karavas, "Weltrecht: Ein Derridasches Monster," in Graf-Peter Calliess, Andreas Fischer-Lescano, Dan Wielsch, and Peer Zumbansen (eds.), *Soziologische Jurisprudenz. Festschrift für Gunther Teubner zum 65. Geburtstag* (Berlin: Walter de Gruyter, 2009), 645–672.

Andreas, Peter, "Illicit Globalisation Myths and Misconceptions," in Valsamis Mitsilegas, Peter Alldridge, and Leonidis Cheliotis (eds.), *Globalisation, Criminal Law and Criminal Justice* (Oxford: Hart, 2015), 45–64.

Ankersmit, Laurens J. and Wessel W. Geursen, "Ruiz Zambrano: De Interne Situatie Voorbij," (2011) 4 *Asiel & Migrantenrecht* 156–164.

Applbaum, Arthur Isak, *Ethics for Adversaries: The Morality of Roles in Public and Professional Life* (Princeton, NJ: Princeton University Press, 1999).

Appleton, Arthur E., "PIL and IEL: Will Seal Deaths Resurrect the Dream of International Legal Coherence?" (2014) 9 *Questions of International Law* 5–18.

Aquinas, Thomas, *Quaestiones*, available at www.corpusthomisticum.org/sth2090.html

Treatise on the Virtues (Notre Dame, IN: University of Notre Dame Press, 1984, Oesterle trans.).

Arangio Ruiz, Gaetano, "International Law and Interindividual Law," in Janne Nijman and André Nollkaemper (eds.), *New Perspectives on the Divide between National and International Law* (Oxford: Oxford University Press, 2015), 15–51.

Arato, Julian, "Subsequent Practice in the Whaling Case and What the ICJ Implies about Treaty Interpretation in International Organizations," *EJILTalk!*, 31 March 2014.

Arcari, M. and S. Ninatti, Exploring Counter-Constitutionalism: The Backlash Effect of Constitutional Vocabulary of the European Court of Justice and the European Court of Human Rights, Workshop Draft Paper, July 2017.

Archibugi, Daniele and David Held, *Cosmopolitan Democracy: An Agenda for a New World Order* (Cambridge: Polity Press, 1995).

Arcuri, Allessandra and Sara Poli, What Price for the Community Enforcement of WTO Law? EUI Working Papers, Law, 2010/2011.

Arendt, Hannah, *Eichmann in Jerusalem: A Report on the Banality of Evil* (London: Penguin, 2006 [1962]).

On Revolution (London: Penguin, 1963).

Aristotle, *The Nicomachean Ethics* (Penguin: New York, 1976, Thomson trans.).

Politics, translated by Benjamin Jowett, available at classics.mit.edu/Aristotle/politics.3.three.html
The Politics (London: Penguin, 1962, Sinclair trans.).
Arnardóttir, Oddný Mjöll, "*Res Interpretata, Erga Omnes* Effect and the Role of the Margin of Appreciation in Giving Domestic Effect to the Judgments of the European Court of Human Rights," (2017) 28 *European Journal of International Law* 819–843.
Arraiza, José-Maria, "Good Neighbourliness as a Limit to Extraterritorial Citizenship: The Case of Hungary and Slovakia," in Dimitry Kochenov and Elena Basheska (eds.), *Good Neighbourliness in the European Legal Context* (Leiden: Martinus Nijhoff, 2015), 114–135.
Austin, John L., *How to Do Things with Words*, 2nd edn. (Oxford: Clarendon Press, 1962).
Austin, John, *The Province of Jurisprudence Determined* (Cambridge: Cambridge University Press, 1995 [1832]).
Azoulai, Loic, "Transfiguring European Citizenship: From Member State Territory to Union Territory," in Dimitry Kochenov (ed.), *EU Citizenship and Federalism: The Role of Rights* (Cambridge: Cambridge University Press, 2017), 178–203.
Baars, Grietje et al., "The Role of Law in Global Value Chains: A Research Manifesto," (2016) 4 *London Review of International Law* 57–79.
Babar, Zahra, "Free Mobility within the Gulf Cooperation Council," (2011) Center for International and Regional Studies Occasional Paper 8.
Backer, Larry Catá, "Are Supply Chains Transnational Legal Orders? What We Can Learn from the Rana Plaza Factory Building Collapse," (2016) 1 *UC Irvine Journal of International, Transnational and Comparative Law* 11–66.
"Economic Globalization and the Rise of Efficient Systems of Global Private Lawmaking: Wal-Mart as Global Legislator," (2007) 39 *University of Connecticut Law Review* 1739–1784.
"Theorizing Regulatory Governance within its Ecology: The Structure of Management in an Age of Globalization," (2018) 24 *Contemporary Politics* 607–630.
Baird, Rachel, "The Antarctic Treaty System and Japan's Scientific Whaling in the Southern Ocean – Is There an Obligation to Protect the Antarctic Marine Ecosystem?" (2008) 11 *Asia Pacific Journal of Environmental Law* 193–206.
Balkin, J. M., "Agreements with Hell and Other Objects of Our Faith," (1997) 65 *Fordham Law Review* 1703–1738.
"The Proliferation of Legal Truth," (2003) 26 *Harvard Journal of Law & Public Policy* 5–16.
Barral, Virginie and Pierre-Marie Dupuy, "Sustainable Development through Integration," in Jorge Vinuales (ed.), *The Rio Declaration on Environment and Development. A Commentary* (Oxford: Oxford University Press, 2015), 157–180.
Barroche, Julien, *Etat, Libéralisme et Christianisme – Critique de la Subsidiarité Européenne* (Paris: Dalloz, 2012).
Bartels, Lorand, "Applicable Law in WTO Dispute Settlement Proceedings," (2001) 35 *Journal of World Trade* 499.
Basch, Fernando et al., "La Efectividad del Sistema Interamericano de Protección de Derechos Humanos: Un Enfoque Cuantitativo sobre su Funcionamiento y sobre

el Cumplimento de sus Decisiones," (2010) 7 *Sur: Revista Internacional de Derechos Humanos* 9–36.

Battini, Stefano, *Amministrazioni senza Stato. Profili di Diritto Amministrativo Internazionale* (Milan: Giuffrè, 2003).

Baude, William and Ryan D. Doerfler, "Arguing with Friends," available at https://papers.ssrn.com/sol3/papers.cfm?abstract_id=2985032

Bellamy, Richard, *Political Constitutionalism: A Republican Defence of the Constitutionality of Democracy* (Cambridge: Cambridge University Press, 2007).

Benton, Lauren, *Law and Colonial Cultures: Legal Regimes in World History, 1400–1900* (Cambridge: Cambridge University Press, 2002).

Benvenisti, Eyal, *The Law of Global Governance* (The Hague: Hague Academy of International Law, 2014).

Berman, Paul Schiff, "Global Legal Pluralism," (2007) 80 *Southern California Law Review* 1155–1237.

"The Globalization of Jurisdiction," (2002) 151 *University of Pennsylvania Law Review* 311–545.

Global Legal Pluralism: A Jurisprudence of Law beyond Borders (Cambridge: Cambridge University Press, 2012).

Bernstein, Steven and Benjamin Cashore, "Can Non-State Global Governance be Legitimate? An Analytical Framework," (2007) 1 *Regulation & Governance* 347–371.

Bernstorff, Jochen von, *Der Glaube an das universal Recht: zur Völkerrechtstheorie Hans Kelsens und seiner Schüler* (Baden-Baden: Nomos, 2001).

Besson, Samantha, "The Authority of International Law: Lifting the State Veil," (2009) 31 *Sydney Law Review* 343–380.

"Community Interests in International Law: Whose Interests are They and How does One Identify Them?" in E. Benvenisti and G. Nolte (eds.), *Community Obligations in Contemporary International Law* (Oxford: Oxford University Press, 2018), 36–49.

"Community Interests in the Identification of International Law: With a Special Emphasis on Treaty Interpretation and Customary Law Identification," in Eyal Benvenisti and Georg Nolte (eds.), *Community Obligations in Contemporary International Law* (Oxford University Press, 2018), 50–69.

"Deliberative Demoi-cracy in the European Union. Towards the Deterritorialization of Democracy," in Samantha Besson and José Luis Marti (eds.), *Deliberative Democracy and Its Discontents* (Aldershot: Ashgate, 2006), 181–214.

"European Legal Pluralism after Kadi," (2009) 5 *European Constitutional Law Review* 237–264.

"The Extraterritoriality of the European Convention on Human Rights. Why Human Rights Depend on Jurisdiction and What Jurisdiction Amounts To," (2012) 25 *Leiden Journal of International Law* 857–884.

"Fédéralisme et droits de l'homme: une introduction thématique," in Samantha Besson and Eva Maria Belser (eds.), *La Convention Européenne des Droits de l'Homme et les Cantons* (Zurich: Schulthess, 2014), 7–39.

"Human Rights and Democracy in a Global Context – Decoupling and Recoupling," (2011) 4 *Ethics and Global Politics* 19–50.

"Human Rights as Transnational Constitutional Law," in Anthony Lang and Antje Wiener (eds.), *Handbook on Global Constitutionalism* (Cheltenham: Edward Elgar, 2017), 234–247.

"Individual and State Liability for an International Organization's Responsibility – The Challenge of Fairness Unveiled," (2017) 6 *Italian Journal of Legal Philosophy* 51–78.

"International Law's Relative Authority, Review of Nicole Roughan's Authorities. Conflicts, Cooperation and Transnational Legal Theory," (2015) 6 *Jurisprudence* 169–176.

"L'extra-territorialité des droits de l'homme internationaux: juridictions concurrentes, obligations conjointes et responsabilités partagées," in Pierre d'Argent (ed.), *Droit des Frontières Internationales* (Paris: Pedone, 2016).

"Law Beyond the State: A Reply to Liam Murphy," (2017) 28 *European Journal of International Law*, 233–240.

"Shared Responsibilities under the ECHR: Concurrent Jurisdictions, Duties and Responsibilities," in J. Motoc et al. (eds.), *The ECHR and General International Law* (Oxford: Oxford University Press, 2018).

"Sovereignty," in Rüdiger Wolfrum (eds.), *Max Planck Encyclopedia of Public International Law*, Vol. 9 (Oxford: Oxford University Press, 2012) 366–391.

"State Consent and Disagreement in International Law-Making: Dissolving the Paradox," (2016) 29 *Leiden Journal of International Law* 289–316.

"Subsidiarity in International Human Rights Law – What is Subsidiary about Human Rights?" (2016) 61 *American Journal of Jurisprudence* 69–107.

"The Truth about Legal Pluralism, Review of Nico Krisch's Beyond Constitutionalism: The Pluralist Structure of Postnational Law," (2012) *European Constitutional Law Review* 354–361.

"Theorizing the Sources of International Law," in Samantha Besson and John Tasioulas (eds.), *The Philosophy of International Law* (Oxford: Oxford University Press, 2010), 164–185.

Bethlehem, Daniel, "The End of Geography: The Changing Nature of the International System and the Challenge to International Law," (2014) 25 *European Journal of International Law* 9–24.

Bettelheim, Bruno, *A Good Enough Parent* (New York: Vintage, 1988).

Bianchi, Andrea, "Reply to Professor Maier," in Karl Matthias Meessen (ed.), *Extraterritorial Jurisdiction in Theory and Practice* (The Hague: Kluwer, 1996), 74–102.

Blake, Judith and Kingsley Davis, "Norms, Values, and Sanctions," in Robert E. L. Faris (ed.), *Handbook of Modern Sociology* (Chicago: Rand-McNally, 1964), 456–484.

Bleckmann, Albert, "The Personal Jurisdiction of the European Community," (1980) 17 *Common Market Law Review* 467–486.

Boisson de Chazournes, Laurence, "Plurality in the Fabric of International Courts and Tribunals: The Threads of a Managerial Approach," (2017) 28 *European Journal of International Law* 13–72.

Boisson de Chazournes, Laurence and Philippe Sands (eds.), *International Law, The International Court of Justice and Nuclear Weapons* (Cambridge: Cambridge University Press, 1999).

Bos, Maarten, "Preliminary Report on the Extraterritorial Jurisdiction of States," (1993) 65 *Yearbook of the International Law Institute* 14.

Bosniak, Linda, "Citizenship Denationalized," (2000) 7 *Indiana Journal of Global Legal Studies* 447–510.

"Persons and Citizens in Constitutional Thought," (2010) 8 *International Journal of Constitutional Law* 9–29.

Bourdieu, Pierre, "The Force of Law: Toward a Sociology of the Juridical Field," (1987) 38 *Hastings Law Journal* 805–853.

Boxer, Karin E., *Rethinking Responsibility* (Oxford: Oxford University Press, 2013).

Bredbenner, Candice L., *A Nationality of Her Own: Women, Marriage, and the Law of Citizenship* (Berkeley: University of California Press, 2018).

Brölmann, Catherine, "Deterritorializing International Law: Moving Away from the Divide between National and International Law," in Janna Nijman and André Nollkaemper (eds.), *New Perspectives on the Divide between National and International Law* (Oxford: Oxford University Press, 2007), 84–109.

Bronckers, Marco, "From 'Direct Effect' to 'Muted Dialogue': Recent Developments in the European Courts' Case Law on the WTO and Beyond," (2008) 11 *Journal of International Economic Law* 885.

Brown, Chester, *A Common Law of International Adjudication* (Oxford: Oxford University Press, 2007).

Brubaker, Rogers, *Citizenship and Nationhood in France and Germany* (Cambridge, MA: Harvard University Press, 1992).

Brunkhorst, Hauke, *Critical Theory of Legal Revolutions: Evolutionary Perspectives* (London: Bloomsbury, 2014).

"Dialectical Snares: Human Rights and Democracy in the World Society," (2009) 2 *Ethics and Global Politics* 219–239.

Brunnée, Jutta and Stephen Toope, *Legitimacy and Legality in International Law: An Interactional Account* (Cambridge: Cambridge University Press, 2010).

Buck-Morss, Susan, *Hegel, Haiti, and Universal History* (Pittsburgh, PA: University of Pittsburgh Press, 2009).

Buhmann, Karin, "Business and Human Rights: Understanding the UN Guiding Principles from the Perspective of Transnational Business Governance Interactions," (2015) 6 *Transnational Legal Theory* 399–434.

Bull, Hedley, *The Anarchical Society* (Basingstoke: Palgrave, 1977).

Burton, Stephen, *Judging in Good Faith* (Cambridge: Cambridge University Press, 1992).

Buxbaum, Hannah, "Territory, Territoriality and the Resolution of Jurisdictional Conflict," (2009) 57 *American Journal of Comparative Law* 631–675.

Caddell, Richard, "'Only Connect'? Regime Interaction and Global Biodiversity Conservation," in Michael Bowman, Peter Davies, and Edward Goodwin (eds.), *Research Handbook on Biodiversity and Law* (Cheltenham: Edward Elgar, 2016), 443–446.

Calliess, Gralf-Peter and Peer Zumbansen, *Rough Consensus and Running Code: A Theory of Transnational Private Law* (Oxford: Hart, 2010).

Cannizzaro, Enzo, "Margin of Appreciation and Reasonableness in the ICJ's Decision in the Whaling Case," in Pierre d'Argent, Beatrice Bonafé, and Jean Combacau, (eds.), *Les Limites du Droit International. Essais en l'Honneur de Joe Verhoeven* (Brussels: Bruylant, 2014), 449–455.

Cardesa-Salzmann, Antonio, "Constitutionalizing Secondary Rules in Global Environmental Regimes: Non-Compliance Procedures and the Enforcement of Multilateral Environmental Agreements," (2012) 24 *Journal of Environmental Law* 103–132.
Cardozo, Benjamin N., *The Nature of the Judicial Process* (New Haven, CT: Yale University Press, 1991 [1921]).
Carens, Joseph, "Aliens and Citizens: The Case for Open Borders," (1987) 49 *Review of Politics* 251–273.
The Ethics of Immigration (Oxford: Oxford University Press, 2013).
Carrara, Francesco, "Delitti commessi all'estero," in *Opuscoli di Diritto Criminale*, 2nd edn. (Lucca: Tipografia Giusti, 1870).
Carta, Andrea and Laurens Ankersmit, "AG Wathelet in C-284/16 Achmea: Saving ISDS?" available at https://europeanlawblog.eu/tag/ag-wathelet-in-c-28416-achmea.
Cassese, Antonio, Paola Gaeta, and Salvatore Zappalà (eds.), *The Human Dimension of International Law: Selected Papers of Antonio Cassese* (Oxford: Oxford University Press, 2012).
Cassese, Sabino, "Administrative Law without the State – The Challenge of Global Regulation," (2005) 37 *New York University Journal of International Law and Politics* 663–694
The Global Polity. Global Dimensions of Democracy and the Rule of Law (Sevilla: Global Law Press, 2012).
I Tribunali di Babele (Roma: Donzelli, 2009)
Il Diritto Globale. Giustizia e Democrazia Oltre lo Stato (Torino: Einaudi, 2009).
"Lo spazio giuridico globale," (2002) 52 *Rivista trimestrale di diritto pubblico* 323–339.
"Nel labirinto delle globalizzazioni," (2007) 4 *Rivista Trimestrale di Diritto Pubblico* 921–930
"Shrimps, Turtles and Procedures: Global Standards for National Administrative Procedure," (2005) 68 *Law & Contemporary Problems* 109–126.
Castrucci, Emanuele, *On the Idea of Potency: Juridical and Theological Roots of the Western Cultural Tradition* (Edinburgh: Edinburgh University Press, 2016).
Chamberlain, Lesley, *The Philosophy Steamer: Lenin and the Exile of the Intelligentsia* (London: Atlantic Books, 2006).
Chan, Johannes M. M., "The right to a Nationality As a Human Right. The Current Trend towards Recognition," (1991) 12 *Human Rights Law Journal* 1–14.
Chanock, Martin, *Law, Custom, and Social Order: The Colonial Experience in Malawi and Zambia* (Cambridge: Cambridge University Press, 1985).
Chayes, Abram and Antionia Handler Chayes, *The New Sovereignty: Compliance and International Regulatory Agreements* (Cambridge, MA: Harvard University Press, 1995).
Chehtman, Alejandro, *Philosophical Foundations of Extraterritorial Punishment* (Oxford: Oxford University Press, 2010).
Chimni, B.S., *International Law and World Order: A Critique of Contemporary Approaches*, 2nd edn. (Cambridge: Cambridge University Press, 2017).
Chiti, Edoardo, "Decentralized Implementation: European Agencies," in Robert Schütze and Takis Tridimas (eds.), *Oxford Principles of European Union Law* (Oxford: Oxford University Press, 2018), 748–776.
L'Amministrazione Militare (Milan: Giuffrè, 2007).

"The European Security and Defense Administration within the Context of the Global Legal Space," (2007) *NYC School of Law Jean Monnet Working Paper* 7.

Chiti, Edoardo and Ramses A. Wessel, "The Emergence of International Agencies in the Global Administrative Space," in Richard Collins and Nigel D. White (eds.), *International Organizations and the Idea of Autonomy* (London: Routledge, 2011), 142–159.

Christiano, Thomas, "A Democratic Theory of Territory and Some Puzzles about Global Democracy," (2006) 37 *Journal of Social Philosophy* 81–107.

"Democratic Legitimacy and International Institutions," in Samantha Besson and John Tasioulas (eds.), *The Philosophy of International Law* (Oxford: Oxford University Press, 2010), 119–137.

Claes, Monica and Maartje de Visser, "Are You Networked Yet? On Dialogues in European Judicial Networks," (2012) 8 *Utrecht Law Review* 100–114.

Clausen, Jens, Michael Keil, and Martin Jungwirth, "The State of EMAS in the EU. Eco-Management as a Tool for Sustainable Development," (2002) Literature Study (for EMAS II Conference, 26–27 June 2002, Brussels, Belgium).

Cohen, Gerald, "Beliefs and Rôles," (1966–67) 67 *Proceedings of the Aristotelian Society* 17–34.

Cohen, Jean, *Globalization and Sovereignty: Rethinking Legality, Legitimacy and Constitutionalism* (Cambridge: Cambridge University Press, 2012).

Cohen, Michael, James March, and Johan Olsen, "A Garbage Can Model of Organizational Choice," (1972) 17 *Administrative Science Quarterly* 1–25.

Cohen, Stanley, "Crime and Politics: Spot the Difference," (1996) 47 *British Journal of Sociology* 1–21.

Colangelo, Anthony, "Spatial Legality," (2012) 107 *Northwestern University Law Review* 69–126.

Confucius, *The Analects* (London: Penguin, 1979, Lau trans.).

Cortese, Ennio, *La Norma Giuridica. Spunti Teorici nel Diritto Comune Classico* (Milan: Giuffrè, 1962).

Cotterrell, Roger, "The Concept of Crime and Transnational Networks of Community," in Valsamis Mitsilegas, Peter Alldridge, and Leonidis Cheliotis (eds.), *Globalisation, Criminal Law and Criminal Justice* (Oxford: Hart, 2015), 7–24.

"Comparative Law and Legal Culture," in Reinhard Zimmermann and Mathias Reimann (eds.), *Oxford Handbook of Comparative Law* (Oxford: Oxford University Press, 2008), 709–738.

"Does Global Legal Pluralism Need a Concept of Law?" in Upendra Baxi, Christopher McCrudden, and Abdul Paliwala (eds.), *Law's Ethical, Global and Theoretical Contexts. Essays in Honour of William Twining* (Cambridge: Cambridge University Press, 2015), 303–319.

Living Law: Studies in Legal and Social Theory (Farnham: Ashgate Publishing, 2008).

Cottier, Thomas, "International Trade Law: The Impact of Justiciability and Separation of Powers in EC Law," (2009) 5 *European Constitutional Law Review* 307.

Cover, Robert, "The Supreme Court 1982 Term. Foreword: Nomos and Narrative," (1983) 97 *Harvard Law Review* 4–68.

Craig, Paul, "Global Networks and Shared Administration," in Sabino Cassese (ed.), *Research Handbook on Global Administrative Law* (Cheltenham: Edward Elgar, 2016), 153–173.

"The Nature of the Community: Integration, Democracy, and Legitimacy," in Paul Craig and Gráinne de Búrca (eds.), *The Evolution of EU Law* (Oxford: Oxford University Press, 1999), 3.

Crawford, James, *Brownlie's Principles of International Law*, 8th edn. (Oxford: Oxford University Press, 2012).

Cremona, Marise, "Member States as Trustees of the Union Interest: Participating in International Agreements on Behalf of the European Union," in Anthony Arnull, Catherine Barnard, Michael Dougan, and Eleanor Spaventa (eds.), *A Constitutional Order of States? Essays in Honour of Alan Dashwood* (Oxford: Hart, 2011), 435–457.

Culver, Keith and Giudice, Michael, *Legality's Borders: An Essay in General Jurisprudence* (Oxford: Oxford University Press, 2010).

Curtin, Deirdre, "Civil Society and the European Union: Opening Spaces for Deliberative democracy," (1999) *Collected Courses of the Academy of European Law* 185.

Dahl, Robert A., "Federalism and the Democratic Process," in J. R. Pennock and J. W. Chapman (eds.), *Nomos XXV: Liberal Democracy* (New York: New York University Press, 1983), 95–108.

Dang, Tum Lam, "Relation associative: les États Fédérés de Micronésie: les spécificités de l'association," in Jean-Yves Faberon et al. (eds.), *Destins des Collectivités Politiques d'Océanie*, Vol. 1, (Marseille: Presses Universitaires d'Aix-Marseille, 2011), 373–376.

Davies, Gareth T., "The Humiliation of the State as a Constitutional Tactic," in Fabian Amtenbrink and Peter van den Berg (eds.), *The Constitutional Integrity of the European Union* (The Hague: TMC Asser Press, 2010), 147–174.

"'Any Place I Hang My Hat?'" (2005) 11 *European Law Journal* 43–56.

de Búrca, Gráinne, "The ECJ and the International Legal Order: A Re-Evaluation," in Gráinne de Búrca and Joseph H. H. Weiler (eds.), *The Worlds of European Constitutionalism* (Cambridge: Cambridge University Press, 2012), 105–149.

"The European Court of Justice and the International Legal Order after *Kadi*," (2010) 51 *Harvard International Law Journal* 1.

de Groot, Gerard-René, "Overwegingen over de *Janko Rottman* – Beslissing van het Europese Hof van Justitie," (2010) 5–6 *Asiel & Migrantenrecht* 293–300.

"Towards a European Nationality Law," (2004) 8 *Electronic Journal of Comparative Law*.

de Sousa Santos, Boaventura, "Beyond Neoliberal Governance: The World Social Forum as Subaltern Cosmopolitan Politics and Legality," in Boaventura de Sousa Santos and César A. Rodríguez-Garavito (eds.), *Law and Globalization from Below* (Cambridge: Cambridge University Press, 2005), 29–63.

"Law: A Map of Misreading. Toward a Postmodern Conception of Law," (1987) 14 *Journal of Law and Society* 279–302.

Toward a New Common Sense: Law, Science and Politics in the Paradigmatic Transition (London: Routledge, 1995).

Toward a New Legal Common Sense, 2nd edn. (London: Butterworths, 2002).

de Wet, Erika, "Judicial Challenges to the Security Council's Use of Sanctions," in Jeremy Farrall and Hillary Charlesworth (eds.), *Strengthening the Rule of Law through the UN Security Council* (London: Routledge, 2016), 193–206.

del Mar, Maksymilian, "System Values and Understanding Legal Language," (2008) 21 *Leiden Journal of International Law* 29–61.

del Ponte, Carla and Chuck Sudetic, *Mevrouw de Aanklager* (Amsterdam: Bezige Bij, 2008, Van der Waa trans.).

del Vecchio, Giorgio, "On the Statuality of Law," (1937) 19 *Journal of Comparative Legislation and International Law* 1–20.

Delwaide, Jacobus, "The Return of the State?" (2011) 19 *European Review* 69–91.

Deva, Surya and David Bilchitz (eds.), *Human Rights Obligations of Business: Beyond the Corporate Responsibility to Respect?* (Cambridge: Cambridge University Press, 2013).

Dewey, John, "The Quest for Certainty," reproduced as *John Dewey, The Later Works, 1925–1953*, Vol. 4 (Carbondale: Southern Illinois University Press, 1988, Boydston ed.).

Dickson, Julie, "Towards a Theory of European Union Legal Systems," in Julie Dickson and Pavlos Eleftheriadis (eds.), *Philosophical Foundations of European Union Law* (Oxford: Oxford University Press, 2012), 25–53.

Dimitrov, Ivaylo, "Digesting the AG Wathelet Opinion in Case C-284/16 *Slowakische Republik v Achmea BV*. Is It a Trap?" available at http://arbitrationblog.kluwerarbitration.com/2017/10/07/digesting-ag-wathelet-opinion-case-c-28416-slowakische-republik-v-achmea-bv-trap.

Dimopoulos, Angelos, *EU Foreign Investment Law* (Oxford: Oxford University Press, 2011).

Dothan, Shai, "How International Courts Enhance Their Legitimacy," (2013) 14 *Theoretical Inquiries in Law* 455–478.

Downie, R. S., *Roles and Values: An Introduction to Social Ethics* (London: Methuen and Co., 1971).

Driessen, Bart, "Interinstitutional Conventions and Institutional Balance," (2008) 33 *European Law Review* 550.

Dryzek, John and Simon Niemeyer, "Discursive Representation," (2008) 102 *American Political Science Review* 481–493.

Dugard, John, "South Africa's Independent Homelands: An Exercise in Denationalization," (1980) 10 *Denver Journal of International Law and Policy* 11–36.

Dumont, Louis, *Homo Aequalis I. Genèse et Épanouissement de l'Idéologie Économique*, 2nd edn. (Paris: Gallimard, 1985).

Dunoff, Jeffrey L., "A New Approach to Regime Interaction," in Margaret A. Young (ed.), *Regime Interaction in International Law: Facing Fragmentation* (Cambridge: Cambridge University Press, 2012), 136–174.

Dunoff, Jeffrey L. and Joel P. Trachtman (eds.), *Ruling the World? Constitutionalism, International Law, and Global Governance* (Cambridge: Cambridge University Press, 2009).

Duve, Thomas, "Was ist 'Multinormativität'? – Einführende Bemerkungen," (2017) 25 *Rechtsgeschichte – Legal History* 88–101.

Dworkin, Ronald, "A New Philosophy for International Law," (2013) 41 *Philosophy and Public Affairs* 2–30.

Law's Empire (London: Fontana, 1986).

Taking Rights Seriously (Cambridge, MA: Harvard University Press, 1978).

Dyer, L., "Anglo-Saxon Citizenship: A Proposition by Professor Dicey Looking to This End," (1897) 3 *The Barrister* 107–110.

Eckert, Julia, "What is the Context of 'Law in Context'?" in Sean Patrick Dolan and Lukas Heckendorn Urscheler (eds.), *Concepts of Law: Comparative, Jurisprudential, and Social Science Perspectives* (London: Routledge, 2014), 225–236.

Eckes, Christina, *EU Counter-Terrorist Policies and Fundamental Rights: The Case of Individual Sanctions* (Oxford: Oxford University Press, 2009).

Edward, David, "National Courts: The Powerhouse of Community Law," (2002–2003) 5 *Cambridge Yearbook of European Legal Studies* 1–13.

Eeckhout, Piet, *EU External Relations Law*, 2nd edn. (Oxford: Oxford University Press, 2011).

Ehrlich, Eugen, *Grundlegung der Soziologie des Rechts, 4. Aufl.* (Berlin: Duncker & Humblot, (1989 [1913]).

"Montesquieu and Sociological Jurisprudence," (1916) 26 *Harvard Law Review* 582–600.

Ekins, Richard, "Judicial Supremacy and the Rule of Law," (2003) 119 *Law Quarterly Review* 127–152.

Elholm, Thomas and Renaud Colson, "The Symbolic Purpose of EU Criminal Law," in Renaud Colson and Stewart Field (eds.), *EU Criminal Justice and the Challenges of Diversity. Legal Cultures in the Area of Freedom, Security and justice* (Cambridge: Cambridge University Press, 2016), 48–64.

Elias, Norbert, *Über den Prozeß der Zivilisation, Band 2* (Frankfurt am Main: Suhrkamp, 1976 [1938]).

Eller, Klaas H., "Private Governance of Global Value Chains from Within: Lessons from and for Transnational Law," (2017) 8 *Transnational Legal Theory* 296–329.

Ellickson, Robert C., *Order without Law: How Neighbors Settle Disputes* (Cambridge, MA: Harvard University Press, 1991).

Endicott, Timothy, "The Logic of Freedom and Power," in Samantha Besson and John Tasioulas (eds.), *The Philosophy of International Law* (Oxford: Oxford University Press, 2010), 245–260.

Engle-Merry, Sally, "From Law and Colonialism to Law and Globalization," (2003) 28 *Law and Social Inquiry* 569–590.

"Legal Pluralism," (1988) 22 *Law and Society Review* 869–896.

Eser, Albin, "Book Review: Comparative Concepts of Criminal Law," (2016) 23 *Maastricht Journal of European and Comparative Law* 375–382.

"Grundlagen und Grenzen "stellvertretender Strafrechtspflege," (§ 7 Abs. 2 Nr. 2 StGB) – Zur Problematik der "identischer Tatnorm" bei Auslandstaten, insbesondere bei Amnestierungen am Tatort," (1993) *Juristenzeitung* 875.

Eser, Albin and Brigitte Heilmann (eds.), *Comparative Criminal Law: Development, Aims, Methods* (Munich and Oxford: Beck-Hart-Nomos, 2017).

Eser, Albin, Otto Lagodny, Christopher L. Blakesley (eds.), *The Individual as Subject of International Cooperation in Criminal Matters* (Baden-Baden: Nomos, 2002).

Esty, Daniel C., "The World Trade Organization's Legitimacy Crisis," (2002) 1 *World Trade Review* 7.

Evans, Andrew, "Nationality Law and European Integration," (1991) 16 *European Law Review* 190–215.

Everling, Ulrich, "The European Union as a Federal Association of States and Citizens," in Armin von Bogdandy and Jürgen Bast (eds.), *Principles of European Constitutional Law* (Oxford: Hart, 2006).

Fabbrini, Federico, "The Political Side of EU Citizenship in the Context of EU Federalism," in Dimitry Kochenov (ed.), *EU Citizenship and Federalism: The Role of Rights* (Cambridge: Cambridge University Press, 2017), 271–293.

Fahrmeir, Andreas F., "Nineteenth-Century German Citizenships: A Reconsideration," (1997) 40 *The Historical Journal* 721–752.

Fischer-Lescano, Andreas and Gunther Teubner, *Regime-Kollisionen: Zur Fragmentierung des globalen Rechts* (Frankfurt am Main: Surhkamp, 2006).

"Regime-Collisions: The Vain Search for Legal Unity in the Fragmentation of Global Law," (2004) 25 *Michigan Journal of International Law* 999–1046.

Fitzmaurice, Andrew, *Sovereignty, Property and Empire, 1500–2000* (Cambridge: Cambridge University Press, 2014).

Fitzmaurice, Malgosia and Dai, Tamada (eds.), *Whaling in the Antarctic: Significance and Implications of the ICJ Judgment* (Leiden: Martinus Nijhoff, 2014).

Fletcher, George, *Basic Concepts of Criminal Law* (Oxford: Oxford University Press, 1998).

Fossum, John E. and Agustin J. Menéndez, *The Constitution's Gift: A Constitutional Theory for a Democratic European Union* (Lanham, MD: Rowman & Littlefield, 2011).

Francq, Stephanie, "The Scope of Secondary Community Law in the Light of the Methods of Private International Law – Or the Other Way Around?" (2006) 8 *Yearbook of Private International Law* 333–374.

Frankfurter, Felix, *The Case of Sacco and Vanzetti: A Critical Analysis for Lawyers and Laymen* (New York: Little, Brown & Co., 1961 [1927]).

Freestone, David, "Responsibilities and Obligations of States Sponsoring Persons and Entities with Respect to Activities in the Area," (2011) 105 *American Journal of International Law* 755–760.

French, Duncan, "From the Depths: Rich Pickings of Principles of Sustainable Development and General International Law on the Ocean Floor – The Seabed Disputes Chamber's 2011 Advisory Opinion," (2011) 26 *International Journal of Marine and Coastal Law* 525–568.

Friedman, Thomas L., *The World Is Flat: The Globalized World in the Twenty-First Century* (New York: Penguin, 2006).

Frison-Roche, Marie-Anne, "Penser le monde à partir de la notion de 'donnée'," in Marie Anne Frison-Roche (ed.), *Internet, Espace d'Interrégulation* (Paris: Dalloz, 2016), 7–16.

Frydman, Benoit, "Comment penser le droit global?" in Jean-Yves Chérot and Benoit Frydman (eds.), *La Science du Droit dans la Globalisation* (Brussels: Bruylant, 2012), 17–48.

Fuller, Lon L., *Anatomy of the Law* (New York: Praeger, 1968).

The Morality of Law, 2nd edn. (New Haven, CT: Yale University Press, 1969).

"On Legal Education," reproduced in Kenneth I. Winston (ed.), *The Principles of Social Order: Selected Essays of Lon L. Fuller* (Oxford: Hart, 2001), 293–303.

"Positivism and Fidelity to Law – A Reply to Professor Hart," (1958) 71 *Harvard Law Review* 630–672.

Gadamer, Hans-Georg, *Truth and Method*, 2nd edn. (New York: Continuum, 1988).

Gaius, *Institutiones* (London: John W. Parker & Son, 1859, Collett Sanders trans.).

Gallant, Kenneth, *The Principle of Legality in International and Comparative Criminal Law* (Cambridge: Cambridge University Press, 2009).
Gambaro, Antonio, "Western Legal Tradition," in Peter Newman (ed.), *The New Palgrave: A Dictionary of Economics and the Law* (New York: Groves Dictionaries Inc., 1998), 687.
Gattinara, G., "Consistnt Interpretations of WTO Rulings in the EU Legal Order," in Enzo Cannizzaro, Paolo Palchetti, and Ramses Wessel (eds.), *International Law As Law of the European Union* (Leiden: Martinus Nijhoff), 2012), 269.
Gautier, Philippe, "Le vertus pratiques des obligations générales relatives à l'environnement dans la Convention des Nations Unies sur le droit de la mer," in Nerina Boschiero, Cesare Pitea, Chiara Ragni, and Tullio Scovazzi (eds.), *International Courts and the Development of International Law* (Dordrecht: Springer, 2013), 365–382.
George, Robert P., *Making Men Moral: Civil Liberties and Public Morality* (Oxford: Clarendon Press, 1993).
Gibney, Matthew, "The Rights of Non-Citizens in Political Thought," in Caroline Sawyer and Brad K. Blitz (eds.), *Statelessness in the European Union* (Cambridge: Cambridge University Press, 2011), 41–68.
Gogarty, Brendan, "Conceptions and (Mis)Conceptions of Science in International Treaties: The ICJ Whaling Case in Context," (2015) 62 *Yearbook of Polar Law* 607–622.
Gogarty, Lawrence, "The ICJ Whaling Case: Missed Opportunity to Advance the Rule of Law in Resolving Science-related Disputes in Global Commons?" (2017) 77 *Zeitschrift für auslandisches öffentliches Recht und Völkerrecht* 161–197.
Goldsmith, Jack and Tim Wu, *Who Controls the Internet? Illusions of a Borderless World* (Oxford: Oxford University Press, 2006).
Gongora-Mera, Manuel, *Inter-American Judicial Constitutionalism: On the Constitutional Rank of Human Rights Treaties in Latin America through National and Inter-American Adjudication* (San José: Inter-American Institute of Human Rights, 2011).
Gordley, James, "Is Comparative Law a Distinct Discipline?" (1998) 46 *American Journal of Comparative Law* 607–615.
Grandmaison, Olivier, "The Exception and the Rule: On French Colonial Law," (2006) 53 *Diogenes* 34–53.
Griffiths, John, "Legal Pluralism," in James David Wright (ed.), *International Encyclopedia of the Social & Behavioral Sciences*, Vol. 13, 2nd edn. (Amsterdam: Elsevier, 2015), 757–761.
Grimm, Dieter, *Constitutionalism: Past, Present, and Future* (Oxford: Oxford University Press, 2016).
Grossi, Paolo, *L'Ordine Giuridico Medievale* (Bari: Laterza, 2000).
Grotius, Hugo, *The Law of War and Peace* (Oxford: Clarendon, 1925 [1625] Kelsey trans.).
Guerrero-Peniche, Juan, "La opinión consultiva del Tribunal Internacional del Derecho del Mar: Aspectos relativos a la determinación del vínculo efectivo entre los Estados y las personas jurídicas a las que patrocinan para llevar a cabo actividades en la Zona," (2012) 5 *Anuario Colombiano de Derecho Internacional* 153–218.

Guèvremont, Véronique, "Traités multilatèraux: nouvelles perspectives relatives à l'articulation," in Vincent Tomkiewicz (ed.), *Les Sources et les Normes dans le Droit de l'OMC* (Paris: Pedone, 2012), 27.

Habermas, Jürgen, "The Constitutionalization of International Law and the Legitimation Problems of a Constitution for World Society," (2008) 15 *Constellations* 444–455.

Between Facts and Norms (Cambridge, MA: MIT Press, 1996, Rehg trans.).

A Theory of Communicative Action (Boston, MA: Beacon Press, 1987, McCarthy trans.).

Zwischen Naturalismus und Religion (Frankfurt: Suhrkamp, 2005).

Hafner, Gerhard, "Pros and Cons Ensuing from Fragmentation of International Law," (2004) 25 *Michigan Journal of International Law* 849–864.

"Risks Ensuing from the Fragmentation of International Law," in *Official Records of the General Assembly*, 566 session, Supplement no. 10, 321 (UN Doc A/55/10).

Hage, Jaap, "Law and Coherence," (2004) 17 *Ratio Juris* 87–105.

Hale, Brenda, "What's the Point of Human Rights?" *Warwick Law Lecture* 2013, 28 November 2013.

Hallevy, Gabriel, A *Modern Treatise on the Principle of Legality in Criminal Law*, (Berlin-Heidelberg: Springer, 2010).

Handl, Gunther, "Extra-Territoriality and Transnational Legal Authority," in Gunther Handl, Joachim Zekoll, and Peer Zumbansen (eds.), *Beyond Territoriality: Transnational Legal Authority in an Age of Globalization* (Leiden: Brill, 2012), 3–12.

"Responsibilities and Obligations of States Sponsoring Persons and Entities with Respect to Activities in the Area: The International Tribunal of the Law of the Sea's Recent Contribution to International Environmental Law," (2011) 20 *Review of European, Comparative and International Environment Law* 208–2013.

Harpaz, Yossi, "Compensatory Citizenship: Dual Nationality as a Strategy of Global Upward Mobility," (2018) 36 *Journal of Ethnic and Migration Studies* 1–20.

Hart, H. L. A., *The Concept of Law* (Oxford: Clarendon, 1994).

"Positivism and the Separation of Law and Morals," (1958) 71 *Harvard Law Review* 593–629.

Punishment and Responsibility (Oxford: Clarendon, 1968).

Held, David, *Cosmopolitanism: Ideals and Realities* (Cambridge: Polity, 2010).

Heller, Kevin Jon and Marcus Dubber (eds.), *The Handbook of Comparative Criminal Law* (Stanford, CA: Stanford University Press, 2011).

Henckels, C., "GMOs in the WTO: A Critique of the Panel's Reasoning in EC–Biotech," (2006) 12 *Melbourne Journal of International Law* 278.

Henkin, Louis, *How Nations Behave* (New York: Praeger, 1968).

Hernandez, Angel, "El principio de integración de los aspectos económicos, sociales y medioambientales del desarrollo sostenibile," (2012) 64 *Revista Española de Derecho Internacional* 133–161.

Hernandez, Gleider I., "A Reluctant Guardian: The International Court of Justice and the Concept of International Community," (2013) 83 *British Yearbook of International Law* 13–60.

Hinarejos, Alicia, "Extending Citizenship and the Scope of EU Law," (2011) 70 *Cambridge Law Journal* 309–312.

Hindelang, Steffen, "The Autonomy of the European Legal Order: EU Constitutional Limits to Investor–State Arbitration on the Basis of Future EU Investment-related Agreements," (2013) 4 *European Yearbook of International Economic Law* 187–198.
Hobbes, Thomas, *The Elements of Law* (Oxford: Oxford University Press, 1994).
"Of the Laws of Nature," in *De Cive* (1642), available at unilibrary.com.
Leviathan (London: Penguin, 1981, MacPherson ed.).
Leviathan, 3 vols. (Oxford: Clarendon, 2012, Malcolm ed.).
Hoekema, André, "European Legal Encounters between Minority and Majority Culture: Cases of Interlegality," (2005) 51 *Journal of Legal Pluralism & Unofficial Law* 1–55.
Hoffmann, Leonard H., "Judicial Studies Board Annual Lecture," 19 March 2009, available at www.brandeis.edu/ethics/pdfs/internationaljustice/biij/BIIJ2013/hoffmann.pdf
Hoffmann, Stefan-Ludwig, "Human Rights and History," (2016) 232 *Past and Present* 279–310.
Hogg, Peter W. and Allison A. Bushell, "The Charter Dialogue between Courts and Legislatures (or Perhaps the Charter of Rights Isn't Such a Bad Thing After All)," (1997) 35 *Osgoode Hall Law Journal* 75–124.
Honohan, Iseult, *Civic Republicanism* (London: Routledge, 2002).
Hovell, Devika, *The Power of Process: The Value of Due process in Security Council Sanctions Decision-Making* (Oxford: Oxford University Press, 2016).
Howse, Robert, "Democracy, Science and Free Trade: Risk Regulation on Trial at the World Trade Organization," (2000) 98 *Michigan Law Review* 2329.
"Human Rights, International Economic Law and 'Constitutional Justice': A Reply by Robert Howse to Ernst-Ulrich Petersmann's Article," *EJILTalk*!, 9 December 2008.
"Montesquieu on Commerce, Conquest, War, and Peace," (2006) 31 *Brooklyn Journal of International Law* 693–708.
"The World Trade Organization 20 Years On: Global Governance by Judiciary," (2016) 27 *European Journal of International Law* 9–77.
Howse, Robert and Ruti Teitel, "Cross-Judging: Tribunalization in a Fragmented but Interconnected Global Order," (2009) 41 *NYU Journal of International Law and Politics* 959–990.
Howse, Robert, Joanna Langille, and Katie Sykes, "Pluralism in Practice: Moral Legislation and the Law of the WTO after *Seal Products*," (2015) 48 *George Washington International Law Review* 81.
Hume, David, "On the Standards of Taste," in Eugene F. Miller (ed.), *Hume: Essays Moral, Political and Literary* (Indianapolis, IN: Liberty Fund, 1985), 11–37.
Hunt, Lynn, *Inventing Human Rights: A History* (New York: W.W. Norton & Company, 2007).
Hunter-Henin, Myriam, "Living Together in an Age of Religious Diversity: Lessons from *Baby Loup* and SAS," (2015) 4 *Oxford Journal of Law and Religion* 94–118.
Huntington, S., *The Third Wave: Democratization in the Late Twentieth Century* (Norman: University of Oklahoma Press, 1991).
Husak, Douglas, "The Philosophy of Criminal Law: Extending the Debates," (2013) 7 *Criminal Law and Philosophy* 351–365.
Hutchinson, Allan C., *Laughing at the Gods: Great Judges and How They Made the Common Law* (Cambridge: Cambridge University Press, 2012).
Iglesias Sánchez, Sara, "Hacia una nueva relación entre la nacionalidad estatal y la cuidadanía europea?" (2010) 37 *Revista de Derecho Comunitario Europeo* 933–950.

Ignatieff, Michael, *The Ordinary Virtues: Moral Order in a Divided World* (Cambridge, MA: Harvard University Press, 2017).

International Bar Association, *Report of the Task Force on Extraterritorial Jurisdiction* (2009).

Ioannidis, M., "Deference Criteria in WTO Law and the Case for a Procedural Approach," in L. Gruszczynski and W. Werner (eds.), *Deference in International Courts and Tribunals: Standard of Review and Margin of Appreciation* (Oxford: Oxford University Press, 2014), 91.

Isin, Engin and Greg Nielsen (eds.), *Acts of Citizenship* (New York: ZED Books, 2008).

Iwawata, Y., "Constitutional Problems Involved in Implementing the Uruguay Round in Japan," in John H. Jackson and Alan O. Sykes (eds.), *Implementing the Uruguay Round* (Oxford: Oxford University Press, 1997), 137.

Jackson, John H., "The Great 1994 Sovereignty Debate: United States Acceptance and Implementation of the Uruguay Round Results," in John H. Jackson, *The Jurisprudence of GATT and the WTO* (Cambridge: Cambridge University Press, 2000), 367.

Japp, Klaus-Peter, "Zur Funktion der Menschenrechte in der Weltgesellschaft," in Bettina Heintz and Britta Leisering (eds.), *Menschenrechte in der Weltgesellschaft. Deutungswandel und Wirkungsweise eines globalen Leitwerts* (Frankfurt am Main: Campus Verlag, 2015), 65–97.

Jaremba, Urszula, *National Judges as EU Law Judges: The Polish Civil Law System* (Leiden: Martinus Nijhoff, 2014).

Jensen, Steven L. B., *The Making of International Human Rights: The 1960s, Decolonization, and the Reconstruction of Global Values* (Cambridge: Cambridge University Press, 2016).

Jessup, Philip, *Transnational Law* (New Haven, CT: Yale University Press, 1956).

Jessurun d'Oliveira, Hans Ulrich, "Europees burgerschap: Dubbele nationaliteit?" in Wouter van Ballegooij (ed.), *Europees Burgerschap* (The Hague: TMC Asser Press, 2004), 91.

"Ontkoppeling van nationaliteit en Unieburgerschap?" (2010) *Nederlandsch Juristenblad* 1028–1033.

Joerges, Christian and Jurgen Neyer, "From Intergovernmental Bargaining to Deliberative Political Processes: The Constitutionalization of Comitology," (1997) 3 *European Law Journal* 273.

Joerges, Christian, Poul F. Kjaer, and Tommi Ralli, "A New Type of Conflicts – Law as Constitutional Form in the Postnational Constellation," (2011) 2 *Transnational Legal Theory* 153–166.

Johnson, Tana, *Organizational Progeny: Why Governments Are Losing Control over the Proliferating Structures of Global Governance* (Oxford: Oxford University Press, 2014).

Joppke, Christian, *Citizenship and Immigration* (Cambridge: Polity, 2010).

"The Instrumental Turn of Citizenship," (2018) *Journal of Ethnic and Migration Studies* 1–21.

Kalicki, Jean E. and Anna Joubin-Bret (eds.), *Reshaping the Investor–State Dispute Settlement System – Journeys for the 21st Century* (Leiden: Martinus Nijhoff, 2015).

Kant, Immanuel, *Kritik der Reinen Vernunft*, available at archive.org.

Kant, Immanuel, *Perpetual Peace*, in *Immanuel Kant, Political Writings*, 2nd edn. (Cambridge: Cambridge University Press, 1991, Reis ed.), 93–130.

Kayaoglu, Turan, "The Extension of Westphalian Sovereignty: State Building and the Abolition of Extraterritoriality," (2007) 51 *International Studies Quarterly* 649–675.
Keiler, Johannes and David Roef (eds.), *Comparative Concepts of Criminal Law*, 2nd edn. (Antwerp: Intersentia, 2016).
Keitner, Chimène and W. Michael Reisman, "Free Association: The United States Experience," (2003) 39 *Texas International Law Journal* 1–64.
Kelemen, R. D., "The Dangers of Constitutional Pluralism," in Matej Avbelj and Gareth Davies (eds.), *Handbook on Legal Pluralism in the EU* (Cheltenham: Edward Elgar, 2018), 392–406.
Kelsen, Hans, *Principles of International Law* (New York: Rinehart & Company Inc., 1952).
Pure Theory of Law (Berkeley: University of California Press, 1967, Knight trans.).
Kennedy, David, *A World of Struggle: How Power Law and Expertise Shape the Global Economy* (Princeton, NJ: Princeton University Press, 2016).
Kenny, Mel, "Globalization, Interlegality and Europeanized Contract Law," (2002) 21 *Pennsylvania State International Law Review* 569–620.
Keohane, Robert, "Social Norms and Agency in Global Politics," (2010) *NYU Straus Institute Working Paper* 7.
Keohane, Robert and David Victor, "The Regime Complex for Climate Change," (2010) 10–33 *Harvard Kennedy School, Discussion Paper*, available at www.belfercenter.org/sites/default/files/legacy/files/Keohane_Victor_Final_2.pdf.
King, Jeff, *The Doctrine of Odious Debts in International Law: A Restatement* (Cambridge: Cambridge University Press, 2016).
Kingsbury, Benedict, "Global Regulation and the New *Jus Gentium*," draft paper, available at www.iilj.org/wp-content/uploads/2016/11/Kingsbury-A-New-Jus-Gentium-2006.pdf.
Kingsbury, Benedict, "The Concept of 'Law' in Global Administrative Law," (2009) 20 *European Journal of International Law* 23–57.
"International Law as Inter-Public Law," in Henry R. Richardson and Melissa S. Williams (eds.), *Nomos XLIX: Moral Universalism and Pluralism*, 167–204.
Kingsbury, Benedict and Megan Donaldson, "From Bilateralism to Publicness in International Law," in Ulrich Fastenrath, Rudolf Geiger, Daniel-Erasmus Khan, Andreas Paulus, Sabine von Schorlemer, and Christoph Vedder (eds.), *Essays in Honour of Bruno Simma* (Oxford: Oxford University Press, 2011), 79–89.
Kingsbury, Benedict and Nico Krisch, "Introduction: Global Governance and Global Administrative Law in the International Legal Order," (2006) 17 *European Journal of International Law* 1–13.
Kingsbury, Benedict, Nico Krisch, and Richard B. Stewart, "The Emergence of Global Administrative Law," (2005) 68 *Law and Contemporary Problems* 15–62.
Kirk, Elizabeth, "The Ecosystem Approach and the Search for an Objective and Content for the Concept of Holistic Ocean Governance," (2015) 46 *Ocean Development and International Law* 33–49.
Kjaer, Poul F., "Claim-Making and Parallel Universes: The Legal Pluralism of Church, State and Empire in Europe," in Gareth Davies and Matej Avbelj (eds.), *Research Handbook on Legal Pluralism and EU Law* (Cheltenham: Edward Elgar Publishing, 2018), 11–21.

Constitutionalism in the Global Realm: A Sociological Approach (Abingdon: Routledge, 2014).
"Constitutionalizing Connectivity: The Constitutional Grid of World Society," 45 *Journal of Law and Society* 114–134.
Between Governing and Governance: On the Emergence, Function and Form of Europe's Post-national Constellation (Oxford: Hart, 2010).
"The Transnational Constitution of Europe's Social Market Economies. A Question of Constitutional Imbalances?" (2018) 57 *Journal of Common Market Studies*, 143–158.
"Why Justification? The Structure of Public Power in Transnational Contexts," (2017) 8 *Transnational Legal Theory* 8–21.
Klabbers, Jan, "Constitutionalism as Theory," in Jeff Dunoff and Mark Pollack (eds.), *International Legal Theory* (Cambridge: Cambridge University Press, forthcoming)
"Doing Justice? Bureaucracy, the Rule of Law and Virtue Ethics," (2017) 6 *Rivista di Filosofia del Diritto* 27–50.
"The EJIL Foreword: The Transformation of International Organizations Law," (2015) 26 *European Journal of International Law* 9–82.
"Executing Mr Breard," (1998) 67 *Nordic Journal of International Law* 357–364.
"In Defense of the Realm," in Robert Schütze and Takis Tridimas (eds.), *Oxford Principles of EU Law* (Oxford: Oxford University Press, 2018), 1208–1233.
International Law (Cambridge: Cambridge University Press, 2013).
"Legal Education in the Balance: Accommodating Flexibility," (2006) 56 *Journal of Legal Education* 196–200.
"The Passion and the Spirit: Albert Camus as Moral Politician," (2016) 1 *European Papers* 13–28.
"Principled Pragmatist? Bert Röling and the Emergence of International Criminal Law," in Frédéric Mégrét and Immi Tallgren (eds.), *The Dawn of a New Discipline* (forthcoming).
"The Reception of International Law in the EU Legal Order," in Robert Schütze and Takis Tridimas (eds.), *Oxford Principles of European Union Law* (Oxford: Oxford University Press, 2018), 1208–1233.
"Setting the Scene," in Jan Klabbers, Anne Peters, and Geir Ulfstein, *The Constitutionalization of International Law* (Oxford: Oxford University Press, 2009) 1–44.
"The Sources of International Organizations' Law: Reflections on Accountability," in Samantha Besson and Jean d'Aspremont (eds.), *The Oxford Handbook of the Sources of International Law* (Oxford: Oxford University Press, 2017), 987–1006.
"Beyond the Vienna Convention: Conflicting Treaty Provisions," in Enzo Cannizzaro (ed.), *The Law of Treaties Beyond the Vienna Convention* (Oxford: Oxford University Press, 2011), 192–205.
Klabbers, Jan, Anne Peters, and Geir Ulfstein, *The Constitutionalization of International Law* (Oxford: Oxford University Press, 2009)
Klabbers, Jan and Touko Piiparinen, "Normative Pluralism: An Exploration," in Jan Klabbers and Touko Piiparinen (eds.), *Normative Pluralism and International Law: Exploring Global Governance* (Cambridge: Cambridge University Press, 2013), 13–34.
Klabbers, Jan and Touko Piiparinen (eds.), *Normative Pluralism and International Law: Exploring Global Governance* (Cambridge: Cambridge University Press, 2013).

Knox, John, "A Presumption against Extrajurisdictionality," (2010) 104 *American Journal of International Law* 351–396.

Kochenov, Dimitry, "Annotation of Case C-135/08, *Rottman*," (2010) 47 *Common Market Law Review* 1831–1846.

Citizenship (Cambridge, MA: MIT Press, forthcoming).

"Citizenship of Personal Circumstances in Europe," in Daniel Thym (ed.), *Reinventing European Citizenship* (Oxford: Hart, 2017), 97–136.

"Double Nationality in the EU: An Argument for Tolerance," (2011) 17 *European Law Journal* 323–343.

"*Ius Tractum* of Many Faces: European Citizenship and the Difficult Relationship between Status and Rights," (2009) 15 *Columbia Journal of European Law* 169–238.

"Neo-Mediaeval Permutations of Personhood in the European Union," (2016) *European University Institute Working Paper* 13.

"Pre-Accession, Naturalization, and 'Due Regard to Community Law': The European Union's 'Steering' of Citizenship Policies in Candidate Countries During the Fifth Enlargement," (2004) 4 *Romanian Journal of Political Science* 71–88.

"A Real European Citizenship: A New Jurisdiction Test: A Novel Chapter in the Development of the Union in Europe," (2011) 18 *Columbia Journal of European Law* 55–110.

"Rounding Up the Circle: The Mutation of Member States' Nationalities under Pressure from EU Citizenship," (2010) 23 *EUI RSCAS*.

"On Tiles and Pillars: EU Citizenship as a Federal Denominator," in Dimitry Kochenov (ed.), *EU Citizenship and Federalism: The Role of Rights* (Cambridge: Cambridge University Press, 2017), 3–82.

Kochenov, Dimitry (ed.), *EU Citizenship and Federalism: The Role of Rights* (Cambridge: Cambridge University Press, 2017).

Kochenov, Dimitry and Justin Lindeboom, "Pluralism through Its Denial: The Success of EU Citizenship," in Matej Avbelj and Gareth Davies (eds.), *Research Handbook on Legal Pluralism and EU Law* (Cheltenham: Edward Elgar, 2018), 179–198.

"Empirical Assessment of the Quality of Nationalities," (2017) 4 *European Journal of Comparative Law* 314–336.

Kochenov, Dimitry and Justin Lindeboom (eds.), *Henley and Partners – Kochenov Quality of Nationality Index*, 3rd edn. (Zürich: Ideos, 2018).

Kochenov, Dimitry and Uladzislau Belavusau, "Kirchberg – Dispensing the Punishment: Inflicting 'Civil Death' on Prisoners in the Recent Case-Law," (2016) 40 *European Law Review* 557–577.

Kolb, Robert, "The Relationship between the International and the Municipal Legal Order: Reflections on the Decision no 238/2014 of the Italian Constitutional Court," (2014) *Questions of International Law* 5–16.

"Short Reflections on the ICJ's Whaling Case and the Review by International Courts and Tribunals of 'Discretionary Powers'," (2014) 132 *Australian Yearbook of International Law* 135–144.

Koller, David, "The End of Geography: The Changing Nature of the International System and the Challenge to International Law: A Reply to Daniel Bethlehem," (2014) 25 *European Journal of International Law* 25–29.

Koskenniemi, Martti, "Colonial Laws: Sources, Strategies and Lessons?" (2016) 18 *Journal of the History of International Law* 248–277.

"Empire and International Law: The Real Spanish Contribution," (2011) 61 *University of Toronto Law Journal* 1–36.

Fragmentation of International Law: Difficulties Arising from the Diversification and Expansion of International Law. Report of the Study Group of the International Law Commission (Helsinki: Erik Castrén Institute, 2007).

"Global Governance and Public International Law," (2004) 37 *Kritische Justiz* 241–254.

"Global Legal Pluralism: Multiple Regimes and Multiple Modes of Thought," 5 March 2005, Lecture at Harvard University, available at www.helsinki.fi/eci/Publications/Koskenniemi.

"The Lady Doth Protest Too Much: Kosovo, and the Turn to Ethics in International Law". Reprinted in Martti Koskenniemi (ed.), *The Politics of International Law* (Oxford: Hart, 2011), 112–130.

The Politics of International Law (Oxford: Hart, 2011).

Kostakopoulou, Dora, "European Union Citizenship and Member State Nationality: Updating or Upgrading the Link," in Jo Shaw (ed.), *Has the European Court of Justice Challenged the Member State Sovereignty in Nationality Law?* (Florence: EUI Robert Schuman Centre for Advanced Studies , 2011), 21–26.

Kotze, Louis, "Constitutional Conversations in the Anthropocene: In Search of Environmental *Jus Cogens* Norms," (2015) 46 *Netherlands Yearbook of International Law* 241–271.

Koutrakos, Panos, *EU International Relations Law*, 2nd edn. (Oxford: Hart, 2015).

"The European Union in the Global Security Architecture," in Bart van Vooren, Steven Blockmans, and Jan Wouters (eds.), *The EU's Role in Global Governance* (Oxford: Oxford University Press, 2013), 81–94.

"The Relevance of EU Law for Arbitral Tribunals: (Not) Managing the Lingering Tension," (2016) 17 *Journal of World Investment and Trade* 873–894.

Krajewski, Markus, "The Reform of the Common Commercial Policy," in Andrea Biondi, Piet Eeckhout, and Stefanie Ripley (eds.), *EU Law after Lisbon* (Oxford: Oxford University Press, 2012), 292–311.

Kratochwil, Friedrich, "Making Sense of 'International Practices'," in Emanuel Adler and Vincent Pouliot (eds.), *International Practices* (Cambridge: Cambridge University Press, 2011) 36–60.

Praxis: On Acting and Knowing (Cambridge: Cambridge University Press, 2018).

"Re-Thinking Inter-Disciplinarity by Re-Reading Hume," in Nikolas Rajkovic, Tanja Aalberts, and Thomas Gammeltoft-Hansen (eds.), *The Power of Legality* (Cambridge: Cambridge University Press, 2016).

Rules, Norms, and Decisions: On the Conditions of Practical and Legal Reasoning in International Relations and Domestic Affairs (Cambridge: Cambridge University Press, 1989).

The Status of Law in International Society: Meditations on the Role and Rule of Law (Cambridge: Cambridge University Press, 2014).

Krisch, Nico, *Beyond Constitutionalism: The Pluralist Structure of Postnational Law* (Oxford: Oxford University Press, 2010).

"The Decay of Consent: International Law in an Age of Global Public Goods," (2014) 108 *American Journal of International Law* 1–40.

"Who Is Afraid of Radical Pluralism? Legal Order and Political Stability in the Postnational Space," (2011) 24 *Ratio Juris* 386–412.
Kristeva, Julia, "Open Letter to Harlem Desir," in Julia Kristeva (ed.), *Nations without Nationalism* (New York: Columbia University Press, 1993).
Küçük, Esin, "The Principle of Solidarity and Fairness in Sharing Responsibility: More than Window Dressing?" (2016) 22 *European Law Journal* 448–469.
Kuisma, Mikko, "Nordic Models of Citizenship: Lessons from Social History for Theorising Policy Change in the 'Age of Globalisation'," (2007) 12 *New Political Economy* 87–95.
Lacey, Nicola, *In Search of Criminal Responsibility: Ideas, Interests and Institutions* (Oxford: Oxford University Press, 2016).
Ladeur, Karl-Heinz, "The Emergence of Global Administrative Law and Transnational Regulation," (2011) *NYU Institute for International Law and Justice Working Paper* 1.
Lamy, Pascal, "The Place of the WTO and Its Law in the International Legal Order," (2007) 17 *European Journal of International Law* 7.
Larik, Joris, "EU Counter-Terrorism and the 'Strict Observance of International Law: Sewing the Seamless Coat of Compliance'," in Ester Herlin-Karnell and Claudio Matera (eds.), *External Dimension of the EU Counter-terrorism Policy* (2014) *CLEER Working Paper* 2.
Latu, Alex, "Public Procurement and Private Certification: The Case of the UK TPP," (2013) *Comparative Research in Law & Political Economy. Research Paper* 53, available at https://ssrn.com/abstract=2360264.
Lautenbach, Geranne, *The Concept of the Rule of Law and the European Court of Human Rights* (Oxford: Oxford University Press, 2013).
Lauterpacht, Hersch, *The Function of Law in the International Community* (Oxford University Press, 2011 [1933]).
Lavranos, Nikolaos, "The Solange-Method as a Tool for Regulating Competing Jurisdictions among International Courts and Tribunals," (2008) 30 *Loyola Los Angeles International & Comparative Law Review* 275–334.
Le Golf, Pierrick, "Global Law: A Legal Phenomenon Emerging from the Process of Globalization," (2007) 14 *Indiana Journal of Global Legal Studies* 119–45.
Leebron, D., "Implementation of the Uruguay Round Results in the United States," in John H. Jackson and Alan O. Sykes (eds.), *Implementing the Uruguay Round* (Oxford: Oxford University Press, 1997), 175.
Legendre, Pierre, *Leçons X, Dogma: Instituer l'Animal Humain* (Paris: Fayard 2017).
Legrand, Pierre, *Fragments on Law as Culture* (Deventer: Tjeenk Willink, 1999).
Lenaerts, Koen and Amaryllis Verhoeven, "Institutional Balance as a Guarantee for Democracy in EU Governance," in Christian Joerges and Renaud Dehousse (eds.), *Good Governance in Europe's Integrated Market* (Oxford: Oxford University Press, 2002) 35.
Lester, Anthony, "Thirty Years On: The East African Case Revisited," (2002) 47 *Public Law* 52–72.
Letsas, George, "Harmonic Law: The Case against Legal Pluralism," in Julie Dickson and Pavlos Eleftheriadis (eds.), *Philosophical Foundations of European Union Law* (Oxford: Oxford University Press, 2012), 77–108.
Lhuilier, Gilles, *Le Droit Transnational* (Paris: Dalloz, 2016).

Liberski-Bagnoud, Danouta, *Les Dieux du Territoire – Penser Autrement la Généalogie* (Paris: Centre national de la recherche scientifique/Édition de la Maison des sciences de l'homme, 2002).

Liberski-Bagnoud, Danouta, "Règne de la loi, régime des interdits," in Giuseppe Longo (ed.), *Loi des Dieux, des Hommes et de la Nature* (Paris: Fayard, forthcoming).

Lindahl, Hans, *Fault Lines of Globalization: Legal Order and the Politics of A-Legality* (Oxford: Oxford University Press, 2013).

Liivoja, Rain, "Book Review of *Jurisdiction in International Law* by Cedric Ryngaert," (2008) 19 *Finnish Yearbook of International Law* 397–401.

Loughlin, Martin, "The Misconceived Search for Global Law," (2017) 8 *Transnational Legal Theory* 353–359.

Loureiro Bastos, Fernando, "Some Notes on the Advisory Opinion of 1 February 2011 of the Sea-Bed Disputes Chamber. Are We in the Presence of a Glimpse of the Future Evolution of the Jurisprudence of the International Tribunal for the Law of the Sea?" in José Manuel Sobrino Hereira (ed.), *The Contribution of the United Nations Convention on the Law of the Sea to Good Governance of the Oceans and Seas*, Vol. 1, (Naples: Editoriale Scientifica, 2014), 343–362.

Lowe, Vaughan, "Jurisdiction," in Malcolm Evans (ed.), *International Law*, 2nd edn. (Oxford: Oxford University Press, 2006), 335–360.

Lowenfeld, Andreas, "International Litigation and the Quest for Reasonableness: General Course on Private International Law," (1994) 245 *Collected Courses of the Hague Academy of International Law* 1–319.

Lowry, Michele and Susanne Luedemann (eds.), *Exemplarity and Singularity: Thinking through Particulars in Philosophy, Literature and Law* (Abingdon: Routledge, 2015).

Luban, David, *Lawyers and Justice: An Ethical Study* (Princeton, NJ: Princeton University Press, 1988).

Luban, David and W. Bradley Wendel, "Philosophical Legal Ethics: An Affectionate History," (2017) 30 *Georgetown Journal of Legal Ethics* 337–364.

Luhmann, Niklas, *Soziale Systeme* (Frankfurt: Suhrkamp, 1984).

Luther, Martin, *De Servo Arbitrio*, available at chapellibrary.org.

MacCormick, Neil, "Beyond the Sovereign State," (1993) 56 *Modern Law Review* 1–18.

Legal Reasoning and Legal Theory (Oxford: Oxford University Press, 1978).

Questioning Sovereignty: Law, State, and Nation in the European Commonwealth (Oxford: Oxford University Press, 1999).

"Risking Constitutional Collision in Europe?" (1998) 18 *Oxford Journal of Legal Studies* 517–532.

"The Maastricht-Urteil: Sovereignty Now," (1995) 1 *European Law Journal* 259–66.

MacIntyre, Alasdair, *After Virtue: A Study in Moral Theory*, 2nd edn. (London: Duckworth, 1985).

Madsen, Mikael Rask, "Sociological Approaches to International Courts," in Cesare P. R. Romano, Karen J. Alter, and Yuval Shany (eds.), *The Oxford Handbook of International Adjudication* (Oxford: Oxford University Press, 2013), 388–412.

Magnus, Albertus, *Summa de Bono*, available at www.albertus-magnus-online.de.

Maier, Hans Gerhard, "Extraterritorial Jurisdiction at a Crossroads: An Intersection between Public and Private International Law," (1982) 76 *American Journal of International Law* 280–320.

"Jurisdictional Rules in Customary International Law," in Karl Matthias Meessen (ed.), *Extraterritorial Jurisdiction in Theory and Practice* (London: Kluwer, 1996), 64–74.

Maine, Henry S., *Ancient Law* (1917 edn., Project Gutenberg, 2007).

Majone, Giandomenico, *The European Community as a Regulatory State* (Dordrecht: Nijhoff, 1995).

Regulating Europe (London: Routledge, 1996).

Maljean-Dubois, Sandrine, "L'enjeu de protection de l'environnement dans l'exploration et l'exploitatione de la Zone: l'apport de l'avis de la Chambre du Tribunal international du droit de la mer du 1er Février 2011," (2011) 16 *Annuaire du Droit de la Mer* 367–380.

Mann, Frederick A., "The Doctrine of International Jurisdiction Revisited after Twenty Years," (1984) 186 *Recueil des Cours* 1–116.

"The Doctrine of Jurisdiction in International Law," (1964) 111 *Recueil des Cours* 1–162.

Manning, Patrick, "The Slave Trade: 'The Formal Demographics of a Global System'," in Joseph E. Inikori and Stanley L. Engerman (eds.), *The Atlantic Slave Trade: Effects on Economies, Societies and Peoples in Africa, the Americas, and Europe* (Durham, NC: Duke University Press, 1992), 117–44.

Marceau, Gabrielle, "A Call for Coherence in International Law: Praises for the Prohibition against 'Clinical Isolation' in WTO Dispute Settlement," (1999) 33 *Journal of World Trade* 87.

"Conflict of Norms and Conflict of Jurisdictions: The Relationship between the WTO Agreement and the MEAs and Other Treaties," (2001) 35 *Journal of World Trade* 1081–1131.

"The Primacy of the WTO Dispute Settlement System," (2015) *Questions of International Law* 23.

Markesinis, Basil and Jorg Fedke, *Engaging with Foreign Law* (Oxford: Hart, 2009).

Judicial Recourse to Foreign Law: A New Source of Inspiration? (London: Routledge, 2006).

Marshall, Thomas H., *Class, Citizenship, and Social Development* (Chicago: University of Chicago Press, 1977).

Martin-Bidou, Pascale, "L'affaire de la chasse à la balaine dans l'Antarctique: droit des traités ou protection des especes?" (2015) 119 *Revue Générale de Droit International Public* 403–417.

Martinez, Jenny, *The Slave Trade and the Origins of International Human Rights Law* (Oxford: Oxford University Press, 2014).

Martini, Chiara, "'States' Control Over New International Organization," (2006) 6 *Global Jurist Advances* 1–25.

Martinico, Giuseppe and Oreste Pollicino, *The Interaction between Europe's Legal Systems: Judicial Dialogue and the Creation of Supranational Laws* (Cheltenham: Edward Elgar, 2012).

Maupin, Julie, "Transparency in International Investment Law: The Good, the Bad, and the Murky," in Andrea Bianchi and Anne Peters (eds.), *Transparency in International Law* (Cambridge: Cambridge University Press, 2013), 142–171.

Mazower, Mark, *Governing the World. The History of an Idea: 1815 to the Present* (London: Penguin, 2013).

Mbengue, Makane, "Between Law and Science: A Commentary on the Whaling in the Antarctic Case," (2015) 14 *Questions of International Law* 3–12.

McGinnis, John O., "The Appropriate Hierarchy of Global Multilateralism and Customary International Law: The Example of the WTO," (2003) 42 *Virginia Journal of International Law* 229.

McLachlan, Campbell, *Lis Pendens in International Litigation* (The Hague: Hague Academy of International Law, 2009).

Mégrét, Frédéric, "International Judges and Experts' Impartiality and the Problem of Past Declarations," (2011) 10 *The Law and Practice of International Courts and Tribunals* 31–66.

Meili, Friedrich, *Die internationalen Unionen über das Recht der Weltverkehrsanstalten und des gesitigen Eigentums* (Leipzig: Duncker & Humblot, 1889).

Mengozzi, Paolo, "Private International Law and the WTO Law," (2001) 292 *Recueil des Cours* 249.

Merli, R., M. C. Lucchetti, M. Preziosi, and G. Arcese, "Motivations behind the EMAS Stagnation and Enabling Measures to Stimulate New Registrations: Characterization of Public Administrations and Private-Owned Organizations," (2017) available at www.advancesincleanerproduction.net/sixth/files/sessoes/6B/8/merli_r_et_al_academic.pdf.

Michaels, Ralf, "Law and Recognition: Towards a Relational Concept of Law," in Nicole Roughan and Andrew Halpin (eds.), *In Pursuit of Pluralist Jurisprudence* (Cambridge: Cambridge University Press, forthcoming).

Michaels, Ralf, "Territorial Jurisdiction after Territoriality," in Piet Jan Slot and Mielle Bultermann (eds.), *Globalisation and Jurisdiction* (Leiden: Kluwer, 2004), 105–130.

Milanovic, Branko, *Global Inequality* (Cambridge, MA: Harvard University Press, 2016).

Milanovic, Marko, *Extraterritorial Application of Human Rights Treaties: Law, Principles, and Policy* (Oxford: Oxford University Press, 2011).

ICJ Decides the Whaling in the Antarctic Case: Australia Wins, EJILTalk!, 31 March 2014.

Miller, David, "Territorial Rights: Concept and Justification," (2012) 60 *Political Studies* 252–68.

Mitchell, Andrew D., "Good Faith in WTO Dispute Settlement," (2006) 7 *Melbourne Journal of International Law* 339–371.

Mitsilegas, Valsamis, "The European Union and the Global Governance of Crime," in Valsamis Mitsilegas, Peter Alldridge, and Leonidis Cheliotis (eds.), *Globalisation, Criminal Law and Criminal Justice* (Oxford: Hart, 2015), 153–198.

"Managing Legal Diversity in Europe's Area of Criminal Justice: The Role of Autonomous Concepts," in Renaud Colson and Stewart Field (eds.), *EU Criminal Justice and the Challenges of Diversity. Legal Cultures in the Area of Freedom, Security and justice* (Cambridge: Cambridge University Press, 2016), 125–159.

Montesquieu, *L'Esprit des Lois in Montesquieu, Oeuvres Complètes*, Vol. 2 (Paris: Gallimard La Pléiade, 1951).

My Thoughts (Indianapolis, IN: Liberty Fund, 2012, Clark trans.).

Moore, Sally Falk, "Law and Social Change: The Semi-Autonomous Social Field as an Appropriate Subject of Study," (1973) 7 *Law and Society Review* 719–743.

Morgenthau, Hans J., *La Réalité des Normes: En Particulier Normes du Droit International. Fondement d'une Théorie des Norms* (Paris: Félix Alcan, 1934).

Mowbray, Alastair, "Subsidiarity and the European Convention on Human Rights," (2015) 15 *Human Rights Law Review* 313–341.
Moyn, Samuel, *The Last Utopia: Human Rights in History* (Cambridge, MA: Harvard University Press, 2010).
Neuman, Gerald, "Fédéralisme et citoyenneté aux Etats Unis et dans l'Union européenne," (2003) 21 *Critique Internationale* 161–169.
Ninatti, S., "How Do Our Judges Conceive of Democracy? The Democratic Nature of the Community Decision-Making Process under Scrutiny of the European Court of Justice," Jean Monnet Working Paper 10/03.
Nollkaemper, André, "Inside or Out: Two Types of International Legal Pluralism," in Jan Klabbers and Touko Piiparinen (eds.), *Normative Pluralism and International Law: Exploring Global Governance* (Cambridge: Cambridge University Press, 2014), 220–239.
"International Adjudication of Global Public Goods: The Intersection of Substance and Procedure," (2012) 23 *European Journal of International Law* 769–791.
Note, "Constructing the State Extraterritorially: Jurisdictional Discourse, the National Interest, and Transnational Norms," (1990) 103 *Harvard Law Review* 1273–1305.
O'Brien, Charlotte, "I Trade Therefore I Am," (2013) 50 *Common Market Law Review* 1643–1684.
O'Neill, Onora, "The Dark Side of Human Rights," in Thomas Christiano and John Christman (eds.), *Contemporary Debates in Political Philosophy* (Chichester: Blackwell-Wiley, 2009), 425–436.
Oakeshott, Michael, "Rationalism in Politics," reproduced in Michael Oakeshott (ed.), *Rationalism in Politics and Other Essays* (London: Methuen and Co., 1962), 1–36.
Oakley, Justin and Dean Cocking, *Virtue Ethics and Professional Roles* (Cambridge: Cambridge University Press, 2001).
Oellers-Frahm, Karin, "Multiplication of International Courts and Tribunals and Conflicting Jurisdictions: Problems and Possible Solutions," (2001) 5 *Max Planck Yearbook of United Nations Law* 67–104.
Oomen, Barbara, Martha F. Davis, and Michele Grigolo, *Global Urban Justice: The Rise of Human Rights Cities* (Cambridge: Cambridge University Press, 2016).
Osterhammel, Jurgen (ed.), *Colonialism: A Theoretical Overview*, 2nd edn. (Princeton, NJ: Princeton University Press, 2005).
Padovani, Tullio, "Il crepuscolo della legalità nel processo penale. Riflessioni antistoriche sulle dimensioni processuali della legalità penale," (1999) 2 *L'Indice Penale* 527–543.
Palombella, Gianluigi, "The (Re-)Constitution of the Public in a Global Arena," in Cormac MacAmlaigh, Claudio Michelon, and Neil Walker (eds.), *After Public Law* (Oxford: Oxford University Press, 2013), 286–308.
E Possibile una Legalità Globale? Il Rule of Law e la Governance del Mondo (Bologna: Il Mulino, 2012).
"German War Crimes and the Rule of International Law," (2016) 14 *Journal of International Criminal Justice* 607–613.
"Global Law and the Law on the Globe," (2012) 1 *Italian Journal of Public Law* 53–92.
"*Senza identità*. Dal diritto internazionale alla Corte costituzionale tra consuetudine, *Jus cogens* e principi 'supremi'," (2015) 35 *Quaderni Costituzionali* 815–30.

"The Principled and Winding Road to *Al Dulimi*: Interpreting the Interpreters," (2014) *Questions of International Law* 16.
"The Rule of Law as an Institutional Ideal," in Leonardo Morlino and Gianluigi Palombella (eds.), *Rule of Law and Democracy. Internal and External Issues* (Leiden: Brill, 2010), 1–37.
"The Rule of Law at Home and Abroad," (2016) 8 *Hague Journal on the Rule of Law* 1–23.
Parsons, Talcott, *The Structure of Social Action: A Study in Social Theory with Special Reference to a Group of Recent European Writers* (New York: Free Press, 1968 [1937]).
Pascal, Blaise, *Thoughts*, Vol. 48 (New York: P.F. Collier and Son Company, 1909).
Paulus, Andreas, "National Courts and the International Rule of Law (Remarks on the Book by André Nollkaemper)," (2012) 4 *Jerusalem Review Legal Studies* 5–18.
Pauwelyn, Joost, *Conflict of Norms in Public International Law: How WTO Law Relates to Other Rules of International Law* (Cambridge: Cambridge University Press, 2003).
Pavlakos, George and Joost Pauwelyn, "Principled Monism and the Normative Conception of Coercion under International Law," in Malcolm Evans and Panos Koutrakos (eds.), *Beyond the Established Legal Orders: Policy Interconnections between the EU and the Rest of the World* (Oxford: Hart, 2011), 317–341.
Payandeh, Mehrdad, "The Concept of International Law in the Jurisprudence of H.L.A. Hart," (2010) 21 *European Journal of International Law* 967–995.
Payne, Cymie, "Biodiversity in High Seas Areas: An Integrated Legal Approach," (2017) 21 *American Society of International Law Insights*.
Peters, Anne, "How to Make the Best out of Sentenza no. 238 of the Italian Constitutional Court for a Global Legal Order," available at https://verfassungsblog.de/let-not-triepel-triumph-make-best-sentenza-no-238-italian-constitutional-court-global-legal-order-2.
"Humanity as the A and Ω of Sovereignty," (2009) 20 *European Journal of International Law* 513–544.
"The Refinement of International Law: From Fragmentation to Regime Interaction and Politicization," (2017) 15 *International Journal of Constitutional Law* 671–704.
Petersmann, Ernst-Ulrich, "Human Rights and International Economic Law in the 21st Century: The Need to Clarify Their Interrelationships," (2001) 4 *Journal of International Economic Law* 3.
"Human Rights, International Economic Law and 'Constitutional Justice'," (2008) 18 *European Journal of International Law* 769.
Pettit, Philip, *Republicanism: A Theory of Freedom and Government* (Oxford: Oxford University Press, 1997).
Pineschi, Laura, "The Duty of Environmental Impact Assessment in the First ITLOS Chamber's Advisory Opinion: Toward the Supremacy of the General Rule to Protect and Preserve the Marine Environment as a Common Value?" in Nerina Boschiero, Cesare Pitea, Chiara Ragni, and Tullio Scovazzi (eds.), *International Courts and the Development of International Law* (Dordrecht: Springer, 2013), 425–439.
Pitea, Cesare, "Multiplication and Overlap of Non-Compliance Procedures and Mechanisms: Towards Better Coordination?" in Tullio Treves, Laura Pineschi,

Attila Tanzi, Cesare Pitea, Chiara Ragni, and Francesca Romanin Jacur (eds.), *Non-Compliance Procedures and Mechanisms and the Effectiveness of International Environmental Agreements* (The Hague: T.M.C. Asser Press, 2009), 439–450.

Plakokefalos, Ilias, "Seabed Disputes Chamber of the International Tribunal for the Law of the Sea: Responsibilities and Obligations of States Sponsoring Persons and Entities with Respect to Activities in the Area," (2011) 24 *Journal of Environmental Law* 133–143.

Pogge, Thomas, "Fighting Global Poverty," (2017) 13 *International Journal of Law in Context* 512–526.

Poisel, Tim, "Deep Seabed Mining: Implications of Seabed Disputes Chamber's Advisory Opinion," (2012) 19 *Australian International Law Journal* 212–233.

Polakiewicz, Jörg, "International Law and Domestic (Municipal) Law, Law and Decisions of International Organizations and Courts," in Rüdiger Wolfrum (ed.), *Max Planck Encyclopedia of Public International Law* (Oxford: Oxford University Press, 2012).

Pomponius, *Digest*, available at https://droitromain.univ-grenoble-alpes.fr/Anglica/D1_Scott.htm#XIV.

Posner, Eric, "Liberal Internationalism and the Populist Backlash," (2017) *University of Chicago Public Law Working Paper* 606.

Posner, Eric and Adrian Vermeule, "The Votes of Other Judges," (2016) 105 *Georgetown Law Journal* 159–190.

Posner, Richard, *How Judges Think* (Cambridge, MA: Harvard University Press, 2008).

Post, Robert, "The Challenge of Globalization to American Public Law Scholarship," (2001) 2 *Theoretical Inquiries in Law* 323–336.

Powell, Jefferson H., *Constitutional Conscience: The Moral Dimension of Judicial Decision* (Chicago: University of Chicago Press, 2008).

Pulkowski, Dirk, *The Law and Politics of International Regime Conflict* (Oxford: Oxford University Press, 2014).

Putnam, Hilary, *Ethics without Ontology* (Cambridge, MA: Harvard University Press, 2004).

Radbruch, Gustav, *Einführung in die Rechtswissenschaft*, 13th edn. (Stuttgart: Koehler Verlag, 1980, Zweigert ed.).

Ragni, Chiara, "Interpretazione dei trattati e standard of review nella giurisprudenza della Corte internazionale di giustizia: riflessioni sull'affare della caccia alla balena nell'Antartico," (2014) *Rivista di Diritto Internazionale* 725–760.

Raustiala, Kal, "Empire and Extraterritoriality in Twentieth Century America," (2011) 40 *Southwestern Law Review* 605–615.

"Governing the Internet," (2016) 110 *American Journal of International Law* 491–503.

Raustiala, Kal and David Victor, "The Regime Complex of Plant Genetic Resources," (2004) 58 *International Organization* 277–309.

Rawls, John, *The Law of Peoples* (Cambridge, MA: Harvard University Press, 2001).

Raz, Joseph, *The Authority of Law* (Oxford: Clarendon, 1979).

"The Problem of Authority: Revisiting the Service Conception," (2006) 90 *Minnesota Law Review* 1003–1044.

"Why the State," (2014) *King's College London Dickson Poon School of Law Legal Studies Research Paper Series* 38.

Reinisch, August, "Articles 30 and 59 of the Vienna Convention on the Law of Treaties in Action: The Decisions on Jurisdiction in the *Eastern Sugar* and *Eureko* Investment Arbitrations," (2012) 39 *Legal Issues of Economic Integration* 157–177.

"The Proliferation of International Dispute Settlement Mechanisms: The Threat of Fragmentation vs. the Promise of a More Effective System? – Some Reflections from the Perspective of Investment Arbitration," in Isabelle Buffard, James Crawford, Alain Pellet, and Stephan Wittich (eds.), *International Law between Universalism and Fragmentation: Festschrift in Honour of Gerhard Hafner* (Leiden: Martinus Nijhoff, 2008), 107–125.

Repetto, Giorgio (ed.), *The Constitutional Relevance of the ECHR in Domestic and European Law: An Italian Perspective* (Antwerp: Intersentia, 2013).

Robert-Cuendet, Sabrina, "Responsabilités et obligations des États qui patronnent des personnes et des entités dans le cadre d'activités menées dans la Zone," (2011) 57 *Annuaire Français de Droit International* 439–476.

Roberts, Anthea "Pledging American Exceptionalism? US Supreme Court Justice Gorsuch on International Law," available at http://opiniojuris.org/2017/05/23/33125.

Robinson, Paul H., "Four Distinctions that Glanville Williams Did Not Make: The Practical Benefits of Examining the Interrelation among Criminal Law Doctrines," in Dennis J. Baker and Jeremy Horder (eds.), *The Sanctity of Life and the Criminal Law: The Legacy of Glanville Williams* (Cambridge: Cambridge University Press, 2015), 106–125.

Robinson, Paul H., Stephen P. Garvey, and Kimberly Kessler Ferzan (eds.), *Criminal Law Conversations* (Oxford: Oxford University Press, 2009).

Rödl, Florian, "Democratic Juridification without Statisation: Law of Conflict of Laws Instead of a World State," (2011) 2 *Transnational Legal Theory* 193–213.

Rodrik, Dani. *The Globalization Paradox: Democracy and the Future of the World Economy* (New York: W. W. Norton, 2011).

Roele, Isabel, "The Vicious Circle of Habermas' Cosmopolitanism," (2014) 25 *Law and Critique* 199–229.

Röling, B. V. A. and Antonio Cassese, *The Tokyo Trial and Beyond* (Cambridge: Polity, 1993).

Rolland, Sonia, "Whaling in the Antarctic (Australia v. Japan: New Zealand Intervening)," (2014) 108 *American Journal of International Law* 496–502.

Rothwell, Donald and Tim Stephens, "The Regulation of Southern Ocean Whaling: What Role for the Antarctic Treaty System?" (2009) *The University of Sydney Law School Legal Studies Research Paper* 09.

Roughan, Nicole, *Authorities: Conflict, Cooperation, and Transnational Legal Theory* (Oxford: Oxford University Press, 2013).

"Mind the Gaps: Authority and Legality in International Law," (2016) 27 *European Journal of International Law* 329–335.

Rubenstein, Kim and Adler, Daniel, "International Citizenship: The Future of Nationality in a Globalized World," (2000) 7 *Indiana Journal of Global Legal Studies* 519–548.

Ruggie, John Gerard, "Territoriality and Beyond: Problematizing Modernity in International Relations," (1993) 47 *International Organization* 139–174.

Rundle, Kristen, "The Impossibility of an Exterminatory Legality: Law and the Holocaust," (2009) 59 *University of Toronto Law Journal* 65–126.

Russo, Deborah, "Addressing the Relation between Treaties by Means of 'Saving Clauses'," (2015) 85 *British Yearbook of International Law* 1–9.

Sabel, Charles F. and Jonathan Zeitlin (eds.), *Experimentalist Governance in the European Union: Towards a New Architecture* (Oxford: Oxford University Press, 2010).

Sacco, Rodolfo, "Diversity and Uniformity in the Law," (2001) 49 *American Journal of Comparative Law* 171–190.

Sadurski Wojciech, "Partnering with Strasbourg: Constitutionalisation of the European Court of Human Rights, the Accession of Central and East European States to the Council of Europe, and the Idea of Pilot Judgments," (2009) 9 *Human Rights Law Review* 397–453.

Sajó, András, "Liberty and its Competitors," in Renata Uitz (ed.), *Freedom and Its Enemies: The Tragedy of Liberty* (The Hague: Eleven International Publishing, 2015).

Sajó, András and Renata Uitz, *The Constitution of Freedom* (Oxford: Oxford University Press, 2017).

Sajó, András and Sergio Giuliano, "Is the Decline of Globalization the End of Human Rights (as We Believe to Know Them)?" (2017) *Annuario di Diritto Comparato e Studi Legislativi* 517–536.

Salamanca Agaudo, Esther, "La contribución de la opinión consultiva de la Sala de controverdsias de fondos marinos del Tribunal internacional del derecho del mar a la interpretación y aplicación de la Parte XI de la Convención de Naciones Unidas sobre el Derecho del mar de 1982 y su Acuerdo de 1994," in José Manuel Sobrino Hereira (ed.), *The Contribution of the United Nations Convention on the Law of the Sea to Good Governance of the Oceans and Seas*, Vol. 1, (Naples: Editoriale Scientifica, 2014), 385–406.

Sartre, Jean Paul, "Existentialism is a Humanism," in Walter Kaufman (ed.), *Existentialism from Dostoyevsky to Sartre* (New York: Plume Books, 1975).

Sassen, Saskia, "The State and Globalization," in Rodney Bruce Hall and Thomas J. Biersteker (eds.), *The Emergence of Private Authority in Global Governance* (Cambridge: Cambridge University Press, 2002), 91–113.

Territory, Authority, Rights: From Medieval to Global Assemblages (Princeton, NJ: Princeton University Press, 2006).

Savino, Mario, "Linkages between Global Regimes and Interactions with Civil Society," in Sabino Cassese (ed.), *Research Handbook on Global Administrative Law* (Cheltenham: Edward Elgar, 2016), 131–152.

Schabas, William, *The European Convention on Human Rights: A Commentary* (Oxford: Oxford University Press, 2015).

Schaltegger, Stephan, Martin Bennett, Roger L. Burritt, and Christine Jasch (eds.), *Environmental Management Accounting for Cleaner Production* (Heidelberg: Springer, 2008).

Schiek, Dagmar, "Perspectives on Social Citizenship in the EU," in Dimitry Kochenov (ed.), *EU Citizenship and Federalism: The Role of Rights* (Cambridge: Cambridge University Press, 2017), 341–370.

Schlesinger, Rudolph (ed.), *Schlesinger's Comparative Law. Cases–Text–Materials*, 4th edn. (Mineola NY: The Foundation Press, 1980).

Schmitt, Carl, *Der Nomos der Erde. Im Völkerrecht des Jus Publicum Europaeum* (Berlin: Duncker & Humblot, 1950).

Ex Captivitate Salus: Experiences, 1945–1947 (Cambridge: Polity, 2017, Hannah trans.).
Schönberger, Christoph, "European Citizenship as Federal Citizenship," (2007) 19 *European Review of Public Law* 61–81.
Unionsbürger. Europas föderales Bürgerrecht in vergleichender Sicht (Heidelberg: Mohr Siebeck, 2006).
Schultz, Thomas "Carving up the Internet: Jurisdiction, Legal Orders, and the Private/Public International Law Interface," (2008) 19 *European Journal of International Law* 799–839.
Transnational Legality: Stateless Law and International Arbitration (Oxford: Oxford University Press, 2014).
Schütze, Robert, "The 'Succession Doctrine' and the European Union," in Anthony Arnull, Catherine Barnard, Michael Dougan, and Eleanor Spaventa (eds.), *A Constitutional Order of States? Essays in Honour of Alan Dashwood* (Oxford: Hart, 2011), 459–484.
Scoditti, Enrico, "Corti e Carte dei diritti," (2013) 2 *Rivista di Filosofia del Diritto* 379–400.
Scott, James C., *Seeing like a State* (New Haven, CT: Yale University Press, 1998).
Scott Joanne, "The GATT and Community Law: Rethinking the 'Regulatory Gap'," in Jo Shaw and Gillian More (eds.), *New Legal Dynamics of European Union* (Oxford: Clarendon Press, 1995), 147.
"The New EU 'Extraterritoriality'," (2014) 51 *Common Market Law Review* 1343–1380.
Scott, Karen, "International Environmental Governance: Managing Fragmentation through Institutional Connection," (2011) 12 *Melbourne Journal of International Law* 1–40.
Scovazzi, Tullio, "Between Law and Science: Some Considerations Inspired by the Whaling in the Antarctic Judgment," (2015) 14 *Questions of International Law* 13–30.
Searle, John, *Speech Acts* (Cambridge: Cambridge University Press, 1969).
The Construction of Social Reality (London: Penguin, 1995).
Selznick, Philip, "Sociology and Natural Law," (1961) 6 *Natural Law Forum* 84–108.
Sen, Amartya, *The Idea of Justice* (Cambridge, MA: Harvard University Press, 2009).
Senden, Linda, "Soft Law and Its Implications for Institutional Balance in the EC," (2005) 1 *Utrecht Law Review* 79.
Shachar, Ayelet, *The Birthright Lottery* (Cambridge, MA: Harvard University Press, 2009).
Shaffer, Gregory, "International Law and Global Public Goods in a Legal Pluralist World," (2012) 12 *European Journal of International Law* 669–693.
Shaffer, Gregory and Tom Ginsburg, "The Empirical Turn in International Legal Scholarship," (2012) 106 *American Journal of International Law* 1–46.
Shamir-Borer, Eran, "Legitimacy without Authority in Global Standardisation Governance: The Case of the International Organization for Standardization (ISO)," in S. Cassese et al. (eds.), *Global Administrative Law: The Casebook* (e-book, 2012), available at www.irpa.eu/en/gal-section/global-administrative-law-the-casebook-2.
Shany, Yuval, *Assessing the Effectiveness of International Courts* (Oxford: Oxford University Press, 2014).
The Competing Jurisdictions of International Courts and Tribunals (Oxford: Oxford University Press, 2004).

Shapiro, Martin, "The Globalization of Law," (1993) 1 *Indiana Journal of Global Legal Studies* 37–64.
Sherman, Gordon E., "*Jus Gentium* and International Law," (1918) 12 *American Journal of International Law* 56–63.
Shklar, Judith, *Legalism: Law Morals and Political Trials* (Cambridge, MA: Harvard University Press, 1986).
Simester, Andrew, Antije Du Bois-Pedain, and Ulfrid Neumann (eds.), *Liberal Criminal Theory: Essays for Andreas von Hirsch* (Oxford: Hart, 2014).
Simon Thomas, Marc, *The Challenge of Legal Pluralism: Local Dispute Settlement and the Indian-State Relationship in Ecuador* (Abingdon: Routledge, 2017).
Simon, Roberts, "After Government? On Representing Law without the State," (2005) 68 *Modern Law Review* 1–24.
Sinclair, Guy Fiti, *To Reform the World: International Organizations and the Making of Modern States* (Oxford: Oxford University Press, 2017).
Sironi, Alice, "Nationality of Individuals in Public International Law," in Serena Forlati and Alessandra Annoni (eds.), *The Changing Role of Nationality in International Law* (Abingdon: Routledge, 2014), 54–76.
Skinner, Quentin, *Reason and Rhetoric in the Philosophy of Hobbes* (Cambridge: Cambridge University Press, 1996).
Skordas, Achilles, "Völkerrechtsfreundlichkeit as Comity and the Disquiet of Neoformalism: A Response to Jan Klabbers," in Panos Koutrakos (ed.), *European Foreign Policy: Legal and Political Perspectives* (Cheltenham: Edward Elgar, 2011), 115–144.
Slaughter, Anne-Marie, "Judicial Globalization," (2000) 40 *Virginia Journal of International Law* 1103–1124.
Smiley, Marion, *Moral Responsibility and the Boundaries of Community* (Chicago: University of Chicago Press, 1992).
Snyder, Francis, "The Construction of Relations between Sites of Governance: The European Courts and WTO Law," in Francis Snyder (ed.), *The EU, the WTO and China: Legal Pluralism and International Trade Regulation* (Oxford: Hart, 2010), 151–208.
Solum, Lawrence B., "A Virtue-Centered Account of Equity and the Rule of Law," in Colin Farrelly and Lawrence B. Solum (eds.), *Virtue Jurisprudence* (New York: Palgrave MacMillan, 2008), 142–166.
Song, Nianshen, "'Tributary' from a Multilateral and Multilayered Perspective," (2012) 5 *Chinese Journal of International Politics* 155–182.
Sousa, Pedro Caro, "Is a Unified Approach to EU Fundamental Freedoms Justified?" (2014) 20 *European Law Journal* 499–519.
Spano, Robert, "Universality or Diversity of Human Rights? Strasbourg in the Age of Subsidiarity," (2014) 14 *Human Rights Law Review* 487–502.
Spiro, Peter J., *At Home in Two Countries* (New York: New York University Press, 2016).
"Dual Nationality and the Meaning of Citizenship," (1997) 46 *Emory Law Journal* 1411–1486.
"Stakeholder Theory Won't Save Citizenship," in Rainer Baubock et al. (eds.), *Democratic Inclusion* (Manchester: Manchester University Press, 2017), 204–224.
Staker, Christopher, "Jurisdiction," in Malcolm Evans (ed.), *International Law*, 4th ed., (Oxford: Oxford University Press, 2014), 309–335.

Steger, Debra, "Canadian Interpretation of the Agreement Establishing the World Trade Organization," in John H. Jackson and Alan O. Sykes (eds.), *Implementing the Uruguay Round* (Oxford: Oxford University Press, 1997), 243.

Stephan, Paul, "Competing Sovereignty and Laws' Domains," (2017) *Virginia Public Law and Legal Theory Research Paper* 4.

Stewart, Richard B., "Global Standards for National Societies," in Sabino Cassese (ed.), *Research Handbook on Global Administrative Law* (Cheltenham: Edward Elgar, 2016), 175–196.

Stewart, Richard B. and Michelle Ratton Sanchez Badin, "The World Trade Organization and Global Administrative Law," (2009) *NYU Institute for International Law and Justice Working Paper* 7.

Strik, Philip, *Shaping the Single European Market in the Field of Foreign Direct Investment* (Oxford: Hart, 2014).

Strumia, Francesca, "Citizenship and Free Movement: European and American Features of a Judicial Formula for Increased Comity," (2006) 12 *Columbia Journal of European Law* 713–750.

Supiot, Alain, *Homo Juridicus: Essai sur la Fonction Anthropologique du Droit* (Paris: Points, 2005).

"L'inscription territoriale des lois," (2008) 11 *Esprit* 151–170.

"The Territorial Inscription of Laws," in Graf-Peter Calliess, Andreas Fischer-Lescano, Dan Wielsch, and Peer Zumbansen (eds.), *Soziologische Jurisprudenz. Festschrift für Gunther Teubner zum 65. Geburtstag am 30. April 2009* (Berlin: Walter de Gruyter, 2009), 375–393.

Surak, Kristin, "Global Citizenship 2.0. The Growth of Citizenship by Investment Programs," (2016) *Investment Migration Working Paper* 3.

Szpunar, Maciej and Maria Esther Blas López, "Some Reflections on Member State Nationality: A Prerequisite of EU Citizenship and an Obstacle to Its Enjoyment," in Dimitry Kochenov (ed.), *EU Citizenship and Federalism: The Role of Rights* (Cambridge: Cambridge University Press, 2017), 107–124.

Tabau, Anne-Sophie and Sandrine Maljean-Dubois, "Non-Compliance Mechanisms: Interaction between the Kyoto Protocol System and the European Union," (2010) 21 *European Journal of International Law* 749–763.

Taekema, Sanne, "Fragments and Continuities of Law and ICT: A Pragmatist Approach to Understanding Legal Pluralism," in Wouter de Been, Payal Arora, and Mireille Hildebrandt (eds.), *Crossroads in New Media, Identity and Law: The Shape of Diversity to Come*, (London: Palgrave Macmillan, 2015), 80–92.

"Private Law as an Open Legal Order: Understanding Contract and Tort as Interactional Law," (2014) 43 *Netherlands Journal of Legal Philosophy* 140–149.

Taekema, Sanne and Wibren van der Burg, "Towards a Fruitful Cooperation between Legal Philosophy, Legal Sociology and Doctrinal Research: How Legal Interactionism May Bridge Unproductive Oppositions," in Richard Nobles and David Schiff (eds.), *Law, Society and Community: Socio-Legal Essays in Honour of Roger Cotterrell* (Farnham: Ashgate, 2014), 129–145.

Tanaka, Yoshifumi, "Obligations and Liability of Sponsoring States Concerning Activities in the Area: Reflections on the ITLOS Advisory Opinion on 1 February 2011," (2013) 60 *Netherlands International Law Review* 205–230.

Tancredi, Antonello, "OMC et coutume(s)," in Vincent Tomkiewicz (ed.), *Les Sources et les Normes dans le Droit de l'OMC* (Paris: Pedone, 2012), 81.

"On the Absence of Direct Effect of the WTO Dispute Settlement Body's Decisions in the EU Legal Order," in Enzo Cannizzaro, Paolo Palchetti, and Ramses Wessel (eds.), *International Law as Law of the European Union* (Leiden: Martinus Nijhoff, 2012), 249.

Taylor, Peter James, "The State as Container: Territoriality in the Modern World-System," (1994) 18 *Progress in Human Geography* 151–162.

Teitel, Ruti, *Humanity's Law* (Oxford: Oxford University Press, 2011).

Transitional Justice (Oxford: Oxford University Press, 2000).

Terris, Daniel, Cesare Romano, and Leigh Swigart, *The International Judge: An Introduction to the Men and Women Who Decide the World's Cases* (Oxford: Oxford University Press, 2007).

Teubner, Gunther, "Global Bukowina: Legal Pluralism in the World Society," in Gunther Teubner (ed.), *Global Law without a State* (Aldershot: Dartmouth, 1997), 3–28.

"Legal Irritants: Good Faith in British Law or How Unifying Law Ends Up in New Divergencies," (1998) 61 *Modern Law Review* 11–32.

Teubner, Gunther (ed.), *Global Law without a State* (Aldershot: Dartmouth, 1997).

Timmermans, Christiaan W. A., "Lifting the Veil of Union Citizens' Rights," in Ninon Colneric et al. (eds.), *Festschrift für Gil Carlos Rodríguez Iglesias* (Berlin: Berliner Wissenschafts-Verlag, 2003), 195–206.

Toner, Helen, "Case C-192/99, R v. Secretary of State for the Home Department, Ex Parte Kaur," (2002) 39 *Common Market Law Review* 881–893.

Toth, Orsolya, *The Lex Mercatoria in Theory and Practice* (Oxford: Oxford University Press, 2017).

Toulmin, Stephen J., *The Place of Reason in Ethics* (Chicago: University of Chicago Press, 1986 [1950]).

Trachtman, Joel P., "Bananas, Direct Effect and Compliance," (1999) 10 *European Journal of International Law* 660.

"The Domain of WTO Law," (1999) 40 *Harvard International Law Journal* 333.

Treves, Tullio, "Vue d'ensemble sur l'avis consultatif du 1er Février 2011," (2011) *Annuaire du Droit de la Mer* 343–350.

Triepel, Heinrich, *Völkerrecht und Landesrecht* (Leipzig: Hirschfeld, 1899).

Trnavci, Genc, "The Meaning and Scope of the Law of Nations in the Context of the Alien Tort Claims Act and International Law," (2005) 26 *University of Pennsylvania Journal of International Economic Law* 193–266.

Trubek, David and Patrick Cottrell, "Robert Hudec and the Theory of International Economic Law: The Law of Global Space in Developing Countries," in Chantal Thomas and Joel P. Trachtman (eds.), *Developing Countries in the WTO Legal System* (Oxford: Oxford University Press, 2009), 129–150.

Tryfonidou, Alina, "Redefining the Outer Boundaries of EU Law: The Zambrano, McCarthy and Dereci Trilogy," (2012) 18 *European Public Law* 493–526.

Tushnet, Mark, *Taking the Constitution Away from the Courts* (Princeton, NJ: Princeton University Press, 1999).

Twining, William, "Diffusion and Globalization Discourse," (2006) 47 *Harvard International Law Journal* 507.

Twining, William, *Globalisation and Legal Scholarship* (Nijmegen: Wolf Legal Publishers, 2009).
Globalisation and Legal Theory (London: Butterworths, 2000).
Tzanakopoulos, Antonios, *Disobeying the Security Council: Countermeasures against Wrongful Sanctions* (Oxford: Oxford University Press, 2011).
Unger, Roberto Mangabeira, *What Should Legal Analysis Become?* (London: Verso, 1996).
Valverde, Mariana, *Chronotopes of Law: Jurisdiction, Scale and Governance* (Abingdon: Routledge, 2015).
van der Burg, Wibren, *The Dynamics of Law and Morality. A Pluralist Account of Legal Interactionism* (Farnham: Ashgate, 2014).
van der Mei, Anne P., "Freedom of Movement for Indigents: A Comparative Analysis of American Constitutional Law and European Community Law," (2002) 19 *Arizona Journal of International and Comparative Law* 803–862.
van Domselaar, Iris, *The Fragility of Rightness: Adjudication and the Primacy of Practice* (doctoral thesis, University of Amsterdam, 2014).
"Moral Quality in Adjudication: On Judicial Virtues and Civic Friendship," (2015) 44 *Netherlands Journal of Legal Philosophy* 24–46.
"A Neo-Aristotelian Notion of Reciprocity: About Civic Friendship and (the Troublesome Character of) Right Judicial Decision," in Liesbeth Huppes-Cluysenaer and Nuno M.M.S. Coelho (eds.), Aristotle and the Philosophy of Law: Theory, Practice and Justice (Dordrecht: Springer, 2013), 223–248.
van Elsuwege, Peter, "Shifting Boundaries? European Union Citizenship and the Scope of Application of EU Law," (2011) 38 *Legal Issues of Economic Integration* 263–276.
van Hoof, Luc, "Fisheries Management, the Ecosystem Approach, Regionalisation and the Elephants in the Room," (2015) 60 *Marine Policy*, 20–26.
van Rossum, Wibo, "Religious Courts alongside Secular State Courts: The Case of the Turkish Alevis," (2008) 2 *Social Justice & Global Development Journal*.
Varella, Marcelo D., *Internationalization of Law: Globalization, International Law and Complexity* (Berlin: Springer, 2014).
Varese, Federico, *Mafias on the Move. How Organized Crime Conquers New Territories* (Princeton, NJ: Princeton University Press, 2011).
Veitch, Scott, *Law and Irresponsibility: On the Legitimation of Human Suffering* (Abingdon: Routledge, 2007).
Verdross, Alfred, "*Jus Dispositivum* and *Jus Cogens* in International Law," (1966) 60 *American Journal of International Law* 55–63.
Visek, Richard C., "Creating Ethnic Electorate through Legal Restorationism: Citizenship Rights in Estonia," (1997) 38 *Harvard International Law Journal* 315–374.
Voeten, Erik, "Competition and Complementarity between Global and Regional Human Rights Institutions," (2017) 8 *Global Policy* 119–123.
von Liszt, Friedrich, Gutachten für die internationale kriminalistische Vereinigung," (1893), reprinted in Friedrich von Liszt (ed.), *Strafrechtliche Aufsätze und Vorträge*, Vol. II (Berlin: De Gruyter, 1905).
Voronina, Natalia, "'Sojuznoje gosudarstvo Rossija – Belarus': opyt pravovogo regulirovanija," (2013) 3 *NB: Mezhdunarodnoje Parvo* 52.

Wagner, Markus, "Regulatory Space in International Trade Law and International Investment Law," (2015) 35 *University of Pennsylvania Journal of International Law* 57.

Waibel, Michael et al. (eds.), *The Backlash against Investment Arbitration: Perceptions and Reality* (The Hague: Kluwer, 2010).

Waldron, Jeremy, "The Core Case against Judicial Review," (2006) 115 *Yale Law Journal* 1346–1406.

"Foreign Law and the Modern *Ius Gentium*," (2005) 119 *Harvard Law Review* 129–147.

"International Law: 'A Relatively Small and Unimportant' Part of Jurisprudence?" (2013) *NYU Public Law and Legal Theory Working Papers* 427.

"*Ius Gentium*: A Defense of Gentili's Equation of the Law of Nations and the Law of Nature," (2008) *Public Law and Legal Theory Research Papers Series* 08/34.

"Legal Pluralism and the Contrast between Hart's Jurisprudence and Fuller's," in Peter Cane (ed.), *The Hart–Fuller Debate in the Twenty-First Century* (Oxford: Oxford University Press, 2010).

"Special Ties and Natural Justice," (1993) 22 *Philosophy and Public Affairs* 3–30.

Walker, Neil, "Beyond Boundary Disputes and Basic Grids: Mapping the Global Disorder of Normative Orders," (2006) 8 *International Constitutional Law Journal* 373–396.

Intimations of Global Law (Cambridge: Cambridge University Press, 2014).

Wang, Dong, "The Discourse of Unequal Treaties in Modern China," (2003) 76 *Pacific Affairs* 399–425.

Warbrick, Colin, "The Jurisdiction of the Security Council: Original Intention and New World Order(s)," in Patrick Capps, Malcolm Evans, and Stratos Konstadinidis (eds.), *Asserting Jurisdiction: International and European Perspectives* (Oxford: Hart, 2003), 127–143.

Web, Philippa, *International Judicial Integration and Fragmentation* (Oxford: Oxford University Press, 2013).

Weil, Patrick, *The Sovereign Citizen* (Philadelphia: University of Pennsylvania Press, 2012).

Weiler, Joseph H. H., "The Geology of International Law: Governance, Democracy and Legitimacy," (2004) 64 *Zeitschrift für ausländisches öffentliches Recht und Völkerrecht* 547–562.

Weinrib, Ernest J., *The Idea of Private Law* (Oxford: Oxford University Press, 2012).

Wenk, Michael S., *The European Union's Eco-Management and Audit Scheme* (Dordrecht: Springer, 2005).

Whelan, Frederick, "Prologue: Democratic Theory and the Boundary Problem," in J. Roland Pennock and John W. Chapman (eds.), *Nomos XXV: Liberal Democracy* (1983) 13–47.

White, Jonathan, "Authority after Emergency Rule," (2015) 78 *Modern Law Review* 585–610.

Whitehead, Tom, "Cameron Vows to Defy Europe on Prisoner Voting," *The Telegraph*, 24 May 2012, available at www.telegraph.co.uk/news/politics/9285408/Cameron-vows-to-defy-Europe-on-prisoner-voting.html.

Wijffels, Alain, "Bringing Peripheries into Focus," in Pierre d'Argent (ed.), *Droit des Frontières Internationals* (Paris: Pedone, 2016), 43–55.

Willems, Vera (2017), "International Courts and Tribunals and Their Linguistic Practices: A Communities of Practice Approach," (2017) 30 *International Journal for the Semiotics of Law* 181–199.

Williams, Bernard, *Ethics and the Limits of Philosophy* (Cambridge, MA: Harvard University Press, 1985).

"Justice as a Virtue," in Amélie Oksenberg Rorty (ed.), Essays on Aristotle's Ethics (Berkeley: University of California Press, 1980), 189–199.

Wittgenstein, Ludwig, *Philosophical Investigations* (Oxford: Blackwell, 1953).

Wolfrum, Matz, Conflicts in International Environmental Law (Berlin: Springer, 2003).

Worster, William Thomas, "Competition and Comity in the Fragmentation of International Law," (2009) 34 *Brooklyn Journal of International Law* 119–150.

Xifaras, Mikhail, "The Global Turn in Legal Theory," (2016) 29 *Canadian Journal of Law and Jurisprudence* 215–243.

Yee, Sienho, "A Call for a More Rigorous Assessment of Universal Jurisdiction," (2013) 107 *ASIL Proceedings* 242–5.

Zekoll, Joachim, "Jurisdiction in Cyberspace," in Gunther Handl, Joachim Zekoll, and Peer Zumbansen (eds.), *Beyond Territoriality: Transnational Legal Authority in an Age of Globalization* (Leiden: Brill, 2012), 341–369.

Zhang, X., *Implementation of the WTO Agreements in China* (London: Wildy, Simmons and Hill Publishing, 2005).

Zimmermann, Andreas, "International Law and 'Cyber Space'," (2014) 3 *ESIL Reflections*.

Zincone, Giovanna and Marzia Basili, "Country Report: Italy," RSCAS/EUDO-CIT-CR 2010/35 (2010).

Zoppo, Laura, *La Soluzione delle Controversie Commerciali tra Stati tra Multilaterismo e Regionalismo* (Naples: Jovene, 2013).

Zuleeg, Manfred, "Demokratie und Wirtschaftsverfassung in der Rechtsprechung des Europäischen Gerichtshofs," (1982) 16 *Europarecht* 21.

Zumbansen, Peer, "The Regulatory Landscape of Global Governance and Transnational Legal Authority," in Gunther Handl, Joachim Zekoll, and Peer Zumbansen (eds.), *Beyond Territoriality: Transnational Legal Authority in an Age of Globalization* (Leiden: Brill, 2012), 551–558.

Zurn, Michael, "Global Governance and Legitimacy Problems," in David Held and Mathias Koenig-Archibugi (eds.), *Global Governance and Public Accountability* (Oxford: Blackwell, 2005), 260–287.

"Introduction: Law and Compliance at Different Levels," in Michael Zurn and Christian Joerges (eds.), *Law and Governance in Postnational Europe: Compliance Beyond the Nation-State* (Cambridge: Cambridge University Press, 2005), 1–39.

Index